Essential Psychotherapies

Essential Psychotherapies
Theory and Practice

Edited by
ALAN S. GURMAN
STANLEY B. MESSER

THE GUILFORD PRESS
New York   London

© 1995 The Guilford Press
A Division of Guilford Publications
72 Spring Street, New York, NY 10012

Printed in the United States of America

This book is printed on acid-free paper.

Last digit is print number: 9   8   7   6   5   4   3

Library of Congress Cataloging-in-Publication Data
Essential psychotherapies : theory and practice / edited by
   Alan S. Gurman, Stanley B. Messer.
        p.   cm.
   Includes bibliographical references and index.
   ISBN 1-57230-018-3
   1. Psychotherapy.   I. Gurman, Alan S.   II. Messer, Stanley B.
   [DNLM: 1. Psychotherapy—methods.   WM 420 E78 1995]
   RC480.E69   1995
   616.89'14—dc20
   DNLM/DLC
   for Library of Congress   95-297
                                                          CIP

To our children,
Jesse and Ted Gurman,
Elana, Leora, and Tova Messer

Contributors

Arthur C. Bohart, PhD, Department of Psychology, California State University–Dominguez Hills, Carson, CA

James F. T. Bugental, PhD, Private practice, Novato, CA

Marianne P. Celano, PhD, Department of Psychiatry and Behavioral Sciences, Emory University School of Medicine, Atlanta, GA

Olga Cheselka, PhD, The William Alanson White Institute, New York, NY

Robert R. Dies, PhD, Department of Psychology, University of Maryland, College Park, MD

Victoria M. Follette, PhD, Department of Psychology, University of Nevada, Reno, NV

William C. Follette, PhD, Department of Psychology, University of Nevada, Reno, NV

Arthur Freeman, EdD, Department of Psychology, Philadelphia College of Osteopathic Medicine, Philadelphia, PA

Jay Greenberg, PhD, The William Alanson White Institute, New York, NY

Alan S. Gurman, PhD, Department of Psychiatry, University of Wisconsin Medical School, Madison, WI

Steven C. Hayes, PhD, Department of Psychology, University of Nevada, Reno, NV

Michael F. Hoyt, PhD, Kaiser Permanente Medical Center, Hayward, CA; University of California School of Medicine, San Francisco, CA

Muriel James, EdD, Private practice, Lafayette, CA

Nadine J. Kaslow, PhD, Department of Psychiatry and Behavioral Sciences, Emory University School of Medicine, Atlanta, GA

Stanley B. Messer, PhD, Graduate School of Applied and Professional Psychology, Rutgers University, Piscataway, NJ

James O. Prochaska, PhD, Cancer Prevention Research Consortium, University of Rhode Island, Kingston, RI

Mark A. Reinecke, PhD, Child and Adolescent Psychiatry, University of Chicago School of Medicine, Chicago, IL

Molly M. Sterling, PhD, Private practice, Novato, CA

David L. Wolitzky, PhD, New York University Psychology Clinic, Department of Psychology; New York University Postdoctoral Program in Psychotherapy and Psychoanalysis, New York, NY

Gary M. Yontef, PhD, Gestalt Therapy Institute of Los Angeles, Los Angeles, CA

Contents

1

Essential Psychotherapies: An Orienting Framework

ALAN S. GURMAN
STANLEY B. MESSER

As the title indicates, this is a book about the theory and practice of essential psychotherapies. In using the term "essential," we are excluding those psychotherapies that may generate faddish enthusiasm but soon pass from the therapeutic scence. Essential psychotherapies, in our view, are those that form the conceptual and clinical bedrock of the field. They are also therapeutic systems that are indispensible in the training and education of psychotherapists. We use the term "essential" to connote two categories of contemporary approaches to psychotherapy. First, there are those treatments that have been developed relatively recently; have had demonstrably powerful effects on practice, training, and research; and are likely to endure for a very long time. Examples include the brief, cognitive, family, and integrative psychotherapies. Second, the "essential" psychotherapies considered here include several whose origins are found in the earlier, and even earliest, phases of the history of psychotherapy. Although the core of each of these methods has endured

through several generations of psychotherapists, they have been considerably revised and refined over the years. Examples are traditional and relational approaches to psychoanalytic psychotherapy, existential–humanistic and person-centered psychotherapy, Gestalt, group, behavior therapy, and Transactional Analysis.

This volume is intended to serve as a primary reference source for comprehensive presentations of the most prominent conceptual and clinical influences in the field today. While there may exist hundreds of differently labeled psychotherapies (Garfield & Bergin, 1994), we believe that they can be subsumed by a mere dozen genuinely discriminable types. As editors, we have challenged our contributors to convey not only what is fundamental to their ways of working, but also what is innovative and forward-looking in theory and practice. We believe that the contributors, all eminent clinical scholars and noted representatives of their treatment approaches, have collaborated on a volume that is well suited to expose advanced under-graduates, beginning graduate students or trainees in all the mental health professions, and more experienced psychotherapists to the major schools and methods of modern psychotherapy. Each chapter offers a clear sense of the history, current status, assessment approach, and methods of the therapy reviewed, along with its foundational concepts of personality and psychopathology. Regarding the latter, we have attempted to balance practice and theory, and to emphasize the interplay between them. As academicians and practicing psychotherapists, we agree with Kurt Lewin that "there is nothing so practical as a good theory."

Before presenting and discussing our organizing framework for the chapters, two comments about the content of this book are in order. First, while *Essential Psychotherapies* provides substantive presentations of the major "schools" of psychotherapeutic thought and general guidelines for practice, it does not include treatment prescriptions for specific disorders or populations. Although there is presently a movement to specify particular techniques for particular disorders and populations, we believe that the vast majority of practitioners continue to approach their work from the standpoint of theory as it informs general techniques of practice.

Second, there is today a thrust toward integration of principles of psychotherapy across "schools," one illustration of which is presented in Chapter 11. While we value the search for integrative and common factors that transcend given therapies (Gurman, 1992; Messer, 1992), we endorse the current practice of teaching about distinct schools or systems of psychotherapy. It would be irrational to teach therapists about therapeutic integration without their first understanding the foundational theories of the field. In addition, theoretical integration cannot advance without

these basic theories remaining intact (Liddle, 1982).

Indeed, the separate models can be seen to stem from different views of human nature, about which there is no universal agreement. Schools also embrace fundamentally different ways of getting to know clients, which stem from different epistemological outlooks (e.g., introspective vs. extraspective; Messer & Winokur, 1980). Furthermore, the therapies encompass distinct visions of reality, such as the extent to which they incorporate the belief that fundamental change is possible, or even what constitutes that change (e.g., tragic vs. comic views of life; Messer & Winokur, 1984). As such, it is important for the field, and a volume such as this one, to respect the search for common principles in theory or practice while continuing to appreciate and highlight the different perspectives each model or school of therapy exemplifies.

A FRAMEWORK FOR DESCRIBING THE PSYCHOTHERAPIES

It is not the answer that enlightens, but the questions.

—EUGENE IONESCO

An important feature of *Essential Psychotherapies* is the comprehensive set of "Authors' Guidelines" that served as a point of reference for the contributors. They were adapted from those used by Gurman and Kniskern in their *Handbook of Family Therapy* (1981, 1991). Such guidelines may facilitate the reader's comparative study of the major models of contemporary psychotherapy (and may also be used by the student as a template for studying systems of therapy not included here).

In offering these guidelines to the chapter authors, we hoped to steer a course between constraining the authors' creativity, and providing the reader with anchor points for comparison across chapters. We believe that our contributors have succeeded in adhering to these guidelines while describing their therapeutic approaches in a lively way. We encouraged authors to sequence the material within chapter sections according to their own preferences. Authors were also advised that they need not limit their presentations to the matters raised in the guidelines, or even include every point, but that they should address these matters in some fashion if they were relevant to the clinical approach being described. It was also acceptable for the authors to collapse or merge sections of the guidelines, if that seemed warranted, in order to communicate their ideas meaningfully and fluidly.

In the end, we believe that the contributors' flexible adherence to the guidelines has helped to make clear to the reader how theory helps to organize clinical work and facilitates case conceptualization. It has also allowed authors to convey the variety that exists even within a given clinical model. The inclusion of clinical case material in each chapter serves to illustrate the constructs and methods described previously.

Rather than summarize each chapter, we will present the Authors' Guidelines we have been alluding to, along with the rationale for each section included.

I. Background of the Approach

History is the version of past events that people have decided to agree on.
　　　　—NAPOLEON BONAPARTE

Purpose: To place the approach in historical perspective within the field of psychotherapy.

Points to include:

1. Cite the major influences that contributed to the development of the approach (e.g., people, books, research, theories, conferences). What were the sociohistorical forces or *Zeitgeist* that shaped the emergence and development of this approach (e.g., Victorian era, American pragmatism, modernism, etc.)?
2. The therapeutic forms, if any, that were forerunners of the approach (e.g., psychoanalysis, learning theory, organismic theory, etc.).
3. Types of patients with whom the approach was initially developed, and speculations as to why.
4. Early theoretical speculations and/or therapy techniques.

Understanding the professional roots and historical context of psychotherapeutic methods is an essential part of therapy education. Without such awareness, therapeutic theories and methods remain disembodied abstractions, seeming to rise from nowhere, and for no discernible reason. An important component of a therapist's persuasiveness is found in his/her belief not only in the technical aspects of an approach but also in the world view that is implicit in that approach (Frank & Frank, 1991). One cannot comprehend the worldview of a therapy without an appreciation of its origins. Just as being emotionally cut off from one's own biological family of origin may sow the seeds for current relationship difficulties, not being connected to one's therapeutic origins may lead to a mechanized and affectless therapy-by-the-numbers. The reader interested in a more detailed study of the history of the first 100 years of psychotherapy may wish to consult the volume edited by Freedheim et al. (1992).

In addition to appreciating the professional roots of therapeutic methods, it is always fascinating to understand why particular methods appear on the scene at particular historical junctures. The intellectual, economic, and political contexts in which therapy methods arise often provide meaningful clues about the emerging social values that frame clinical encounters, and may have a subtle but powerful impact on the staying power of new approaches. We firmly believe that systems of therapy are no more value free or free of societal forces than are therapists themselves.

II. The Concept of Personality

Children are natural mimics—they act like their parents in spite of every attempt to teach them good manners.
                                   —ANONYMOUS

Purpose: To describe within the theoretical/therapeutic framework the conceptualization of personality and/or behavior.

Points to include:

1. Is the concept of "personality" meaningful within your approach, or is there some other unit that is more meaningful?
2. What are the basic psychological concepts used to understand the person/family/group? (Discuss whichever unit is most appropriate for your chapter here and elsewhere.)
3. What is the theory of development of the person/family/group?
4. Is there a concept of the healthy, well-functioning, adaptive personality/family/group?

III. The Pathological or Dysfunctional Individual/ Family/Group

Utopias will come to pass when we grow wings and all people are converted into angels.
                                   —FYODOR DOSTOYEVSKI

Purpose: To describe the way in which pathological functioning is conceptualized within the approach.

Points to include:

1. Describe any formal or informal system for diagnosing or typing individuals/families/groups.
2. What leads to individual/family/ group dysfunction?
3. How do symptoms or problems develop? How are they maintained?
4. What determines the type of symptom or character style to appear?
5. Why are some people symptomatic and not others?
6. Are there other dimensions that need to be considered in describing dysfunctional individuals, families, or groups?

These two sections of the Authors' Guidelines deal with two questions: (1) What is your approach's understanding of the essence of personality formation and of the psychologically "healthy" person? (2) In your approach, what constitutes pathological or "unhealthy" behavior, and how is it established and maintained? The first question begs the issue somewhat in that, as Messer and Warren (1990) have pointed out, "Not all theories of personality explain the process of personality change, nor are all efforts to effect psychological change supported by a personality theory" (p. 371). Some theories of psychotherapy are virtually mute on the matter of how personality develops, or indeed, assert that the concept of personality is not needed for effective clinical practice. Yet even those theories that steadfastly avoid the use of language and labels that pathologize human experience speak clearly about what constitutes "maladaptive" behavior. Thus, even schools of therapy that do not formally judge the "health" of a person based on criteria external to that person (or family or group), do attend to the consequences of behavior in terms of that person's welfare and interest, phenomenologically defined.

Messer and Warren (1990) go on to note that "the terms of a personality theory and the goals of its related system of psychotherapy are not neutral . . . they are embedded in a value structure that determines what is most important to know and change . . ." (p. 372). Even schools of psychotherapy that attempt to be neutral with regard to what constitutes healthy (and, therefore, desirable) and unhealthy (and, therefore, undesirable) behavior inevitably, if unwittingly, reinforce the acceptability of some kinds of patients' strivings more than others. Not even Carl Rogers, the originator of "nondirective" therapy (as it was called in the past) was able to provide facilitative therapeutic conditions, such as empathic understanding and unconditional positive regard, uniformly, but responded differently to certain categories of client speech (Truax, 1966).

IV. The Assessment of Dysfunction

If you are sure you understand everything that is going on, you are hopelessly confused.
—WALTER MONDALE

Purpose: To describe the methods, whether formal or informal, used to gain understanding of a particular individual/family/group's style or pattern of interaction, symptomatology, and adaptive resources.

Points to include:

1. At what *unit* level is assessment made (e.g., individual, dyadic, triadic, family system, group)?
2. At what *psychological* levels is assessment made (e.g., intrapsychic, behavioral, systemic)?
3. What tests, devices, questionnaires, or observations are typically used?
4. Is assessment separate from treatment or integrated with it (e.g., what is the temporal relation between assessment and treatment)?
5. Are the individual/family/group's strengths/resources a focus of your assessment? If so, in what way?
6. What other dimensions or factors are typically involved in assessing dysfunction?

Up to this point in our guidelines, the therapist has not yet met the patient, so to speak. Equipped with particular views of normal and abnormal human psychological functioning, the therapist now encounters the patient. The therapist is obligated to take some purposeful action with regard to understanding the nature and parameters of whatever problems, symptoms, or complaints are presented. Therapists typically will be interested in understanding what previous steps patients have taken to resolve their difficulties and what adaptive resources the patient (and possibly others in the patient's everyday world) has for doing so.

How therapists go about engaging in a clinical assessment will vary from approach to approach, but all will include face-to-face clinical interviews. A smaller number will also observe the problem directly, apart from conversations between patient and therapist *about* the problem. Still fewer will call upon specific tests and questionnaires to complement interviews and observations.

The major dimension along which clinical assessments will vary is the intrapersonal–interpersonal. Some approaches will emphasize "intrapsychic" process and events while others will emphasize social transaction and interaction. But note that there is a constant interplay between clients' "inner" and "outer" lives and that emphasis on one domain "versus" another reflects arbitrary punctuation of human experience that says as much about the theory of the perceiver as it does about the client who is perceived.

V. The Practice of Therapy

*All knowledge is sterile which does not lead
to action and end in charity.*
            —CARDINAL MERCIER

Purpose: To describe the typical structure, goals, techniques, strategies, and the process of a particular approach to therapy and their tactical purposes.

Points to include:

Basic structure of therapy

1. How often are sessions typically held?
2. Is therapy time-limited or unlimited? Why? How long does therapy typically last? How long are typical sessions?
3. Who is typically included in therapy? Are combined formats (e.g., individual plus family or group sessions) ever used?
4. How structured are therapy sessions?

Goal setting

5. Are there treatment goals that apply to all or most cases for which the treatment is appropriate (see "Treatment Applicability," below) regardless of presenting problem or symptom?
6. Of the number of possible goals for a given person/family/group, how are the central goals selected for this unit? How are they prioritized?
7. Do you distinguish between intermediate or mediating goals and ultimate goals?
8. Who determines the goals of treatment? Therapist, individual, both, or other? How are differences in goals resolved? To what extent and in what ways are therapist values involved in goal setting?
9. Is it important that treatment goals be discussed with the individual/family/group explicitly? If yes, why? If not, why not?
10. At what level of psychological experience are goals established (e.g., are they described in overt behavioral terms, in affective–cognitive terms, etc.)?

Techniques and strategies of therapy

11. Identify, describe, and illustrate major commonly used techniques.
12. Are psychotropic medications ever used within your method? What are the indications/contraindications for their use?
13. Are "homework" or other out-of-session tasks used?
14. How is the decision made to use a particular technique or strategy at a particular time? Are different techniques used for different individual/family/group problems?

Process of therapy

15. What techniques or strategies are used to create a treatment alliance?
16. What are the most commonly encountered forms of resistance to change? How are these dealt with?
17. What are both the most common *and* the most serious technical errors a therapist can make operating within your therapeutic approach?
18. On what basis is termination decided and how is termination effected?

VI. The Stance of the Therapist

*It is only an auctioneer who can equally and
impartially admire all schools of art.*
            —OSCAR WILDE

Purpose: To describe the stance the therapist takes with the individual/family/group.

Points to include:

1. To what degree does the therapist overtly control sessions? How active/directive is the therapist?
2. Does the therapist assume responsibility for bringing about the changes

desired? Is responsibility left to the individual/family/group? Is responsibility shared?

3. Does the therapist use self-disclosure? What limits are imposed on therapist self-disclosure?
4. Does the therapist "join" the individual/family/group or remain more "outside"?
5. Does the therapist's role change as therapy progresses? Does it change as termination approaches?
6. Is countertransference recognized or employed in any fashion?
7. What are the clinical skills or other therapist attributes most essential to successful therapy in your approach?

Section V, "The Practice of Therapy," and Section VI, "The Stance of the Therapist," taken together, reflect the core considerations in the actual practice of psychotherapy. They subsume the large majority of technical and relational factors operating in treatment. The kinds of essential facets of therapy considered in these sections, in aggregate, make up what therapists refer to when they identify their primary therapeutic orientation. And just how do therapists choose their therapeutic orientations, their preferred ways of working? For better or for worse, therapists do not advocate or practice different approaches mainly on the basis of their relative scientific status. For example, Norcross and Prochaska (1983) found that the four most influential factors in orientation choice were one's clinical experience, values and personal philosophy, graduate training, and personal life experiences. Therapists are attracted to different approaches on the basis of a large number of both rational and irrational factors. The choice of a favorite method of psychotherapy often derives from personal factors. For example, therapists with a "take charge" personal style may be better suited to practice clinical methods requiring a good

deal of therapist activity and structuring than those requiring a more reflective style. Given the presumed equivalence of effectiveness of the major methods of psychotherapy (Garfield & Bergin, 1994), it is not surprising that idiosyncratic personal variables should exert such an influence on therapists' preferred ways of practicing. As Robin Skynner (personal communication, March 1982) has quipped, we need "different thinks for different shrinks."

In addition to the personal meaning to therapists of adopting particular models of therapy, the meaning of a given technique within a particular context also deserves our attention. While all therapeutic techniques are born within an originating "home theory," so to speak, these techniques are often exported for use within other clinical frameworks. While potent techniques may not lose their effectiveness when "exported," their introduction into a given course of therapy may significantly alter the nature of the patient–therapist relationship and, therefore, the thrust of the therapy (Messer, in Lazarus & Messer, 1991). A technique is an intervention, but it is also a communication within a specific context.

VII. Curative Factors or Mechanisms of Change

You can do very little with faith, but you can do nothing without it.
— SAMUEL BUTLER

Purpose: To describe the factors, that is, mechanisms of change, that lead to change and to assess their relative importance. Include research findings if possible.

Points to include:

1. What are the proposed curative factors or mechanisms of change from the standpoint of your theoretical approach?

2. Do patients need insight or understanding in order to change? (Differentiate between historical–genetic insight and interactional insight.)
3. Are interpretations of any sort important and, if so, do they take history (genetics) into account? If interpretations of any kind are used, are they seen as reflecting a psychological "reality," or are they viewed rather as a pragmatic tool for effecting change?
4. Is the learning of new interpersonal skills seen as an important element of change? If so, are these skills taught in didactic fashion, or are they shaped as approximations occur naturalistically in treatment?
5. Does the therapist's personality or psychological health play an important part in bringing about change?
6. How important are techniques as opposed to just "being with" the person/family/group?
7. Is change in an "identified patient" (where relevant) possible without interactional or systemic change? Does systemic change necessarily lead to change in symptoms?
8. What factors or variables enhance or limit the probability of successful treatment in your approach?
9. To what extent does the management of termination of therapy determine outcome?
10. What aspects of your therapy are *not* unique to your approach, that is, common to all therapy?
11. Can you give an example of the kind of research that backs up the proposed mechanisms of change?

VIII. Treatment Applicability

Society has always seemed to demand a little more from human beings than it will get in practice.

—GEORGE ORWELL

Purpose: To describe those individuals/families/groups for whom your approach is particularly relevant.

Points to include:
1. For what kinds of individuals/families/groups is your approach particularly relevant?
2. For whom is your approach either not appropriate or of uncertain relevance? For example, is it less relevant for severely disturbed individuals/families/couples/groups? For marital and/or sexual problems? Why?
3. What is the applicability of your approach to children, adolescents, and the elderly?
4. What kinds of modifications are typically introduced in treating any or all of these age groups?
5. When, if ever, would a referral be made for another (i.e., different) type of therapy?
6. When would *no* treatment (of any sort) be recommended?
7. Are there aspects of your approach that raise particular ethical issues that are different from those raised by psychotherapy in general?
8. How is the outcome, or effectiveness, of therapy in this model evaluated in clinical practice?
9. What are the data supporting the value of the approach?

Taken together, Section VII, "Mechanisms of Change," and Section VIII, "Treatment Applicability," ask two fundamental questions: (1) How effective is this method of therapy, and for whom? and (2) When change occurs in this method of therapy, through what processes does that come about? Ultimately, such important questions are best answered through painstaking research rather than by testimonials, appeals to authority and tradition, and other unsystematic methods. Psychotherapy is far too complex to track the interaction among, and impact of, the most relevant factors in effectiveness via individuals' participation in the process alone. The relative contributions to the outcomes of psychotherapies of therapist factors, patient factors, and technique factors probably vary from method to method. Moreover, it is unlikely that many of these factors by themselves exert strong, reliable effects on treatment outcomes, other than in interaction with other variables.

Yet, as noted previously, most psychotherapists are not easily persuaded to adopt unfamiliar treatment methods simply because research suggests they are helpful, or to stop using more familiar methods because research casts doubt on their helpfulness or because relevant research barely exists. While we would personally be pleased to see research findings affecting practice to a greater extent, there is another prominent way in which research can influence and enhance clinical practice, namely through clinicians learning the practical importance of critical thinking. Psychotherapists should be very concerned about the quality of evidence they accept in their daily clinical decision making. Some common errors in critical thinking among therapists (and among the members of many other helping professions, as well!) are the following: confusing description and naming with explanation; mistaking correlation for causation; ignoring alternative plausible explanations; failing to identify, or incorrectly identifying, implicit assumptions; failing to operationally define key concepts and terms; and reasoning only by analogy. Two outstanding recent books we recommend to therapists to hone their critical reasoning skills are by Browne and Keeley (1994), written for all disciplines, and Gambrill (1990), written especially for psychotherapists.

IX. Case Illustration

A good example is the best sermon.
—YANKEE PROVERB

Purpose: To illustrate the clinical application of this model by detailing the major assessment, structural, technical, and relational elements of the process of treating a unit viewed as typical, or representative, of the kinds of individuals/families/groups for whom this approach is appropriate.

Points to include:

1. Relevant case background (e.g., presenting problem, referral source, previous treatment history).
2. Description of relevant aspects of, your clinical assessment (e.g., functioning, structure, dysfunctional interaction, resources, individual dynamics/characteristics), including how this description was arrived at.
3. Description of the process and content of goal setting.
4. Highlight the major themes, patterns, etc., of the therapy over the whole course of treatment. Describe the structure of therapy, the techniques used, the role and activity of the therapist, etc.

Note: Do *not* describe the treatment of a "star case," in which therapy progresses perfectly. Select a case which, while successful, also illustrates the typical course of events in your therapy.

Someone once said that the main function of professional psychotherapy workshops is to help clinicians feel more confident by watching renowned experts fail in demonstrations with "impossible" patients. Conversely, published case illustrations not infrequently seem designed to showcase the clinical genius of their authors, resulting in reader demoralization and feelings of relative ineptitude. It was with such thoughts in mind that we cautioned our contributors to elucidate rather than intimidate.

X. Suggestions for Further Reading

A professor is someone who talks in someone else's sleep.

—W. H. AUDEN

Purpose: To aid the instructor in assigning relevant readings as a supplement to the text.

Points to include:

1. Two articles or accessible book chapters that give detailed, extensive clinical case studies.
2. Two research oriented articles or chapters, preferably one of which includes an overview of findings or research issues pertinent to your approach.
3. Two books that serve as reference volumes for the student.

CONCLUSION

In editing *Essential Psychotherapies*, we have brought together a collection of systematic and extensive expositions of important treatment methods that we expect will have enduring value both in the education of students and in the continuing education of more seasoned clinicians. We hope that *Essential Psychotherapies* aids the process of clinical growth of therapists as much as therapists and therapy themselves aid the process of change.

REFERENCES

Browne, M. N., & Keeley, S. M. (1994). *Asking the right questions: A guide to critical thinking.* Englewood Cliffs, NJ: Prentice-Hall.

Frank, J. D., & Frank, J. B. (1991). *Persuasion and healing.* Baltimore: Johns Hopkins University Press.

Freedheim, D. K., Freudenberger, H., Kessler, J., Messer, S., Peterson, D.,

Strupp, H., & Wachtel, P. (Eds.). (1992). *History of psychotherapy: A century of change.* Washington, DC: American Psychological Association.

Gambrill, E. (1990). *Critical thinking in clinical practice.* San Francisco: Jossey-Bass.

Garfield, S. L., & Bergin, A. E. (Eds.). (1994). *Handbook of psychotherapy and behavior change* (4th ed.). New York: Wiley.

Garfield, S. L., & Bergin, A. E. (1994). Introduction and historical overview. In S. L. Garfield & A. E. Bergin (Eds.), *Handbook of psychotherapy and behavior change* (4th ed., pp. 3–18) New York: Wiley.

Gurman, A. S. (1992). Integrative marital therapy: A time-sensitive model for working with couples. In S. Budman, M. Hoyt, & S. Friedman (Eds.), *The first session in brief therapy* (pp. 186–203). New York: Guilford Press.

Gurman, A. S., & Kniskern, D. P. (1981). *Handbook of family therapy.* New York: Brunner/Mazel.

Gurman, A. S., & Kniskern, D. P. (1991). *Handbook of family therapy* (Vol. 2). New York: Brunner/Mazel.

Lazarus, A. A., & Messer, S. B. (1991). Does chaos prevail? An exchange on technical eclecticism and assimilative integration. *Journal of Psychotherapy Integration, 1,* 143–158.

Liddle, H. A. (1982). On the problems of eclecticism: A call for epistemologic clarification and human scale theories. *Family Process, 21,* 81–97.

Messer, S. B. (1992). A critical examination of belief structures in integrative and eclectic psychotherapy. In J. C. Norcross & M. R. Goldfried (Eds.), *Handbook of psychotherapy integration* (pp. 130–165). New York: Basic Books.

Messer, S. B., & Warren, S. (1990). Personality change and psychotherapy. In L. A. Pervin (Ed.), *Handbook of personality: Theory and research* (pp. 371–398). New York: Guilford Press.

Messer, S. B., & Winokur, M. (1980). Some limits to the integration of psychoanalytic and behavior therapy. *American Psychologist, 35,* 818–827.

Messer, S. B., & Winokur, M. (1984). Ways of knowing and visions of reality in psychoanalytic therapy and behavior therapy. In H. Arkowitz & S. B. Messer (Eds.), *Psychoanalytic therapy and behavior therapy: Is integration possible?* (pp. 53–100). New York: Plenum Press.

Norcross, J. C., & Prochaska, J. O. (1983). Clinicians' theoretical orientations: Selection, utilization and efficacy. *Professional Psychology, 14,* 197–208.

Truax, C. B. (1966). Reinforcement and nonreinforcement in Rogerian psychotherapy. *Journal of Abnormal Psychology, 71,* 1–9.

2

The Theory and Practice of Traditional Psychoanalytic Psychotherapy

DAVID L. WOLITZKY

BACKGROUND OF THE APPROACH

The aim of this chapter is to introduce the theory and practice of Freudian psychoanalysis and the psychoanalytic psychotherapy that derived from it. The term "psychoanalysis" refers to (1) a theory of personality and psychopathology, (2) a method of investigating the mind, and (3) a theory of treatment. I shall be concerned primarily with the theory of treatment, but will need to present some of the basic theoretical and methodological concepts as the context for understanding the theoretical rationale for therapeutic intervention.

Sigmund Freud (1856–1939) was the founder of psychoanalysis and the father of modern psychotherapy. Although he was confronted with the exigencies of the clinical situation, Freud's primary aspiration was to develop psychoanalysis as a theory of the human mind and secondarily as a therapeutic modality. Accordingly, his theoretical writings con-

sume the bulk of the 23 volumes of his collected works, published as the definitive *Standard Edition*. There are relatively few papers on the theory of technique or on basic technical precepts.

As a comprehensive theory of personality and psychopathology, psychoanalysis has had a profound impact on 20th-century thought and culture, an impact that is unrivaled by any other conception of personality. Psychoanalytic theorizing not only has aimed at understanding and explaining the nature of adult psychopathology, but has also addressed the broader domain of normal personality functioning and the development of personality. In this sense it can be regarded as a general psychology. As such, it ranges from biologically based explanations of key aspects of mental life (e.g., cognition, affect, and motivation) to sociocultural, historical theorizing about the origins of society and the family. Attempts to understand art, literature, music, religion, and virtually all other aspects of human experience according to psychoanalytic principles (so-called "applied psychoanalysis") have filled innumerable journals and books for nearly a full century.

The origins of psychoanalysis can be traced back to the last two decades of the 19th century in the cultural context of turn-of-the-century Vienna. It has evolved throughout the past century and spread throughout the world, particularly to the rest of Europe, the United States, and South America. Freud's life and the psychoanalytic movement he inspired and led have been the subject of a multitude of books and articles through the years.

In the past century, we have seen many developments of psychoanalytic theory and practice. All of them have taken their point of departure from Freud, either by extending or modifying a line of thought implicit or undeveloped in Freud's work or by rejecting essential Freudian assumptions yet referring to their alternate conceptions by the term "psychoanalytic." Indeed, there have been many heated professional squabbles through the years about whether one should call certain "deviations" from the original theory and practice of psychoanalysis by that name. For instance, the so-called neo-Freudians (e.g., Adler, Jung, and Horney) have been called deviant in that each departs from Freud's emphasis on the importance of childhood sexuality. Whether a new school of psychoanalytic thought evolves and becomes assimilated into the mainstream of the prevailing psychoanalytic paradigms or whether it becomes a "deviant" school often has more to do with the existing sociohistorical *Zeitgeist* than with the extent to which the theory advanced departs from Freud's views. A most recent case in point is Kohut's self psychology which departs in fundamental ways from basic Freudian tenets yet did not create the kinds of schisms that characterized earlier theoretical differences (Eagle, 1987).

There is by now significant diversity within what has been termed "the common ground of psychoanalysis" (Wallerstein, 1990). Therefore, it is no longer accurate to refer to *the* psychoanalytic theory of personality or of treatment. Rather, we need to specify the particular theoretical perspective from which we are approaching the topic. In this chapter, I shall focus primarily on traditional Freudian theory and its ego-psychological extensions. That is, I shall provide an account of Freud's core concepts and their implications for treatment as well as a brief reference to the contributions of later theorists who sought to extend Freud's thinking. Together, this body of thought constitutes what has been called traditional Freudian theory and forms the basis for the so-called "classical" psychoanalytic approach to treatment.

For present purposes, we may follow Pine (1990) and divide theoretical changes in psychoanalytic thinking into four main eras. First, of course, was Freud's theory of unconscious motivation with its ultimate postulation of *libidinal and aggressive drives* as the prime movers of mental life and behavior. The second wave of theorizing was the development of *ego psychology* with its focus on the defensive and coping devices used to deal with conflicted wishes. Third, we saw the evolution of versions of *object relations theory* with its focus on the mental representation of objects, the relationship of the self to one's world of inner objects, and the repetitive reenactment of this internal world in the context of ongoing interpersonal relationships and fantasies of such relationships. The fourth, and most recent change in psychoanalytic thinking is the advent of *self psychology*, as created by Heinz Kohut (1984), in which the cohesion and fulfillment of the self came to be regarded as the individual's primary aim.

This chapter focuses on the first and second eras of psychoanalytic theorizing and on the contemporary extensions, revisions, and understandings of those views. It should be noted that this categorization is somewhat oversimplified in that within traditional Freudian theory there have been important contributions to our understanding of ego development that have included a major emphasis on the development of selfhood (e.g., Jacobson, 1964; Mahler, 1968). At the same time, some object relations theorists (e.g., Klein, 1921–1945) retained significant aspects of Freud's drive theory. It is also important to point out that many contemporary Freudian analysts often incorporate, at least informally and implicitly, aspects of object relations theories and self psychology. The whole question of the relationship between theory and practice is an interesting one, which I touch on later.

Having created an orienting context with this brief overview of theoretical developments in psychoanalytic thinking, I will proceed to focus on the origins and the current application of traditional psychoanalytic theory to the treatment of psychopathology.

The kinds of patients first treated by Freud were usually late adolescent women who presented with hysterical symptoms. The kinds of hysterical symptoms prevalent in the Victorian society in which Freud worked were disturbances in the senses and/or the musculature: for example, blindness, paralyses, mutism, convulsive-like motor actions (e.g., trembling), and anesthesia (i.e., loss of or diminished sensation in one or more parts of the body). These symptoms came to be regarded as psychological when no organic basis for them could be found. Undoubtedly, some organic conditions were mistaken for neurotic ones and vice versa.

Prior to the development of any form of psychoanalytic therapy, the main methods of treating emotional and mental disturbances were rest, massage, hydrotherapy (warm baths), faradic therapy (the application of low-voltage electrical stimulation to areas of the body that were symptomatic), and hypnosis. As we shall see later, psychoanalysis evolved from attempts to treat symptoms via hypnosis (Bernheim, 1886; Charcot, 1882; Janet, 1907).

Dissatisfied with the existing methods of treating these "nervous conditions," Freud became particularly interested in the potential of hypnotic suggestion as a therapeutic tool. He began to employ hypnosis in his practice, at first using the direct suggestion that the symptom(s) disappear. This approach generally met with limited success. Some patients could not readily be hypnotized; in others, symptoms would dissipate but return. These early clinical experiences led Freud to become more curious about the causes and mechanisms of symptom formation and to search for more effective therapeutic methods. With regard to the latter, Freud sometimes used the so-called "pressure technique" in which he placed his hand on the patient's forehead and gave the strong suggestion that the patient would remember the original experience associated with the onset of the symptoms. These early variations in technique evolved into the method of *free association* in which the patient is asked to say whatever comes to mind without the usual editing and inhibition characteristic of typical social interactions.

The patient known as Anna O provided a critical turning point for Freud and for the development of psychoanalysis. Anna O was suffering from a variety of hysterical symptoms for which she was being treated by Josef Breuer, an eminent Viennese physician. Breuer attempted to hypnotize her and to suggest away her symptoms. However, she wanted to talk (to have a "catharsis") and as he allowed her to do so, she began to recall the memories and affective states that turned out to be the context in which the symptoms originated. This was the birth of the "talking cure."

In the intimate setting of recounting emotionally vivid and meaningful experiences, patients developed an attachment to the doctor. At one point in the course of her treatment with Breuer, Anna O developed a pseudocyesis (a fantasy of being pregnant) which featured the fantasy that Breuer was the father. Breuer, unsettled by this development, left for vacation with his wife. These kinds of emotional reactions by the patient and the therapist led to the development of the central concepts of transference and countertransference (discussed later).

Breuer and Freud published their ideas about their early cases in *Studies in Hysteria* (1895), the key idea contained in this work being that "hysterics suffer from reminiscences." That is, a painful memory is dissociated from the mass of conscious experience and the "quota of affect" associated with that memory is converted to a bodily symptom. The release of the dammed-up affect via talking about the memory allows for the "associative reabsorption" of the blocked idea and causes the symptom to disappear. Breuer and Freud (1895) offered a two-factor theory as to why the memory and its affect were not in consciousness in the first place. The first factor was that the experience in question occurred in an altered state of consciousness (a so-called hypnoid state) so that it failed to connect with the dominant mass of conscious ideas. The second factor was a motivational one, namely, the person did not want to remember the experience.

Here we have the beginnings of a *dynamic* point of view. In this view, the patient is seen as being motivated to keep an idea and its associated affect out of awareness. This defensive effort arises because the idea and its associated affect are considered by the person to be incompatible with the dominant mass of ideas making up the ego. *Repression*, that is, the motivated forgetting of the disagreeable idea or conflicted wish, is a way of repudiating or disavowing impulses that are anxiety arousing or repugnant to one's sense of morality. A key accomplishment of successful defense is self-deception. But, such efforts always weaken the personality by impairing its integrated functioning.

THE CONCEPT OF PERSONALITY

In this early phase of Freud's work, the focus was on the symptom. Symptoms were regarded as circumscribed, disembodied foreign objects to be excised, not unlike an impacted wisdom tooth. The nature of the person in whom the symptoms resided was not considered important. However, Freud soon realized that patients' symptoms were meaningful expressions of their character and overall personality functioning. Over the next several decades Freud evolved his theory of personality development and psychopathology. His followers have extended and modified his ideas, sometimes within the spirit of Freud's core concepts, at other times with significant rejection of those core concepts. Freud himself changed central aspects of his theory many times in the course of his long career. Obviously, I cannot present a complete account of all these theoretical developments but must content myself with a brief statement of the essential concepts. The interested reader should consult Brenner's (1973) *An Elementary Textbook of Psychoanalysis* or Waelder's (1960) *Basic Theory of Psychoanalysis.*

For Freud, the basic unit of study was the intrapsychic life of the individual. He realized that psychic structure is formed in the context of social interaction. The biological helplessness of the infant requires, as a matter of survival, that the mother serve as the supplier and homeostatic regulator of the infant's basic needs. Thus, from the start the infant had to relate to the social world.

Freud believed that there were two basic tendencies governing mental life, the *pleasure principle* and the *reality principle*. According to the pleasure principle, the basic tendency of the organism is to maximize pleasure and to minimize pain and to do so in as rapid and automatic a way as possible. Increases in endogenous excitation were regarded as unpleasant, while decreases were associated with pleasure. Hence, the aim of the organism was to rid itself of excitation as soon as possible. Reality forces the organism to give up sole reliance on the pleasure principle. For example, if the hungry infant hallucinates the mother's breast, it learns that it can achieve a partial, temporary satisfaction. But, it also learns that this gratification is short lived and turns to pain if its hunger pangs continue for any length of time. Thus, "finding" the breast, that is, turning to reality, is essential for satisfaction and survival. In other words, the infant has to adopt the reality principle, if only as an expedient, if it is to find pleasure and survive.

As the infant perceives, thinks, and lays down memories, we have the beginnings of what is called psychic structure. In his paper *Formulations on the Two Principles of Mental Functioning*, Freud (1911) distinguished between two kinds of thinking, primary-process thinking and secondary-process thinking. *Primary-process thinking* is governed by the pleasure principle. It is not governed by the rules of logic but is primitive and directed by the desire for immediate drive discharge. *Secondary-process thinking* is reality oriented and based on a conceptual organization of memories.

The memory of previous experiences of satisfaction forms the basis for wishes. A *wish*, according to Freud, is a desire to reinstate a condition of "perceptual identity"; that is, to have a current experience that matches the memory of a prior experience of satisfaction. To the extent that the wish is pursued without regard to reality considerations, the cognitive elaboration of it should show hallmarks of primary-process thinking. The symbolization, condensation, and displacement seen in dreams and/or in hallucinatory wish fulfillment are instances of primary-process thinking. Even in dreams, however, we see the residual operation of secondary-process thinking. For example, the choice of a symbol is not arbitrary but is based on the structural and functional similarity of the symbol and the thing symbolized.

What are the basic tensions that one must reduce in order to avoid unpleasure? This question brings us to Freud's basic theory of motivation. Freud always postulated two major classes of instinctual drives. At first, the two drives were the sexual or *libidinal* and the self-preservative or *ego instincts*. Later, Freud theorized that the two major drives were the *libidinal* (or sexual) drive and the *aggressive* drive. According to the theory, a drive is the psychical representative of the instinct. It is a demand made on the mind for work. It impels the organism to mental and physical activity the aim of which is to discharge the nervous system excitation produced by the drive. According to Freud, sexuality (broadly conceived as sensual) and aggression were the two basic human motivational sources of behavior.

There are four main characteristics of an instinctual drive; it has a source (a bodily tension), an impetus (a degree of intensity), an aim (to lessen the drive tension), and an object (the means whereby the drive tension is reduced, e.g., sucking one's thumb, milk from mother's breast). The object is the most variable aspect of the drive (i.e., the drive can be more or less satisfied in a number of ways). We do not directly observe drives but infer them on the basis of "drive derivatives" (i.e., wishes). The energy that derives from the instinctual drives is *psychic energy*. The term "cathexis" refers to the amount of sexual or aggressive drive or psychic energy invested in a particular idea, wish, or unconscious fantasy. These energic concepts have been cogently criticized in the past two decades as pseudoscientific explanations that are at best descriptive metaphors designed to capture the force and quantitative aspects of behavior and experience (Holt, 1989).

At first Freud believed that accumulated drive pressure that was not discharged was transformed into anxiety. For example, the practice of coitus interruptus was believed to lead to anxiety. In this connection, he made a distinction between the *actual neuroses* and the *psychoneuroses*. Neurasthenia, anxiety neurosis, and hypochondria were classified as actual neuroses. These syndromes, each of which has clear somatic aspects, were distinguished from the psychoneuroses on the grounds that the latter have a primarily psychological etiology.

Although Freud never quite abandoned the idea of actual neuroses, the concept of *intrapsychic conflict* became the core notion of Freudian theory. If the person believes that the satisfaction of a wish, or even the desire to satisfy it, is dangerous, an approach–avoidance situation is created. This formulation assumed certain typical danger situations in childhood. In developmental order, they are loss of the object, loss of the object's love, castration anxiety, and guilt (the latter two presume the loss of the object's love).[1]

The anticipation of each of these dangers gives rise to signal anxiety and leads to a *defense* against a potentially traumatic anxiety. For example, suppose a young boy has incestuous wishes toward his mother but believes and fears that such wishes will lead to castration by the fa-

ther. The boy, who loves the father as well as fears him and resents him as an unwanted rival, now needs to defend against his sexual wishes toward his mother. This, of course, is the classic *Oedipal conflict* so central to Freudian theory.

Freud's theory has a very strong developmental emphasis. The nature of the child's wishes and preoccupations, and therefore of the corresponding anxieties, differs at different ages. There is an invariant sequence of phases or *stages of psychosexual development*. These stages are the oral, anal, phallic, and genital. Each stage is influenced by the preceding one. As the name implies, the *oral* stage centers on concerns with hunger and maternal care, with the mouth as the chief bodily zone involved. At this stage the primary fear is loss of the object. In the *anal* phase, the focus is on toilet training and the major anxiety is loss of the parent's love. In the *phallic* phase, the boy is subject to castration anxiety, and in the *genital* stage, guilt is the major danger.

There are two other concepts that need to be noted here, *fixation* and *regression*. According to Freud, excessive frustration or satisfaction could lead to a rigid clinging to a particular mode of satisfaction characteristic of that stage. For example, excessive oral satisfaction (or frustration) could lead to the persistence of thumb-sucking long after it is age appropriate. Regression refers to the reinstatement of a mode of seeking satisfaction that is no longer age appropriate. If, for example, the birth of a sibling leaves the older sibling feeling terribly unloved he/she might revert to thumb-sucking. Freud believed that the major modes of adaptation to the environment and to the regulation of tension states are well developed by the time a child is 6 years old and change relatively little after that.

Given this sketch of personality functioning, we may say that the mind is always in a state of dynamic equilibrium as it tries to secure for itself maximum satisfaction with a minimum of pain. Another way of stating this point is that there is always a balance between the attempt to express and satisfy wishes and the attempt to defend and disguise those wishes that are considered likely to arouse more anxiety than pleasure. If we listen to someone free associate in therapy, we can expect to see indications of the expression of and the defense against wishes. That is, we expect to observe the ways in which a person deals with conflict.

Following are some of the core, interrelated propositions of traditional Freudian theory:

1. The principle of psychic determinism states that there is a lawful regularity to mental life; that is, even seemingly random or "accidental" mental phenomena have causes.

2. A substantial part of mental life takes place outside conscious awareness. Unconscious wishes and motives exert a powerful influence on conscious thought and behavior and can explain seemingly random or "accidental behaviors" (e.g., slips of the tongue and many other kinds of parapraxes described by Freud, 1901, in his *The Psychopathology of Everyday Life*).

3. All behavior is motivated by a desire, first, to avoid being rendered helpless by excessive stimulation and, second, to maximize pleasure and minimize pain (the pleasure principle).

4. Inner conflict is inevitable and ubiquitous; all behavior reflects efforts at effecting a compromise among the various components of the personality, principally one's desires for instinctual drive gratification (sexual and aggressive) and the constraints against such gratification (physical reality, social constraints, and superego prohibitions). This proposition takes its fullest form in Freud's (1923, 1926) structural theory of id, ego, and superego.

5. Anxiety in small doses (i.e., signal anxiety) is a danger signal that triggers defensive measures designed to avoid awareness and/or behavior geared toward gratification of unconscious wishes in order to avoid an anticipated full-blown traumatic experience of anxiety which would totally overwhelm the ego and flood the organism with an unmanageable amount of excitation.

6. A complete explanation of psychological phenomena should include multiple points of view, or what has been called metapsychology (Rapaport & Gill, 1959): genetic (i.e., developmental), adaptive, dynamic, topographical, economic, and structural. These terms refer, respectively, to the psychosexual stages of development (with their corresponding *zones* of pleasures and *modes* of behavior); the coping devices and defensive measures by which the ego mediates between the motivational drive pressures, external reality, and superego prohibitions; the nature of the conflicts involved; the relation of mental contents to consciousness; the energic and quantitative aspects of the dynamic interplay of forces in the mind; and the organization of the tripartite psychic apparatus (id, ego, and superego). It should be noted that id, ego, and superego are hypothetical constructs by which the observer organizes the aspects of behavior that are likely to conflict with one another; they are not concrete entities doing battle with one another, even though in the analytic literature it often sounds like they are.

7. The principle of multiple determination (sometimes misleadingly called overdetermination) refers to the facts of divergent and convergent causality; that is, the same motive can give rise to myriad behaviors and a given behavior is a function of multiple motives.

8. Finally, Freud's notion of a "complementary series" makes room for the joint contribution and interaction of ge-

netic/constitutional and environmental factors as determinants of behavior.

Psychoanalytic ego psychology, aspects of which were clearly implied by Freud, was further developed by Anna Freud (1937), Hartmann, Kris, and Loewenstein (1946), and others. As seen by these theorists, ego capacities (e.g., cognition, delay of gratification, reality testing, and judgment) have an innate, autonomous basis independent of instinctual drives. In Hartmann's (1939) terms, there are ego apparatuses that have "primary autonomy" (i.e., originate and evolve independently of the drives) and there are ego functions that achieve "secondary autonomy" (i.e., are implicated at some point in conflict but later function as "conflict-free spheres of the ego"). This theoretical thrust was an attempt to flesh out the ego's role in adaptation and to balance Freud's strong emphasis on the primacy and dominance of the instinctual drives with a recognition that there are behaviors, interests, and motives that are not always or simply indirect expressions or sublimations of sexual or aggressive wishes.

Mahler's (1968) studies of separation–individuation and Jacobson's work on the self (1964) and on psychotic depression (1967) have contributed significantly to our understanding of the development of the self, a topic not directly dealt with in early psychoanalytic writings. In more recent years, issues of self-esteem and disturbances in the sense of self have been a prominent focus of psychoanalytic theorizing, particularly in borderline and narcissistic conditions (Kernberg, 1975; Kohut, 1971, 1977, 1984). These theoretical developments owe much to Freud's (1914) paper *On Narcissism*, which contains numerous implications for our conceptions of psychosis, character development, and object relations.

THE PATHOLOGICAL OR DYSFUNCTIONAL INDIVIDUAL

Behavior is dysfunctional or pathological to the extent that the compromise formations among the constituents of the personality are "maladaptive." That is, they create more pain than pleasure, bring the person into significant interpersonal conflict, create undue anxiety and/or guilt and depressive affects, lead to significant inhibitions in personal functioning, and thereby impair the person's capacity to love and/or work. In this view, there is no sharp demarcation between "normal" and "abnormal" functioning.

Stated in the psychoanalytic language of ego psychology, one may ask: How well does the individual adapt to the "average expectable environment"? How adaptive versus maladaptive or pathological are the person's compromise formations? *Pathological compromise formations* refer to outcomes of psychic conflict in which the ego is ineffective in arriving at a solution to the problem of dealing with drive pressures and opposing superego demands. The appearance of symptoms or the development of ego inhibitions are indications of ineffective coping with inner conflict. Thus, the onset of agoraphobia (fear of open spaces) can represent the person's failed defense against the anxiety attached to desires to separate and function in a more autonomous manner, desires that may be experienced as arousing separation anxiety as well as reflecting wishes to rid oneself of the maternal object and thereby induce feelings of guilt. The onset of hysterical blindness in a mother who harbors hostile wishes toward her son, who then has a bad accident because his mother was not watching him, would be understood, in part, as a self-punishment for her hostile wishes. In another example, impotence in a male in relation to certain women but not others may be due to the fact that the women with whom the impotence occurs are unconsciously regarded as incestuous objects, and the impotence is an inhibition of unacceptable and anxiety-ridden Oedipal wishes.

The psychoanalytic formula for the formation of symptoms is that there is a wish that is too strong and/or defenses that are too weak to contain it in a sufficiently disguised form. In this drive-defense model, symptoms appear as a second line of defense to help ward off the awareness and/or expression of wishes (drive derivatives) that are deemed too threatening and/or unacceptable. Symptoms vary with respect to the extent to which they show evidence of the underlying wish or show more clearly the defensive side of the conflict.

The maintenance of symptoms is due to the *primary* and *secondary* gain they provide. The primary gain is the relative freedom from anxiety that is achieved while partially satisfying a wish in a compromise form. Secondary gain refers to the fringe benefits of a symptom (e.g., justifiable escape from normal responsibilities and increased satisfaction of needs for nurturance).

The drive-defense model also is used as part of the explanation for the development of personality or character styles. For example, a pattern of noncommitment in relationships may protect the person against the feared consequences of intimacy in instances in which intimacy might give rise to claustrophobic anxiety, which in turn signifies a sense of danger about what may be seen as an "Oedipal triumph."[2] To avoid this anxiety, the person chooses to enter relationships that are at some level "known" to preclude the possibility of a serious commitment. When this is repeated on an unconscious basis, the person may have the experience of feeling frustrated and puzzled at the failure of any of his/her relationships to last. Thus, the persistence of even maladaptive behavior patterns reflects the powerful tendency to keep alive the painful as well as the pleasurable aspects of internalized object relations.

With respect to "choice" of symptoms, Freud, early on, held the simplistic belief that the nature of infantile sexual experience determined the type of symptoms that would appear later. He thought, for example, that a passive sexual experience led to hysterical symptoms while an active sexual experience led to obsessional symptoms. With the abandonment of the *seduction theory* (i.e., the idea that hysterical symptoms would not occur unless the patient had experienced a sexual seduction as a child), Freud, in 1897, came a long way in recognizing that there was no simple correspondence between a particular external event and the type of symptom that might ensue. The question of the "choice" of symptom became as complex as the determinants of personality development and the individual's psychic reality.

It is worth noting that although Freud has been criticized for giving up the seduction theory, Freud clearly never gave up his belief that sexual and other environmental trauma took place. However, and this was decisive for the evolution of psychoanalytic thinking, what was significant for psychological development was what the individual did with what happened to him/her. That is, not everyone reacts to the same external trauma in the same way and individual differences in the way people do react affect and are affected by the conflicts and means of coping and defending they bring to the situation.

It should be apparent thus far that psychoanalytic theory does not make a sharp distinction between symptom neuroses and character neuroses, nor does it posit a sharp dividing line between what is regarded as "normal" versus "pathological." With respect to the distinction between symptoms and character traits, it is true that the former refer to discrete, circumscribed impairments in functioning that the patient usually, but by no means always, experiences as ego alien. However, more subtle, behavioral patterns that are not classified as symptoms may and often do cause distress and can be experienced as ego alien. For example, the person who "engineers" one rejection after another in work and/or in love would be seen as having a character style with significant masochistic components. Such a person unconsciously seeks suffering, which is associated with pleasure, even while consciously claiming to want to change. The usual formulation that symptoms are always ego alien and that maladaptive character traits are always ego syntonic is too simple.

Since these formulations and the early contributions by Abraham (1927), Reich (1933), and others, there has been an increasing interest in studying character and character pathology. This interest is due to the apparently growing number of patients who present with character pathology, particularly narcissistic and borderline personalities, rather than symptom neuroses, and to the idea that dealing with symptoms in treatment is impossible without addressing the character issues in which they are embedded.

By personality or character we mean the unique psychological organization (of traits, conflicts, defensive and coping strategies, attitudes, values, cognitive style, etc.) that characterizes the individual's stable, enduring modes of adaptation across a wide range of conditions encountered in the individual's "average expectable environment" (Hartmann, 1939). The multiple determinants of character include biological, psychological, and sociocultural factors. The complex interactions of these factors are best described in Erikson's (1950) *Childhood and Society.*

Two major psychological paths to character formation, which of course are influenced by biological and sociological factors, are one's identifications with significant others and one's style of coping and defense. Maladaptive patterns of dealing with conflict tend to become rigidified and repeated in vicious cycles, as will be seen in the case presented later. By definition, personality structure changes at a slow rate. This is one reason why meaningful personality change through psychotherapy generally takes a long time.

THE ASSESSMENT OF DYSFUNCTION

The unit of study is the individual or, more specifically, his/her inner world. Although the clinician will want to know a great deal about the individual's actual functioning in different social contexts (family, friends, work groups, etc.), the relevance of this information is its value in understanding the intrapsychic world of the individual.

The primary means of conducting the assessment of the individual's psychopathology is through the clinical interview. The interview serves simultaneously to assess the prospective patient's suitability and motivation for treatment. In earlier years, if the first few interviews did not reveal any gross contraindications to the start of treatment, clinicians began with a *trial analysis* in order to have an extended period in which to assess suitability for analytic treatment. In recent years, this decision is generally made after two or three consultations.

Referrals for psychological testing are relatively rare, both at the stage of the initial assessment as well as later on. Testing is more likely to be recommended when there is little treatment progress or marked unclarity regarding diagnosis (e.g., if organicity or a learning disability is suspected).

In the course of the clinical interview, the therapist attempts to form an initial picture of the patient's current and past level of functioning, including the nature, onset, duration, intensity, and fluctuation of symptoms. The therapist also begins to get a sense of the patient's character style, his/her principal defenses, and the core, unconscious conflicts presumed to underlie manifest aspects of behavior. The clinician will also want to develop some hypotheses concerning the psychodynamic significance of the current stresses faced by the prospective patient, the manner and effectiveness with which they are handled, and the patient's decision to seek treatment at this time. Part of this broad assessment of the patient's psychopathology and personality functioning includes an appraisal of the person's ego interests, areas of and capacity for pleasure and achievement, and quality of interpersonal relations.

The clinician also attempts to appraise the prospective patient's suitability for psychoanalysis or psychoanalytic psychotherapy. Among the main qualities evaluated are the person's motivation for change, ego resources, including capacity to regress in the service of the ego, and degree of psychological-mindedness. The latter refers to the patient's capacity for self-reflective awareness, for an introspective tuning in on one's inner experiences, fantasies, and dreams. Because analysis requires that the patient oscillate between verbalizing his/her subjective experience and, in collaboration with the analyst, reflecting on the multiple meanings of those experiences, an inability or disinclination to view experience and behavior in psychological terms does not bode well for this form of treatment.

Because an implicit and explicit condition for meaningful introspection, and a value undergirding the therapeutic situation, is self-examination, the capacity to tolerate frustration and not act impulsively is considered a prognostically favorable sign. As indicated earlier, there is a vital collaborative aspect to the analytic work. Therefore, the patient's history of sustained, satisfying interpersonal relationships and reasonably intact reality testing are relevant predictors of the collaborative quality of the prospective therapeutic relationship.

In addition to the kinds of assessments mentioned, the analyst should also conduct a self-assessment to try to get a sense of whether there are particular personality conflicts, personal biases (e.g., with respect to value systems), or other factors that might preclude the possibility of maintaining the objectivity and attitudes necessary to be helpful to the patient. If there are such potential problems, referral to another clinician is indicated.

Finally, the therapist will need to assess the patient's reality situation to determine whether matters of money, time, and/or immediate crises in the patient's life would interfere significantly with the possibility of a sustained, unhurried exploration of his/her core conflicts. In the event that such factors are present to a strong degree, an alternative approach is recommended (e.g., a delay in the beginning of treatment, crisis intervention, and/or a more supportive, less challenging therapy).

There is no universally accepted, formal psychoanalytic system for diagnosing different varieties of dysfunction. Originally, Freud focused primarily on three symptom pictures: hysterical, obsessional, and phobic. Other psychiatric syndromes soon received attention (e.g., depression, paranoid conditions, bipolar disorder, schizophrenia, and perversions). In recent years, narcissistic and borderline conditions have been the focus of intense interest, as such patients are increasingly common in psychoanalytic practice.

Psychoanalysts have contributed to and generally follow the diagnostic system of the fourth edition of the *Diagnostic and Statistical Manual of Mental Disorders* (DSM-IV; American Psychiatric Association, 1994) even though its successive versions have become increasingly atheoretical and less sympathetic to a psychoanalytic viewpoint. However, many analysts do not place much value on an initial, formal diagnosis beyond the gross classification of the patient as psychotic, borderline, or neurotic. Many, if not most, patients seen in private analytic practices rarely meet all the DSM-IV criteria for a given diagnostic category but frequently approximate, especially as the treatment unfolds, the criteria for several diagnostic categories. That is, rarely do we see pure types and, in any case, the focus is more on the underlying dynamics than on the changing symptom picture. Furthermore, a purely descriptive classification that does not attempt to address etiological and dynamic factors is of limited interest or clinical utility to psychoanalytic clinicians.

THE PRACTICE OF THERAPY

Basic Structure of Therapy

Before discussing the basic structure of therapy, we have to address the distinction between psychoanalysis and psychoanalytically oriented psychotherapy. There are those who would make a very sharp, qualitative distinction between these two forms of treatment and those who view the differences as relatively unimportant. The field is beset with often heated and endless arguments regarding what should properly be called "psychoanalysis." In these controversies it has been easiest to fall back on simple external criteria for what is "really" analysis as opposed to therapy. The implication, of course, is that psychoanalysis, whenever it is applicable, is the superior form of therapeutic intervention. It is regarded as a deeper, more thorough approach to the patient's problems. Freud and traditional Freudians have maintained that whenever a patient is suitable for standard psychoanalysis it is the treatment of choice as the other forms of treatment mix the "pure gold of psychoanalysis" with the "copper of suggestion" (Freud, 1919, p. 168). Thus, the common clinical maxim that has guided psychoanalysts is to be as supportive as necessary and as exploratory as possible.

Relying on external criteria, psychoanalysis is defined in large part by the frequency of sessions and the use of the couch. Sessions typically are held three or four times per week, for 45 or 50 minutes, over a period of many years. Psychoanalytic psychotherapy usually takes place at a frequency of once or twice a week in the face-to-face position and can last as long as psychoanalysis or may be as short as 12 sessions (e.g., Crits-Christoph & Barber, 1991; Malan, 1976).

A more meaningful distinction between psychoanalysis and psychoanalytic psychotherapy, as well as between these forms of treatment compared with others, would focus on intrinsic rather than extrinsic features (Gill, 1984). In this regard, the nature of the therapist's focus in psychoanalysis is on transference and resistance (to be described later). Such a focus is considered to be the most emotionally meaningful and therefore most effective way of helping patients become aware of how and why they are reenacting conflicts from the past in the present, particularly in relation to the therapist. Although such explorations go on in psychoanalytic psychotherapy, they are not as prolonged or detailed, nor do they focus as systematically on the past and on the transference.

The range of psychoanalytically informed treatment can be ordered on a continuum from classical psychoanalysis at one end to psychoanalytic psychotherapy (or expressive therapy) in the center to supportive psychotherapy at the other end. These modalities are best regarded as overlapping and distinguishable from one another to the extent that they focus on the interpretation of transference resistances. The greater the reliance on interpretation and the less the emphasis on suggestion and on healing through the direct benefits of the therapeutic relationship per se, the more closely the treatment can be said to be psychoanalysis. The powerful and innovative feature of psychoanalysis is the attempt, paradoxical in nature, to use the therapist's authority to free the patient from excessive reliance on suggestion and authority. This is less the case in expressive therapy and even less in supportive treatment, where the therapist capitalizes on his/her authority and uses direct suggestions more freely.

It should be clear that none of the three, overlapping modalities arranged on the continuum outlined above are pure types; rather, it is matter of emphasis. There are both deliberately supportive and inherently supportive elements in classical psychoanalysis, and, interpretations, though not central, are found in supportive treatments. It is also the case that a treatment that begins with an intent to use one modality will, given certain clinical indications, shift to another modality.

In what follows I shall talk primarily about psychoanalysis with the understanding that a good deal of what is said is more or less applicable to psychoanalytic psychotherapy.

The Conduct of the Sessions

Who determines what the patient talks about? Although sessions in psychoanalytic psychotherapy generally are relatively less unstructured than in psychoanalysis, in both approaches, compared with supportive psychotherapy based on psychoanalytic principles, the sessions are essentially unstructured. That is, the patient determines the content of the session. The goal of encouraging the patient to free associate is a mediating or process goal. That is, it is assumed that the nondirected verbalization of thoughts and feelings will reveal the patient's core issues, with respect both to content and to the manner in which the patient institutes defensive maneuvers in the face of actual or anticipated anxiety or other dysphoric affect. The analyst wants to encourage the free expression of thoughts and feelings because this will enable the patient to get an increasingly clear sense of how his/her mind works and how these workings are shaped by unconscious factors.

Rarely is a time limit imposed on the therapy. The main exception is brief, psychoanalytically oriented treatments in which the patient is explicitly informed that the treatment will last only for a limited number of sessions (see Sifneos, 1987, and Mann, 1973, for such approaches).

In individual treatment, significant others in the patient's life typically are not seen by the patient's therapist. Sometimes combined formats are used. For example, a patient in individual treatment may also be seen as part of a couple, family, or group therapy. In these circumstances, it generally is not considered proper practice for the patient's individual therapist to treat the patient in one of the other modalities as well. To do so would interfere with the optimal development and resolution of the transference.

Goal Setting

Stated in general terms, the ultimate goal of treatment is to increase the patient's adaptive functioning by ameliorating the disabling symptoms and crippling inhibitions that have plagued the patient. As the patient gradually reduces the neurotic vicious cycles that characterized his/her prior adaptive efforts, he/she will experience this change as involving an expanded sense of personal agency and freedom. Usually, this goal is assumed to be so basic and obvious as to not require explicit verbalization.

Although this is the patient's presumed goal, it is one that can contradict the patient's often unconscious need to suffer. It is not surprising to a psychoanalytic clinician to observe that after a period of improvement in treatment the patient may deteriorate. Freud called this the "negative therapeutic reaction" and regarded it as a serious obstacle to some treatments.

In the final paragraph of *Studies on Hysteria*, Freud, in response to a patient's query, stated, "No doubt fate would find it easier than I do to relieve you of your illness. But you will be able to convince yourself that much will be gained if we succeed in transforming your hysterical misery into common unhappiness" (Breuer & Freud, 1895, p. 305). At first he thought that this transformation was achieved by "making the unconscious conscious." His later epigrammatic statement of the goal of psychoanalysis, consistent with the replacement of the topographic theory (conscious, preconscious, unconscious) by the structural theory (id, ego, superego), was "where id was, there shall ego be" (Freud, 1933, p. 80). In other words, awareness was still a necessary but no longer sufficient condition for change. The patient must also be able to *integrate* previously disavowed, split-off aspects of his/her personality. This is another way of talking about the resolution of conflict.

As stated in his 1923 paper, Freud indicated the goal of analysis as follows:

It may be laid down that the aim of the treatment is to remove the patient's resistances and to pass his repressions in review and thus to bring about the most far-reaching unification and strengthening of his ego, to enable him to save the mental energy which he is expending on internal conflicts, to make the best of him that his inherited capacities will allow and so to make him as efficient and as capable of enjoyment as is possible. The removal of the symptoms of the illness is not specifically aimed at, but is achieved, as it were, as a by-product if the analysis is properly carried through. (p. 251)

It should be clear that the resolution of conflict is far from an all-or-none, once-and-for-all matter. In this sense, analysts do not expect to "cure" their patients. This point is depicted humorously in a cartoon in which the first picture, titled "Before Therapy," shows a man riding a motorcycle with a monkey on his back; the second picture is captioned "After Therapy" and shows the man riding his motorcycle and the monkey seated in the sidecar. If we can help the patient avoid tripping over his/her own feet, we have accomplished a lot.

Support for this point of view is found in a series of studies by Luborsky and his colleagues (e.g., Luborsky & Crits-Christoph, 1990). They have examined treatment protocols to identify core conflictual relationship themes (CCRTs) based on an assessment of relationship episodes described by the patient. A CCRT consists of a wish expressed by the patient, the response by the person to whom the wish is directed, and the patient's reaction to the response of the other. Patients typically show a few key CCRTs that remain fairly stable over the course of treatment in the sense that the same themes continue to be expressed. What changes is that the patient handles his/her issues in a more adaptive manner and with less subjective distress.

Techniques and Strategies of Therapy

The main strategy in the conduct of psychoanalytic treatment is the analysis of the resistances and transferences that emerge from the patient's "free associations." For the most part, I shall have to ask the reader to wait until the "Case Illustration" section (below) for concrete examples of the application of strategies and techniques of treatment.

We can frame our discussion here by citing Gill's (1954) often quoted definition: "Psychoanalysis is that technique which, employed by a neutral analyst, results in the development of a regressive transference neurosis and the ultimate resolution of this neurosis by techniques of interpretation alone" (p. 775). I shall defer a discussion of neutrality until the next main section of the chapter and focus on the two other key elements of the definition, regressive transference neurosis and interpretation. First, however, I need to define the term "transference."

Transference

Transference, according to Greenson (1967) is the "experience of feelings, drives, attitudes, fantasies, and defenses toward a person in the present which do not befit that person but are a repetition of reactions originating in regard to significant persons of early childhood, unconsciously displaced onto figures in the present" (p. 155). In describing transference as a "new edition of an old object relationship," Freud (1912, p.116) was aware that the repetition need not be literal.

Transference reactions to emotionally significant persons in the present are fairly ubiquitous and are not restricted to experiences in analysis. In fact, in everyday life they often are a source of considerable difficulty in interpersonal relationships. What is distinctive about psychoanalytic treatment is that they are *analyzed*.

Freud originally classified transference reactions into three kinds: the positive (erotic) transference, the negative (hostile), and the unobjectionable (i.e., aim inhibited or nonerotic), positive transference necessary for cooperating and collaborating in the analytic work. We have come to see that transference reactions typically are ambivalent, as are reactions to significant others in any relationship. The other characteristics of transference reactions, which essentially follow from Greenson's definition, are that they show evidence of inappropriateness, tenacity, and capriciousness. In this sense, whatever germs of veridicality they may contain, transference reactions are considered inaccurate, distorted attributions about the emotional experience, behavior, intentions, and other aspects of the analyst's behavior.

The intense concentration of the patient's core conflicts on the person of the analyst in the form of feelings, fantasies, and marked preoccupation in an increasingly regressive manner has been termed the "transference neurosis." It should also be noted that the patient's readiness for the emergence of a regressive transference neurosis (Macalpine, 1950) is facilitated by certain features of the analytic situation (e.g., the relative anonymity of the analyst, the withholding of deliberate transference gratifications, the invitation to free associate, and the supine position of the patient).

In the traditional Freudian account, the analysis of the transference neurosis reveals the *infantile neurosis* (the central conflicts of childhood, whether or not they were clinically manifest at that time). However, Cooper (1987) believes that "the concept of the transference neurosis has lost its specificity and efforts to clarify it no longer expand our vision. The concept should be abandoned" (p. 587). Although most analysts appear reluctant to discard the concept, it is increasingly recognized that (1) the transference neurosis does not *replace* the patient's ongoing neurosis, (2) not all patients regularly develop a clearly identifiable transference neurosis, and (3) effective analytic work occurs in the absence of a fully formed transference neurosis.

It is sufficient for our present purposes to think in terms of a continuum of intensity of transference reactions. The greater the degree to which the patient's current and infantile conflicts center on the person of the analyst and, correspondingly, the more intense and pervasive the preoccupation with the analyst, the more closely does the patient's state approximate what has been called transference neurosis. As a practical matter, our clinical approach is essentially the same whether we call the patient's reactions a "transference neurosis" or refer to them as "significant transference reactions." Issues of terminology are not as significant as stressing the affectively charged, vivid reliving of past relationships in the patient's current experience with the therapist that makes eventual awareness of these experiences emotionally meaningful and convincing and gives transference interpretations a particularly mutative impact. As Freud (1912) observed, one cannot slay anyone "*in absentia* or *in effigy*" (p. 108).

In concluding this section, I would like to make two points regarding transference. First, transference is not simply a matter of bringing the past into the present. Thus, the analytic relationship is simultaneously a new experience as well as a reenactment of earlier experiences. The "modernist" view of transference (Cooper, 1987) stresses the aspect of new experience; the "historical" view emphasizes the aspect of reliving the past. In the historical view, the experiencing of the "here-and-now" transference is important not only in its own right but as a path toward the revival and recovery of childhood memories and the reconstruction of the past through genetic transference interpretations. In the modernist view, successfully analyzing the "here-and-now" transference is equivalent to dissipating the neurosis. Keep in mind that these are matters of emphasis, not either–or distinctions.

Second, in recent years Gill (1982) has challenged the traditional view of transference as a distortion or an "inappropriate" reaction because that view creates the danger that the therapist will fail to recognize that the patient's reactions often are plausible responses to the therapist's behavior and technique. The classical conception of transference is seen as one rooted in an outmoded, positivistic, so-called "one-person psychology" (Modell, 1984).

However, the contemporary Freudian analyst (Boesky, 1990; Jacobs, 1986; McLaughlin, 1991) is comfortable in recognizing his/her contribution to determining the content, intensity, and form of the patient's transference *while* inferring that the patient is "distorting" (overreacting to, exaggerating, or selectively reading) the analyst's contributions for reasons deriving primarily from the patient's past. Boesky (1990), for example, writes: "I am quite convinced that the transference as *resistance* in any specific case is unique and would never, and could never, have developed in the identical manner, form, or sequence with any other analyst" (p. 572).

Interpretation

Turning now to interpretation, we may say that interpretation (particularly though not exclusively of the transference) leading to insight is regarded as the major curative factor in psychoanalytic treatment. Interpretation, broadly conceived, refers both to meanings attributed to discrete aspects of the patient's behavior and experience and to constructions that attempt to offer a more comprehensive account of portions of the patient's history.

Schematically stated, the optimal interpretation, though not necessarily presented comprehensively at one time, would take the form of "what you are doing (feeling, thinking, fantasizing, etc.) with me now is what you also are doing with your current significant other (spouse, child, boss, etc.), and what you did with your father (and/or mother) for such and such reasons and motives and with such and such consequences." In the convergence of the past and the present (both in the treatment relationship as well as other current relationships) the recognition of repetitive, pervasive, and entrenched patterns of relating and of personal functioning can have maximum emotional and cognitive impact.

Although interpretation of transference resistances is "the single most important instrument of psychoanalytic technique" (Greenson, 1967, p. 97), other interventions are necessary prerequisites to interpretation. For example, *confrontation* and *clarification* are preparatory to interpretation. Confrontation points to the fact of resistance (e.g., "I notice that when you are reminded of your mother, you quickly change the subject"). Clarification refers to exploration of why the patient is resisting (e.g., "Talking about your mother that way seems to have made you uncomfortable"). This line of inquiry blends into interpretations of the unconscious fantasies and motives for the resistance (e.g., "You think that wishing to be alone with your mother was wrong and that I will chastise you for feeling that way"). A detailed exposition of these techniques can be found in Greenson (1967).

It should be noted that when Gill (1954) speaks of "interpretation *alone*" (italics added), he means that although many other interventions occur in psychoanalysis, in addition to confrontation and clarification, the reliance on interpre-

tation leading to insight is the key element. The power of the transference is used to resolve the transference through interpretation rather than through suggestion (i.e., the direct manipulation of the transference; for example, praising the patient or telling the patient how to act). At the same time, it is recognized that the effect of interpretations is to some extent carried by the positive transference. According to Freud (1940) the positive transference "becomes the *true motive force* of the patient's collaboration . . . he leaves off his symptoms and seems apparently to have recovered—merely for the sake of the analyst" (p. 175; italics added).

Thus, the overarching therapeutic strategy is to foster and maintain the conditions necessary for interpreting the transference. However, there will be occasions, particularly with the so-called nonclassical analytic patient, when one will knowingly and advisedly employ nonanalytic interventions, including advice, active support, suggestions, and so on. These deviations from classical technique have been termed "parameters" (Eissler, 1953) and should be used whenever the patient's ego cannot tolerate adherence to the standard procedures. Ideally, such parameters should be as minimal and as temporary as possible, their meaning and impact should be subsequently analyzed, and they should not preclude the possibility of returning to an analytic process. For example, if the patient is in a state of panic and fears being overwhelmed by sexual and/or aggressive impulses and the therapist thinks that such fears are realistic, the therapist will need to reassure the patient that attempts will be made to make sure that the patient does not harm him/herself or the therapist. At such times, measures such as medication and/or hospitalization may be indicated. In all instances, the guiding consideration is the survival and welfare of the patient, even if this means that psychoanalysis or psychoanalytic psychotherapy is no longer the treatment of choice and that a more supportive treatment is required.

Psychoanalysis and psychoanalytically oriented psychotherapy have been differentiated from other forms of psychotherapy on the grounds that the effects of psychotherapy rest on the impact of the interaction, for example, the explicit and implicit suggestions offered by the therapist, rather than on interpretations (Oremland, 1991). It should be clear that everything that transpires between the patient and therapist, including interpretations, constitutes an interaction. Thus, as Oremland (1991) reminds us, the distinction is really between interactions that emphasize interpretations and interactions that do not. Thus, interpretations are particular kinds of interactions. Therefore, to say that an interpretation is a relational event, as several object relations clinicians have stressed lately, is not a statement that any contemporary Freudian would question.

In fact, from a psychoanalytic perspective, Freudian or otherwise, a vital focus of interpretive work is the patient's experience of an interpretation. The analyst is as interested in this aspect of the process as in the content of the interpretation. For example, does the patient experience an interpretation as an instance of feeling empathically understood (and how does he/she feel if it is not such an instance)? Is the fact and/or the content of an interpretation experienced as a humiliation, a gift, a sexual penetration, or all of the above?

By maintaining such a focus on the patient's reaction to the fact as well as the content of the analyst's interpretation, the analyst reduces the possibility of unanalyzed interactions. Let me illustrate this point with an example, taken from Basescu (1990), that seems to be an instance of an unanalyzed interaction:

One woman said, "I had a bad weekend. Other people are stable. I'm so up and down. I hide my rockiness." I said, "Don't we all." She: "You too?" I: "Does that surprise you?" She: "Well, I guess not. You're human too." I understood that to mean she also felt human, at least for the moment." (p. 54)

Wachtel (1993) cites this example approvingly as "a forthright approach to conveying a version of Sullivan's 'we are all much more simply human than otherwise.'" He regards this kind of interchange as "one of the many small increments in reappropriated humanity that in their sum constitute a successful therapy" (p. 217).

The traditional Freudian, as well as many analysts of other persuasions, would view Basescu's remark as a noninterpretive, supportive effort to soothe the patient's self-denigration instead of exploring the meanings of the patient's statement. What does it mean to her that she feels unstable and has a need to hide it? Does she find it shameful? If so, why and in what contexts? Is she envious of others, including the therapist? Why does she idealize the therapist and what implications does this have for her interpersonal relationships? Is she complaining that the therapist has not yet helped her reach a more stable existence? These are a few of the possible lines of exploration that the analytic therapist would want to pursue in an effort to facilitate an understanding of the motives, origins, and functions of her self-denigration. Unless the patient is in a dire situation, to reassure her by his self-disclosure, to directly dissuade the patient of her self-denigrating attitude and of her idealization of the therapist, is to run the serious risk of not getting to an awareness and an understanding of the patient's underlying conflicts.

A few final comments are in order before we leave the topic of interpretation. The shifting cultural attitude away from a positivistic, objective, knowable reality toward a more relativistic, pluralistic, constructivist stance has had a significant impact on psychoanalysis, particularly with regard to its views of interpretation. This change has been referred to as the "hermeneutic turn" in psychoanalysis. From this perspective, interpretations are regarded much more as constructions than as discoveries of an underlying psychic reality. Parallel to this view is an altered conception of transference–countertransference in which two subjectivities are in constant interaction, in which the transference is decisively shaped by the analyst's countertransference and thus not to be viewed simply as a distortion. Lines of interpretation are considered to be as much the analyst's preferred story lines and narratives as they are veridical readings of the patient's psychic reality (Schafer, 1992). In part, this view is an antidote to an analytic stance in which the analyst thinks that he/she possesses something akin to interpretive infallibility, a countertransference danger that can plague any analyst regardless of theoretical persuasion.

Resistance

As the patient attempts to free associate and the analyst offers interpretations, the patient will inevitably show evidence of *resistance* both to the awareness of warded-off mental contents and to the behavioral and attitudinal changes that might be attempted based on the awareness of previously repressed material. Resistance, following Gill (1982), can be defined as defense expressed in the transference, though Freud (1900) defined it more broadly as "anything that interferes with the analysis."

Because the patient fears the anxiety and/or depressive affect (e.g., humiliation, shame, and guilt) that is anticipated as an accompaniment to the awareness of certain wishes and fantasies, the natural tendency is to defend against and to avoid becoming aware of those mental contents. At the same time, the analytic situation has been deliberately designed to maximize the possibility of such awareness. Two main features expected to facilitate expanded awareness are the "fundamental rule" of free association and the interpretive activity of the therapist. The more freely the patient talks, the more he/she is able and willing to suspend the normal inhibitions and editing processes that are part and parcel of our usual dialogues with others, the more introspective and self-disclosing the person will be, and the easier it will be for previously repressed or suppressed feelings and thoughts to come under analytic scrutiny. (This is also the rationale for the use of the couch.) Although the patient seeks greater self-understanding and indeed sought this form of treatment knowing that its goal was to undo self-deception, there is at the same time a reluctance to fully open up to another person even when one is reasonably trusting of that person.

Resistance can and does take many forms, both blatant (e.g., a deliberate refusal to say what is on one's mind) and subtle (e.g., filling every silence quickly out of fear that the analyst would be critical of "resistance"). I chose this last example to make two points: (1) The patient's resistance will usually be connected to the analyst and it is these transference resistances that are the major focus of analytic attention, and (2) patients (and, unfortunately also many therapists) think of resistance as something bad, as something to be overcome. This pejorative connotation doubtless derives from the early days of psychoanalysis in which Freud used hypnosis, pressure techniques, and the insistence on complete candor ("You *must* pledge to tell me *everything* that comes to mind") in the initial formulation of the "fundamental rule." However, as Freud (1912) also said, "The resistance accompanies the treatment step by step. Every single association, every act of the person under treatment must reckon with the resistance and represents a compromise between the forces that are striving towards recovery and the opposing ones" (p. 103).

Thus, resistance naturally and inevitably includes "opposition to free association, to the procedures of analysis, to recall, to insight, and to change" (Eagle & Wolitzky, 1992, p. 124). In this sense, to refer to resistance is to say little more than people defend themselves against anxiety and other dysphoric affects in an analytic situation that fosters free association and the uncovering of repressed conflicts. The underlying sources of the clinical manifestations of resistance, according to Freud (1937), include the constitutional strength of the instinctual drives, rigid defenses, and powerful, repetitive attempts to seek particular, familiar forms of drive gratification.

Finally, it should be noted that the affirmative, as well as the obstructive, aspects of resistance need to be recognized. For instance, resistance can be used in the service of forestalling a feared regression, asserting one's autonomy, or protecting the therapist from one's destructive impulses.

Process of Therapy

According to Freud, in psychoanalysis, which he likened to chess, the opening moves and the end game are fairly standard, but the long middle phase is not predictable and is open to many variations. In psychoanalytic treatment, clinicians distinguish between an opening phase, the extended, middle phase of "working through," and the termination phase.

In general, we are describing the psychoanalytic treatment of the average expectable neurotic patient. Patients with serious borderline and narcissistic conditions require other considerations which we cannot cover within the confines of a single chapter. The interested reader should see Druck (1989).[3]

The primary emphasis in the opening phase is on the establishment of rapport and a good working relationship. This aspect of the therapeutic process has been called the "working alliance" (Greenson, 1965), the "therapeutic alliance" (Zetzel, 1956), and the "helping alliance" (Luborsky, 1984). Although there are differences in these similar-sounding concepts, I will, for present purposes, regard them as equivalent and restrict myself to Greenson's conception.

Working Alliance

According to Greenson (1967), the working alliance is the "relatively nonneurotic, rational relationship between patient and analyst which makes it possible for the patient to work purposefully in the analytic situation" (p. 45). The patient achieves this attitude through an identification with, or at least an adoption of, the clinician's analytic stance in which he/she fosters a collaborative spirit in the interests of facilitating the patient's self-understanding. This alliance between the analyst's analytic attitude and the patient's reasonable ego is not a once-and-for-all achievement but one that is readily disrupted by the patient's transference reactions.

The patient's neurotic suffering and the alliance provide the incentive to embark on and to stay the course of the lengthy analytic journey. The underlying motivation for maintaining the alliance (as well as the willingness to change) is said to be based in large measure on the patient's positive transference to the therapist.

Some authors (e.g., Brenner, 1979; Curtis, 1980) have cautioned that an emphasis on promoting and maintaining the alliance runs the risk of providing the patient with unanalyzed transference gratification and is thus counterproductive. However, virtually all analysts would agree that the patient's capacity to listen to, reflect on, and make effective use of transference interpretations requires the presence of a good working relationship. In empirical studies of psychoanalytic psychotherapy, Luborsky and Crits-Christoph (1990) have found that the strength of the helping alliance, measured early in treatment, is a significant predictor of treatment outcome.

How does one foster the treatment alliance? The primary answer is that one listens empathically and nonjudgmentally, is alert to countertransference reactions, explains, to the extent necessary, the rationale for the rules and the framework of the treatment (e.g., why one does not routinely answer questions), and offers interpretations with proper timing and dosage. By the latter, we mean that we develop a sense of the patient's optimal level of anxiety and his/her vulnerabilities to narcissistic injury (blows to self-esteem). We function in a way that is aimed at not traumatically exceeding these levels. These considerations come under the heading of, for want of a better term, "clinically informed common sense," "clinical wisdom," or "tact" and take precedence over technical rules and precepts for the handling of the opening phase of treatment (or any phase for that matter). Thus, the usual precepts of analyzing defenses before impulses, beginning with the surface, allowing the patient to determine the subject of the session, and so on, are all liable to be suspended if clinical judgment so dictates.

From the perspective described above, the most common and serious technical errors a therapist can make are to function with attitudes or offer interventions that reflect rigid, unconscious, countertransferential, unempathic responsiveness to the patient and that thereby fail to respect the patient's individuality, integrity, and autonomy. Any specific, discrete technical error (e.g., intervening too rapidly and fostering premature closure instead of giving the patient the opportunity to express his/her feelings and thoughts more fully) is considered relatively minor when compared to the kind of retraumatization that will occur if the therapist acts in the manner described above. Thus, common technical errors such as failing to leave the initiative with the patient; frequent interruptions and questions (especially those that call for a simple "yes" or "no" rather than encouraging exploration); offering far-fetched, intellectualized or jargon-filled interpretations; an excess of therapeutic zeal; attitudes of omniscience and grandiosity; dogmatism; the need to be seen as clever; engaging in power struggles with the patient; failure to begin or end the session on time; and being punitive or overly apologetic all derive their potentially adverse effects from the extent to which they express undetected and therefore unmanaged countertransference.

Working Through

In the extended, middle phase of treatment, the focus is on the analysis of transference and resistance with the aim of having the patient "work through" the transference neurosis. Working through refers to "the repetitive, progressive and elaborate explorations of the resistances which prevent insight from leading to change" (Greenson, 1967, p. 42).

In the early days of psychoanalysis, Freud reported some dramatic "cures" in which hysterical symptoms disappeared, at least temporarily, following the recall of the traumatic memories of the experiences that first gave rise to the symptoms. Patients, even fairly sophisticated ones, often have the fantasy that a single, blinding insight will free them to take the path previously not taken because it was unseen or too frightful to pursue. In fact, as patients become aware of their core conflicts they appreciate that they have been repeatedly reenacting many variations of the same theme in ways that they regard as vital, even though such actions also cause them pain and suffering. Becoming aware of one's patterns of maladaptive living in the context of the transference, recalling their similarity to childhood reactions and modes of relating to significant others, and realizing the unconscious fantasies on which they are based rarely in and of themselves lead to rapid changes in behavior.

Recall that Gill (1982) made the distinction between resistance to the awareness of transference and resistance to the resolution of transference. It is particularly this latter resistance that often can be slow to dissolve. The main approach to dealing with this resistance is to help the patient examine the motives for persisting in attitudes and behaviors that maintain the status quo. Fear and guilt concerning the consequences of change (e.g., feelings that one does not deserve to be happy, feeling that changing means that one is abandoning or being disloyal to a parent, and the reluctance to relinquish long cherished fantasies and beliefs) continue to be analyzed so that the secondary as well as the primary gain of the symptoms or neurotic patterns may be lessened.

The repeated exploration and elaboration of the patient's key, unconscious conflicts and the defenses against them as they become expressed in the context of the therapeutic relationship and in other aspects of the patient's life are the core of the analytic process. More specifically, the analytic process can be viewed as consisting of numerous sequences of (1) the patient's resistance, (2) the analyst's interpretation of the resistance, and (3) the patient's responses to the interpretation (Weinshel, 1984).

Termination

Relatively little has been written regarding termination compared with the literature on other aspects of treatment. It is generally agreed that termination should not be forced (as in setting a specific time limit), unilateral, premature, or overdue. It has been claimed that a poorly planned and handled termination phase can practically destroy an otherwise good analysis.

As the work proceeds, therapist and patient periodically implicitly and explicitly assess the degree of progress made toward achieving the therapeutic goals. Ideally, the idea of termination emerges naturally in the minds of both participants as they recognize that the therapeutic goals (both those articulated at the start and ones that developed later on) have been essentially met and that the treatment therefore has reached the point of diminishing returns. Unfortunate but realistic reasons for termination include the judgment that little or no progress has been made over a significant period of time.

Although I am not aware of any systematic studies of the way termination decisions are reached, it is my impression that they are not always "natural" in the sense indicated above; that is, not infrequently they are due to a relocation of the therapist or patient, patient dissatisfaction or premature departure, or the lack of sufficient funds.

In any case, actual termination is ideally planned to commence at some specified time after a mutual decision has been made. The rationale for a planned termination phase rather than an abrupt ending includes the idea that separation from the analyst is a significant psychological event that will evoke feelings, fantasies, and conflicts that require analytic attention. It is not unusual that once a target date for termination is set, feelings emerge that previously had been latent and not dealt with, particularly around issues of loss, separation, abandonment, and incomplete mourning. In addition, the temporary recrudescence of symptoms in the termination phase is not uncommon.

In summary, the optimal criteria for termination, following Berger (1987) and Ticho (1972), are the reduction of the transference, the achievement of the main treatment goals, an acceptance (or at least tolerance) of the futility of perfectionistic strivings and childhood fantasies, an increased capacity for love and work (Freud's succinct statement of the goals of analysis), a reduction in the intensity and poignancy of core conflicts, the attainment of more stable and less maladaptive compromise formations, a reduction in symptoms, and the development of a self-analytic capacity. This latter quality is considered an important, new ego function, built on the patient's psychological mindedness and on his/her identification with and internalization of the analyst's analytic attitude. It should help the person during the posttermination consolidation of the analytic work and subsequently as well. Patient and analyst part on the understanding that the door is open for a return for more analytic work at some time in the future. The analyst goes on analyzing into the last session. Self-understanding is never complete or final. Treatment does not resolve conflict completely or immunize the patient from future psychological difficulties.

THE STANCE OF THE THERAPIST

The analyst's stance is best described as one in which the primary aim is to maintain an analytic attitude (Schafer, 1983). A major component of the analytic attitude is the analyst's genuine interest in helping the patient, expressed, in part, through the creation of a safe, caring, nonjudgmental therapeutic atmosphere.

Analytic Neutrality

Analytic neutrality is considered an essential feature of the proper analytic attitude. Neutrality is here understood not in the sense of indifference but in the sense of *not* taking sides in the patient's conflicts. In other words, the analyst attempts to be objective in the context of offering an empathic understanding of the patient. This stance has also been called a benevolent neutrality or a technical neutrality. As stated by Anna Freud (1954), the analyst adopts a position equidistant between the id, ego, and superego.

In addition, the analyst respects the uniqueness and individuality of the patient and does not attempt to remake the patient to fit any particular image or set of values. The analyst does not exploit the patient to meet his/her own needs. The analyst does not try to rescue the patient, to play guru, to become engaged in power struggles with the patient, to seek the patient's adulation or to feel critical or impatient toward the patient. The analyst appreciates that patients both seek and are frightened by the prospect of change and that ambivalence is a ubiquitous feature of human experience.

This description may begin to sound like an impossible ideal. It should be kept in mind that it is an ideal to be aspired to with the recognition that one can only approximate it and should not be unduly self-critical when the approximation is inevitably less than one would wish.

The concept of neutrality is closely linked to the idea that the analyst should function like a surgeon, a mirror, or a blank screen, metaphors used by Freud to depict the proper analytic stance as one of optimal abstinence and relative anonymity. These metaphors, which often have been misconstrued both by practitioners and by students of psychoanalysis, do *not* mean that the analyst functions with an attitude of a cold, detached, silent observer.[4] It does mean that the primary, deliberate attitude of the analyst is to analyze and that the analysis is best facilitated by certain conditions. Foremost among these conditions are a genuinely nonjudgmental attitude on the part of the therapist and a situation in which the patient's transference reactions can emerge in a relatively uncontaminated manner. The analytic restraint that the analyst imposes on him/herself is intended to facilitate the clear expression of the patient's transference.

Although there cannot be a truly "uncontaminated" transference, the analyst's technical neutrality and relative anonymity will bring the patient's contribution into bolder relief. The analyst, of course, gives cues, witting and unwitting, about his personality and values from the location and furnishing of the office, the manner of dress, and so forth. However, there is still a very large realm of nondisclosure that allows many degrees of freedom for the patient to "construct" the analyst. The patient's appreciation of his/her own needs and motives for making particular attributions or selective readings of the analyst will be more emotionally convincing when it is based on minimal cues.

Critics of Freudian analysis not infrequently misconstrue the position described above as indicating that Freudian analysts think that they should or somehow can take a position as observers of a process and yet remain outside the interaction. This is obviously impossible and it would be undesirable even if it were somehow possible. What is possible is for the analyst to *subordinate* his/her personality in the service of the analytic work by staying, relatively speaking, in the background in the sense of a certain restraint of one's narcissistic needs or a

muted emotional responsiveness of the kind not necessary in an ordinary social relationship. Nonetheless, the patient and the analyst mutually influence one another. The particular transference–countertransference configurations that emerge are unique to each analytic relationship. At the same time, both parties bring to the analytic situation a preexisting set of unconscious conflicts and fantasies, aspects of which are likely to be activated in any, or most, analytic dyads.

Another aspect of the notion of neutrality is the idea of abstinence, which means not yielding to the patient's wishes for transference gratification. The rationale for this principle is that providing direct transference gratification would at best create a temporary satisfaction but risk reducing the patient's motivation for treatment and make the analysis of the transference and the resistances all the more difficult. The analyst thus imposes a relative deprivation of gratification on both participants in the process. This is not to say that there are no gratifying aspects to the patient's experience of the analytic process. On the contrary there are several silent factors inherent in the situation that can be powerful sources of satisfaction and security. Foremost among these elements is the sense of steady support that comes from the sustained, genuine interest of a benign listener over a long course of regular and frequent contacts. This sense of support has been referred to as a "holding environment" (Winnicott, 1965). This term is a metaphor that derived from Winnicott's (1965) view that the analytic setting bears a similarity to features of the mother–child interaction in which the child is not only literally held as a means of soothing but is cared for and loved more generally and comes to rely on the provision of this protection.

What enables the analyst to provide a good holding environment, an environment that includes a shifting but optimal degree of abstinence with respect to the patient's transference wishes? To answer this question, we have to discuss the concepts of empathy and countertransference.

Empathy

In the evolving narrative of the patient that characterizes psychoanalytic work (Schafer, 1959, 1983, 1992), the analyst obviously does not begin with a completely blank or open mind. Based on the amalgam of past clinical experience, knowledge of human development, general models of human behavior, and particular psychoanalytic theories, the analyst will hear and organize the material in particular ways so as to develop a working mental model of the patient.

The crucial listening process described above is guided by the analyst's empathy. By empathy we mean that the analyst forms a partial, transient identification with the patient in which he/she attempts to apprehend in a cognitive–affective manner what it is like for the patient to experience his/her world in a particular manner. On one level, the analyst is always imagining what the patient's experiential world is like. The analyst oscillates between relating to patients in this way and stepping back as an observer and reflecting on why patients are experiencing their inner world as they are. These reflections serve as the basis for interpretation. Offered with proper timing, tact, and dosage, interpretations attempt to convey empathic understanding and explanation of patients' difficulties.

Countertransference

Countertransference can be thought of as empathy gone awry. That is, to the extent that the analyst's feelings or actions

toward, and understanding of, the patient are influenced by the analyst's unconscious, unresolved conflicts and needs, the analyst is being biased and thereby not functioning in the best interests of the patient.

At first, countertransference was thought of as the direct counterpart to the patient's transference (i.e., as the analyst's transference to the patient's transference, or to the patient more generally). By this definition, countertransference was regarded as an undesirable, potentially serious obstacle to effective treatment. Freud (1910) held that the therapist's countertransference limited the degree to which the patient could progress in treatment. Some authors (e.g., Langs, 1982) go so far as to assert that *all* treatment failures are due to unrecognized and/or unmanaged countertransference reactions.

In more recent years, influenced in large part by work with more disturbed patients, the concept of countertransference has been broadened to include all the analyst's emotional reactions to the patient, not just his/her transference reactions to the patient's transference. This definition has been called totalistic, in contrast to the earlier "classical" definition. The therapist's emotional reactions, whether based primarily on his/her own conflicts or due mainly to the fact that the patient's behavior would likely evoke the same reaction in virtually all analysts, came to be regarded both as inevitable and as potentially quite useful. They are useful in pointing to feelings that the patient might be "pulling for" from the therapist and therefore can serve as one important guide to the interpretations offered by the therapist. One needs to be careful, however, and not assume automatically that just because one is feeling a certain way, the patient was trying to evoke that particular reaction. To make such an automatic assumption (as one unfortunately encounters in some recent psychoanalytic literature) is to ignore the possibility that one's conflict-based countertransference is responsible for what one thinks the patient is trying to make one feel.

As noted above, countertransference-transference enactments are inevitable even though the analyst has been analyzed. What is considered crucial is to be able to recognize such enactments before they become too intense, disruptive, or traumatic for the patient and to step back, reflect on, and utilize one's understanding of them in the service of interpretation.

Some countertransference reactions are blatant, but most are subtle and therefore potentially more insidious. Some are readily recognized by the analyst; others are brought to the analyst's attention by the patient. Here is an example from Greenson (1967) of a subtle kind of countertransference reaction brought to the analyst's awareness by the patient.

A patient of Greenson's whose symptoms of depression and stomach ulcers intensified during an unproductive period in his analysis, also showed changes in his attitude and behavior toward Greenson. He became sullen and stubborn in place of his previous joking and teasing. As Greenson (1967) describes it:

> One day he told me he had dreamed of a jackass and then lapsed into a sullen silence. After a period of silence on my part, I asked him what was going on. He answered with a sigh that he had been thinking maybe the two of us were jackasses. After a pause he added, "I won't budge and you won't either. You won't change and I won't change [silence]. I tried to change but it made me sick." I was puzzled, I had no idea what he was referring to. I then asked him how he had *tried* to change. The patient answered that he had tried to change his political beliefs in accordance with mine. He had been a lifelong Republican (which I had known), and he

had tried, in recent months, to adopt a more liberal point of view, because he knew I was so inclined. I asked him how he knew that I was a liberal and anti-Republican. He told me that whenever he said anything favorable about a Republican politician, I always asked for associations. On the other hand, whenever he said anything hostile about a Republican, I remained silent, as though in agreement. Whenever he had a kind word for Roosevelt, I said nothing. Whenever he attacked Roosevelt, I would ask who did Roosevelt remind him of, as though I was out to prove that hating Roosevelt was infantile.

> I was taken aback because I had been completely unaware of this pattern. Yet, the moment the patient pointed it out, I had to agree that I had done precisely that, albeit unknowingly. We then went to work on why he felt the need to try to swallow my political views. (pp. 272–273)

The prescription for dealing with countertransference reactions is self-analysis, informed by the analyst's own prior training analysis and, if necessary, facilitated by consultations with colleagues and/or by the resumption of treatment. In the example above, Greenson presumably reflected on why he responded to the patient as he did, wondered whether his response was unique to this patient, whether there were other subtle ways in which he was critical of the patient, and so on.

The presumption is that undetected (and therefore unmanaged) countertransference reactions always have a detrimental impact on the treatment. The literature is replete with clinical vignettes demonstrating that a bogged-down analysis resumed its forward thrust following the analyst's awareness of a countertransference trend and the new interpretation to which it led. Although these accounts generally are persuasive, it is not clear how much undetected countertransference the average patient could, in fact, tolerate and still have a reasonably successful analysis.

It is also not clear to what extent and under what circumstances the analyst should disclose to the patient the fact of his/her countertransference and the presumed basis for it. Some analysts regard it as essential for the egalitarian spirit of the analytic process and for affirming the patient's sense of reality, whereas others feel that it unnecessarily burdens the patient and should be employed quite sparingly.

Virtually all therapists do agree that the analytic ideal would require that self-analysis be a constant, silent, background accompaniment to the conduct of each analytic session. The process would be heightened at moments when the analyst recognizes a change in the baseline of his/her typical attitudes and reactions to the patient (e.g., a shift in mood or a train of personal associations). Such attention to one's own experience can provide vital data concerning lines of exploration and interpretation that may previously have been avoided.

CURATIVE FACTORS OR MECHANISMS OF CHANGE

Since the inception of psychoanalysis, there has been continual discussion and debate concerning its curative ingredients. By now, it is clear that there is no single factor that can be said to be the major element in therapeutic change for all patients. Broadly speaking, the curative factors in treatment have been divided into two main categories—insight and the relationship. This is a potentially misleading distinction because insight based on interpretation can only take place in the context of a relationship. Thus, an interpretation leading to an emotionally meaningful insight can be, and often is, simultaneously experienced as a profound feeling of being understood (perhaps the strongest expression of a solid holding environment). None-theless, the distinction between insight and relationship factors is retained in order to assign relative influence to the element of enhanced self-understanding versus the benefits of the relationship per se. Among the benefits of the latter one can include the support inherent in the therapeutic relationship, the experience of a new, benign object relationship with a significant person (i.e., one who does not re-create the traumatic experiences that the patient suffered in relation to the parents), and identification with the analyst and the analytic attitude, including a softening of superego self-punitiveness.

Among traditional analysts, these relationship elements are still regarded as necessary, but secondary, background factors, which give interpretations their mutative power. In some contemporary views, particularly some versions of object relations theory and Kohut's self psychology, the relationship is regarded as directly therapeutic in its own right. Kohut (1984), for example, argues that the main impact of interpretations is that they strengthen the empathic bond between patient and therapist.

Some writers have suggested that a comprehensive theory of curative factors would have to consider that the relative therapeutic efficacy of insight and relationship factors may depend on the type of patient being treated. The generalization has been offered that, relatively speaking, patients whose early history was marked by serious disturbances in the mother–child relationship would benefit more from the healing aspects of the relationship, whereas patients who struggle primarily with Oedipal problems would find insight a more potent factor.

All analysts believe that insight is most effective when it is emotionally meaningful and includes both current and past experiences. Thus, as noted earlier, an insight in which the patient sees how he/she is repeating in the here-and-now transference to the analyst an experience that occurs with contemporary significant others, *and* that took place with one or another or both parents is convincing, in part, because of the convergence of these three domains.

Such insights both presuppose a degree of change and point the way to further changes. The patient, for example, can recognize the tendency to invite rebuff or to undermine him/herself in certain ways. Although this awareness does not automatically result in behavioral change, it can set the stage for it.

In summary, and at the risk of oversimplification, one can discern two main, but not mutually exclusive, models of how therapeutic change occurs. Following Cooper (1992), we can refer to these as the growth model and the repair model. In the growth model, the analytic situation fosters the resumption of an arrested or thwarted development by providing the benign, facilitative conditions insufficiently present in the course of development. Kohut's (1984) approach is a good example of this model. The repair model is more the model of traditional Freudians who, relatively speaking, would place greater emphasis on interpretation leading to insight and, "having less faith in the patient's healthy impulses" (Cooper, 1992, p. 247), would likely be more active in focusing on the patient's distortions of reality, self-defeating patterns, and resistance to change. As Cooper (1992) correctly points out, the necessity of a safe holding environment is assumed in both models. The repair model would stress that this is a necessary but not sufficient condition for change.

TREATMENT APPLICABILITY

Psychoanalysis originated as a treatment for individual adult patients. Over the years, psychoanalytically oriented approaches have been developed for the treatment of couples, groups, and families. The psychoanalytic treatment of children and of adolescents has also been an active area. In the treatment of couples, groups, families, children, and adolescents, clinicians continue to be guided by their understanding of personality dynamics and development and its pathological variations. The specific techniques employed differ in these different situations. A separate chapter would be required to begin to do justice to the range and complexity of the factors involved in these treatment applications. Given the limitations of space and the fact that most psychoanalytic treatments still focus on the individual, adult patient, the material in this chapter is deliberately restricted to a discussion of adults.

For what kinds of adults is psychoanalysis or psychoanalytic psychotherapy suitable? I began to answer this question in "The Assessment of Dysfunction" (above) and can now add to those remarks.

Individuals seeking psychoanalysis or psychoanalytic psychotherapy usually do so at a time of anticipated or actual loss, typically the loss of an important personal relationship. Other common reasons for entering treatment at a particular point include the outbreak of symptoms (e.g., panic attacks), diminution of self-esteem, and the unavailability of usual social or emotional supports at times of life transition (e.g., graduating from college, being fired from a job, or the birth of a child). The latter normal life changes often create significant stress which, when superimposed on chronic, unresolved conflicts, can give rise to disabling symptoms. In other words, patients typically seek treatment in a state of disequilibrium.

Research on Efficacy

Analysts attempt to maximize their effectiveness by bringing to their work their accumulated "clinical wisdom," which is an amalgam of the received wisdom of their supervisors and teachers, theory, and common sense. But, what do we know about the efficacy of psychoanalytic treatment on the basis of systematic, empirical inquiry? Unfortunately, we know very little. There are no well-controlled outcome studies of long-term treatment from which clinicians can draw knowledge. This is not to say that a few properly conducted outcome studies would alter clinical practice. In fact, for a variety of reasons, such outcome data probably would have little impact on clinical work. Nonetheless, it is essential that we obtain reliable information about the outcome of long-term treatment.

The several available meta-analytic psychotherapeutic outcome studies (in which the results of many studies are combined statistically) are irrelevant to the issue of the efficacy of long-term treatment. To my knowledge, there are only four outcome studies of long-term psychoanalytic treatment (Bachrach, Galatzer-Levy, Skolnikoff, & Waldron, 1991). Each has a number of methodological weaknesses; most notably, none of them employed a control group. Yet, what kind of control group could feasibly and ethically be employed in a study of long-term treatment? An untreated group, a wait-list control, or an attention–placebo control obviously are inappropriate. The best we can do is to use comparison groups of patients who, although deemed suitable for psychoanalysis, are assigned to another form of long-term treatment. To my knowledge, no study has employed this design.

The study closest to this design, and the most ambitious long-term treatment and follow-up study ever undertaken, is the Menninger Foundation Psychotherapy Research Project (PRP), initiated more than three decades ago. Five books and more than 60 articles have been based on this project, including follow-up studies and a detailed write-up of each of the cases (Wallerstein, 1986).

In the PRP study, 42 patients were seen in either psychoanalysis (22) or psychotherapy (20). Overall, the outcome for the two groups was similar; about 60% of patients in both groups showed at least moderate improvement. Most of the analyses had to be modified and all the treatments contained more supportive elements than originally intended. In fact, half of the 42 patients showed positive therapeutic changes without evidence of having obtained insight into their core conflicts. The supportive elements appear to have been necessary for the treatment and yielded long-term benefits. By the criteria of durability and effective coping in the face of conflict and stress the supportive elements were no less significant than insight in generating structural change. Wallerstein (1986) concludes that there has been "a tendency to overestimate the necessity of the expressive–analytic treatment mode, and of its central operation via conflict resolution based on interpretation, insight, and working through, to achieve therapeutically desired change" (p. 723).

How shall we understand these findings? Do they contradict the idea that psychoanalysis achieves better results? Might the common factors in all these treatments (e.g., the provision of a good "holding environment") (Modell, 1976) be the significant elements (assuming, of course, that these patients were better off than a comparable, "no treatment" control group). Although this is certainly a possibility, the point is that we cannot reach a definite conclusion on the basis of one study, ambitious and detailed as it was. Furthermore, many of these patients had failed in prior treatments (e.g., about "one third of the analytic patients had to be hospitalized at some point during their treatment") (Bachrach et al., 1991, p. 879). This suggests that psychoanalysis probably was not the treatment of choice in the first place.

Let us now turn from the presumed basis of therapeutic change to the fact of change per se. Based on a detailed review of the PRP and the only three other large-scale studies (the Columbia Psychoanalytic Center Research Project, the Boston Psychoanalytic Institute Prediction Study, and the New York Psychoanalytic Institute Studies), Bachrach et al. (1991) conclude that "the majority of patients selected as *suitable* for analysis derive substantial therapeutic benefit: improvement rates are typically in the 60–90% range, and effect sizes, when they have been calculated, are significant" (p. 904). The main predictor of outcome was initial ego strength. Again, we need appropriate comparison groups to evaluate these findings.

In conclusion, I believe it is fair to state that there is no reliable, quantitative, research evidence concerning the outcome of psychoanalysis or long-term psychoanalytic psychotherapy compared with other forms of treatment. There is a body of findings concerning changes in process variables and these are generally consistent with what one would expect on the basis of theory (e.g., Kantrowitz, Katz, Paolitto, Sashin, & Solomon, 1987).

In the absence of a body of research findings on the relative efficacy of different psychoanalytic treatment approaches (or of findings comparing psychoanalytic approaches with other forms of treatment), the effectiveness of long-term therapy is evaluated on the basis of clinical experience. In this era of accountability, clinicians should be increasingly aware of the limitations of this informal means of evaluating treatment outcome. Thus, when Kohut (1979) presents his two analyses of Mr. Z as evidence of the alleged superiority of his second, new self psychology view over the traditional Freudian position, one should regard this as little more than a self-congratulatory testimonial.

Challenges to Traditional Psychoanalysis

The reader should realize that the Freudian approach to treatment has been criticized on a number of grounds, including its limitations when applied to seriously disturbed narcissistic and borderline patients (Druck, 1989). Underlying many criticisms of traditional theory is the view that Freudian drive theory and the tripartite, structural theory of mind constitutes a Procrustean bed that fails to account adequately for the richness and variety of human motivation and experience (Sandler, 1988). Furthermore, the emphasis on tension reduction and the depiction of human beings as more apt to seek a regressive path rather than a more progressive alternative and the stress on aggression as a fundamental drive reflect a generally pessimistic view of the human condition. It assumes, for example, that patients prefer the stagnating safety of familiar patterns of behavior and that they will be more inclined to seek from the analyst the satisfaction of dependent and sexual wishes than the more independent direction of insight, risk taking, and potential satisfaction with suitable objects in the real world. It is argued that the theory of technique that derives from the Freudian view is limited, even with neurotic patients. For example, the emphasis on interpretation, particularly in the context of a strict adherence to the principle of abstinence in an overconcern with the possible dangers of excessive transference gratification, is said to be unnecessarily adversarial and depriving, and apt to result in an iatrogenic (i.e., treatment-induced) regression.

I cannot take the space here to explicate these issues further and to present a rebuttal to these critiques. The interested reader should see Lasky (1993) and Weinshel (1990).

CASE ILLUSTRATION

At the request of the editors, I have not selected a case that proved to be an outstanding success. On a scale including "deterioration," "no change," "minimal improvement," "mild improvement," "moderate improvement," and "marked improvement," I chose a case that showed a moderate degree of improvement. Obviously, I can only present a highly condensed account of some aspects of the case.

Mr. T started treatment at the age of 27. He had been referred to the university counseling service because he was on the verge of being dropped from the university for an increasingly long string of incompletes that began in his freshman year (age 18) and snowballed such that he was adding new incompletes at a faster rate than he was undoing the backlog of those he had already accumulated. After three sessions with the university counseling service, which offered only short-term therapy, he was referred to me. Not surprisingly, he was late to each of the three sessions he had at the counseling service. His most vivid memory of those three sessions, and one he would call up early in our work together, was being chided for this lateness by the female therapist and feeling intense resentment toward her. I took his comments as an expression of his concern about how I might react to his lateness as well as to other aspects of his violation of our arrangements.

The patient grew up in an upper-middle-class Jewish family. His father, a man of seemingly indefatigable energy, was a manufacturer who, along with his main business, was always engaged in several other, unrelated business ventures, was actively involved in the life of his community, and contributed to a variety of Jewish causes. He would frequently take his son to his office and to various community functions. The boy was awed by and envious of his father's accomplishments. He was deeply moved by witnessing the respect and esteem accorded his father by the community in general, and by its religious leaders in particular. His admiration of and identification with his father was one important basis for (1) his feeling that he wanted to be similarly recognized as well as his serious doubts that he ever would be held in such high regard, and (2) his belief that to devote his energies exclusively to only *one* major goal or project, no matter how impressive or successful, was to be second-rate and to forgo the possibility of successfully competing with his father for recognition and respect.

His parents, particularly his mother, led him to believe that he had the ability, the potential, and the *obligation* to achieve greatness as an adult; all that was required was the proper motivation. These messages from his mother contributed to his sense of having a special destiny that he ought to fulfill. Together with the model of his father described above, this sense of a duty to perform motivated him to involve himself in several activities simultaneously. During college, for example, he usually was working at three different jobs while taking a full course load and trying to lead an active social life.

An image that we often used to refer to this style of overextending himself, complicating his life, and never completing any project until faced with a truly unavoidable deadline, was that of a frequent guest on *The Ed Sullivan Show* who would attempt to spin and balance plates on top of long sticks. He would start with one and keep adding several others while running back and forth continuously to each stick in order to further increase the spin on the plate before it came crashing down on the floor. The absurd, futile aspect of the incessant activity in this feat of respinning each plate just before it was about to fall is that this activity, somewhat like chasing one's tail, absorbs all one's time and energy in the constant effort to stave off disaster. In the patient's case, it served his need to be active on several fronts simultaneously and his desire to avoid dealing with substantive matters. Thus, this image served as an apt, evocative metaphor for the way the patient conducted his life. I say the way the patient "conducted his life," but it should not come as a surprise to the reader that Mr. T hardly experienced himself as actively directing his life. Rather, he viewed himself as the passive victim of an unremitting barrage of impersonal, environmental impingements and hassles (e.g., bills and taxes that he was expected to pay on a timely basis) and interpersonal expectations, which he experienced as onerous obligations (e.g., being on time for sessions and dates).

The patient's mother, whose budding career as an actress was aborted by marriage, was experienced by the patient, from early on, as an extremely demanding, controlling, manipulative, hostile and unempathic person who derived sadistic pleasure from always taking advantage of her power over him. For example, she would often be the last mother to arrive to pick him up after school, sometimes making him wait a half hour or more after the other children had left. On the one occasion when he took matters into his own hands and walked home, she severely berated him.

One could listen to Mr. T for a year or more and not know that he had a sister 3 years his junior. On the face of it, she did not seem to figure prominently in his psychic life. I had the impression that he obliterated her in this manner in the service of making himself an only child. The little he said about her indicated that they never got along very well as children and rarely spoke to one another as adults.

Given the entrenched nature of Mr. T's behavioral problems and his characterological difficulties, I recommended, after three or four initial interviews, that we embark on psychoanalysis at a frequency of four sessions per week. Mr. T was somewhat hesitant and fearful of the commitment but nonetheless accepted my recommendation. I reviewed with him the material of the initial interviews and summarized the main presenting issues to be dealt with: his severe procrastination and his problems with time; his feelings of anxiety, depression, and low self-esteem; his turbulent, sticky relationship with his mother; his difficulties with women; and his problems in concentration.

We then turned to the contractual aspects of our working relationship; we agreed on a fee and arranged a schedule. I informed him about my usual vacation times and told him about my fee policy regarding missed sessions: I would charge him for missed sessions but would try to arrange make-up sessions when I could. I then offered a brief description of how I thought we could best work together. Because he had no prior experience in treatment, save for the three sessions in the college counseling service (and a few sessions when he was an unhappy high school student), I told him that he should feel free to say what comes to mind and that he should to try to do so without editing or withholding any thoughts or feelings that he might regard as tangential or irrelevant. I added that my role would be to facilitate his self-exploration by making comments and observations from time to time.

The treatment involved an elaboration of the themes and conflicts outlined above. However, I will restrict my account almost exclusively to his problems with time and with concentration. Fairly quickly, these conflicts began to be expressed in his relationship with me. For instance, and to put it rather mildly, the patient had a great deal of difficulty getting to the sessions on time. Not infrequently, he would arrive *exactly* at the midpoint of the session, seemingly without conscious intent to do so. Sometimes, he would show up when there were 10 minutes or less left in the session; on a couple of occasions he arrived with 2 or 3 minutes left, explaining that the idea of missing the session altogether was more troubling than the frustration of traveling 40 minutes each way for 2 or 3 minutes of his session with me. Once on the couch, he showed little awareness that the end of the session was approaching, continuing to talk in a way that made my stopping the session feel to both of us like an intrusive interruption rather than a somewhat natural ending.

Time was a bitter enemy in *every* aspect of his life. He would resist doing things until he inevitably was coerced into action, even though he consciously hated being coerced. Thus, he came within a hair's breadth of finally being dismissed forever from college for his long list of incompletes; his telephone and electrical service were regularly threatened with termination for delinquent payment of bills; he was *never* on time to a date, a dance, a concert. He even missed airline flights to go off on vacations he planned for himself.

He recalled that as a child, he had a strong resistance to going to sleep, exceeded by his even more powerful resistance to getting up on time to go to school. (Any and all transitions from one activity to another were extremely difficult for him.) He was able to engage his father in the game of "5 more minutes" in which his father would tug at his leg to urge him to get out of bed and the patient would plead for "5 more minutes." This playful encounter (with its homoerotic overtones) became a morning ritual for many years and resulted in frequent lateness to school, as his father readily gave in to his son's entreaties (in

contrast to the mother who was a harsh taskmaster). For this patient, simply to be awake and conscious was to feel a profound sense of the impingement of reality and an aversive sense of burden and responsibility in relation to all his unfinished daily tasks, to say nothing of the grand accomplishments he felt were his burden to achieve. In fact, so profound were his passive yearnings that to stand up straight and carry himself erect, as opposed to being in a slouched or supine position, often felt effortful and was experienced as a hardship to be endured and resented.

The patient experienced the passage of time during which he avoided chores, school assignments, or other obligations as but a temporary reprieve from feeling coerced. Of course, his stance was an invitation to others to cajole him. Therefore, it was hard to relax. As he put it, "My ability to resist the passage of time is an expression of my need for freedom. Wasting time to me feels freeing." The patient also had fantasies of teleportation in which he pictured himself getting from his apartment to my office in a split second. The harsh, tyrannical time limits his mother constantly imposed on him were never far from his awareness.

For a long time he was unable to assume responsibility for his lateness, attributing it to a variety of external causes and denying that it expressed anything about how he felt toward me. He felt that this characteristic of his had achieved a kind of functional autonomy, like a well-ingrained habit, and that I should not take it personally. Similarly, the patient was also consistently late in paying his bill, a fact that, early on, he also attributed to his general tardiness with bills.

Material relevant to the patient's problems with time emerged over many months and became one main focus of the analysis. These problems were intimately intertwined with his problems in concentration. I will draw on this material from several points in the treatment to create a composite vignette in order to illustrate some of the technical precepts that guided my overall approach to this patient and to demonstrate the actual interventions derived from these precepts.

By my listening, by my periodic, general requests for elaboration of his associations (e.g., "What comes to mind?"), by occasional, specific, but open-ended questions designed to elicit further associations, I attempted to understand and to interpret the meanings of his behavior and experiences in relation to time and to the matter of concentration as expressions of unconscious, core conflicts, particularly as they were expressed in the transference.

Some months into the analysis I pointed out to the patient that he had been late a lot, something that, of course, he knew. (Recall that he was confronted with this early on in the few sessions he had with the female therapist who had referred him to me and that he felt chastised by her.) He replied that it was difficult for him to get anywhere on time, that I should, therefore, not take it personally, and that he does not keep track of time enough to focus on when he would have to leave to show up on time. The tone of his remarks suggested to me that he took my observation as a criticism. Rather than respond directly to the content of what he said, I focused on the affect-laden manner of his reply. The technical precept guiding this choice was the idea of emphasizing the implicit affective aspects of the "here-and-now" transference.

From the perspective of technique, my reference to his lateness is what Greenson (1967) would call a *confrontation*. It conveys the message: "Both the fact of your repeated lateness and your affective–cognitive response to my calling attention to it are matters of psychological import that we might profitably examine together." By inquiring whether he might have experienced my observation as a criticism I was engaging in the technical intervention that Greenson calls *clarification*. As indicated earlier, confrontation and clarification are preparatory to *interpretation*, which searches for the *meanings* of behavior and experience. My confrontation and clarification already hint at the possibility of a transferential response while trying to maintain a positive working alliance by implicitly suggesting that we look at our interchange. As the therapist, I also need to be aware of why and how I am choosing to intervene at the time I do: What attitudes, affects, and conflicts have been activated in me, including the questions of how I feel about his lateness (e.g., Am I irritated and sounding critical in the content, tone, syntax, or other aspects of my remarks?). In short, I need to monitor, manage, and get interpretive clues from my own countertransference reactions.

Not surprisingly, the patient replied that he did feel somewhat chastised by my comment and that it reminded him of a similar reaction to the female therapist he saw initially and who referred him to me. His thoughts next turned to his mother and her almost invariable lateness in picking him up from elementary school in the afternoon. He felt angered at what he felt was the power differential and double standard in their relationship; she constantly chided him for being late in getting ready for school, yet she apparently had no compunction about keeping him waiting in all sorts of situations (e.g., she would drag him to stores and would take her time shopping while he waited impatiently and with much frustration). After listening to him elaborate these memories and feelings, I interpreted one meaning of his lateness with me to be a desire to keep me waiting as his mother had kept him waiting, to right the humiliating, infuriating wrong that he felt she had imposed on him. This desire for revenge was expressed in this manner both with me and with others. I later rephrased and amplified my interpretation by stating that he wished to reverse roles with me by having me suffer helplessly as he had and that he found this desire to be legitimate in some sense. But, I added, it also was something that he felt was wrong, just as his mother regarded his attempts to defy her as evidence of his badness and lack of respect for her. I wondered whether he heard his mother's critical voice in my initial observation of his lateness and whether his feeling criticized by me was something that he seemed to feel was in some sense justified and in some sense unfair. In making this kind of interpretation I was communicating the view that while he bitterly resented his mother's accusations and criticisms, he also felt that they had a certain degree of merit and that this contributed to his feeling that he was being a "bad boy."

Variations and elaborations of this line of interpretation were offered repeatedly in contexts where issues of control, autonomy, and sense of obligation were prominent in the patient's associations. For instance, during the period of the analysis when he frequently arrived *exactly* at the midpoint of the session, seemingly without conscious intent to do so, I eventually offered the interpretation that he seemed to be effecting a precise compromise between his sense of obligation to be on time and his need to assert his autonomous control and to thwart and defy what he experienced as my stern expectation that he be prompt. The patient agreed with this interpretation and his associations led to fantasies that the powerful can and do exercise great control over others. For instance, in being late to catch a plane he came to realize that he had the fantasy that if he were a famous politician or head of state, the plane would be held until he arrived. In

other sessions, this line of exploration led to a host of childhood memories associated with the issue of surrender versus defiance (e.g., the time when, as a preadolescent, he deliberately acted on the inexplicable urge to defecate in the woods surrounding his house; his guilt-tarnished glee in playing behind his locked bedroom door when his mother thought that he was doing his homework; his guilt-laden pleasure in seeking out nude beaches as a young adult; and his conflicts around prayer and religious observance—e.g., "cheating" by leaving synagogue during portions of the service).

As indicated earlier, the patient's problems with time were closely linked to his difficulties in concentration, a problem also connected to his conflict over autonomy and defiance (which meant much the same thing to him) versus humiliating surrender. For example, it was evident that Mr. T had a great deal of difficulty listening to my comments and interpretations. Not infrequently, he would remark, "Could you say that again? I completely lost track of what you said." (These lapses occurred mainly when I said something unpalatable and in sessions when he was present more out of obligation than desire.) Rather than simply repeat what I had said, I asked what came to mind about his not retaining it in the first place. He replied, "As you know, I've always had trouble paying attention to what I'm doing. I can't concentrate and often don't realize that I'm not concentrating until some time later. If I'm reading an assigned chapter in a textbook I find that after a few pages I turn to some unassigned portion of the text and I start to read without any problem in concentration or in remembering what I read. Of course [said with a knowing chuckle], if the unassigned portion became the assignment I would wander to some other part and forget what I had read. I engage in my shutdown procedure without realizing it at the time." I then said, "It seems that you often experience what I say in here as carrying the demand that you pay attention and do your 'homework' here immediately." The patient, struggling to retain my comment, replied that he did feel that it was coercive to pay attention to what I had to say. In this context, as earlier in relation to the issue of time and being kept waiting by his mother, he again recalled ignoring his mother's entreaties to do his homework, the incident of defecating in the woods around his house, and struggles with his mother around toilet training and cleanliness training in general. The patient spontaneously acknowledged that there was something gratifying in defying what he felt was required or expected. For example, he again recalled times when his mother thought that he was in his room studying and he was playing instead, feeling good (but also guilty) that he was getting away with something. He also recounted that he would graciously accept a dinner invitation, but as the hour of his expected arrival approached, he increasingly felt the invitation to be a burden. What began as a freely chosen, pleasant anticipation became transformed into an onerous obligation.

We were able to see that not hearing what I said was not some meaningless, momentary memory lapse but a significant here-and-now transference marker of his conflict between obedience and defiance. When I spoke, his mind "wandered to the unassigned portion" and he engaged in his "shutdown procedure" with me. His emotional insights into the nature, origins, and pervasiveness of this conflict were facilitated by so-called genetic transference interpretations linking his resistance to aspects of the analytic process to his struggles with his mother.

It should be emphasized that what I am describing here is a tiny fragment of a long process. It is not that the patient and analyst suddenly arrive at one all-encompassing, blinding insight in which everything heretofore cloudy and obscure gels such that long-standing conflicts suddenly become fully and forever resolved. This image, still a common fantasy, is a holdover from the rapid, usually short-lived, dramatic "cures" in the early days of psychoanalysis in which the retrieval of an unconscious, traumatic memory appeared to play a decisive role. Instead, the process often proceeds in terms of a two-steps-forward, one-step-back model. Insights are gained, lost, and regained. The working alliance is to some extent repeatedly ruptured in the face of the negative transference and then repaired. There are strong resistances against translating insight into action. This is why analysts talk about the importance of working through. At times, working through is written about as though it were a special process or phase within the analysis. It is more accurate to say that working through *is* the analysis.

It should be clear in this case that just one interpretation of the patient's lateness did not change this behavior. The interpretations needed to be expanded, modified in the light of new information, applied to multiple variations on the same major theme, and integrated with related interpretations. For example, to this point I have discussed the dynamics of the patient's lateness in pre-Oedipal terms, centering on his anal conflicts. Although the constraints of space do not permit an account of the clinical evidence, interpretations regarding his lateness, procrastination, and problems in concentration eventually addressed his oral and his Oedipal conflicts and their role in his symptoms.

In summary, the diagnostic picture that emerged over the course of treatment was of an obsessive–compulsive character structure, with narcissistic, depressive, and passive–aggressive features. Dynamically, his core conflicts centered on (1) his passive wishes for symbiotic union with his mother and his guilt over such wishes, as well as his autonomous strivings to free himself from enmeshment with his mother; (2) his rage at, and desire to defy, parental authority and his feeling that he should obediently yield to it in order to be a good boy; and (3) his Oedipal rivalry with his father, contributing to his grandiose wishes to be mother's favorite through some great achievement, along with his love for his father and desire not to hurt him. While these conflicts interacted with one another in synergistic ways, it was the second conflict listed that was the most significant one and the one that contributed most to his impaired functioning. That is why I focused on this aspect of his personality in this brief presentation. It should be noted, however, that the three conflicts listed above, originating, respectively, from the oral, anal, and phallic stages of psychosexual development, interact synergistically. That is, the same behavior can simultaneously express aspects of each conflict and the conflicts themselves are related to one another.

I shall illustrate very briefly. One particularly prominent manifestation of Mr. T's obsessive–compulsive style was his severe preoccupation with the idea of lost or missed opportunities, particularly with respect to his search for the perfectly gratifying female. He would always arrive at a dance late and then be unable to let go of the idea that the girl of his dreams had been there and left. When he was embracing a woman in the middle of his living room he strained to look into the window of the apartment across the street in order to catch a glimpse of a woman in a partial state of undress.

In general, whatever he had or was experiencing at a given moment was, by definition, at least mildly disappointing; perfection was an elusive, future possibility for which he had to keep his options open. When he opened a gift-wrapped package he was invariably disappointed because, however nice the gift was, it immediately stirred his fantasy of the perhaps truly special contents of the other package that was still gift-wrapped.

This material was elaborated in further sessions and eventually led to interpretations to the effect that he was seeking a blissful merger with a perfect, omnipotent woman who would immediately recognize and happily satisfy all his needs, promptly and without his having to verbalize them; that he had a marked sensitivity to feeling controlled and trapped by a powerful woman; and that he constantly yearned for an elusive, special, but unattainable woman. Thus, conflicts at the oral, anal, and phallic levels, respectively, were expressed in the above clinical material as well as in his difficulties in making commitments to a woman and to his career.

Focusing again on his conflict between obedience and defiance, over time Mr. T came to experience both in the transference and in his other, concurrent relationships, the repetition of his struggles with his mother and the self-defeating and self-punitive consequences of his many displaced attempts to take revenge against her tyranny over him. At the same time, we also recognized in his resistances and acting out the attempt to secure for himself some sense of personal agency and freedom. However, he was imprisoned in this scenario with his mother. Mr. T came to appreciate that his relationships with women were modeled on this sadomasochistic prototype and regularly ended in bitter power struggles. As suggested above, this central pattern also had strong dynamic links to his passive–oral yearnings as well as to his Oedipal conflicts.

The reenactment, eventual understanding, and working through of these conflicts in a context of empathy and support contributed to a much greater sense of personal agency and to increased self-esteem based on a diminution of the superego pressures that he fulfill his alleged potential for greatness. Eventually, his battles with time diminished. He made considerable progress in coming to terms with his rage against his mother and his fear and guilt about relinquishing her as a manipulative, persecutory object. There was a reduction in his anger and in the self-directed aggression he practiced on himself in atonement for his guilt over his defiant rage and "misbehavior." He also came to uncouple the idea of his success with the notion of his father's demise. In these ways he freed himself to take more genuine control over his own life.

The awareness and working through of these issues was a slow, steady process that included the realization of the many ways in which the "5 more minutes" procrastination game that originated with his father was being played out (including its underlying homoerotic components) in his relationship with me, with others in his life, and in relation to life in general (e.g., with respect to commitment to career and to marriage).

During the analysis, I attempted to use my countertransference reactions to guide my understanding of his experience and behavior. For example, I saw in my reactions to his marked lateness in arriving for the sessions and in paying his bill how he likely felt himself to be the passive victim of his mother's arbitrary exercise of power and control. I could also begin to see how his provocativeness in these and other ways invited the harsh responses that he also wanted to avoid. I would repeatedly try to explore with him how these patterns were developing in the treatment relationship and how his reactions to the fact of my interpretations as well as their content reflected the same dynamic issues.

The treatment lasted for 8 years. The patient finished college, obtained an advanced degree, and, after several turbulent relationships with women modeled on his relationship with his mother, became engaged to a woman who was refreshingly different from his mother. However, relative to others he had a lower threshold for feeling coerced by others and still showed a tendency to procrastinate.

CONCLUSION

I have used this case material to illustrate some aspects of the traditional theory of psychoanalytic treatment which holds that the resolution of the transference leads to positive personality change. Accordingly, the aim of therapy is to establish and maintain conditions conducive to the achievement of this goal. Stated succinctly, these conditions include the following: (1) a person who (a) is suffering emotionally, (b) is motivated to change, (c) shows some degree of psychological-mindedness, (d) has sufficient ego strength, and (e) has a decent enough history of gratifying interpersonal relationships to form and maintain a reasonable working alliance in the face of the inevitable frustrations involved in the treatment; and (2) a therapist who (a) can provide an optimal "holding environment," (b) can facilitate and maintain the working alliance in the face of its inevitable ruptures, (c) is relatively free of unmanaged countertransference reactions, and (d) provides accurate, empathically based interpretations of transference and extratransference behaviors with the timing, tact, and dosage necessary to facilitate insight into the unconscious conflicts that influence the patient's symptoms and maladaptive patterns of behavior.

These conditions promote increased self-understanding and self-acceptance. They help free the patient from reliance on maladaptive defenses and facilitate more effective functioning in work, in love, and in play.

I shall conclude with McDougall's (1985) quasi-poetic chararacterization of the ideal psychoanalytic outcome:

> Psychoanalysis is a theater on whose stage all our psychic repertory may be played. In these scenarios the features of the internal characters undergo many changes, the dialogues are rewritten and the roles recast. The work of elaboration leads analysands to the discovery of their internal reality and their inner truth, once all the different parts of themselves and all the people who have played important roles in their lives have had a chance to speak their lines. Accounts are settled with the loved–hated figures of the past; the analysands now possess them in all their aspects, good and bad, instead of being possessed by them, and now are ready to take stock of all they have received from those who brought them up and of what they have done with this inheritance. Whatever their conclusions may be, they recognize their place in this inner universe and claim that which is their own. (p. 284)

NOTES

1. While the term "object" sounds quite impersonal and strange when applied to a person, it is used in psychoanalytic theory as a general term to indicate that wishes can be directed to inanimate objects and, especially, to so-called internalized objects (mental representations of the person).

2. This term refers to any wish, attitude, or action that signifies (usually on an unconscious, symbolic level), the son's desire to win the competition with his father for his mother's love. Such desires typically are conflicted, due, in part, to a fear of the father's retribution. The daughter experiences a similar conflict vis-à-vis her mother.

3. In these days of biologically oriented psychiatry many, but not all, therapists have come to believe that there is no inherent contradiction between psychoanalysis and psychopharmacological treatment. Therefore, where there are fairly clear indications of a biological predisposition to aspects of the patient's emotional disturbance, medication that will take the edge off these disturbances actually may facilitate the treatment. Of course, the psychological meanings of taking medication, including the question whether it is prescribed by the therapist or a psychopharmcologist, will have to be carefully explored, particularly in its transference implications.

4. Freud's use of these metaphors to depict the desired attitude of technical neutrality and relative emotional muteness helped give rise to the perception of the classical analyst as creating an austere, aloof ambience and showing a minimal humaneness. This perception also is encouraged by those analysts who are inhibited, stiff, and minimally friendly in their interactions with patients. However, as Lipton (1977) points out, Freud did not set such a tone in his own work with patients. Therefore, as Lipton (1977) suggests, one should make a distinction between "classical" technique, as practiced by Freud, and "standard" technique, or "neoclassical" technique (Stone, 1961, 1967), as practiced by subsequent generations of analysts. Stone's writings (1961, 1967) are a useful corrective to the unnecessary rigidities of orthodox practitioners in the 1950s and the 1960s.

SUGGESTIONS FOR FURTHER READING

Brenner, C. (1982). Transference and countertransference. In *The mind in conflict* (pp. 194–212). New York: International Universities Press.

Cooper, A. M. (1989). Concepts of therapeutic effectiveness in psychoanalysis: A historical review. *Psychoanalytic Inquiry*, *9*(1), 4–25.

Dewald, P. A. (1982). Psychoanalytic perspectives on resistance. In P. L. Wachtel

(Ed.), *Resistance* (pp. 45–68). New York: Plenum Press.

Eagle, M. N. (1987). Theoretical and clinical shifts in psychoanalysis. *American Journal of Orthopsychiatry*, *57*(2), 175–184.

Eagle, M. N., & Wolitzky, D. L. (1981). Therapeutic influences in dynamic psychotherapy: Overview and synthesis. In S. Slipp (Ed.), *Curative factors in dynamic psychotherapy* (pp. 349–378). New York: McGraw-Hill.

Eagle, M. N., & Wolitzky, D. L. (1992). Psychoanalytic theories of psychotherapy. In D. K. Freedheim (Ed.), *History of psychotherapy: A century of change* (pp. 109–158). Washington, DC: American Psychological Association.

Gill, M. M. (1982). *Analysis of transference: Vol. 1. Theory and technique.* New York: International Universities Press.

Greenson, R. R. (1974). The theory of psychoanalytic technique. In S. Arieti (Ed.), *American handbook of psychiatry* (pp. 765–788). New York: Basic Books.

Greenson, R. R. (1978). Empathy and its vicissitudes. In R. R. Greenson (Ed.), *Explorations in psychoanalysis* (pp. 147–161). New York: International Universities Press.

Peterfreund, E. (1975). How does the analyst listen? On models and strategies in the psychoanalytic process. In D. P. Spence (Ed.), *Psychoanalysis and contemporary science* (pp. 59–102). New York: International Universities Press.

Reich, A. (1973). On countertransference. In A. Reich (Ed.), *Psychoanalytic contributions* (pp. 136–154). New York: International Universities Press.

Schafer, R. (1979). The appreciative attitude and the construction of multiple histories. *Psychoanalysis and Contemporary Thought*, *2*(1), 3–24.

Schafer, R. (1982). The analytic attitude: An introduction. In *The analytic attitude* (pp. 3–13). New York: Basic Books.

Schwaber, E. (1981). Empathy: A mode of analytic listening. *Psychoanalytic Inquiry*, *1*, 357–392.

Storr, A. (1979). *The art of psychotherapy.* New York: Methuen.

Usher, S. F. (1993). Starting out. *Introduction to psychodynamic psychotherapy technique*

(pp. 27–38). New York: International Universities Press.

REFERENCES

Abraham, K. (1927). *Selected papers of Karl Abraham.* London: Hogarth Press, 1948.

American Psychiatric Association. (1994). *Diagnostic and statistical manual of mental disorders* (4th ed.). Washington, DC: Author.

Bachrach, H., Galatzer-Levy, R., Skolnikoff, A., & Waldron, S. (1991). On the efficacy of psychoanalysis. *Journal of the American Psychoanalytic Association*, *39*, 871–916.

Basescu, S. (1990). Show and tell: Reflection on the analyst's self-disclosure. In G. Stricker & M. Fisher (Eds.), *Self-closure in the therapeutic relationship* (pp. 47–59). New York: Plenum Press.

Berger, D. M. (1987). *Clinical empathy.* Northvale, NJ: Jason Aronson.

Bernheim, H. (1886). *De la suggestion et de ses applications à la thérapeutique.* Paris. (2nd ed., 1887)

Boesky, D. (1990). The psychoanalytic process and its components. *Psychoanalytic Quarterly*, *59*, 550–584.

Brenner, C. (1973). *An elementary textbook of psychoanalysis.* New York: International Universities Press.

Brenner, C. (1979). Working alliance, therapeutic alliance and transference. *Journal of the American Psychoanalytic Association*, *27* (Suppl.), 137–157.

Breuer, J., & Freud, S. (1895). Studies on hysteria. *Standard Edition*, *2*, 1–305. London: Hogarth Press, 1955.

Charcot, J. M. (1882). Physiologie pathologique: Sur les divers états nerveux déterminés par l'hypotization chez les hystériques. [Pathological physiology: On the different nervous states hypnotically induced in hysterics.] *CR Academy of Science Paris*, *94*, 403–405.

Cooper, A. M. (1987). Changes in psychoanalytic ideas: Transference interpretation. *Journal of the American Psychoanalytic Association*, *35*, 77–98.

Cooper, A. M. (1992). Psychic change: Development in the theory of psychoanalytic techniques: 37th IPA Congress overview. *International Journal of Psycho-Analysis, 73,* 245–250.

Crits-Christoph, P., & Barber, S. P. (1991). *Handbook of short-term dynamic psychotherapy.* New York: Basic Books.

Curtis, H. (1980). The concept of therapeutic alliance: Implications for the widening scope. In H. Blum (Ed.), *Psychoanalytic explorations of technique: Discourse on the theory of therapy* (pp. 159–192). New York: International Universities Press.

Druck, A. (1989). *Four therapeutic approaches to the borderline patient: Principles and techniques of the basic dynamic stances.* Northvale, NJ: Jason Aronson.

Eagle, M. (1987). Theoretical and clinical shifts in psychoanalysis. *American Journal of Orthopsychiatry, 57*(2), 175–184.

Eagle, M., & Wolitzky, D. (1992). Psychoanalytic theories of psychotherapy. In D. K. Freedheim (Ed.), *History of psychotherapy: A century of change* (pp. 109–158). Washington, DC: American Psychological Association.

Eissler, K. R. (1953). The effect of the structure of the ego on psychoanalytic technique. *Journal of the American Psychoanalytic Association, 1,* 104–143.

Erikson, E. H. (1950). *Childhood and society* (rev. ed.). New York: Norton, 1963.

Freud, A. (1937). *The ego and the mechanisms of defence.* New York: International Universities Press.

Freud, A. (1954). Problems of technique in adult analysis. *Bulletin of the Philadelphia Association for Psychoanalysis, 4,* 44–69.

Freud, S. (1900). The interpretation of dreams. *Standard Edition, 4,* 1–338; *5,* 339–627. London: Hogarth Press, 1953.

Freud, S. (1901). The psychopathology of everyday life. *Standard Edition, 6,* 1–310. London: Hogarth Press, 1960.

Freud, S. (1910). The future prospects of psychoanalytic therapy. *Standard Edition, 11,* 139–151. London: Hogarth Press, 1957.

Freud, S. (1911). Formulations on the two principles of mental functioning. *Standard Edition, 12,* 218–226. London: Hogarth Press, 1958.

Freud, S. (1912). The dynamics of transference. *Standard Edition, 12,* 97–108. London: Hogarth Press, 1953.

Freud, S. (1914). On narcissism: An introduction. *Standard Edition, 14,* 73–102. London: Hogarth Press, 1957.

Freud, S. (1919). Lines of advance in psychoanalytic therapy. *Standard Edition, 17,* 135–144. London: Hogarth Press, 1955.

Freud, S. (1923). The ego and the id. *Standard Edition, 18,* 12–66. London: Horgarth Press, 1961.

Freud, S. (1926). Inhibitions, symptoms and anxiety. *Standard Edition, 20,* 77–174. London: Hogarth Press, 1959.

Freud, S. (1933). The dissection of the psychical personality. *Standard Edition, 17,* 57–81. London: Hogarth Press, 1964.

Freud, S. (1937). Analysis terminable and interminable. *Standard Edition, 23,* 216–253. London: Hogarth Press, 1964.

Freud, S. (1940). An outline of psycho-analysis. *Standard Edition, 23,* 144–207. London: Hogarth Press, 1964.

Gill, M. M. (1954). Psychoanalysis and exploratory psychotherapy. *Journal of the American Psychoanalytic Association, 2,* 771–797.

Gill, M. M. (1982). *Analysis of transference.* New York: International Universities Press.

Gill, M. M. (1984). Psychoanalysis and psychotherapy: A revision. *International Journal of Psycho-Analysis, 11,* 161–179.

Greenson, R. R. (1965). The working alliance and the transference neurosis. *Psychoanalytic Quarterly, 34,* 155–181.

Greenson, R. R. (1967). *The technique and practice of psychoanalysis* (Vol. 1). New York: International Universities Press.

Hartmann, H. (1939). *Ego psychology and the problem of adaptation.* New York: International Universities Press, 1958.

Hartmann, H., Kris, E., & Loewenstein, R. M. (1946). Comments on the formation of psychic structure. In *Papers on psychoanalytic psychology* (pp. 27–55). (*Psychological Issues, 4.* Monograph No. 14). New York: International Universities Press.

Holt, R. R. (1989). *Freud reappraised: A fresh look at psychoanalytic theory.* New York: Guilford Press.

Jacobs, T. (1986). On countertransference enactments. *Journal of the American Psychoanalytic Association, 34,* 289–307.

Jacobson, E. (1964). *The self and the object world.* New York: International Universities Press.

Jacobson, E. (1967). *Psychotic conflict and reality.* New York: International Universities Press.

Janet, P. (1907). *The major symptoms of hysteria.* New York: Macmillan.

Kantrowitz, J., Katz, A. L., Paolitto, F., Sashin, J., & Solomon, L. (1987). Changes in the level and quality of object relations in psychoanalysis: Follow-up of a longitudinal prospective study. *Journal of the American Psychoanalytic Association, 35,* 23–46.

Kernberg, O. (1975). *Borderline conditions and pathological narcissism.* Northvale, NJ: Jason Aronson

Klein, M. (1921–1945). *Love, guilt, and reparation and other works.* New York: Delta, 1975.

Kohut, H. (1971). *The analysis of the self.* New York: International Universities Press.

Kohut, H. (1977). *The restoration of the self.* New York: International Universities Press.

Kohut, H. (1979). The two analyses of Mr. Z. *International Journal of Psycho-Analysis, 60,* 3–27.

Kohut, H. (1984). *How does analysis cure?* Chicago: University of Chicago Press.

Langs, R. J. (1982). Countertransference and the process of cure. In S. Slipp (Ed.), *Curative factors in dynamic psychotherapy* (pp. 127–152). New York: McGraw-Hill.

Lasky, R. (1993). *Dynamics of development and the therapeutic process.* Northvale, NJ: Jason Aronson.

Lipton, S. D. (1977). The advantages of Freud's technique as shown in his analysis of the Rat Man. *International Journal of Psycho-Analysis, 58,* 255–274.

Luborsky, L. (1984). *Principles of psychoanalytic psychotherapy: A manual for supportive–expressive (SE) treatment.* New York: Basic Books.

Luborsky, L., & Crits-Christoph, P. (1990). *Understanding transference: The CCRT method.* New York: Basic Books.

Macalpine, I. (1950). The development of the transference. *Psychoanalytic Quarterly, 19,* 501–539.

Mahler, M. (1968). *On human symbiosis and the vicissitudes of individuation: Vol. I.* *Infantile psychosis.* New York: International Universities Press.

Malan, D. (1976). *The frontier of brief psychotherapy.* New York: Plenum Press.

Mann, J. (1973). *Time-limited psychotherapy.* Cambridge, MA: Harvard University Press.

McDougall, J. (1985). *Theaters of the mind.* New York: Basic Books.

McLaughlin, J. (1991). Clinical and theoretical aspects of enactment. *Journal of the American Psychoanalytic Association, 39,* 595–614.

Modell, A. (1976). The "holding environment" and the therapeutic action of psychoanalysis. *Journal of the American Psychoanalytic Association, 24,* 285–307.

Modell, A. (1984). *Psychoanalysis in a new context.* New York: International Universities Press.

Oremland, J. (1991). *Interpretation and interaction.* Hillsdale, NJ: Analytic Press.

Pine, F. (1990). *Drive, ego, object, and self.* New York: Basic Books.

Rapaport, D., & Gill, M. M. (1959). The points of view and assumptions of metapsychology. *International Journal of Psycho-Analysis, 40,* 153–162.

Reich, W. (1933). *Character analysis: Principles and techniques for psychanalysis in practice and training* (3rd ed.). New York: Orgone Institute Press, 1945.

Sandler, J. (1988). Psychoanalytic technique and "Analysis terminable and interminable." *International Journal of Psycho-Analysis, 69,* 335–345.

Schafer, R. (1959). Generative empathy in the treatment situation. *Psychoanalytic Quarterly, 28,* 342–373.

Schafer, R. (1983). *The analytic attitude.* New York: Basic Books.

Schafer, R. (1992). *Retelling a life.* New York: Basic Books.

Sifneos, P. (1987). *Short-term dynamic psychotherapy.* New York: Plenum Press.

Stone, L. (1961). *The psychoanalytic situation.* New York: International Universities Press.

Stone, L. (1967). The psychoanalytic situation and transference: Postscript to an earlier communication. *Journal of the American Psychoanalytic Association, 15,* 3–58.

Ticho, E. (1972). Termination of psychoanalysis: Treatment goals and life goals. *Psychoanalytic Quarterly, 41,* 315–333.

Wachtel, P. (1993). *Therapeutic communication: Principles and effective practice*. New York: Guilford Press.

Waelder, R. (1960). *Basic theory of psychoanalysis*. New York: International Universities Press.

Wallerstein, R. S. (1986). *Forty-two lives in treatment: A study of psychoanalysis and psychotherapy*. New York: Guilford Press.

Wallerstein, R. S. (1990). Psychoanalysis: The common ground. *International Journal of Psycho-Analysis, 71*, 3–20.

Weinshel, E. M. (1984). Some observations on the psychoanalytic process. *Psychoanalytic Quarterly, 53*, 63–92.

Weinshel, E. M. (1990). How wide is the widening scope of psychoanalysis and how solid is its structural model? Some concerns and observations. *Journal of the American Psychoanalytical Association, 38*, 275–296.

Winnicott, D. W. (1965). *The maturational processes and the facilitating environment*. London: Hogarth Press and Institute of Psycho-Analysis, 1987.

Zetzel, E. R. (1956). Current concepts of transference. *International Journal of Psycho-Analysis, 37*, 369–378.

3

Relational Approaches to Psychoanalytic Psychotherapy

JAY GREENBERG
OLGA CHESELKA

BACKGROUND OF THE APPROACH

Freud's psychoanalytic method was rooted in a mode of thought that dominated the intellectual climate of the 19th century. Impressed by what had emerged from the study of the natural world—from Darwin's observations that led to the theory of evolution to discoveries in medicine that promised control of previously disastrous biological processes—he constructed what he hoped would be a similar approach to problems of human psychology.

Why, Freud reasoned, could we not study the mind in the same way that had been so fruitful for other disciplines? All we need do is to engage patients in mental activity—through the method of free association—and then to observe it with the objectivity that characterizes any scientific endeavor. All the technical procedures that he developed were designed to promote this objectivity. The analyst was to be open-minded and accepting of whatever the patient said (what Freud called the analyst's "neutrality"); he was to create a benign distance between himself and the patient (which Freud compared to the surgeon's detachment); he was to intrude as little of himself as possible into the patient's experience (Freud suggested that the analyst could be a blank screen or reflecting mirror).

Ironically, however, as Freudian psychoanalysis flowered the philosophy of science on which it was based faded. Objective observation, many scientists came to believe, was a wishful (if at times also useful) myth. Einstein's theory of relativity and Heisenberg's uncertainty principle exposed the weakness of the idea that any observer could stand completely outside his observational field. There is no such thing, Heisenberg insisted, as studying without influencing. If this was true in the world of particle physics, how could it not be decisive in the relationship between two people, one a therapist, the other a patient?

Freud had focused his own attention on what went on *within* one person and on how this could be studied and modified by an outside observer. How did the changing intellectual climate affect the theory and practice of psychoanalysis? Now, for many therapists, the emphasis shifted to what went on *between* people. We are, from the moment of birth, immersed in relationships with other people. The qualities of these relationships must be decisive determinants of who we become, how we think about ourselves, how we negotiate the course of our lives. Both healthy personality and psychopathology reflect the influence of these relationships. Similarly, attempts to intervene therapeutically rest on the possibility of creating a new sort of relationship, one that has the power to alter the course that the patient has been following.

The new emphasis on relationship, on interaction, on communication emerged independently in far-flung quarters of the psychoanalytic world. In the United States, Harry Stack Sullivan (1953) developed his "interpersonal psychiatry," with its emphasis on psychopathology as a personal method for coping with terrifying relationships and on the therapist as a "participant-observer" offering a new, mutative quality of relatedness. In Great Britain, W. R. D. Fairbairn (1952) built on the work of Melanie Klein (1935, 1946) to create what he called an "object relations theory of personality" that was couched in language vastly different from Sullivan's but that contained similar insights. Similar sensibilities informed the work of Karen Horney (1937, 1939), Erich Fromm (1941), Clara Thompson (1964), D. W. Winnicott (1965) and, later, the "psychology of the self" developed by Heinz Kohut (1971, 1977). The "relational model" of psychoanalysis (Greenberg & Mitchell, 1983) is defined by a shared belief in the developmental, structural, and therapeutic importance of relationships.

The relational model did not simply offer a new way of thinking about personality and psychopathology. Each of its proponents suggested that rethinking familiar psychoanalytic teaching would make treatment available to groups of patients traditionally thought to be unreachable. Freud had developed both his theory and his therapy on the basis of work with highly functional people who requested treatment for disturbing but relatively circumscribed psychogenic difficulties. The instrusive symptoms of conversion hysteria or obsessive–compulsive neurosis were the targets of his method.

As early as the 1920s it became apparent, however, that a therapy focused narrowly on symptoms had limited applicability. Accordingly, over a period of several decades, clinicians intrigued by Freud's insights (and more or less identified with the psychoanalytic movement) have experimented with applying psychoanalytic principles to a range of patients previously considered "too disturbed" to benefit from treatment. Sullivan worked psychodynamically with schizophrenics; Fairbairn analyzed profoundly traumatized and frightened "schizoid" patients; Winnicott treated those deeply regressed patients who had never become what he called "a whole person among whole people"; and, most recently, Kohut developed a method for analyzing severely impaired patients with "narcissistic character disorders."

The early relational analysts lived and worked in different times and different places. They were not necessarily aware of each others' ideas or clinical findings. Nevertheless, two common themes emerged from their efforts. First, there was a consensus that the theory developed by Freud and his followers within classical psychoanalysis cannot adequately explain the psychopathology of this new group of patients. These people were not simply struggling with conflicts between forbidden sexual and aggressive impulses on the one hand and repression enforced by the demands of society on the other. Rather, their difficulties were the result of severe disturbance in their early relationships with the important people in their lives. Although different analysts emphasized different aspects of the early interactions, they converged in their appreciation of the importance of environment in shaping personality and its disturbance. What kinds of people were the parents, the siblings, or members of the extended family? What were their own needs, defenses, and emotional difficulties? And how did these qualities affect the growing child?

In addition to noticing the etiological force of early relationships, relational analysts arrived at a second shared sensibility: They saw that the success of treatment depended on there being something reparative in the new relationship that develops between therapist and patient. Therapeutic action does not depend simply on the information that the analyst conveys to the patient through interpretations. The various relational analysts emphasized different facets of the patient–therapist relationship. Sullivan stressed the therapist's interest in and respect for the patient, especially for his/her fears and anxieties. Winnicott talked at length about the need for therapists to create a *holding environment* for the patient, within which past traumas could be relived. Kohut described the therapist's empathy: his/her willingness to meet and to understand the patient's own point of view. Running through these various formulations is the belief that being in therapy is a new interpersonal experience for the patient. The quality of this experience—intensified by patients investing the process with their hope for an improved life and also with fears about changing—profoundly influences the outcome of treatment.

Although it is a fair generalization to say that relational psychoanalysis and psychotherapy developed out of attempts to treat "new" and more severely disturbed patients, each relational theorist quickly asserted the value of the new method for all patients. Today, the heirs of Sullivan's interpersonal psychiatry, of the object relations tradition of Fairbairn and Winnicott, and of Kohut's self psychology practice psychotherapies based on relational premises across the entire diagnostic spectrum. All relational approaches have outgrown their origins; each contains a comprehensive model of treatment. This method of psychoanalytic psychotherapy is the treatment of choice for anyone who wishes to address problems in living by exploring his/her experience in depth, within the context of a relationship that facilitates emotional openness and risk taking.

Because each evolved independently, the various relational approaches are not identical and may not even be fully compatible. They share the fundamental assumptions about psychopathology and its treatment, not specific techniques or rules of procedure. In this chapter, we develop a model of therapy that is based as much as possible on these shared premises. We note when our presentation departs notably from the specific techniques that are central to one or another of the individual theories that make up the relational model.

THE CONCEPT OF PERSONALITY

All psychoanalytic theory and therapy is based on the premise that throughout the course of life peoples' experience shapes their personality, and that the impact of experience is greatest in the impressionable years of childhood. The concept of personality—the more typical terms in the psychoanalytic literature are "character" or "psychic structure"—points to a continuity that makes a particular person identifiable over a range of circumstances that are externally dissimilar. This continuity covers many aspects of psychological functioning: personal needs and desires, including the way priorities among them are set; anxieties and fears; ways of pursuing goals and defending against fears, both interpersonally and intrapsychically; beliefs and assumptions about oneself and others; ways of reacting to life circumstances; and so on. The psychoanalyst assumes that people bring themselves into every situation in which they become involved, and that there are demonstrable patterns to their behavior. For example, a man may react in a particular way to all relationships with people he sees as authority figures. We would, then, expect to find similarities running through his interactions with his boss, his tennis instructor, his father, his wife, and eventually his therapist. These patterns reflect his hopes, fears, and expectations with authorities as they have developed over the course of his life. Characterological patterns are at the center of psychoanalytic therapy; we work with what is stable and continuous in our patients' lives.

One of the important functions of psychoanalytic theory has been to draw "maps" of the personality that can guide therapists in their efforts to understand the forces that shape character and its psychopathology. Freud's division of the mind into *id*, *ego*, and *superego* is one example of such a map. For Freud, the *id* contains everything that is most primitive, even bestial, in our personalities; it is the repository of untamed, unsocialized sexual and aggressive urges that are passed down to us from our evolutionary past. The *superego*, in contrast, develops largely on the basis of our interaction with the external world; it contains the prohibitions against the sort of instinctual expression that the id demands but that society cannot tolerate. The task of the *ego* is to adjudicate among the competing demands of the id, the superego,

and the external world; it must find a route to some satisfaction of id instincts without unduly compromising our capacity to live in a world of other people. Individual character, in Freud's model, is determined by the nature of these three psychic structures, by the conflicts that arise among their often incompatible goals, and by the kinds of solutions to these conflicts that the individual adopts.

Just as there are many different ways to map a particular geographic area, so there are many ways to map psychic structure. Because relational psychoanalysis evolved simultaneously in the work of many different theorists, there is no one consensually agreed upon alternative to Freud's model. There is, however, general agreement among relational theorists that Freud drew too sharp a distinction between biologically determined and socially determined aspects of the personality. Everything about us, the relational theorist asserts, is shaped by our experience in the interpersonal world (even if everything is also influenced by our organismic nature). Accordingly, maps of character structure reflect different aspects of our relationships with others.

In constructing their maps, relational psychoanalysts rely heavily on the concept of *mental representation*. These representations contain the psychic residue, the imprint of interpersonal living as it is experienced by the individual. A simple example from early in life will help clarify the concept. Imagine a child playing contentedly by himself while his mother reads. After a while, the child becomes bored and approaches his mother to join him in a game. Mother, who is ready for company herself, is pleased that the child wants to be with her, and the two find something that they can enjoy together.

The child's mental representation of this experience will have three components: a representation of the self, a representation of the mother, and a representation of the interaction between the two of them. The child will represent himself as needing something from another person but as comfortable in approaching somebody who can meet the need and capable of asking effectively for what he needs. The mother will be represented as available, interested, capable of meeting a need, and able to enjoy the child's presence. The interaction itself is satisfying, both participants are able to give and to get something from the other, and both are competent and powerful at fulfilling their roles.

Mental representations are not memories, nor are they established by single events. Rather, they are summaries of interactions that have taken place over the course of life. These summaries are structuralized; they become mental templates that give later experience its shape. Staying with our example, we can see that the representation growing out of this event—if it is powerful enough to influence the child's subsequent experience—would lead to an optimistic streak in his personality. He would assume that having a need is good because it tends to lead to satisfying interactions with others. He would also have faith in the interest and generosity of other people, so that approaching them would be comfortable for him.

Of course, it is unlikely that the mother in our example will always be as available to the child as she was in this instance. At other times she may be preoccupied, tired, anxious, depressed, or perhaps just involved in some other activity. The child himself will not always be so unambivalently interested in his mother; often he will wish that his father was there instead, or that he could go over to a friend's house, or that he had a sibling. The quality of the interaction is highly variable and will depend on the mesh between the mental states of the two participants. There are multiple representations of all sorts of relational expe-

riences. Some of these are complementary, some conflictual, some are easily accessible to conscious awareness, others are so threatening that they must be repressed, denied access to consciousness. Although representations are stable structures, the particular representations that guide our experience at any given moment are influenced by contemporary circumstances and are thus subject to change.

It is important to emphasize that mental representations are not veridical renderings of interpersonal events; they are not like mental photographs of something that an outside observer could have seen happening. The "represented" father, for example, will necessarily not look like the father who is experienced by his friends, his boss, his employees, or his own father. Consider the change in the way people appear to us—even in the simplest physical sense—as we grow up. To the small child, all adults are giants; this alone is enough to convey an impression of enormous strength and potency. All of us carry around old mental representations in which we are small and weak, while the people who are most important to us are huge and strong. The stability and persistence of these archaic representations explains why it is so difficult to change peoples' impressions of their parents (or of others like them), even when there is "objective" contemporary proof that the impressions are distorted.

The way both self and other are experienced and represented is highly influenced not only by perceptual factors (e.g., the way adults appear to children gazing up at them) but also by the needs of the individual subject. Freud became aware of this very early in his career and suggested that we experience other people virtually exclusively as *objects* of our biologically based, phylogenetically determined sexual and aggressive drives. Relational psychoanalysts argue that this

Freudian "dual instinct theory" is too narrow to account adequately for the broad range of human relational experience. They have not, however, developed any unified motivational theory to replace it. But there is some consensus among psychoanalysts working with this model that we can specify two broad categories of need that may be considered universal. Each of us needs to feel secure both emotionally and physically, free from anxiety, unthreatened by external trauma. Although we all strive to maintain this sense of safety, it is not all that we want. Sometimes, in fact, we will sacrifice security for excitement: Mountain climbers, parachutists, and intellectual risk takers do this all the time. From this, relational analysts infer an equally powerful need for self-expression, competence, or what some have called "effectance" (White, 1963; Greenberg, 1991). These two sets of needs may be complementary or they may conflict with each other; their state at any moment will be an important element in determining the tone of interpersonal experience and its mental representation.

Like all psychoanalysts, adherents of the relational model believe that mental health and psychopathology lie on a continuum. This is inherent in any system that emphasizes personality and difficulties in living rather than the presence or absence of discrete symptoms. The concepts of mental representation and the ubiquitous needs for safety and effectance help to define the healthy individual, at least in broad strokes. Health requires the person to integrate, express, and satisfy his/her various needs in a way that maintains a positive sense of self (a generally good self-representation) and realistically positive feelings about other people (generally good representations of others). This will make it possible for the individual to have solid interpersonal relationships and also to use his/her own capacities fully. A person living in this way

will feel emotionally strong, in control of things, and generally in a positive emotional state. Such a person will not, of course, be immune to buffeting by life's circumstances or by the stresses that are often inherent in pursuing one's goals.

THE PATHOLOGICAL OR DYSFUNCTIONAL INDIVIDUAL

Relational psychoanalysts are, like all psychotherapists, concerned with the sorts of disabling symptoms that frequently bring people to treatment. The early sessions of any therapy will be partially devoted to ascertaining the presence and severity of such focal symptoms: mood disorders, phobias or other anxiety-related states, obsessions or compulsions, psychotic symptoms, and so on. However, as our discussion of the healthy personality suggests, the deeper understanding of these symptoms—and of psychopathology generally—hinges on their relation to the patient's underlying personality structure. Assessment, then, is geared to getting a sense of the stable patterns that characterize a person's functioning across a wide range of specific circumstances.

Because relational therapists believe that character is forged in experiences with other people, the diagnostic process will focus significantly (although not exclusively) on the quality of the patient's relationships, current and past. A great deal of attention is paid to the way interpersonal experience is described and to the patient's manner of talking about important people in his/her life. The therapist will infer from the account of these experiences the sorts of relationships that have been benign and growth enhancing for the patient and those that have led to difficulties of various sorts. This will indicate areas of contemporary functioning that need work and will also provide a clue about where to look for the source of trouble in the patient's life history.

A particularly important source of diagnostic information for the relational therapist is the quality of the transference that the patient develops. The emphasis on using transference as a diagnostic tool is unique to psychoanalytic psychotherapy and is relied on most heavily by therapists with a relational orientation. Virtually from the first session, patients have characteristic ways of experiencing and behaving with the therapist. The range of possibilities is limitless. Just to suggest two extremes, some patients see the therapist as an interested professional who wants to be helpful; others see the therapist as a punitive authority figure eager to humiliate or to harm in some other way. Every psychotherapist who is open to the full force of the patient's transference has had such experiences with patients. It is clear that the transference can be disruptive to treatment, especially when the feelings that get stirred up are powerfully negative. However, it is also the only relationship that the therapist can experience directly. It is, therefore, a crucial source of information about the nature of the patient's relationships and about the formative experiences that led to current difficulties in living.

A key hypothesis of the relational psychoanalytic model is that psychopathology, like healthy character, is forged in the crucible of the child's experience with important people in his/her life. These early interactions give rise to mental representations that shape subsequent beliefs, feelings, and behavior. In the previous section we described an exchange between a child and his mother that could lead to positively toned, sustaining representations. We also suggested that for a variety of reasons involving the mother's state of mind or availability, or the child's mood, the result might be quite different emotionally. Imagine, for example, that the child was feeling particularly needy and that the mother was depressed and wanting to be left alone. Under such circumstances, the mother would regard the child's approach as a troublesome imposition, and the child would experience his mother's reaction as a harsh rebuff. If this type of experience were repeated often enough, the child would develop a mental representation in which he was demanding, intrusive, and unappealing. Mother would be represented as unavailable and rejecting. Finally, the child will come to believe that others are uninterested in him, especially when he needs them most, and perhaps that his needs themselves are bad.

We suggested in the previous section that the quality of experience as it is represented depends in large measure on the needs that children bring to their interactions. A central hypothesis of relational psychoanalysis is that as people develop, the types of relationships that they need change continuously. These changing needs give rise to different types of interaction with others. There are many ways of conceptualizing the flow of development; perhaps the most general is W. R. D. Fairbairn's (1952) idea that we all move from the need for absolute dependence on others to what he called "mature dependence," in which there is intimacy but also considerable autonomy. It is easy to see that the quality of interpersonal experience and the nature of the mental representations deriving from it depend on the needs that a person is experiencing at his/her particular developmental level. During early infancy, for example, the child requires the nearly constant presence of a caretaking adult who will be able to anticipate and respond to needs before the child can express them explicitly. Representations of such experiences will be positively toned and will contribute to what D. W. Winnicott (1965) called a healthy feeling of omnipotence and to what Erik Erikson (1963) called "basic trust" in the goodness of others.

But quickly, children develop the need to spread their own wings, to be able to do for themselves. If the adult fails to adjust to this change, the child is likely to feel intruded upon and stifled. Representations of a hovering adult's constant presence later in development will have an aversive tone; the child will feel too weak to resist the adult and afraid of the possibility of being overwhelmed by others. All of us have had both positive and negative experiences with our caretakers; the conflicting mental representations to which they give rise account for ambivalent feelings about both ourselves and others when we think of ourselves as dependent.

The concept of conflicting representations is central to the understanding of psychopathology in the relational model. In the course of development, we come to experience ourselves and other people in some ways that are so different from what we would like to believe that we cannot admit them into conscious awareness. Just which experiences will be unacceptable itself depends on our early relationships. The list is endless: Some people cannot fully acknowledge their own anger, dependency, sexuality, ambitions, or competitiveness. Some people cannot accept insights that they have about important people in their lives: An admired older brother was frightened of life and self-destructive; a mother was less devoted and more depressed than she wanted known; a father was covertly critical and undermining of his wife and his children.

When experiencing a representation consciously leads to powerfully negative feelings (anxiety, guilt, depression, shame, etc.), the representation will be subject to repression. When this happens, although it will be banished from awareness, the representation will not disappear. Repression underlies both symptoms and character pathology because the rejected representations continue to influence the person's experience and behavior. People who cannot see themselves as dependent, for example, will seek to gratify their dependency indirectly and covertly. They will not *be* less dependent because of repression, but their attempts to get even their quite normal needs met will be tortured and fraught with unpleasant feelings.

People who have had to ward off certain kinds of perceptions of others will continue to have such perceptions but will try (typically without success) to hide them. Consider a man who grew up with a father who wanted to be seen as benign and supportive but who was actually quite competitive with his son. The son would sense the competitiveness but be too anxious to address it directly. We would expect that later in life he would react to male authorities as potential competitors, probably in some veiled manner. His behavior is likely to antagonize others and get him into trouble with teachers and bosses. All this would go on without either party being fully aware of what was happening. A man who had this underlying character problem might come to a therapist complaining that he does not seem to be getting ahead professionally as much as his abilities suggest he could.

THE ASSESSMENT OF DYSFUNCTION

Assessment is carried out informally and automatically in the course of getting to know the patient and why the patient wants to be in therapy. The early phase of treatment is characterized by focused inquiry and observation of the patient. Several factors need immediate attention. First, the therapist must consider whether the patient has a mood or thinking disorder (e.g., schizophrenia or depression) that will affect how well he/she can use therapy and whether medication will be required. It is especially important to evaluate the suicide potential of a depressed patient.

In addition, a general assessment is made of the diagnostic category that best describes the patient in terms of cognitive and personality style so that the therapist can quickly begin working on the most effective way to engage and help the patient. For example, if the patient has an hysterical style, the therapist might have difficulty getting specific details and would automatically begin to try to teach the patient how to communicate in a less impressionistic and more informative way. Or, with a paranoid patient the therapist would realize that a casual, joking therapeutic style might be inappropriate and would respect the aloofness in the relationship that the patient might need.

Assessment of the strengths and weaknesses of the patient continues as the therapist gains more information in the course of treatment. Three general areas of functioning are directly relevant to working on psychological problems in treatment: cognitive abilities, which include the person's judgment and reality-testing and decision-making abilities; emotional capabilities, which include the person's capacity for relationships and the ability to handle fluctuations in feelings, moods and energy levels; and self-defeating factors, which include the unconscious components of the personality that might create conflict and lead to actions or lack of actions that are not in line with stated goals. (In other words, how free is a person to act in a way that will lead to the results that are desired?)

The positive aspects of patients' functioning are also assessed. People usually operate successfully in some areas of their lives and are dissatisfied about other areas. Patients' resources can be used to improve aspects of functioning that need bolstering. Also, these strengths can be an important source of motivation and

fortification when the patient is feeling frustrated or discouraged about the problems he/she is experiencing. Consider the case of Peter, who came into therapy at the age of 25 when he decided to return to college. He had dropped out 8 years earlier because he was anxious about being able to develop a relationship with a woman. The social discomfort preoccupied him to the point that he just wanted to get away from the scrutiny and pressure of his dorm mates, even though he was doing well academically. When he finally did return to school and started treatment, he spent much of his time discussing the reasons for his problems with relationships, stemming from difficult relationships he had with an overly involved and intrusive mother and a critical and distant father. The therapist helped Peter use his good cognitive skills that were an aid scholastically to sort out what had been happening in his family relationships, and how that was distorting his ability to relate to people in the present. When—as frequently happened—Peter felt overwhelmed and hopeless about rejections in relationships, the therapist reminded him of his intelligence and talents, which were appreciated by others if not by his parents. Over time these reminders helped Peter to detach himself from his parents' criticisms, and to hold on to his self-esteem. Peter did well in therapy, eventually going on to graduate school and becoming involved in a serious relationship with a woman.

Assessment is made at different levels of functioning; it includes the patient's emotional and mental state, his/her behavior in a variety of situations, and the nature of repetitive relational patterns that get played out. The therapist asks about how the patient acts in many different situations, takes note of the how the patient thinks, and also examines the interaction between them. The therapist is looking for areas of distress or success in relationships, work, and sense of self. Those areas that are defined as problems need to be looked at from the point of view of inconsistencies or contradictions. These are clues as to what conflict is preventing realization of the patient's acknowledged goals. For instance, one woman insisted that she wanted to leave an unsatisfying relationship but had not taken any of the necessary steps to achieve this goal. The therapist pointed out what this woman's behavior was saying and looked for the underlying causes of the contradiction. Perhaps she felt that her boyfriend would be devastated or inconsolable. Or perhaps she had questions about her own ability to manage outside of the relationship, or maybe both reasons contributed to the impasse. The assessment of the underlying problems or conflicts helps determine the direction of the therapy.

The relationship between patient and therapist becomes one of the best sources of information for the therapist because it reveals the transference and countertransference reactions of the participants. The *transference* reflects the way patients feel about and behave toward the therapist and is based on experiences drawn from other relationships. It is a customary and reflexive way of interacting that the patient has adopted to deal with various circumtances. For this reason, it reflects both what the patient is like as a person and what the therapist is like. What is happening in the transference is a guide to what happens in general for that patient.

For example, somebody who has an unconscious belief that the way he really feels is unacceptable or irrelevant to other people will present a false, compliant self in his/her relationships. It might be difficult for the therapist to know how ungenuine the patient feels because the patient cannot articulate something that is still unconscious and may not describe his/her outside relationships in a way that will make this clear to the therapist. However, it will be much more readily detectable in the therapy relationship, because the therapist will feel the effects of this firsthand. For instance, the patient will be a "good" patient who makes few demands and is accommodating. But the therapist will sense that there are times the patient is angry or discouraged, or the therapist may feel the lack of a depth or intensity in their relationship and will bring this up for discussion. The goal in this case would be to help the patient recognize the underlying feeling of being unacceptable, examine it for its validity or usefulness, and then uncover the more genuine aspects of the self which would then, it is hoped, be better integrated into the person's conscious outward presentation.

The *countertransference*, those of the therapist's feelings that are a reaction to the particular patient, are a source of information in much the same way. Therapists distinguish countertransference from feelings that they have that are not a response to the patient by knowing themselves well so that they know what is typical and likely to occur in reaction to a particular stimulus. Feelings that seem to be evoked by the patient can then be used to understand what usually goes on between the patient and another person. For example, if the therapist notices that he always feels sleepy during the session of a certain patient, at a time of day that he usually is not tired, and does not feel bored or sleepy in any of his other sesssions, it would become clear that the patient is doing something to keep the therapist away from him or to prevent an intensification in their relationship. The therapist would then bring this up for exploration.

THE PRACTICE OF THERAPY

In general, relational therapy is considered a treatment for people who are experiencing difficulties in living. This may be in terms of specific problems or critical situations, or it may be in more general terms of dissatisfactions or failure to actualize one's potential. Typically, people come into treatment because they are unhappy about relationships, career, or problems or suffer from anxiety or depression without necessarily being able to identify the causes. Usually, people start working on a specific or concrete problem, and as they continue in treatment they shift their focus to other concerns that may be of a more general nature (e.g., someone might start with the problem of a breakup with her boyfriend and go on to discuss what in her personality has made it difficult to stay in any long-term relationship).

Basic Structure

Sessions are usually held once or twice a week for 45 or 50 minutes. Under optimal circumstances, treatment begins with an open-ended commitment; the therapist does not set a time limit in advance. Occasionally, patients know that they will only be able to stay in therapy for a certain amount of time; they may, for example, be planning a move to another city in a year. This does not rule out the possibility of beginning treatment, but the therapist will inform the patient that there may not be enough time to achieve his/her stated goals. When it is open-ended, the total time spent in relational therapy is variable but typically can last anywhere from one year to several years, and in some cases longer.

The kind of treatment that psychoanalytic psychotherapy is and the nature of its goals explain the difficulty of setting time limits. Because the focus is on expanding patients' knowledge of previously disavowed aspects of themselves and their life circumstances, the concept of a predetermined end point—and even

the concept of cure itself—is not applicable. Instead, the work is defined by the problems the patient wants to resolve and by the interest in increasing self-awareness.

Because relational psychotherapy is exploratory, there is a flexibility inherent in its structure, so that goals themselves change or are enlarged as a result of the process itself. The situation is comparable to what happens in exploratory surgery, where it cannot be fully predicted what the extent of the work will be until there is a clear picture of what the problem is. In psychotherapy, of course, the patient's own interest in deepening his/her experience will be an important determinant of how far treatment goes.

One patient, Alice, entered treatment because she was not sure why she hesitated about making a commitment to her boyfriend, who was pressing her for one. As she talked about their relationship over a period of weeks she realized that she had qualms about some things she had noticed about him. She felt that he was overly dependent on his mother, who seemed to be too involved and too influential in his decision making. But becoming aware of these misgivings was not the end of the work for Alice. When questions were raised about why she had difficulty taking seriously what she had dimly noticed all along, she began to think about her relationship with her own parents. She had the same worries about her dependent relationship with them, she realized, as she had about her boyfriend's involvement with his mother. She then began talking about why she had not been able to move out of their house into her own place, even though she was 28 years old. Eventually she became interested in working on what she began to see as her limited aspirations for herself, and the goals of therapy broadened considerably beyond the concern that had brought her to treatment in the first place.

The privacy of the two person situation is crucial in creating an atmosphere of safety and acceptance that can lead to a complete and honest appraisal of oneself. Accordingly, there is an emphasis on individual therapy in this approach. Sometimes, however, either patient or therapist feels that it would be helpful to include an important "other" for a limited number of sessions, as a way of acquiring additional information about the patient's most important relationships. These changes in format are thoroughly discussed both in advance and as sessions are held so that the patient's thoughts and feelings about them can be fully expressed.

There are two basic principles in relational psychoanalytic theory that are relevant in discussing why there is a preference for leaving sessions as unstructured as possible: unconscious processes and resistance. Because the *unconscious* contains much information—including a lifetime of memories and thoughts and feelings that are deemed irrational, illogical, or too unconventional—it is considered to be a valuable source of data in attempting to know one's self, to unveil hidden potential, and to help the personality expand. Therefore, what is contained in the unconscious is extremely important; without it one has knowledge of only a limited aspect of the personality.

Unconscious ideas are kept out of awareness for different reasons. One reason is that the unconscious provides a safe place for feelings and thoughts that are anxiety provoking, so there is some protection from the debilitating effects of anxiety. However, as the unconscious is seen as a necessary adjunct or aid to the work being done in therapy the therapist wants to provide an atmosphere that will enhance the emergence of unconscious material. A good way of "catching" the elusive unconscious is by recognizing it and defining it when it slips into consciousness for a moment. The more some unconscious thought is talked about the more it becomes available to the patient as something that can be worked on.

The opportunity for the patient to be spontaneous and to say whatever comes to mind (which is a simplified way of utilizing free association) are aids in providing an atmosphere that is more conducive to the emergence of unconscious material. Therefore, the therapist usually waits to hear what the patient says at the beginning of the session rather than starting the session him/herself. Similarly, the therapist waits for the patient to choose the topics of the session rather than imposing his/her own thoughts on the patient.

The British psychoanalyst Masud Khan described the therapist as a slave to the patient's process. This means that the therapist must wait for certain material to emerge. What the therapist is looking for is material that will be helpful in understanding and resolving the issues the patient has designated as areas of interest or concern. Unlike other forms of psychoanalytically oriented therapy, the therapist does not take the role of the expert who knows better than the patient him/herself what needs to be addressed, so the therapist waits to hear what is on the mind of the patient.

Resistance is another facet of the unconscious that needs to be understood in working from a relational viewpoint, and another reason that therapists avoid structuring sessions. The belief is that conflict permeates all mental processes. Another way to say this is that for every thought there is an opposing thought. For any situation there is a positive and a negative aspect, and a conscious and an unconscious aspect. An example of conscious ambivalence is the idea of going on a vacation. Although for many people this is a positive decision, there are also concerns that are evoked, such as how much the trip will cost, what will happen during the time the person is gone, how much work will be piling up at the office, and so on.

Indications of unconscious conflict become clear when what the person says is at odds with what the person does. For instance, in the example of Alice given earlier, Alice said she wanted to be in a serious relationship but when the opportunity arose she found it difficult to make a commitment. On a conscious level she may have felt comfortable in her view of herself as independent and ready to deal with the anxiety that would develop for both her and her parents when she moved out of their house. However, unconsciously there were many other considerations. For one, she sensed but could not let herself know fully that her parents were very dependent on her emotionally, and they dreaded the loss of the closeness in the relationship with her. They had been so good to her that it was difficult to think about disappointing and hurting them. In addition, she knew that although there were many benefits to the relationship with her boyfriend there were ways in which he was demanding, and she did not want to get involved in another relationship where she felt somebody else was controlling her, as she had felt for many years with her parents.

When the thought of exploring a particular issue becomes anxiety producing, aspects of the personality that are security seeking will come into play, and the person may avoid dealing with the very issue for which he/she has come into treatment. Or the resistance may take the form of not being able to really hear what the therapist is saying or reacting to the interventions in an oppositional way. The therapist wants to leave open the possibility for the resistance to be expressed by the patient. One way to increase this possibility is for the therapist to hear what is on the mind of the patient—whatever that might be. The

more structured the session, the less likely oppositional thoughts that are not fully in awareness will be revealed and subsequently worked through.

Although relational analysts avoid structuring sessions too rigidly, there are times when some structure is imposed, either by the therapist or by the patient. For example, patients sometimes have specific topics that they want to cover in a particular sesssion. They may have procrastinated and failed to finish some important work for a boss, or they may have neglected to make plans for the weekend, which always leads to a despondency and loneliness on days off. If the patient then does not discuss what he/she initially stated was important, the therapist may remind the patient of what his/her goal was, and ask whether the patient wants to change it. This guidance by the therapist is a way of helping the patient fight against the resistance he/she might feel to discussing something. Similarly, even if the patient has not made a specific statement about what he/she wants to talk about but seems to be wasting time, talking about trivial matters, or repeating things he/she has already gone over, the therapist may ask questions to help the patient address what seems to be a more productive line of thought.

Another way in which the therapist structures the time is by asking about something he/she feels is important that has not been brought up by the patient. The simplest example is that of a subject that is obviously a big part of the patient's life but which is not talked about (e.g., "You've told me a great deal about your mother, but you rarely mention your father. Why is that?"). Another important area that patients are often reluctant to bring up and which the therapist will question is the relationship between them. For instance, the therapist might say, "I noticed that you seemed annoyed that I have to cancel our next two sessions, but you didn't say anything about it. What was your reaction?"

Goal Setting

There is a two-tier system of working on goals that applies to any treatment in relational therapy; the general or underlying goals that are the foundation of all the work that is done, and the specific goals that the particular patient brings to the treatment. First we will discuss the general goals in detail and then give examples of how these apply to the specific issues that the patient addresses in treatment.

The underlying goals reflect the values of the therapist who believes that what will be most helpful to the person is an attempt to help a person achieve a richer experience of living by expanding the conscious and unconscious aspects of the mind, in both the cognitive and emotional spheres. In less abstract terms, this can be seen as helping the patient gain a better and deeper understanding of the patient's "self," relationships with others, and repetitive patterns in living, while minimizing the limiting effects of anxiety and psychic conflict.

How is this done? Let us look at each aspect of the mind that is potentially influenced by therapy and see how the goal to expand it can apply.

First, it is helpful to distinguish between conscious and unconscious, both of which play a part in the above-mentioned cognitive and emotional aspects of the mind. What is conscious is usually known to the patient but may not be as utilizable until there is an attempt to focus on it (e.g., the ability to analyze information in one's environment, or the ability to be more assertive with people). What is unconscious is that part of the mind that is usually not available to the person but contains information and feelings that form the basis for the beliefs,

attitudes, and behavioral patterns the person recognizes consciously. These include the themes and myths that the person has absorbed over time, which lead to the "rules" the person lives by (e.g., "you shouldn't trust anybody," or "if you treat people right they'll treat you right"). It also includes ideas that are troubling in some way because they are contradictory, shameful, or unconventional so that the person feels more comfortable suppressing them, making them something that is out of awareness. However, in order for people to have more understanding of themselves and others they need to know what is in the unconscious, for often it contains information that leads to ambivalent feelings or motivations that direct or even dictate their behavior.

What is the goal in terms of the cognitive area? The capacities for questioning and analyzing, for problem solving, for tolerating ambiguity, for learning about psychology (human nature), and for developing a story about one's self are all addressed here, in terms of both conscious and unconscious application. Improved ability to question is desirable because it enables patients to look more carefully at themselves and their situation, to recognize the complexity of their lives, and to address problems without feeling that nothing can be done about them. This leads to the ability to look for previously unacknowledged meanings of events in peoples' lives, and to the assumption that there are multiple ways of looking at things. Problem solving is a process that leads to change and a skill that people can develop. The aim is to provide patients with tools that they can use after leaving therapy, including the ability to define a problem, assess its severity or extent, formulate an understanding of what conflict or motivation underlies the problem, develop options, make decisions, and tolerate ambiguity.

Another interesting development of work in therapy is the creation of a story about one's life. Usually, patients spend part of their time in treatment going over their history: what their families were like, their experience of childhood, how they did in school, their friendships, and other important circumstances (e.g., a major illness, frequent moving around, and financial instability). Then patients integrate what they know about events and circumstances with what they can now understand about themselves or about people who were important to them (e.g., the birth of a sibling with a critical illness imposed certain burdens on the family, which resulted in the mother's becoming depressed or the father's emotional distance, etc.). The story that evolves with the help of the therapist becomes an important aid in making sense of one's past and one's personality. This can be seen as another cognitive tool that the patient develops that forms the base of a cognitive structure to help explain things in a person's life. Much as scientists use theory to assemble data and make sense of them, and to enable them to make predictions about future events, patients can use knowledge of their history in the same way.

The emotional aspects of the mind are also expected to expand during treatment in the sense that the person is able to be in touch with a greater array of feelings and also able to recognize more subtle feelings. For many people, feelings are placed into acceptable and unacceptable categories, and they deny or avoid those feelings that they think are not acceptable (a common example is anger). Or, they may feel threatened by the presence of certain feelings (e.g., dependency) so they are not acknowledged. With the opportunity to look at these feelings in a safe environment the individual can learn to accept them. At the same time, he/she can have a sense of control over them because they are part of his/her con-sciousness and can be regulated more effectively. A range of emotions enlivens and enriches the experience of living.

Linked to both the cognitive and the emotional aspects of the mind is creative ability, which can be enhanced by a therapeutic involvement. The possibility for a person to be more in touch with feelings and fragments of thoughts that are different or even slightly odd and the ability to see something new that other people have not seen are critical parts of the creative process. By affording opportunities for patients to see the nuances and complexities of their own mind, relational therapy helps them develop a more creative approach to life.

The above is a summary of the underlying goals. The specific problems that the patient brings into therapy provide the focus and content for the therapeutic work, and the underlying goals are the means by which the problems are solved. Therefore, there is no question as to who determines the goals; patients are free to choose whatever they feel is meaningful to them, and in fact are expected to make the choice. The therapist's goal is to add to self-knowledge, not to interfere with the patient's choice of focus.

In working on these problems, the therapist tries from the beginning of the treatment to harness the potential of both the conscious and the unconscious aspects of the mind in a way that will increase the information that can be gathered from both spheres and at the same time allow for an enriching integration of both spheres. Exploration is carried on in the three areas mentioned previously: *the self* (e.g., Who am I? How do I characteristically react? How was I different in childhood, and would I like to reclaim some of that former way of being? Is my motivation so conflicted in certain areas that I can't set clear goals and pursue them successfully? etc.); *relationships* (e.g., What are my interactions with others like? Are there predictable conflicts that usually evolve in my relationships? Am I satisfied with the level of intimacy I have in my important relationships? What people in my mind still have a hold on me? etc.); and *repetitive patterns* (e.g., Why do I always sabotage myself when I'm on the verge of success? Why do I choose the same kind of boy/girlfriend over and over again even though it's a problematic match? Why do I always find something to worry about instead of enjoying myself? etc.).

From the previous discussion about the two categories of goals, underlying and specific, it follows that the way goals are set for the treatment is through an interaction. The specific goals the patient states become the central goals for the manifest content of the work in the sessions. The patient also decides what is most important to work on, and, as in the example given earlier, the definition and prioritization of the goals are expected to change as the work continues. Although in some way this can be construed as the difference between intermediate and ultimate goals, in fact it is not. Because the underlying goals are very general and focus on the attainment and expansion of self-knowledge, all the efforts of the patient in this direction are equally important.

Techniques and Strategies of Therapy

Before describing the various techniques used in relational treatment, it is important to have an overview of the use of technique in all of psychoanalytic therapy. There are two different approaches that determine how decisions about technique are made, the technique-driven approach (exemplified by classical psychoanalysis, in which "correct" technique is clearly specified) and the interaction-driven approach (exemplified by relational psychoanalysis). Although this is

a simplification, the two approaches can be described as differing on the basis of whether content or process is being emphasized when the therapist is trying to understand the patient. Content refers to what is thought to be innate or predetermined in the patient, for instance, the need for mirroring by the parent or the aggressive drive that leads to competitiveness between father and son. Process refers to the events that occur in the relationships that are being talked about, including that between therapist and patient. For example, the process would include a discussion of the repetitive ways of acting toward and reacting to people that the patient also replays in the treatment.

The technique-driven approach emphasizes content. It is used by therapists who work from a theoretical model that makes certain assumptions: that there are drives that dictate human behavior and that much of what constitutes personality is derived from innate or biologically determined factors. The theory prescribes what should happen between the therapist and patient. For example, the classical theory specifies that the therapist should create an atmosphere that will promote the emergence (from the unconscious to the conscious) of repressed infantile wishes. To accomplish this, the therapist uses techniques that will enable his/her personality to recede to the background of the interaction, to propel that of the patient to come forward to the greatest extent possible so that it can be thoroughly analyzed. The therapist remains anonymous and asks the patient to say everything that comes to mind (*free association*). The therapist is listening for material that reflects the primitive sexual and aggressive drives that need to be tamed (renounced by the patient and exchanged for more appropriate goals). The therapist, through the process of transference, also acts like a conduit through which the wishes are channeled and acted out. This means that the patient will have feelings about the therapist that are feelings that have developed in other important relationships. These feelings get carried over, or transferred, to the therapist and are an important source of information about how the patient feels and acts toward people in general. There are certain techniques that are considered helpful in uncovering the transference, such as neutrality, abstinence (not gratifying the patient), and anonymity. So the technique-driven therapist obeys these specific rules with the expectation that the force of the drives will always create the situation that is described above, as long as the therapist does not interfere in this naturally occurring course of events.

By contrast, the interaction-driven therapist, working from a theoretical model that focuses on the process between patient and therapist, does not have specified rules about what the content of the therapy work should be. Instead, he/she starts with a more general goal: to expand cognitive and emotional capacities by making the unconscious conscious. For example, the theory behind relational theory does not depend on examining the content (e.g., sexual, aggressive, or need for idealization) behind the problem being talked about but rests on the expectation that exploration and discussion of the interactions between the patient and others, and the new experiences resulting from the therapeutic relationship, will help expand the patient's knowledge of him/herself.

Any number of techniques might be used, but they would be chosen with a certain strategy in mind. For example, if a particular patient had very intrusive, overinvolved parents, the therapist might be seen in the same light if she were active, responsive, and self-revealing to the patient. If this made it difficult for the patient to engage in a process of self-exploration, the therapist might decide to be quieter and more restrained than she typically is with patients. For another patient, whose parents were aloof and uninterested, the therapist might have to extend herself more to be present and self-disclosing in order to facilitate the patient's participation in treatment. Therefore, it would be hard to specify in advance what particular interventions or techniques would be used by the therapist. What is most important to the relational therapist is to create an atmosphere in which there is a balance between a comfortable, familiar, secure feeling and a new and challenged feeling for the patient. The goal is for patients to feel safe enough to experiment, but not so comfortable that they feel passive and unstimulated.

In the repertoire of techniques that the relational therapist uses, a further distinction can be made between those by which the therapist "joins" with the patient and those by which the therapist "separates from" the patient. The joining techniques are those that emphasize the therapist's alliance and agreement with the patient, with the expectation that this will increase security, openness, and depth in what the patient is talking about because a feeling of safety is achieved. These techniques include such things as empathy, support, understanding, mirroring or reflecting the patient's experience, joining the defenses of the patient, and entering the patient's world. Those techniques that enhance the separation or distance from the patient are thought to challenge the patient, to offer a bridge to a way of thinking that is different, yet not threatening. Some examples are reality testing (i.e., making personal judgments about the circumstances of a patient's life or about the patient's behavior), reframing, curiosity, detailed inquiry, clarification, interpretation, and uncovering the unconscious. There are also techniques that can be used in either a joining or separating way, such as silence, free association, and the use of the therapist's own marginal or fleeting thoughts.

How is the decision made to use a particular technique? There are some cases in which there would be a need to modify the overall strategy of the treatment. For instance, with more seriously disturbed patients, the therapist would most likely want to decrease the amount of regression the patient experiences in the treatment, so the therapist would be more structured and more active. In some cases, for example, when time is limited or the patient is not able to articulate his/her problems, there would be more direction given to the patient in the form of "assignments" (e.g., to read something, or keep a written record of events or thoughts, or to try a new experience in order to overcome a fearful inhibition). In certain circumstances, such as severe depression or anxiety, a consultation for an evaluation for medication might be suggested.

In general, decisions about technique in relational therapy are being made continuously, in an ongoing assessment. An important aspect of this is the matter of the treatment alliance, which refers to the part of the therapist–patient relationship that enables them to work collaboratively. As is true of the treatment work in general, the alliance is established through the therapist's efforts to create an environment that offers a balance between safety and a novel and challenging experience. The alliance has to be established early on in treatment and has to be maintained in order for the work to progress. Because there is a commitment in relational therapy to examine the relationship continuously, whether it seems to be going smoothly or not, there is an automatic focus on what is happening with the therapeutic alliance. Sometimes the naturally occurring resistance that the patient experiences from time to time will become more intense, or a negative transference will develop that erodes the

alliance. An example of this would be the emergence of a new suspicion that the therapist is not really concerned about what is good for the patient but wants the patient just to work out his problems in the most expedient way so that the therapist can feel gratification about good results. A different scenario would be the case in which there seems to be little resistance or negativism. The therapist would still explore the relationship and question whether the patient is maintaining an artificially friendly feeling because he/she is afraid to confront his/her own doubts or mistrust or is afraid to anger the therapist. In either case these issues would be discussed.

Resistance to change is a normal part of the process of therapy. Although there are many ways in which people act out their resistances in the treatment, from a relational perspective, patients are seen as transforming the relationship with the therapist into a familiar but stultifying one, similar to an older relationship. So patients create situations in which they feel less anxiety but at the same time are not growing or making changes because they are not allowing themselves the opportunity for a new experience.

How is this dealt with by the therapist? Again, the theory of technique suggests that if the therapist steps back and scrutinizes what is happening in the dyad of therapist and patient, and not just in the content of what is being said, a break in repetitive patterns can be made. In this way the therapist does not get caught up in the "dance" (Levenson, 1972) that the patient initiates. However, this is more easily said than done, and the most common and most serious mistake that therapists can make is to allow themselves to be transformed into figures from the patient's previous experiences without analyzing this process and pointing it out to the patient. It is not an error to be caught up in the reenactments of old experiences by the patient, because that is inevitable, but the error is in losing sight of the fact that this is occurring. In addition, therapists need to look at their own participation and contribution to the reenactment or repetitive pattern to see how they perpetuate the cycle. It is especially difficult to analyze and be aware of one's own behavior, so a special effort must be made to keep this in the forefront of the therapist's thinking.

Termination

How is the decision made to terminate in relational therapy? Usually at the point when the defined goals have been met and the patient is not arriving at new goals, the therapist or patient will bring up the question of termination. (Obviously, there are situations in which a termination occurs because reality factors dictate the necessity for ending, but here we are talking about a choice based on the preference to end rather than to continue.) There are always issues that remain that patients feel need more attention, but at some point they recognize that they no longer need the help or the structure of the treatment to accomplish these goals. There may also be further goals that the therapist thinks about which might seem worthy of pursuit, and he/she would bring this up with the patient for discussion. It is then up to the patient to decide whether these new goals (or old goals that have been only partially met) require additional time in treatment. The expectation is that both the therapist and the patient will have an opinion about the advisability of terminating, and both will feel free to express their views. Ultimately the decision rests with the patient, of course.

In relational therapy the ideal situation for termination to occur is when there has been a significant amount of time to prepare for the ending, perhaps several weeks or several months. It is recognized that the time from the decision to the actual ending is a unique and important experience. They are also particularly poignant issues that arise for everybody in their relationships, very often with little opportunity to work out the feelings that accompany leave taking with the other person. Issues of separation, sadness, grieving, indepencence, excitement, and confusion are all present in a way that they are at no other time during the therapy. Therefore, this situation is given special attention.

THE STANCE
OF THE THERAPIST

Effective psychoanalytic psychotherapy depends on the patient's ability to risk knowing thoughts and feelings so distressing that they have had to be kept away from consciousness for many years. Psychoanalysts believe that what we are afraid to know about ourselves and about our life experience compromises our ability to live life fully or to enjoy what we have. Accordingly, our patients must be helped to get on speaking terms with their deepest hopes, fears, wishes, beliefs, memories, and fantasies.

But there is a paradox here: The therapist's job is to help the patient to know the unknowable, to speak the unspeakable. How is this possible, in the face of all the fears and the sorrows that led to repression in the first place? Freud instructed his patients to "free associate"—to say aloud whatever came into their minds. He believed that if they did so, the analyst—an expert at reading between the lines and decoding hidden meanings in the patient's words—would be able to see through to the repressed and to fill in the gaps in the patient's conscious experience. All the analyst would need to do was to listen objectively, to appreciate both what was being said and what was being left unsaid, and to interpret what he/she understood in a way that the patient could assimilate. This is a difficult enough task in light of the powerful feelings that get stirred up when people are talking so personally about themselves.

From the beginning, relational psychoanalysts and psychotherapists have seen that treatment demands even more of the patient than Freud had imagined. What makes it possible for people to face nameless terrors that they have spent a lifetime avoiding? Simply wanting to change cannot be enough; if it were, nobody would need therapy in the first place. There must be, then, something that happens in the consulting room—in the relationship with the therapist—that makes self-disclosure and eventually psychological growth possible. Therapists working within the model of relational psychoanalysis have focused a great deal of attention on what the clinician can do to help patients feel safe and comfortable enough to take the risks that treatment requires. Accordingly, everything that the therapist does is guided by the goal of facilitating the patient's awareness of previously repressed ideas and feelings.

But one of the most important insights that relational psychoanalysts have achieved is that each of us has lived through highly personal experiences that have shaped what we believe to be safe and what we sense might be dangerous. This suggests that there is no one therapeutic stance that can be effective with all patients. Some patients, for example, will be comfortable with the benign distance, even the aloofness, of the classical psychoanalyst that Freud described. They will be able to experience a quiet, unintrusive interest that encourages the freedom to express themselves spontaneously. But this same posture will remind other patients of, say, a depressed, unavailable parent. These people learned to stifle their spontaneity to avoid disturbing such parents and to maintain whatever tenuous connection with them was possible. Accordingly, they may need an active therapist who talks more and who freely offers reassurance and support. We also know that these needs change over time, so that the patient–therapist relationship is always in a dynamic flux. Some patients need more activity at the beginning of treatment but later need the therapist to pull back in a way that helps them to feel more independent. Others start therapy with a need for distance but require more activity as they become able to tolerate fuller engagement and emotional intimacy with another person.

In light of these variations, a great deal of the training of the psychoanalytic psychotherapist goes toward building sensitivity to the relational needs of individual patients in a way that permits drawing on personal emotional potential to facilitate the work of treatment. This is one area in which the history of the relational model—its evolution in different places and within different traditions—comes to the therapist's aid, because there is no one "approved" method. Sullivan, for example, advocated the active use of probing, even challenging questions. Kohut suggested empathically reflecting what the patient had in mind in a way that stayed close to conscious experience. Many relational analysts of the British School believe that maintaining a traditional interpretive posture, moving quickly into what is most deeply buried in the unconscious, works best. As a result, the modern relational therapist has a range of alternatives to choose from. The clinician can be more active or directive when doing so facilites the patient's feelings of safety and willingness to take risks; he/she can be quieter and more receptive when that stance will work better. Similarly, there are no hard and fast rules about the therapist's self-disclosure; the decision whether to do so will be determined by what is most useful at any point in treatment.

There are some general principles that guide the therapist's thinking about what to do with particular patients. Psychotherapy is a collaborative enterprise in which the therapist can help the patient to clarify his/her experience but then respects the patient's right and responsibility to decide what to do with what has been learned. One woman, Ms. L, entered treatment because she was having difficulty completing work in a doctoral program and because she was feeling ambivalent about whether to go through with a marriage to her fiancé. Ms. L was the daughter of an extremely successful, charismatic, self-absorbed businessman who, when she was a child, would take her to conventions and meetings so that he could show off his brilliant, beautiful daughter. In the course of therapy, this patient learned both how exciting and how stifling these early experiences were for her. She also learned how similar her fiancé was to her father; he was in a similar line of work, he had similar ambitions, and he wanted a wife who would serve him in much the same way that she had served her father. Her fiancé disdained her professional goals and demanded a kind of attentiveness that interfered with the patient's full commitment to them, but he offered her the possibility of feeling connected to another powerful, exciting man.

When these issues were clarified in treatment, Ms. L was aware of and free to choose between the conflicting demands of marriage and career. The therapist believed deeply that these conflicts were the patient's own, that both reflected aspects of her life history that were simultaneously attractive and aversive to her. The therapist did not believe that it was his responsibility to make a choice or even to negotiate a compromise. Illuminating the issues involved is the goal of therapy; using what has been learned to shape life decisions is the responsibility of the patient.

Leaving choices to the patient does not, of course, mean that the therapist has no feelings about them. It is not possible to work closely with people's deepest hopes and fears without experiencing powerful countertransference reactions. The relational therapist accepts the inevitability of countertransference and believes that his/her feelings are a valuable clue to what is going on in the treatment process. Accordingly, the therapist will attend carefully to the countertransference rather than attempting to overcome it. In this case, for example, the therapist experienced a strong negative reaction to the patient's father and to her fiancé; he felt an urge to advise her to develop herself professionally and to fight against men's efforts to dominate her. But he also recognized that his own feelings reflected one side of Ms. L's own conflict, and that if he acted on them he would be playing out the role of yet another controlling man in her life. Realizing this, he was able to use the countertransference feelings to promote further exploration of the patient's own conflicts and of their expression in the therapy itself. This way of understanding and using countertransference is a natural application of the fundamental premises of relational psychoanalysis.

CURATIVE FACTORS OR MECHANISMS OF CHANGE

We have seen that relational psychoanalytic theory holds that personality and psychopathology are decisively shaped by the quality of early experiences with others. These experiences are perpetuated in subsequent relationships because they are familiar, exciting, and safe even though they may also be stifling. Ms. L's relationships with her father and fiancé fit this pattern, which the patient will attempt to reestablish in the treatment itself. If this happens—if the patient's transference and the therapist's countertransference mesh in a way that re-creates familiar patterns—the patient will be locked into old modes of experience, old satisfactions, old frustrations. Growth will not occur.

If there is to be change, then, there must be new qualities of relatedness. Ms. L, for example, must be able to experience the therapist as different from her father and her fiancé; she must be able to feel that she is with a man who is not interested in controlling and exploiting her. If she cannot feel this, her old beliefs will just be reconfirmed. For treatment to work, the patient must be able to feel a difference between what has always seemed inevitable and what could happen in the present. The nature of the therapeutic relationship—the determined scrutiny of the patient's transferential experience and the therapist's equally intense self-examination—makes this possible.

But it is not enough simply to offer the patient something different. Everybody encounters such offers as they live their lives. Ms. L, for example, certainly met many men who were not interested in dominating her, but because of her history she wound up either rejecting them or eliciting whatever potential they had for acting in the familiar pattern. The work of therapy revolves around helping the patient to become aware of the tension between the novel relationship that is offered and the old relationship that threatens to engulf it. Ms. L had to see how hard she worked to transform a therapist who was interested in clarifying her own conflicts into one who had a stake in her decision, and in controlling the course of her life. This is where insight—the central concept in psychoanalysis as Freud developed it—enters the picture. The patient must be made aware of the way the therapeutic relationship is developing and of the quality of the patient–therapist interaction. The

therapist's interpretations are the primary means for communicating this sort of understanding. When Ms. L would insist that the therapist say what he believed she should do, or even predict what he thought she might decide, he would respond by interpreting. He would say something like: "The idea of being left alone with a tough choice frightens you. You would prefer that I take the lead, even though that would put me in charge of directing your life."

This sort of interpretation reflects the patient's current experience, which for the relational therapist is the most important route to broadening self-understanding. For most patients, the process does not stop there, however. Understanding is deepened and consolidated when what is going on in the present can be connected with earlier patterns, providing a context within which apparently self-defeating behavior can be understood. Ms. L, for instance, might have felt ashamed of herself if things had been left with her attempts to transform and even to undermine the therapist's good intentions. Helping her to see the roots of this in a compelling relationship with her controlling father makes it apparent that she is doing what—until now—has been the best that she could possibly do. This promotes not only insight into the past but also an acceptance and even an appreciation of the struggles that she has gone through.

As patients become aware of the relational patterns on which they have relied throughout their lives, patterns that have simultaneously sustained and limited them, they begin to develop the ability and the courage to try out new ways of engaging the world. Relational therapists expect their patients to become better observers of themselves and others, and to be more confident and creative in organizing and valuing their own experience. As patients' emotional and interpersonal reality testing improves, they become able to act more effectively and affirmatively to achieve personal goals. Because change is a highly individual matter, there is no way of specifying what these new skills might look like for any particular patient: Some patients become more assertive, some less suspicious, some less anxiously controlling with others, and some more tolerant of intimate relationships. The list is virtually endless.

The acquisition of new skills is essential to the process of change because without them the patient remains locked into old, pathogenic patterns. We have already described the importance of insight in bringing about change, but for the relational therapist insight is never enough. Patients also need to experience new ways of being, both with the therapist and with other important people in their lives. In fact, there is a reciprocal relationship between insight and behavioral change—insight may lead to change, and change generates new insights.

Despite the importance of these new skills, they are rarely taught didactically in a relational psychotherapy. Typically, giving this sort of instruction would be seen as infringing unnecessarily on the patient's autonomy and as encouraging feelings of dependence that will compromise growth in the long run. Patients' failure to learn interpersonal skills (assertiveness, courtesy, fairness, etc.) is caused by underlying anxieties and conflicts; addressing these in the context of an affirmative therapeutic relationship makes new learning possible.

In some circumstances, when it seems that the patient needs only a small push to be able to use what he/she has learned in treatment, the therapist may make a didactic suggestion to help the patient get moving. This would be unusual, however, and before intervening in this way the therapist would give considerable thought to why doing so seemed necessary or useful at the moment. This is one example of how the therapist's analysis of his/her countertransference reactions plays an important role in the treatment process. Ms. L, for example, frequently asked the therapist for advice about how to deal with her fiancé. She felt that if only the therapist told her what to do she would be able to cope more effectively with his demands and to negotiate the conflict between her interest in the relationship with him and her professional ambitions. In this case the therapist had to allow himself to become aware of his feelings about Ms. L and her request. He was not immune to her suggestion that he could save her from a difficult situation; the idea that he could be "better" than the other men in her life was flattering and appealing. But because he also saw that this would ultimately work against Ms. L's capacity to grow on her own, he resisted the offer despite knowing that doing so would frustrate and anger her. One of the most important reasons that relational therapists are required to undergo a personal analysis is to help them avoid getting into interactions with their patients that seem gratifying to both participants but that inhibit change in the long run. Therapists must, as much as possible, keep their own needs out of the treatment process.

TREATMENT APPLICABILITY

Relational therapy can be used with many different types of patients and problems. However, there are certain types of people for whom relational therapy seems particularly effective. Rather than defining this group in terms of diagnostic categories, it makes more sense to describe the characteristics necessary for a person to receive maximum benefits. At the most basic level a person needs to have the interest and motivation to explore him/herself in a diligent, risk-taking, and flexible manner. There also has to be some basic trust and hope that the therapist can be helpful in the search for greater satisfaction. In addition, the person has to have some tolerance for the fact that life's problems that are precipitants for starting therapy often have complex and multifaceted roots, which require patience and hard work to unravel. Self-understanding and self-expansion are goals that are reachable, but usually in a way that is not as expedient or as complete as people would like.

Relational therapy can relatively easily be applied to groups of patients that some Freudian psychoanalysts would deem inappropriate. The various theories that predated the emergence of relational therapy were developed because there seemed to be a need for treatments that would be psychoanalytic in clinical application but based on different theoretical concepts. As stated earlier, severely disturbed individuals were treated by Sullivan (1962), Fairbairn (1952), and Kohut (1971, 1977). In addition, more recently there has been an expansion of treatments using the underlying principles of relational therapy in the areas of child and adolescent therapy and marital and family therapy (see Lionells, Fiscalini, Mann, & Stern, 1995).

In working with people who have less verbal facility (children, adolescents), or whose personality traits lead them to be less successful in interpersonal situations (paranoid or borderline patients) appropriate modifications in therapeutic technique are made. Sometimes more education or guidance seems advisable, or the use of free association or interpretation is curtailed.

There are times, however, when a patient will be referred for another kind of therapy. This occurs when a patient has a specific and concrete problem for which he/she wants relief without a consideration of other factors such as underlying personality determinants or rela-tionship complications. Examples of this would be phobias, sexual dysfunction, or the wish to stop smoking. (This does not imply that personality or relationship issues are not important in these areas, only that some people are reluctant to engage in the broad exploratory process that any psychoanalytic psychotherapy requires.) There are also certain circumstances under which a relational therapist would recommend that a person not be in therapy for some time. For instance someone might profit from not being in treatment because their life circumstances would interfere with being able to maintain an ongoing consistent relationship with the therapist (e.g., a hectic travel schedule for business, or frequent absences from therapy because of family responsibilities). Psychoanalytic psychotherapy requires a commitment to attend sessions regularly over a relatively prolonged period of time.

CASE ILLUSTRATION

A 45-year-old physician came to treatment because he was unable to maintain a satisfying relationship with a woman. He met women easily and would date them for periods ranging up to several months. Inevitably, however, one or the other would lose interest and break off the relationship. Dr. B had a successful medical practice, had an active social life with many friends, and pursued a wide range of hobbies and interests. None of this, however, was as satisfying to him as it might have been; he felt lonely and was sure that something crucial was missing in his life. In the initial consultation the therapist summarized his sense of what Dr. B was describing by saying that despite all his accomplishments, it sounded as if Dr. B moved through life dragging an anchor behind him. The remark was particularly striking to Dr. B; throughout 2½ years of twice-weekly therapy he referred back to it frequently. For him, it was a sign that the therapist had listened carefully, had cared, and had understood. It was something of a surprise to Dr. B that a person could react to him like that.

But despite this good start, being in treatment was not easy for Dr. B. He was typically amiable, respected the "rules" of therapy (coming to sessions regularly and punctually, paying his bill promptly, etc.), and made no unusual demands on the therapist. This behavior not only reflected his fundamental decency as a person but also revealed his caution in the role of patient. Both his posture and his tone of voice were stiff; he spoke slowly, in a low monotone. Frequently, he repeated stories that he had told once or even several times before. When he finished a particular train of thought he would look expectantly to the therapist, waiting for a sign that he was doing the "right" thing. Fairly quickly it became apparent that talking about himself was painful. He wondered whether it was really a good idea for him to continue the treatment.

Because Dr. B's reaction to therapy was both powerful and paradoxical (he wanted treatment but was afraid to ask for help or to embrace it fully), the initial phase of the work focused on what it was like for Dr. B to be a patient. When that was addressed directly, Dr. B acknowledged that he was ashamed of many things about himself and found it hard to believe that anybody could listen to him without feeling contempt. He was especially sure that he would be disdained or even rejected outright if he expressed any dependent or angry feelings. He could be certain of acceptance only if he was exquisitely attentive to the needs and feelings of the other person, even if this meant squelching himself. The feelings of being weighted down that we identified early on were not only a defense against more painful emotions.

They were a key to Dr. B's belief that he had to renounce his own needs for the sake of maintaining benign relationships with other people.

Although these feelings could easily have disrupted the therapy, viewing them as powerful transference reactions was the key to exploring Dr. B's personality and the problems that he had encountered. Working with the transference clarified both his experience of the treatment and his ways of coping with it. In the course of doing so, Dr. B brought in new information about his relationships outside treatment. Although he got along well with others and knew he was generally liked, he frequently was told that people did not feel that they knew him very well. The comments struck a chord for Dr. B. He was aware that he was a good listener, somebody who was easy to talk to. But he could also see the other side of that coin—that he said very little about himself. He was a good friend to others, but his interest and generosity concealed a personal reserve.

Articulating this relational theme allowed us to link a number of apparently unrelated facets of Dr. B's life. His decision to become a physician—a choice that he had never fully understood and that had never seemed entirely right to him—became clearer. Being a doctor allowed him to be close to people, even intimate with them, and to be helpful. But it permitted, even required, that he maintain some distance. It also meant that he was always giving more to the people he worked with than he was asking from them. This allowed him to create a safe space within which to conduct his relationships.

The discussion led Dr. B to describe another pattern that he had never been quite able to put his finger on before. From a very early age, he reported, he was always eager to leave situations he was involved in and to move on to something new. He felt no anxiety about facing the unfamiliar; in fact, doing so felt like a relief. When he was 13 years old he asked his parents to send him to boarding school. They agreed to do so, evidently with little discussion of what the change would mean to them or to him. The transition to the new school went remarkably well; unlike the other boys at the school, Dr. B never felt homesick at all. He stayed at the boarding school until graduation. When it was time to choose a college, he decided to pick a school far from home, in a very different part of the country. He went to a university thousands of miles away, once again never feeling the loss. He went through the rest of his training repeating the pattern: Medical school was far from college, internship was in another distant city, and so on.

As he talked about his eagerness to leave familiar places quickly, Dr. B began to think in a new way about a symptom that had troubled him a number of years before and for which he had received behavioral treatment. Beginning in his early 20s, Dr. B had suffered from premature ejaculation. Almost as soon as any sexual activity between him and a woman began, he would reach a climax. As a result, he was unable to have intercourse and remained a virgin until almost 30 years of age. In the several years preceding the behavioral treatment he stopped attempting sexual contact, breaking off dating when such contact seemed inevitable.

The therapy worked, and Dr. B was able to establish and maintain sexual relationships. But as he learned more about his relational patterns, he was able to understand the symptom in a broader context. The premature ejaculation, he could see, was a way of keeping to himself, of avoiding any risk of either intimacy or loss of control with his partner. It was also another sort of abrupt departure; in reaching a climax without the full partici-

pation of his partner, Dr. B took care of himself, eliminating the other person before she could become too important to him.

Dr. B was thus able to find a relational meaning in his symptom. It was a sexual expression of his self-containment and fear of prolonged or uncontrolled contact with other people. This also explained the limitations of his earlier treatment. While it was successful in curing the premature ejaculation, it could not address the underlying characterological problems out of which the sexual symptom arose. Dr. B was able to function sexually after this first therapy but he was no more able to sustain or to enjoy fully the relationships of which sexuality was a part.

The early phase of Dr. B's psychoanalytic psychotherapy was devoted to illuminating these relational patterns, both within the transference and in his life outside the treatment. Particularly important were moments when the work of therapy itself bogged down. Dr. B would feel that he had nothing to say, that the therapist should take the lead or be more active in giving advice, or that progress was too slow. These moments of disappointment, frustration, and irritation with the therapist were extremely difficult for Dr. B. He could not imagine sustaining a relationship while feeling such troublesome and "messy" emotions. It did not seem possible to be openly angry, or even to acknowledge that he would like the therapist to do something differently. A considerable amount of work focused on helping Dr. B to talk freely about what he wanted from the therapist and about his reactions to the give and take in the sessions.

About 6 months after he began treatment, Dr. B met a woman whom he found interesting. A professional of similar age and background, she was attracted to Dr. B and was interested in developing their relationship. Dr. B moved cautiously into his involvement with her. He enjoyed her company and they had a great deal of fun together, but he had many doubts. Consciously he wondered whether she was the right person for him, whether she was attractive enough, whether he was passionate enough about her. As time went on, it became apparent that he was concerned that having a relationship with her or with any other woman would threaten a carefully—although entirely unconsciously—contrived way of life. He was afraid that he would no longer have time for his friends, his hobbies, or even his work. He was spending so much money on dates, on weekend trips, and on renting a summer house with his girlfriend that he would not be able to afford therapy. He worried that he would have to give up much of what was most important to him in his life.

These thoughts led Dr. B to recall a fantasy that had plagued him throughout his adolescence and early adulthood, but that he had never fully understood. He had always believed, he said, that he would never be able to marry while his mother was still alive. He did not know why this should be true, but he was once sure it was, and even now wondered whether marriage would be possible. As his mother, although aging, was in good health, the belief cast a shadow on his developing relationship. With some work, Dr. B was able to see that the fantasy lay behind his concerns about how much of his life he would have to give up for the sake of his girlfriend.

The new information opened up important data about Dr. B's early experience. His mother was an angry, frightened, and depressed woman who felt only marginally capable of meeting the demands of family life. His father—ambitious, self-absorbed, and aloof—was preoccupied with business ventures that never quite succeeded and had little time for or interest in other people. A brother, 4 years younger than Dr. B, was a rebellious child who had behavior problems at home and in school from a very early age. Much of mother's limited energy and of father's limited interest were devoted to coping with the stress created by this boy's difficulties.

For Dr. B, the only way to get along in this situation was to stifle his natural boyish energy and enthusiasm, to weigh himself down with burdensome feelings of obligation to others and with depression. Two memories from childhood illustrated the problems with which he was faced. Once, when he was about 7, the family planned a trip to a national park a few hundred miles away from their home. Dr. B was excited to be there; it was one of the few outings the family had undertaken and he was an active child who loved the outdoors. Next door to the motel where they were staying there was a softball diamond, and in the afternoon Dr. B walked over to it and started running around the bases. His mother came out and told him to stop, but he continued to run. She told him again, with the same result. When the sequence repeated a third time, his mother became enraged, said, "That's it, you never listen, we're going home!" They packed their bags and drove back to the city, ending their short vacation 2 days early.

When Dr. B described this incident, the therapist wondered where his father had been and why he seemed to have nothing to say about the decision. This led to the second memory, dating back to a few years earlier. Dr. B had a longstanding conviction that his father had never liked him very much, certainly that he had never enjoyed spending time with his son. He could not remember the two of them ever doing anything alone with each other, except for one time when he had begged his father to come into the front yard and throw a ball around. Father agreed, and Dr. B was thrilled, but just as they were about to start their catch a neighborhood boy walked by and Dr. B's father invited him to join them. The terrible hurt of that moment lingered in Dr. B's memory throughout his life; the event confirmed that his father had little or no use for him.

As these memories emerged in the therapy, Dr. B was able to see that although he was disappointed and angry with his parents, he was also tied to them in a powerful way. He had not been able to give up his hopes that he could still get some of what he wanted from them, and he could not renounce the relational patterns that had been established in his early years. The "anchor" that he dragged through his life was the continuing attachment to an early way of being and feeling; he continued to stifle and to isolate himself as an adult, much as he had as a child. This was particularly true of his relationships with women. He had lived out the terror of his early fantasy: Not only was he unable to marry while his mother was alive, he was unable to establish any kind of relationship that would threaten her at all. He came to see his abrupt, irreversible departures in a new way: By wiping out connections to others he was also preserving the crucial tie to his mother. The relationship with his mother, Dr. B realized, had been the most dependable and even the most gratifying relationship of his early years, despite its frustrations and despite the limitations it imposed on his potential.

As these ideas got worked through in treatment, Dr. B's relationship with his woman friend intensified and deepened. About 1½ years into the therapy they became engaged, and they were married 6 months later. At this point, Dr. B had achieved the goal that brought him to treatment in the first place. A few months after the marriage he arrived at a therapy session, said that things were going quite well for him and that he was feeling happier than he had ever felt, and suggested that it was time to end treat-

ment. He thought it would be a good idea to have one more session, or perhaps a few to say good-bye. There was a clear sense of urgency to the idea.

The therapist fully agreed that Dr. B had gotten what he had come for out of treatment. But he also knew that this was a very important moment in the work. Dr. B was suggesting yet another abrupt departure; he was on the verge of enacting, in the transference to the therapist, the pattern of leaving things behind that had characterized so much of his life. The therapist was faced with a dilemma: He wanted to acknowledge and support the growth that had occurred, but he also knew that it was crucial to address the wish to terminate treatment so suddenly. Accordingly, he said, "You have worked hard over the past 2 years and have made a great deal of progress. Perhaps it is time to think about stopping, but I can't help noticing that you want to do it very quickly. That reminds me of the way you've left important relationships in the past. It makes me wonder whether you think doing that would help you to avoid some uncomfortable feelings about me and about what we have accomplished."

Dr. B was somewhat taken aback and even annoyed by the therapist's comment. Thoughts of staying without a defined task that could serve as the focus of attention and discussing feelings about leaving were not pleasant. He said that the therapist seemed self-absorbed and was out of line to think that any work needed to be done on their relationship. For several sessions there was a great deal of tension, with Dr. B thinking that he would be better off quitting the treatment immediately. But he did respect the therapist's judgment, and he could see that the way he imagined terminating repeated a long-standing pattern. That got him to wondering about the sense of urgency in his idea. It occurred to him that he dreaded facing the therapist knowing that he would be leaving in the foreseeable future. He was afraid that the therapist would be disappointed or angry with him for wanting to leave. This reminded him of the women with whom he had been involved over the years and the way he would lose interest in them or they in him. The easiest way to avoid unpleasantness, he had decided, was to get out as quickly as possible. He could never be sure of friends' feelings either, and his insecurity led to wanting to leave others before he was left himself.

Discussing these concerns over the course of a few weeks provided a context for Dr. B's idea about stopping. He still felt that he had achieved what he had wanted, but also saw that working on his feelings about leaving would help consolidate what he had gained. Accordingly, he and the therapist set a termination date 3 months ahead. Arranging a termination phase—during which the patient–therapist relationship is no longer open-ended but instead has a fixed stopping point—is important in any psychoanalytic psychotherapy; this was especially true in light of Dr. B's history of urgent departures and because of the way this reflected his personality structure.

Anticipating rather than abruptly enacting a departure slowed things down enough that Dr. B could catch and hold on to feelings that previously he would have swept under the rug. For the first time he said that he could anticipate thinking about the therapist after termination; he imagined missing the sessions and wishing he could come in to talk things over when the need arose. The therapist was moved by this and pleased that for the first time Dr. B seemed able to imagine holding on to a relationship indefinitely. He was also concerned, however, that in thinking about the possibility of future contact Dr. B was denying the need for any true ending. Accordingly, he was careful to point out that although termination did not mean closing doors that could never be opened again, there was some real finality involved. Dr. B could come back if he needed to, of course, but he also needed to face the inevitability of a powerful and perhaps painful separation.

As Dr. B and the therapist discussed the end of treatment, some new feelings emerged. Dr. B noticed that he felt sad about leaving the therapist, toward whom he felt considerable gratitude and a even a good deal of personal affection. He also had some sense of dread, a vague anxiety that he would not be able to manage life "on his own" as well as he had during the treatment. His old defenses of an exaggerated self-reliance combined with projecting his own dependency onto others and then taking care of them no longer worked as well as they had before. The therapist suggested that these fears dated back a long time, originating at a time in Dr. B's life when he lacked both the emotional capacities and the relationships to recognize and to meet his own needs.

Realizing how much he would miss the therapist and even the therapy itself helped Dr. B to catch on to similar feelings from other times in his life. He began to remember intimate and sustaining times with friends and even with his parents. This did not always feel good; Dr. B experienced a powerful sense of missed opportunity and loss. Much that had happened, he realized, could never be made up for or recovered; some sadness is inevitable. But he also had a sense of possibility for the future. He had friends, with whom he now shared himself more fully than he had ever been able to in the past, and he had an intimate, deepening relationship with his wife. Therapy was ending and so was, in an important way, his childhood. But Dr. B could look forward to life without the anchor he had been dragging around behind him, and that was more than an adequate replacement for what he had to renounce.

SUGGESTIONS FOR FURTHER READING

Bromberg, P. (1983). The mirror and the mask: On narcissism and psychoanalytic growth. *Contemporary Psychoanalysis, 19,* 349–387.

Mitchell, S. (1988). *Relational concepts in psychoanalysis, Part 2.* Cambridge, MA: Harvard University Press.

Ogden, T. (1989). The initial analytic meeting. In *The primitive edge of experience* (pp. 169–194). New York: Jason Aronson.

Weiss, J., Sampson, H., & the Mount Zion Psychotherapy Research Group. (1986). *The psychoanalytic process: Theory, clinical observations, and empirical research.* New York: Guilford Press.

REFERENCES

Erikson, E. (1963). *Childhood and society* (2nd ed.). New York: Norton.

Fairbairn, W. R. D. (1952). *An object-relations theory of the personality.* New York: Basic Books.

Fromm, E. (1941). *Escape from freedom.* New York: Irvington.

Greenberg, J. (1991). *Oedipus and beyond: A clinical theory.* Cambridge. MA: Harvard University Press.

Greenberg, J., & Mitchell, S. (1983). *Object relations in psychoanalytic theory.* Cambridge, MA: Harvard University Press.

Horney, K. (1937). *The neurotic personality of our time.* New York: Norton.

Horney, K. (1939). *New ways in psychoanalysis.* New York: Norton.

Klein, M. (1935). A contribution to the psychogenesis of manic–depressive states. In *Contributions to psychoanalysis, 1921–1945.* New York: McGraw-Hill, 1964.

Klein, M. (1946). Notes on some schizoid mechanisms. In *Envy and gratitude and other works, 1946–1963.* New York: Delacorte Press, 1975.

Kohut, H. (1971). *The analysis of the self.* New York: International Universities Press.

Kohut, H. (1977). *The restoration of the self.* New York: International Universities Press.

Levenson, E. (1972). *The fallacy of understanding.* New York: Basic Books.

Lionells, M., Fiscalini, J., Mann, C., & Stern, D. (1995). *Handbook of interpersonal psychoanalysis.* Hillsdale, N.J.: The Analytic Press.

Sullivan, H. (1953). *The interpersonal theory of psychiatry.* New York: Norton.

Sullivan, H. (1956). *Clinical studies in psychiatry.* New York: Norton.

Sullivan, H. (1962). *Schizophrenia as a human process.* New York: Norton.

Thompson, C. (1964). *Interpersonal psychoanalysis.* M. Green, Ed. New York: Basic Books.

Winnicott, D. W. (1965). *The maturational process and the facilitating environment.* New York: International Universities Press.

White, R. W. (1963). *Ego and reality in psychoanalytic theory* (*Psychological Issues,* Monograph 11). New York: International Universities Press.

4

The Person-Centered Psychotherapies

ARTHUR C. BOHART

"Person-centered therapy" is an umbrella term chosen to refer to the variety of approaches grounded in a theoretical view of the nature of human beings and their interactions originally developed by Carl Rogers in the 1940s and 1950s (Brodley, 1988). Rogers first developed his ideas in the form of *client-centered therapy.* Since then there have been many offshoots from Rogers's basic formulations. Two of these offshoots, the *experiential psychotherapy* of Eugene Gendlin (1979) and the *process−experiential psychotherapy* of Leslie Greenberg, Laura Rice, and Robert Elliott (1993), are also covered in this chapter. I first describe the general person-centered perspective on human beings, psychopathology, and therapeutic change. I then describe the specific therapeutic practices of client-centered, experiential, and process−experiential therapy.

BACKGROUND OF THE APPROACH

Several influences led Carl Rogers to begin to develop the person-centered view of humans and therapy. As a youth, Rogers spent much of his time on a farm where he was particularly interested in the processes of facilitating growth, and where he studied scientific experimentation with respect to agriculture. Growth facilitation and a hypothesis-testing, experimental attitude toward both life and theoretical constructs are basic characteristics of Rogers's views.

Later, when Rogers was already working as a child guidance counselor, he was exposed to the ideas of Otto Rank. Rankian ideas that influenced Rogers included an emphasis on creativity and potential, the aim of therapy as acceptance of the self as unique and self-reliant, the belief that the client must be the central figure in the therapeutic process and that the client is his/her own therapist, and an emphasis on present experience in therapy (Raskin & Rogers, 1989).

Another influence was the *Zeitgest* of the 1930s (Barrett-Lennard, 1991), the "Roosevelt years." Some of the features of these times that Barrett-Lennard speculates influenced Rogers include a focus on empowering people, on learning through trial and error, and on openness to new thought and solutions. Roosevelt also emphasized participation in appraisal and decision making by those affected. He encouraged and accepted divergent thinking and pressed for the integration of opposites. His supervision style was a supportive one in which he tried to release the creativity of his subordinates. Roosevelt held an optimistic view of human nature in that people were to be treated as basically trustworthy and reasonable, even if their behavior was not always rational.

However, for Rogers, the most formative influences came from his experience with clients. To quote one example:

> I had been working with a highly intelligent mother whose boy was something of a hellion. The problem was clearly her early rejection of the boy, but over many interviews I could not help her to this insight. . . . Finally I gave up. I told her that it seemed we had both tried, but we had failed, and that we might as well give up our contacts. She agreed . . . and she walked to the door of the office. Then she turned and asked, "Do you ever take adults for counseling here?" When I replied in the affirmative, she said, "Well then, I would like some help." She came to the chair she had left, and began to pour out her despair about her marriage, her troubled relationship with her husband, her sense of failure and confusion. . . . Real therapy began then, and ultimately it was very successful. This incident was one of a number which helped me to experience the fact . . . that it is the *client* who knows what hurts, what directions to go in, what problems are crucial. (Rogers, 1961a, pp. 11–12)

Rogers formulated an early version of client-centered therapy, called nondirective therapy, in the 1940s. This stage was characterized by a fundamental emphasis on the therapist's nondirectiveness: The goal was to create a permissive, nonin-terventive atmosphere. The major therapeutic "interventions" were acceptance and clarification. In the 1950s, empathic understanding of the client increasingly came to be emphasized. In the 1960s the emphasis shifted to the congruence or genuineness of the therapist.

Rogers's interests later expanded beyond the field of psychotherapy. He began to work increasingly in group settings to facilitate growth in nonpatient populations and, in his last years, focused his energy on using the group format to foster world peace. He studied the potential of bringing together warring political factions to promote open, constructive dialogue. Groups were run, for instance, with blacks and whites from South Africa and with Protestants and Catholics from Northern Ireland.

The client-centered perspective was also extended to education (Rogers, 1983) and medicine (cf. Levant & Shlien, 1984; Lietaer, Rombauts, & Van Balen, 1990). Rogers renamed his approach *person-centered* to reflect this shift from a focus on the individual in psychotherapy to the nature of people and their interactions in general.

There have been many other innovations and derivations that have flowed from the client-centered/person-centered philosophy, including communication skills training (Goodman, 1984; Cash, 1984). Programs for training parents, leaders, and teachers and for enhancing relationships have been devised (Gordon, 1984; Guerney, 1984).

One of the most important innovations was Gendlin's (1964) concept of experiencing, which led to the development of experiential psychotherapy. Another important innovation was the attempt to translate client-centered ideas into the language of cognitive science (Wexler & Rice, 1974), a precursor of process–experiential psychotherapy (Greenberg et al., 1993).

Types of Clients on Which the Approach Was Originally Developed

Client-centered therapy was developed from work with a wide range of clients in a number of different settings. Carl Rogers's first clinical work was at a psychoanalytically oriented child guidance clinic in Rochester, New York, where he began to develop his approach with underprivileged children and their families. Later, at the University of Chicago Counseling Center, he and his colleagues saw clients from both the community and the college campus. Client-centered therapists worked with problems of all types, including depression, anxiety, personality disorders, and psychosis. During the late 1950s a major research project with schizophrenics resulted in additions to both theory and practice.

Research Tradition

Carl Rogers has been called the "founder of psychotherapy research" and was the first to record psychotherapy interviews for research study. During the 1940s and 1950s Rogers and his graduate students carried out a series of studies on psychotherapy research (e.g., Rogers & Dymond, 1954), and many studies have been conducted since then. This tradition has continued with the work of modern researchers such as Rice and Greenberg (1984).

Current Status

In a poll conducted by Smith (1982), Carl Rogers was rated as the most influential psychotherapist, even over Freud, despite the fact that fewer than 9% of the therapists identified themselves as client-centered. On the other hand, most thera-pists currently consider themselves to be eclectic, and over a third of those combine client-centered and other humanistic approaches with some other orientation (Norcross & Prochaska, 1988). The influence of the person-centered approach is increasing in Europe, and Bankart, Koshikawa, Nedate, and Haruki (1992) have noted that "among Japanese psychotherapists the work of Carl Rogers is probably more highly regarded than [that of] any other Western theorist . . . " (p. 144).

THE CONCEPT OF PERSONALITY

Personality as Process

Is personality fixed, like the structure of a building or a sculpture, or is it constantly changing, more like the improvisations of a melody as played by a jazz musician? Person-centered theory holds that personality is more like the themes in a piece of music, which a person can "play" differently at different times in his/her life, rather than like a fixed inner structure that "holds us up" much as the structure of a building bolsters it. That is, people are "structures-in-process." Person-centered theory does not deny that structures, such as personality traits, may exist. Nor does it deny that there is continuity in personality over time. But of greater importance is that personality structures are continually *evolving*, even while they may stay the same in some respects. People change all the time, most of the time making small, subtle adjustments, sometimes major ones. As an analogy, consider the coastlines of the continents from the viewpoint of a space satellite. They look the same as they did 20 years ago. Yet from a closer perspective they are continually changing.

Similarly, personality structures may stay "the same" over time, although a closer look reveals that their manifestations have shifted (Cantor, 1990; Caspi, Elder, & Herbener, 1990). Caspi et al., for instance, found that men who were dependent in childhood still showed signs of it as adults but in very different forms (e.g., being interpersonally nurturant themselves or stable marital partners). Dependency had evolved into more mature ways of relying on and maintaining supportive relationships. The theoretical ideas of Carl Rogers and Sigmund Freud are also examples of structure-in-process: Their perspectives continually evolved and grew, although neither fundamentally ever shifted their perspectives.

What is true for intellectual frameworks also applies to personal frameworks such as traits, core beliefs, basic values, and personality organizations. This emphasis on personality as process is compatible with a view of personality traits as action strategies rather than as fixed characteristics (Cantor, 1990).

The following description of the person-centered view of personality, therefore, focuses on aspects of the person as a living process: moment-by-moment living, learning, growth, creativity, future orientation, interaction, the self-in-context, agency, the multiplicity of personal reality, communication, self–self relationships, experiencing and feeling, and the self-as-process.

Moment-by-Moment Living

It is commonly held that our personality traits, core schemata, and the like determine how we will act in a given situation. The "reappearance hypothesis," as Anderson (1974) has referred to it, holds that "the individual learns and stores percepts, images, memories, and acts, which then are simply reactivated upon

need or demand as exact replicas or duplicates of those earlier events" (p. 30).

By contrast, person-centered theory emphasizes the *moment-by-moment* nature of personal functioning. General frames, personality traits, or rules that people use to help themselves cope in a given situation are *never* specific enough to concretely determine what the individual actually does. Actual behavior in any given situation is a creative application of the general structure to the specific circumstances in that particular situation, always resulting in something slightly new and different than before.

Neisser (1967), a cognitive scientist, has noted concerning the reappearance hypothesis that "this assumption is so ingrained in our thinking that we rarely notice how poorly it fits experience. If Reappearance were really the governing principle of mental life, repetition of earlier acts or thoughts should be the natural thing, and variation the exception. In fact, the opposite is true" (p. 282). Similarly, Epstein (1991), a radical behaviorist, has noted, "The behavior of organisms has many firsts, so many, in fact, that it's not clear that there are any seconds. We continually do new things, some profound, some trivial . . . when you look closely enough, behavior that appears to have been repeated proves to be novel in some fashion. . . . You never brush your teeth exactly the same way twice" (p. 362).

As an example of this principle, I believe that one of my personality traits is a capability to be sensitive, and one of my values is being empathic. Yet, as I interact with my 13-year-old daughter I am continually challenged to find new and different ways to be empathic and sensitive with her that differ from how I tried to be these things with her brother when he was a teenager. My personality traits, general beliefs about parenting, and prior experience both as a parent and as a child myself act only as rough guides to influence the continually improvisatory nature of the decisions I make with this new and different person.

Learning Potential

To function fully, people have to learn continually on a moment-by-moment basis. They incorporate feedback to make adjustments as they interact with persons or tasks. For instance, therapists must continue to learn from one moment to the next as they try out approaches with clients. Therefore, people function most fully when they are operating intelligently, and client-centered therapy has been found to work by strengthening clients' ability to think clearly and intelligently (Van Balen, 1990; Zimring, 1990). Learning operates to constantly flesh out generalized beliefs, concepts, schemata, constructs, and operating traits. This will lead over time either to gradual evolution of these broader, longer-term frameworks or, on occasion, to major, significant shifts.

Growth Potential

Carl Rogers originally discussed an *actualizing tendency* in living things and later expanded this idea by suggesting that it was merely an individual form of a broader *formative* tendency found in the universe at large. This formative tendency is for things (such as crystals, as well as living creatures) to move toward greater order, complexity, and interrelatedness. This process includes the subprocesses of differentiation and integration.

On the level of the individual person, the actualizing tendency is, therefore, the inherent tendency of individuals to develop by forming more differentiated and integrated personal life structures. This does not necessarily mean that people are basically "good." Shlien and Levant (1984), for instance, note that "we

are basically both good and bad. . . . What is fundamentally assumed is the *potential to change*" (p. 3).

I think of the actualizing tendency as the person's inherent *self-righting* tendency (Masten, Best, & Garmazy, 1990). Based on their research on children who grow up and survive in adverse circumstances, these authors suggest that "studies of psychosocial resilience support the view that human psychological development is highly buffered and self-righting" (p. 438).

Emphasis on Creativity

To be fully functioning, individuals will be creative in everyday life because each situation is a little different from the past and presents the challenge to creatively incorporate old learning into what is different and new about this particular situation. In the course of any given day, people are continually exploring and discovering new ways of being and behaving, even though many of these new ways represent relatively minor creative adjustments.

Future Orientation

An organism that is continually exploring and learning will be oriented toward the future and toward its open possibilities. Humans are forward-looking in that their behavior is guided by what they imagine will be there in the next moment more so than by what is there in this moment (Markus & Nurius, 1987). Even being effectively present in the here and now is, like a surfer riding a wave, based on having a sense of what may be immediately coming next. The basketball player Larry Bird once noted that he was always playing "one step ahead" of what was actually happening.

It is our anticipation of where we want to go, how likely we think it is that we can get there, our estimation of our talents and skills for getting there, and what we believe the obstacles will be that determine our behavior. Shlien (1988) has argued that "the future is more important than the past in determining present behavior." The past influences us because we use it to make predictions about the future, not because it gets "wired" into us and then mechanistically drives behavior.

Interaction

Humans are interactional in nature. Persons are always "persons-in-contexts," and their behavior arises both from their personalities and from their relationships in their "ecological niches." It is meaningless to talk about individuals as if they were completely free of contexts. A person's ecological niche includes the family and other interpersonal situations as well as the broader network of neighborhoods, social support networks, and cultural variables and values. Also included are occupational and economic circumstances, religious and political affiliations, and so on. There is a continual dynamic interplay between self and situation. We "configure ourselves," so to speak, partially in response to what is important and present in each moment. Thus, some "sides" of ourselves come out in some situations, and other sides in other situations. This is a "field" view of human behavior and is compatible with a systems perspective (see Kaslow & Celano, Chapter 10, this volume).

Selves-in-Context, Autonomy, and Individualism

For Carl Rogers, becoming autonomous was a major goal of human development, as it has been for most theories of personality developed in the West. Rogers thought that the fully functioning person had an internal locus of control and operated on the basis of personally chosen values, rather than by rigidly conforming to the dictates of society.

Some person-centered theorists, however, have recently criticized the emphasis on individualism and autonomy in Rogers's work as well as in Western thought in general (Holdstock, 1990; O'Hara, 1992). They note that these values are highly specific to Western culture and are even more specifically masculine in nature and lead to other concepts, such as codependency, which are also highly Western (Bishop, 1992). They have noted that in other cultures the boundary of the self does not stop at the skin of the person but is extended to the family or the group. Fluid boundaries are emphasized over the firm self-boundaries emphasized in Western psychology. The determinants of behavior are seen as located in a field of forces, which includes the self, in contrast to Western psychology in which causes are located inside the individual.

What O'Hara (1992) argues for is the view of a self-in-context, which stresses the interconnected, interdependent nature of humans. Barrett-Lennard (1993) has noted that "individual selves are only one of the forms human life takes; other forms include relationships, families and living communities" (p. 1). O'Hara and Wood (1983) note that in some of the large group experiments conducted by person-centered theorists in recent years, "the individual achieves an integration with all of his or her own inner world. Individuals achieve integration with other group members and with the collective mind [as well]. . . . The individuals do not lose their identity to the group, they integrate the 'I' with the 'We'" (p. 109).

Agency

I believe that the operative ingredient in Rogers's emphasis on *autonomy* is a sense of *agency*: A sense that one can confront challenge. A sense of ableness or effectance may be more important than a sense of self-sufficiency. Because challenge is an inherent part of doing most things worthwhile in life (careers, relationships, childrearing), having a sense of ableness that one can confront and cope with challenges is fundamental to effective functioning (Dweck & Leggett, 1988). An orientation toward confronting challenges leads to a focus on the process of doing more so than on the outcome and means that failure is viewed as information to learn from rather than as information about one's inadequacies.

Multiple Personal Realities

The recognition that different cultures have different concepts of the self is part of a larger recognition that personal and social reality are fundamentally multiple (O'Hara & Anderson, 1991; Rogers, 1980). Individuals and cultures find many different viable but workable ways of constructing personal realities. Individuals, based on their cultural background, gender, and history, live in different "perceptual universes" (O'Hara, 1992). Therefore, therapists must respect the growth potential available within each person's personal perceptual universe rather than try to impose an objectively "correct" way of being on them.

Communication

It is assumed that there is some "sense" in each individual's perceptual universe. Therefore, facilitating communication among different people's perceptual universes, such as those between therapist and client, is more important than judging who has the correct view. Open sharing of feelings and perspectives in a mutually respecting and accepting atomosphere will facilitate movement toward congruence among the parties involved and mobilize

the "wisdom of the group or dyad." This is an important process for couples, families, and the workplace and between ethnic groups and among nations.

Congruent Self–Self Relationships

An open *internal* process of communication in which all aspects of the self are respected and listened to is equally important. Open, "friendly" listening to all aspects of thoughts, feelings, and experiences (including any internalized "voices" from parents and society) allows one's "internal community within" to move toward creative synthesis. All internal voices may have something to contribute.

Congruence is precisely this inner openness (Lietaer, 1991). Congruence does not always mean inner harmony. An inner sense of harmony comes and goes. However, if one is being congruent—open and receptive to all inner voices—the creative synthesizing process of the individual can move forward.

Experiencing, Feelings, and Emotion

Person-centered therapists value both intellectual, rational thinking and feelings and experience as important sources of information about how to deal with the world creatively.

However, experiencing is a different, more fundamental way of knowing self and world than is rational, conceptual thinking. Experiencing is also different from emotion (Bohart, 1993). Experiencing is the direct, nonverbal sensing of patterns and relationships in the world, between self and world, and within the self. It includes what is often called "intuitive knowing." However, there is nothing mysterious about it. We can sense or perceive relationships that we cannot easily describe in words. People can, for instance, sense or "feel" when a human face is drawn out of proportion long before they can cognitively and intellectually identify what is wrong with it (Lewicki, 1986).

The meanings that are acquired through direct experiencing are much more powerful than meanings acquired through conceptual thought. The *experience* of feeling loved in a relationship is a complex, whole-bodied sense of interaction that has much more to it than any intellectual or conceptual description can convey. Infants can tell from their interactions with their mothers whether the latter are empathically attuned to them. This does not mean they have a "concept" of empathic attunement. Rather, they sense directly an attuned pattern of interaction between themselves and the mother (Stern, 1985).

Gendlin (1964, 1969) believes experiencing can be more complex than conscious verbal–conceptual thought and is the source of creativity. We can sense more complex patterns experientially than we can put into words. Einstein, for instance, had a nonverbal sense of relativity theory before he had spelled it out in concepts. We can sense that something is wrong in our relationship long before we can conceptually spell out what it is.

Internally we have a "felt sense" of how our lives are going and how each specific situation is presenting itself to us. It is at the level of felt sense that therapeutic change must take place, according to Gendlin. Therapy must lead to a directly felt shift in how we relate to the world, rather than merely to intellectual change.

Feelings

Person-centered therapists have been well-known for advocating "getting in touch with" and "trusting" feelings. Feelings, from a person-centered view, are more than emotions. While we can feel anger and sadness, we also feel or sense complex meaning patterns. To be aware of feelings, therefore, is to be aware of both emotions and of sensed patterns of relationships between self and world at a given moment. We can "feel that something is wrong in our relationship" and "feel that our life is out of balance." To "trust one's feelings" means to listen to them as a source of information. It does not mean to do what they say.

A client came to me after seeing another therapist. Her problem was that she was *feeling* that her husband did not love her. Yet intellectually, when she thought about it, she could identify no logical reason for that feeling. Her husband claimed he loved her, and the other therapist had concluded that she was misperceiving the situation based on childhood problems with her father. A month or 2 after she had started to see me her husband suddenly announced that he was leaving her. He admitted that he had been having an affair for months and was in love with someone else. Clearly my client's feeling had been based on the apprehension of a set of subtle changes in her husband's manner of relating, which were so subtle that her intellectual, rational side could not identify them. If she had been able to trust her feelings, she would have explored her experience more carefully and might have been able to identify the subtle cues involved.

Feelings are not always correct, however, and sometimes we are misled because something "feels right" when it is not. It could have been that my client's feelings about her husband were wrong. If, in that case, she had been able to trust her feelings, she would have been able to continuously check them against her ongoing experience with her husband and would have discovered they were wrong. The legacy from her childhood was not so much that she projected lack of love onto her husband but that she had learned to distrust her feelings.

Person-centered theorists believe that fully functioning people use *all* their faculties. They use both their ability to think rationally and problem-solve and their ability to experientially sense what is personally meaningful to the self. Either source of information can be mistaken: Full functioning takes both into account.

The Self as Process

For person-centered theory the self is not an internal thing or agent but the experience of ourselves as a whole person in any given moment. At the same time, we form *concepts* of ourselves to help us organize our knowledge about reality, just as we form concepts of other things. The self-concept is a knowledge structure we use as a "map" to help us navigate reality (Shlien, 1970). It is multidimensional, but there are two aspects of prime importance: the "real self-concept" and the "ideal self-concept." The real self-concept is our image of who we think we actually are, and the ideal self-concept is our image of who we would like to be or think we should be. When they are fully functioning, people hold both aspects of the self-concept tentatively. It is not healthy to have too firm a self-concept, as selves are growing and changing, and one must be able to modify one's self-concept to incorporate new experience just as one must revise other concepts to fit with experience.

Theory of Development

Although Rogers offered some views on psychological development, person-centered theory has not emphasized it. However, person-centered theory implies a view of development. First, the infant at birth is an active, curious, exploratory organism, interested in learning about the world and intrinsically interested in developing its own capacities. The child will listen to and learn from all its experiences: parents, peers, relatives, teachers, neighbors, cultural stories, and so on. It will be particularly interested in learning that results from its own efforts and exploratory activity.

As a growing organism, the child will not be "finished" within the first few years of life. Whereas in psychoanalytic theory early experience is "foundational," seen as the primary shaping influence on all later constructions of personal reality, person-centered theory assumes that people continually develop. As they do so, they incorporate what was learned earlier into broader and more inclusive frameworks for understanding themselves and their world. This view is more compatible with Piaget's theory than with Freud's. In Piaget's view, development is an expanding process in which later stages involve a transcending and reorganizing of what has come before. Earlier ideas and experience are retained but are incorporated in newer, more sophisticated constructions of reality in such a way that the form in which they were originally learned is altered.

Freudian models view development as being like a pyramid, with early learnings forming a broad base for what comes later. Person-centered theory sees development more like a series of Chinese boxes. Early childhood is like the smallest box, which gets incorporated into the next largest box, and so on. Each new developmental experience forms a broader and more coherent framework for personal integration than the previous one.

Furthermore, humans are more oriented toward exploring and confronting challenge than they are toward avoiding pain and frustration. Psychodynamic theorists assume that humans have a "ubiquitous tendency to avoid pain" (Strupp & Binder, 1984, p. 32) and that children commonly avoid, deny, and repress painful experiences or emotions. In contrast, I am constantly amazed by my clients' courage and persistence in confronting pain and challenge and their attempts to master them. Children also repeatedly face up to painful events and frustrating experiences in attempts at mastery. Humans only avoid pain and frustration when they feel incompetent to deal with them (Bandura, 1986), as might occur with overwhelming experiences such as early childhood abuse.

When One Is Functioning Fully

Rogers and his colleagues developed a Process Scale to measure change in therapy from "dysfunctional" to more "fully functional" ways of being. Rogers describes the scale thus: "it commences at one end with a rigid, static, undifferentiated, unfeeling, impersonal type of psychologic functioning. It evolves through various stages to, at the other end, a level of functioning marked by changingness, fluidity, richly differentiated reactions, by immediate experiencing of personal feelings, which are felt as deeply owned and accepted" (Rogers, 1961b, p. 33). When people are functioning fully they are therefore fluid and flexible: holding constructs tentatively, testing them against experience, open to and accepting of feelings, listening to and learning from feedback, dialoguing with themselves and their surroundings, and experiencing themselves as able to direct their own lives.

Fully functioning simply means that, at a given moment, a person is operating as an evolving process. This does not mean the person is fulfilled, content, or even happy (Rogers, 1961a). Nor is there such a thing as a "fully functioning *person*" who is *always* operating optimally. Even when functioning fully, people may periodically feel blocked, incompetent, inadequate, or frustrated. However, being in process they struggle with

problems, try to learn, and continue onward.

Extensions to Family and Group

Person-centered ideas have been extended to family therapy (cf. Lietaer et al., 1990; Levant & Shlien, 1984) and to groups (O'Hara & Wood, 1983). The general principles are the same: Fully functioning familes and groups are ones in which there is open communication so that all voices can be heard. Decisions are made through a process of dialogue rather than by appealing to rigidified rules, concepts, and "shoulds." Open dialogue and communication can mobilize the "wisdom of the group." In contrast, groups and families in which dialogue is closed in order that the family or group can maintain a rigidified set of rules and concepts may be prone to dysfunction. This brings us to the topic of dysfunction in individuals, families, and groups.

THE PATHOLOGICAL OR DYSFUNCTIONAL INDIVIDUAL

From a person-centered perspective, abnormal behavior is likely to arise if a person is unable to operate in an ongoing, evolving way. Psychological problems are neither faulty beliefs or perceptions nor inadequate or inappropriate behavior per se. As humans confront challenges in life they will periodically misperceive, operate on mistaken beliefs, and behave inadequately. Dysfunctionality occurs if we *fail to learn* from feedback and therefore remain stuck in our misperceptions or inadequate behavior. Dysfunctionality is really a failure to learn and change. There are three interrelated explanations in the person-centered literature for how this occurs: incongruence, failure to be in process, and difficulties in information processing.

Incongruence

The most pervasive view of dysfunctionality in the person-centered literature is that abnormal behavior arises from a disparity between aspects of the self-concept and experience. For example, Janet was a premed student I knew in college. Her self-image was that she would be a doctor. Yet she was experiencing classes in biology and chemistry as alien and unfulfilling, and this disparity troubled her.

However, it is not disparity per se that creates dysfunctionality but how the person responds to and tries to resolve the disparity. All people experience such disparities periodically. If constructs are held tentatively then one will be able to work toward integrating disparate aspects of the self, and it is from such integration that creativity arises. However, if any aspects of the self-concept are held rigidly, integration and synthesis will be blocked.

People learn to hold parts of their self-concept rigidly when parents, teachers, or culture impose *conditions of worth* on them. That is, they are made to feel that they are worthwhile only when they conform to others' standards and values. This leads to the adoption of rigid "shoulds" about how they are supposed to be. When incongruence between rigid shoulds and experience occurs they are unable to challenge their shoulds and so may respond by trying to ignore their experience or by misinterpreting it. Being unable to listen to their own experience, they disempower themselves. They then must rely exclusively on the rigid shoulds to guide their choices. And when that does not resolve anxiety and incongruence they feel helplessness and may become depressed.

Janet had been "programmed" for years by herself, her parents, and her teachers to become a doctor. In order to follow this program she had to ignore any inconsistent feelings, which is what she did with her feelings toward her chemistry and biology classes. This appeared to affect her personality as well: I experienced her as a distant and guarded person. One day, however, she came to class and was different: open, warm, and friendly. She told me she had made a major personal decision and had changed her major to art. She disclosed that she had finally begun to listen to her experience and had realized that she really did not want to be a doctor. Trusting that part of her experience allowed her to "open up" in other ways.

Janet's problem was that she was holding her belief that she was to be a doctor rigidly. When she was able to hold it tentatively and evaluate it against her experience, she chose to change her major. However, she could have gone in the opposite direction: choosing to become a doctor even though she did not like chemistry and biology. What was important was that she be open to question and challenge her constructs.

Incongruence can come in many shapes and forms. Some people have generalized negative self-concepts and judge themselves harshly in all areas. This may lead to serious problems, such as antisocial behavior or personality disorders. Others may feel incongruent only in specific areas—for instance being unable to accept an emotion such as anger. Recently, Speierer (1990) tried to specify the different kinds of incongruences found in different psychological disorders. He argued that depressive clients are particularly likely to be plagued by rigidly held perfectionistic self-concepts, while "hysterical" clients rigidly hold exaggeratedly positive self-images in an effort to appear a certain way to others. However, person-centered therapists believe that individuals are unique and there are no invariable rules about what kinds of incongruences cause what kinds of problems.

Failure to Be in Process

This view can be thought of as an extension of the idea of incongruence. As Rogers's thought evolved, he focused more and more on the idea that dysfunctionality related to the degree to which a person was not functioning as a person in process. A person at the low end of the Process Scale, for instance, is described as functioning in a "rigid, static, undifferentiated, unfeeling . . . " way (Rogers, 1961b, p. 33).

Gendlin also held that psychopathology resulted from a failure to be in process. Individuals who are experiencing psychological problems are not "focusing" (Gendlin, 1969). That is, they are not attending inwardly to the flow of their experience in a manner that promotes creatively working on their problems. Instead of engaging in internal empathic listening, they harshly criticize their own feelings and reactions by lecturing themselves, analyzing themselves, or trying to "self-engineer" (Gendlin, 1964). In extreme cases, such as with schizophrenia (Gendlin, 1967), individuals may come to feel that their own inner life is so chaotic and "sick" that they turn away from it altogther, assuming that there is nothing there to be trusted.

Information-Processing Views

In 1974, Wexler and Rice published a seminal volume presenting several information-processing perspectives on client-centered therapy. The ideas of Rogers and Gendlin were recast in the language of cognitive psychology. Indi-

viduals are held to develop schemata for organizing information about the world. Full functioning consists of continual assimilation of information into these schemata, creating more differentiated and integrated knowledge structures. Psychopathology results from rigid, undifferentiated systems of schemata that fail to integrate new information. An important process in the creation of more differentiated and integrated knowledge structures is that of *attention*. Failure to productively attend to new information results in the rigid persistence of old knowledge structures (Anderson, 1974). Toukmanian (1990) has pointed out that individuals with problems often fail to suspend their prior conceptions and so do not notice new, potentially enriching information. Further, they also fail to generate alternative hypotheses.

Greenberg et al. (1993) have developed an integrative cognitive theory of personal functioning based in person-centered theory. For them a person's experience in a given moment is a product of a complex integration of cognitive schemata, motivation, and action tendencies. These are synthesized and result in both a holistic sense of ourselves in a given situation and specific emotional reactions, which organize us for action. Psychological problems occur either because individuals fail to attend to and symbolize their own internal reactions or because their reactions come out of rigid "emotion schemes" (*not* "schemata")— ways of reacting emotionally that have been previously learned but are not currently appropriate.

These authors particularly emphasize the importance of emotional reactions in human functioning. Emotions reflect action tendencies, which inform people as to how they are experiencing a given moment. Therefore, the failure to be aware of or to access emotional information interferes particularly with adaptive capabilities. This failure may lead to a persistence in dysfunctional reactions and an inability to flexibly choose new behaviors to meet the demands of a situation.

Interactive View of Psychopathology

Psychological problems are not viewed as entities *within* the person but are considered to exist in interaction with life situations and are transactions with the world. Problems develop when people encounter situations that challenge their abilities to respond in flexible, integrative, problem-solving ways. Some people have been less prepared by life than others to effectively process and learn in situations that pose a challenge. However, any of us is capable of becoming temporarily dysfunctional if we encounter a challenge that overwhelms our resources to cope. Extreme stress due to economic circumstances or illness may disrupt our ability to openly relate to and integrate problematic experience. Being part of a group that is operating dysfunctionally, such as a family or a committee at work, might also disrupt that ability.

Dysfunctional Families and Groups

Dysfunctionality in families and groups occurs for the same reasons that it does in individuals. Organizations and groups, like individuals, are dynamic "living" entities capable of intelligent functioning if their internal communication processes are open. Pathological behavior results when internal communication is blocked. Janis's (1972) work on "groupthink" in government is a good illustration of how groups operate dysfunctionally if communication channels both within the group and between the group and the world are blocked.

THE ASSESSMENT OF DYSFUNCTION

Person-centered therapists generally do not find traditional diagnosis or assessment procedures useful. Such procedures encourage an "outside" perspective on the client, as if the client is being put under a microscope and dissected. This is antithetical to the person-centered empathic stance in which the therapist tries to feel him/herself into the client's unique experience. Categorizing people tends to bias the therapist toward treating the individual as a member of a *class* rather than as a unique being. As a person-centered therapist I am interested in understanding and relating to Jack or Carolyn, not Jack-the-borderline or Carolyn-the-narcissist. However, because the mental health field uses diagnostic labels, person-centered therapists will sometimes employ them for communication purposes (as I have done in this chapter).

Process–experiential therapists (Greenberg et al., 1993) do make "process diagnoses" in therapy. A process diagnosis is an assessment by the therapist of the presence of some dysfunctional emotional scheme that the client needs to change, and of the client's readiness to work on it, at a given moment in therapy. It is important to note that the therapist does not focus on the *content* of this emotional scheme (e.g., anger toward one's father) but merely on evidence that the client is experiencing some block in the process of resolving a personal problem. Process–experiential therapists look for "markers," which are specific verbal, behavioral, or emotional signs that a client is struggling with a particular kind of emotional-processing problem. For instance, a marker for a "problematic reaction point" is that clients are describing an incident in which they found themselves reacting to some situation or person in a way that puzzles them. This puzzlement may consist of feeling that their reactions to the situation or person were unreasonable, dysfunctional, exaggerated, or unexpected. A process diagnosis of a specific kind of marker will suggest to the therapist what kind of procedure could be best used at that moment to foster and deepen the client's exploration.

THE PRACTICE OF THERAPY

Client-centered therapy in its traditional or "pure" form is highly nondirective. The therapist's goal is primarily to be a companion on the client's journey of self-discovery. By being a certain kind of companion, namely, a warm, empathic, and genuine one, the therapist provides an atmosphere in which the client's own thrust toward growth can operate.

However, in the 1960s a trend developed among some client-centered therapists to treat client-centered therapy more as a philosophy of therapy than as a specific way of doing it. It was argued that if therapists were warm, empathic, and genuine and respected the client's own growth process, they could be more active and even use techniques from other therapies (Holdstock & Rogers, 1983). For many, client-centered therapy became a "person-centered" philosophy in the context of which therapists could practice in eclectic ways. As a result, some modern person-centered therapists have incorporated behavioral, hypnotic, Gestalt, and confrontational techniques into their practice. Natalie Rogers (Toms, 1988) includes art and dance in her "person-centered expressive therapy." Similarly, Gendlin's experiential therapy and Greenberg et al.'s process–experiential therapy hold that the therapist can systematically try to facilitate exploratory processes that help clients grow.

Other, more traditional client-centered therapists (Brodley, 1993) disagree with this development. They believe that to use any technique systematically is to violate the basic "nondirective attitude" of follow-

ing the client and letting the client find his/her own pathway to growth. Below I consider three different approaches to psychotherapy grounded in person-centered philosophy. These are "pure" client-centered therapy, Gendlin's experiential therapy, and Greenberg et al.'s process–experiential psychotherapy. I then consider the controversy over whether the latter two are "really person-centered."

Philosophy of Therapy

Person-centered therapies are based on the belief that it is the clients who "heal" themselves and who create their own self-growth. Growth and healing happen from within the person, though external processes can facilitate or retard that growth. As analogies to the person-centered view, plants and children both grow themselves, though farmers and parents can foster or retard that growth.

Person-centered therapies are relatively unique in how much they emphasize the self-righting, self-healing tendencies of the person. Although there are other approaches that agree that humans have positive potential within, they believe people may not use this potential unless guided to do so by the therapist. This may be because clients are supposedly so motivated by their desires to avoid pain and to gain security that they avoid dealing with issues that will unlock that potential. Or, it is because they are trapped in faulty thinking from which they must be freed by the therapist. The therapist becomes the "expert guide" on *what* issues the client needs to face in order to grow.

In contrast, the job of the person-centered therapist is to provide optimal conditions under which the intrinsic self-organizing and self-transcending capabilities of the person can operate. Under supportive conditions the client's thrust toward growth will override any tendencies toward avoidance of pain. People are adept at facing up to and bearing a great deal of pain while continuing to function, as long as they feel they have a chance of productively mastering painful circumstances. They will only avoid pain and seek security at the expense of growth if they feel helpless (Dweck & Leggett, 1988) or low in self-efficacy (Bandura, 1986) to deal with the pain.

Consider the example of my daughter when she first learned to swim. Initially, she was frightened and went slowly, first paddling around with a life vest on for several months. I did not try to cajole or pressure her to "face her fears" and to go farther, as some parents might have done. One day she spontaneously decided to take off the life vest and to try swimming on her own. I trusted her process, and she was motivated eventually to face her fears in order to move forward, but in her own time.

Therapists do not have to make clients face up to even extremely repressed, painful experiences such as those of early childhood abuse. If conditions are provided under which clients can begin to begin to develop a sense of self-efficacy in their own capacity for self-righting and growth, they will come to want to face up to such experiences when necessary for their continued development. At that point such experiences will begin to emerge slowly as a part of the process of self-healing.

Person-centered therapists take clients where they are when they come into therapy. If the client's problem is that he/she is chronically feeling tense, the person-centered therapist will work with what the client focuses on and will not assess whether there are "deeper issues" to confront. This is due to person-centered therapists' belief that clients' development of their capacities for self-direction and self-regulation are the most important aspect of therapy and that cli-

ents will move deeper on their own when necessary.

Basic Structure of Person-Centered Therapies

Person-centered therapists are flexible in how the therapy interaction is structured. Although they most typically meet with the client for a 1-hour session on a once-a-week basis, person-centered therapists modify this format if needed to conform to the needs of working with a particular client. A client might be seen either more or less than once a week, sessions might last either longer or shorter than 1 hour, and meetings might or might not be held in the therapist's office. Gendlin (1967) talks about taking hospitalized patients for a walk down to the hospital cafeteria as therapy. I worked with a young hospitalized "paranoid" client by meeting with him on the hospital lawn.

Although at least several sessions will typically be needed, person-centered therapists believe that occasionally, important change can occur in a single session (Rogers & Sanford, 1984). There is no meaningful "average length" that can be prescribed for person-centered therapy. I have seen clients for one session and for well over 100 sessions.

Person-centered therapists might utilize any or all of individual, couple, family, or group therapy formats. The choice would be jointly decided by the therapist and all participants.

Goal Setting

Person-centered therapists believe that it is the client who knows what hurts and what needs to be changed (though this knowing is often of a felt, intuitive nature). Therefore, person-centered therapists do not set goals for what changes clients need to undergo in order to improve (e.g., "become more assertive," "stop thinking irrationally," or "get out of your dysfunctional relationship"). Rather, the goal is to provide the conditions under which the client's own intrinsic tendencies to confront problematic experiences, explore them, extract new and important meanings, and creatively reorganize ongoing experience in more productive ways can operate.

Why can't the therapist simply tell the client "the answer"? I argued earlier that people live in different perceptual universes of which therapists can know only little bits. In a famous film of Carl Rogers working with Gloria (Shostrom, 1965), Gloria's problem was that she had lied to her daughter about the fact that she was having sexual relationships although she was not married. She wanted Rogers to tell her whether or not to tell her daughter the truth. Rogers refused to do so and helped Gloria arrive at her own answer. In watching the film, some of my students have expressed frustration: Why can't Rogers just tell her to be honest?

One reason is that only Gloria knows the true subtleties and complexities of her life and of her relationship with her daughter. Only she knows the intricate "web" of relationships that constitutes her "ecological niche." What might seem wise from an outside perspective might not be wise from an inside one. Therefore, only she will know how, ultimately, to reorganize and synthesize all the factors in her perceptual universe to provide a solution that is "ecologically wise" within that universe. By "ecologically wise" I mean a solution that best takes into account this complex web of relationships. If Rogers were to give generalized advice ("Yes. It's better to be honest.") it might work. However, it also is possible that if Gloria simply followed this advice without working out its "ecological wisdom" within her universe it might backfire.

Although all person-centered therapists agree on not setting goals for *what* the client needs to change, they differ on whether to have goals regarding *how* to best help the client find his/her own answers. Pure client-centered therapists set no goals for their clients or for the therapy process at all. Although client-centered therapists believe that therapy leads to outcomes such as people being more open to experience, more fluid, and more differentiated, they believe that these changes will best occur if they do not try to make them happen but rather focus on how they as therapists can best be present with their clients. That is, pure client-centered therapists' goals are ones they set for *themselves:* to be empathic, accepting, respectful, and congruent. The therapist, in some sense, works on *him/herself* in therapy rather than on the client. If the therapist feels that he/she is not understanding the client, the therapist struggles to do so. If the therapist feels incongruent, he/she struggles to be more so.

Experiential and process–experiential therapists do not adopt this nondirective attitude as thoroughly as do client-centered therapists. They believe that the therapist can have "process" goals; that is, they hold that helping facilitate certain kinds of processes of exploration with clients can more efficiently help clients find their own answers. I will describe this in more detail when I discuss these two therapies later.

Techniques and Strategies

Client-Centered Therapy

For client-centered therapy, the establishment of a facilitative therapeutic relationship is itself the therapeutic technique and strategy. The process of "being with" the client in the sense of accepting the client as he/she is, entering imaginatively into the client's world of perception and feelings, and being authentic is sufficient for the facilitation of a process of change.

What the therapist primarily does is express his/her struggles to understand the client's experience. This will often come out in the form of what have been called "reflections." Reflection is a way of responding in which the therapist tries to express his/her attempt at understanding what the client is experiencing and trying to say. Therapists can reflect feelings, meanings, experiences, emotions, or any combination thereof. They often go beyond what the client has explicitly *said* to try to grasp what the client is also experiencing but has been left unsaid. However, the therapist tries to grasp only what is within the client's current range of awareness of experiencing. The therapist does not try to grasp possible unconscious aspects of the client's experience. This is the main theoretical difference between a reflection and a psychodynamic interpretation. Following is an example of a reflection compared to an interpretation:

Client: "I'm feeling so lost in my career. Every time I seem to be getting close to doing something really creative, which would lead to a promotion, I somehow manage to screw it up. I never feel like I am really using my potential. There is a block there."

Reflection: "It's really *frustrating* to screw up and kill your chances; and it feels like it's something in *you* that's making that happen again and again."

A psychodynamic interpretation: "It sounds like every time you get close to success you unconsciously sabotage yourself. Perhaps success means something to you that is troubling or uncomfortable, and you are not aware of what that is."

Notice that this interpretation might in fact be true but is an attempt to bring to the client's attention something that is *not* currently in the client's awareness. This is the key difference between reflections and interpretations.

For client-centered therapists it is important to react in a therapeutically spontaneous manner to whatever is happening in the moment between themselves and the client. Although reflection has been the traditional form for expressing empathy, spontaneous expressions of empathy may take many other forms (Bozarth, 1984), such as the self-disclosure of the therapist's own experience in "resonance" to client experience. At a given moment, the sense of sharing between therapist and client might also lead the therapist to spontaneously suggest a technique. Client-centered therapists are not banned from suggesting techniques. It is *how* they suggest techniques that is important. A technique would only be suggested when to do so is to further the process of being together with the client in a real, empathic relationship (Bohart & Rosenbaum, 1995). It is not an attempt to "do anything" to the client or "make anything happen." The client is always free to reject the technique. However, techniques are used relatively infrequently by client-centered therapists.

Experiential Psychotherapy

In the field of psychotherapy in general the term "experiential therapy" is used to refer to a range of approaches whose focus is on emotions or experiencing. However, in the person-centered "camp," experiential psychotherapy primarily refers to Gendlin's (1979) approach. Gendlin, Beebe, Cassens, Klein, and Oberlander (1967) interpreted a number of research findings as suggesting that therapy only "happens" when an experiencing process is present. Clients grow when they are actively referring inwardly to their experience and feelings and articulating that experience in words. They do not grow if they talk about their problems in distanced intellectual ways or focus externally on the situations in their lives. Based on this premise, Gendlin and other experiential psychotherapists try to facilitate this experiencing process in psychotherapy in three basic ways. First, they utilize a variant of empathic responding, which they call "experiential" responding (Gendlin, 1968). Experiential responses more specifically focus on the felt aspects of the client's present experience and often rely on metaphors. An experiential response to our client above might be, "It sounds like you're feeling really up against it, like up against a big wall, which you're trying to push aside and you don't know how to."

A second technique utilized by experiential therapists is the sharing of their own immediate experience in the therapy relationship with their clients (Gendlin, 1967). The therapist focuses on his/her own immediate experience in the situation and tries to explicate it in words. This helps clarify the nature of what is going on between therapist and client and provides a model for clients of how to relate inwardly to their own experience. For instance, the therapist might say to a silent, sad client who has just suffered a loss, "Part of me wants to reach out and contact you, and talk to you about the loss, and part of me feels like I just want to sit in silence with you and keep you company in your pain. I'm not sure what you want but I want you to know that I'm here if you want to talk, and I'm here even if I just stay silent with you for a while."

The third technique is called "focusing" (Gendlin, 1981). Clients are asked to focus inwardly and to "clear a space" by imagining that they have set all their problems aside for the moment. Then they take one problem and try to focus on how all the problem feels inside. While people can think about only parts of a problem at any given moment, they can feel all those parts together. They then wait and listen to see whether some words or concepts come from the feeling. This process often leads to a "felt shift" in which the sense of the problem reorganizes so that the person can get a better "handle" on what the crux of it is.

Any concept or technique from other therapies might be used by an experiential therapist if it helped facilitate contacting, exploring, and articulating inner experiencing. Experiential therapists have used Gestalt role-playing, body techniques, and relaxation. They can talk about object relations or dysfunctional cognitions if these concepts help clients directly refer to their immediate felt experience. Thus, Gendlin's theory of experiencing has provided a theoretical rational for eclectic therapeutic practice (Gendlin, 1979).

Process–Experiential Psychotherapy

Process–experiential psychotherapy is an integrative psychotherapy based in a person-centered view of the nature of the human being but draws on ideas from both cognitive theory and Gestalt psychotherapy.

Carrying forward work by Wexler, Rice, and others (cf. Wexler & Rice, 1974), process–experiential therapists (Greenberg et al., 1993) view clients' problems as a result of the failure to productively explore certain classes of cognitive–affective information. The goal of the process–experiential therapist is to facilitate different types of cognitive-affective operations in the client at different times to best enhance deeper exploration. The job of the therapist is to (1) select the intervention that will best facilitate work on a given emotional task at a given moment, and (2) systematically guide the client through the operations involved in the chosen intervention. Different client behaviors serve as therapeutic markers to guide the therapist in choosing which intervention to use.

Greenberg et al. identify five basic therapeutic markers. I will briefly describe three. The first is what is called a "problematic reaction point." A problematic reaction point refers to the client's having behaved in some way that strikes the client as exaggerated, inappropriate, or unexpected. For instance, the client may have said something in anger which he/she feels ashamed about. The therapist uses "evocative unfolding" and guides the client to explore both "edges" of the problematic experience: The situation in which the problematic reaction occurred and the person's inner experience at the time. Evocative unfolding consists of empathic responses designed to be highly vivid and emotionally evocative (e.g., "That superioristic smirk on his face really made you boil"). This process leads clients to discover how they were construing the situation and how that led to their reaction. Typically, clients feel better when they realize that their behavior, no matter how dysfunctional, had some "sense" behind it, and this discovery allows for the possibility of new options to develop. Often clients also spontaneously recognize how this way of construing a situation has played a role in other problematic situations in their lives.

The second client marker is that of an experienced *split*: The client is in conflict about something. Usually there is a "should" side saying "do this," and a "want" side saying "I don't want to." With this marker, the Gestalt two-chair exercise (Yontef, Chapter 8, this volume) is used. The client role-plays both sides, speaking from the "should" side and then switching chairs to speak from the "want" side. The client goes back and forth until some integration is reached. This integration occurs because both sides begin to see some "sense" in the other side. Changes in the "should" side particularly facilitate integration because the should side moves from talking in "shouldistic" language to expressing hopes and fears. Instead of "You should study harder," it says, "I'm worried that if you don't study harder you won't achieve your goals."

A third marker occurs when the client has "unfinished business" with another person. For this problem another version of the Gestalt two-chair exercise is used. Clients role-play dialogues between themselves and the other person, taking both roles. This allows the client to arrive at a personal resolution with the emotional problems created by the relationship with the other person. For instance, a sexually abused daughter role-plays a dialogue between herself and her father. In her chair she expresses her rage, guilt, and sadness over what her father has done to her. She may play her father as someone whom she can ultimately come to forgive, or she may play him as an "unrepentant bastard." In either case she becomes able to let go of her guilt and of the past and reclaim a sense of her own worth and potency.

Would the Real "Person-Centered Therapy" Please Stand Up?

Can one systematically try to facilitate experiencing, work through problematic reaction points, and resolve unfinished business and still be consistent with the person-centered philosophical emphasis on people finding their own solutions? Many traditional client-centered therapists say "no." They believe that to act in these ways is to no longer be truly nondirective. They believe that being directive, even if only by suggesting an exercise such as focusing, takes some of the power away from the client for finding his/her own self-directed way of changing. Further, they believe that by so doing the therapist is relating to a part of the client rather than to the whole client.

On the other hand, experiential and process–experiential therapists argue that they deeply respect the internal wisdom of their clients and strongly believe in clients' ability to find their own personally wise solutions. They deeply value providing a warm, empathic, and genuine relationship. However, they believe that the therapist is a "process expert" who can structure things so that clients can more creatively and optimally explore. They do not believe it is incompatible with person-centered theory to systematically use interventions to mobilize clients' exploratory capacities.

My belief is that person-centered theory can support a number of different ways to practice. I agree with Brodley's (1988) proposal that there is a family of "person-centered therapies," of which the experiential and process–experiential approaches are members. However these newer approaches should be distinguished from pure client-centered therapy because of their relatively more process-directive nature.

Process of Therapy

For the person-centered therapies, the therapeutic process is one of staying closely with the moment-to-moment "flow" of what is happening in the session. Therapists focus on what clients bring up to talk about and do not try to guide the conversation toward topics the therapist thinks are important. For instance, Gloria shifted topics several times over the course of her half-hour session with Carl Rogers. He stayed with her shifts, and it is clear that there was a kind of intuitive wisdom to these shifts as they led Gloria to deepen her exploration.

What is talked about is not nearly as important as the moment-by-moment process: Are clients relating to themselves in a productive, self-evolutionary way no matter what is being talked about? The process of therapy will have, therefore, its own intrinsically structured flow, and clients will often recycle topics several times before they are resolved.

From a person-centered perspective, "resistance" is not a useful concept. What other therapists call resistance may be defined as occurring when the *therapist* thinks the client should be talking about something, feeling something, or doing something other than what the *client* is doing. When clients are "resisting" they are trying to follow what they feel will best help them maintain or grow at that time. As with anything else the client is doing, the person-centered therapist will try to empathize with "where the client is coming from" at that moment. This is the best way to facilitate the process of moving forward. Clients will grow out of resistance if the therapist remains in empathic and genuine contact but may get stuck in resistance if therapists (or anyone else) relate to them in a "superior" manner—correcting them or imparting "truth" to them.

Because person-centered therapists invest so much trust in clients' ability to direct their process of growth, termination of therapy is rarely a problem. In my experience, clients are motivated to move away from being dependent on the therapist and to "try their wings" when they are ready. They do not need to be "fully healed" with all problems resolved (who is?) in order to try to live on their own. Problems are a part of life and clients sometimes leave because they now feel they can manage the problems on their own. Sometimes clients ease themselves into termination by deciding to come every other week instead of every week for a time, before they decide to stop altogether. In other instances, clients just decide they are ready to stop.

When a client decides to stop therapy, the therapist and client talk over the decision. If the therapist has reservations about the client's terminating, these may be expressed, especially if the client asks for the therapist's opinion. But contrary to the "expert therapist" model, in which clients are sometimes told that they are avoiding or resisting because they want to stop therapy, a person-centered therapist would confine him/herself to a *personal* self-disclosure (e.g. "I worry that we didn't quite work through that issue, and I wonder if it might bother you again, but you know I'm here if you ever do feel a need for further work").

Virtually all the errors a person-centered therapist could commit would come out of either failing to be warm, empathic, and genuine or imposing an agenda upon the client. Even Carl Rogers was capable of committing such an error. Raskin (1991) has pointed out that, early in the interview with Gloria, the value Rogers placed on people trusting their own organismic wisdom interfered with his ability to empathically hear all of Gloria's concern about being honest with her daughter, although he did become more empathic later on. Zimring (1991) has pointed out that so-called transferential reactions in which the client begins to focus on the therapist rather than on his/her own experience occur when the therapist is not being sufficiently empathic.

THE STANCE OF THE THERAPIST

The therapeutic relationship is the single most important factor in any of the person-centered approaches. The three primary conditions of a good therapeutic relationship are unconditional positive regard or warmth, empathy, and genuineness or congruence. Carl Rogers (1957) postulated that these basic relationship conditions were "necessary and sufficient" for therapeutic growth to oc-

cur, although Bozarth (1993) has recently suggested these conditions are sufficient but not absolutely necessary. This is because the self-actualization tendency may sometimes facilitate growth even without a therapeutic relationship.

The implications of Rogers's (1957) statement were (and are) radical: Any therapist who is warm, empathic, and genuine will be therapeutic no matter what point of view he/she adopts or what techniques he/she uses (as long as they do not conflict with being warm, empathic, and genuine); and any *person*, regardless of professional training, will be therapeutic if he/she can provide this kind of relationship. Strupp and Hadley (1979), for instance, found that untrained college professors chosen for their sensitivity were, on the average, as therapeutic as professional therapists.

Warmth or unconditional positive regard has also been called "acceptance," "respect," "liking," "prizing," or even "nonpossessive love." The quality is a basic attitude of liking, respecting, or prizing directed at the client as a whole person. It rests on a distinction between the client as a person and the client's behavior (Lietaer, 1984). Just as good parents continue to like and prize their children even while disliking specific behaviors (e.g., writing on the walls with crayons), the person-centered therapist continues to prize the client as a person even when the client's behavior is dysfunctional. Unconditional regard does not mean the person-centered therapist conveys support or approval for dysfunctional behavior.

Holding an attitude of unconditional positive regard toward others precludes neither feeling angry at them nor setting limits (although person-centered therapists generally tend not to set limits). Good parents set limits while prizing and respecting their children. Good relationships in which both partners generally like and prize one another include times when either or both of the participants become angry with one another. Good therapy relationships as well may include moments in which the therapist must set limits (e.g., if the client is tearing up the therapist's office), or in which the therapist may experience anger or dislike toward some of the client's behavior. I will discuss how this is handled when I discuss genuineness and congruence.

Feeling liked and prized as people, clients begin to feel safe to explore their experience and to take a more objective look at their behavior. Clients are able to distinguish between their intrinsic worth as persons and the dysfunctionality of current ways of experiencing and behaving.

Empathy is the ability to intuit oneself inside the client's perceptual universe, to come as close as one can to seeing and feeling as the client sees and feels. From an "outside" perspective, client behavior often seems irrational, self-destructive, manipulative, narcissistic, rigid, infantile, or egocentric. However, from an "inside" perspective behaviors that seemed so dysfunctional and irrational from the outside usually make "sense" in terms of how the client is experiencing the world. This does not mitigate the behavior's dysfunctionality. Rather, it suggests that from within the client's skin, there is a "positive thrust" underlying it (Gendlin, 1967).

A client of mine was arrested for exposing himself to his 13-year-old stepdaughter. As I struggled to understand him from inside his perceptual universe it became clear that he felt totally helpless and impotent in his dealings with this girl whom he experienced as ignoring him and consistently treating him with disrespect. Exposing himself was an extreme (albeit dysfunctional) reaction to one particularly hurtful show of disrespect on her part, and a way of his expressing his helplessness, anger, and rage. I shall describe later what happened in this case.

There are a number of different positive therapeutic effects of empathy. First, the experience of being known seems to be intrinsically therapeutic. When I feel fully known by someone, it is as if I feel I come into focus. I feel better able to sort things out and to make choices for myself. Second, finding that there is some sense in my experience, even when I have acted dysfunctionally, makes me feel generally less crazy or dysfunctional. I begin to have some confidence in my own inner experience. Increased confidence allows me to look at things more carefully and to confront painful experience.

Third, therapist empathy provides a model for a "friendly" way for clients to listen to their own experience. This will allow them to accept and hear meanings that they were previously afraid of because they seemed "unfriendly" to the self. This allows clients to begin to find more productive and less dysfunctional ways of dealing with those feelings and meanings. As my client began to listen to his own experience in a friendly manner, he began to realize there was some "sense" in his impulsive act of exposing himself to his stepdaughter. He decided that what he wanted to do was to develop more proactive and less hurtful ways of asserting himself and expressing his anger, which is what we worked on.

Genuineness or congruence refers to the degree to which a therapist is "being him/herself" in therapy. Being oneself does not mean that one acts out one's feelings or says whatever is on one's mind. Genuineness and congruence are matters of *inner* connection (Lietaer, 1991). They have to do with the degree to which therapists are in touch with the flow of their inner experience, and the extent to which their outward behavior reflects some truly felt aspect of their inner experience. For instance, as I listen to my client describe his exposing himself to his stepdaughter, I may experience both empathy for him and dislike of what he did. At one moment in therapy it may feel more congruent to express my empathy; at another moment to let my client know I disliked his action. Being genuine does not mean that I "dump" what is on my mind at any given moment into the therapy session.

Lietaer (1991) has distinguished between congruence and *transparency*. Congruence is attending inwardly to one's experience and working to sort out its meanings. Transparency is the open self-disclosing of what is within the therapist. Person-centered therapists value self-disclosure in therapy. However, they only value therapeutically relevant self-disclosure. Rogers has argued that therapists should only self-disclose their reactions when (1) they are persistent, and (2) they are getting in the way of the therapeutic relationship itself.

Gendlin (1967) has noted that therapists must self-disclose in more effective and productive ways than does the person in the street. The way people in the street are "honest" is often to label, criticize, and judge (e.g., "You're boring"). If I have a reaction to my client (such as anger) which I wish to share, I first must work with it myself before I self-disclose. I tune inwardly and try to sort out the degree to which my reaction is "mine" from the degree to which it belongs in the relationship. If I conclude that it belongs in the relationship, I will share it. However, I then share it as *my* reaction, not as the "truth."

If I experience anger and disgust as my client tells me how he exposed himself to his daughter, I do not disclose as the person in the street might: "Oh! That's disgusting and repulsive! You are really being a selfish and insensitive person by doing that!" I try to figure out how much the disgust reaction belongs in our relationship and how much it is "just me." As I explicate my reaction to myself I

may discover that what is really bothering me is that when my client described the act of exposure, his whole tone was one of self-protection rather than of any concern for its effect on his stepdaughter. I might decide what is bothering me belongs in the relationship and say, "What I find myself experiencing as you describe that is a great deal of concern for your daughter, and I feel dismayed because I don't experience you right now as feeling that concern yourself. I feel angry with you because I want you to be concerned about her, and I feel stuck because I want to be on your side, and usually I am on your side, but right now in this moment I don't feel on your side."

Such a self-disclosure is neither a criticism nor an act of blame. Rather, it is an invitation to my client to explore with me the consequences of his actions for both himself and for his daughter. I am hoping that he will be enlisted as a collaborator to explore this *problem*, which, in some sense, we both have (i.e., how can *we* help *him* to behave in a way that is better for both him and his daughter). In contrast, the "person on the street" disclosure given above merges the client and the problem so that the client is liable to experience *himself as the problem*. The "person on the street" disclosure makes it "me versus the client" rather than "me and the client versus the problem."

Genuineness as a Basis for Therapeutic Eclecticism

From the 1960s on, many person-centered therapists increasingly emphasized genuineness as the most important of the therapeutic conditions, although only in the context of warmth, empathy, and a belief in the client's intrinsic self-directive capacities. For many, the emphasis on genuineness provided a basis for eclectic therapeutic practice. First, it encouraged therapists to find their own styles for expressing empathy instead of expressing it primarily in the form of reflection. Responding empathically in the moment might sometimes mean backing off and allowing the client some distance, being silent, asking a question, sharing a thought or feeling, or even suggesting a technique. Genuinely expressed empathy became a matter of tuning in and timing rather than a specific kind of response.

One of my clients, for instance, did not experience reflections as empathic, and I soon gave up sharing my understanding with him in that way. He felt more comfortable with my expressing my own reactions to what he said, and he experienced me as "really understanding him" when I responded in that manner. With other clients my empathy has sometimes come out in a light, humorous way of interacting.

Second, the emphasis on genuineness provided a philosophical basis for therapists to disclose their views, share their opinions, and suggest techniques. If I as a therapist have an opinion or a thought or know of a technique, and I deliberately withhold it in order to "play my role as a nondirective therapist," then I am not being genuine. The issue is not whether a technique is suggested but how. Is it suggested as the expert trying to fix the client or as one human sharing his/her own experience with another human? In the latter, the implicit message is: This is something from my experience that you may find useful; however, it is up to you to evaluate its usefulness and to use it if you wish. With this modification, many person-centered therapists have incorporated hypnosis, dreamwork, Gestalt techniques, and behavioral techniques.

For instance, Swildens (1990) has argued that in treating borderline clients the person-centered therapist must utilize anxiety-reducing strategies, confronting and interpreting strategies, and counseling, support, and advice. He also suggests that while the therapist must be empathic, it is better not to use traditional empathic reflections with these clients.

How can one confront while still being person-centered? After all, confrontation often entails the provision by a therapist of an alternative perspective to the client. Some therapists hold that confrontation is particularly important with borderline personality disorder because such clients have "immature ego structures." Therapists who adopt this point of view confront clients from a position of superior knowledge. As they are presumably more mature, have stronger egos, and so on, they feel they can provide a more realistic perspective.

Although person-centered therapists might also "confront," they do so from a completely different philosophical base. When I challenge clients' behavior that I perceive as self-destructive, my goal is to be genuinely in contact with them. I am not trying to play "the expert" who is going to "correct them" but rather another human being who wants to share my experience and my perspective with them. I am very careful to "own" what I say as my perspective and to invite clients to think about it and reject it if they do not agree.

In sum, the shift toward genuineness allowed many person-centered therapists to practice in a more flexible, eclectic way that suited their individual personalities. It also allowed greater flexibility in "tailoring" the relationship to suit different clients. However, as was true in the advent of experiential and process–experiential therapy, this change has not been welcomed by some client-centered therapists, who believe that clients grow best when they are in the company of someone who empathically follows the client's lead in self-exploration and self-growth.

Transference and Countertransference

Many person-centered therapists such as Shlien (1984) and myself do not find the concepts of transference and countertransference either meaningful or therapeutically helpful. These terms originate in psychoanalytic theory. Transference refers to the tendency of the client to read things into the therapist's behavior based on the client's past experience (primarily with parents). Countertransference refers to the tendency of the therapist to read things into the client's behavior based on the therapist's past experience and unresolved problems.

My view is that these concepts are not helpful because they do not make meaningful distinctions between different kinds of experiences. In order to understand the present we *always* "transfer" past experience onto it. You are "transferring" right now when you read these words as if they were in "English." Whenever we use past experience to interpret the present there is the possibility of error. For instance, in some other cultures people stand much closer to one another when they talk than they do in our culture. Based on our past experience we might misinterpret someone from such a culture as being intrusive or overly familiar were we to meet them. We might continue to feel uneasy around them, even when we know intellectually that we are just dealing with a cultural difference. We might also make dysfunctional decisions about the person based on our erroneous interpretation.

The key is not whether we use our past experience to understand the present—we always do that. It is whether or not we attend to the *discrepancies* between what is new and different in the present from our past experience and use that to learn and to adjust our perceptions. Clients often appear to persist in their "misreadings" of the therapist, but that

is not because they are "transferring." Rather, their ability to openly listen to corrective information, both from others and from their own inner experiencing, has been compromised by a lack of self-trust. As they come to trust themselves and the therapist, and as they learn how to listen to their feelings, they become better and better at correcting misreadings of situations.

Therapists also always "countertransfer" (i.e., they use preconceptions based on their past experience to try to understand their present client). Therapists' preconceptions arise from far more than the therapist's personal problems. They are also based on cultural norms and stereotypes, and on the therapist's professional training. Therapists countertransferentially see clients through the eyes of both psychiatric diagnoses and their pet theories. For a psychodynamic therapist, *seeing* a client's response as transference may be an example of the therapist's countertransference!

As I have already noted, therapists' personal reactions can be productively used in therapy if they are expressed therapeutically and owned as the therapists' own reaction rather than presented as objective truth about the client. Therapists need to listen to clients to see whether their perceptions and reactions are fitting with the client's experience. In other words, therapists need to notice discrepancies between their perceptions of their clients and their clients' actual reactions, whether these perceptions are based on theory, cultural background, or personal experience.

What is important is that both therapists and clients engage in a *process* of getting to know what is unique and different about this person and this situation compared to the past. The question is: Is the individual exploring preconceptions in order to modify them over time and truly get to know *this* person or situation? This process is crucial for effective coping in life. This is the process the therapist must develop for him/herself and the process that person-centered therapy models for the client through its emphasis on acceptance and open exploration.

The concepts of transference and countertransference grow out of a traditional medical view of psychotherapy in which the personal is kept separate from the professional. However in person-centered theory the personal *is* the professional in a very important sense. If I, as the therapist, have a personal reaction to my client, the issue is how can I use that therapeutically, not "can I eliminate it?" If I have the same unfinished problem that my client has, this will harm my therapeutic relationship only if it blinds me to how my client is uniquely experiencing the problem. On the other hand, I can use my struggle with the problem to help me empathize. There is no need to resolve the problem in order to be therapeutic as long as I continue to check my perceptions and listen. Sometimes it is therapists who have resolved their problems who are *most* likely to impose *their* solutions on the client.

CURATIVE FACTORS OR MECHANISMS OF CHANGE

For the person-centered therapies, therapy is more a process of creation than of repair. Some therapies focus on repairing damage from the past. However, for the person-centered therapies the focus is on forging creative new ways of synthesizing old experience, which carry one forward beyond old ways of being. As part of that process, old traumatic experiences will be related to in new ways, allowing them to be worked through and more productively incorporated into personal functioning. A person who was abused as a child may come to appreciate and value the processes whereby she managed to preserve herself and survive. She

may gain from that a sense of strength rather than one of weakness. She may use her experience to develop her own sensitivity and capacity for caring. Working through past trauma is therefore not really repairing damage so much as it is learning how to assimilate and reorganize traumatic experience in order to mobilize potential.

Because the therapy process is creative, therapists will often have no idea of the new solutions that will emerge from the therapy process. Mahoney (1991) and others have talked about Ilya Prigogine's research in chemistry and physics, which has found that systems confronted with disorganization will sometimes spontaneously jump to entirely new, more sophisticated levels of organization. Person-centered therapists believe this is what often happens in therapy.

The therapist does not therefore have to be the expert who knows the answer. Rather, the therapist must be a "process expert" who can facilitate this creative process. In developmental psychology those who follow the Piagetian approach do not believe that children can be taught to go from one developmental level to another. Yet if children who are at the same developmental level are brought together to discuss a problem, their collaboration often moves both of them to a higher level (Perret-Clermont, Perret, & Bell, 1991). Similarly, person-centered therapists try to provide a dialogical *process* that will result in the emergence of new, creative, and more sophisticated ways of functioning. Two heads are better than one, even if neither "knows" the solution—or even the path—in advance.

The provision by person-centered therapists of an engaged, experientially supportive and empathic relationship will provide a "conflict-free zone" that mobilizes the client's "critical intelligence." Clients will begin to become curious about their own experience and perceptions and begin to explore them.

This exploratory process will lead to the creative synthesis of incongruencies between different thoughts and perspectives or thoughts and experiences. It will lead to clients learning to incorporate and include all their experience. Clients will feel free to try out new behaviors, and to fail with them, before they refine them so that they become truly effective.

A sense of *efficacy* develops: I can learn and change and move my life forward. One learns that one can struggle with something one is up against and make some productive accommodation with it, no matter how awful the problem. For instance, a client may learn to live productively even if paralyzed. One learns that life is a process of continual confrontation of problems and challenges and of moving onward—the goal of life is not necessarily personal fulfillment or happiness, in contrast to what some other humanistic therapies hold.

Person-centered therapists do not explicitly teach life skills, as do some behavioral approaches. Nevertheless the process of person-centered therapy is one in which such skills as learning to explore and to listen to one's experience, as well as good communication skills, are modeled and experienced. The client learns that there is something valuable and trustworthy in everyone's experience and that it is better to listen to others than it is to impose one's will and values upon them. Dialoguing in an open, cooperative way about mutual problems is the best way to find a solution and mobilizes the "wisdom of the group." Respecting different ways is not only interpersonally important but fosters the creativity that comes from openness to difference.

Insight

The acquiring of insight is not the primary change mechanism in person-cen-

tered therapies, although clients often may attain it. Change often occurs without insight (Meyer, 1981). It is the direct experience of the therapy relationship itself that has the most impact. *What* one learns about oneself is less important than *the changes that come about in how* one relates to oneself, to others, and to problematic experience. These are complex, lived, whole-bodied changes that occur in an experiential manner rather than being guided "from above" by insight.

Because *self*-exploration is the important key, interpretations are generally not used in person-centered therapies. The therapist does not try to bring "news" to the client or to give the client insights.

The Role of the Therapist's Personality

I have previously described how the therapist's ability to be congruent and to be a real person in therapy is crucial to the change process. Good therapists would seek out their own therapy whenever it appeared that their problems or personalities were getting in the way of providing a therapeutic environment for the client.

Factors That Limit the Success of Person-Centered Therapies

First, although person-centered therapists have developed ways of working with unmotivated clients (Gendlin, 1967), the therapy's effectiveness is limited by low client motivation. Clients who are in therapy against their will, such as those who are court-referred or adolescents brought by their parents, are more difficult to work with. The establishment of a good relationship becomes even more central with such populations.

Second, clients with whom it is difficult to establish a relationship will limit the effectiveness of person-centered therapy. Some clients labeled with "borderline personality disorder," for instance, are difficult to work with not because their personality structure is primitive but because some have difficulty staying with the frustrations that are a normal part of the working environment of therapy. If a strong therapeutic alliance can be formed, I believe these clients can be worked with effectively.

It has been asserted at times that person-centered therapy is not useful with "nonverbal" clients. However, person-centered therapists have had success with nonverbal schizophrenics (Gendlin, 1967). Prouty (1990) recently developed techniques for working with both severely regressed schizophrenics and mentally retarded persons. Sometimes when people talk about nonverbal clients what they mean are lower-class clients. Aside from the fact that this is a "classist" position and that lower-class people are every bit as verbal as anyone else, Lerner (1972) has found evidence that client-centered therapy can help with lower-class clients as well.

Aspects Shared
with Other Approaches

A number of aspects of person-centered therapies are shared by other therapies. The emphasis on the relationship has been adopted by most therapy approaches. Empathy is now valued by virtually all approaches, although different therapies mean different things by it (Bohart, 1991). The idea of using one's personal reactions in therapy rather than trying to exclude them is now being emphasized in psychoanalytic object relations therapy, and therapist self-disclosure has become more highly emphasized by many psychodynamic therapists as well. The importance of accessing emotion and experiencing is becoming more and more emphasized in cognitive therapy.

Research

Because I am considering three different "person-centered therapies" I will briefly consider research examples of each. Tomlinson and Hart (1962) hypothesized that successful clients in therapy would score higher on the Process Scale at termination than would unsuccessful clients. The Process Scale measures the degree to which the client is functioning in a fluid, flexible, and open manner. Ten cases from the files of the University of Chicago Counseling Center were selected as representative of the kinds of cases treated there. Five were rated on multiple criteria as being more successful, and five were rated as less successful. Two-minute samples from both early and late interviews were selected and given to judges to rate. More successful cases were rated significantly higher on the Process Scale than were less successful cases. Similarly, later interviews were rated as significantly higher than were earlier interviews. There was a nonsignificant trend for more successful clients to show larger changes on the Process Scale over the course of therapy than did less successful cases.

From an experiential perspective, Gendlin and Berlin (1961) had college subjects focus on external matters, such as school friends, or internally on a specific aspect of a personal problem. Galvanic skin responses were measured and it was found that internal focusing led to significantly greater tension-reduction patterns than did external focus.

From a process–experiential perspective, Rice and Saperia (1984) studied the use of evocative unfolding with problematic reactions. Therapists worked with undergraduate subjects who had done something they felt self-critical about. The therapists used evocative unfolding in one session and nonspecific client-centered therapy in another. Some subjects received evocative unfolding first, while others received nonspecific client-centered therapy first. Subjects' ratings found that evocative unfolding was rated as significantly more helpful than nonspecific client-centered therapy. Intensive studies of tapes supported the hypothesized process of change: Evocative unfolding helped clients identify the specific meaning—construction that led to their problematic reaction, and this discovery often generalized to clarify other areas of the client's life.

TREATMENT APPLICABILILITY

Person-centered therapies have been used with a wide range of client problems, including alcoholism, schizophrenia, anxiety disorders, and personality disorders such as borderline personality disorder (Bohart, 1990; Swildens, 1990). They have also been used with mentally handicapped individuals and the elderly (cf. Lietaer et al., 1990). Process—experiential therapy is currently being successfully applied to the treatment of depression (Elliott et al., 1990). Experiential psychotherapy and focusing have been used with a variety of problems, including borderline personality disorders and cancer (cf. Greenberg, Elliott, & Lietaer, 1994). A number of person-centered therapists have been developing models for working with families and couples (cf. Levant & Shlien, 1984; Lietaer et al., 1990). Client-centered therapy was originally developed in a child guidance clinic and has been used successfully with children (Axline, 1947).

With children, a good relationship in which the child learns that he/she is valuable, understandable, and acceptable through the therapist's empathy, congruence, and acceptance is even more a primary change agent than in adult psychotherapy. The therapy format is one in which the child and the therapist play, and feelings are talked about in that context. Similarly, establishing a good therapeutic bond is the primary treatment goal with adolescents. Many adolescents are in therapy against their will and do not trust adults. Establishing a trustful empathic relationship in which the therapist is willing to be open is already therapeutic, regardless of what issues are talked about. Santen (1990) has also used focusing with traumatized children and adolescents.

The philosophy of person-centered therapy makes it particularly appropriate for the treatment of women, minorities, people of different cultural backgrounds, or people of alternative sexual orientations. This is because the therapist is not an "expert" who is going to impose the "right way of being" on the client but rather is a "fellow explorer" who tries to enter the life world of the client in a curious, interested, accepting, and open way. The therapist tries to work from the frame of reference of what the client thinks is important. Paradoxically, this might lead a person-centered therapist to become somewhat more directive with a client who might want directiveness based on his/her cultural background. Working with people who come from experiential backgrounds different from the therapist, however, imposes a particular burden on therapists to continually check to make sure their perceptions of their clients' experience are not being colored by their own backgrounds and preconceptions.

None of the person-centered therapies discussed in this chapter would be the treatment of choice for problems where the teaching and learning of specific skills is important, as is the case in sex therapy. I would refer clients if there were specific skills that I do not have that could help them. Certain problems are best treated by behavioral methods, for instance. I would not require a client to obtain medication, but with certain kinds of problems (such as major affective disorders), I would make them aware of the availability of medication and tell them there is a good possibility that their problem would be alleviated by it.

As a person-centered therapist I would neither recommend nor not recommend that potential clients enter therapy. I would talk it over to help them arrive at their own decision.

There are no particular ethical issues unique to the use of person-centered therapy. However, the egalitarian, democratic stance of the person-centered therapist, along with the belief in clients' self-healing potential, can sometimes create a disparity with the perspectives of other professionals. The problem is that person-centered therapists do not adopt an "expert" stance vis-à-vis the client. Although they may have expertise, they share it with their clients in a collaborative, nonauthoritarian way and do not perscribe treatment for the client. For instance, they would not decide for a client who had been sexually abused as a child that the number one priority of therapy must be working with the abuse (as many abuse therapists hold). Yet the field of psychotherapy is currently increasingly adopting a "medical" view in which the therapist is the "expert/professional" who decides on the course of treatment. Because a crucial part of person-centered therapy is to trust the client's judgment, if a client chose not to explore their childhood abuse, the person-centered therapist would go along with that decision. This might bother therapists who believe it is the expert professional's role to decide what focus is best.

This does not mean a person-centered therapist would go along with *any* decision a client made. There are cases when a person-centered therapist has to choose

to impose his/her judgment upon the client, though this is avoided as often as possible. Person-centered therapists have loyalties to society as well as to their clients and would take action to protect others from a client's choices if necessary. As a member of society I would also make a personal choice to have an acutely suicidal client hospitalized, even against my client's judgment. However, I would take the responsibility for my decision—I did it because *I* wanted to save the client's life—rather than because I the expert know what is "best for" my client.

Generally there are a number of different indicators that a person-centered therapist might look for as signs that therapy is being effective. These include greater client access to and acceptance of feelings and experiencing; a greater sense of client self-acceptance and self-trust; signs of the client showing more initiative in making personal choices; signs that the client is beginning to relate more as an equal to the therapist; more client comfort with personal self-disclosure; and signs that the client can better tolerate, face up to, and continue to try to master adversity. Ultimately, the single most important criterion of effectiveness is if the client feels he/she has made progress.

RESEARCH

Research on Therapy Outcome

A meta-analysis of research on the outcome of psychotherapy carried out by Smith, Glass, and Miller (1980) found that client-centered therapy was, on the average, about as effective as other approaches to therapy. More recently, Greenberg et al. (1994) have conducted a meta-analysis of over 20 studies on "experiential" therapies in general, which included Gestalt (see Yontef, Chapter 8, this volume) and other feeling-oriented approaches in the category of experiential therapy, along with the person-centered therapies covered in this chapter. However, the bulk of the studies included were on person-centered therapies. They found general equivalence in effectiveness for experiential treatments compared to nonexperiential treatments, such as cognitive therapy, for a variety of disorders. In contrast to certain biases in the field that experiential/person-centered approaches are not useful with certain disorders (e.g., depression), they concluded that there is no evidence contraindicating the use of an experiential approach with any disorder.

To give some specific examples of research findings, Ends and Page (1957, 1959) conducted two studies that suggested that client-centered group therapy may hold promise as an adjunct to inpatient treatment of alcoholism. Patients who received client-centered therapy had the highest rates of abstinence (58%) at an 18-month follow-up in comparison to two other therapy approaches (40% and 7%, respectively) and to a control group (18%), and the differences between client-centered therapy and the less effective of the other therapy approaches and the control group were statistically significant. Significantly positive changes in self-concept from client-centered therapy were also found.

Borkovec and colleagues have used a nondirective, client-centered therapy approach as a comparison to cognitive therapy in the treatment of anxiety disorders. Borkovec and Mathews (1988) gave anxiety-disordered clients training in relaxation. In addition, each received nondirective therapy, cognitive therapy, or a behavioral desensitization therapy. Nondirective therapy was equivalent in effectiveness to the cognitive and behavioral treatments. Borkovec et al. (1987) found nondirective therapy to be effective with anxiety-disordered clients who had also received relaxation training, though in this study not as effective as cognitive

therapy. Teusch and Boehme (1991), in a study without a control group, found 75–80% success rate with agoraphobics based on a 10-week treatment program with individual and group client-centered therapy.

Studies by Meyer and his colleagues (Meyer, 1981) comparing client-centered therapy to psychodynamic treatment of psychosomatic clients found general equivalence in effectiveness between the two approaches. Another study (Grawe, Caspar, & Ambuhl, 1990) compared client-centered therapy to several variants of behavioral therapy with clients experiencing interpersonal problems and once again found general equivalence in effectiveness. Eckert and Biermann-Ratjen (1990) compared inpatient programs utilizing client-centered or psychodynamic group therapy in the treatment of severely neurotic or personality-disordered clients (typically with suicidal symptomatology) and once again found equivalence in effectiveness. In a carefully screened sample of schizophrenics seen in a client-centered inpatient treatment program, Teusch (1990) found a 75% improvement rate.

Preliminary research data show that process–experiential psychotherapy created positive changes in depressives at a level equivalent to that achieved by cognitive therapy (Elliott et al., 1990). Focusing interventions have been shown to be effective for coping with cancer, dealing with weight problems, and working with public speaking anxiety (cf. Greenberg et al., 1994).

In sum, there is a growing body of evidence to support the effectiveness of client-centered, experiential, and process-experiential approaches with a wide range of problems.

Research on Therapy Process

Many researchers have investigated Rogers's hypothesis that therapist warmth, empathy, and genuineness are "necessary and sufficient conditions" for psychotherapeutic change. Early research, primarily on client-centered therapy, appeared to support the importance of these therapeutic conditions. However, recent research reviews have pointed out a number of methodological problems with earlier research and have been more cautious in drawing conclusions (e.g., Lambert, De Julio, & Stein, 1978).

In a recent review, Orlinsky and Howard (1986) concluded that *patients'* perceptions of both their therapists' warmth and their empathy were strongly related to positive change in therapy, with genuineness related to change but less consistently so. However, when the presence or absence of warmth, empathy, and genuineness was measured in other ways (for instance, by having objective raters rate tape-recorded therapy sessions), the results were less consistently positive. Recently, Greenberg et al. (1994) reviewed several new studies which found positive correlations between these conditions and therapeutic change.

In summary, there is evidence suggesting a positive relationship between therapist warmth, empathy, and genuineness and change in therapy. However, it cannot be said at the present time that research has shown the therapeutic conditions to be either absolutely necessary or sufficient as Rogers claimed.

For experiential psychotherapy, Gendlin et al. (1967) reviewed a number of studies in which samples of tape-recorded therapy sessions were rated for the degree to which the client was actively experiencing and exploring their experiencing. It was found that higher levels of experiencing predicted positive therapeutic change. Further research utilizing the Experiencing Scale (Klein, Mathieu-Coughlan, & Kiesler, 1986) has found significant correlations between levels of experiencing and positive change in a number of different approaches to psychotherapy, although the results are not always supportive.

CASE ILLUSTRATION

Andrea, a 36-year-old, white woman, was referred to me by a urologist whom she had seen because she had been having chronic urinary pain. Although initially she had had an infection, the urologist believed that the chronicity of the problem might be based on psychological factors.

Andrea was currently on welfare, studying to be a computer programmer. Prior to this she had been hospitalized for several months with a depressive reaction, following the breakup of a relationship with a man named Lance. She had been diagnosed by other professionals with both a major depressive disorder and a borderline personality disorder.

Andrea had been married once in her 20s to an alcoholic. Between her marriage and relationship with Lance, she had had several other failed relationships. Andrea saw herself as having a problem with commitment, blaming the breakup of all her relationships on herself. For example, when engaged to her first fiancé in her early 20s, she slept with one of his friends. She had recently become involved in a fundamentalist Christian church but was having difficulties following its rules about sex outside marriage. She had had a couple of casual sexual relationships, which she believed had contributed to her urinary difficulties. At the moment she was not involved with anyone.

The problems as defined by Andrea were as follows: First, she felt debilitated by her urinary problems—unable to hold a job as long as she had to go to the bathroom so frequently. Second, she felt depressed and empty about her life. Third, she had no career and was living on welfare. Fourth, she had no current relationship. Fifth, she felt she was over-weight and was having no luck in dieting.

In the first session I started where Andrea wanted to start—on her relationship with Lance. Earlier that week Lance had reappeared in her life. He had called her and they had met for dinner. He wanted to resume their relationship and Andrea was tempted. Specifically, she felt sexually tempted. Andrea had held off sexually that night because of her newfound religious beliefs, but she was unsure whether she would be able to hold off if she saw Lance again.

Andrea began to explore the various "threads" of her former relationship with Lance. As she did so, I empathically reflected her experience and its two prongs: On the one hand, she was alone and wanted a relationship, and she really had liked Lance before he had gotten sick with a circulatory problem; on the other hand something was holding her back from getting involved with him again. Complicating the problem was that she felt under pressure to make some kind of decision because she was going to see Lance again the next night.

First, Andrea focused on what had been good about the relationship, getting to know her own perceptual universe better. She articulated how important she had felt to him and was able to clarify this sense of importance: "I was the only one he could talk to. I really provided emotional support for him. That felt good. He had a lot of problems with his ex-wife."

After she had explored some of the ties to Lance, she began to shift her attention to the problems. Lance had two grown sons who resented Andrea's presence and she felt caught in a triangle between them and Lance. This situation had become unbearable for Andrea when Lance got sick and had to go into the hospital. At that point he increasingly gave into his sons and Andrea experienced no support

from him, which led her to break off the relationship.

Then Andrea's attention shifted to the present: "I'm tired of being alone, Dr. Bohart. I'd really like to be married. And we did love each other. But I want to make the right decision for myself. I'm afraid that I might go to bed with him and get involved with him again just 'cause I'm lonely. So maybe it's good that something in me feels like holding back. But I'm afraid I might hold back when I shouldn't and blow it too." I empathized with the vulnerability Andrea was feeling: "It feels so lousy to be alone. You'd really like to have someone to love you. And here he is again. And yet you're really not sure its good for you. And you're afraid that either way you go might be the wrong decision."

Later in the session Andrea asked me whether I thought she should get reinvolved with Lance. I certainly did not know and disclosed my empathic sense of her confusion: "If I were in your shoes I think I'd feel as confused as you. The scary part for me would be the fear I might make make a wrong choice. I sense that may be true for you but I'm not sure. And you don't even know what's holding you back or whether or not it can be trusted."

As Andrea further explored her experience she had a growing sense of danger about getting reinvolved with Lance too quickly. Part of the reluctance concerned having sex with him outside marriage because of her newfound religious beliefs. More important, however, she began to get in touch with a deep sense that she did not entirely trust him anymore. Her reluctance began to make more sense to her and she began to get a sense that maybe her feelings were trustworthy.

With a more differentiated sense of her own experience, Andrea was able to listen and explore when she met with Lance. She discovered that she did indeed have deep reservations as to how much she could trust him. Further, she was able to identify one of the sources of that distrust as a sense that Lance allowed himself too easily to be torn in different directions by the demands of various people. Another source of the distrust was that Andrea had an increasingly clear sense that the relationship with him had been, and would likely continue to be, imbalanced, with her taking care of him but not with him taking care of her.

At first these discoveries were more like hypotheses. However, Andrea met with Lance several more times, and we continued to discuss that experience in therapy. Her sense of what was wrong in her relationship with Lance became clearer and more specific, and Andrea ultimately chose not to get reinvolved with him. This was an important learning experience because Andrea found that out of her own self she was able to choose to be alone rather than be in a relationship that might not have been entirely good for her. Further she had been able to choose to forgo a sexual relationship for the same reason. These experiences empowered her. She had begun to learn that (1) her own feelings were trustworthy, (2) she could make good choices for herself—she did not have to fear that her own needs would lead her astray, and (3) she could *choose* to be alone.

Evocative Unfolding

As she began to trust her inner capacity for choice, Andrea also began to focus on the self-perception that she had an "evil tendency" inside to sabotage a relationship whenever it began to get too serious, though she was now clear that ending the relationship with Lance had been a good thing. She brought up the example of ruining her first engagement by sleeping with one of her fiancé's friends. She was very self-critical for having done this. However, by now Andrea had

learned the value of exploration and wanted to explore this apparently self-destructive reaction in more detail. I thought that this might be a point where she could use the evocative unfolding technique for problem reaction points. In this way, I was making available to Andrea a process for self-discovery. Its use is an example of what Greenberg et al. (1993) call being "process-directive," although I would consider it being "process-suggestive." Andrea decided to try it.

In the evocative unfolding procedure the therapist helps the client to reenter a situation in which a problematic reaction occurred in as much vivid, experiential detail as possible. Then, using highly vivid empathic reflections helps the client explore his/her reaction. As we worked to get a vivid sense of the circumstances surrounding her decision to sleep with the friend, Andrea remembered that the friend was commiserating with her over her fiancé's mistreatment of her. In the session, she began to remember having felt very mistreated and unloved by her fiancé and very comforted and taken care of by this friend. The specific incident of mistreatment had been that her boyfriend had gotten angry with her and had hit her the day before. As she recalled this she also accessed other vivid experiences of how he had mistreated her.

The picture of her relationship with her fiancé emerged as one in which he constantly criticized and mistreated her, but she continually blamed herself for it. The friend had been supportive and constant over several weeks, and that night, they ended up sleeping together. She remembered vividly wanting some caring, connected contact. Suddenly her decision to sleep with the friend began to make sense.

This experience broadened out with Andrea reevaluating other relationships. She realized that there were sensible reasons for her ending other relationships—

she had left because she was not getting what she really wanted and needed. She began to shift her self-perception from "I am not currently in a relationship because there is something horribly wrong with me" to "I am not in a relationship because I haven't yet gotten involved with someone I could really work things out with."

Two-Chair Technique

In an early session Andrea had once mentioned in passing that her father had physically abused her. Many therapists would have become directive at that point and focused Andrea's attention on the abuse. This is an example of being *content-directive*—the therapist decides what content the client will focus on. In contrast, I followed Andrea's process. I believed that as she explored the topics of immediate relevance to her, and as she gained more and more of a sense of self-trust and self-efficacy, she would come to explore the abuse experience if and when it became meaningful for her to do so to further her self-evolution.

Sometime later Andrea started talking about her feelings of negative self-worth. She brought up an example of feeling very self-critical because she was not married, had no children, and did not have a solid career. Once again, growing out of the collaborative sense of our sharing in the exploration process, I said, "You know, like that evocative unfolding technique we tried a few sessions back, there's another technique that people can sometimes use to help them sort out where they stand when they're feeling split. In this technique the person puts one side of themselves in one chair, and talks from that side, and then switches chairs and puts the other side in the second chair and talks from *that* side. They go back and forth and make up a dialogue. Some people don't like this

technique. Others do. But I thought I'd share it with you."

Andrea decided she wanted to try it. In one chair she forcefully expressed her criticisms: "You really have mismanaged your life. Here you are age 36 and you're not even married yet. And you don't even have a stable career. You really need to get your act together."

Then Andrea switched chairs. In the other chair a remarkable thing happened. Her whole demeanor and tone of voice changed. She looked and sounded like a little girl. Experientially she had become herself as a little girl. She began to relate to the critical side as if it were her father. She said, "I'm sorry daddy. I really try to be a good girl. Don't hurt me daddy."

At this point Andrea stopped the exercise and began to spontaneously explore her physical abuse experiences with her father. She recalled several incidents, one in which he had become angry with her for something and had picked her up by her hair and thrown her into a corner. She was spontaneously experiencing the terror she felt around her father, and how frightening it was when what she did did not please him.

She began to experience directly how her attention in that relationship had been so exclusively focused on pleasing her father that she had not had any left over to focus on what *she* wanted or what *she* thought, thereby paralyzing her own ability to think critically. As she focused on her reactions of fear and fright she also began to recognize directly how she had lost a sense of herself in that relationship. She began to experience herself as now being able to take care of herself.

A Theoretical Note

It would be instructive to contrast a person-centered view of how Andrea's childhood affected her with a psychodynamic view. A psychodynamic view might assume that Andrea's pattern of poor relationships with men was due to her choosing men, albeit unconsciously, in order to re-create the kind of relationship she had with her father. However, from a person-centered perspective Andrea was not trying to re-create her relationship with her father. Rather, her motives were the same motives everyone has in trying to form a relationship: wanting intimacy, sharing, sex, and support.

Yet she had impulsively and prematurely entered such relationships and, when she had left abusive relationships, she criticized herself for intimacy problems, overlooking problems in the relationships themselves. Why? From a person-centered perspective, her childhood experiences with her father had created an extreme form of self-distrust in Andrea. She was afraid of men and unable to trust her feelings and critically evaluate the men with whom she got involved. Having no sense of self-trust, she had leapt into relationships without "looking" very carefully. The result was that she had chosen several poor partners, usually basing her decision on some superficial characteristic that seemed initially promising. Even if she had fortuitously made a good choice, her fear and her lack of self-trust made her think all problems were her fault. This paralyzed her ability to discuss and solve problems that did come up in the relationship.

As Andrea began to trust her own feelings and judgmental capacity, she became more and more adept at evaluating the men in her life in terms of whether or not they truly met her needs. A distinct felt shift had occurred. She now had a direct sense of herself trying to take care of herself in relationship contexts, rather than of herself as a negative force ruining her relationships. She began to feel more proactive and more hopeful about making good choices in the future.

As therapy progressed, Andrea shifted her attention to career issues. She began to question her choice of working with computers. As she was able to hold more tentatively what she thought she "should" do (i.e., computer work), she began to get more in touch with something she thought she would really enjoy: working with people.

Conclusion

I saw Andrea 36 times on a once-a-week basis over a period of about 11 months. In general, how did she do and why did we terminate? Did we stop because she was completely cured, no longer showing any borderline symptoms, as slim as she wanted to be, no longer depressed, urinary problem completely gone, relationship problems all solved, and Andrea safely ensconced in a stable, high-paying job?

Things did not turn out *this* rosy. Generally, in terms of her presenting problem, Andrea's urinary problems improved significantly but had not completely disappeared. When she first came she was experiencing pain on almost a daily basis. When she terminated she was having pain only occasionally (maybe once every 3 or 4 weeks). But she had learned that this pain was associated with the experience of significant stress in her life. Because she was generally better able to manage stressful problems, the periods of pain were not as long lasting.

As is typical of my experience with person-centered therapy, termination was not a problem. At first Andrea cut down from once a week to once every 2 weeks. Then she decided to go for a while without coming in. Several months later I heard from her by phone that she was doing okay and that she would come back "if needed." It has now been a year since that telephone call and I have not seen her again.

When she left, Andrea was finishing up her computer course. She still did not know what she was going to do. However, she had become a volunteer at a local convalescent hospital, where she spent several afternoons a week taking wheelchair patients out for walks, reading to them, and playing games with them. There was a possibility that this might turn into a paying job. She also had begun to study to be a minister in her church. As of the time she terminated she had still not found a relationship. However she was generally doing well alone and practicing her ability to "just say no" when a relationship was not in her best interest. Generally she was not feeling depressed, although she still had occasional moments when she felt lonely and depressed. She was still struggling with her weight.

In terms of my personal assessment from a person-centered perspective, Andrea had moved away from self-criticism toward greater self-trust. She had gotten a positive sense of herself. She was better able to "think and feel through" what she wanted on her own. She was "more in touch with herself" and had developed a greater sense of what she valued and what she wanted. She was less a creature buffeted by the winds.

I do not believe Andrea was "cured" or that she may never again need therapy. I would have liked to work with her longer to consolidate the gains she had made and to explore more thoroughly the impact of her early abuse on her. However, I trust Andrea to take care of herself and to return if she feels the need to. I know she will still be bothered by occasional bouts of depression (aren't many of us?). However, when she left she seemed better able to ride out and transcend these periods rather than to sink into them.

ACKNOWLEDGMENTS

I gratefully acknowledge the help given by Barbara Brodley, Ph.D., and Leslie Greenberg, Ph.D., both of whom read several drafts of the chapter and provided extensive feedback on their approaches to person-centered therapy. I would also like to acknowledge the helpful feedback received from Stanley Messer, Ph.D., Fran Miller, M.S., and Suzanne Browner, B.A., on the chapter in general.

SUGGESTIONS FOR FURTHER READING

General Reference Books

Levant, R. F., & Shlien, J. M. (Eds.). (1984). *Client-centered therapy and the person-centered approach: New developments in theory, research, and practice.* New York: Praeger. This book has articles on the nature of unconditional positive regard, empathy, family and couple therapy, Gendlin's theory of experiencing, Rice's cognitive approach, applications to medicine and education, pastoral counseling, person-centered approaches to research, and an article coauthored by Carl Rogers on his peace work, as well as an afternote on what happened to Gloria after the Rogers–Gloria film.

Lietaer, G., Rombauts, J., & Van Balen, R. (Eds.). (1990). *Client-centered and experiential psychotherapy in the nineties.* Leuven, Belgium: Leuven University Press. This book has articles on the debate over whether client-centered therapy should remain purely nondirective; on how to combine it with other approaches; several articles on the use of focusing; client-centered dream therapy; work with schizophrenics, borderlines, and mentally retarded persons; applications to health psychology; use in groups and with couples and families; as well as several research studies.

Case Studies

Corsini, R. J. (1991). *Five therapists and one client.* Itasca, IL: Peacock. This book has a detailed case history by Fred Zimring, with comment by Nathanial Raskin.

Greenberg, L. S., Rice, L. N., & Elliott, R. (1993). *Facilitating emotional change: The moment-by-moment process.* New York: Guilford Press. This book on process–experiential psychotherapy has detailed case histories at the end.

Rogers, C. R., & Dymond, R. F. (Eds.). (1954). *Psychotherapy and personality change.* Chicago: University of Chicago Press. This book has lengthy case histories, including transcriptions.

Research

Greenberg, L. S., Elliott, R., & Lietaer, G. (1994). Research on humanistic and experiential psychotherapies. In A. Bergin & S. Garfield (Eds.), *Handbook of psychotherapy and behavior change* (4th ed., pp. 509–542). New York: Wiley. This chapter summarizes a number of research findings.

Greenberg, L. S., & Pinsof, W. M. (Eds.). (1986). *The psychotherapeutic process: A research handbook.* New York: Guilford Press. Has chapters by Greenberg, Toukmanian, Robert Elliott, and William Stiles on research projects related to client-centered therapy, as well as on the Experiencing Scale and on Barrett-Lennard's Relationship Inventory for measuring quality of the therapeutic relationship.

Rice, L. N., & Greenberg, L. S. (Eds.). (1984). *Patterns of change: Intensive analysis of psychotherapy process.* New York: Guilford Press. Has articles on research on aspects of process–experiential therapy and on experiencing.

Rogers, C. R., & Sanford, R. C. (1984). Client-centered psychotherapy. In H. I. Kaplan & B. J. Sadock (Eds.), *Comprehensive textbook of psychiatry* (4th ed., pp. 1374–1388). Baltimore: Williams & Wilkins. This chapter summarizes a number of research findings.

REFERENCES

Anderson, W. (1974). Personal growth and client-centered therapy: An information-processing view. In D. A. Wexler & L. N. Rice (Eds.), *Innovations in client-centered therapy* (pp. 21–48). New York: Wiley.

Axline, V. M. (1947). *Play therapy.* New York: Ballentine.

Bandura, A. (1986). *Social foundations of thought and action: A social–cognitive analysis.* Englewood Cliffs, NJ: Prentice Hall.

Bankart, C. P., Koshikawa, F., Nedate, K., & Haruki, Y. (1992). When west meets east: Contributions of eastern traditions to the future of psychotherapy. *Psychotherapy, 29,* 141–149.

Barrett-Lennard, G. T. (1991). *Carl Rogers' helping system: Journey and substance.* Manuscript in preparation.

Barrett-Lennard, G. T. (1993). The phases and focus of empathy. *British Journal of Medical Psychology, 66,* 3–14.

Bishop, B. (1992). *Codependency theory and immigrant populations who embrace familism: Mental illness or clashing cultural values and norms?* Unpublished manuscript, California State University Dominguez Hills.

Bohart, A. C. (1990). A cognitive client-centered perspective on borderline personality development. In G. Lietaer, J. Rombauts, & R. Van Balen (Eds.), *Client-centered and experiential psychotherapy in the nineties* (pp. 599–622). Leuven, Belgium: Leuven University Press.

Bohart, A. C. (1991). Empathy in client-centered therapy: A contrast with psychoanalysis and self psychology. *Journal of Humanistic Psychology, 31,* 34–48.

Bohart, A. C. (1993). Experiencing: The basis of psychotherapy. *Journal of Psychotherapy Integration, 3,* 51–67.

Bohart, A., & Rosenbaum, R. (1995). The dance of empathy: Empathy, diversity, and technical eclecticism. *The Person-Centered Journal, 2,* 5–29.

Borkovec, T. D., & Mathews, A. M. (1988). Treatment of nonphobic anxiety disorder: A comparison of nondirective, cognitive, and coping desensitization therapy. *Journal of Consulting and Clinical Psychology, 56*, 877–884.

Borkovec, T. D., Mathews, A. M., Chambers, A., Ebrahimi, S., Lytle, R., & Nelson, R. (1987). The effects of relaxation training with cognitive or nondirective therapy and the role of relaxation-induced anxiety in the treatment of generalized anxiety. *Journal of Consulting and Clinical Psychology, 55*, 883–888.

Brodley, B. T. (1988). Responses to person-centered versus client-centered? *Renaissance, 5*, 1–2.

Brodley, B. T. (1993). Response to Patterson's "Winds of change for client-centered counseling." *Journal of Humanistic Education and Development, 31*, 139–143.

Bozarth, J. D. (1984). Beyond reflection: Emergent modes of empathy. In R. F. Levant & J. M. Shlien (Eds.), *Client-centered therapy and the person-centered approach: New directions in theory, research, and practice* (pp. 59–75). New York: Praeger.

Bozarth, J. D. (1993). Not ncessarily necessary but always sufficient. In D. Brazier (Ed.), *Beyond Carl Rogers: Toward a psychotherapy for the 21st century* (pp. 287–310). London: Constable and Co.

Cantor, N. (1990). From thought to behavior: "Having" and "doing" in the study of personality and cognition. *American Psychologist, 45*, 735–750.

Cash, R. W. (1984). The human resources development model. In D. Larson (Ed.), *Teaching psychological skills: Models for giving psychology away* (pp. 245–270). Monterey, CA: Brooks/Cole.

Caspi, A., Elder, G. H., & Herbener, E. S. (1990). Childhood personality and the prediction of life-course patterns. In L. E. Robins & M. Rutter (Eds.), *Straight and devious pathways from childhood to adulthood* (pp. 13–35). New York: Cambridge University Press.

Dweck, C. S., & Leggett, E. L. (1988). A social–cognitive approach to motivation and personality. *Psychological Review, 95*, 256–273.

Eckert, J., & Biermann-Ratjen, E.-M. (1990). Client-centered therapy versus psychoanalytic psychotherapy: Reflections following a comparative study. In G. Lietaer, J. Rombauts, & R. Van Balen (Eds.), *Client-centered and experiential psychotherapy in the nineties* (pp. 457–468). Leuven, Belgium: Leuven University Press.

Elliott, R., Clark, C., Wexler, M., Kemeny, V., Brinkerhoff, J., & Mack, C. (1990). The impact of experiential therapy of depression: Initial results. In G. Lietaer, J. Rombauts, & R. Van Balen (Eds.), *Client-centered and experiential psychotherapy in the nineties* (pp. 549–577). Leuven, Belgium: Leuven University Press.

Ends, E. J., & Page, C. W. (1957). A study of three types of group psychotherapy with hospitalized male inebriates. *Quarterly Journal of Studies in Alcoholism, 18*, 263–277.

Ends, E. J., & Page, C. W. (1959). Group psychotherapy and concomitant psychological change. *Psychological Monographs, 73* (Whole No. 480).

Epstein, R. (1991). Skinner, creativity, and the problem of spontaneous behavior. *Psychological Science, 2*, 362–370.

Gendlin, E. T. (1967). Therapeutic procedures in dealing with schizophrenics. In C. R. Rogers, E. T. Gendlin, D. J. Kiesler, & C. B. Truax (Eds.), *The therapeutic relationship and its impact* (pp. 369–400). Madison: University of Wisconsin Press.

Gendlin, E. T. (1968). The experiential response. In E. Hammer (Ed.), *Use of interpretation in treatment*. New York: Grune & Stratton.

Gendlin, E. T. (1969). Focusing. *Psychotherapy: Theory, research and practice, 6*, 4–15.

Gendlin, E. T. (1970). A theory of personality change. In J. T. Hart & T. M. Tomlinson (Eds.), *New directions in client-centered therapy* (pp. 129–174). Boston: Houghton Mifflin. [Reprinted from P. Worchel & D. Byrne (Eds.). (1964). *Personality change*. New York: Wiley.]

Gendlin, E. T. (1979). Experiential psychotherapy. In R. Corsini (Ed.), *Current psychotherapies* (2nd ed., pp. 340–373). Itasca, IL: F. E. Peacock.

Gendlin, E. T. (1981). *Focusing*. New York: Bantam.

Gendlin, E. T., Beebe, J., Cassens, J., Klein, M., & Oberlander, M. (1967). Focusing ability in psychotherapy, personality, and creativity. In J. M. Shlien (Ed.), *Research in psychotherapy* (Vol. 3, pp. 217–241). Washington, DC: American Psychological Association.

Gendlin, E. T., & Berlin, J. (1961). Galvanic skin response correlates of different modes of experiencing. *Journal of Clinical Psychology, 17,* 73–77.

Goodman, G. (1984). SASHAtapes: Expanding options for help-intended communication. In D. Larson (Ed.), *Teaching psychological skills: Models for giving psychology away* (pp. 271–286). Monterey, CA: Brooks/Cole.

Gordon, T. (1984). Three decades of democratizing relationships through training. In D. Larson (Ed.), *Teaching psychological skills: Models for giving psychology away* (pp. 151–170). Monterey, CA: Brooks/Cole.

Grawe, K., Caspar, F., & Ambuhl, H. (1990). Differentielle psychotherapieforschung: Vier therapieformen im Vergleich. *Zeitschrift für Klinische Psychologie, 19,* 287–376.

Greenberg, L. S., Elliott, R., & Lietaer, G. (1994). Research on humanistic and experiential psychotherapies. In A. Bergin & S. Garfield (Eds.), *Handbook of psychotherapy and behavior change* (4th ed., pp. 509–542). New York: Wiley.

Greenberg, L. S., Rice, L. N., & Elliott, R. (1993). *Facilitating emotional change: The moment-by-moment process.* New York: Guilford Press.

Guerney, B. G. (1984). Contributions of client-centered therapy to filial, marital, and family relationship enhancement therapies. In R. F. Levant & J. M. Shlien (Eds.), *Client-centered therapy and the person-centered approach: New directions in theory, research, and practice* (pp. 261–277). New York: Praeger.

Holdstock, T. L. (1990). Can client-centered therapy transcend its monocultural roots? In G. Lietaer, J. Rombauts, & R. Van Balen (Eds.), *Client-centered and experiential psychotherapy in the nineties* (pp. 109–121). Leuven, Belgium: Leuven University Press.

Holdstock, T. L., & Rogers, C. R. (1983). Person-centered theory. In R. J. Corsini

& A. J. Marsella (Eds.), *Personality theories, research, and assessment* (pp. 189–228). Itasca, IL: Peacock.

Janis, I. L. (1972). *Victims of groupthink.* Boston: Houghton Mifflin.

Klein, M. H., Mathieu-Coughlan, P., & Kiesler, D. J. (1986). The experiencing scales. In L. S. Greenberg & W. M. Pinsof (Eds.), *The psychotherapeutic process: A research handbook* (pp. 21–72). New York: Guilford Press.

Lambert, M. J., De Julio, S. S., & Stein, D. M. (1978). Therapist interpersonal skills: Process, outcome, methodological considerations, and recommendations for future research. *Psychological Bulletin, 85,* 467–489.

Lerner, B. (1972). *Therapy in the ghetto.* Baltimore: Johns Hopkins University Press.

Levant, R. F., & Shlien, J. M. (Eds.). (1984). *Client-centered therapy and the person-centered approach: New directions in theory, research, and practice.* New York: Praeger.

Lewicki, P. (1986). *Nonconscious social information-processing.* New York: Academic Press.

Lietaer, G. (1984). Unconditional positive regard: A controversial basic attitude in client-centered therapy. In R. F. Levant & J. M. Shlien (Eds.), *Client-centered therapy and the person-centered approach: New directions in theory, research, and practice* (pp. 41–58). New York: Praeger.

Lietaer, G. (1991, July). *The authenticity of the therapist: Congruence and transparency.* Paper presented at the 2nd International Conference on Client-centered and Experiential Psychotherapy, Stirling, Scotland.

Lietaer, G., Rombauts, J., & Van Balen, R. (Eds.). (1990). *Client-centered and experiential psychotherapy in the nineties.* Leuven, Belgium: Leuven University Press.

Mahoney, M. (1991). *Human change processes.* New York: Basic Books.

Markus, H., & Nurius, P. (1987). Possible selves: The interface between motivation and the self-concept. In K. Yarddley & T. Honess (Eds.), *Self and identity: Psychosocial perspectives* (pp. 157–172). New York: Wiley.

Masten, A. S., Best, K. M., & Garmazy, N. (1990). Resilience and development: Contributions from the study of children who overcome adversity. *Development and Psychopathology, 2,* 425–444.

Meyer, A.-E. (Ed.). (1981). The Hamburg Short Psychotherapy Comparison Experiment. *Psychotherapy and Psychosomatics, 35,* 81–207.

Neisser, U. (1967). *Cognitive psychology.* New York: Appleton-Century-Crofts.

Norcross, J. C., & Prochaska, J. O. (1988). A study of eclectic (and integrative) views revisited. *Professional Psychology: Research and Practice, 19,* 170–174.

O'Hara, M. M. (1992, April). *Selves-in-context: The challenge for psychotherapy in a postmodern world.* Invited Address at the Conference of the Society for the Exploration of Psychotherapy Integration, San Diego, CA.

O'Hara, M., & Anderson, W. T. (1991, September/October). Welcome to the postmodern world. *The Family Therapy Networker,* pp. 19–25.

O'Hara, M. M., & Wood, J. K. (1983). Patterns of awareness: Consciousness and the group mind. *The Gestalt Journal, 6,* 103–116.

Orlinsky, D. E., & Howard, K. I. (1986). Process and outcome in psychotherapy. In S. L. Garfield & A. E. Bergin (Eds.), *Handbook of psychotherapy and behavior change* (3rd ed., pp. 311–384). New York: Wiley.

Perret-Clermont, A.-N., Perret, J.-F., & Bell, N. (1991). The social construction of meaning and cognitive activity in elementary school children. In L. B. Resnick, J. M. Levine, & S. D. Teasley (Eds.), *Perspectives on socially shared cognition* (pp. 41–62). Washington, DC: American Psychological Association.

Prouty, G. F. (1990). Pre-therapy: A theoretical evolution in the person-centered/experiential psychotherapy of schizophrenia and retardation. In G. Lietaer, J. Rombauts, & R. Van Balen (Eds.), *Client-centered and experiential psychotherapy in the nineties* (pp. 645–658). Leuven, Belgium: Leuven University Press.

Raskin, N. J. (1991, August). *Rogers and Gloria: Listening, respectful, and congru-ent—Response to Weinrach.* Presentation as part of a symposium on "Carl Rogers and Gloria—Interpreting or listening therapist?" American Psychological Association Convention, San Francisco, CA.

Raskin, N. J., & Rogers, C. R. (1989). Person-centered therapy. In R. J. Corsini & D. J. Wedding (Eds.), *Current Psychotherapies* (4th ed., pp. 155–194). Itasca, IL: Peacock.

Rice, L. N., & Greenberg, L. S. (Eds.). (1984). *Patterns of change: Intensive analysis of psychotherapy process.* New York: Guilford Press.

Rice, L. N., & Saperia, E. P. (1984). Task analysis of the resolution of problematic reactions. In L. N. Rice & L. S. Greenberg (Eds.), *Patterns of change: Intensive analysis of psychotherapy process* (pp. 29–66). New York: Guilford Press.

Rogers, C. R. (1957). The necessary and sufficient conditions of therapeutic personality change. *Journal of Consulting Psychology, 21,* 95–103.

Rogers, C. R. (1961a). *On becoming a person.* Boston: Houghton Mifflin.

Rogers, C. R. (1961b). The process equation of psychotherapy. *American Journal of Psychotherapy, 15,* 27–45.

Rogers, C. R. (1980). *A way of being.* Boston: Houghton Mifflin.

Rogers, C. R. (1983). *Freedom to learn for the 80's.* Columbus, OH: Merrill.

Rogers, C. R., & Dymond, R. F. (Eds.). (1954). *Psychotherapy and personality change.* Chicago: University of Chicago Press.

Rogers, C. R., & Sanford, R. C. (1984). *Client-centered psychotherapy.* In H. I. Kaplan & B. J. Sadock (Eds.), *Comprehensive textbook of psychiatry* (4th ed., pp. 1374–1388). Baltimore: Williams & Wilkins.

Santen, B. (1990). Beyond good and evil: Focusing with early traumatized children and adolescents. In G. Lietaer, J. Rombauts, & R. Van Balen (Eds.), *Client-centered and experiential psychotherapy in the nineties* (pp. 779–796). Leuven, Belgium: Leuven University Press.

Shlien, J. M. (1970). Phenomenology and personality. In J. T. Hart & T. M. Tomlinson (Eds.), *New directions in client-*

centered therapy (pp. 95–128). Boston: Houghton Mifflin.

Shlien, J. M. (1984). A countertheory of transference. In R. F. Levant & J. M. Shlien (Eds.), Client-centered therapy and the person-centered approach: New directions in theory, research, and practice (pp. 153–181). New York: Praeger.

Shlien, J. M. (1988, September). The future is more important than the past in determining present behavior. Paper presented at the 1st International Conference on Client-centered and Experiential Psychotherapy, Leuven, Belgium.

Shlien, J. M., & Levant, R. F. (1984). Introduction. In R. F. Levant & J. M. Shlien (Eds.), Client-centered therapy and the person-centered approach: New directions in theory, research, and practice (pp. 1–16). New York: Praeger.

Shostrom, E. L. (Producer). (1965). Three approaches to psychotherapy [Film]. Orange, CA: Psychological Films.

Smith, D. (1982). Trends in counseling and psychotherapy. American Psychologist, 37, 802–809.

Smith, M. L., Glass, G. V., & Miller, T. I. (1980). The benefits of psychotherapy. Baltimore: Johns Hopkins University Press.

Speierer, G. W. (1990). Toward a specific illness concept of client-centered therapy. In G. Lietaer, J. Rombauts, & R. Van Balen (Eds.), Client-centered and experiential psychotherapy in the nineties (pp. 337–360). Leuven, Belgium: Leuven University Press.

Stern, D. N. (1985). The interpersonal world of the infant: A view from psychoanalysis and developmental psychology. New York: Basic Books.

Strupp, H. H., & Binder, J. L. (1984). Psychotherapy in a new key: A guide to time-limited dynamic psychotherapy. New York: Basic Books.

Strupp, H. H., & Hadley, S. W. (1979). Specific versus nonspecific factors in psychotherapy: A controlled study of outcome. Archives of General Psychiatry, 36, 1125–1136.

Swildens, J. C. A. G. (1990). Client-centered psychotherapy for patients with borderline symptoms. In G. Lietaer, J. Rom-

bauts, & R. Van Balen (Eds.), Client-centered and experiential psychotherapy in the nineties (pp. 623–636). Leuven, Belgium: Leuven University Press.

Teusch, L. (1990). Positive effects and limitations of client-centered therapy with schizophrenic patients. In G. Lietaer, J. Rombauts, & R. Van Balen (Eds.), Client-centered and experiential psychotherapy in the nineties (pp. 637–644). Leuven, Belgium: Leuven University Press.

Teusch, L., & Boehme, H. (1991). Results of a one-year follow up of patients with agoraphobia and/or panic disorder treated with an inpatient therapy program with client-centered basis. Psychotherapie-Psychosomatik Medizinische Psychologie, 41, 68–76.

Tomlinson, T. M., & Hart, J. T. (1962). A validation study of the Process Scale. Journal of Consulting Psychology, 26, 74–78.

Toms, M. (1988, January/February). Expressive therapy: Creativity as a path to peace. A conversation with Natalie Rogers. New Realities, 13–17.

Toukmanian, S. G. (1990). A schema-based information processing perspective on client change in experiential psychotherapy. In G. Lietaer, J. Rombauts, & R. Van Balen (Eds.), Client-centered and experiential psychotherapy in the nineties (pp. 309–326). Leuven, Belgium: Leuven University Press.

Van Balen, R. (1990). The therapeutic relationship according to Carl Rogers: Only a climate? A dialogue? Or both? In G. Lietaer, J. Rombauts, & R. Van Balen (Eds.), Client-centered and experiential psychotherapy in the nineties (pp. 65–86). Leuven, Belgium: Leuven University Press.

Wexler, D. A., & Rice, L. N. (Eds.). (1974). Innovations in client-centered therapy. New York: Wiley.

Zimring, F. (1990). Cognitive processes as a cause of psychotherapeutic change: Self-initiated processes. In G. Lietaer, J. Rombauts, & R. Van Balen (Eds.), Client-centered and experiential psychotherapy in the nineties (pp. 361–380). Leuven, Belgium: Leuven University Press.

Zimring, F. (1991, August). *Rogers and Gloria: Genuine and prizing but insufficiently empathic.* Presentation as part of a symposium on "Carl Rogers and Gloria— Interpreting or listening therapist?" American Psychological Association Convention, San Francisco, CA.

5

Behavior Therapy: A Contextual Approach

STEVEN C. HAYES
WILLIAM C. FOLLETTE
VICTORIA M. FOLLETTE

BACKGROUND OF THE APPROACH

The behavior therapy movement can be divided into several historical periods. The first period marked the shift of focus in psychology from the study of mind to the study of behavior. Applied behavioral work during this period was infrequent and, when it occurred, was often used more to demonstrate the applicability of behavioral principles than to develop a robust applied technology. The second period was characterized by the application of neobehavioristic and behavior analytic theory to applied problems. The third period was characterized by the reascendance of the psychology of mind and the rise of cognitive therapy. The final period, is marked by two maturing traditions. On the one hand, the cognitive and neobehaviorist streams of behavior therapy have combined into an empirical clinical mainstream. On the other, there is a reinvigorated contextualistic behavioral approach to behavior *and* that form of behaving called "mind."

This chapter is placed squarely in that final period, and examines behavior therapy from a "contextualistic" point of view, which we describe in detail later. As such, it is designed both as a review and as a reformulation. Cognitive and social learning perspectives, presented in another chapter in this volume (Freeman & Reinecke, Chapter 6) are more known, more popular, and perhaps more accessible to general readers. Contemporary contextualistic forms of behavior therapy have shown notable overlaps with other points of view and thus it seems possible that the entire distinction between behavior therapy and other forms of therapy is in transition.

Periods in the Development of Behavior Therapy

The First Period: A Science of Behavior

The first period was most influenced by John B. Watson. Presenting a mix of views drawn from American pragmatism, evolutionary biology, functionalism, and reflexology, Watson's impact was on the focus of psychology—its mission and its purpose. Watson rejected mind as the subject matter of psychology and introspection as the method of its investigation (Watson, 1913, 1924, pp. 2–5). The rejection of the psychology of mind was based on two lines of argument: one metaphysical and one methodological. Watson's (1924) metaphysical claim was that mind did not exist, and thus all that psychologists can study is overt behavior. He defined "behavior" largely on the basis of its form: Behavior was muscle movements and glandular secretions (e.g., see p. 14). Even when studying "private events" (Watson, 1920), Watson's view was openly peripheralist (e.g., he believed that thinking was subvocal speech).

Watson's methodological claim was that psychology as a science could not study mind, even if mind existed, because there was no scientifically acceptable method to do so. For methodological reasons, behavior (defined as movements and secretions) had to be the subject matter of psychology. This methodological claim had an enormous impact on psychology. "Behavioristic" methods were adopted in nearly every area of psychology.

Paradoxically, although this first period of behaviorism succeeded for a time in establishing psychology as the science of behavior, it did so at the cost of providing philosophical grounds for more sophisticated forms of mentalism. If mental events exist but cannot be scientifically studied directly, perhaps they can be scientifically studied indirectly. By leaving the door open in this way, methodological behaviorism undermined the behavioral agenda over the long term.

Watson himself was quite interested in applied topics and conducted several studies demonstrating the applicability of behavioral principles (e.g., Watson & Raynor, 1920). These did not lead to a robust applied technology, but they do show the natural alliance within the behavioral movement between basic theory and applied research.

From the early part of the century until a decade or more past World War II the learning theorists busied themselves developing and testing behavioral principles. Because much of this work included contextual and situational variables, the analyses that resulted were well suited as theoretical foundations for applied work. It was quite possible to use behavior theory to identify manipulable variables that might give rise to behavior change in applied populations.

The principles of *classical conditioning* and *operant conditioning* were especially important in that regard. Many responses, particularly emotional reactions, could be conceptualized as elicited behavior produced by a temporal–spacial contingency between neutral and behaviorally effective events. Watson looked with great favor at the work of Pavlov and used principles of direct association to explain a great deal of human behavior.

Other, more instrumental actions, were conceptualized via a multiterm contingency, usually containing three terms:

$$S^D \cdot R \to S^R$$

The S^D, or *discriminative stimulus*, is a stimulus in the presence of which the probability of a reinforcing consequence for a given behavior is greater than in its absence. The response to this stimulus is not elicited as in classical conditioning—rather, the contingency influences the probability that the response will be emitted or evoked. For example, suppose a child notices her mother putting away a newly purchased box of candy after dinner. In the past asking for candy has not always produced it—often none is in the house, and if requests are made before dinner they are rarely honored. Conversely, requests made after dinner and when it is available often produce candy. Given such a history, the time of day and seeing the candy being put away may function as an S^D because the probability of a receiving candy when it is requested is greater given the presence of these cues than in their absence.

The S^R term, or *reinforcer*, is a stimulus that increases the probability of a given response in a given situation when it is presented following and contingent upon that response. The arrow refers to such a contingency. In our simple example, if receiving the candy when it is requested has increased the probability of requests for candy in these circumstances, the candy is functioning as a reinforcer for that response.

Many other divisions were developed within this simple "three-term contingency" framework. Consequences were divided into several classes (unconditioned reinforcers, conditioned reinforcers, positive reinforcers, negative reinforcers, punishers, etc.), as were the other terms. Other terms were added by some, such as motivational variables, setting factors, or conditional stimuli in the presence of which the entire contingency was more or less operative.

The Second Period: Behavioral Treatment

In this period, behavior theory was systematically applied to human problems. Applied behavioral work defined itself as a distinct subdisciplinary area. Beginning in 1963, with the establishment of the first behavior therapy journal (*Behaviour Research and Therapy*), followed by the first applied behavior analysis journal (*Journal of Applied Behavior Analysis*, founded in 1968) and the first U.S.-based behavior therapy journal (*Behavior Therapy*, founded in 1970 by the fledgling As-

sociation for Advancement of Behavior Therapy), the number of applied behavioral journals and societies increased rapidly over the next 15 years.

There were two distinguishable traditions within the applied behavioral group. The first began in the United States and was more closely related to operant psychology and the radical behaviorism of B. F. Skinner. It included early leaders such as Donald Baer, Todd Risley, Teodoro Ayllon, and Nathan Azrin. Professionals within this tradition were more likely to describe themselves as "applied behavior analysts" or, at times, "behavior modifiers." They tended to work more with children and institutionalized clients than with outpatient adults, in part because their techniques relied heavily on the direct manipulation of environmental contingencies. For example, Ayllon and Azrin formed the first token economy at Anna State Hospital in Illinois in 1961.

Operant theory is an inherently interactive and developmental perspective. Actions of organisms are situated, both historically and by the current context—they evolve over time and emerge in certain specific circumstances. The position is epigenetic: The relevant context for behavior includes the structure of the organism itself, but no one part of the situational features of an interaction eliminate the importance of other features.

The second tradition emerged in Britain and South Africa, and was more closely associated with the neobehaviorism of stimulus–response (S–R) learning theory. It included such people as Joseph Wolpe, Arnold Lazarus, Stanley Rachman, Hans Eysenck, M. B. Shapiro, and others. These professionals were more likely to call themselves behavior therapists (even though this term was apparently coined by Ogden Lindsley, a student of B. F. Skinner's) and to work with adults in outpatient settings.

The early forms of intervention from this tradition focused on how old associations can be replaced with new ones (e.g., through systematic desensitization) and problems that yielded most readily to this approach (e.g., anxiety disorders) were given the most attention.

The neobehavioristic tradition is behavioral more in Watson's methodological sense than in a philosophical sense. In the S–R tradition, definitions of behavior tend to emphasize public observability and other methodological requirements. Philosophically, the approach is mechanistic: Systems are analyzed in terms of discrete parts, relations, and forces that are presumed to preexist as part of a grand mechanical system.

Each of these traditions was committed both to the application of clearly specified and replicable techniques, made available by well-designed and systematic experimental research, and to learning theory (Eysenck, 1972). For example, Franks and Wilson (1974) argued that the common element in behavior therapies was an adherence to "operationally defined learning theory and conformity to well established experimental paradigms" (p. 7). Of the two traditions, the operant tradition had fewer adherents: "Methodological behaviorism [being behavioral in a methodological sense] is much more characteristic of contemporary behavior modifiers than is radical behaviorism [the more philosophically behavioral approach of B. F. Skinner]" (Mahoney, Kazdin, & Lesswing, 1974, p. 15).

The Third Period: Cognitive Therapy

By the early 1960s basic S–R learning theory had crumbled as a coherent position, but the effect within applied areas was delayed. In the basic area, S–R behaviorists gradually began to adopt more flexible associationistic principles, based on the computer as a metaphor. That is, mechanistic behaviorism began to transform itself into a similarly mechanistic science of mind: cognitive psychology. By the late 1960s, cognitive psychology had emerged as the mainstream of experimental psychology. The new science of mind used behavioristic methods, but in an attempt to assess the functioning of the mind. Reaction time replaced performance as the primary metric. Increasingly elaborate mediational models were developed of the hypothetical "internal machinery" that was presumed to bridge the gaps between an event and a response to it.

As if lit by a time-delayed fuse, a similar explosive transition began in the 1970s within behavior therapy. Early cognitive mediational accounts of behavior change (e.g., Bandura, 1969) blossomed into the cognitive therapy movement (e.g., Mahoney, 1974; Meichenbaum, 1977). Despite protests from some neobehaviorists that these cognitive ideas had been present all along (e.g., Wolpe, 1980), the very vitality of the movement suggested that many therapists felt otherwise. The cognitive movement sought not just the addition of a range of verbal psychotherapies to the technical armamentarium of behavior therapy, but also the addition of modern cognitive mediational constructs to mediational learning theory concepts already in place. Mediationalism (the attempt to bridge temporal and spacial gaps by modeling internal machinery) became a uniting theme that would ultimately tie together neobehavioristic and cognitive perspectives as variants of methodological behaviorism: "One can study inferred events or processes and remain a behaviorist as long as these events or processes have measurable and operational referents" (Franks & Wilson, 1974, p. 7).

The Fourth Period: Maturing Traditions

Like S–R behaviorism itself, the neobehavioristic wing of behavior therapy largely folded into the cognitive wing. The "behavioral" commitment of behavior therapy weakened noticeably, so much so that in the hands of many, behavior therapy became simply empirical clinical psychology. What was important, adherents argued, was not any given philosophical or theoretical approach but rather empirically verified technologies. This new mainstream is not, however, free of philosophical and theoretical commitments—the philosophy is largely mechanistic, and the theorizing is largely mediational. Many adherents criticize "behavioral" conceptions and contrast these with what is claimed to be more current or progressive cognitive ideas. The "behavioral" ideas they criticize, however, are the largely discredited ideas of neobehaviorists or purely direct contingency analyses from the behavior-analytic stream.

While the neobehavioristic/cognitive/social-learning tradition has matured into the empirical clinical mainstream of behavior therapy, the behavior-analytic tradition has also matured, and it is from that point of view that this chapter is being written. The change involves a questioning of mechanism, the development of contextualistic behavioral models (e.g., Hayes, Hayes, & Reese, 1986; Jacobson, 1991a, 1991b; Kohlenberg & Tsai, 1987; Morris, 1988), and a set of new findings regarding the analysis of human verbal events (Hayes & Hayes, 1992a).

Definition of Behavior Therapy

In our view, behavior therapy is simply the application of the techniques, methods, principles, and assumptions of modern behavior theory and science to human problems. There are both mechanistic and contextualistic forms of behavior theory, and thus of behavior therapy, but we will limit our analyses to the contextualistic variety as defined earlier.

THE CONCEPT OF PERSONALITY

Basic Concepts and the Unit of Analysis

Philosophical Assumptions

Contextualistic behaviorism has several defining assumptions:

1. The psychological level of analysis is the study of whole organisms interacting in and with a context. At this level of analysis, behavior cannot be separated from context, and parts of the organism cannot be separated from the whole. All forms of interactive activity, including thoughts and feelings, are included as "behavior."

2. Because the unit is considered to be fundamentally indivisible and interactive, contextualists hold that psychological events can never fully be explained by events at other levels of analysis. For example, a psychological act-in-context cannot be explained by appeal to actions of various parts of the organism involved in the interaction (e.g., its brain and glands). Similarly, an act alone and cut off from a context is not considered a psychological act at all.

3. All verbal abstractions of distinct features are considered to be themselves acts that are occurring in and with a context. This means that selecting among certain scientific constructs over others can only be justified on the basis of utility—the achievement of some end that the analyst is seeking in doing the analysis.

4. Causality is viewed as a useful way of speaking about the accomplishment of one's scientific goals, but causality as an ontological matter (as a matter of what

exists) is rejected. That is, it is useful to speak of causes but one should not assume that causes exist independently in the world.

5. The particular goals of contextualistic behaviorism are increasingly organized systems of verbal rules that permit the description, prediction, influence, and interpretation of interactive activity. It seeks empirically based analyses that achieve all these goals jointly (not any one in isolation), and with precision (a restricted set of constructs apply to any particular event), scope (a wide number of events can be analyzed with these constructs), and depth (analytic constructs at the psychological level cohere with those at other levels). It is, thus, a psychological variety of what has been termed "functional contextualism" (Biglan & Hayes, in press) as distinguished from other, more descriptive forms of contextualism that seek simply an understanding of the various participants in a psychological interaction (e.g., Rosnow & Georgoudi, 1986).

6. Given these goals, all explanations of behavior that appeal only to other forms of behavior are viewed as incomplete. To accomplish the goal of influence, and to remain true to the psychological event as defined above, contextual features outside of the behavioral domain must be included in the analysis. Thus, for example, thoughts or feelings do not *cause* overt actions (nor do overt actions cause other overt actions); at best, a thought–overt action relation is a behavior–behavior relation to be analyzed contextually (Hayes & Brownstein, 1986).

Behavioral Principles

The core of a contextual behavioral approach is this: *Behavior is understood in terms of its function, not its form.* Behaviors that accomplish the same goal are equivalent even if the topography or form of the behaviors is different. An example

may help clarify the idea. Suppose a woman is asked to go out on a date but wishes to decline. A wide variety of actions might accomplish this end. She might try to change the subject, get into an argument, leave, claim a lack of time, pretend to be involved with someone else, decline directly, and so on. Even though the *topography* of all of these actions are different the *function* is equivalent.

More is involved, however. In a behavioral approach, *functions are understood both historically and situationally.* Thus, while all these actions may avoid the date in the current situation, we need to know more about the history of the person so that we can determine why avoiding the date is important. The person might be getting over a hurtful relationship in which her partner left her for someone else quite unexpectedly, thus causing her to be wary of future relationships. She might be attracted to her pursuer and still decline. The consequence of avoiding a date in this case might be important because of the need to avoid emotional pain. Conversely, she might be attracted to the person but is extremely dedicated to her job and helping members of the community such that she believes she has no time or emotional energy to invest in a potential relationship. In this case, the consequence of avoiding a date might be important because it increases access to alternative positive consequences. In a third instance, the person may remind her of a hated boy from her childhood, and avoiding the date avoids further aversive stimulation. Thus, as behavior is viewed in its historical and situational context, the specific functions involved are quite different.

The functions of many forms of behavior are based on what organisms have experienced directly. All nonverbal organisms acquire behavioral functions in this way, and in these cases the "function" of behavior refers largely to its direct consequences. As we will discuss shortly, however, verbal organisms can construct response–consequence relations that have never been experienced directly. In these cases, function can also refer to what other psychological traditions call purpose (see Hayes & Wilson, 1993, for a more detailed discussion of this point). Purpose, used in this way, refers to the guidance of behavior by verbal rules that specify consequences for this behavior.

One of the most common misconceptions of behavior therapy is that all that is important is the management of overt behavior—what are viewed by other traditions as "symptoms." In fact, the focus on symptoms without an understanding of why they exist and how they function makes no sense at all to contextualistic behavior therapists, even though some forms of behavior therapy have traditionally been far too interested in behavior topographically defined (Jacobson, 1991b, makes a similar point).

The principles used to understand behavioral functions can be divided into two categories. First, there are a wide variety of well-known *direct contingency principles* drawn from classical and operant conditioning such as positive and negative reinforcement, schedules of reinforcement, stimulus control, establishing operations (i.e., "motivation"), and so on. For example, declining the date either to avoid emotional vulnerability or to avoid being reminded of a loathed acquaintance are both forms of negative reinforcement—avoiding the date avoids a negative consequence and it is thereby strengthened. Conversely, avoiding a desirable date to have time for a more highly preferred activity is the result of a concurrent schedule of reinforcement in which access to one reinforcer precludes access to another.

Second, contemporary behavior analysis has developed a variety of *indirect contingency principles* or principles of *verbal control* (Hayes & Hayes, 1992a). These

principles—which are essentially the contextual behavioral reply to cognitive psychology—are little known outside of behavior analysis, and thus we will discuss them at more length.

When humans are taught unidirectional relations, they readily derive bidirectional relations. Imagine a triangle formed by three events. If humans are taught relations in one direction of any two sides, they will derive relations in all directions for all sides (e.g., Sidman, 1971; Sidman, Cresson, & Willson-Morris, 1974). Suppose the three points of the triangle are a written word, oral name, and object. When a child learns any two relations among these three things, the remaining four can be readily derived. For example, a child taught to say "dog" given the letters D-O-G, and to point to actual dogs given that same written word, will now probably be able to say "dog" when seeing an actual dog. The six relations formed by the three sides of the triangle are shown in Table 5.1.

If just one relation from each of two sides is trained, all six will emerge without additional training (e.g., Dixon & Spradlin, 1976; Sidman, 1971; Sidman & Tailby, 1982; Sidman, Kirk, & Willson-Morris, 1985; Spradlin & Dixon, 1976). This is true regardless of the actual events that define this triangle.

This emergence of bidirectional relations has been shown with children 16 months to 2 years old (Devany, Hayes, & Nelson, 1986; Lipkens, Hayes, & Hayes, 1993), but such derived relations are quite difficult to get with nonhumans (D'Amato, Salmon, Loukas, & Tomie, 1985; Kendall, 1983; Sidman et al., 1982; Lipkens, Kop, & Matthijs, 1988). In the example above, the particular relation involved is one of coordination or similarity ("this object is called *x*"), but the same phenomenon occurs when other relations are involved. For example, if you are told that "A" is the opposite of "B" and "B" is the opposite of "C," you will

TABLE 5.1. The Relations among Written Names, Objects, and Oral Names

Side 1	Written name → Object	Reading with understanding
	Object → Written name	Writing
Side 2	Oral name → Object	Hearing with understanding
	Object → Oral name	Naming
Side 3	Written name → Oral name	Reading aloud
	Oral name → Written name	Dictation

derive relations of oppositeness between B and A, and C and B, but a relation of sameness between A and C and C and A. Such contextually controlled derived relational responding defines what we mean by *verbal events* (Hayes & Hayes, 1989, 1992a).

What is most important about *derived stimulus relations* is that they enable a new form of behavioral regulation: *rule governance* (see Hayes, 1989, for a review). Skinner originally distinguished direct contingency control from rule governance (Skinner, 1966), but it is only recently that the distinct behavioral processes involved are understood. Rules are verbal formulae where by "verbal" we mean processes such as the above. Rule governance involves the transfer of antecedent psychological functions among these relational networks (Hayes, 1989; Hayes & Hayes, 1989). Suppose a child is trained that the written word D-O-G is called "dog" and that the written word goes with actual dogs. Later the child plays with a dog for the first time and is scratched, pushed down, and nipped by the dog. Actual dogs would probably now have several functions: They would elicit fear or serve as a discriminative stimulus for avoidance or escape responses. Later, the child hears his mother say "Oh, dogs" from another room. He may cry and hide under the bed, even though he has no negative history with the words "oh, dogs." Many fears and phobias seem to be indirect; even careful interviews can reveal no direct history that could account for the fear, and this process provides a working model for such indirectly acquired functions.

This kind of effect has been shown in many studies. When functions are trained with one member of an equivalence class, the other members tend to acquire the same function regardless of what it is (Catania, Horne, & Lowe, 1989; De Rose, McIlvane, Dube, Galpin, & Stoddard, 1988; Gatch & Osborne, 1989; Hayes, Brownstein, Devany, Kohlenberg, & Shelby, 1987; Hayes, Kohlenberg, & Hayes, 1991; Kohlenberg, Hayes, & Hayes, 1991; Lazar, 1977; Lazar & Kotlarchyk, 1986; Wulfert & Hayes, 1988).

It is now known that rules greatly alter how direct contingencies operate, both because they alter how contingencies are contacted and because they increase the impact of social and conventional histories. In addition, verbal control is a much more specific and indirect form of behavioral regulation than is direct contingency control (Hayes, 1989, 1991).

To return to the example of a woman avoiding a date, many of the important functions involved may be verbally established rather than directly acquired. The woman may have constructed a response–consequence relation based on a verbal history (e.g., "If I get too involved I will feel cornered and that will make me unhappy"). In fact, this contingent relation may never have been experienced and might even be incorrect if it were tested. The rule may have been acquired in various ways (e.g., she may have heard similar rules from her mother, who may have felt cornered and unhappy in her marriage). What is important is that some functions of behavior are indirect and may not involve directly experienced consequences. Avoiding dates to avoid being cornered may be purposive only in a verbal sense.

Personality from a Behavioral Perspective

Traditional notions of personality imply that a person is prone to act in a relatively consistent fashion across a variety of situations because of constitutional reasons that may be unspecified developmental factors or genetic and physiological factors. The focus of personality theories is to understand behavior as being primarily a function of the individual regardless of circumstances. Furthermore, personality is generally represented as being fixed and intractable once it is formed. Once one forms an introverted personality, there is little in personality theory to suggest how change might come about.

Given the goals of contextualistic behaviorism, such a view is necessarily incomplete. It is not enough to develop categories of particular forms of behavior, even if they are situationally or temporally pervasive. What must be understood is the historical and situational context that completes the functional behavioral unit. For example, it is not enough to know that Frank is passive—we must also know what functions this passivity serves, and how these functions were acquired. For this reason, personality as traditionally conceived is not a centrally important topic within behavior therapy.

There are, however, several behavioral ideas that overlap with the traditional domain referred to by personality. Behavior therapists might well say that Frank is introverted or passive, but what would immediately be at issue is the actual function and history of the behaviors of interest. Various possibilities might be considered.

Perhaps this passivity is a matter of a limited repertoire. A person has only a limited number of ways of interacting with the world at any given time—their behavioral repertoire is always finite. The "introverted" person may have a limited behavioral repertoire with which to interact with the environment. No other forms of behavior are likely because no others have been learned.

Conversely, perhaps our introverted individual has not had a history such that he adequately discriminates situations calling for different forms of behavior. He may know how to behave as an extrovert—and in some very limited situations (e.g., parties) he may behave in this way—but most situations appear to him to call for passive behavior. It is easy to model such a lack of discrimination in the animal operant laboratory simply by failing to provide reliable cues in the presence of which alternative forms of behavior are reinforced.

Perhaps only certain events may function as reinforcers for Frank. If he does not find social stimulation to be reinforcing, he may appear passive simply because there is little in the social environment that would lead to more active behavior.

Perhaps Frank contacted early and severe social punishers, and thus outgoing behavior may bring him into contact with aversive consequences. He may "feel uncomfortable."

Rule governance provides another way to induce pervasive and persistent forms of behavior. Our introvert might have been taught specific verbal rules ("be seen, not heard") that have induced an insensitivity to direct consequences that might have otherwise led to more extroverted styles. Similarly, he might be deficient in generating or following rules that include behavioral alternatives.

When we describe action in personality terms, historical sources of action are obscured in favor of a more descriptive topology. Such conceptualizations of others and of ourselves may reduce the degree of behavioral variability that would otherwise occur. Much of this is probably not to the good. Therapists tend to supply personality trait explanations when they know little about the variables controlling some instance of behavior. Paradoxically, these very conceptualizations could reduce the possibility of client change by blinding the therapist to a more complex and detailed account rooted in the client's history.

While both traditional personality theorists and behavior therapists recognize the importance of history in shaping behavior, behavior therapists see behavioral tendencies as ever evolving. Behaviors can and do change as a person's history is altered with new experiences. The idea that one could literally have a fixed personality type makes little sense from this perspective. Behaviorists believe that personalities can indeed change fundamentally. They recognize that many behavioral patterns are, in fact, difficult to change because our histories with regard to these patterns become ever more extensive and elaborated and the person may act to maintain the very conditions that extend an original history. For example, a child may have been punished for assertive behavior. As an adult she may now seek out dependent relationships to avoid having to be assertive, but such dependent relationships may also lead to little reinforcement for the more assertive behaviors that do occur. Early histories can lead to behavior that produce more extended histories of the same kind, and thus "personality" is surely difficult to change, but it is nevertheless changeable. In radically different contexts entirely new forms of behavior may emerge and under the right conditions may be maintained.

Healthy Development from a Behavioral Perspective

Contextual behavior therapy is neutral with respect what is "normal" development and adjustment. All forms of behavioral development—whether they are considered to be healthy or deviant—are analyzed in the same way: as a matter of the evolution of interactions between a given person, with a given structure, and nonverbal and verbal environments. If there were different circumstances, behavior would be different. Within limits, normal and abnormal development are viewed as statistical phenomena. Behavior therapists would point to the vast cultural differences around the world to demonstrate that what is normal in one culture is not in another.

There are, however, structural and historical commonalities that rather universally act to produce homogeneity in common environments. For example, people are reinforceable, people can form verbal rules, people can make subtle environmental discriminations, and they do. Imagine someone who was for many years the victim of severe child physical and sexual abuse by a stepfather who threatened her with harm if the abuse was revealed. She may certainly grow up to be mistrusting of men, guarded, emotionally avoidant, and ambivalent about sex. In one sense of the term, there is nothing "abnormal" about such a development because the adult behavior is understood to result from a dangerous and confusing environment. One of the virtues of behavior therapy is that clients are never blamed for their behavior, and relatively little importance is attached to the diagnostic label given to behavioral effects removed from its historical context.

There is a negative side to this aspect of behavior therapy, however: It has not adequately considered what psychological adjustment or well-being actually means. Even though health involves a values statement, there is no reason behaviorists cannot specify more clearly the degree to which particular behavioral patterns are adaptive. Some efforts have been made, incorporating such concepts as a flexible behavioral repertoire (Goldiamond, 1974), increasing access to reinforcers (Skinner, 1974), or decreasing control by purely arbitrary verbal rules (Hayes, Kohlenberg, & Melancon, 1989). Increased conceptual and research attention is being given to these topics within behavior therapy (e.g., Follette, Bach, & Follette, 1993), but it still must be admitted that no well-agreed-upon definition of psychological health exists within behavior therapy.

As a result, behavior therapists usually say that they are fairly open to any client treatment goals, as long as these goals are not proscribed by legal or ethical concerns, and as a field behavior therapy probably follows client preferences more closely than most other orientations. In complex cases, however, having an overarching set of beliefs about psychological health provides needed coherence, and over time many behavior therapists seem to develop their own conceptions of psychological health and to try to move clients in these directions even if the client has not explicitly specified these goals. For example, a cognitive-behavioral therapist may believe that black and white thinking is unhealthy, and if it is detected, steps will be taken to reduce it, even if the specific client goals do not necessitate this effort. The problem with these ad hoc definitions of psychological health is that they are often relatively hidden from view, and clients may not know beforehand what the underlying agendas may be in therapy. In addition, ad hoc goals may be relatively intuitive and less well thought out, which undermines their primary value, which is to provide increased coherence for behavior

change efforts. It may be impossible for behavior therapy as an enterprise to agree on a definition of psychological health, but it seems ethically and practically crucial for individual behavior therapists to be very clear and explicit about their own beliefs in this area.

THE PATHOLOGICAL OR DYSFUNCTIONAL INDIVIDUAL

Because normal and abnormal development are on a continuum within a behavioral point of view, more emphasis is given to the understanding of behavioral principles than to the categorization and modeling of pathology. Indeed, historically one of the dominant behavioral interests in pathology and classification was an attack on classification itself.

Concerns with Traditional Syndromal Classification

Contextualistic behaviorists worry about classification per se because any classification is an analytic fiction that can threaten appreciation of the whole act-in-context (Pepper, 1942). For example, it is said that psychiatric labels blur the important differences between one individual and another (Ullmann & Krasner, 1976), and that a more individualized approach might be more valuable (e.g., Cone, 1988). Concerns over the stigmatization caused by syndromal labels (e.g., Rosenhan, 1973) reflect a similar issue.

Based on an embrace of a pragmatic truth criterion, the major contextualistic concern with syndromal classification is this: "To put it bluntly, what purpose is served by such diagnostic practice?" (Garfield, 1986, p. 106; Hersen, 1976; Nathan, 1981). Meehl (1959) phrased it this way: "In what way and to what extent does this . . . information help us in treating the patient?" (p. 117). Meehl called this question "ultimately the practically significant one by which the contributions of our [assessment] techniques must be judged" (p. 116).

The link between syndromal assessment and actual differential treatment has long been known to be weak (e.g., Adams, 1972; Bannister, Salmon, & Lieberman, 1964; Blatt, 1975; Daily, 1953; Hayes, Nelson, & Jarrett, 1987; Korchin & Schuldberg, 1981; McReynolds, 1985). This weak link necessarily means that syndromal classification has little treatment utility, although studies on its utility are quite feasible (Nelson, 1991). It is instructive that many treatments are applied to many different classes of syndromes, often without significant modification. For example, entire books have been written showing how cognitive therapy applies equally well to depression (Beck, Rush, Shaw, & Emery, 1979), anxiety disorders (Michelson & Ascher, 1987), personality disorders (Beck, Freeman, & Associates, 1990), and several other syndromes. To the extent that this is true, the treatment utility of the relevant syndromal distinctions is undermined.

If syndromes are thought of merely as covarying sets of behaviors (e.g., Nelson & Barlow, 1981), identifying a syndrome might be a helpful place to begin. Some kind of nomothetic categories seem to be needed early in assessment to guide the process of individual analysis. Even to talk about cases seems to require some categorization (the talk itself). But syndromal categories are more than empirically identified clusters of characteristics. It is quite possible to have two people diagnosed the same way, without sharing even a single characteristic (Frances, Pincus, Widiger, Davis, & First, 1990). For example, the internal consistency of symptoms in personality disorders according to the revised third edition of the *Diagnostic and Statistical Manual of Mental Disorders* (DSM-III-R; American Psychiatric Association, 1987) ranges from .10 to .29 (Morey, 1988).

The Development of Psychological Problems

Behavior therapists suppose that psychological problems exist on a continuum with more "normal" behaviors and are differentiated verbally and conventionally. The psychological processes that are supposed to lead to abnormal behavior are the same as those that lead to the development of normal behavior. The combination of the structure of the organism, its history, and current behavioral, motivational, and environmental context together lead to behavior regardless of its form or effect. When contextualistic behaviorists are asked why are some people symptomatic and not others, the answer will always be found in the interaction among these elements.

For example, take the case of a person with a simple phobia. It is known that such phobias tend to run in families, and at least part of this seems genetic and not merely cultural. Many variables could be relevant at the level of biological structure. For example, some persons may be more prone to react strongly to aversive events or to associate such events with given contextual features. Note that this feature is not alone thought to be a cause of phobias; rather, it may make certain historical events more or less impactful: Behavioral views tend strongly toward epigenetic rather than simple genetic accounts. At the level of history, phobic persons tend to have a greater likelihood of direct aversive experiences with the feared object or situation or of having observed such a phobia in others. They may have learned rules about feared events ("Be careful when you play! There might be snakes out there."), or about fear itself (e.g., that fear is to be feared). These various experiences or rules would be interpreted in terms of behavioral principles such as those described earlier. At the level of current context, a phobic person may have limited behavioral alternatives relevant to a feared situation (e.g., the person may not be manually skilled enough to trust that he/she can catch and handle a wiggling object), may be in a social context that fosters or inhibits the phobia (e.g., phobia is expected because "girls are always afraid of snakes"), and, of course, may be in the presence of the feared event itself or events that relate to it either experientially or verbally. These classes of events, working together, explain the phobia and explain why this person has it and not others.

One of the major criticisms of behavioral accounts by nonbehaviorists is that different people "in the same environments" act differently, or that people raised "in the same environment" are still unique. Behaviorists do not deny the importance of structural differences between people, so even on its own terms such statements are not troubling to behavior therapists, but there is a more fundamental objection. Behaviorists view environments historically and functionally, not structurally. A stimulus is not an object, alone and cut off from behavior—it is a way of speaking about a locus of historically situated behavioral functions. In that sense, people with different histories are literally in different environments even when the environment is the same from the point of view of the observer. For that reason, the analysis of psychological problems is very much a historical exercise for behavior therapists. It is not the dead past that behaviorists are interested in—that already occurred and will never occur again. It is the past that is alive and in the present. For example, a teacher tells a class how to do something, and one child is immediately resistant while another complies. A behavior therapist might suppose that the functional properties of the teacher and her statement differed for two children. For one child, with a history of reliable and reasonable statements from adults about the natural contingencies, the teacher's statement is a description. For another, with a history of selfish and unreasonable demands from adults to engage in behaviors that have no real utility to the child, the teacher's statement is an aversive demand. The "same statement" from the teacher is thus the same only for an observer—it is quite literally a different stimulus for each child.

This kind of thinking makes behavioral analysis an inherently idiothetic enterprise—nomothetic principles emerge only on the basis of the aggregation of idiothetic analyses. It also means that few a priori theories exist about behavioral development.

That does not mean that there are no analytic guidelines for the interpretation of pathology. The unit of analysis is a situated action: In a given context (composed of historical, motivational, and verbal features; a behavioral repertoire; direct and indirect stimulus functions; and other features), an organism with a current structure engages in an interaction with the world and the world is thereby changed in some way. By applying principles of operant conditioning, classical conditioning, and verbal control, myriad specific possible problems emerge. For example, behavior problems can emerge from *inappropriate behavioral regulation*. Some specific types might include:

1. *Weak, strong, or inappropriate stimulus control.* A person might engage in behaviors that are perfectly appropriate in some settings but inappropriate in others, because the discriminative stimuli regulating the response are faulty. For

example, a first visitor to a facility for retarded persons may be approached by a resident who says "I love you" and gives the person a hug. It is good to know how to display affection toward others, but the mere presence of another person is not the proper cue for such a response.

2. *Weak, strong, or inappropriate consequential control.* A person might engage in behaviors that are inappropriate because the functional effects of the consequences these behaviors produce are odd. For instance, sensory stimulation functions as a reinforcer for most of us, but only to a degree—humming, tapping fingers, twirling hair, rubbing eyes, scratching, and so on are common in normal populations because of the stimulation these behaviors produce. Some individuals, however, respond inordinately to these sensory consequences to the point that other consequences (e.g., social approval) have no functional effect. Autistic children commonly tap fingers, rock, or twirl objects most of their waking day because primitive forms of sensory stimulation are such powerful reinforcers for them.

3. *Weak, strong, or inappropriate motivational conditions that alter the effects of given consequences.* A person might engage in behaviors that are inappropriate because the functional effects of the consequences these behaviors produce are temporarily increased or decreased to an unusual degree by certain setting factors. For example, most people will act aggressively if sufficiently provoked. Aggressive behavior is reinforced by its effects on others, by the sensory stimulation it provides, and by other consequences. When we are especially motivated to produce such consequences we usually say we "feel angry." But some people are moved to anger and anger-induced aggression by even the slightest offense—for them minor aversive events have enormous motivative properties.

4. *Weak, strong, or inappropriate rule control.* Behavior analysts have distinguished several types of rule control. For example, in one case (*tracking*) rules are followed because they have led to contact with natural contingencies in the past, while in another (*pliance*) they are followed or not followed because of a history of socially mediated consequences for rule following. For example, suppose a child is told by a parent, "It is cold outside, wear your jacket." If the jacket is put on to avoid cold, this is an instance of tracking; if it is put on to avoid a scolding, this is an instance of pliance; if it is not put on "to show Mom I can't be pushed around" it is also functionally an instance of pliance (though to acknowledge its formal dissimilarity with pliance it is called counterpliance). With some histories, however, even routine descriptions of contingencies can result in pliance—either in the form of the excessive and rigidly hyperconventional rule following or in the form of rebellion and resistance.

In other cases, the problem is not deficient regulatory processes but in specific response forms. This might include such things as a lack of established appropriate behaviors (e.g., a limited social repertoire or weak rule-generation skills) or the presence of inappropriate behaviors established through normal means such as learned inappropriate social behaviors.

This idea was prevalent early in the behavioral movement (e.g., Bandura, 1968; Kanfer & Grimm, 1977), but the lists of functional relations that resulted were more in the spirit of a menu than a road map. Many alternatives were supplied but there was no ready means of selecting among them. In addition, the categories included almost no connection to the characteristic forms of behavior clients actually bring to a session. For example, Kanfer and Grimm's major categories were things like "behavioral excesses" or "problems in environmental stimulus control." Virtually every category could in principle be applied to any given case. Today, many of the specific types of problems (e.g., anxiety disorders) have known characteristic patterns of behavioral regulation or response forms.

In addition, behavior therapists distinguish very clearly between etiological factors and maintaining factors. An action may have emerged from a historical pattern that is no longer present. Behavior may have developed because it served one function, while it may be maintained because it serves another. For example, a depressed women may have originally displayed negative emotion because it was elicited by aversive circumstances—say abuse from a parent. Negative emotional displays by women also reduce aggression and abuse from men, however, and depressive expressions may thus eventually occur because they restrain an abusive spouse. The use of behavioral principles in the analysis of practical problems is a dynamic process that must be fitted to the purposes of the analysis.

THE ASSESSMENT OF DYSFUNCTION

The integral and ongoing role that assessment plays in therapy is a distinguishing feature of behavior therapy.

The Level of Assessment and the Unit of Analysis

Behavioral assessment is directed toward an understanding of the whole person functioning within a particular context. The study of isolated behavior, without understanding the conditions that give rise to the behavior and the consequences that follow and maintain the behavior, is

bound to be limited at best and completely useless at worst.

An example should clarify the point. Consider the disruptive behavior of Johnny, an 8-year-old student in a third-grade classroom. One could observe Johnny and count the number of times that Johnny gets out of his chair without first getting permission from the teacher. Perhaps one could devise an intervention to eliminate this behavior (e.g., time-out procedures, in which disruptive behavior reliably lead to a brief period in a relatively barren environment), but on average this kind of shotgun approach seems unlikely to succeed.

We need to know why Johnny gets out of his chair in the first place—what function did it serve for him? Did Johnny get out of the chair because it was the only way to get attention from an otherwise overworked teacher? Did Johnny get out of the chair because when he did so he was able to avoid getting called on to answer a question that he did not know? The answers to these question would lead to different understandings of the problem and certainly to different interventions.

There is empirical evidence showing that taking the time to understand the function of disruptive behavior rather than simply counting the problem behavior leads to greater treatment success. If children are disruptive to avoid working on a difficult task, it helps to teach them to ask for help. If they are disruptive to seek attention, it helps to teach them to attract attention appropriately. Treatments that do not match the functional problem do not work as well (Carr & Durand, 1985; see also Durand & Carr, 1991).

Behavioral assessment of clinical problems concerns itself not only with action but also with the context in which it occurs because examining behavior cut off from its context can lead to a completely useless analysis. To understand behavior, it must be examined and interpreted at a psychological level, and for a contextual behaviorist, that level is contextual by its very essence.

A Behavioral Approach to Assessment: Functional Analysis

Understanding the context in which behavior occurs can be a massive undertaking. The process of identifying these behavioral and contextual features of a psychological situation is termed "functional analysis" (Kanfer & Saslow, 1969). Functional analysis has had a wide variety of meanings within behavior analysis and therapy (Haynes & O'Brien, 1990), including an experimental demonstration of behavioral control, however achieved, an experimental demonstration of control by factors that are hypothesized to have produced past problematic behavior, and the conceptualization of such factors prior to intervention. Classical functional analysis has the following components:

1. *Identify potentially relevant characteristics of the individual client, his/her behavior, and the context in which it occurs via broad assessment.* The purpose of the step is simply to collect data from which the beginnings of analysis might emerge. Exactly what occurs at this step is dictated by the philosophical and theoretical assumptions (usually implicit) of the assessor and informal prejudgments made about the case based on referral information, preliminary interviews, and the like.

2. *Organize the information collected in step 1 into a preliminary analysis of the client's difficulties in terms of behavioral principles so as to identify important causal relationships that might be changed.* The process of functional analysis has been described as a funnel (Hawkins, 1979). The opening is wide at the top but then begins to narrow down. Step 2 in functional analy-

sis, traditionally conceived, is to begin to narrow the focus of assessment. Certain features (e.g., forms of behavior, motivational operations, and contexts in which behavior occurs) are tentatively selected as more important than others. Characteristics of the case are organized into classes. The guiding principles are behavioral in the catholic sense of that word, but with a special emphasis not simply on the structure of the phenomena observed but on their function—what they do or affect in a dynamic system.

3. *Gather additional information based on step 2 and finalize the conceptual analysis.* As features of the case coalesce, additional information is gathered relevant to the analysis. Specific assessment devices may be selected or created to examine particular features of the case as conceptualized in step 2. In this process, the analysis may be refined and modified. Eventually the assessor has a stable conceptual analysis of the relation between actions of the client and its context (Hawkins, 1986), with measurement data on the primary components of that analysis and assessment procedures in place for a continuing evaluation of the case.

4. *Devise an intervention based on step 3.* One dominant characteristic of behavioral assessment is the close link, at least conceptually if not often empirically, between assessment and treatment (Kanfer & Saslow, 1969). Because behavioral principles are explicitly pragmatic (their confirmation is usually based on the ability to predict and influence behavioral events through their use), a functional analysis often points to concrete events in the life of the clients that have established and are maintaining the problem of interest. If these events are manipulable in the practical world of clinical intervention, a thoroughgoing functional analysis often directly suggests a particular intervention. Thus, in step 4 a treatment is devised that is linked to step 3.

5. *Implement treatment and assess change.* Assessment, to most behavioral assessors, is not something done only at the beginning of treatment. It is an ongoing process. Thus, a functional analysis contains within it the ongoing assessment of clients' progress.

6. *If the outcome is unacceptable, recycle back to step 2 or 3.* If treatment is not successful, usually this is taken as an indication that the conceptualization phase of the functional analysis itself is flawed. Thus, a failure to see the kinds of changes that are desired leads directly to a reexamination of the conceptualization, in the form of either a minor adjustment or, at times, a complete overhaul of the analysis.

While only a very few studies have evaluated the actual empirical utility of functional analysis (Haynes & O'Brien, 1990; for an example, see McKnight, Nelson, Hayes, & Jarrett, 1984), there can be little doubt that there is at least a link between functional analysis and differential treatment decisions. Such a link is necessary, though not sufficient, for treatment utility to occur.

Some have gone so far as to *define* functional analysis in terms of this link. For example, Haynes and O'Brien defined functional analysis as "the identification of important, controllable, causal functional relationships applicable to a specified set of target behaviors for an individual client" (1990, p. 654). As this definition is deconstructed, it becomes clear that the words "important, controllable, causal" are there both because these features are what makes a functional analysis relevant to treatment and because treatment impact is the best way to evaluate whether a variable is important, controllable, and causal.

The difficulty with a functional analytic approach is that there are no well-researched guidelines for how to decide what factors should be studied, in what order they should be studied, and when

one has conducted a sufficiently detailed analysis that the assessment process can stop and treatment begin (see Hayes & Follette, 1992, for a more detailed discussion of these problems and possible alternatives).

Nevertheless, there have been proposals about how to assess the adequacy of a functional analysis. Hayes, Nelson, and Jarrett (1987) have argued that assessment should be judged as to whether it possesses "treatment utility." The assessment is guided by asking oneself, "Does the assessment information I have gathered indicate a specific course of action which I would otherwise not know to take if I did not have this information?" Implicit in this statement is that the treatment based on the assessment will produce *better outcomes* than if the information were not present. A second set of recommendations was offered by Haynes and O'Brien (1990), who suggested that a functional analysis should attend to those factors that were (1) causally related to the clinical problem at hand, (2) important (i.e., variables or characteristics that when manipulated produced significant changes in the clinical problem), and (3) changeable by the therapist.

While these guides may seem obvious, it is surprising how much assessment information does not lead to changes in treatment strategy or is not relevant to better outcomes. For example, assessment interviews are used by therapists of all persuasions, but they often lead to information that is not particularly important, is historical in nature but not changeable, or that is not actually currently related to the problems at hand. Very often therapists will adopt the same approach regardless of assessment content.

Functional analysis, however, is done in the service of case conceptualization and treatment planning. When the therapist has conceptualized the case properly, the intervention is often self-evident and treatment proceeds. A fundamental principle in behavior therapy is that assessment is a dynamic, ongoing process. Because clients are not willing to stay in therapy indefinitely, therapy must sometimes begin without one being certain that his/her case conceptualization is perfectly correct. Because data are continually gathered during behavior therapy, case conceptualizations are often expanded and modified during the course of therapy.

Assessment Techniques

There are no specific assessment devices that are used only by behavior therapists. Any procedures that allow one to better understand the circumstances that determine the behavior of interest are potentially useful. (There are, however, devices and procedures that are characteristic of behavioral assessment and we will note these below.)

Assessment often begins with a clinical interview, particularly in step 1 above. A history of the problems would be taken with special emphasis on when and under what circumstances the problem started, what made it better or worse, and what happens after the problem behavior is emitted. Other behavioral strengths and weaknesses would be identified. During such an interview, the behavior therapist is trying to generate hypotheses about the controlling variables. Assessment data gathered to support or disconfirm initial hypotheses could come from many sources, but behavior therapists seem more prone than most practitioners to examine action directly in its context and to use self-monitoring and self-report procedures with high face validity. For instance, one may ask the client or someone in his/her family to monitor the behavior of interest and note the corresponding circumstances. One may set up conditions in the therapy setting to elicit

the problem behavior (e.g., role playing) and score the results. The therapist may even accompany the client into the setting in which the behavior is most problematic and perform naturalistic observations. Interactions may be observed and the behavior may be systematically coded by raters applying a prescribed set evaluative criteria. The use of these assessment devices varies from setting to setting. In institutional settings, for example, direct observation and coding are common, but in outpatient settings the primary reliance is on self-report and self-monitoring.

A number of specific procedures have been developed of this kind. We will describe a few as examples of the general character of a behavioral assessment approach.

Written Self-Report Instruments

The Pleasant Events Schedule (PES) is a self-report behavioral inventory that assesses the frequency of occurrence and degree of subjective pleasure involved in a series of potentially reinforcing events and behaviors (Lewinsohn, Munoz, Youngren, & Zeiss, 1978; MacPhillamy & Lewinsohn, 1972, 1973). It is commonly used to assess the activity of depressed persons and is based on the behavioral view that depression is in part the result of decreased levels of positive activity (MacPhillamy & Lewinsohn, 1974). Acceptable levels of reliability and validity have been established for the PES as a whole, and it is considered to be a useful measure of the frequency of positively reinforcing events (MacPhillamy & Lewinsohn, 1982).

The Fear Questionnaire (FQ) is a brief self-report measure monitoring change in phobic patients (Marks & Mathews, 1979). This one-page fear survey asks individuals to rate their degree of anxiety-related affective disturbance and avoidance of their main phobic stimulus (described in their own words) and a list of all common phobic stimuli on a 0–8 scale. The FQ yields scores for main phobia, global phobia, total phobia, and anxiety/depression, as well as subscales for agoraphobia, social phobia, and blood and injury phobias. The FQ is one of the most frequently used self-report instruments for anxiety disorders (Trull, Nietzel, & Main, 1988). It has good test–retest reliability (Marks & Mathews, 1979; Michelson & Mavissakalian, 1983) and can discriminate client subgroups in a valid manner (Mavissakalian, 1985; Van Zuuren, 1988). Normative data are available for clinical, community, and collegiate populations, providing target levels for assessing clinical significance (Jacobson, Follette, & Revenstorf, 1984).

What is worth noting is that the both the PES and the FQ approach their topical areas directly and with specificity. Rather than assessing fears by asking oblique questions, FQ clients are asked directly how afraid they are of specific items. Rather than inferring that depressives have decreased levels of activity, the PES asks how often specific activities occur and has the client rate how pleasant these activities were. It is also worth noting that traditional psychometric analyses (e.g., reliability, validity, and normative levels) have been applied to these instruments as they have to most behavioral assessment devices. Psychometrics is to some degree a different tradition than behavioral assessment because psychometric criteria emphasize structure over function, but these criteria and traditions can be harmonized to a large degree (Silva, 1993).

Structured Clinical Interview

The Anxiety Disorders Interview Schedule—Revised (ADIS-R) is a structured clinical interview developed to distinguish among different syndromal classifications (DiNardo et al., 1985). Clients are asked many very specific questions about their overt behavior, feelings, and thoughts. Questions are arranged into a kind of tree such that positive answers in a given area may lead to a whole series of more detailed questions in the same domain, while negative answers will lead to questions about other topics. ADIS-R is commonly used as an initial screening interview between a therapist and client, so that programs can be applied that are designed for a specific disorder. Again, what is especially noteworthy is that this instrument is highly specific and asks questions directly related to the problems at hand.

Idiosyncratic Self-Monitoring Methods

The relatively idiographic approach of behavioral assessment leads to the frequent use of self-monitoring or other instruments that are designed for specific individuals and are not standardized. For example, when working with a client with panic disorder, behavior therapists may ask clients to carry a pocket-size notebook assessing daily anxiety. Information included in the diary might include an overall daily anxiety rating on a 1 to 10 scale; a list of situations, if any, that they avoided that day; the number of panic attacks, if any, experienced that day (e.g., as defined by the occurrence of at least four of the DSM-IV [American Psychiatric Association, 1994] criteria for panic attacks); a symptom checklist to mark the anxiety symptoms that were present that day; and a list of activities or situations that they typically would have avoided but participated in today. The specific content of the diary could be modified on a case-by-case basis. The diary would be examined at the beginning of each therapy session.

Direct Assessment of Behavior

Staying with the example of a client with panic attacks and agoraphobic avoidance, a behavior therapist might periodically ask the client to complete a standardized walk. It might consist of a 1-mile course, divided by approximately 20 equidistant stopping points or "stations." Clients would be instructed to walk alone as far as possible on the course, while stopping at each station to rate their anxiety. The number of stations completed would provide an estimate of anxiety-related phobic avoidance.

One may notice from these brief descriptions that the problem behaviors identified by the client and/or therapist (and the behavioral strengths and weaknesses that serve as context for these problems) are of direct interest in and of themselves. That is, assessment focuses on direct samples of behavior and the behavioral context and assumes that what one sees is the clinical problem. This assessment philosophy stands in contrast to traditional personality assessment which has viewed information gathered from assessment to be a sign of other underlying psychopathological processes. For example, behavioral assessment would directly focus on examples of aggressive behaviors exhibited during videotaped social interactions, while traditional assessment may choose to use projective techniques such as the Rorschach test to infer some underlying problem from the responses given to the Rorschach cards. This sign versus sample distinction between behavioral and traditional assessment approaches sets behavior therapy apart from many other therapy schools (Nelson & Hayes, 1981).

The Analysis of Complex Cases

Many clients do not fit well-described syndromal classifications, and many do not display a single well-defined target behavior for intervention, even after careful assessment. Several different problems are abstracted, and the relation between them is unclear. Thus, there are many possible foci of treatment.

In these instances, the clinician attempts to organize the data into a more coherent whole. Often one problem has led to another—one is primary and another is secondary. For example, a person might have originally been socially withdrawn because of social skills deficits, but this withdrawal in turn has produced difficulty in acquiring and maintaining employment. In this case, it might make sense to target the underlying social skills deficit first rather than the employment difficulty.

It may be the case that one problem, while not primary in the sense just described, is preventing successful remediation of another problem. For example, a socially backward person who is 30 years old and living at home may become depressed following the death of his only parent, who has taken care of him since birth. His social skills deficit may not have caused the depression, but it now prevents the actions that might alleviate the depression. In this case, it might make sense to target the social skills deficit first rather than the depression per se.

Sometimes problems can be organized into those that are easiest to treat and those that are likely to be more difficult. Clinicians will often treat the former first in order to establish a sense of progress and to gain the trust of the client.

THE PRACTICE OF THERAPY

Behavior therapy is not a unidimensional set of techniques that can be described in one broad brush stroke. Rather, it is composed of a number of diverse forms of treatment, based on behavioral principles, that address a variety of clinical problems. An elaboration of the set of overarching principles common to most behavioral therapies will be presented. Some of the major treatment formats will be reviewed with special emphasis on innovative therapies that are based on contemporary behavioral thinking.

The Basic Structure of Therapy

Number of Sessions

Because behavior therapies have been the subject of a great deal of empirical research, treatment manuals exist to address a number of clinical issues. When treatment is manualized, therapy is often quite structured and generally time-limited. To some degree, this is an artifact of research considerations and not a result of clinical decision making. As we stated earlier, ongoing idiographic assessment is an integral part of behavior therapy. When the therapist is not constrained by participation in a research protocol, the length of therapy is ideally determined by the attainment of goals that were agreed to by the therapist and client and that have been continuously monitored and modified as therapy has progressed. Behavior therapy is, however, pragmatically driven, and thus the fewer sessions needed to reach a given goal the better. Many of the best known behavior therapy methods have shown effects even when delivered in a very limited course of treatment.

Formats

Behavior therapy uses individual, couple, family, and group formats and combinations of these. Behavior therapists are more likely than most others to conduct therapy in natural settings, or to use approaches other than verbal psychotherapy, but the traditional "1 hour per week in the office" structure is probably the modal format. Behavior therapists are also more likely than most therapists

to have relatively specific treatment plans and treatment goals, and many forms of behavior therapy are rather structured as a result. However, relatively unstructured forms also exist.

Homework

Whether one spends 1 hour a week in treatment or several hours, the experiences that occur in therapy will always be a relatively small proportion of a client's total experience. Behavior therapists recognize that for effective behavior change to occur, therapeutic activity must occur outside the session. Thus, homework is a critical component of many types of behavior therapy. The goal of homework is to bring the client in contact with the actual events that naturally affect the behavior of interest. Behavior therapists are also quite willing to use significant others as part of the therapy. For example, a spouse, friend, or parent might be involved in assessing progress, managing contingencies, or other such activities.

Goal Setting

Picking the Problem

Historically, behavior therapy has been relatively client-focused in its treatment goals. Higher-functioning clients are virtually always involved in the collaborative establishment of treatment goals. The client's presenting problems, while they may be reinterpreted and reframed in terms that fit within a behavioral approach, are still an important emphasis of most behavior therapy work. This does not mean that a therapist would uncritically accept the client's first conceptualization of what the treatment should accomplish. In the case of couple therapy, for example, many clients initially present with either the stated or the unstated goal that the therapist "fix" their partner. Most commonly, the therapist's assessment of the case will lead to a dyadic conceptualization of the problems that will involve change on the part of both partners. The therapist does not impose this conceptualization on the couple but rather works with the couple on both the conceptualization of the problem and treatment goals. It should be remembered that the word "behavior" in behavior therapy does not refer to motor activity but to all psychological events conceptualized from the point of view of behavior theory. The goals of behavior therapy, therefore, need not be overt behavioral goals—all psychologically relevant goals can be encompassed within a behavioral approach.

Outcome and Process Goals

The outcome goal of behavior therapy across the specific techniques and modalities has been to produce behavior change that will generalize beyond therapy and that will maximize positive outcomes for the client while minimizing aversive consequences, particularly over the long term and in the context of the good of the larger social units in which the client participates. That is, the goal is to increase client function in the environments in which clients find themselves—recognizing that increasing functioning may depend on altering these environments themselves. The therapist may identify a number of intermediate goals that are successive approximations of the ultimately desired goal, but these intermediate goals are valuable only if they promote the outcome goal itself.

Fitting Goals to the Natural Environment

Behavior therapists believe that maintenance and generalization of treatment gains depend in parts on the degree to which therapy taps into positive natural contingencies. Many clinical behaviors that are discussed in the confines of a therapy setting are quite different than how they are experienced in the natural environment. For example, the behavioral rehearsal of relevant skills to remediate social anxiety can occur in the therapist's office. However, the stimulus conditions that give rise to significant amounts of anxiety are much more likely to occur outside the safety of the therapist's office. Likewise, a therapist's positive feedback for a successful rehearsal may be qualitatively different from consequences of a successful social interaction in the real world (cf. Ferster, 1967).

This interest in natural arrangements leads to a concern over arbitrariness and artificiality. If arbitrary events are used to establish behavior change, behavior therapists are concerned that improvements might not be maintained. For example, if arbitrary consequences are presented contingent upon behavior x and, as a result, behavior x changes, this change might disappear when more natural consequences are allowed to follow behavior x.

Behavior therapists feel most comfortable, therefore, when the natural contingencies of interest occur in the therapy environment. For example, in the case of couple therapy, often the real life antecedent and consequent conditions relevant to behavior change are present in therapy—the reactions and feelings of the other. This enables both an increased opportunity for making an accurate functional analysis of the problematic interactional style and a chance to change the consequences of interest directly.

Techniques and Strategies of Therapy

Table 5.2 provides a sample of problems and treatments that might be conceptual-

TABLE 5.2. Examples of Problems and Treatments as Conceptualized from a Behavior Therapy Perspective

Functional problem	Description	Specific problem example	Intervention example
Defective stimulus control	Response OK but emitted under wrong conditions	Client reveals personal information prematurely to people	Social skills training
Deficient behavioral repertoire	Does not have behaviors that will lead to reinforcement	Assertion deficits, insufficient social skills, poor parenting, poor academic skills	Assertion training FAP (Functional Analytic Psychotherapy)
Aversive behavioral repertoire	Exhibits behavioral excesses that others find aversive	Aggressive behavior	Self-control training
Behavior controlled by defective or ineffective reinforcement	Normal contingencies do not sufficiently reinforce or restrict behavior	Antisocial behavior	Establishment of conditioned reinforcers
Inappropriate contingent control	Reinforcers socially unacceptable or lead to bad outcomes for client	Substance abuse, pedophilia	Self-control training; social skills training
Insufficient available reinforcement	Client does not have sufficient access to reinforcement of appropriate behaviors	Client lives in social situation where education is not encouraged or valued or is inadequate	Pleasant activities planning and social skills training
Behavioral excess	Client exhibits excess behavior that interferes with optimal functioning or learning	Anxiety, obsessive–compulsive behavior	Systematic desensitization; flooding; Panic Control Therapy
Inappropriate self-generated stimulus control—poor self-labeling	Self-generated cues for behavior lead to negative outcomes	Person inappropriately limits behavior by underestimating ability	Behavioral rehearsal
Excessive schedule dependence	Client's behavior is too dependent on constant reinforcement	One is too easily frustrated and gives up too easily (e.g., studying behavior is too fragile)	Self-control procedures; contingency management procedures
Excessive self-monitoring of behavior	Person is overly concerned with form of behavior rather than function	Perfectionism that impairs efficiency	Thought stopping

TABLE 5.2. (*Continued*)

Functional problem	Description	Specific problem example	Intervention example
Ineffective arrangement of contingencies	Person does not arrange immediate environment to usefully control their behavior	Inefficient work performance; problems with time management	Problem solving
Overly rigid rule-governance	Client is not under contingent control of the environment	Client does not see actual relationship between behavior and consequences	ACT (Acceptance and Commitment Therapy)
Discrimination deficits of private events	Person does not accurately label their feelings	Client mislabels anger as some other feeling	Training in self-labeling
Restricted range of reinforcement	Person finds only a limited set of stimuli reinforcing	Overly dependent relationships; vulnerability to depression at loss of reinforcement	Reinforcer sampling
Noncontingent reinforcement	Person receives significant reinforcement for inadequate performance	Narcissism, spoiled	Parent training
Overly punitive environment	Person's behavior is under aversive control rather than positive control	Mistrust, overcaution, misses opportunity for expanding behavioral repertoire	Social skills training; relationship-oriented approach
Aversive self-reinforcement strategies	Person sets standards excessively high	Constant disappointment in self or others	Self-instructional training
Inappropriate conditioned emotional response	Person has a classically conditioned response	Phobia, excessive fear	Exposure; modeling

ized from a behavior therapy perspective. In the left-hand column is an abstract behavioral concept that could be the source of clinical difficulties. This concept is rephrased more discursively in the next column. In the third column, an example or two is given of a clinical problem that might arise because of these behavioral processes. In the last column, one or two behavioral treatments that might address these difficulties are listed. This table is not meant to be comprehensive in terms of principles, problems, or treatments, but it gives a small sample of some of the kinds of problems and procedures that are relevant to behavior therapy. Because of space limitations, it is not possible to describe in detail these procedures, but we will consider a few examples.

Exposure-Based Interventions

Exposure-based treatments designed to treat a variety of anxiety based conditions have had a central place in behavior therapy for more than 30 years (Wolpe, 1958). Exposure techniques can involve actual or imaginary experiencing of the feared stimuli for either a long or a short period. The treatment may involve either high or low levels of arousal or fear in the client and may be graduated or initially intense.

Systematic desensitization is the classic example of a graduated exposure treatment. It involves three key steps: the construction of an anxiety hierarchy, training of an alternative response, and gradual exposure in imagination.

Detailed assessment is important to the successful implementation of systematic desensitization because the therapist must identify the nature of the aversive stimuli and any themes that are relevant to the problem in order to construct an anxiety hierarchy. The list of situations, usually a dozen or more, is concretely specified and sufficiently detailed to allow for vivid imagery. An individual with a fear of flying, for example, might describe the following list of situations.

Reading about planes.
Going to the airport to pick up a friend.
Seeing a plane fly overhead.
Making a flight reservation.
Packing baggage for travel.
Going to the airport to take a flight.
Boarding an airplane.
Waiting in the airport to board the plane.
Waiting on the runway for departure.

The list should be a rather extensive one that the therapist orders in terms of aversiveness to the client. This can be done using a simple rating process, with each item being assigned a number from 0 to 100 to reflect the amount of anxiety it occasions. The therapist then checks that imaging the specified situations does indeed produce anxiety. If the anxiety was not present, it has been proposed that the desensitization process would be likely not to have much utility (Goldfried & Davison, 1976).

Clients are then taught to relax, usually using progressive muscular relaxation. There are several methods of relaxation training such as tension reduction, letting go, sensory awareness, and hypnotic inductions (Goldfried & Davison, 1976). In general, the process is one in which the client learns to actively relax and release all tensions from all the parts of the body, progressing from the hands, up the arms, shoulders, and so on. The therapist actively directs the client through the process, attending to breathing and reminding the client to enjoy the calm feelings as they spread through the body. The client practices relaxation between sessions until he/she has mastered the skill.

Finally, the therapist works with the client, exposing the client to the hierarchy of feared stimuli while in the relaxed state. The client works up the hierarchy only after having tolerated lower-level scenes without becoming significantly anxious. Clients are asked to imagine the least intense item while using their relaxation skills. If the client experiences significant anxiety, the image is terminated. Over time, more and more intense items are imagined, as the anxiety connected to each becomes more manageable.

Desensitization has been used successfully for a wide variety of problems, including negative emotions other than anxiety, such as anger. Initially desensitization was hypothesized to reduce anxiety through counterconditioning (Goldfried & Davison, 1976), but it appears that—like all exposure-based treatments—the key element is exposure itself in the absence of actual negative consequences. For example, the empirical data suggest that the rank ordering of the hierarchy and the presence of anxiety may not be essential to the procedure (Emmelkamp, 1982).

In vivo exposure has become increasingly popular, especially the inclusion of interoceptive cues to avoidance or escape as in David Barlow's *Panic Control Therapy* (Barlow & Craske, 1989; Barlow, Craske, Cerny, & Klosko, 1989). Like desensitization, the procedure relies on graduated exposure, but direct methods are used to produce the avoided events. For example, a panic-disordered person who responds intensely to feelings of dizziness and rapid heartbeats, may be asked to run up several flights of stairs and then twirl around until dizzy. A person with a fear of heights may be asked to climb higher and higher fire-escape stairs. With severe problems, such as agoraphobia, *in vivo* exposure of a prolonged nature produces better outcome than imaginal exposure (Emmelkamp, 1982).

Other exposure treatments are prolonged and intense. An obsessive–compulsive client, for example, might be exposed to a feared event (e.g., dirt) for long periods without an opportunity to wash. Imaginal procedures have also been developed that present feared images in an intense way.

While all these forms of exposure definitely work, it is still not clear how they work. Many models exist, but none are yet supported unequivocally.

The procedures used in contingency management have been modified successfully for use by individuals themselves in what are usually termed *self-control procedures*. These procedures are usually most helpful when the short-term consequences of an action differ from the long-term consequences. For example, the short-term consequences of illegal drug use may be highly reinforcing, but the long-term consequences can include incarceration, poverty, loss of one's family, and so on. This kind of situation is termed a "behavioral trap" because the short-term conse-

quences lure people into damaging behavior. Similarly, the short-term consequences of studying are aversive but the long-term consequences include increased income, a richer intellectual life, or a more valued career. This kind of situation is termed a "behavioral fence" because the short-term consequences make it more difficult to engage in the desired behavior.

To overcome such problems, clinicians might try to arrange for discriminative cues that will strengthen the desired response. For example, a person having a difficult time studying might be asked to schedule studying time at the same time and place each day and to make sure that all materials are available and no distractions are present in that setting.

Similarly, the clinician might try to arrange short-term consequences that are more harmonious with the long-term consequences. To continue with our studying example, the client might give a trusted friend $100 and have $10 returned every day in which there was at least 2 hours of studying.

A major component underlying the effectiveness of self-control procedures appears to be social contingencies. For example, it is known that stating a goal publicly can have powerful effects, even though the same goals stated entirely privately (so that literally no one else knows that the goal exists) tend to have minimal effects. Publicly stated goals change the short-term contingencies because others will respond differently to behaviors if they know a goal is being kept or broken (Hayes et al., 1985).

Direct Manipulation of Contingencies

The direct use of contingencies has been most common in the treatment of children and chronically institutionalized mental patients. These *contingency management* procedures include reinforcement therapy, time out, contingency contracting, token economies, and the like.

For example, suppose a child has tantrums in class. A functional analysis may suggest that the child is seeking the teacher's attention in this inappropriate manner. A behavioral program might be established with two components: time out and shaping appropriate attention getting. Time out consists of the presentation of an uninteresting environment contingent upon unacceptable behavior: When tantrums occur, the child might be placed in a small empty room for 3 or 4 minutes. Because it is known that these kind of behavior-decreasing strategies work best in conjunction with repertoire-building strategies, the child also simultaneously might be trained to ask the teacher to come and look at things achieved throughout the day. The child might be prompted at first, and even a poor request (but not a tantrum) would at first lead to attention. Over time, only completely appropriate requests would reliably lead to teacher attention.

The actual target should depend on a functional analysis. If the child is having tantrums in order to escape from an aversive task, for example, time out might actually increase the tantrums. In this case the child needs to be taught how to deal with a difficult task (e.g., ask for help).

The evidence supporting the effectiveness of direct contingency manipulation is voluminous. In 1968, Allyon and Azrin were able to bring about dramatic behavioral improvements in what were thought to be chronically psychotic patients in the back ward of a state mental hospital. They altered staff behaviors so that the staff reinforced appropriate and ignored inappropriate patient behavior using a token economy procedure where useful behaviors earned tokens redeemable for items sold in a small patient-run store and special privileges. The result

was that patients who had been institutionalized for an average of 13 years were able to function at much higher levels than previously thought. In this case, the behavioral intervention was more on the staff than on the patients, but the benefits accrued to both.

In 1987, Ivar Lovaas reported the most dramatic results to date in treating autistic children. Lovaas has been working with this population for over 25 years and his work is characterized by the application of operant principles to teaching autistic children language and social behavior. Prior to the application of the operant principles, children with severe forms of this condition frequently had to be tied to their beds or else they would engage in such self-destructive behavior that they could make themselves blind, deaf, or severely brain damaged. They rarely learned language. Mortality was high in these individuals as a result of complications from having to be restrained. Following years of very intensive behavior therapy, Lovaas reported examples of autistic children who became essentially indistinguishable from nonautistic children. Others improved on many of the criteria but were admittedly still "different" (e.g., in interpersonal skills). Although their results were not perfect, the outcomes overall were strikingly positive, especially when compared to the generally dismal outcomes that occurred without behavioral treatment.

Both of these examples show how therapists can significantly control and alter the way clients are reinforced. In the case of psychotic patients, the wards of the hospital were completely controlled by the staff, and thus how patients were reinforced with tokens was also under staff control. With autistic children, either Lovaas had the children available in a clinic for many hours a day where he and his staff could control when behaviors were reinforced or he sent staff to the client's home where more direct control over the environment was possible.

Innovative Verbal Psychotherapies in the Contextualistic Behavioral Tradition

The impact of traditional forms of behavior therapy was substantial, but many clinicians reported that behavior therapy was not relevant to much of their case load. The problems of the average adult outpatient client did not always seem to fit neatly into the behavioral treatment methodologies (Jacobson, 1991b). Cognitive therapy emerged in part out of this frustration, and most of the currently well-developed verbal psychotherapies in behavior therapy are cognitive-behavioral. These are addressed in Chapter 6. It is quite possible, however, to develop verbal psychotherapies based solely on principles of operant and classical conditioning and verbal control. We will give two examples.

Functional Analytic Psychotherapy (FAP) has its basis in a behavioral analysis of the therapeutic relationship (Kohlenberg & Tsai, 1987). FAP is meant to be used either in conjunction with more straightforward and traditional behavioral technologies or when the client's presenting issues are such that the interpersonal aspects of the client's ability to relate are, in fact, the problem that needs to be treated.

Kohlenberg and Tsai focus on clinically relevant behaviors (CRBs). There are three kinds. The first is instances of the clinical problem that occur during the therapy session. For example, suppose a woman with a sexual abuse history dissociates when she is feeling frightened in intimate situations. If she now dissociates in session when discussing difficult and intimate topics, she is displaying a CRB1. The second type of CRB includes behaviors or groups of behaviors that need to be established but that are not apparent early in the treatment. An ex-ample of this using our client with the abuse history might be experiencing certain feelings (e.g., anger toward her abuser) that had previously been suppressed. If such anger emerged, it would be an instance of CRB2. The third type of CRB involves the adoption of an agreed on verbal repertoire for describing her own CRBs.

Kohlenberg and Tsai suggest following five rules that comprise the therapeutic technique. The first and most critical of these rules is to *develop a repertoire for noticing the occurrence of CRBs in session.* Although at first glance this might seem obvious, mastery of this component of the therapy is difficult. Often, a therapist becomes so involved in talking about the problems that bring the client to treatment that she does not notice actual instances of the behavior in session. If, for example, a client presents for job difficulties that involve an acquiescent manner and a failure to perform the tasks assigned, the therapist might at first miss the clinical relevance of coming late to a session and apologizing for the tardiness.

The second guideline for the therapist is to *structure the therapy environment to increase the likelihood of CRBs.* The idea is that it is much easier to deal with clinically relevant material if it is occurring in session rather than merely be described.

The third rule is to *reinforce CRB2s as they occur.* There are two important aspects to this rule: The reinforcers must be natural, and approximations toward healthy behavior must be discerned and reinforced.

Behavior therapists have often relied on *arbitrary reinforcers*—ones that are not likely to occur in the natural environment in response to the behavior of interest. Arbitrary reinforcers have many disadvantages, however. They seem manipulative to adults, and gains they produce may disappear when therapy is terminated because they are unlikely to occur (by definition) in the natural environment. Thus it becomes critical that the therapist has in her repertoire an ability to reinforce CRB2s in a natural manner. For example, suppose an unassertive client asks the therapist to change an appointment. It may be more important for the therapist to change the appointment (the *natural consequence*) than to praise the client for assertiveness (an unusual and arbitrary consequence).

It is also important for the therapist to discern steps in the right direction. Suppose a client who has difficulty expressing anger tells the therapist that she is upset with the advice given her last week, that it did not work well. The therapist might defend her advice and attempt to analyze what the client did to determine whether she accurately complied with the instructions. These responses, however, are not based on the progress the client made: She is expressing her anger. Even small steps in the right direction must be supported.

The fourth rule is that therapists should *observe how their own behavior influences their client's CRBs,* and the final rule is that the therapist should *describe the client's CRBs in functional terms.* In order to develop and maintain this therapeutic strategy, it is useful to observe and describe contingencies and to develop a similar repertoire in the client.

FAP is best done in the context of a long-term, intense psychotherapeutic relationship. It requires significant commitment by both the client and the therapist to be willing to examine aspects of their relationship that will at times be painful and conflictual.

FAP is a behavioral, interpersonal treatment based on direct contingency principles. We described it here because it shows one way the contextual behavioral approaches can address issues that are dealt with in traditional psychotherapy approaches. We will give one more such example.

Acceptance and Commitment Therapy (ACT; originally termed "comprehensive distancing") (see Hayes, 1987; Hayes et al., 1989; Hayes & Melancon, 1989; Hayes & Wilson, 1994; Kohlenberg, Hayes, & Tsai, 1993) also has its roots in the contextual behavioral tradition but is more based on principles of verbal control than is FAP.

The core idea of ACT is that the relationship between private events such as thoughts (or other private events) and overt behavior is contextually established and maintained. Rather than try to change the *content* of private antecedents (e.g., thoughts and emotions), the *context* that relates them to undesirable overt behavior is challenged. Several processes are argued to be involved: *Literality* refers to the idea that due to the transfer of functions seen in verbal control, words are confused with events they describe. Clients having the thought "I am bad" may perceive themselves to be in a situation of being bad, not in a situation of having the thought of being bad. *Reason giving*, a context so fundamental to our culture that it is hard to see it as a problem, describes the phenomenon of appealing to our reactions as causes of behavior. For example, feelings are said to explain overt action ("I was too anxious to go") when from an ACT perspective there is no necessary link between these described emotions and action ("I felt anxious *and* I went"). Finally, we are taught that it is possible and necessary to *control private events* so that we can change behavior ("Just stop worrying about it!"). From an ACT point of view, private events serve as controlling variables not because they necessarily control behavior but because maladaptive social–verbal contexts exist that establish such a relationship. The end result is that humans try to avoid and manipulate their own emotions instead of feeling them.

ACT deals with this problem by confronting clients with the hopelessness and futility of a struggle with their own history, by distinguishing individuals from their behavioral reactions, by loosening the literal meaning of language, and by encouraging emotional acceptance in the service of behavior change.

In ACT, if a client has feelings of depression or negative thoughts, instead of trying to change them, ACT encourages the client to feel sadness (when sadness is there) and to observe the occurrence of "negative" thoughts without either believing or disbelieving them. For example, clients may be asked to repeat negative thoughts out loud over and over, so that their literal meaning may diminish. The goal is not to get rid of thoughts but to deliteralize them—to contact self-talk as words, not just to view the world as structured by these words.

Deliteralization is based on a contextual view of thinking (Hayes & Hayes, 1992b). The relation between a thought and overt behavior idea is conceived of as behavior–behavior relation (where "behavior" is defined as psychological activity), and *such a relation itself is viewed as contextually situated.* The meaning of any verbal event derives in part from its derived relations with other events, but these derived relations occur in a social–verbal context. Thus, for example, when a thought is repeated over and over, the dominance of the functions that come from the derived relation between the verbal events and other events diminishes, and the direct auditory functions become more dominant. The reader can try a simple exercise to see how this works. First, say the word "milk" out loud. Come back to this part of the page after you do so. Most people will have noticed not just that they said the word "milk" but also that they contacted the functions of actual milk—you may have thought of white creamy liquid that tastes a certain way, feels cold, and makes a glugging sound when you drink

it fast. These functions occur directly when milk is actually contacted, but they also occur via derived stimulus relations with the word "milk."

Now say the word "milk" out loud but repeat it over and over, very quickly, for a minute or so. Come back to this part of the page after you do so. Most people will have noticed that after half a minute or so that white creamy liquid that tastes a certain way, feels cold, and makes a glugging sound when you drink it fast *disappears psychologically*—instead one begins to notice only the rather odd sound of the word "milk." Deliteralization is thus the weakening of derived stimulus relations and the functions produced by them. Repeating a word over and over is only one trivial example of dozens of deliteralization methods that are possible, such as paradox, confusion, and the like.

When presented in an individual format, ACT has been shown to be more effective than Beck's cognitive therapy in the treatment of depression (Zettle, 1984). When conducted in a group format ACT was still superior, but only marginally so (Zettle & Raines, 1989). ACT has been used to treat the emotional distress of families with severely physically handicapped children—a situation in which removal of the stressor is not possible (Biglan, 1989). ACT has also been found to be effective with several different anxiety disorders (Hayes, 1987; Hayes, Afari, McCurry, & Wilson, 1990).

In line with theoretical expectations, process research has shown that ACT clients show a slower drop in the frequency of depressive beliefs than do cognitive therapy clients but show a much more rapid drop in the believability of those thoughts (Zettle & Hayes, 1986). Similar differences have been shown in other studies (Zettle, 1984; Zettle & Raines, 1989). Also in line with ACT theory, beneficial outcomes have been shown to be related to reductions in emotional avoidance, both self-reported and directly observed in session (McCurry, 1991; Khorakiwala, 1991).

ACT shares common ground with experiential therapies in that experiencing and feeling are to be accepted and valued, not controlled out of existence. Some of the techniques used in ACT are borrowed from other approaches. The conceptualization, however, is thoroughly behavioral.

ACT and FAP show that "behavior therapy" is not usefully understood in a commonsense manner (e.g., "behavior therapy focuses on overt behavior, not thoughts or feelings") or as a matter of technique (e.g., "desensitization is behavioral, but the empty chair technique is not"). Rather, behavior therapy is a conceptual approach to therapy. It can incorporate forms of treatment that look psychodynamic, experiential, Gestalt, interpersonal, and so on, but the use of these techniques is coordinated within a coherent behavioral account.

The Process of Behavior Therapy

The Therapeutic Alliance

Behavior therapists are acutely aware of the necessity for a positive working alliance. Therapy, conceptualized behaviorally, is largely a social change process. Superficially, this may seem one-sided: A therapist is attempting to use his/her social influence to change another. If a one-sided approach would work to help accomplish the agreed on goals of therapy, behavior therapists would consider it, but in fact a one-sided approach is largely unworkable. Clients do not like to be manipulated, and they will not seriously examine the ideas of untrustworthy or unlikable people. The reinforcing effectiveness of a therapist's response depends on the warmth, empathy, and genuineness of this response. The effective-

ness of verbal antecedents presented by therapists depends on the relationship between the client and therapists.

Behavior is an interaction of an organism with the historical and current context. In this view, persons with problems are not "at fault" for their actions, and thus the behavior therapist is well positioned to accept the client as he/she comes to therapy. At the same time, behavior therapists recognize the responsibility of clients for their lives in the original sense of that term: People have an "ability to respond" and what they get comes from what they do. Thus, responsibility involves identifying and being guided by the contingent relationship between action and outcome: the essence of operant behavior. The goal is not to fix broken people but to construct successful ways of producing valued outcomes. This very attempt assumes that, ultimately, the client is able to respond (is "responsible").

In the initial phases of treatment, it is important for the behavior therapist to enlist the client as a collaborator in the identification of problematic behaviors and positive behavioral goals. The behavior therapist develops a plan for treatment that is shared with the client in an open manner. Many behavioral treatments have a great deal of empirical support for their efficacy and some of this information is often shared with the client. As treatment proceeds, ongoing assessment is used to evaluate not only change in the client's presenting problem but also his/her satisfaction with the course of therapy. Thus, for both pragmatic and ethical reasons, behavior therapy is collaborative, not hierarchical. The focus remains on developing new, more adaptive behavioral repertoires, not on the labeling and the identification of pathology in the client.

Resistance

In one sense of the term, "resistance" is assumed by behavior therapists. In general, organisms naturally do what works instead of what does not work. Thus, whenever a behavioral system is leading to undesirable consequences, it must be because other aspects of that system are preventing successful behavioral development. This kind of resistance, however, is in the behavioral system, not in the person cut off from the historical and situational context. Placing resistance inside a person is a nonsensical notion to a contextualistic behaviorist. If the client is not achieving treatment goals, according to behavior theory, either the analysis of controlling variables is incorrect or incomplete or the intervention is not adequately implemented. While the client is always assumed to be "able to respond" (response-able), so, too, is the therapist. By accepting a therapeutic role, a therapist also accepts the centrality of the contingent relationship between therapeutic actions taken and the outcomes these actions produce. In a sense, the therapist and the client are each 100% response-able for the course and outcome of therapy, because the outcomes apply 100% to the therapist's behavior and 100% to the client's behavior.

Common Errors

Errors are endemic. In many areas, we simply do not know how best to help people, and thus even the most careful, skilled, and caring therapist will occasionally inadvertently hurt people and will regularly fail to help them. The easiest way for a behavior therapist to make a theoretically preventable mistake is to do an incomplete or incorrect functional analyses. This kind of error is also impossible to avoid entirely, but the ongoing, systematic, idiographic assessment characteristic of behavior therapy at least makes it more likely that such errors will be detected.

Behavior therapy has other characteristic types of errors. Behaviorists recognize that some behavior is best guided by experience (i.e., "direct contingencies") rather than by verbal formulae. Thus, while we can have a science *of* everything, we cannot have science *do* everything. A science of art does not do art; a science of sex is not itself sex. Some things cannot be learned from or fully captured by rules, no matter how valid these rules may be. If psychotherapy is one of those things—at least to a degree—then any perspective or point of view about psychotherapy carries with it the danger that theoretical conceptualizations will dominate even when rule-governed therapy is not what is needed. This error is perhaps more likely within behavior therapy because it is an approach that so actively pursues and values the development of scientifically established rules (e.g., carefully described and empirically tested forms of treatment or the development of behavioral analyses of complex clinical phenomena). On the positive side, this interest holds out the promise of a progressive science of psychotherapy. If rules can help therapists, behavior therapists hope to find them. Even if psychotherapy is in part an art, it may be possible to develop rules that describe how best to train this art. On the negative side, unsophisticated behavior therapists may show the downside of rule-governed behavior—insensitivity to the current situation (e.g., client feelings) (see the preceding section, "The Therapeutic Alliance").

A good example of the limitations of rule-based treatment is in the area of social skills development. Social skills training has been driven by the idea that socially ineffective people have specific deficits in particular skill areas. Because behavior therapists often assume that they must treat specific behaviors directly (e.g., instruct specific behavior change and provide feedback about performance) they also assume that these specific social deficits must be identified and described in detail. But after 20 years of trying, and literally hundreds of studies, there is still is no useful list of the specific components of "social skill."

Social behavior involves myriad specific response forms (facial expressions, gestures, verbal requests, movements, etc.) in myriad specific contexts (different audiences, social setting, types of interaction, etc.). Even a few dozen response forms and contextual factors can quickly lead to billions of specific combinations and sequences. It seems unlikely that a comprehensive list of social skills will be identified or trained. Furthermore, it seems clear that in most areas social skills are originally learned more by experience than by direct verbal instruction, as children try out various social behaviors and note the results. Verbally guided social behavior may seem rigid or artificial as a result (as when an adolescent boy repeats a "pick-up line" he learned from "How to Pick Up Girls").

There is an alternative, however: Shape the behavior directly by presenting and amplifying its consequences (Follette, Dougher, Dykstra, & Compton, 1992; Hayes, 1993; Hayes et al., 1989). In the first study of this kind (Azrin & Hayes, 1984), male subjects were asked to view a videotape of a female conversing with an unseen male and each minute to rate how interested they thought she was in the unseen other. In the original taping, the female had actually given such ratings each minute and by using these as criteria, the male subjects' ratings could be assessed for accuracy. Treatment consisted simply of giving subjects feedback on the accuracy of their guesses. Thus, this strategy allowed both assessment and training of sensitivity to social interest cues, even though we had no idea what these cues were (as we would need to if we were developing a rule-based intervention). The results showed that with feedback, subjects improved in their ability to discriminate social interest, that this ability generalized to previously unviewed females and led to improvements in actual social skills in subsequent role-play situations.

In another study (Rosenfarb, Hayes, & Linehan, 1989) subjects repeatedly role-played social situations. The therapist stated his "gut reaction" about the overall quality of the role-played performance without any description of the behaviors the therapist liked or disliked. This was compared to interventions consisting of therapist- or client-generated rules about effective social behaviors. The results suggested that subjects receiving experiential feedback improved more and were more likely to generalize improvements to new situations.

What is noteworthy about this approach is that experiential methods can be developed and tested scientifically without turning treatment itself into a rule-based enterprise. There may be many examples in which therapists would be more effective if their own therapy behaviors were shaped rather than instructed—indeed the method just described might be used to train such therapist behaviors.

Termination

In the most typical case in behavior therapy, termination is viewed as a time to fade out any distinctive characteristics of therapy and to accentuate the aspects of the natural environment that might maintain treatment gains. Without the generalization and maintenance of new behaviors, therapy would not be considered successful. Thus, termination is most often a gradual process so as to facilitate the transfer of the gains made in therapy to the client's daily environment. For example, as the client and therapist recognize the attainment of the mutually agreed on therapy goals, the temporal space between sessions often becomes greater. Many behavior therapists will use periodic booster sessions in order to increase the likelihood of maintaining treatment gains. The client is encouraged to see these booster sessions not as a failure but rather as an opportunity for some maintenance work, similar to a regular dental check-up.

In some particular circumstances, termination may have another dimension. If a client has a history of abandonment, for example, termination may replicate some aspects of the original traumatic situation and thus bring into therapy some of the original forms of responding. "Transference"—in a behavioral view— refers simply to the shared behavioral functions for a client of current and historical contexts due either to their formal similarity (the behavioral process known as *stimulus generalization*) or to verbal relations that tie the current event to past events ("he wants to dominate me just like Mom did"). As our earlier discussion of FAP shows, transference is not a problem from a behavioral viewpoint, but rather an opportunity to establish new, more effective responses in the presence of psychologically powerful contextual cues. If termination taps into strong feelings of abandonment, for example, a sophisticated behavior therapist will— with the client's agreement—turn therapeutic attention to this very issue and use termination as a context within which to work on it.

THE STANCE OF THE THERAPIST

There is a great deal of research within behavior therapy on the impact of clinical techniques, but relatively little on how behavior therapists should behave more generally to best bring about behavior change. The most important guides become those that flow from a general behavioral perspective.

Directiveness

It is false to place structure and freedom at opposite poles. Behavior is contextu-

ally sensitive both in and out of therapy—it is never literally "free." In general, behavior therapists tend to be more directive than humanistic or psychodynamic therapists, if "directive" is taken to mean more verbal during sessions, and more specific with their suggestions. In many instances, the therapist may be in the role of instructor or may suggest possible "experiments" for the client to try in order for the client to contact experientially the relevant behavioral determinants. In adult outpatient therapy, the client is often the only one who has the opportunity to alter the relevant aspects of the behavioral context so that behavior change is possible.

In some clinical settings, such as institutions or family settings, where the main sources of reinforcement can be directly altered, the behavior therapist may be quite direct in his/her instructions about how to control behavior. For example, parent training is often conducted didactically with homework given and progress monitored by having parents collect data on children's behavior.

Responsibility for Change

Human language makes the analysis of responsibility a difficult one. As described earlier, for contextualistic theorists truth is a matter of successful action—of reaching one's goals. The scientific goal of contextualistic behavioral theory is to predict and influence behavioral interactions. Given that goal, principles and analysis must start and end in the environment—the world outside behavior that is, at least in principle, manipulable. This is because it is impossible to alter the behavior of another without altering the context of that behavior. Thus, behavior therapists locate the source of behavioral influence in the environment when speaking scientifically. The responsibility for behavior and behavior changes rests neither with the therapist nor with the client directly. It emerges from the interaction between the behavior of the client and the therapist in a historical and situational context. The rule of therapy is to create an environment where appropriate behaviors can be emitted, shaped, and reinforced naturally.

In many cases, therapy is presented in a psychoeducational framework, utilizing a similar analysis. Relevant behavioral principles may be paraphrased and presented to the client, and the therapist may simply facilitate the client in creating conditions in which these principles will work to the advantage of the client. For example, if one were treating a client with a fear of flying, a simple version of classical conditioning and extinction may be explained to the client, and an exposure-based treatment may begin. In this simple clinical example, the therapist and the client are often collaborators in creating the conditions where exposure is palatable and possible for the client. The client is not viewed as passive or active, but as interactive.

At times, however, a behavior therapist may speak quite differently. For example, a behavior therapist may reason with a client that she faces a "choice to change" or has "responsibility for her life." This way of speaking helps restrict the ready excuses and reasons humans give for their difficulties—especially when the main purpose of this reason giving is to deflect the natural contingencies for action. Thus, on behavioral grounds, it is often useful to speak clinically in ways that literally conflict with behavioral assumptions.

As noted earlier, however, responsibility is never confused with blame. If one is being consistent with a behavioral perspective on clinical problems, the notion of "abnormal or psychopathological" behavior often makes little sense to the behavior therapist. As pointed out earlier, there would be nothing "abnormal" about a young female client presenting with mistrust of men, fear of intimacy, and sexual difficulties if one knew she had a long-standing physical and sexual abuse history as a child where the perpetrators were male family members. This would be a perfectly explainable consequence of such a behavioral history. In fact, it would be hard to imagine what set of psychological principles would allow one to predict that a person with such a history should have a different outcome.

The result of the above assumptions and beliefs is that the therapist and the client are viewed in some basic ways as equals in therapy. Power differentials are minimized and collaboration rather than hierarchical doctor–patient roles is sought by behavior therapists. This does not mean that the clinician does not have expert knowledge, but rather that the universal applicability of that knowledge puts all humans, including the clinician, swimming together in the same stream of behavioral processes.

Process Variables: Self-Disclosure and Joining In

Until recently, behavior therapy has not focused much attention on process variables in therapy. For example, there are no behavioral principles that dictate whether or not a therapist should self-disclose. Likewise, therapists are neither enjoined from nor encouraged to "join in the therapy change process" versus remaining outside. In making a decision about such issues, data sometimes exist that can serve as a guide, but, more often, behavior therapists must analyze their own in-session behavior using the same set of principles they use to understand their client's behavior.

For example, at times therapist self-disclosure might help develop the relationship between the therapist and client. We analyzed earlier why a therapeutic relationship is important from a behavioral point of view, and when self-disclosure promotes this relationship, behavior therapists would encourage self-disclosure. Self-disclosure could also have negative effects, however. It could take advantage of a power imbalance between client and therapist, for example.

Transference and Countertransference

We earlier defined "transference" as the shared behavioral functions of the client's current and historical contexts due to their formal or verbally produced similarity. Countertransference is viewed the same way—only the agent involved is changed. Consider the following exchange:

THERAPIST: How did things go this last week?

CLIENT: Terrible. By now I figure I should be getting a lot better.

THERAPIST: Let's see, am I correct that this is our third session together?

CLIENT: Sometimes I feel as though you don't care about me. It is only 3 weeks, but that's a long time in the hell I'm in. When are you going to help me? I'm beginning to wonder if you even can.

THERAPIST: (*Feeling intensely angry, defensive, and hurt, the therapist notices a strong tendency to withdraw entirely but nevertheless says . . .*) It must be frightening to feel out so out of control and yet have to depend upon a person you are just getting to know.

From a behavioral perspective, in this example the client seems to have unrealistic expectations of the therapist. Suppose we knew that the client had a notably cold and distant father, and that the main way the client produced attention was to attack him verbally. With such a history, it is possible that the behavioral functions (attack over failure to fulfill unreasonable expectations) of a historical context (a parental relationship) occur now in a current context (the therapeutic relationship) because of formal and verbal similarities between the two. Both environments involve "authority figures," for example. This "transference" would be useful in therapy if the client wanted to work on parental relationships, or perhaps other relationships with authority figures, because it means that the behavior of direct interest is occurring in therapy.

Similarly, the therapist's affective response of feeling angry or wanting to withdraw upon hearing the client's diatribe might be a response based not just on the therapeutic relationship itself but on its similarity to other relationships—perhaps the criticism reminded the therapist of what it felt like as a child to be expected to know more than a child could know. Noticing possible instances of "countertransference" could be therapeutically useful, primarily because it might help reveal the function of the client's behavior, not just its form. In the natural social environment, people have little reason to distinguish countertransference from the demands of the current situation per se. Thus, noticing how one responds is a clue to how others may respond (assuming that the therapist's historical context is not too idiosyncratic) and thus to the social functions of a client's actions.

The therapist's noticing a tendency to withdraw, for example, suggests that the client may attack to chase people away. It is well-known that signaled and controllable aversive events are less aversive than unsignaled and uncontrollable ones. Chasing away a cold and distant father might be preferable to being ignored by one. Noting the presence of defensiveness might suggest that the client attacks in part to elicit defensive verbal explanations for an apparent lack of caring—itself a kind of caring. Given such an analysis, a therapist might work with the client over ways to build intimacy or tolerate vulnerability, rather than, for example, simply trying to reassure the client or simply trying to get the client not to make unreasonable demands.

Thus, a well-trained, well-adjusted therapist can, under the right circumstances, use his/her reactions to client behaviors as a guide to determine the functions of particular response topographies. The utility of this approach is completely dependent on two things.

First, it is dependent on a well-trained, well-adjusted therapist who has learned to distinguish reactions that are idiosyncratic and those that are normative. If the therapist's responses bear little relation to those of others, or if these responses are misinterpreted, the therapist will reach the wrong conclusion about the functional units involved in a client's behavior. This is why dynamic therapists are often very concerned about countertransference—if the response of their therapist is based on idiosyncratic elements of the clinician's history, they may be harmful or at least of little use. For example, a therapist may note that there is sexual tension in the therapy room. If this is solely because the client looks like the therapist's ex-spouse, and the therapist cannot discriminate the source of the reaction, serious miscommunication may result. The therapist may pursue sexual themes that are not characteristic of the client's behavior and its effect on others. Furthermore, if the therapist acts out on historically produced reactions without regard to their clinical utility, countertransference can do great harm, as when clients and therapists become sexually involved.

Second, it is dependent on unconditional acceptance of the client. In the real world, someone being attacked as the therapist was might naturally respond by escalating the conflict, telling the client off, making the client wrong, or some other peremptory response. This cannot

be the response of the therapist because it is logically inconsistent to blame the client for engaging in the behaviors that brought them into therapy. Therapy must be a place where the client is free to try alternative behaviors that may sometimes fail. The therapist must be accepting of clients, complete with their assets and liabilities, and at the same time respond differentially to client actions. From a behavioral point of view, unconditional positive regard is not helpful if that is taken to mean that anything the client does is reinforced by the therapist. Some behaviors work better than others. But the therapist can accept the client while differentially evaluating the client's behavior.

CURATIVE FACTORS OR MECHANISMS OF CHANGE

Mechanisms

A great strength of behavior therapy is the consistent approach taken to the analysis, treatment, assessment, and interpretation of behavior change. The curative mechanisms of behavior therapy are the behavioral principles of classical and operant conditioning and verbal control that together establish effective forms of interaction with the environment.

Insight

In the early days, behavior therapists were fond of distinguishing between behavior therapy and insight-oriented treatment (e.g., Wolpe & Rachman, 1960), but, in fact, behavioral principles suggest that insight may at times be important. Insight, from a behavioral point of view, involves contacting controlling contingencies verbally and emotionally. Insight is an inherently verbal process in that by "contacting" contingencies we do not simply mean being controlled by them—we mean responding self-reflectively, symbolically, or "consciously" to them. It might involve an appreciation of the relevance of history—as when a client realizes that her current fear is like the fear she had when being abused as a child. It may be interactional, as when a client appreciates that the current function of resistance in therapy is to be right and make the therapist wrong. The difference between the two involves the controlling contingencies that have been contacted.

Insight can be important for at least two reasons. First, when an event becomes verbally accessible it allows verbal rules to be applied to the event. Via a transfer of functions, these verbally established functions then may change the functions of the current environment. For example, a client remembering an abuse history for the first time may say, "I used to think I just didn't love my husband even though he was good to me, but now I see how terrified I am of being vulnerable because it reminded me deep down of the abuse." Such an insight might alter dramatically the psychological functions of the husband or of intimate interactions with him. When the client feels afraid around her husband she may be able to approach rather than withdraw because the fear is no longer verbally linked to "not loving my husband." Second, contact with controlling contingencies can enable extinction of established unadaptive stimulus functions. A person reexperiencing an abuse history is contacting some of the original event (via verbal relations). If many of the original functions are aversive and are present, this can be a very emotional experience (thus the phrase "emotional insight"). But unlike the original event, the vivid memory is unlikely to be followed by actual trauma, and so the thoughts, emotions, bodily sensations, and so on, that were associated with the original events lose some of their behavioral functions. In other words, insight involves both the alteration of verbal rules and the extinction of previous behavioral functions.

While insight can be important, there is nothing in behavior theory to suggest that it must be important. Not all behavior change is usefully rule-governed, and not all involves extinction. In these cases, insight may be less relevant.

Interpretation

As noted above, behavior therapists often use interpretations that describe possible contingencies and historical factors that might be operating in a given bit of client behavior. Some of these may be virtually identical to those given by other kinds of therapists ("perhaps you are just angry with me because I remind you of your father"), but the analysis that underlies the interpretation will be behaviorally sensible. At times, behavioral terms might be used directly ("perhaps you are just angry with me because you have come to expect certain kinds of reinforcers from authority figures and I am not delivering them"). In all cases, however, interpretations are merely pragmatic tools in therapy. They carry no necessary ontological meaning. Therapy is not a science class; it is more like a football game. The object is to help the client win, not to show the client who is right.

Interpersonal Skills and the Role of the Therapist's Personality or Health

Behavior analysts have long believed that it is easier to build repertoires than to remove them. The two are not symmetrical. For example, while reinforcement can shape entirely new response forms, punishment or extinction weakens the probability of the emission of response forms but does not truly eliminate them. Thus, permanent therapeutic changes always involve efforts to construct more effective ways of dealing with the world.

To build a repertoire one must (1) start from where the client currently is, and (2) build from strength. Thus, behavior therapists are interested in what clients are already doing well, and how they are doing it.

Many behavioral processes that might be involved with such an effort require some degree of adaptiveness on the part of the therapist. A therapist cannot model what he/she does not do; a therapist is unlikely to discriminate and shape skills that he/she does not have; a therapist cannot supply genuine social reinforcers without good interpersonal skills; and so on. Even if traditional social skills training is a sensible way to proceed (we listed our reservations earlier), if it is delivered by a socially incompetent therapist the two processes (verbal instruction and modeling) would compete with each other and perhaps cancel each other out.

Behavioral procedures that shape social effectiveness (e.g., see earlier discussion of FAP or of shaping-based social skills training) are based on genuineness, a sensitivity to the ongoing present actions of clients, a consistent posture of acceptance of the client, and differential consequences. When interpersonal skills are best modeled and shaped by natural social contingencies, the use of an intimate, supportive, ongoing therapeutic relationship is useful. In this case, the ability and interpersonal skill of the therapist are critical.

The Role of Techniques versus "Being with" the Person

Behavior therapy traditionally has been almost the archetype of a technique-ori-ented form of therapy. The rise in the development of "manualized" treatments was driven largely by behavior therapists. There is nothing, however, in the theoretical and philosophical underpinnings of behavior therapy that demands such an approach. While the outcome of scientific analysis is the development of systems of rules, this does not mean that therapy itself must be rule-based. As discussed previously, rules tend to establish a relative lack of sensitivity to direct contingencies. Thus, for example, a person told in detail how to hit a tennis ball may have a more difficult time getting the "feel of the ball" and hitting it effectively. If we were to do a scientific analysis of hitting of tennis balls, one of the rules might be, "Be careful not to follow too many rules in your efforts to learn how to hit the ball." Similarly, a successful scientific analysis of good art would lead to rules, but that does not mean that artists should paint by numbers.

It seems plausible to some degree that some components of therapy with at least some types of clients are best learned by direct experience. "Being with" the client is a way of speaking about therapeutic behaviors that change behavior through the direct contact with natural (largely social) contingencies, rather than through explicit, verbally guided behavior change efforts.

Is Change in an Identified Patient Possible without Systemic Change?

Behavior therapy incorporates an analysis of the social context of behavior, and to the degree that a given undesirable behavior is situated in a social system that fosters and maintains it, change requires change in that social system. There is no a priori commitment, however, to the participation of any given set of factors in a problem area. The issue, for contextual behaviorists, is never limited exclusively to the form of an event. The issue is its function: its history, the conditions under which it occurs, and its effects. While many—even most—clinically relevant behaviors have been socially situated and are maintained by social factors, not all are. In these latter cases, changes in an identified patient are possible without systemic change.

The Probability of Successful Treatment

Behavior therapy is believed to be effective based on the degree to which (1) the problem is modifiable by experience or rules, (2) the client's behavior has been functionally analyzed, (3) the maintaining contextual variables are available for modification, (4) methods for modifying these variables are developed, and (5) these methods are matched to the underlying functional analysis.

What Is Not Unique

Behavior therapy is more a theoretical and methodological approach to therapy than a specific set of technologies; in other words, what is unique is the general approach, not necessarily the specific treatments. If behavioral principles are meant to describe all forms of situated actions, they aspire to describe all the phenomena reliably found within all approaches to therapy. The analysis might differ, and the concern for empirical demonstration may differ, but the actual treatment technologies may not in a given instance.

This is not to say that behavior therapy does not have a compendium of treatment technologies that have developed within its tradition. It has many of these, and because placing new technologies within the behavioral armamentarium requires passing through methodological and theoretical filters, these homegrown technologies by definition are more likely to be viewed as "adequate" than would technologies from alternative traditions. But the behavior therapy approach itself dictates that ultimately there is nothing that works reliably from alternative traditions that is or should be excluded from behavior therapy.

Research on Mechanisms of Change

Behavior therapy is the most empirically oriented approach to applied psychology. Its journals are usually experimental journals, based on rigorous scientific data. But this is not just a methodological commitment; it is also a theoretical one.

Unlike almost every other tradition within applied psychology (with a few exceptions such as neuropsychology), behavior therapy was based originally on the application of basic psychological knowledge. The contextualistic wing of behavior therapy has maintained that contact and the principles of classical and operant conditioning and verbal control are themselves voluminous literatures within basic psychology. The earlier section on verbal control, for example, would have been as appropriate in a book on basic psychology as it is in a volume such as this.

TREATMENT APPLICABILITY

The scope of problems that have been addressed by the application of behavioral principles to clinical problems is enormous. For example, in children behavior therapy has been used to treat enuresis, autism, retardation, conduct disorders, and phobias. In adolescents, it has been used to treat social skills deficits and most major categories found in DSM-IV. Additionally, in adults it has been studied and used to treat depression, severe psychotic disorders, sexual dysfunction, agoraphobia, marital distress, sleep disorders, chronic pain, eating disorders, and family problems. This is just a partial list of some of the areas to which behavior therapy has been successfully applied and empirically studied.

The broad applicability of behavior therapy to clinical problems is sensible in terms of its operating assumptions: If humans are governed by behavioral principles, a therapy that applies those principles to the understanding of clinically interesting situated action is likely to have some impact. Behavior therapists do not always understand the relevant controlling variables that operate to influence behavior in a given instance, nor do they always have access to the important controlling contingencies even when their role is appreciated. In addition, the current set of behavioral principles is hardly a complete set. Thus, behavioral treatment technologies have far to go, but behavior therapy admits of no intractable domains and obvious progress has been made in many areas.

When Behavior Therapy Is Most Successful

In general, behavior therapy is most effective when therapists have the ability to control the delivery of the natural reinforcers that control the clinically relevant behavior. For example, in young children, institutionalized patients, and geriatric clients, it is often possible to have someone in the client's environment monitor and deliver reinforcers that can shape client behavior.

In some cases of outpatient psychotherapy, effective control over the variables that shape behavior is also suffi-

ciently available to allow profound behavior change. For example, in the case of the treatment of simple phobias or agoraphobia, it is possible to accompany the client to make sure that he/she comes into contact with the phobic situation to a sufficient degree where the clinically relevant fear and avoidance response can be extinguished or altered in such a way as to affect very significant improvement. Similarly, avoidance of interoceptive cues can be addressed directly because it can be discerned in the therapy environment.

Difficulties for Behavior Therapy

The types of clinical problems that are least well understood and treated by behavior therapists fall into two major classes. The first problematic area arises when the variables that originally led to the formation of the maladaptive behavior are remote in time, or when the elements of the environment that are currently maintaining the behavior are not directly under the control of the therapist or someone cooperating with the therapist. The second circumstance occurs when the clinically relevant behavior is a problem due to the lack of motivation on the part of clients to either change their behavior or cooperate in treatment, especially if the therapist does not control many important consequences.

Remote Histories

It is common for clients to have problems based on remote histories. For example, "personality disorders" are relatively fixed patterns of behavior, typically emerging in young adulthood or even before. The contingencies that originally shaped the problem behaviors may not themselves be currently operating—behaviorists assume that if the behavior persists in the present, it is because of currently operating contingencies or rules. The task of the behavior therapist is to identify what those currently operating factors are.

For example, if a client presents for therapy with a long-standing pattern of suspicion, mistrust, and hostility that began after she was sexually abused as a child, we can certainly understand the conditioning and shaping events that would lead to such behavior. But if the pattern is maintained years or even decades after the initial events, one must look to more current circumstances to explain the maintenance of the behavior. It could be that the initial behavior pattern itself leads to people becoming disappointed in interactions with the client and leaving her. The exit of people from her life reinforces the mistrust and produces hostility, producing a pattern of interaction that is difficult to change.

Lack of Motivation

A second problem circumstance for behavior therapy is when motivation for change is absent, especially in adult outpatient settings. A clinical example that would be familiar to many is that of marital therapy. Behaviorally based marital therapies are among the best researched and frequently lead to significant improvement (Jacobson, 1991a). Successful cases are those in which couples suffer from behavioral deficits such as inability to communicate, sexual dysfunction, childrearing problems, or poor management of their life so that they do not have sufficient time for each other. In such cases, building better and more complete behavioral repertoires that are naturally maintained by the contingent improvement in marital satisfaction is relatively straightforward. However, such success requires that couples would find an improved relationship reinforcing if circumstances were better. Sometimes this is not the case. Perhaps one partner is no

longer "in love" with his/her spouse, or is having an affair with someone else. A similar problem occurs in disorders of sexual desire where one partner is simply not interested in sex.

Ethics and Indication for Treatment

There has been a long-standing concern about the ethics of behavior modification and behavior therapy, especially over the use of behavior-regulating technologies. From a behavioral point of view, the concern is somewhat misplaced. Whether one employs behavior therapy or any other sort of intervention, one must change behavior using the psychological principles that shape it. Behaviorists could be wrong about which principles are most important, but it is not a matter of escaping the psychological regularities of the natural world.

Oddly, in the language of free choice and freedom, society accepts a great deal of coercive control. Our society codifies its social mores almost entirely by using the aversive control strategies of punishment and negative reinforcement. Overburdened teachers in overcrowded classrooms use threats and punishment because they are not trained adequately to engineer a positive environment, and if they are, they do not have the time or consulting available to make it actually happen.

For the most part, the same ethical dilemmas face behavior therapy as any other therapeutic school. But because behavior therapy is a powerful means of changing behavior in circumstances where the environment can be highly structured, special problems can occur. Of all the ethical issues in the area, aversive control is the most difficult.

Consider the case of a self-destructive, retarded child who cannot be left alone in an institution because he will bang his head until he does serious physical damage. One alternative is to put such a child in restraints and limit his mobility and ability to use his limbs. A second alternative is to fit him with a head strap that senses each head bang and administers an aversive electrical shock each time this behavior occurs with the result that he quickly and greatly reduces head banging and is allowed to move about freely. The ethical dilemma is twofold. First, should aversive contingencies be applied to individuals who cannot provide informed consent for themselves? The use of punishment or aversive control is not as problematic when an adult consents to this approach (e.g., to pay for a smoking cessation program that uses a rapid smoking technique that makes one nauseous in order to reduce smoking). But, in the case of the severely retarded child, informed consent can come only from a legal guardian. In addition, some well-known behaviorists (e.g., Sidman, 1990) have argued that aversive control simply represents a failure to adequately analyze a situation to find a positive control strategy that would accomplish the same end. Punishment is often effective and does stop behavior in the short run. It is cost-effective when only dollars are evaluated. The problem is that in many cases punishment is used by unskilled staff as a first rather than a last resort. This has led some states to pass laws restricting the use of punishment in institutional settings.

Another example of ethical dilemmas in behavior therapy that is more subtle brings us back into contact with behavior therapy's limited ability to manipulate motivational factors in normal adults. Consider a married couple who seeks treatment to resolve distress in their marriage. In the course of therapy, the following hypothetical dialogue could occur after a couple has learned *some* communication and behavioral exchange principles.

MALE: One thing I am unhappy with is our sex life. I would like to have sex more often.

FEMALE: I don't like sex that much but I suppose I could be talked into having it more often.

MALE: What would it take to have you be willing to have more sex?

FEMALE: Well, if you bought me a new piano for the parlor I would let you have sex with me more often.

The problem is that the couple has learned to use rudimentary arbitrary reinforcement as a kind of barter rather than learning to construct an environment in which each person pleases the other because pleasing the other person is reinforcing itself. If it were allowed to stand, the above interaction would be poor therapy at the least and perhaps unethical because each person is learning to see the other as a commodity rather than as a person.

A final example of an ethical dilemma is the use of behavioral principles to modify the behavior of a group without each member specifically consenting to be "in treatment." If the mayor of a small city asked a behavior therapist to create an environment in which smoking is actively discouraged, most behaviorists would probably not object on ethical grounds. If the mayor wanted to create an environment where people were more likely to report the nonmarital sexual behavior of others, the response would probably be less positive. Such an intervention might lower the unplanned pregnancy rate and lead to lower rates of sexually transmitted diseases, but this is an example of a significant intrusion into the lives of people who have not specifically invited behavior change.

Of course, nonpsychologists do this sort of thing all the time. Advertising companies try to alter behavior in ways that cause disease or death. They try to increase smoking and drinking, sometimes using the same behavioral principles a behavior therapist would use to reduce the problem if an individual wanted to alter his/her behavior.

When to Refer

Behavior therapists refer clients for the same reasons any other therapist would: for nonimprovement. Excluding conditions requiring medications, we can find no clinical problem presented in meta-analytic literature (e.g., Sadish & Sweeney, 1991) that is not treated with behavior therapy at least as effectively as with any other method.

Behavior therapy is not a bag of tricks. Our personal clients would probably do worse than chance at guessing our therapeutic orientation. The process of behavior therapy relies on many of the same interpersonal factors as any therapy. It is the behavior therapist's job to conceptualize the case using behavioral principles, but the direct clinical task is to present an intervention in way that fits the history of the client and uses a language and style comfortable for that client.

CASE ILLUSTRATION

Bob was a 28-year-old single male who came to therapy complaining of intense and frequent panic attacks in which he experienced his heart beating very rapidly, hyperventilated, felt dizzy or faint, had chest pains, and thought he was going to die or go crazy. His struggles with panic had been going on since age 14 when he saw a fatal traffic accident and developed an intense fear of death and had trouble staying in school as a result.

He had a long history of previous treatment, including the use of beta-blockers (which slow the heart), minor tranquilizers, biofeedback, relaxation and breathing control training, and other forms of psychotherapy, including cognitive therapy. His main method of coping with the panic was avoidance. As a result, he traveled little and never alone or without tranquilizing drugs. He normally was not more than a dozen miles from home. He avoided restaurants, bridges, tunnels, shopping malls or other busy stores, and almost any other setting in which escape would be difficult. Over the years his life had become increasingly constricted. He had not worked in years but lived frugally off successful investments.

His relationships were difficult in many areas of his life. His mother was an alcoholic and was overinvolved with her son. She told her son her personal problems and even at a young age had him serve as a go-between with her husbands. She wanted to know every detail of Bob's life and used guilt to control him (in the first session he said "she could afflict guilt on the Pope"). His biological father was distant, domineering, and extremely critical and had left the family while Bob was young. He avoided contact with Bob ever since but when there was contact, he criticized Bob for his perceived inadequacies. His stepfather was kind to him but was thrown out of the house after sexual abuse of his sister was discovered.

His school history had been traumatic. He was picked on mercilessly. A slight and somewhat sickly child, he was always on the outside looking in. As an adult, Bob appeared shy, even withdrawn. He was consistently pleasant but showed little genuine humor, adopting instead a kind of resigned, depressed, and inwardly angry stance. He was very rarely overtly angry (saying "if I stand up for my rights I'll have a panic attack later") and said he had not cried in years. Bob avoided dating and intimate relationships and could not imagine ever having a family. He wanted to travel and participate actively in life but viewed that as a near impossibility because of the panic.

Bob had many notable strengths, however. He was intelligent, likable, and good looking. He had some financial security as a result of his investments, even though he had dropped out of college because of his panic disorder and agoraphobic avoidance. He could work hard. For example, had achieved local notoriety as an outstanding stunt pilot (he did not mind anxiety in that situation "because it is normal").

It is not difficult to imagine why Bob might be anxious. His early history was filled with pain in almost every area. What is more difficult to understand is why this anxiety gradually consumed his life.

Our analysis was as follows: Bob experienced many strong, negative emotions as a result of his difficult history. When someone is hurt by criticism, abandonment, and manipulation, it is natural to feel anger, sadness, and anxiety. Bob had been unsuccessful in creating a more positive and supportive life for himself, in part because he did not have all the skills needed to build and maintain successful social relationship, but also because most of the overt actions he might take were associated not just with the normal fears anyone with such a history would face, but also with intense guilt from on overbearing mother who had kept this adult man suffocated under her wing. For example, when he went to college 100 miles away, his mother called almost every day (often speaking of her intense loneliness now that he was gone), and when he felt panicky there she encouraged him to move back home so that she could take care of him. Thus, his major source of social support and reinforcement encouraged childish and dependent behaviors and actively punished his attempts to create an independent and successful adult life. He felt trapped and was angry about it, but he learned to avoid almost every form of

human emotion from anger to sadness because all were associated with additional aversive consequences, both historically and currently. Only anxiety remained, but that too he ran from with all his might and gradually learned to avoid everything associated with it, from bodily sensations to external situations. As a result, his life had become increasingly restricted. Suicide seemed the only way out. He described himself "at the end of my rope. If this [therapy] doesn't work I can't see any hope for me."

According to his formulation, we had several goals in therapy:

1. *Undercut the avoidance of anxiety and fearful thoughts.* We felt that the anxiety struggle prevented increased independence and disguised other, even more difficult but in a sense more "natural" emotions such as sadness and anger. In this analysis, anxiety was a kind of avoidance maneuver that had become functionally autonomous from its original antecedents.

2. *Watch for the emergence of other emotions as struggling with anxiety becomes less dominant and undercut the avoidance of these as well.* We felt that the original responses to a history such as Bob's would be hurt, anger, and sadness and that it was diagnostic that he showed almost a complete absence of such emotions at the overt level. We felt Bob had learned a general pattern of emotional avoidance and that it was creating a box around his life because almost any change would initially be emotionally difficult.

3. *Help him face the fear of death.* This was one of the original private events that Bob began to struggle with. It is a natural fear for any verbal organism because we can verbally construct futures in which we do not exist. We felt he needed to face this fear; not to overcome it but to incorporate it into a positive approach to life.

4. *Find positive behavioral steps that would lead to greater independence.* Bob had

learned to lie low in life. He avoided many of the normal challenges people face, such as having a regular job, going to school, leaving home, developing permanent relationships, having children, and so on. He was excessively entangled with his mother. Any steps toward independence would be scary and difficult and might evoke retribution from his mother. He had to start small, with short trips, more assertiveness, and so on.

5. *Build on small behavioral changes to increasingly demanding behavioral changes that fit within his underlying values and desires.* As behavior change began to occur we would look to encourage actions that undermined agoraphobic avoidance and began to create a life that he would have if it were a free choice. For example, Bob wanted to travel and to establish successful intimate heterosexual relationships.

In other words, we would focus initially on anxiety, then the range of private events he was experiencing, and finally we would work on successful living.

To assess progress, we created several idiosyncratic scenes that described situations Bob found especially anxiety provoking and assessed his level of anxiety in association with these scenes periodically. We also asked him regularly about his level of behavioral avoidance in significant areas. We went with him to phobic situations and examined his willingness to expose himself to these situations. Our treatment included the following:

1. *Exposure to the futility of emotional avoidance.* We tried, through images, metaphors, paradox, and confusion, to break down the verbal system that had Bob in its grip. This system led to emotional avoidance as the only course of action, but that step itself prevented true progress.

2. *Deliberate emotional exposure exercises at first in imagination and then in vivo.* For example, in imagination we created situations from Bob's childhood that were painful or anxiety provoking and attempted to relive these without any attempt to avoid the emotions that were present. In an *in vivo* exercise, we went several miles into the desert to see how it felt to be so far from help. We worked on exposure to the interoceptive cues associated with anxiety. For example, we walked up hills to create a rapid heart rates and practiced letting go of any struggle with that sensation.

3. *Deliteralization exercises.* We tried to help Bob experience thoughts as thoughts rather than as the situations the thoughts described. We tried to undermine reason giving ("I did this because . . .") in favor of a more open approach that admitted to confusion and ignorance when that was present.

4. *Small commitments to behavior change.* We began to construct homework exercises that pushed out the envelope slightly (e.g., taking short trips or confronting a business partner).

5. *Larger commitments to behavior change.* As opportunities arose, we supported Bob in dramatic new initiatives as they arose. For example, late in the course of therapy he was offered a free ticket on an extensive ocean cruise. After a lot of soul searching, he accepted the offer and went on the trip. We practiced every step of the journey in imagination, making room for even the most frightening thoughts, feelings, or bodily sensations that might emerge. The trip itself, as we expected, created a great deal of anxiety at times, but he generally did not try to defeat the anxiety and instead rode the emotional roller coaster his history presented him with. The trip as a huge success even with the anxiety. Bob was learning to carry the anxiety with him as he made behavior changes.

Through an iterative process, more and more difficult emotional material emerged, but our strategy remained the same: abandonment of the emotional avoidance agenda, exposure, deliteralization, and behavior change. As his behavior began to change, Bob realized he had to confront such issues as resolving his relationship with his father, which he did to a large degree. We practiced in therapy what he might say, feel, or do, so that this step would not seem to large. He became seriously involved with a woman who cared for him and was herself fairly together. He traveled more frequently and stopped taking tranquilizers. We periodically agreed on willingness exercises, such as leaving the pills home for a day (rather than carrying them with him).

After about 40 sessions Bob could no longer be diagnosed as an agoraphobic, and panic attacks were rare and nontraumatic. He still had a hard time with many emotional situations, but increasingly less so. Anxiety was still very much present, but it gradually became less intense across the board and in any case did not lead to destructive behavior. Therapy gradually faded out. He checked in periodically, but he increasingly progressed on his own. He got married, took a job in human services for a time, and made a conscious choice to have children—steps that originally he thought were simply impossible.

Bob came to a class of clinical psychology students one day to talk about his journey in therapy (itself a difficult exposure exercise). Here is a section of the transcript from that class:

STUDENT: Has it . . . has it spread over into other things in your life? This . . . the therapy?

CLIENT: Oh, sure yeah, it's more than just a specific therapy, at least in my life. I look at it more as just a philosophy or a way of life. I don't really see it as just a therapy for a phobia. So I see it more as just a life philosophy.

STUDENT: How, can you think of a way that your life feels different in addition to the agoraphobia?

CLIENT: Oh, sure. Umm, it's like I've been given color. Seeing black and white your whole life and it's like I see rainbows now and stuff. A lot of the emotions I thought I couldn't have and wasn't willing to have I can get as much enjoyment out of those now as anything else. . . . I had several key areas. Sadness was one, embarrassment was another, and then anxiety. And the anxiety is one that I still focus on the most because it does have that life-threatening quality. I'm very in touch now with mortality, and like I said when you get a stabbing chest pain, numbness, and can't breathe and, you know, that catches your attention. But the other ones, I've had those, and, uh, I enjoy them very much really. . . . Sadness used to be a thing that was, it wasn't life-threatening, but it was. . . . Well, in a sense it was. . . . It was so overwhelming that I felt that it almost felt like it was life threatening in itself. I would come up against a few issues in my life and it was so sad that I thought if I was to have that, you know, fully, that I really wasn't sure *what* would happen. I couldn't *conceive* of being that sad.

A little later in the transcript he explained:

CLIENT: I had never conceived or even dreamed possible that it was okay to have your thoughts and your feelings. I began to consider that I didn't need to run or hide from my own thoughts and feelings and bodily sensations, that I didn't need to be afraid of them, things like that, and it was okay, and there's as much life and living in a moment of pain as there is in happiness or whatever. To me that was a revelation. Just I never even considered it. And so it was things like that that would just leave me reeling. It just really start breaking the ice.

STUDENT: Before that had you consciously thought about "well my thoughts and feelings are not okay, I should try to control them."

CLIENT: Oh, absolutely. Yeah, I mean, I would be "better" or "fixed" as soon as I quit having these thoughts and these feelings and so that was my mission in life was to get rid of these and so, umm, it was really a 180 to consider having all that instead. As I learned I can't get rid of it anyway, and then to go on with it, uh, I just found that to be absolutely just a revelation.

This description fits the experience of most of our successful clients whom we treat with emotional exposure as part of the ACT approach. This case mixed many elements, including steps that experiential or dynamic therapists might feel comfortable with, but it is still recognizably a behavioral approach, rationalized in terms of contemporary behavior theory.

CONCLUSION

It is useful to distinguish between approaches at the level of philosophy, theory, methodology, and technique. The heart and soul of an approach are found at the level of philosophy and theory. It is there that the most reliable distinctions can be made because clinicians can, do, and should borrow techniques drawn from other traditions and reinterpret them in their own terms. We have presented behavior therapy as an approach based in contextualistic philosophy that analyzes clinical problems using established, empirically based behavioral principles. We have tried to show that this approach can deal with some of the most thorny clinical issues in ways that maintain contact with the true issues on the one hand while staying true to known behavioral principles on the other. Methodologically, behavior therapy is an approach that is commited to empirical analysis of its terms and techniques, which is one of its great strengths. Finally, we have given several examples of the assessment and intervention techniques that have emerged from this tradition.

Behavior therapy is a vital and vibrant corner of the clinical universe. We believe it is made even more so by grounding this work firmly in the best philosophical and theoretical aspects of the behavioral tradition.

SUGGESTIONS FOR FURTHER READING

Behavioral Philosophy

Hayes, S. C., Hayes, L. J., Reese, H. W., & Sarbin, T. R. (Eds.). (1993). *Varieties of scientific contextualism.* Reno, NV: Context Press.

Leigland, S. (Ed.). (1992). *Radical behaviorism: Willard Day on psychology and philosophy.* Reno, NV: Context Press.

Skinner, B. F. (1974). *About behaviorism.* New York: Knopf.

Behavioral Methodology

Barlow, D. H., Hayes, S. C., & Nelson, R. O. (1984). *The scientist-practitioner: Research and accountability in clinical and educational settings.* New York: Pergamon.

Basic Behavioral Theory

Hayes, S. C. (Ed.). (1989). *Rule-governed behavior: Cognition, contingencies, and instructional control.* New York: Plenum Press.

Skinner, B. F. (1953). *Science and human behavior.* New York: Free Press.

Assessment Theory

Nelson, R. O., & Hayes, S. C. (Eds.). (1986). *Conceptual foundations of behavioral assessment.* New York: Guilford Press.

Intervention Technology

Barlow, D. H. (1993). *Clinical handbook of psychological disorders* (2nd ed.). New York: Guilford Press.

Spiegler, M. D. & Guevremont, D. C. (1993). *Contemporary behavior therapy* (2nd ed.). Pacific Grove, CA: Brooks/Cole.

REFERENCES

Adams, J. (1972). The contribution of the psychological evaluation to psychiatric diagnosis. *Journal of Personality Assessment, 36,* 561–566.

American Psychiatric Association. (1987). *Diagnostic and statistical manual of mental disorders* (3rd rev. ed.). Washington, DC: Author.

American Psychiatric Association. (1994). *Diagnostic and statistical manual of mental disorders* (4th ed.). Washington, DC: Author.

Ayllon, T., & Azrin, N. H. (1968). *A motivating environment for therapy and rehabilitation.* New York: Appleton-Century-Crofts.

Azrin, R. D., & Hayes, S. C. (1984). The discrimination of interest within a heterosexual interaction: Training, generalization, and effects on social skills. *Behavior Therapy, 15,* 173–184.

Bandura, A. (1968). A social learning interpretation of psychological dysfunctions. In P. London & D. Rosenhan (Eds.), *Foundations of abnormal psychology* (pp. 293–344). New York: Holt, Rinehart, & Winston.

Bandura, A. (1969). *Principles of behavior modification.* New York: Holt, Rinehart & Winston.

Bannister, D., Salmon, P., & Lieberman, D. M. (1964). Diagnosis and treatment relationships in psychiatry—A statistical analysis. *British Journal of Psychiatry, 129,* 726–732.

Barlow, D. H., & Craske, M. G. (1989). *Mastery of your anxiety and panic.* New York: Graywind.

Barlow, D. H., Craske, M. G., Cerny, J. A., & Klosko, J. S. (1989). Behavioral treatment of panic disorder. *Behavior Therapy, 20,* 261–282.

Beck, A. T., Freeman, A., & Associates (1990). *Cognitive therapy of personality disorders.* New York: Guilford Press.

Beck, A. T., Rush, A. J., Shaw, B. T., & Emery, G. (1979). *Cognitive therapy of depression.* New York: Guilford Press.

Biglan, A. (1989). A contextual approach to treating family distress. In G. Singer & L. Irvin (Eds.), *Supporting the family: Enabling a positive adjustment to children with disabilities* (pp. 299–311). Baltimore: Paul H. Brookes.

Biglan, A., & Hayes, S. C. (in press). Should the behavioral sciences become more pragmatic? The case for functional contextualism in research on human behavior. *Applied and Preventive Psychology.*

Blatt, S. J. (1975). The validity of projective techniques and their research and clinical contribution. *Journal of Personality Assessment, 39,* 327–343.

Carr, E. G., & Durand, V. M. (1985). Reducing problem behaviors through functional communication training. *Journal of Applied Behavior Analysis, 18,* 111–126.

Catania, A. C., Horne, P., & Lowe, C. F. (1989). Transfer of function across members of an equivalence class. *Analysis of Verbal Behavior, 7,* 99–110.

Cone, J. D. (1988). Psychometric considerations and the multiple models of behavioral assessment. In A. S. Bellack & M. Hersen (Eds.), *Behavioral assessment: A practical handbook* (3rd ed., pp. 42–66). New York: Pergamon.

Daily, C. A. (1953). The practical utility of the clinical report. *Journal of Consulting and Clinical Psychology, 17,* 297–302.

D'Amato, M. R., Salmon, D. P., Loukas, E., & Tomie, A. (1985). Symmetry and transitivity of conditional relations in monkeys (*Cebus apella*) and pigeons (*Columba livia*). *Journal of the Experimental Analysis of Behavior, 44,* 35–47.

De Rose, J. T., McIlvane, W. J., Dube, W. V., Galpin, V. C., & Stoddard, L. T. (1988). Emergent simple discrimination established by indirect relation to differential consequences. *Journal of the Experimental Analysis of Behavior, 50,* 1–20.

Devany, J. M., Hayes, S. C., & Nelson, R. O. (1986). Equivalence class formation in language-able and language-disabled children. *Journal of the Experimental Analysis of Behavior, 46,* 243–257.

DiNardo, P. A., Barlow, D. H., Cerny, J. A., Vermilyea, B. B., Vermilyea, J. A., Himadi, W. G., & Waddell, M. T. (1985). *Anxiety Disorders Interview Schedule—Revised (ADIS-R).* Albany, NY: Center for Stress and Anxiety Disorders.

Dixon, M. H., & Spradlin, J. E. (1976). Establishing stimulus equivalences among retarded adolescents. *Journal of Experimental Child Psychology, 21,* 144–164.

Durand, V. M., & Carr, E. G. (1991). Functional communication training to reduce challenging behavior: Maintenance and application in new settings. *Journal of Applied Behavior Analysis, 24,* 251–264.

Emmelkamp, P. M. G. (1982). *Phobic and obsessive–compulsive disorders: Theory, research, and practice.* New York: Plenum Press.

Eysenck, H. J. (1972). Behavior therapy is behavioristic. *Behavior Therapy, 3,* 609–613.

Ferster, C. B. (1967). Arbitrary and natural reinforcement. *Psychological Record, 22,* 1–16.

Follette, W. C., Dougher, M. K., Dykstra, T. A., & Compton, S. N. (1992, November). *Teaching complex social behaviors to subjects with schizophrenia using contingent feedback.* Paper presented at the meeting of the Association for Advancement of Behavior Therapy, Boston.

Follette, W. C., Bach P. A., & Follette, V. M. (1993). A behavior analytic view of psychological health. *The Behavior Analyst, 16,* 303–316.

Frances, A., Pincus, H. A., Widiger, T. A., Davis, W. W., & First, M. B. (1990). DSM-IV: Work in progress. *American Journal of Psychiatry, 147,* 1439–1448.

Franks, C. M., & Wilson, G. T. (1974). *Annual review of behavior therapy: Theory and practice.* New York: Brunner/Mazel.

Garfield, S. L. (1986). Problems in psychiatric classification. In T. Millon & G. L. Klerman (Eds.), *Contemporary directions in psychopathology* (pp. 99–114). New York: Guilford Press.

Gatch, M. B., & Osborne, J. G. (1989). Transfer of contextual stimulus function via equivalence class development. *Journal of the Experimental Analysis of Behavior, 51,* 369–378.

Goldfried, M. R., & Davison, G. C. (1976). *Clinical behavior therapy.* New York: Holt, Rinehart & Winston.

Hawkins, R. P. (1979). The functions of assessment: Implications for selection and development of devices for assessing repertoires in clinical, educational, and other settings. *Journal of Applied Behavior Analysis, 12,* 501–516.

Hawkins, R. P. (1986). Selection of target behaviors. In R. O. Nelson & S. C. Hayes (Eds.), *Conceptual foundations of behavioral assessment* (pp. 331–385). New York: Guilford Press.

Hayes, S. C. (1987). A contextual approach to therapeutic change. In N. Jacobson (Ed.), *Psychotherapists in clinical practice: Cognitive and behavioral perspectives* (pp. 327–387). New York: Guilford Press.

Hayes, S. C. (1989). (Ed.). *Rule-governed behavior: Cognition. contingencies and instructional control.* New York: Plenum Press.

Hayes, S. C. (1991). A relational control theory of stimulus equivalence. In L. J. Hayes & P. N. Chase (Eds.), *Dialogues on verbal behavior* (pp. 19–40). Reno, NV: Context Press.

Hayes, S. C. (1993). Rule-governance: Basic behavioral research and applied implications. *Current Directions in Psychological Science, 2,* 193–197.

Hayes, S. C., Afari, N., McCurry, S. M., & Wilson, K. (1990, May). *The efficacy of Comprehensive Distancing in the treatment of agoraphobia.* Paper presented at the meeting of the Association for Behavior Analysis, Nashville, TN.

Hayes, S. C., & Brownstein, A. J. (1986). Mentalism, behavior–behavior relations and a behavior analytic view of the purposes of science. *The Behavior Analyst, 9,* 175–190.

Hayes, S. C., Brownstein, A. J., Devany, J. M., Kohlenberg, B. S., & Shelby, J. (1987). Stimulus equivalence and the symbolic control of behavior. *Mexican Journal of Behavior Analysis, 13,* 361–374.

Hayes, S. C. & Follette, W. C. (1992). Can functional analysis provide a substitute for syndromal classification? *Behavioral Assessment, 14,* 345–365.

Hayes, S. C., & Hayes, L. J. (1989). The verbal action of the listener as a basis for rule-governance. In S. C. Hayes (Ed.), *Rule-governed behavior: Cognition, contingencies, and instructional control* (pp. 153–190). New York: Plenum Press.

Hayes, S. C., & Hayes, L. J. (1992a). Verbal relations and the evolution of behavior analysis. *American Psychologist, 47,* 1383–1395.

Hayes, S. C., & Hayes, L. J. (1992b). Some clinical implications of contextualistic behaviorism: The example of cognition. *Behavior Therapy, 23,* 225–249.

Hayes, S. C., Hayes, L. J., & Reese, H. W. (1988). Finding the philosophical core: A review of Stephen C. Pepper's *World Hypotheses. Journal of the Experimental Analysis of Behavior, 50,* 97–111.

Hayes, S. C., Kohlenberg, B. S., & Hayes, L. J. (1991). Transfer of consequential functions through simple and conditional equivalence classes. *Journal of the Experimental Analysis of Behavior, 56,* 119–137.

Hayes, S. C., Kohlenberg, B. S., & Melancon, S. M. (1989). Avoiding and altering rule-control as a strategy of clinical treatment. In S. C. Hayes (Ed.), *Rule-governed behavior: Cognition, contingencies, and instructional control* (pp. 359–385). New York: Plenum Press.

Hayes, S. C., & Melancon, S. (1989). Comprehensive distancing, paradox, and the treatment of emotional avoidance. In M. Ascher (Ed.), *Paradoxical procedures in psychotherapy* (pp. 184–218). New York: Guilford Press.

Hayes, S. C., Nelson, R. O., & Jarrett, R. (1987). Treatment utility of assessment: A functional approach to evaluating the quality of assessment. *American Psychologist, 42,* 963–974.

Hayes, S. C., Rosenfarb, I., Wulfert, E., Munt, E., Zettle, R. D., & Korn, Z. (1985). Self-reinforcement effects: An artifact of social standard setting? *Journal of Applied Behavior Analysis, 18,* 201–214.

Hayes, S. C., & Wilson, K. G. (1993). Some applied implications of a contemporary behavior analytic account of verbal events. *The Behavior Analyst, 16,* 283–301.

Hayes, S. C., & Wilson, K. G. (1994). Acceptance and commitment therapy: Altering the verbal support for experiential avoidance. *The Behavior Analyst, 17,* 289–303.

Haynes, S. N., & O'Brien, W. H. (1990). Functional analysis in behavior therapy. *Clinical Psychology Review, 10,* 649–668.

Hersen, M. (1976). Historical perspectives in behavioral assessment. In M. Hersen & A. S. Bellack (Eds.), *Behavioral assessment: A practical handbook* (pp. 3–22). New York: Pergamon Press.

Jacobson, N. S. (1991a). To be or not to be behavioral when working with couples: What does it mean. *Journal of Family Psychology, 4,* 436–445.

Jacobson, N. S. (1991b, November). *Acceptance and change.* Presidential address delivered to the meeting of the Association for Advancement of Behavior Therapy, New York.

Jacobson, N. S., Follette, W. C., & Revenstorf, D. (1984). Psychotherapy outcome research: Methods for reporting variability and evaluating clinical significance. *Behavior Therapy, 15,* 336–352.

Kanfer, F. H., & Grimm, L. G. (1977). Behavioral analysis: Selecting target behaviors in the interview. *Behavior Modification, 1,* 7–28.

Kanfer, F. H., & Saslow, G. (1969). Behavioral diagnosis. In C. M. Franks (Ed.), *Behavior therapy: Appraisal and status* (pp. 417–444). New York: McGraw-Hill.

Kendall, S. B. (1983). Tests for mediated transfer in pigeons. *Psychological Record, 33,* 245–256.

Khorakiwala, D. (1991). *An analysis of the process of client change in a contextual approach to therapy.* Unpublished doctoral dissertation, University of Nevada, Reno.

Kohlenberg, B. S., Hayes, S. C., & Hayes, L. J. (1991). The transfer of contextual control over equivalence classes through equivalence classes: A possible model of social stereotyping. *Journal of the Experimental Analysis of Behavior, 56,* 505–518.

Kohlenberg, R. J., Hayes, S. C., & Tsai, M. (1993). Radical behavioral psychotherapy: Two contemporary examples. *Clinical Psychology Review, 13,* 579–592.

Kohlenberg, R. J., & Tsai, M. (1987). Functional analytic psychotherapy. In N. Jacobson (Ed.), *Psychotherapists in clinical practice: Cognitive and behavioral perspectives* (pp. 388–443). New York: Guilford Press.

Korchin, S. J., & Schuldberg, D. (1981). The future of clinical assessment. *American Psychologist, 36,* 1147–1158.

Lazar, R. (1977). Extending sequence-class membership with matching-to-sample. *Journal of the Experimental Analysis of Behavior, 27,* 381–392.

Lazar, R. M., & Kotlarchyk, B. J. (1986). Second-order control of sequence-class equivalences in children. *Behavioural Processes, 13,* 205–215.

Lewinsohn, P. M., Munoz, R. F., Youngren, M. A., & Zeiss, A. M. (1978). *Control your depression.* Englewood Cliffs, NJ: Prentice Hall.

Lipkens, R., Hayes, S. C., & Hayes, L. J. (1993). Longitudinal study of derived stimulus relations in an infant. *Journal of Experimental Child Psychology, 56,* 201–239.

Lipkens, R., Kop, P. F. M., & Matthijs, W. (1988). A test of symmetry and transitivity in the conditional discrimination performances of pigeons. *Journal of the Experimental Analysis of Behavior, 49,* 395–409.

Lovaas, O. I. (1987). Behavioral treatment and normal intellectual and educational functioning in autistic children. *Journal of Consulting and Clinical Psychology, 55,* 3–9.

MacPhillamy, D. J., & Lewinsohn, P. M. (1972, September). *The measurement of reinforcing events.* Paper presented at the meeting of the American Psychological Association, Honolulu.

MacPhillamy, D. J., & Lewinsohn, P. M. (1973). *A scale for the measurement of positive reinforcement.* Mimeo, University of Oregon.

MacPhillamy, D. J., & Lewinsohn, P. M. (1974). Depression as a function of levels of desired and obtained pleasure. *Journal of Abnormal Psychology, 83*(6), 651–657.

MacPhillamy, D. J., & Lewinsohn, P. M. (1982). The pleasant events schedule: Studies on reliability, validity and scale intercorrelation. *Journal of Consulting and Clinical Psychology, 50*(3), 363–380.

Mahoney, M. J. (1974). *Cognition and behavior modification.* Cambridge, MA: Ballinger.

Mahoney, M. J., Kazdin, A. E., & Lesswing, N. J. (1974). Behavior modification: Delusion or deliverance? In C. M. Franks & G. T. Wilson (Eds.), *Annual review of behavior therapy: Theory and practice* (pp. 11–40). New York: Brunner/Mazel.

Marks, I. M., & Mathews, A. M. (1979). Brief standard self-rating for phobic patients. *Behaviour Research and Therapy, 17,* 236–267.

Mavissakalian, M. (1985). Male and female agoraphobia: Are they different? *Behaviour Research and Therapy, 23*(4), 469–471.

McCurry, S. M. (1991). *Client metaphor use in a contextual form of therapy.* Unpublished doctoral dissertation. University of Nevada, Reno.

McKnight, D. L., Nelson, R. O., Hayes, S. C., & Jarrett, R. B. (1984). Importance of treating individually-assessed response classes in the ame lioration of depression. *Behavior Therapy, 15,* 315–335.

McReynolds, P. (1985). Psychological assessment and clinical practice: Problems and prospects. In J. N. Butcher & C. D. Spielberger (Eds.), *Advances in personality assessment* (Vol. 4, pp. 1–30). Hillsdale, NJ: Erlbaum.

Meehl, P. E. (1959). Some ruminations on the validation of clinical procedures. *Canadian Journal of Psychology, 13,* 102–128.

Meichenbaum, D. H. (1977). *Cognitive-behavior modification: An integrative approach.* New York: Plenum Press.

Michelson, L., & Ascher, L. M. (1987). *Anxiety and stress disorders: Cognitive-behavioral assessment and treatment.* New York: Guilford Press.

Michelson, L., & Mavissakalian, M. (1983). Temporal stability of self-report measures in agoraphobia research. *Behaviour Research and Therapy, 21*(6), 695–698.

Morey, L. C. (1988). Personality disorders in DSM-III and DSM-III-R: Convergence, coverage, and internal consistency. *American Journal of Psychiatry, 145,* 573–577.

Morris, E. K. (1988). Contextualism: The world view of behavior analysis. *Journal of Experimental Child Psychology, 46,* 289–323.

Nathan, P. E. (1981). Symptomatic diagnoses and behavioral assessment: A synthesis. In D. H. Barlow (Ed.), *Behavioral assessment of adult disorders* (pp. 1–11). New York: Guilford Press.

Nelson, R. O. (1991). DSM-IV: Empirical guidelines from psychometrics. *Journal of Abnormal Psychology, 100,* 308–315.

Nelson, R. O., & Barlow, D. H. (1981). An overview of behavioral assessment with adult clients: Basic strategies and initial procedures. In D. H. Barlow (Ed.), *Behavioral assessment of adult disorders* (pp. 13–43). New York: Guilford Press.

Nelson, R. O., & Hayes, S. C. (1981). Theoretical explanations for the reactive effects of self-monitoring. *Behavior Modification, 5,* 3–14.

Pepper, S. C. (1942). *World hypotheses: A study in evidence.* Berkeley: University of California Press.

Rosenfarb, I. S., Hayes, S. C., & Linehan, M. M. (1989). Instructions and experiential feedback in the treatment of social skills deficits in adults. *Psychotherapy: Theory, Research, and Practice, 26,* 242–251.

Rosenhan, D. L. (1973). On being sane in insane places. *Science, 179,* 250–258.

Rosnow, R. L., & Georgoudi, M. (Eds.). (1986). *Contextualism and understanding in behavioral science.* New York: Praeger.

Sadish, W. R., & Sweeney, R. B. (1991). Mediators and moderators in meta-analysis: There's a reason why we don't let dodo birds tell us which psychotherapies should have prizes. *Journal of Consulting and Clinical Psychology, 59,* 883–893.

Sidman, M. (1971). Reading and auditory-visual equivalences. *Journal of Speech and Hearing Research, 14,* 5–13.

Sidman, M. (1990). *Coersion and its fallout.* Boston: Author's Cooperative.

Sidman, M., Cresson, O., & Willson-Morris, M. (1974). Acquisition of

matching-to-sample via mediated transfer. *Journal of the Experimental Analysis of Behavior, 22,* 261–273.

Sidman, M., Kirk, B., & Willson-Morris, M. (1985). Six-member stimulus classes generated by conditional-discrimination procedures. *Journal of the Experimental Analysis of Behavior, 43,* 21–42.

Sidman, M., Rauzin, R., Lazar, R., Cunningham, S., Tailby, W., & Carrigan, P. (1982). A search for symmetry in the conditional discriminations of rhesus monkeys, baboons and children. *Journal of the Experimental Analysis of Behavior, 37,* 23–44.

Sidman, M., & Tailby, W. (1982). Conditional discriminations vs. matching-to-sample: An expansion of the testing paradigm. *Journal of the Experimental Analysis of Behavior, 37,* 5–22.

Silva, F. (1993). *Psychometric foundations and behavioral assessment.* Newbury Park, CA: Sage.

Skinner, B. F. (1966). An operant analysis of problem solving. In B. Kleinmuntz (Ed.), *Problem-solving: Research, method, and theory* (pp. 225–257). New York: Wiley.

Skinner, B. F. (1974). *About behaviorism.* New York: Knopf.

Spradlin, J. E., & Dixon, M. (1976). Establishing a conditional discrimination without direct training: Stimulus classes and labels. *American Journal of Mental Deficiency, 80,* 555–561.

Trull, T. J., Nietzel, M. T., & Main, A. (1988). The use of meta-analysis to assess the clinical significance of behavior therapy for agoraphobia. *Behavior Therapy, 19,* 527–538.

Ullmann, L. P., & Krasner, L. (1976). *A psychological approach to abnormal behavior.* Englewood Cliffs, NJ: Prentice Hall.

Van Zuuren, F. J. (1988). The Fear Questionnaire: Some data on validity, reliability, and layout. *British Journal of Psychiatry, 153,* 659–662.

Watson, J. B. (1913). Psychology as a behaviorist views it. *Psychological Review, 20,* 158–177.

Watson, J. B. (1920). Is thinking merely the action of language mechanisms? *British Journal of Psychology, 11,* 87–104.

Watson, J. B. (1924). *Behaviorism.* New York: Norton.

Watson, J. B., & Raynor, R. (1920). Conditioned emotional reactions. *Journal of Experimental Psychology, 3*, 1–14.

Wolpe, J. (1958). *Psychotherapy by reciprocal inhibition.* Stanford, CA: Stanford University Press.

Wolpe, J. (1980). Cognitive behavior: A reply to three commentaries. *American Psychologist, 35*, 112–114.

Wolpe, J., & Rachman, S. (1960). Psychoanalytic "evidence:" A critique based on Freud's case of Little Hans. *Journal of Nervous and Mental Disease, 131*, 135–148.

Wulfert, E., & Hayes, S. C. (1988). The transfer of conditional sequencing through conditional equivalence classes. *Journal of the Experimental Analysis of Behavior, 50*, 125–144.

Zettle, R. D. (1984). *Cognitive therapy of depression: A conceptual and empirical analysis of component and process issues.* Unpublished doctoral dissertation, University of North Carolina at Greensboro.

Zettle, R. D., & Hayes, S. C. (1986). Dysfunctional control by client verbal behavior: The context of reason giving. *Analysis of Verbal Behavior, 4*, 30–38.

Zettle, R. D., & Raines, J. C. (1989). Group cognitive and contextual therapies in treatment of depression. *Journal of Clinical Psychology, 45*, 438–445.

6

Cognitive Therapy

ARTHUR FREEMAN
MARK A. REINECKE

Cognitive therapy has attracted increasing interest from mental health professionals around the world during recent years. The "cognitive revolution" (Mahoney, 1977, 1991), ushered in by a 1956 symposium on information processing at MIT and the publication of seminal works by Bruner, Goodnow, and Austin (1956), Chomsky (1956, 1957), Kelly (1955), Newell and Simon (1956), and Whorf (1956), has matured so that cognitively based therapies have moved to the forefront of professional interest (Smith, 1982). Cognitive therapy has become a meeting ground for therapists from diverse theoretical and philosophical positions ranging from the psychoanalytic to the behavioral. Psychodynamic therapists find in cognitive therapy a dynamic core that involves working to alter tacit beliefs and interpersonal schemata. Behavioral therapists find in the model a brief, active, directive, collaborative, psychoeducational model of psychotherapy that is empirically based and has as its goal direct behavioral change. The merging of cognitive therapy and behavior therapy has become more the rule than the exception. Behavior therapy as-

sociations around the world have added the term "cognitive" to their name and the prestigious journal *Behavior Therapy* now carries the subtitle, "An international journal devoted to the application of behavioral and cognitive sciences to clinical problems."

The literature on cognitive therapy has grown in an almost exponential fashion during the past decade. Rooted in the early work of Aaron Beck on the treatment of depression (Beck, 1972, 1976; Beck, Rush, Shaw, & Emery, 1979), contemporary cognitive therapy has become a broad-spectrum model of therapy and psychopathology and has been applied to a wide range of problems, patient groups, and therapeutic contexts. There are now Centers for Cognitive Therapy in such widely separated locations as Buenos Aires, Stockholm, and Shanghai. The basic model has been adapted to a variety of cultures rather easily. Therapists in both Sweden and China claim that there has been interest and growth in cognitive therapy in their country as the model seemed to suit their national character. Given the differences between these two cultures, this is a most interesting statement. Cognitive approaches appear to be applicable cross-culturally because they are process focused and phenomenologically based. Helping individuals to develop the ability to examine their beliefs (whatever those beliefs might be) appears to be far more helpful cross-culturally than focusing on specific points of content. The model is respectful of the fact that specific, tacit beliefs may be shared by members of particular cultures, and that there are meaningful cross-cultural differences in these beliefs. Cross-cultural differences in tacit beliefs appear to exist with regard to the development of skills or competence, personal responsibility, adaptability or malleability of behavior, and the expression of anger. Western societies, for example, have been characterized by an emphasis on individual autonomy and achievement, whereas Asian societies appear to place a relative emphasis on social cohesion and an individual's responsibility to family and the larger community.

This chapter offers the reader an overview of the theoretical bases and history of cognitive therapy and then discusses specific conceptual and technical issues leading to the various treatment strategies. Finally the chapter presents applications of the cognitive therapy model for treating a broad range of clinical disorders.

BACKGROUND OF THE APPROACH

We begin with a brief review of the philosophical foundations of cognitive psychotherapy. Cognitive theory is founded upon intellectual traditions dating to the Stoic philosophers, such as Epictetus (1983), who in the first century commented, "What upsets people is not things themselves but their judgements about the things. . . . So when we are thwarted or upset or distressed, let us never blame someone else but rather ourselves, that is, our own judgements" (p. 13)

Contemporary cognitive psychotherapy is founded upon the concept of "psychological constructivism." Michael Mahoney (1991) has defined this as "a family of theories about mind and mentation that (1) emphasize the active and proactive nature of all perception, learning, and knowing; (2) acknowledge the structural and functional primacy of abstract (tacit) over concrete (explicit) processes in all sentient and sapient experience; and (3) view learning, knowing and memory as phenomena that reflect the ongoing attempts of body and mind to organize (and endlessly reorganize) their own patterns of action and experience—patterns that are, of course, related to changing and highly mediated engagements with their momentary worlds" (p. 95).

The cognitive–constructivist model of human behavior that has emerged during the past 10 years is very different from traditional psychodynamic theories in that behavior is not viewed as determined by early experiences or mediated by the regulation of unconscious drives. It may also be contrasted with operant behavioral formulations in that our emotional and behavioral reactions are not viewed simply as the products of our reinforcement histories and current environmental contingencies. Rather, our behavior is seen as goal-directed, purposive, active, and adaptive. Constructivism asserts that individuals do not simply react to events. Rather, individuals are proactive and develop systems of personal meaning that organize their interactions with the world. Constructivists suggest that knowledge (both personal and scientific) is relative insofar as it is based on personal and cultural epistemologies and may not be based upon a knowable "objective" reality (Mahoney, 1991; Niemeyer, 1993). In concrete terms, constructivists suggest that there are a virtually limitless number of perspectives or interpretations that can be derived from any given event.

Contemporary cognitive psychotherapy reflects the confluence of several schools of thought and is an extension of the earlier work of Adler (1927, 1968), Arieti (1980), Bowlby (1985), Frankl (1985), Freud (1892), Horney (1936), Sullivan (1953), and Tolman (1949). The influence of psychodynamic theory on the evolution of cognitive psychotherapy is perhaps most apparent in the topographic model of personality and psychopathology that they share. Whereas Freud partitioned the psyche into the conscious, preconscious, and unconscious domains, with an individual's behavior primarily mediated by unconscious motives or drives (the id), cognitivists partition cognitive processes into "automatic thoughts," "assumptions" and "schemata."

Like dynamic psychotherapists, cognitive therapists recognize the importance of attending to internal dialogues and motivations. Although attempts are made to avoid drive-reduction metaphors and the notion that behavior is motivated by the repression of anxiety-laden impulses, the cognitive therapist nonetheless works to give voice to the unspoken. Explicit attempts are made to identify and change unrecognized beliefs and attitudes that contribute to patients' distress. The role of cognitive variables—including intentions, expectations, memories, goals, and cognitive distortions—in the etiology of emotional disorders was, in fact, recognized by Freud (1892). He observed that thoughts or ideas can have an affect attached to them, and that emotional reactions to events are dependent on an individual's goals, the degree of strength or certainty with which they hold their beliefs, and the presence of negative automatic thoughts, which he referred to as distressing antithetical ideas.

The influence of the behavioral school of psychology is reflected in cognitive therapy's focus on behavior change, its recognition of social and environmental determinants of behavior, and its use of empirical research as a means of refining both the theory and clinical technique. An empiricist attitude is encouraged for both the therapist and the patient, and behavioral interventions are employed as an integral part of the treatment. An emphasis is placed on identifying discrete problems whose improvement can be objectively assessed.

Many writers have referred to cognitive therapy as a variant or offspring of behavior modification. This is reflected in the widespread use of the term "cognitive-behavioral therapy." As should be clear, however, this does not do justice to the conceptual richness of the model. Moreover, it does not acknowledge the important contributions of other theoretical orientations to its development.

Cognitive psychotherapy has historically been identified with a specific set of techniques and has been viewed by some as a model whose scope is limited to the treatment of specific emotional disorders. This view, while understandable, reflects an oversimplification of contemporary cognitive theory. The view that the cognitive model is no broader than that which is immediately relevant to the conduct of therapy stems from several historical currents. The model, as it was initially presented, was in fact largely limited to the treatment of major depression among adults. The model was limited in scope, and was not intended as a theory of personality or of developmental psychopathology. Although early treatment outcome studies were positive, it was not until the early 1980s that cognitive models of other disorders were developed and the etiology of maladaptive belief systems became a focus of attention. As such, cognitive therapy reflects an evolving model of psychotherapy, psychopathology, and development whose scope of utility is expanding.

The development of cognitive psychotherapy encompasses early work by Bandura (1973, 1977a, 1977b, 1985), Beck (1970, 1972, 1976), Ellis (1962, 1973, 1979), Goldfried (see Goldfried & Merbaum, 1973), Kelly (1955), A. Lazarus (1976, 1981), Mahoney (1974), Maultsby (1984), Meichenbaum (1977), Mischel (1973), Rehm (1977), and Seligman (1974, 1975). These authors were among the first to incorporate cognitive mediational constructs with behavioral theory. They focused on the role of social learning processes in the development of emotional problems and on the use of cognitive restructuring, the development of social problem-solving capacities, and the acquisition of behavioral skills in resolving them. Although cognitive models of psychopathology and psychotherapy have been refined and elaborated since that time, the techniques described in those early works continue to serve as the basis of clinical practice and so deserve mention. Thoughtful reviews of historical factors contributing to the development of cognitive therapy have been prepared by Dobson and Block (1988), Ellis (1989), and Mahoney (1991). Arguably the first contemporary cognitive-clinical psychologist was George Kelly (1955) who, in proposing his "personal construct theory" of emotional disorders, explicitly recognized the importance of subjective perceptions in human behavior. He proposed that individuals actively perceive or "construe" their behavior and generate abstractions about themselves, their world, and their future. An individual's "constructs," as such, can be quite idiosyncratic or personal and represent the ways in which they systematically categorize their experiences. These contructs, in turn, determine how the individual will respond to events. From this perspective, a goal of

therapy is to understand patients' subjective interpretations or judgments about their experiences and to assist patients to construe them in a more adaptive manner. Kelly's therapeutic techniques, while not widely used today, remain an important forerunner of modern "constructivist" or "structural" schools of cognitive therapy (Guidano & Liotti, 1983, 1985; Guidano, 1987, 1991).

The development of cognitive therapy accelerated during the 1970s as information-processing models of clinical disorders were developed, as therapeutic techniques based on cognitive-mediational models were proposed, and as outcome studies documenting the efficacy of the techniques were published. Meichenbaum (1977), for example, described the role of internalized speech in the development of emotional disorders. Based on earlier theoretical work by Luria (1961) and his student, Vygotsky (1962), Meichenbaum's techniques for "self-instructional training" via the rehearsal of "self-statements," modeling, and self-reinforcement have proven particularly useful in treating depressed or impulsive children.

Bandura (1969, 1977a, 1977b) is perhaps best known for developing social learning models of anxiety and aggression and for identifying the central importance of perceptions of "self-efficacy" or personal competence in guiding human behavior.

In reformulations of traditional behavioral theory, a number of authors argued that human behavior is mediated not only by environmental antecedents and contingencies but also by an individual's beliefs and perceptions. The now familiar "ABC" model of the relationships between "*Antecedent Events*," "*Beliefs*," "*Behavior*," and "*Consequences*" for the individual proposed by Albert Ellis (1962, 1979, 1985; Ellis & Harper, 1961) suggested that neurotic or maladaptive behaviors are learned and are directly related to irrational beliefs that people hold about events in their lives. Ellis developed a typology of common cognitive distortions or errors, as well as a number of directive therapeutic techniques for changing them. His model assumes that by identifying and changing unrealistic or irrational beliefs, it is possible to alter one's behavioral or emotional reactions to events. As irrational beliefs are often tightly held and long-standing in nature, highly focused and, at times, confrontationally expressed interventions are necessary to dispute them. His therapeutic approach is active and pragmatic. Although the basic tenets of rational–emotional therapy (RET) have not, as yet, been subjected to extensive empirical scrutiny (Haaga & Davison, 1993), his clinical techniques for challenging irrational beliefs are now widely used. In developing a behavioral model of depression, Seligman (1974, 1975) proposed that individuals become depressed when they come to believe that they are unable to control important outcomes in their life (including both positive or reinforcing events and negative events or punishments). This "learned helplessness" model of depression was subsequently refined by Abramson, Seligman, and Teasdale (1978) in an "attributional reformulation" of the theory. The model has generated a great deal of empirical interest (Sweeney, Anderson, & Bailey, 1986; Peterson & Seligman, 1984; Abramson, Alloy, & Metalsky, 1988; Alloy, Abramson, Metalsky, & Hartlage, 1988; Abramson, Metalsky, & Alloy, 1989) and suggests that attributions made by depressed patients about the causes of events may be an important target of therapy.

Rehm (1977) proposed a cognitive-behavioral model of depressive disorders focusing on deficits in "self-regulation." Specifically, he suggested that depressed individuals manifest impaired self-monitoring (they selectively attend to negative events, and to the immediate rather than the delayed consequences of their behavior), self-evaluation (they are overly self-critical and tend to make inappropriate attributions about their responsibility for negative events), and self-reinforcement (they do not tend to reward themselves for their successes, and can be highly self-punitive when they fail to meet their goals). Rehm's model extended earlier behavioral self-regulation models (Kanfer, 1971) and is clinically useful in that it directs clinicians' attention to specific cognitive and behavioral problems experienced by depressed patients (Fuchs & Rehm, 1977).

EVIDENCE FOR THE EFFECTIVENESS OF COGNITIVE THERAPY

Does cognitive therapy work? The results of empirical outcome studies have generally been both supportive and promising (Simon & Fleming, 1985). A number of controlled studies have been published during recent years supporting the utility of cognitive therapy for treating depression among adults (Hollon & Najavits, 1988). A meta-analysis of 28 studies completed by Dobson (1989) indicated a greater degree of change for cognitive therapy in comparison to a waiting-list or no-treatment control, pharmacotherapy, behavior therapy, or other types of psychotherapies. Moreover, the results of several studies suggest that relapse rates after cognitive therapy are lower than with antidepressant medications (Evans, Hollon, DeRubeis, & Piasecki, 1992; Hollon, 1990; Hollon, Shelton, & Loosen, 1991; Murphy, Simons, Wetzel, & Lustman, 1984), and that cognitive therapy may have prophylactic effects in preventing a recurrence of depression after the completion of treatment (Beck, Hollon, Young, Bedrosian, & Budenz, 1985; Blackburn,

Eunson, & Bishop, 1986; Kovacs, Rush, Beck, & Hollon, 1981). It should be acknowledged that psychotherapy outcome research can be quite difficult. There is a range of methodological, conceptual, and statistical problems that limit our confidence in outcome studies and meta-analytic reviews (Crits-Christoph, 1992; Garfield & Bergin, 1986). Nonetheless, recent findings regarding the effectiveness of cognitive therapy (and other forms of individual psychotherapy) have been encouraging.

Clinical reports suggest that cognitive therapy and medications can be used together (Wright, 1987, 1992; Wright & Schrodt, 1989). Contrary to expectation, cognitive therapy appears to be effective in addressing "biological" or endogenous symptoms of depression (such as insomnia, loss of appetite, and decreased libido) and has been found useful in treating patients with low IQs and low socioeconomic status patients (Blackburn, Bishop, Glen, Walley, & Christie, 1981; Blackburn et al., 1986; Williams & Moorey, 1989). Cognitive therapy also appears to be effective in treating panic disorder (Beck, Sokol, Clark, Berchick, & Wright, 1992; Sokol, Beck, Greenberg, Berchick, & Wright, 1989) and generalized anxiety disorder (Butler, Fennell, Robson, & Gelder, 1991).

ASSUMPTIONS OF COGNITIVE THERAPY

Like behavioral, psychodynamic, and systemic models of psychotherapy, cognitive therapy might best be described as a "school of thought" rather than a single theory. Cognitive models might usefully be characterized along a continuum ranging from behaviorally oriented rationalism to radical constructivism. Although these approaches are conceptually somewhat distinct, they share a number of fundamental assumptions (Freeman &

Reinecke, 1993). The basic assumptions of cognitive therapy are as follows:

1. The way individuals construe or interpret events and situations mediates how they subsequently feel and behave. Cognitions are postulated to exist in a transactional relationship with affect and behavior and with their consequent effect on events in the individual's environment. As such, human functioning is the product of an ongoing interaction between specific, related "person variables" (beliefs and cognitive processes, emotions, and behavior) and environmental variables. These variables influence one another in a reciprocal manner over the course of time. None, as a result, is viewed as "primary" or a "first cause." Rather, each is seen as both an initiator and a product of a transactional process.

2. This interpretation of events is active and ongoing. The construing of events allows individuals to derive or abstract a sense of meaning from their experiences and permits them to understand events with the goal of establishing their "personal environment" and of responding to events. Behavioral and emotional functioning, as a result, are seen as goal-directed and adaptive. Humans are viewed as "active . . . seekers, creators, and users of information" (Turk & Salovey, 1985).

3. Individuals develop idiosyncratic belief systems that guide behavior. Beliefs and assumptions influence an individual's perceptions and memories and lead the memories to be activated by specific stimuli or events. The individual is rendered sensitive to specific "stressors," including both external events and internal affective experiences. Beliefs and assumptions contribute to a tendency to selectively attend to and recall information that is consistent with the content of the belief system and to "overlook" information that is inconsistent with those beliefs.

4. These stressors consequently contribute to a functional impairment of an individual's cognitive processing and activate maladaptive, overlearned coping responses. A feed-forward system is established in which the activation of maladaptive coping behaviors contributes to the maintenance of aversive environmental events and the consolidation of the belief system. The person who believes, for example, that "the freeway is horribly dangerous" might drive in such a timid manner (20 miles per hour slower than traffic; stopping on the entrance ramp before merging) that he causes an accident, thus strengthening his belief in the danger of freeways and the importance of driving even more defensively.

5. The "cognitive specificity hypothesis" states that clinical syndromes and emotional states can be distinguished by the specific content of the belief system and the cognitive processes that are activated.

The foundation of cognitive therapy is the belief or meaning system. Our knowledge base provides us with a lens through which we interpret our experiences and a set of expectations that guide us in developing plans and goals. Our beliefs may be available to our conscious awareness (as in the case of "automatic thoughts") or may be implicit and unstated (as with schemata). Our use of the term "meaning system" suggests that our knowledge base and ways of processing information are organized and coherent. From this perspective, human behavior is both goal-directed and generative. It is based on rules and tacit beliefs that are elaborated and consolidated over the course of an individual's life. Cognitive processses, like emotional responses and behavioral skills are adaptive. Cognitive processes are seen as playing a central role in organizing our response both to daily events and to long-term challenges. Cognitive processes do not func-

tion independently of emotional regulation and behavioral action. Rather, they form an integrated adaptive system (Leventhal, 1984; R. Lazarus, 1991). Cognitive processes, like emotions and behavior, cannot be divorced from biological and social functioning. Cognitions are dependent on (and influence) the functions of the brain and are acquired in a social context. To understand cognition, then, one must understand action and the uses to which the knowledge will be put. To understand emotion, one must understand cognition and the structure that is imposed by a meaning system.

When we speak of "cognitions" we are not limiting ourselves to "automatic thoughts"—that is, to the thoughts and beliefs that comprise a person's moment-to-momemt stream of consciousness. Rather, cognitions include our perceptions, memories, expectations, standards, images, attributions, plans, goals, and tacit beliefs. Cognitive variables, then, include thoughts in our conscious awareness as well as inferred cognitive structures and cognitive processes (Kihlstrom, 1987, 1988; Meichenbaum & Gilmore, 1984; Safran, Vallis, Segal, & Shaw, 1986).

THE BASIC COGNITIVE THERAPY MODEL

The cognitive therapy model posits that three variables play a central role in the formation and maintenance of the common psychological disorders: the cognitive triad, schemata, and cognitive distortions (Beck et al., 1979; Freeman, Pretzer, Fleming, & Simon, 1990).

The Cognitive Triad

The construct of the cognitive triad was first proposed by Aaron Beck as a means of describing the negativistic thoughts and dreams of depressed inpatients (Beck, 1963). He observed that the thoughts of clinically depressed individuals typically include highly negative views of themselves, their world, and the future. The thoughts of anxious patients, in contrast, tend to differ from those of depressed individuals in each of these domains. They tend to view the world or others as potentially threatening and maintain a vigilant and wary orientation toward their future. The concept of the cognitive triad, then, serves as a useful framework for examining the automatic thoughts and tacit assumptions that patients describe. Virtually all patient problems can be related to maladaptive or dysfunctional beliefs in one of these three areas. When beginning therapy, as a result, it is often helpful to inquire as to your patient's thoughts in each of these areas. As each patient's beliefs and attitudes are quite personal, we should anticipate that the specific content of their thoughts regarding the self, their world, and the future will differ. By assessing the degree of contribution of thoughts in each of these areas to their distress, the therapist can begin to develop a conceptualization of their concerns.

Schemata

The concept of schemata plays an important role in cognitive models of emotional and behavioral problems. The concept was originally proposed by Kant and has more recently been employed by Piagetian psychologists and associative network theorists to refer to organized, tacit cognitive structures made up of abstractions or general knowledge about the attributes of a stimulus domain and the relationships among these attributes (Horowitz, 1991). As Segal (1988) stated, schemata incorporate "elements of past reactions and experience that form a relatively cohesive and persistent body of knowledge capable of guiding subsequent perception and appraisal." Stored in memory as generalizations from specific experiences and prototypes of specific cases, schemata provide focus and meaning for incoming information. Although not in our conscious awareness, they direct our attention to those elements of our day-to-day experience that are most important for our survival and adaptation. Schemata are seen, then, as influencing cognitive processes of attention, encoding, retrieval, and inference. Individuals tend to assimilate their experiences to preexisting schemata rather than to accommodate schemata to events that are unexpected or discrepant (Fiske & Taylor, 1984; Kovacs & Beck, 1978; Meichenbaum & Gilmore, 1984). That is, we tend to make sense of new experiences in terms of what we already believe, rather than by changing our preexisting views. As Paul Simon observed in his song "The Boxer," "A man hears what he wants to hear and disregards the rest."

In addition to representations and prototypic exemplars of specific events, schemata also incorporate emotions or "affective valences" related to the events. From this perspective, the distinction that is often drawn between "cold," cognitive approaches to psychotherapy and "warm," emotion-focused models is misguided. Rather, cognition and emotion are viewed as interacting components of an integrated, adaptive system (Leventhal, 1984). Events in one's life activate both ideational content and an associated affect. Cognitive schemata, as a result, might more accurately be described as cognitive-emotional structures (Bower, 1981; R. Lazarus, 1991; Lazarus & Folkman, 1984; Markus & Nurius, 1986; Mahoney, 1980, 1985; Greenberg & Safran, 1987; Turk & Salovey, 1985). As Flavell (1963) succinctly observed, cognitive and emotional reactions are "interdependent in functioning—essentially two sides of the same coin" (p. 80). This notion is clinically useful in that it guides us to examine a patient's thoughts when a strong emotion is expressed and to elicit a patient's feelings when they describe a strongly held, maladaptive belief.

Schemata are established as individuals abstract similarities between events. They are maintained, elaborated, and consolidated through processes of assimilation and are changed through accommodation to novel experiences (Rosen, 1985, 1989). These adaptive processes underlie the effectiveness of behavioral interventions. Behavioral exposure and training provide individuals with experiences and evidence that are inconsistent with their existing beliefs. Behavioral and emotional change is not seen as stemming from associatively based learning and reinforcement. Rather, it is due to the elaboration or adaptation of existing beliefs and the construction of alternative beliefs. In essence, to change an individual's feelings one must change the individual's thoughts or beliefs. As Kegan (1982) observed, behavioral and emotional change involve "an evolution of meaning" (p. 41).

In addition to beliefs about the world and our social relationships, we also possess relatively stable, unstated beliefs about ourselves. These "self-schemata" include cognitive generalizations that "serve as a template against which individuals perceive and encode information about themselves" (Turk & Salovey, 1985, p. 4). Like other schemata, self-schemata orient one's perception, encoding, retrieval, and utilization of information in a schema-consistent manner. This, along with the fact that they are often highly elaborated and associated with intense affect, can make them difficult to change (Fiske & Taylor, 1984, Mahoney, 1980; Markus, 1977; Turk & Salovey, 1985).

The precise content of schemata is not typically open to introspection or rational disputation. As Guidano and Liotti (1983) concisely observed, "self-knowledge is irrefutable." Nonetheless, basic categories for classifying events can be inferred from monitoring the types of information that are most frequently remembered and used (Kovacs & Beck, 1978; Meichenbaum & Gilmore, 1984).

Highly depressed persons, for example, often maintain schemata that "I'm defective" (self) and "people are unreliable" (social). While these beliefs may be tacit, in that they are not in their conscious awareness, they will, nonetheless, influence their perceptions, memories, and social interactions. Highly angry individuals, in contrast, may or may not believe that they are flawed or defective. They do, however, tend to believe that "the world is dangerous" (social), and that "people are malicious" (social). Although these beliefs may not be part of their daily thoughts, they strongly influence their behavior and emotional reactions toward others.

As noted, schemata are developed and consolidated over the course of an individual's infancy and childhood. While maladaptive schemata rarely stem from single, traumatic experiences, they possess adaptive value and may represent internalizations of ongoing or repetitious parental behavior. The parent who is unsupportive, punitive, or unpredictable toward his/her infant, for example, will likely behave in a similar manner during later years. The child's nascent beliefs that "my needs won't be met by others," "I am flawed or inadequate," and "I must submit to the control of others to avoid punishment" are initially represented nonverbally as subjective encodings of interactive experiences and are elaborated and consolidated by later events. They are reified as procedural memories, tacit beliefs, or representations about the self and the world—they become the "givens" of life.

These beliefs and information-processing styles are later activated by events that are similar to early experiences that surrounded their development (Ingram, 1984). As the activation of the memory spreads throughout the associative links of the schema's network, other memories, exemplars, expectations, and emotions related to the event will be activated. If the schemata are very elaborate, individuals become preoccupied with the event. As thoughts about personal weakness, hopelessness, and unremitting disappointment gain predominance, individuals become less active and socially engaged and their mood becomes increasingly depressed and hopeless. People's observations of themselves in this state only provide further evidence of their inadequacy and contribute to a worsening of their interpersonal problems.

Both behavior and emotions, from this perspective, are adaptive. Individuals behave in terms of outcomes that they desire and expectations that they maintain. Behavior is influenced by the intentions or goals that precede it, the plans or exemplars that accompany and direct it, and the criteria for successful completion against which it is compared. Our behavior, as a result, is responsive to feedback from our environment in that it is compared with a goal or an intended state on an ongoing basis and is adjusted to compensate for discrepancies. Human behavior, from this perspective is structured and organized. It is guided by tacit rules or cognitive structures.

Schemata play a central role in the expression of clinical disorders and are postulated to account for consistencies in behavior over time and for continuities in one's sense of self through one's life. These tacit rules, assumptions, and beliefs serve as the well-spring of the various cognitive distortions seen in patients. Schemata are often strongly held and are seen as essential for the person's safety, well-being, or existence. Schemata that are consolidated early in life and are powerfully reinforced by significant others, are often highly valent in the personality style of the individual (Beck, Freeman, & Associates, 1990; Layden, Newman, Freeman, & Byers, 1993; Young, 1991). Schemata, like other beliefs, rarely function in isolation. Like the cognitive distortions we discuss next, schemata occur in complex combinations and permutations.

Cognitive Distortions

There is a potentially infinite amount of information impinging upon us in our day-to-day lives. As a result, we must selectively attend to those events or stimuli that are most important to our adaptation and survival. Some events will be examined, recalled, and reflected upon; others will be overlooked, ignored, and forgotten as uninteresting or unimportant. As our attentional capacities and ability to process information are limited, some distortion of our experiences necessarily must occur. An individual's perceptions, memories, and thoughts can become distorted in a variety of adaptive and maladaptive ways. Some individuals may, for example, view life in an unrealistically positive way and perceive that they have control or influence that they may not, in reality, possess. They may take chances that most people would avoid—such as starting a new business or investing in a risky new stock. If successful, the individual is vindicated and may be envied for his/her *chutzpah*, or nerve. Such distortions can, however, be problematic in that they may lead individuals to take chances that may eventuate in great danger. They might, for example, experience massive chest pains and not consult a physician due to the belief that "nothing will happen to me. . . . I'm too young and healthy for a heart attack."

It is the negative or maladaptive distortions that typically become the focus of therapy. One task in treatment is to make these distortions manifest and to assist patients to recognize the impact of the distortions on their life. Distortions, as such, represent maladaptive ways of processing information and may become emblematic of particular styles of behaving or of certain clinical syndromes.

The distortions and patient styles are presented here in isolation for the sake of discussion. This is not meant to be a comprehensive list but rather is presented for illustrative purposes. Typical distortions and examples of the common clinical correlates include:

1. *Dichotomous thinking.* "Things are black or white"; "You're either with me or against me." At its extreme, this tendency toward "all-or-nothing" thinking is encountered in borderline and obsessive compulsive disorders.
2. *Mind reading.* "They probably think that I'm incompetent"; "I just know that they will disapprove." This processing style is common to avoidant and paranoid personality disorders.
3. *Emotional reasoning.* "Because I feel inadequate I am inadequate"; "Because I 'feel' uncomfortable, the world is dangerous"; "I'm feeling upset, so there must be something wrong." This distortion is common among individuals suffering from anxiety disorders and panic.
4. *Personalization.* "That comment wasn't just random, I know it was directed toward me"; "Problems always emerge when I'm in a hurry." At the extreme, this is also common in avoidant and paranoid personality disorders.
5. *Overgeneralization.* "Everything I do turns out wrong"; "It doesn't matter what my choices are, they always fall flat." At the extreme, this is common among depressed individuals.

6. *Catastrophizing.* "If I go to the party, there will be terrible consequences"; "I better not try because I might fail, and that would be awful"; "My heart's beating faster, it's got to be a heart attack." At the extreme, this distortion is characteristic of anxiety disorders, especially social anxiety, social phobia, and panic.
7. *"Should" statements.* "I should visit my family every time they want me to"; "They should do what I say because it is right." At the extreme, this is common in obsessive–compulsive disorders and among individuals who feel excessive guilt.
8. *Selective abstraction.* "The rest of the information doesn't matter. . . . This is the salient point"; "I've got to focus on the negative details, the positive things that have happened don't count." At the extreme, this is common in depression.

Other common cognitive distortions include "disqualifying the positive," "perfectionism," and "externalization of self-worth." Fallacies and irrational beliefs often center on the desire for control over events, the value of self-criticism, worrying, and ignoring problems and beliefs about fairness and stability in relationships.

THE PRACTICE OF THERAPY

An element common to the different cognitive-behavioral models is their shared emphasis on helping patients examine the manner in which they construe or understand themselves and their world (cognitions) and to experiment with new ways of responding (behavioral). By learning to understand the idiosyncratic ways in which they perceive themselves, the world, and their prospects for the future, patients can be helped to alter negative emotions and to behave more adaptively.

In practice, cognitive therapy includes all of the following:

- Is structured, active, and problem oriented.
- Is time limited and strategic.
- Employs a collaborative therapeutic relationship.
- Incorporates psychoeducational techniques.
- Assists in skill acquisition.
- Utilizes Socratic questioning.
- Is based on constructivist models of thought and behavior.
- Employs both coping and mastery models.

Perhaps the strongest elements of cognitive therapy are the *structure, focus,* and *problem orientation* of the model. Cognitive therapy attempts to identify specific, measurable goals and move quickly and directly into those areas that create the most difficultly for the patient. The approach is similar in this regard to contemporary short-term dynamic and interpersonal psychotherapy (Crits-Christoph & Barber, 1991).

Moreover, cognitive therapy is *strategic* and often *time limited.* The cognitive therapist views treatment as having a distinct beginning, middle, and end. Each phase of the treatment has specific goals (Beck et al., 1979). By keeping these objectives in mind, the patient's problems can be addressed in a systematic fashion.

Like other forms of psychotherapy, cognitive therapy attempts to ameliorate underlying processes that are maintaining an individual's distress. It differs from psychodynamic psychotherapy, however, in that it can be *psychoeducational* in nature and attempts to provide patients with skills for coping with feelings of anxiety, depression, anger, or guilt as they arise. It does not presume

to protect individuals from experiencing distress in the future. Anxiety, depression, and guilt can play an essential and adaptive role in people's lives. Cognitive therapy endeavors not to alleviate these emotions but to provide patient's with skills for understanding and managing them. Cognitive therapy incorporates both *mastery and coping* models of treatment.

One reason that individuals can experience difficulty coping with internal or external stimuli is a lack of basic skills. Cognitive and behavioral skills for regulating affect typically develop over the course of one's development through structured interactions with supportive caregivers. These skills include the ability to respond adaptively to depressogenic or anxiogenic thoughts, interpersonal skills that make it possible to cope in social situations, the ability to direct and maintain one's attention, and the ability to recognize negative emotions as they begin to emerge so that one might attend to their source and take appropriate action. An important component of cognitive therapy is to *enhance patients' skills* and sense of personal competence so that they can more effectively deal with the exigencies of life and thereby have a greater sense of control and self-efficacy. Social skills training, relaxation training, and anger control exercises are examples.

The Therapeutic Relationship in Cognitive Therapy

As Truax and Carkhuff (1964) observed, therapists who are "nonpossessively warm," empathetic, and genuine achieve greater gains than do those who are not. Cognitive therapy recognizes the central importance of these nonspecific relationship variables in facilitating change but views them as "necessary but not sufficient" for therapeutic improvement. That is, the development of a warm, empathic, and genuine relationship is not, in our view, necessarily accompanied by behavioral or emotional change.

It is proposed that the therapeutic relationship should be collaborative. The term "therapetic collaboration" is used frequently in cognitive therapy and refers to a specific form of patient–therapist relationship. The therapist is viewed as a "coinvestigator"—working with patients to make sense of their experiences and emotions by exploring their thoughts, images, and feelings with them. Guided Socratic questioning is often employed as a means of providing patients with an understanding of their thoughts and the ways their beliefs influence their feelings and actions. As Beck et al. (1979) have stated, "The therapeutic relationship is used not simply as *the* instrument to alleviate suffering but as a vehicle to facilitate a common effort in carrying out specific goals" (p. 54).

This understanding of the therapeutic relationship is also very different from that found in psychodynamic models of psychotherapy. The cognitive therapist does not serve as a blank screen onto which the patient's impulses and wishes are projected through the transferential relationship. Similarly, the cognitive therapist does not unquestioningly accept the objectivity of the patient's views and perspectives. Recognizing that cognitive and perceptual distortions may be at play, the cognitive therapist encourages patients to view their thoughts as an object and to rationally evaluate their validity and adaptiveness. Dysfunctional or maladaptive thoughts are viewed as "hypotheses" that require empirical testing.

The therapist's directiveness can be adjusted over the course of treatment depending on the needs of the patient. With a highly depressed patient who is immobilized by psychomotor retardation and feelings of hoplessness, for example, the therapist may want to adopt a more as-

sertive, directive stance. Behavioral interventions serving to "activate" the patient may be introduced. In contrast, a less directive stance might be employed in working with a highly passive and dependent patient. The man who states, "you're the doctor . . . just tell me what to do," may feel unable to cope with day-to-day problems on his own and so seeks support and guidance from others. In his case one may wish to shift to him a greater proportion of the responsibility for identifying specific problems, identifying and evaluating automatic thoughts and developing homework assignments. Attempts might be made to encourage him to take responsibility for the direction of the therapy and discuss with him his passivity toward the therapist and toward others in his life.

The transference relationship also plays an important role in cognitive therapy (Safran & Segal, 1990). The patient's behavior toward the therapist may reflect the activation of schemata (as might the therapist's behavioral and emotional responses to the patient). The patient's experiences during the therapy hour can, as a consequence, serve as evidence to dispute tacit beliefs. Moreover, schemata activated in the therapeutic relationship can be, in many ways, similar to those activated in the patient's relationships with others. The therapist works, through the use of Socratic questioning, to develop greater awareness in patients of their thoughts, feelings and perceptions—including those about the therapeutic relationship.

Patients' patterns of interaction with others are often recapitulated in their relationship with their therapist. The disorganization, anger, confusion, anxiety, avoidance, envy, helplessness, fear, resentment, and attraction that they exhibit toward the therapist need not be in reaction to specific behaviors on the part of the therapist. In this sense, the cognitive construct of schema activation is similar to the psychodynamic concept of transference. However, cognitive theory does not presume that the elaboration and interpretation of the transference is the principle mechanism of change in therapy, or that patterns of interaction apparent in the therapeutic relationship represent a recapitulation of earlier mother–infant interactions.

Although there may be fundamental similarities between the processes of change in psychotherapy and those in development, cognitive therapy does not assume that therapeutic change is based on a reconstruction of developmental experiences in the context of a supportive therapeutic relationship.

Assessment and Treatment Planning

As a precondition for therapeutic change to occur, it is essential for a trusting therapeutic collaboration to be established. The first goal in cognitive therapy, then, is for rapport to be established through empathic, active listening. Patients need to feel that they have been heard, and that their concerns have been understood and acknowledged by their therapist. As is characteristic of other forms of psychotherapy, the cognitive therapist encourages and facilitates patient speech, promotes the experience of affect in the therapy session, identifies recurrent patterns in the patients behavior and thoughts, points out the use of maladaptive coping strategies or distortions, and draws attention to feelings and thoughts that the patient may find disturbing. Before specific interventions can be made, however, a careful review of their developmental, familial, social, occupational, educational, medical, and psychiatric history should be made. These data are essential in helping to turn a patient's presenting complaints into a working problem list and a treatment conceptualization (Persons, 1989). The establishment of a discrete problem list helps both patient and therapist have an idea of where the therapy is going, a general time frame, and a means of assessing therapeutic progress. Having agreed upon a problem list and a focus for therapy, an agenda is set for each session.

The review of the patient's feelings and experiences since the last session flows seamlessly into the development of an agenda. The identification of an agenda item leads directly into an examination of the patient's emotions and thoughts in a recent situation.

The structuring of sessions through the establishment of an agenda helps to maintain the strategic focus of the therapy. Specific problems or issues can be identified so that the therapist and patient can make the most efficient use of their time. Setting an agenda at the beginning each session allows both patient and therapist to bring out issues of concern for discussion. Moreover, it allows for a continuity between sessions so that sessions are not individual events but rather part of a cohesive whole. A typical agenda might include:

1. Discussion of events during the past week and feelings about the prior therapy session.
2. A review of self-report scales filled out by the patient prior to the session.
3. A review of agenda items remaining from the previous session.
4. A review of the patient's homework. The patient's success or problems in doing the homework are discussed, as are the results of the assignment.
5. Current problems are put on the agenda. This might involve the development of specific skills (e.g., social skills, relaxation training, or assertiveness skills) or the examination of dysfunctional thoughts.

6. A review of what has been accomplished during the current session. This gives the therapist an opportunity to help the patient to clarify the goals and accomplishments of the session. A homework assignment for the next session can then be developed and the session given a closure. Finally, the patient can be asked for his/her response to the session.

Assessment Techniques

Identifying specific problems and objectively evaluating the effectiveness of interventions made to alleviate them is an essential part of cognitive psychotherapy. Assessment instruments, including self-report questionaires, behavior rating scales, and clinician rating scales, can be quite useful in this regard.

A large number of well-validated rating scales have been developed during recent years, and it would be beyond the scope of this chapter to review them. There are several, however, that we have found to be particularly useful and that deserve note. When depression is a primary concern, the Beck Depression Inventory (BDI) is among the most useful tools available to the therapist (Beck, Ward, Mendelson, Mock, & Erbaugh, 1961; Beck & Steer, 1987). It is among the most widely used self-report measures for depression in the world and is well-accepted as reliable and valid measure of depressed mood. The administration of a self-report depression scale such as the the BDI prior to each session can provide objective data regarding therapeutic progress and can assist in identifying the specific focus of a patient's depression. The scale was designed to asssess the full range of symptoms associated with the syndrome of depression, including affective, behavioral, cognitive, motivational, and vegetative components. Representative items include:

"I do not feel like a failure"; "I feel I have failed more than the average person"; "As I look back on my life, all I see is a lot of failures"; "I feel I am a complete failure as a person"; "I have not lost interest in other people"; "I am less interested in other people than I used to be"; "I have lost most of my interest in other people;" and "I have lost all of my interest in other people."

When anxiety is a target symptom, the Beck Anxiety Inventory (BAI), a 21-item self-report symptom checklist designed to measure the severity of anxiety-related symptoms (Beck, Epstein, Brown, & Steer, 1988), the Zung Anxiety Scale, or the State–Trait Anxiety Scale may be employed. Like the BDI, these measures provide a useful, objective measure of the patient's general level of anxiety and can be used both quantitatively and qualitatively as a diagnostic aid.

The Hopelessness Scale (HS) is a brief and highly useful measure of pessimism (Beck, Weissman, Lester, & Trexler, 1974). As levels of hopelessness are often highly correlated with suicidal potential, the HS can be used in conjunction with a measure of depression as a means of estimating suicide risk (Beck, Brown, & Steer, 1989; Drake & Cotton, 1986; Freeman & Reinecke, 1993). Moreover, pessimistic patients often tend to believe that it is not possible for problems in their lives to be resolved and feel personally unable to influence important events. They feel, in short, that they are "ineffective." Given these perceptions and beliefs, such individuals often find it difficult to summon up motivation to participate actively in their treatment. And why should they? They do not perceive that it will be of help. Their hopelessness, then, interferes with their ability to progress. An initial focus of treatment, as a result, might be on the beliefs underlying their hopelessness. As they learn new ways of coping, experience greater self-efficacy, and perceive that change is possible, their level of hopelessness will decrease.

Assessment of Vulnerability Factors

These are circumstances, situations, or deficits that have the effect of decreasing the patient's ability to effectively cope with life stressors, lose options, or fail to see available options. These factors work to lower the patient's threshold or tolerance for life stress situations, and alone or in combination may serve to increase the patient's suicidal thinking or actions, lower threshold for anxiety stimuli, or increase the patient's vulnerability to depressogenic thoughts and situations (Freeman & Simon, 1989). These include:

1. Acute illness
2. Chronic illness
3. Deterioration of health
4. Hunger
5. Anger
6. Fatigue
7. Loneliness
8. Major life stress or loss of an important support
9. Poor problem-solving ability
10. Alcohol, substance abuse, or other maladaptive coping
11. Chronic pain
12. New life circumstance

An assessment of these factors allows for a more comprehensive understanding of experiences that may be exacerbating a patient's distress, and assists in developing a more specific treatment plan. Interventions can be directed toward increasing supports, alleviating specific stressors, and improving coping skills.

Diagnosis and Treatment Planning

An initial step in developing a treatment plan involves the establishment of a working conceptualization of the pa-

tient's problems. This conceptualization will be based on family and developmental histories, test data, interview material, and reports of previous therapists or other professionals.

The conceptualization must meet several criteria. It must (1) be useful, (2) be parsimonious, (3) be theoretically coherent, (4) explain past behavior, (5) make sense of present behavior, and (6) be able to predict future behavior. The conceptualization process begins with the compilation of a specific, behaviorally based problem list, which is then prioritized. A particular problem may be the primary focus of therapy because of its debilitating effect on the individual. In another case, one may focus on the simplest problem first, thereby giving the patient a sense of confidence in the therapy itself as well as practice in basic problem solving. In a third case, the initial focus might be on a "keystone" problem—that is, a problem whose solution will cause a ripple effect in solving other problems. Having set out the treatment goals with the patient, the therapist can begin to develop strategies and the interventions that will help put them into effect.

Cognitive therapy is proactive in that it endeavors to anticipate problems that may arise and provides patients with skills to cope with them. As such, the therapist must develop hypotheses about what reinforces and maintains dysfunctional thinking and behavior. As noted earlier, beliefs are held with varying degrees of strength. In developing a conceptualization of a particular problem, then, it is often useful to discuss with patients the strength with which they believe key automatic thoughts or assumptions. Automatic thoughts containing the phrase "I am _____" can be particularly difficult to change in that they are often regarded as part of the self. As one young woman, whose frequent and vociferous complaining had led her to be fired at work and to be dropped from the lead role in a theatrical production, stated, "I know I make people defensive . . . but it's just who I am, and they have to accept me for that. . . . I'm just identifying problems I see for people who are the authorities, so they have to change them. . . . I *can't* change who I am, even though I know I shoot myself with this. . . . Even back in high school they voted me 'most likely to complain'."

Chronic behavioral and emotional patterns are often seen by patients as "part of me." Like the woman described above, they readily verbalize "this is who I am and this is the way I have always been." Challenges to these core beliefs are often accompanied by anxiety, anger, or avoidance. As such, challenges to these tightly held beliefs should stem from careful, guided discovery based on collaboration rather than on direct confrontation or disputation.

Specific Interventions

A wide range of cognitive and behavioral techniques can be used to identify and to then question both cognitive distortions and the schemata that underlie them. These techniques are taught to the patients to help them respond in more functional ways. The precise mix of cognitive and behavioral techniques used will depend on the patient's abilities, the therapist's skills, the level of pathology, and the specific treatment goals. When working with severely debilitated patients, for example, the initial goals of treatment might focus upon assisting the patient with behavioral self-help tasks. For example, graded task assignments can be used with great success. Starting at the bottom of a hierarchy of difficulty and moving through successively more difficult tasks provides patients with a greater sense of personal efficacy.

Pharmacotherapy may be an important adjunct in the therapy program.

Contrary to popular myth, cognitive therapy and pharmacotherapy are not mutually exclusive but can be integrated into an effective treatment program (Wright & Schrodt, 1989; Wright, 1987, 1992). In addition to its value in modifying dysfunctional thoughts or maladaptive behavior that contribute to patients' feelings of dysphoria, anxiety, or anger, cognitive therapy can also be used to identify and change maladaptive beliefs about taking medications. Such thoughts as "this just proves I'm crazy" and "this means there must be something wrong with my brain" can be quite distressing and can contribute to poor compliance with the treatment regime. Were pharmacotherapy used alone, these beliefs might not be addressed. Antidepressant medications typically take several weeks before improvement is seen. Cognitive therapy, however, can be helpful in a short period and so can provide highly depressed or anxious patients with a sense of relief before the medications can be titrated to an effective dose. Moreover, as Wright (1992) observed, cognitive therapy can "arm the patient with problem-solving techniques that can maximize the chances of good psychosocial functioning . . . and can reduce the risk of non-adherence to a long term pharmacotherapy regimen."

Although the empirical evidence is equivocal, clinical experience suggests that pharmacotherapy may be useful in alleviating biologically based symptoms of depression, such as insomnia, fatigue, and impaired concentration, and so may help the severely depressed patient to participate more actively in the therapy process. The mechanisms of therapeutic change, however, are not well understood. In a provocative early study of pharmacotherapy and cognitive therapy, Simons, Garfield, and Murphy (1984) found that therapeutic improvement following the administration of tricyclic antidepressant medications was accompanied by changes in dysfunctional thoughts. Medications are clearly indicated in combination with psychotherapy for patients with bipolar disorder or psychosis and for patients who are so depressed that they are unresponsive to verbal or behavioral interventions.

Cognitive Techniques

In practice, cognitive therapy may be defined as a set of techniques designed to alleviate emotional distress by directly modifying the dysfunctional cognitions that accompany them. As such, any intervention or technique that alters a patient's perceptions or beliefs might be viewed as "cognitive." The number of techniques that are potentially available is virtually infinite.

A number of years ago, for example, David Burns reported the case of a patient who was disabled by recurring panic attacks. She feared that any exertion whatsoever would trigger a fatal heart attack and so became quite sensitive to her physical state and assiduously avoided all physical activities. As part of her therapy, Burns asked her to stand and raise her hands over her head, which she did with no difficulty. He then requested that she lower them and raise them again. No problem. Within minutes the patient was vigorously doing jumping jacks in his office and recognized that the sensation of her heart pounding need not signify an impending heart attack. The frequency of her panic attacks subsequently declined. While we are not presenting jumping jacks as a model for cognitive therapy, the value of this case example still obtains. The effective cognitive therapist is able to provide patients with experiences in a creative, flexible manner that will refute their maladaptive beliefs.

There are a relatively small number of techniques that have been found to be useful with a wide range of problems.

As with other models of psychotherapy, it is necessary for the skilled cognitive therapist to be aware of the range of available interventions and to be able to skillfully move between various techniques. Therapists will be able to teach these skills to their patients so that they can "become their own therapist." Although these techniques have been described in detail elsewhere (Beck et al., 1979; Freeman et al., 1990; McMullin, 1986; Persons, 1989; Stern & Drummond, 1991), we briefly present them here.

1. *Idiosyncratic meaning.* The meanings attached to the patient's words and thoughts can be explored. The patient who believes, for example, that he will be "devastated" by his spouse leaving might be asked, in a supportive manner, what he means by "devastated." He may be asked to reflect upon exactly how he would be devastated and then on the ways he might be spared from "devastation." All words carry an idiosyncratic or personal meaning. The exploration of these meanings models the need for active listening skills, increased communication, and the value of examining one's assumptions.

2. *Questioning the evidence.* Individuals can be taught the value of questioning the evidence that they are using to maintain and strengthen their beliefs. This would involve systematically examining evidence in support of a belief, as well as evidence that is inconsistent with it. An examination of the reliability of the sources of the information might be made, and the individual might come to recognize that he/she has ignored important pieces of data that are inconsistent with the individual's dysfunctional views.

3. *Reattribution.* Patients often take responsibility for events and situations that are only minimally attributable to them. The therapist can help the patient distrib-

ute responsibility among all relevant parties.

4. *Rational responding.* One of the most powerful techniques in cognitive therapy involves helping the patient to challenge dysfunctional thinking. The Daily Record of Dysfunctional Thoughts is an ideal format for testing dysfunctional thoughts. The process begins with patients identifying the thought, emotion, or situation that causes them difficulty. If the patient presents with an emotional issue (i.e., "I'm very sad"), the therapist needs to inquire as to the situations that might engender the emotion and the attendant thoughts. If the patient presents with a thought (i.e., "I'm a loser"), the therapist needs to ascertain the feelings and the situation. Finally, if the patient presents a situation (i.e., "My husband left me"), the therapist would endeavor to determine the thoughts and emotions that precede, accompany, and follow the event. Statements such as "I feel like a loser" need to be reframed as thoughts and the emotions that are a concomitant of the thought elicited. After the dysfunctional automatic thought has been identified, a "rational response" can be developed. Rational responding involves four steps: (a) a systematic examination of evidence supporting and refuting the belief, (b) the development of an alternative, more adaptive explanation or belief, (c) decatastrophizing the belief, and (d) identifying specific behavioral steps that can be taken to cope with the problem.

5. *Examining options and alternatives.* This involves working with patients to generate additional options. Suicidal patients, for example, often see their options and alternatives as so limited that death becomes a viable solution. Patients can be assisted to develop, and then to evaluate, alternative solutions and avenues.

6. *Decatastrophizing.* This involves helping patients to evaluate whether they are overestimating the nature of a situa-

tion. Patients can be helped to see that the consequences of their life actions are not "all or nothing" and, thereby, are less catastrophic. It is important that this technique be used with great gentleness and care so that the patient does not feel ridiculed by the therapist. Questions that might be asked of the patient include, "What is the worst thing that can happen," or "And if it does occur, what would be so terrible?"

7. *Fantasized consequences.* Patients are asked to describe a fantasy about a feared situation, their images of it, and the attendant concerns. In verbalizing their fantasies, patients can often see the irrationality of their ideas. If the fantasized consequences are realistic, the therapist can work with the patient to assess the danger and develop coping strategies.

8. *Advantages and disadvantages.* By asking the patient to examine both the advantages and the disadvantages of both sides of an issue, a broader perspective can be achieved. This basic problem-solving technique is useful in gaining a perspective and then plotting a reasonable course of action.

9. *Turning adversity to advantage.* There are times that a seeming disaster can be used to advantage. Losing one's job can be, in some cases, the entry point to a new job or career. Having a deadline imposed may be seen as oppressive and unfair but may be used as a motivator. There is a balancing that puts their experience into a perspective.

10. *Guided association/discovery.* In contrast to the psychodynamic technique of free association, guided association or discovery involves the therapist working with the patient to connect ideas, thoughts, and images by means of Socratic questioning. Also referred to as the "vertical" or "downward arrow" technique, the therapist provides conjunctions to patients' verbalizations and so encourages them to identify a series of automatic thoughts. The use of state-

ments like "And then what?" or "And that means, what?" allows the therapist to guide patients toward an understanding of themes within their stream of automatic thoughts and to identify possible underlying schemata.

11. *Use of exaggeration or paradox.* There seems to be room at the extremes for only one position. By taking an idea to its extreme, the therapist can often help to move the patient to a more moderate or adaptive position vis-à-vis a particular belief. Given their sensitivity to criticism, however, some patients may experience paradoxical interventions as making light of their problems. As such, the therapist who chooses to use the paradoxical or exaggeration techniques must have (a) a strong working relationship with the patient, (b) good timing, and (c) the good sense to know when to back away from the technique. The use of paradox in cognitive therapy has been described in some detail by McMullin (1986).

12. *Scaling.* For those patients who see things as all or nothing, the technique of scaling along a continuum can be quite useful. Scaling of emotions, for example, can lead patients to gain a sense of distance and perspective. A depressed patient who believes that he is "incompetent," for example, might first be asked to rate the strength of his belief in this statement on a 100-point scale. He can then be asked to establish anchor points for his belief—identifying the "most incompetent person in the world" (0) and the "most highly skilled and competent person in the world" (100). When asked to rerate himself on the "competence scale" he has developed, he typically would recognize that he is neither incompetent nor the most competent individual, but that, like others, he has strengths and weaknesses and has at least a modicum of competence.

13. *Externalization of voices.* Most individuals, when asked to reflect on their thoughts, can "hear" the voice of their thoughts in their head. When patients are asked to externalize these thoughts, they are in a better position to deal with these "voices" and thoughts. By having the therapist take the part of the dysfunctional voice, the patient can gain experience in responding adaptively. The therapist might begin, for example, by modeling rational responses to patients' verbalizations of their dysfunctional thoughts. After modeling a more adaptive or functional voice, the therapist can, in a graded manner, become an increasingly more difficult and dysfunctional voice for the patient. With practice, patients come to recognize the dysfunctional nature of their thoughts and can become better able to respond adaptively to them.

14. *Self-instruction.* Meichenbaum (1977) and Rehm (1977) developed an extensive battery of self-instruction techniques that are useful in working with depressed or impulsive patients. Patients can be taught, for example, to offer direct self-instructions for more adaptive behavior as well as counterinstructions to avoid dysfunctional behavior.

15. *Thought stopping.* Given the relationship between thoughts and mood, maladaptive automatic thoughts can have a "snowball effect" in that even mild feelings of dysphoria or anxiety can bias subsequent cognitive processes, leading the individual to feel continually more distraught. What started as a small and insignificant problem can easily gather weight, speed, and momentum. Thought stopping is best used when the negative emotional state is first recognized and is less effective after the process has proceeded. Anxious patients, for example, can be taught to picture a stop sign or "hear a bell" at the outset of an anxiety attack. This momentary break in the process can allow them to reflect on the origin of the anxiety and to introduce more powerful cognitive tech-

niques (such as rational responding) before their anxiety escalates.

16. *Distraction.* This technique is especially helpful for patients with anxiety problems. Because it is almost impossible to maintain two thoughts simultaneously, anxiogenic thoughts generally preclude more adaptive thinking. Conversely, a focused thought distracts from the anxiogenic thoughts. By having patients focus on complex counting, addition or subtraction, they are rather easily distracted from other thoughts. Having the patient count to 200 by 13s, for example, can be very effective, as can reading a page of text upside down. When outdoors, counting cars, people wearing the color red, or any cognitively engaging task will suffice. Distraction or refocusing of attention may be achieved by focusing on some aspect of the environment, engaging in mental exercise or imagery, or initiating physical activity. While this technique is a short-term technique, it is useful to allow patients the time to establish some degree of control over their thinking. This time can then be used to utilize other cognitive techniques.

17. *Direct disputation.* There are times when direct disputation is helpful. When there is an imminent risk to the patient, as in the case of suicide, direct disputation might be considered. As these approaches are, in some regard, noncollaborative, the therapist risks becoming embroiled in a power struggle or argument with the patient. Disputation of core beliefs may, in fact, engender passive resistance and a passive–aggressive response. Disputation, argument, or debate must be used carefully, judiciously, and with skill.

18. *Labeling of distortions.* Fear of the unknown and "fear of fear" (Foa, Steketee, & Young, 1984) can be important concerns for anxious patients. The more that can be done to identify the nature

and content of the dysfunctional thoughts and to help label the types of distortions that patients utilize, the less frightening the entire process becomes. Patient can be taught to identify and label specific distortions during the therapy session and can be asked to practice the exercise at home. This can be accomplished with the aid of a "thought record" on which patients record their automatic thoughts on an ongoing basis during the day, or with a counter with which they simply record the frequency of the thoughts.

19. *Developing replacement imagery.* Many anxious patients experience vivid images during times of stress. Inasmuch as their anxiety may be exacerbated by these images, patients can be helped by training in the development of "coping images." For example, rather than imagining failure, defeat, or embarrassment, the therapist assists the patient to develop a new, effective coping image. Once well practiced, patients can substitute these images outside the therapy session.

20. *Bibliotherapy.* Several excellent books can be assigned as readings for homework. These books can be used to educate patients about the basic cognitive therapy model, emphasize specific points made in the session, introduce new ideas for discussion at future sessions, or offer alternative ways of thinking about patients' concerns. Some helpful books include *Love Is Never Enough* (Beck, 1989), *Feeling Good* (Burns, 1980), *Woulda, Coulda, Shoulda* (Freeman & DeWolfe, 1989), and *The 10 Dumbest Mistakes That Smart People Make* (Freeman & DeWolfe, 1992).

Behavioral Techniques

The goals in using behavioral techniques within the context of cognitive therapy are manifold. The first goal is to utilize direct behavioral strategies and techniques to test dysfunctional thoughts and assumptions. By having the patient try feared or avoided behaviors, old ideas can be directly challenged. A second use of behavioral techniques is to practice new, more adaptive behaviors or coping strategies. Specific behaviors can be introduced in the office and then practiced at home. As with cognitive homework assignments, the therapist will want to review the thoughts and emotions experienced by the patient as they attempted the behavioral assignment with them. Commonly employed behavioral interventions include:

1. *Activity scheduling*. Along with rational responding, activity scheduling is, perhaps, the most ubiquitous technique in the therapist's armamentarium. For patients who are feeling overwhelmed, the activity schedule can be used to plan more effective time use. The activity schedule is both a retrospective tool to assess past time utilization and a prospective tool to help plan better time use.

2. *Mastery and pleasure ratings*. The activity schedule can also be used to assess and plan activities that offer patients a sense of personal efficacy or mastery and pleasure. The greater the mastery and pleasure, the lower the rates of anxiety and depression. By discovering the low- or high-anxiety activities, plans can be made to increase the former and decrease the latter.

3. *Social skills or assertiveness training*. If patients lack specific social skills, it is incumbent upon the therapist to either help them to gain the skills or to make a referral for skills training. The skill acquisition may involve anything from teaching patients how to properly shake hands to practicing conversational skills.

4. *Graded tasks assignments*. Graded task assignments involve a series of small sequential steps that lead to the desired goal. By setting out a task and then arranging the necessary steps in a hierarchy, patients can be helped to make reasonable progress with a minimum of stress. As patients attempt each step, the therapist can be available for support and guidance.

5. *Behavioral rehearsal/role-playing*. The therapy session is the ideal place to practice many behaviors. The therapist can serve as teacher and guide offering direct feedback on performance. The therapist can monitor the patient's performance, offer suggestions for improvement and model new behaviors. In addition, anticipated and actual road blocks can be identified and worked on in the session. There can be extensive rehearsal before the patient attempts the behavior *in vivo*.

6. *In vivo exposure*. There are times that therapy must take place outside the consulting room. While often time-consuming, such *in vivo* therapy can be quite powerful. A therapist might, for example, accompany his/her patient into a feared situation, such as a supermarket or crowded shopping center. As noted earlier, the objective of *in vivo* exposure is not solely to allow patients to "habituate" to the feared setting but to provide them with incontrovertible behavioral evidence that is inconsistent with their dysfunctional beliefs.

Example: A 29-year-old graduate student was unable to complete her degree because she feared meeting with a professor to discuss an incomplete grade she had received in a course. She was quite convinced that the professor would "scream at her" and had been unable to complete a homework assignment to call the professor's secretary to arrange a meeting. An *in vivo* task was agreed on in which she called the professor from her therapist's office. Her thoughts and feelings before, during, and after the call were carefully examined. As might be expected, the professor was quite glad to hear from his former student and was pleased to accept her final paper. The origins of her beliefs about how others feel toward her were then reviewed and she was able to see that these beliefs were both maladaptive and erroneous.

7. Relaxation training. Anxious patients often can profit from relaxation training inasmuch as the anxiety response and relaxation are mutually exclusive. Relaxation training can be taught in the office and then practiced by the patient at home. Although relaxation tapes can be purchased from a number of publishers, we have found that therapists can easily tailor a tape for patients that incorporates images that the latter find most relaxing and that focus on symptoms that are most distressing to them.

Homework

No therapy takes place solely within the confines of the consulting room. Insights and skills gained within the therapeutic milieu will, by their nature, be consolidated and employed in the patient's day-to-day life. This consolidation process, while implicit in many models of psychotherapy, is explicitly addressed and exploited in cognitive therapy. It is important for the patient to understand that the extension of the therapy work to the nontherapy hours allows for a greater therapeutic focus and for more rapid gains. As Burns and Auerbach (1992) observed in their review of factors associated with improvement in therapy, "differences in homework compliance are significantly correlated with recovery from depression."

Homework assignments can be either cognitive or behavioral. They might involve having the patient complete an activity schedule (an excellent homework for the first session), complete several "daily thought records," or try new behaviors. The homework assignment should, when appropriately assigned,

flow directly from the session material. It is simply an extension of the therapy hour into the patient's daily life. The more meaningful and collaborative the homework, the greater the likelihood of patient compliance with the therapeutic regimen. If completed homework assignments are not regularly reviewed as part of the session, the patient will quickly come to believe they are unimportant and will stop doing them.

Even assignments that are failed can be useful. A patient with social anxiety, for example, might anticipate rejection were he to talk to an unfamiliar person. A reasonable assignment might be to "talk to the salesclerks at the 7–11 where you buy your coffee each morning, and note their reactions." If the clerks respond positively to him (as one might expect they would) he will have an experience that is inconsistent with his beliefs and will begin to develop a new social skill. Suppose, however, he is not able to talk to the clerk but instead runs from the store, shrieking as the hot coffee spills down his shirt. All is not lost. In his recounting the episode in therapy we will gain access to that most important of information—his "hot cognitions"—the automatic thoughts that occur while he is anxious. These, in turn, are submitted to rational refutation and become further grist for the therapeutic mill.

Common Errors in Conducting Cognitive Therapy

To paraphrase Francis Bacon, it is easier to know a bad cake than it is to bake a good one. So it is with psychotherapy—it is often easier to identify shortcomings or difficulties in a therapy session than it is avoid them. There are, nonetheless, a number of common errors made in conducting cognitive therapy which can be readily addressed. These include:

- Inadequate socialization of the patient to the model.
- Failure to develop a specific problem list.
- Not assigning appropriate homework (and not following-up on homework assignments that have been completed).
- Premature emphasis on identifying schemata.
- Therapist impatience; becoming overly directive during therapy in an attempt to immediately resolve the patient's symptoms.
- Premature introduction of rational techniques (before a comprehensive conceptualization has been completed).
- Lack of attention to developing a solid, collaborative rapport; inadequate attention to the "nonspecific factors" of the therapy relationship.
- Not attending to the therapist's own emotional reactions, automatic thoughts, and schemata—the countertransference.

Termination

Termination in cognitive therapy begins in the first session. As the goal of cognitive therapy is not cure per se but more effective coping, the cognitive therapist does not plan for therapy ad infinitum. As a skills acquisition model of psychotherapy, the therapist's goal is to assist patients in acquiring the capacity to deal with internal and external stressors that are a part of life. When the objective rating scales, patient report, therapist observations, and feedback from significant others confirm improvement and a higher level of adaptive abilities, the therapy can move toward termination.

Although numerous outcome studies have found that cognitive therapy can be highly effective in 12 to 15 sessions, there is no typical duration for the treatment. In assisting patients with more severe or long-standing difficulties (such as borderline personality disorder), for example, we have found that meaningful gains can be achieved within several weeks as patients learn cognitive and behavioral techniques for coping with their feelings of depression, anxiety, and anger. Cognitive therapy can profitably continue for 2 to 3 years, however, as the assumptions and schemata underlying their difficulties are examined and addressed. Nonetheless, recent studies have failed to find a relationship between duration of therapy and effectiveness (Berman, Miller, & Massman, 1985; Miller & Berman, 1983; Shapiro & Shapiro, 1982). Rather, studies suggest that the benefits of continuing treatment beyond 12 to 15 sessions are modest. With this in mind, we have often found it useful to discuss the expected duration of therapy with patients at the outset and negotiate a termination date or a set number of sessions in advance. This encourages both the therapist and the patient to maintain a problem focus and maintains a sense of urgency in the treatment (see Hoyt, Chapter 12, this volume).

Termination in cognitive therapy is accomplished gradually to allow time for ongoing modifications and corrections. Sessions are tapered off from once weekly to biweekly. From that point, sessions can be set on a monthly basis, with follow-up sessions at 3 and 6 months until therapy is ended. Patients can, of course, still call and arrange an appointment in the event of an emergency. Sometimes patients will call simply to get some information or a reinforcement of a particular behavior or to report a success. With the cognitive therapist in the role of a consultant/collaborator, this continued contact is appropriate and important. As the conclusion of treatment nears, the patient's thoughts and feelings about the termination are carefully explored, as are schemata and assumptions regarding separation. The termination of therapy can have important meanings for the patient and can activate memories and schemata about separations from others in the patient's past (Mann, 1973; Safran & Segal, 1990). Termination can afford the therapist an opportunity to explore with patients their thoughts, feelings, and characteristic ways of coping with separations. This is particularly important when working with patients whose histories suggest that they have responded to separations and losses in maladaptive ways. Such reactions are not uncommon among patients with personality disorders.

As noted earlier, it is essential for therapists to attend to their own emotional reactions and thoughts over the course of therapy. This is nowhere more important than during the termination period. In addition to the therapist's feelings and beliefs about separation, one of the difficulties often encountered in doing cognitive therapy is the pressure to achieve significant improvement rapidly. Cognitive therapy, with its focus on strategic, observable gains can leave therapists with the belief that they are responsible for assuring that the goals of the treatment are met. As is so often the case in life, our expectations and goals may not be fully realized, and important work may remain for the patient after the conclusion of treatment. Cognitive therapy views the mechanisms of therapeutic change as essentially similar to those underlying development over the life-span. Cognitive and behavioral skills, insights, and new ways of understanding one's life that are acquired during therapy may sow the seeds of further growth after termination. As Safran and Segal (1990) cogently observed, the thoughts and emotions that emerge as the conclusion of therapy approaches have "significance for the patient's internal working model and for his or her relationship with the therapist"—thus, they should be examined carefully and utilized as an important part of the therapy process.

Noncompliance

Noncompliance, sometimes called resistance, often carries the implication that the patient does not want to change or "get well," for either conscious or unconscious reasons. The resistance may be manifested directly (e.g., tardiness or missing of appointments) or more subtly through omissions in the material reported in the sessions. Clinically, we can identify several reasons for noncompliance. They can appear in any combination or permutation, and the relative strength of any noncompliant action may change with the patient's life circumstance, progress in therapy, relationship with the therapist, and so on. Several reasons for noncompliance are:

1. Lack of patient skill to change his/her behavior.
2. Lack of therapist skill to help the patient change.
3. Environmental or familial stressors preclude changing.
4. Patient cognitions regarding the possibility of failure.
5. Patient cognitions regarding consequences of their changing to others.
6. Patient and therapist distortions are congruent.
7. Poor socialization to the cognitive therapy model.
8. The gain from maintaining a dysfunctional behavior.
9. Lack of collaboration in the therapeutic alliance.
10. Poor timing of interventions.
11. Patient fear of changing.

TREATMENT APPLICABILITY

In this section, the applications of cognitive therapy to anxiety and personality are described.

The Cognitive Specificity Hypothesis

Of particular importance for the clinician is the "cognitive specificity hypothesis"—the postulate that emotional states (and, perhaps, clinical disorders) can be distinguished in terms of their specific cognitive contents and processes. As noted earlier, for example, depression, is characterized by the cognitive triad (Beck, 1976)—a set negative perceptual and cognitive biases regarding the self, the world, and the future. Depressed individuals tend to view themselves as flawed in important ways and lacking the requisite abilities for attaining important goals. They view their future as bleak and foreboding and view others as uncaring and rejecting. Their views of themselves and their world are filtered through the dark prism of negativistic attributions and expectations. The schemata of depressed persons encompass associations related to themes of deprivation, loss, and personal inadequacy (Guidano & Liotti, 1983; Kovacs & Beck, 1978).

Anxiety disorders, in contrast, are based upon a generalized perception of threat in conjunction with a belief that one is unable to cope with the impending danger. Moreover, each of the specific anxiety disorders (obsessive–compulsive disorder, panic disorder, simple phobia, generalized anxiety disorder, social anxiety) can be distinguished by the specific focus of the threat. A general model for anxiety disorders (Freeman et al., 1990) is presented below.

This model suggests how a number of factors interact in the development and treatment of anxiety disorders. As individuals confront a situation (e.g., an upcoming exam), their perceptions of that event are influenced by their existing beliefs, memories, schemata, and assumptions. In evaluating the situation they make two judgments—an assessment of the degree of risk or threat and an assessment of their ability to cope with that risk. If, for example, they believe that they are capable and well prepared and that the exam will have little bearing on their ultimate grade, they will not view the test as a threat but a challenge. If, however, they believe the exam is highly important and that they are not prepared, they will view the situation as threatening and become anxious. Anxiety may be seen as an adaptive response to a perceived threat. Should the individual cope successfully with the threat (by studying strenuously and passing the exam), this experience will enhance his/her sense of self-efficacy and will inspire confidence in his/her ability to cope with future tests. If, however, the individual fails the exam or avoids the threat (by dropping the course), his/her perception of personal efficacy will decline and his/her belief that the situation was a legitimate threat will increase. As a consequence, the individual will become vigilant or wary about similar situations in the future and will become more likely to avoid other threatening situations. Treatment of anxiety disorders, then, involves reexamining beliefs, assumptions, and schemata; developing appropriate coping skills; enhancing perceptions of personal efficacy; decatastrophizing perceived threats; and discouraging avoidance or withdrawal.

Other emotions (including anger, guilt, relief, dissappointment, despair, hope, resentment, jealousy, joy, pity, and pride) and clinical disorders (including personality disorders) can be distinguished in terms of their specific cognitive contents and processes (Beck et al., 1990; Ortony, Clore, & Collins, 1988). The cognitive specificity hypothesis is of central importance in the clinical practice of cognitive therapy in that it directs our attention to specific beliefs and information processing styles that are often found among patients with specific disorders. It allows us to provide patients with a rationale for understanding their emotional experiences that might otherwise be seen as inscrutable and overwhelming, and allows us to target both cognitive and behavioral interventions toward changing specific central beliefs that mediate their distress.

Anxiety

Complaints of anxiety, nervousness, and tension are among the most common problems presented to mental health professionals. Clinical anxiety often presents as a concomitant to a number of other physiological and psychological disorders, including depression and psychosomatic disorders, that may, in fact, mask the anxiety. In still other cases, the presenting symptoms are physiological and may or may not be anxiety-related. Therefore, the incidence and prevalence of anxiety are most likely underestimated in medical and psychotherapeutic practice.

Anxious individuals appear to share a number of beliefs (Deffenbacher, Zwemer, Whisman, Hill, & Sloan, 1986; Mizes, Landolf-Fritsche, & Grossman-McKee, 1987; Zwemer & Deffenbacher, 1984). Research suggests that anxious patients tend to believe that if a risk exists, it is adaptive to worry about it (anxious overconcern), that it is necessary to be competent and in control of situations (personal control/perfection), and that it is adaptive to avoid problems or challenges (problem avoidance). As noted earlier, the common themes shared by each of the anxiety disorders are a perception of a threat and a belief that the threat cannot be managed or avoided. The threats may be real or imagined and are most often directed toward the person or the personal domain. Are all anxiety threats from without? Certainly not. Whereas there are real and present external threats that can contribute to feelings of

anxiety—the possibility of losing one's job or spouse or of failing an exam, the large doberman down the street, an IRS audit, one's brakes on an icy road—there are internal threats as well. These can include somatic sensations and emotions (as occur in panic disorder), and thoughts (as in obsessive–compulsive disorder), as well as images, impulses, and fantasies. All, however, are similar in that they are perceived as endangering our physical, psychological, emotional, or social well-being.

The threat may cause psychological or physical symptoms, all labeled as "anxiety." Perhaps the most striking and distinguishing feature of clinically significant anxiety, is its duration. To meet criteria for generalized anxiety disorder according to the fourth edition of the *Diagnostic and Statistical Manual of Mental Disorders* (DSM-IV; American Psychiatric Association, 1994), the symptoms, which include signs of motor tension, autonomic hyperactivity, apprehensive expectation, vigilance, and scanning, must be present for at least 6 months. Clinical and "normal" anxiety may differ, but not invariably, on the dimension of severity. A final consideration is the individual's degree of dysfunction and incapacitation. Anxiety can affect virtually all response systems—respiratory, muscular, circulatory, dermal, or gastrointestinal—singly or in combination. The manifestations of debilitating anxiety usually include behavioral responses, either by commission (i.e., fight or flight) or omission (i.e., avoidant behavior). There are the physiological sensations that signal the presence of the anxiety, the affective experience of the anxiety, and the cognitive events and processes that stimulate and maintain the anxiety. All these may be disabling in personal, occupational, and social functioning.

The cognitive model of anxiety (Barlow, 1988; Beck, Emery, & Greenberg,

1985; Freeman & Ludgate, 1988; Freeman & Simon, 1989) involves several elements. Anxiety, being an adaptive response to one's environment, begins with the perception of threat in a specific situation. As noted, the meaning individuals attach to the situation is determined by their schemata and by their memories of similar situations in their past. The individual then makes an assessment of the seriousness of the threat and an evaluation of his/her perceived self-efficacy or personal resources for coping with it. If the situation is viewed as very threatening, a sense of danger will ensue. If a mild threat is perceived, the individual will respond to it as a challenge. The individual will feel excitement and enthusiasm. Cognitive and perceptual processes can be affected by an individual's current mood (Bower, 1981). In this case, when an individual begins feeling anxious, he/she is likely to become even more vigilant to perceived threats and will begin to recall threatening experiences in his/her past. The individual may come, as a consequence, to perceive threat where none existed before.

The course of cognitive therapy for anxiety disorders follows from the general principles discussed above. In conceptualizing an individual's anxiety, we begin by assessing his/her "anxiety threshold" or ability to tolerate anxiety. Each person has a general anxiety threshold as well as an ability to tolerate anxiety in specific situations. These thresholds may shift in response to stresses in the individual's day-to-day life and supports that are available to the individual. The therapist begins, then, by asking what specific events, situations, or interactions trigger the individual to become anxious.

Next, an assessment is made of automatic thoughts accompanying the feelings of anxiety. Although the thoughts of anxious individuals often center around themes of threat and vulnerability, their specific content can be quite personal or idiosyncratic and may be related to a specific syndrome.

As the cognitive specificity hypothesis suggests, each of the anxiety disorders can be distinguished on the basis of its accompanying cognitive contents and processes. *Panic disorder*, for example, is characterized by a sensitivity or vigilance to physical sensations and a tendency to make catastrophic interpretations of these somatic feelings. Momentary feelings of dizziness, for example, might be interpreted as evidence of an aneurysm or brain tumor. *Agoraphobia* typically involves a fear of being unable to rapidly reach a "safety zone," such as one's house—leading the individual to avoid cars, planes, crowded rooms, bridges, and other places where ready escape might be blocked. *Phobias*, in contrast, stem from a fear of specific objects (such as a large dog) or a situation (such as speaking in public). *Obsessive–compulsive disorder* is characterized by a fear of specific thoughts or behaviors, whereas *generalized anxiety disorder* involves a more pervasive sense of vulnerability and a fear of physical or psychological danger.

As noted, when people enter a situation they make several evaluations. The first is, "What risk do I perceive for myself in this situation." Second is an assessment of the personal or environmental resources that may be available to the individual. If people perceive their resources as adequate to cope with the risk, they typically do not experience anxiety. Cognitive interventions are directed toward reducing the perception of threat and toward increasing an individual's confidence in his/her ability to cope with the situation. Before intervening, however, it is important to assess whether the threat is "perceived or real," whether the individual actually lacks the skills to cope with the situation, and whether the patient's perception of limited resources is veridical.

Example: A 28-year-old doctoral student in philosophy complained of being unable to study for her upcoming foreign language qualifying exam. She was trembling with anxiety at the outset of the session and began crying and wringing her hands as she described her fear of failing the test. The exam, she felt, would "prove" that she could never finish her degree, and that she was an unfit wife and mother. Catastrophic thoughts included the belief that she would "wind up living on the street" and that "I'd have to depend on others . . . but there'll be no one there." When asked whether she had felt this anxious in the past, she acknowledged that she had "before every exam." When asked whether she had ever failed an exam, she smiled, glanced up, and replied, "No, of course not . . . I've gotten all A's in grad school . . . nothing lower than a B in my life."

Although we cannot predict her performance on the upcoming exam with certainty, her life experience suggests that her perception of her "inability to cope" may be more illusory than real. If, however, there was a skill deficit, behavioral interventions would be appropriate and attempts could be directed toward developing competence and enhancing social supports. Personality traits of autonomy and sociotropy/dependence (Beck, Epstein, & Harrison, 1983) appear to influence the ways in which individuals cope with anxiety-provoking situations. Autonomous individuals typically adopt a goal-oriented stance and prefer to "take action," whereas sociotropic individuals typically seek support, reassurance, or protection from others.

The usual responses to stress are fight, flight, or freeze. Highly autonomous individuals, when stressed, will typically attempt to "solve it themselves." They rarely seek help spontaneously and do not come into therapy willingly. They often describe their anxiety in terms of vague physiological symptoms and may feel trapped and encroached upon during therapy sessions. The therapist who attempts to engender a warm, close rapport with the autonomous patient, or who gives direct recommendations or homework assignments, may find the patient becoming more anxious and possibly leaving therapy.

Dependent or sociotropic individuals, in contrast, enter therapy willingly, again and again. They often feel immobilized by their anxiety and actively seek guidance and support from others. They may ask how often they can come for therapy and may become concerned that if they do not tell the therapist everything, the therapist's ability to help will be impaired. When stressed, dependent patients become vulnerable to feelings of abandonment. They are typically compliant in following therapeutic recommendations and diligent in completing homework assignments. Nonetheless, their tendency to defer to others and to seek reassurance or guidance from others limits their ability to cope with life's problems independently. Thus, a goal of therapy is to encourage them to accept greater responsibility for identifying problems and generating alternative solutions.

Not all anxiety reactions are the same. Rather, symptom patterns vary from person to person. One individual may experience predominantly physical symptoms—such as tachycardia, difficulty breathing, dizziness, indigestion, wobbliness, or hot flashes—necessitating the development of an individualized treatment program. Another individual's anxiety, however, might be characterized by "fears of the worst" happening and thoughts of losing control. Their treatment program would be somewhat different. When treating anxiety disorders, it is helpful to keep this variability in mind and to address each of the component symptoms individually.

Anxiety disorders tend to run in families. Panic disorder, obsessive–compulsive disorder, phobias, and generalized anxiety disorder are more common among first-degree relatives of individuals with each of these disorders than among more distant relatives and the general population. Although research strongly suggests that genetic factors may contribute to the development of these disorders, it is also clear that social learning and environmental factors play a role. An evaluation of family history of anxiety can be useful in that it can provide us with information about early experiences that may have contributed to the development of anxiogenic beliefs. Moreover, it may shed light on the ways in which other family members coped with their feelings of anxiety—coping responses that were modeled for the patient. The objective is to gain insight into the origins of the patient's tacit beliefs and the ways the patient has learned to manage these feelings.

As with other clinically important problems, treatment of anxiety begins with the development of a coherent and parsimonious case conceptualization. By adopting a phenomenolgical stance, we attempt to understand the individual's thoughts, feelings, and behavioral responses as they are confronted with anxiety-provoking situations. Questions to be addressed include:

- Is the patient in real danger, or is his/her response out of proportion to threat? If the patient faces a legitimate threat, reattribution would be inappropriate.
- What attributions does the patient make as to the cause of the anxiety?
- Has the patient accurately assessed his/her own abilities, or does the therapist hold erroneous and distorted views of personal efficacy and competence?
- What expectations does the patient hold regarding his/her behavior and the behavior of others? Are the expectations for self (or therapist) reasonable?
- What are the dysfunctional automatic thoughts and cognitive distortions that accompany the anxiety?
- What are the schemata and assumptions that maintain the patient's anxiety?
- What behavioral skills are needed to cope more effectively?
- Does the patient engage in maladaptive behaviors (e.g., avoidance, drug use, or excessive seeking of reassurance) that may be exacerbating his/her feelings of vulnerability?

Consideration of these questions will guide the therapist toward a more systematic and effective treatment program.

Personality Disorders

Personality disorders refer to enduring patterns of thought, perception, and interpersonal relatedness that are inflexible and maladaptive. They tend to occur in a wide range of settings and are often accompanied by a great deal of distress. More often than not, they greatly impair the individual's social or occupational functioning. They are both chronic and highly pernicious. Personality disorders differ from other clinically important problems (such as major depression or anxiety disorders) in that they do not fluctuate over time and are not characterized by discrete periods of distress.

Like other problems discussed thus far, each of the personality disorders can be described in terms of a specific constellation of cognitive contents and processes (Freeman & Leaf, 1989; Layden et al., 1993). The schemata of a dependent individual, for example, tend to be characterized by schemata of the form, "I am a flawed or incapable person" (self), or, "The world is a dangerous place" (world), and by the assumption, "If I can maintain a close relationship with a supportive person, I can feel secure." As a consequence, the individual with a dependent personality disorder continually seeks relationships with others, fears the loss of relationships, and feels despondent and anxious when deprived of the support of others.

A schizoid individual, in contrast, may also hold the belief that "The world is a dangerous place" (world), but also maintains the schema, "Others are dangerous or malevolent" (world), and the assumption, "If I can avoid intimate relationships with others, I can feel secure." Their behavioral and emotional responses, as a consequence, are quite different. They tend to be indifferent to the praise or criticism of others, maintain few close friendships, and are emotionally aloof from others. As one patient succinctly stated, "My dream is to get through law school so I can get a lot of money . . . then I'd buy an island . . . I'd never have to deal with anyone, that would be ideal."

Personality disorders reflect the activity of maladaptive schemata and assumptions (Beck et al, 1990; Bricker, Young, & Flannagan, 1993; Freeman, 1993; Young, 1991). Although these schemata may have been adaptive in the context in which they were developed, they have long since lost their functional value. As the beliefs underlying personality disorders are tacit, they are not open to refutation. As a consequence, patients tend (at least initially) not to view their perceptions, thoughts, or behavior as a problem. Their difficulties are ego-syntonic. Rather, they believe that the problems reside in others. As the "complaining woman" described earlier remarked, "I'm just identifying problems . . . *they* have to change them." She believed that her behavior was both appropriate and rational, and that she was doing a service to others by pointing out their shortcomings.

Because their difficulties are ego-syntonic, individuals with personality disorders typically seek treatment due to other concerns—most often feelings of depression, anxiety, or anger or difficulties maintaining jobs or relationships. It is important to remember that the patient's goals in seeking treatment may not be shared with others (including the therapist). If a patient is not willing to work on "core" issues, therapy may still prove useful by providing the patient with techniques for controlling his/her feelings of depression or anxiety and by assisting the patient to develop trusting relationships. Although more time-consuming, the gradual uncovering of schemata through guided discovery and the demonstration that they are maladaptive through Socratic questioning can be far more fruitful than direct confrontation.

Cognitive therapy of personality disorders differs from short-term cognitive psychotherapy in that it incorporates a more comprehensive exploration of the developmental origins of the schemata (a "developmental analysis") and examines the ways in which the schemata are expressed in the therapeutic relationship. Unlike psychodynamic psychotherapy, however, the cognitive therapist does not allow a negative transference relationship to develop as a means of permitting interpretation of underlying drives or ego functioning. The development of an angry or depressive relationship with the therapist would undermine the therapeutic collaboration. Rather, the negative perceptions, attributions, or expectations would be challenged directly. The therapeutic relationship would serve as evidence that the tacit belief was not true.

Example: A 39-year-old woman sought treatment due to continuing feelings of depression, anxiety, and emptiness. She had been married several times before, and her current relationship (with a recovering alcoholic and drug addict) was both unsatisfying and unstable. After a particularly strong session she brought an expensive gift for her therapist. When asked why she remarked, "Whenever a man does something for me, I feel I have to reciprocate or he'll leave." She stated that she had been having recurrent thoughts that the therapist would "think I was done and terminate treatment" over the past week, as well as frequent dreams of being left by her boyfriend. When the therapist asked how she would feel if he did not accept the gift, she became highly agitated and began crying. He then asked if there was anything he had said or done to suggest that he would abandon her or terminate treatment. She acknowledged that there was not. "So where did this thought come from, then?" the therapist continued. "It's not you," she responded, "it's from when I was growing up." The session continued with a discussion of how she could identify and cope with emotional reactions based on latent schemata.

As noted in this example, the therapeutic relationship plays a central role in the treatment of personality disorders. The therapeutic relationship serves as a microcosm of the patient's responses to others. The sensitive nature of the relationship means that the therapist must exercise great care. Being even 2 minutes late for a session with the dependent personality may elicit anxiety about abandonment. The same 2-minute lateness will raise the specter of being taken advantage of by the paranoid personality.

It is often valuable to discuss the time frame for treatment with patients at the outset of therapy. Many patients, for example, may have read of cognitive therapy and expect that they will be "cured" in 12 to 20 sessions. Given the greater severity and chronicity of their difficulties, however, a longer time frame might be anticipated. Although patients may expect some symptomatic improvement within a relatively short period of time,

a longer time is necessary to identify and change tacit beliefs (12 to 20 months is a far more reasonable time frame).

Cognitive therapy of personality disorders is a rapidly evolving area for clinical theory and research. Although few controlled outcome studies have yet been completed, our clinical experience suggests that model provides a parsimonious means of understanding a range of persistent and self-defeating patterns of thought, emotion, and behavior. The potential value of cognitive therapy for treating these most challenging patients, while not yet realized, is great.

CASE ILLUSTRATION

Presenting Problems

LV, 20 years of age, was living with his parents at the time of his referral for cognitive therapy. He was working part-time as a box boy at a local parts warehouse, and had recently taken a leave of absence from a prestigious university. LV was mildly obese and although appropriately attired, had an unkempt, disheveled look—as if he had not showered in several days. He walked with a heavy, plodding gait, and he mumbled, making his speech difficult to understand. Eye contact was poor, and his speech was driven and rambling. His diagnoses at the time of his referral were bipolar disorder–depressed and avoidant personality disorder.

LV's presenting concerns included a history of severe depression, suicidality, feelings of worthlessness, social anxiety, manic episodes (characterized by decreased sleep, agitation, constant talking, irrational spending, grandiose delusions, and motoric overactivity), and poor social skills. He had participated in psychoanalysis four times a week for several years and had received trials of a number of medications—all to no avail. Although his episodes of mania were reasonably well-controlled by lithium (which he took regularly), his feelings of depression continued to worsen. LV had been hospitalized twice due to suicidal ideations, and his psychiatrist had recommended he be placed in a residential treatment program due to his deteriorating condition. His parents were interested in a second opinion before placing their son in a long-term treatment facility and felt that cognitive therapy was their "last hope."

Initial Assessment

Complete developmental, social, and medical histories were obtained and a battery of objective rating scales were administered in order to gain a clearer idea of his problems. LV's scores on the BDI, BAI, and HS were 28, 51, and 19, respectively. These scores are indicative of clinically severe depression, anxiety, and pessimism. His responses on the Minnesota Multiphasic Personality Inventory (MMPI) yielded a 2-8-7 profile, with concomitant elevations of scales 3, 4, and 10. That is, his responses on the MMPI were similar to those of persons who are highly anxious, depressed, agitated, and tense. LV was dependent and unassertive in his relationships with others and felt unable to meet the challenges of day-to-day life. His responses on a series of automatic thought questionnaires revealed that he was highly concerned that others like him, that he experienced difficulty being alone, and that he "could not avoid thinking about his past mistakes."

History

LV was the younger of two children and had grown up in an affluent suburb and attended exclusive schools. Although he had done quite well academically during his elementary and high school years, his interpersonal and emotional functioning were quite poor. He was plagued by feelings of self-doubt and worthlessness and made self-critical comparisons with others on an almost continual basis. He believed that others were of "stellar quality" and that he was "stupid and a fraud." When asked to elaborate, LV noted that although he had graduated near the top of his high school class, his father had written many of his papers. While away at college LV began to withdraw. He rarely attended class, and during one fire drill remained in his room "hoping to be killed in the flames." After several weeks of desperate calls to his parents and increasing suicidal ideations, LV returned home. His father, concerned by possible repercussions of leaving the university, devised an elaborate story that LV needed to return home as his mother was having brain surgery. When he returned home, his father was very disappointed and could not tell anyone in the family or community about it. To protect this secret, whenever they left the house LV was required to lie on the floor of the car, covered by a blanket.

Although LV had done well academically and had attempted to be a "perfect child," he struggled internally with feelings of anger, depression, and inadequacy. He reported experiencing sadistic fantasies of attacking children in the neighborhood and recalled having made obscene phone calls to an 8-year-old boy while he was in high school.

Cognitive Conceptualization

LV's depression and anxiety were superimposed on a self-critical and perfectionistic personality style. He maintained high, even grandiose, standards for his own performance (e.g., believing that he needed to earn the Nobel prize in literature) and anticipated rejection from anyone who would come to know him. LV's beliefs and actions were characteristic of many depressed individuals, and fit well with cognitive models of depression. Negative views of the self, world, and future, for example, were readily apparent in LV's thoughts. His social skills were poor, and he tended to behave in ways that led others to withdraw from him. LV's social problem-solving capacities were poorly developed, and he engaged in few activities that would provide a sense of accomplishment or pleasure. When he did do well on a task, he would minimize the significance of his accomplishment and would begin recounting past failures. He tended to respond to feelings of depression and anxiety though rumination and withdrawal, rather than through adaptive coping. Given the information available to this point, one might conceptualize LV's difficulties as follows:

Behavioral coping strategies

Avoidance or withdrawal
Seeking reassurance from others

Cognitive distortions

Dichotomizing (e.g., "If I'm not right, I must be wrong . . . I can't even think right")

Selective abstraction (e.g., "I wasn't comfortable in class that first day, it didn't feel right . . . I knew it, that just tells you I'll never make it in college")

Personalization (e.g., "Everybody was sitting at other tables in the cafeteria . . . it shows nobody likes me")

"Should" statements (e.g., "I should be smarter and do more . . . I *have* to")

Magnification/minification (e.g., "I know he sent me a letter about how much he liked my class, but it doesn't mean anything . . . it doesn't count")

Catastrophizing (e.g., "I'm incompetent at life . . . I have *no* abilities")

Self-critical comparison (e.g., "Everyone is better than me, I can't even blow a bubble")

Automatic thoughts

"I'm so stupid . . . I'm an unintelligent jerk."
"People will discover I'm a fake."
"I'll never be a success."
"My life is meaningless . . . I have no one to share it with."
"I'm really disturbed . . . I have a hollow head."

Assumptions

"If I can avoid others, then I can feel secure."
"If I'm successful, then I can feel good about myself."

Schemata

"I'm fundamentally defective" (self).
"The world is a dangerous place" (world).
"People are unreliable and unsupportive" (social relations).

Course of Treatment

The first goals in treatment were to establish trust and rapport, develop a problem list, and educate LV about the process of cognitive therapy. During the initial sessions, LV invariably appeared sad and anxious. He maintained a very pessimistic outlook and continually sought reassurance from the therapist that he was "OK." LV expressed a great deal of anger about his limited progress in psychoanalysis and was skeptical about cognitive therapy. We began, then, with a discussion of his feelings about therapy, what he had learned in his analysis, and what his goals were for the future. He conceded that he had developed a number of important insights during his analysis, and that he "really didn't know much" about cognitive therapy. LV remarked that he just wanted "to be an average person in college"—a reasonable and appropriate goal—and agreed to read a short book on cognitive therapy before our next session. His first formal homework assignment was to "write down his thoughts when he was feeling upset during the week"—an initial step toward completing a dysfunctional thought record (Beck et al., 1979).

LV's feelings of dysphoria and anxiety became more severe as he became adept at identifying his automatic thoughts. This is not uncommon and appears to reflect patients' increasing sensitivity to thoughts they had been attempting to avoid. Rational responding, a countering technique (McMullin, 1986), was introduced to alleviate these feelings. LV was asked to write down his thoughts when he was feeling particularly depressed or anxious. He then systematically examined evidence for and against each of the distressing thoughts (rational disputation), listed alternative ways of thinking about the evidence (reattribution), and developed more adaptive ways of coping with the concerns (decatastrophizing and search for alternative solutions). As noted, for example, LV felt he was "an unintelligent jerk." A brief review of LV's recent past revealed that, although he had left several schools, he had graduated near the top of his high school class, had received a score of 1580 (out of 1600) on his college entrance exam, and had been admitted to the honors program at an Ivy League university. Taken together, the evidence suggested that LV was not unintelligent. In fact, he was quite bright. A more parsimonious (and reasonable) interpretation of his experiences was that he lacked confidence in his abilities given events during junior and senior high school, and he was unprepared to cope with the anxiety of moving away from his home and parents. A goal of therapy would be to develop skills to accomplish this goal.

Given his low motivation and social isolation, LV next was encouraged to begin completing daily "activities sched-

ules" (Beck et al., 1979). He wrote down his activities on an hour-by-hour basis, then rated them as to their degree of "mastery/sense of accomplishment" and "pleasure/fun." As might be expected, LV engaged in few activites that provided him with a sense of worth, accomplishment, or enjoyment. Depressed patients such as LV often avoid challenging tasks and experience difficulty completing tasks they had accomplished with ease before the onset of their depression. Thoughts that "I can't do it" and "What's the point?" inhibit them from engaging in activities that might provide them with a sense of competence or pleasure. Moreover, their avoidance of tasks and impaired performance serves as further evidence that "there's something wrong with me . . . I can't do it." Activity scheduling serves to directly counteract these processes. LV and his therapist developed a list of simple activities he would attempt each day. He was encouraged, for example, to get out of bed at 10:00 A.M. and take a shower (rather than lounging in bed until midafternoon), to call a friend on the phone, to accept an invitation from a friend to play cards, and to go to the local gym for a swim. As LV began to employ these techniques, his feelings of anxiety and dysphoria began to decline. These gains were reflected in LV's improving scores on several objective rating scales. His scores on the BDI, for example, declined from a 28 (severe) at week 2 of treatment to a 9 (mild) at week 23. His scores on the BAI declined from a 51 (severe) to a 3 (negligible anxiety) during this same period.

To paraphrase Freud, the important goals of life are "to love and to work." With this in mind, we were not content to note reductions in LV's feelings of dysphoria and anxiety but wished to address larger issues in his life—his inability to develop close relationships with others and to live independently from his parents. Behavioral interventions (such as modeling appropriate eye contact and role-playing basic conversational skills) were introduced to develop LV's social skills, and a hierarchy of social activities (beginning with playing cards with his friends and concluding with going on a "date" with a woman) was established. LV was able to progress through the hierarchy over several months but encountered a great deal of anxiety with each new step. Relaxation training, rational responding, guided imagery, and role-playing of the activities were useful in helping LV to develop these skills.

At the same time, LV was encouraged to consider ways of returning to college. As he was highly anxious about leaving home (his last two attempts to live on his own had ended in psychiatric hospitalizations), LV began by taking night classes at a local university. Not suprisingly, he did quite well. His tendency to minimize these accomplishments was addressed directly in therapy, as was the effect of these accomplishmnets on his mood and self-esteem. After aproximately 6 months, LV began discussing the possibility of applying to college once again. His fears of another "breakdown," as well as his uncertainty about possible majors and careers, became the focus of therapy. Once again, he began seeking reassuarance from the therapist that he would "be OK." This provided an opportunity for examining experiences that had contributed to the consolidation of his schemata and the ways they were reflected in the therapy relationship. It was noted, for example, that he frequently sought reassurance and assistance from his mother during his childhood, and that his father's attempts to assist him with his homework during high school had maintained his belief that he was "incompetent" and "stupid." LV acknowledged that reassurance (whether from his therapist or his parents) did little to alleviate these feelings, and that his search

for support precluded him from solving problems on his own. Experiences during his childhood that were inconsistent with these beliefs were examined, and LV was encouraged to "test out" the current validity of the beliefs by completing tasks without seeking support or reassurance.

LV was subsequently accepted at a major university several hundred miles from home. Before leaving for college, however, we felt it would be beneficial for him to have an experience that would give him confidence that he could live alone. Rather than continuing with his job as a box boy, L.V. applied for a position as a relief worker in a small South American village. During his 6 weeks away from home, LV was confronted with numerous challenges that previously he would have felt he could not handle. He returned home with a new (longer) hairstyle, an earring, and a developing sense of identity as an individual who might be able to help others.

LV left for college several weeks later. After a difficult first year, he became a residence hall counselor and his grades began to stabilize. Booster sessions were held aproximately once a month. Therapy was concluded after aproximately 3 years. LV graduated from college, began teaching inner-city children in another state, and has been accepted to graduate school. Although he remained somewhat anxious and self-critical, he has become able to function autonomously. The gains made over the course of treatment are not only reflected in his improved scores on objective rating scales but also in the quality of his life. The goals of therapy were not limited to the alleviation of depression and anxiety but included a focus on latent beliefs and the establishment of an adult identity. Individuation from his parents, a return to school, the development of career goals, and the acquisition of social skills were all important objectives.

This case illustrates how strategic interventions can be employed in treating severe and long-standing psychological difficulties. The treatment of this individual was multifaceted and incorporated traditional cognitive and behavioral approaches, as well as interpersonal interventions focusing on the ways in which unstated beliefs or schemata were expressed in the therapeutic relationship (Safran & Segal, 1990; Safran & McMain, 1992). Social problem solving, rational responding, attributional retraining, behavioral skill development, and the developmental analysis of underlying schemata and assumptions all played a role. With the exception of three family sessions, LV's parents were not included in his treatment. This was explicitly discussed with LV—a goal of therapy was to encourage him to accept responsibility for the course of his treatment and to function more autonomously.

CONCLUSION

The usefulness of cognitive therapy for treating depression and anxiety disorders has been well established. Refined models of depression and the anxiety disorders have been proposed and have generated a great deal of empirical interest. Controlled studies of cognitive therapy's effectiveness in the treatment of other clinically important problems, however, remain to be completed. Moreover, the processes underlying change over the course of therapy are not well understood. What specific cognitive and behavioral techniques, for example, are most closely associated with clinical improvement? Do rationalistic and constructivist variants of cognitive therapy differ with regard to their effectiveness in treating specific disorders? What changes in patients over the course of their treatment? Cognitive models of psychopathology suggest that changes should be apparent in the occurrence of dysfunctional automatic thoughts and maladaptive cognitive distortions, and that changes in schemata should be predictive of a reduced risk of relapse. Can these changes be documented? What is the role of affect and of "behavioral enactment" (Arkowitz & Hannah, 1989) in therapeutic improvement? These are compelling questions, and their answers will serve as an impetus for further refinements of the cognitive model. Cognitive therapy stands as a sophisticated approach to psychotherapy based on the simple truth that maladaptive behavior and emotions stem from maladaptive ways of thinking. In reflecting upon developments in cognitive theory and practice over the past 30 years, Beck (1991) noted that "cognitive therapy is no longer fledgling and has demonstrated its capacity to fly under its own power. How far it will fly remains to be seen." Indeed.

SUGGESTIONS FOR FURTHER READING

Beck, A. T., Rush, A. J., Shaw, B. F., & Emery, G. (1979). *Cognitive therapy of depression.* New York: Guilford Press. The original manual for cognitive therapy of depression and suicide. The cognitive model is outlined and specific techniques are described.

Dobson, K. S. (Ed.). (1988). *Handbook of cognitive-behavioral therapies.* New York: Guilford Press. A well-edited introduction to cognitive-behavioral assessment and treatment. More than a compendium of techniques, the authors offer critical reviews of recent research and suggest areas of inquiry.

Freeman, A., & Reinecke, M. (1993). *Cognitive therapy of suicidal behavior.* New York: Springer. These authors propose an expanded cognitive model of suicidality that incorporates developmental, biological, and social factors. They then offer specific recommendations for assessing and treating depressed and suicidal patients based on this model. The book is practical—it includes numerous case examples and clinical vignettes.

Freeman, A., Simon, K., Beutler, L., & Arkowitz, H. (Eds.). (1989). *Comprehensive handbook of cognitive therapy*. New York: Plenum Press. An expansive text that lives up to its title. It is comprehensive, scholarly, and, as a handbook, clinically useful.

Guidano, V. F., & Liotti, G. (1983). *Cognitive processes and emotional disorders*. New York: Guilford Press. A thoughtful, although sometimes dense, introduction to the constructivist school of cognitive therapy. The discussions of depression and obsessive–compulsive disorder are particularly good.

Mahoney, M. (1991). *Human change processes*. New York: Basic Books. An exceptionally strong discussion of cognitive processes mediating behavior and emotional change. Cognitive therapy is placed in a historical context, and its relationship to the fields of philosophy, evolutionary biology, and developmental psychology are reviewed.

Persons, J. (1989). *Cognitive therapy in practice: A case formulation approach*. New York: Norton. A clear, succinct primer for cognitive case conceptualization.

Safran, J., & Segal, Z. (1990). *Interpersonal process in cognitive therapy*. New York: Basic Books. This book addresses a common criticism of cognitive therapy—that it does not attend to interpersonal factors in psychotherapy. They propose a cognitive-constructivist model for understanding the transference relationship, and provide recommendations for employing the therapeutic relationship to facilitate change.

Scott, J., Williams, J., & Beck, A. (Eds.). (1989). *Cognitive therapy in clinical practice: An illustrative casebook*. London: Routledge. A brief and highly readable casebook. Chapters detail the assessment, conceptualization, and treatment of a range of behavioral and emotional problems.

REFERENCES

Abramson, L., Alloy, L., & Metalsky, G. (1988). The cognitive diathesis–stress theories of depression: Toward an adequate evaluation of the theories' validities. In L. Alloy (Ed.), *Cognitive processes in depression* (pp. 3–30). New York: Guilford Press.

Abramson, L., Metalsky, G., & Alloy, L. (1989). Hopelessness depression: A theory-based subtype of depression. *Psychological Review, 96*(2), 358–372.

Abramson, L., Seligman, M., & Teasdale, J. (1978). Learned helplessness in humans: Critique and reformulation. *Journal of Abnormal Psychology, 87*, 49–74.

Adler, A. (1927). *Understanding human nature*. New York: Fawcett.

Adler, A. (1968). *The practice and theory of individual psychology*. New York: Humanities Press.

Alloy, L., Abramson, L., Metalsky, G., & Hartlage, S. (1988). The hopelessness theory of depression: Attributional aspects. *British Journal of Clinical Psychology, 27*, 5–21.

American Psychiatric Association. (1994). *Diagnostic and statistical manual of mental disorders* (4th ed.). Washington, DC: Author.

Arieti, S. (1980). Cognition in psychoanalysis. *Journal of the American Academy of Psychoanalysis, 8*, 3–23.

Arkowitz, H., & Hannah, M. (1989). Cognitive, behavioral, and psychodynamic therapies: Converging or diverging pathways to change. In A. Freeman, K. Simon, L. Beutler, & H. Arkowitz (Eds.), *Comprehensive handbook of cognitive therapy* (pp. 143–168). New York: Plenum Press.

Bandura, A. (1969). *Principles of behavior modification*. New York: Holt, Rinehart & Winston.

Bandura, A. (1973). *Aggression: A social learning analysis*. Englewood Cliffs, NJ: Prentice-Hall.

Bandura, A. (1977a). Self-efficacy: Towards a unifying theory of behavior change. *Psychological Review, 84*, 191–215.

Bandura, A. (1977b). *Social learning theory*. Englewood Cliffs, NJ: Prentice-Hall.

Bandura, A. (1985). Model of causality in social learning theory. In M. Mahoney & A. Freeman (Eds.), *Cognition and psychotherapy* (pp. 81–100). New York: Plenum Press.

Barlow, D. H. (1988). *Anxiety and its disorders: The nature and treatment of anxiety and panic.* New York: Guilford Press.

Beck, A. T. (1963). Thinking and depression: I. Idiosyncratic content and cognitive distortions, *Archives of General Psychiatry, 9,* 324–333.

Beck, A. T. (1970). Cognitive therapy: Nature and relation to behavior therapy. *The Behavior Therapist, 1,* 184–200.

Beck, A. T. (1972). *Depression: Causes and treatment.* Philadelphia: University of Pennsylvania Press.

Beck, A. T. (1976). *Cognitive therapy and the emotional disorders.* New York: International Universities Press.

Beck, A. (1989). *Love is never enough.* New York: HarperCollins.

Beck, A. T. (1991). Cognitive therapy: A 30-year retrospective. *American Psychologist, 46*(4), 368–375.

Beck, A. T., Brown, G., & Steer, R. (1989). Prediction of eventual suicide in psychiatric inpatients by clinical ratings of hopelessness. *Journal of Consulting and Clinical Psychology, 57*(2), 309–310.

Beck, A. T., Emery, G., & Greenberg, R. (1985). *Anxiety disorders and phobias: A cognitive perspective.* New York: Basic Books.

Beck, A. T., Epstein, N., Brown, G., & Steer, R. (1988). An inventory for measuring clinical anxiety. *Journal of Consulting and Clinical Psychology, 56,* 893–897.

Beck, A. T., Epstein, N., & Harrison, R. (1983). Cognitions, attitudes and personality dimensions in depression. *British Journal of Cognitive Psychotherapy, 1*(1), 1–16.

Beck, A. T., Freeman, A., & Associates. (1990). *Cognitive therapy of personality disorders.* New York: Guilford Press.

Beck, A. T., Hollon, S., Young, J., Bedrosian, R., & Budenz, D. (1985). Combined cognitive-pharmacotherapy versus cognitive therapy in the treatment of depressed outpatients. *Archives of General Psychiatry, 42,* 142–148.

Beck, A. T., Rush, A. J., Shaw, B. F., & Emery, G. (1979). *Cognitive therapy of depression.* New York: Guilford Press.

Beck, A. T., Sokol, L., Clark, D., Berchick, R., & Wright, F. (1992). A crossover study of focused cognitive therapy for panic disorder. *American Journal of Psychiatry, 149*(6), 778–783.

Beck, A. T., & Steer, R. (1987). *Manual for the revised Beck Depression Inventory.* San Antonio, TX: Psychological Corporation.

Beck, A. T., Ward, C., Mendelson, M., Mock, J., & Erbaugh, J. (1961). An inventory for measuring depression, *Archives of General Psychiatry, 4,* 561–571.

Beck, A. T., Weissman, S., Lester, D., & Trexler, L. (1974). The measurement of pessimism: The hopelessness scale. *Journal of Consulting and Clinical Psychology, 42,* 861–865.

Berman, J., Miller, R., & Massman, P. (1985). Cognitive therapy versus systematic desensitization: Is one treatment superior? *Psychological Bulletin, 97,* 451–461.

Blackburn, I., Bishop, S. Glen, A. I., Walley, L., & Christie, J. (1981). The efficacy of cognitive therapy in depression: A treatment using cognitive therapy and pharmacotherapy, each alone and in combination. *British Journal of Psychiatry, 139,* 181–189.

Blackburn, I., Eunson, K., & Bishop, S. (1986). A two year naturalistic follow-up of depressed patients treated with cognitive therapy, pharmacotherapy, and a combination of both. *Journal of Affective Disorders, 10,* 67–75.

Bower, G. (1981). Mood and memory. *American Psychologist, 36,* 129–148.

Bowlby, J. (1985). The role of childhood experience in cognitive disturbance. In M. Mahoney & A. Freeman (Eds.), *Cognition and psychotherapy* (pp. 181–200). New York: Plenum Press.

Bricker, D., Young, J., & Flannagan, C. (1993). Schema-focused cognitive therapy: A comprehensive framework for characterological problems. In K. Kuehlwein & H. Rosen (Eds.), *Cognitive therapy in action: Evolving innovative practice* (pp. 88–125). San Francisco: Jossey-Bass.

Bruner, J., Goodnow, J., & Austin, G. (1956) *A study of thinking*. New York: Wiley.

Burns, D. (1980). *Feeling good*. New York: Morrow.

Burns, D., & Auerbach, A. (1992). Does homework compliance enhance recovery from depression. *Psychiatric Annals, 22*(9), 464–469.

Butler, G., Fennell, M., Robson, P., & Gelder, M. (1991). Comparison of behavior therapy and cognitive behavior therapy in the treatment of generalized anxiety disorder. *Journal of Consulting and Clinical Psychology, 59*(1), 167–175.

Chomsky, N. (1956). Three models for the description of language. *IRE Transactions on Information Theory, 2*(3), 113–124.

Chomsky, N. (1957). *Syntactic structures*. The Hague: Mouton.

Crits-Christoph, P. (1992). The efficacy of brief dynamic psychotherapy: A meta-analysis. *American Journal of Psychiatry, 149*(2), 151–158.

Crits-Christoph, P., & Barber, J. (Eds.). (1991). *Handbook of short-term dynamic psychotherapy*. New York: Basic Books.

Deffenbacher, J., Zwemer, W., Whisman, M., Hill, R., & Sloan, R. (1986). Irrational beliefs and anxiety. *Cognitive Therapy and Research, 10*, 281–292.

Dobson, K. S. (1989). A meta-analysis of the efficacy of cognitive therapy for depression. *Journal of Consulting and Clinical Psychology, 57*(3), 414–419.

Dobson, K. S., & Block, L. (1988). Historical and philosophical bases of the cognitive-behavioral therapies. In K. S. Dobson (Ed.), *Handbook of cognitive-behavioral therapies* (pp. 3–38). New York: Guilford Press.

Drake, R., & Cotton, P. (1986). Depression, hopelessness, and suicide in chronic schizophrenia. *British Journal of Psychiatry, 148*, 554–559.

Ellis, A. (1962). *Reason and emotion in psychotherapy*. New York: Lyle Stuart.

Ellis, A. (1973). *Humanistic psychotherapy: The rational–emotive approach*. New York: Julian Press.

Ellis, A. (1979). The basic clinical theory of rational–emotive therapy. In A. Ellis & R. Grieger (Eds.), *Comprehensive handbook of rational–emotive therapy*. New York: Springer.

Ellis, A. (1985). Expanding the ABC's of RET. In M. Mahoney & A. Freeman (Eds.), *Cognition and psychotherapy* (pp. 313–324). New York: Plenum Press.

Ellis, A. (1989). The history of cognition in psychotherapy. In A. Freeman, K. Simon, L. Beutler, & H. Arkowitz (Eds.), *Comprehensive handbook of cognitive therapy* (pp. 5–20). New York: Plenum Press.

Ellis, A., & Harper, R. (1961). *New guide to rational living*. New York: Crown.

Epictetus. (1983). *The handbook of Epictetus*. (N. White, Trans.). Indianapolis, IN: Hackett.

Evans, M., Hollon, S., DeRubeis, R., & Piasecki, J. (1992). Differential relapse following cognitive therapy and pharmacotherapy for depression. *Archives of General Psychiatry, 49*(10), 802–808.

Fiske, S., & Taylor, S. (1984). *Social cognition*. Reading, MA: Addison-Wesley.

Foa, E., Steketee, G., & Young, M. (1984). Agoraphobia: Phenomenological aspects, associated characteristics, and theoretical considerations. *Clinical Psychology Review, 4*, 431–457.

Flavell, J. (1963). *The developmental psychology of Jean Piaget*. New York: D. Van Nostrand.

Frankl, V. (1985). Cognition and logotherapy. In M. Mahoney & A. Freeman (Eds.), *Cognition and psychotherapy* (pp. 259–276). New York: Plenum Press.

Freeman, A. (1993). A psychosocial approach for conceptualizing schematic development for cognitive therapy. In K. Kuehlwein & H. Rosen (Eds.), *Cognitive therapies in action: Evolving innovative practice* (pp. 54–87). San Francisco: Jossey-Bass.

Freeman, A., & DeWolfe, R. (1989). *Woulda, coulda, shoulda*. New York: HarperCollins.

Freeman, A., & DeWolfe, R. (1992). *The 10 dumbest mistakes that smart people make*. New York: HarperCollins.

Freeman, A., & Leaf, R. (1989). Cognitive therapy of personality disorders. In: A. Freeman, K. Simon, L. Beutler, & H. Arkowitz (Eds.) *Comprehensive handbook of cognitive therapy* (pp. 403–434). New York: Plenum Press.

Freeman, A., & Ludgate, J. (1988). Cognitive therapy of anxiety. In P. Keller & S. Heyman (Eds.), *Innovations in clinical practice* (Vol. 7, pp. 39–60). Sarasota, FL: Professional Resource Exchange.

Freeman, A., Pretzer, J., Fleming, B., & Simon, K. (1990). *Clinical applications of cognitive therapy.* New York: Plenum Press.

Freeman, A., & Reinecke, M. (1993). *Cognitive therapy of suicidal behavior.* New York: Springer.

Freeman, A., & Simon, K. (1989). Cognitive therapy of anxiety. In A. Freeman, K. Simon, L. Beutler, & H. Arkowitz (Eds.), *Comprehensive handbook of cognitive therapy* (pp. 347–366). New York: Plenum Press.

Freud, S. (1892). Treatment by hypnosis. In *Collected works.* London: Hogarth Press.

Fuchs, C., & Rehm, L. (1977). A self-control behavior program for depression. *Journal of Consulting and Clinical Psychology, 45,* 206–215.

Garfield, S., & Bergin, A. (Eds.). (1986). *Handbook of psychotherapy and behavior change: An empirical analysis* (3rd ed.). New York: Wiley.

Goldfried, M., & Merbaum, M. (Eds.). (1973). *Behavior change through self-control.* New York: Holt, Rinehart & Winston.

Greenberg, L. S., & Safran, J. D. (1987). *Emotion in psychotherapy.* New York: Guilford Press.

Guidano, V. F. (1987). *Complexity of the self: A developmental approach to psychopathology and therapy.* New York: Guilford Press.

Guidano, V. F. (1991). *The self in process: Toward a post-rationalist cognitive therapy.* New York: Guilford Press.

Guidano, V. F., & Liotti, G. (1983). *Cognitive processes and emotional disorders: A structural approach to psychotherapy.* New York: Guilford Press.

Guidano, V. F., & Liotti, G. (1985). A constructivist foundation for cognitive therapy. In M. Mahoney & A. Freeman (Eds.), *Cognition and psychotherapy.* New York: Plenum Press.

Haaga, D., & Davison, G. (1993). An appraisal of rational–emotive therapy. *Journal of Consulting and Clinical Psychology, 61*(2), 215–220.

Hollon, S. (1990). Cognitive therapy and pharmacotherapy for depression. *Psychiatric Annals, 20*(5), 249–258.

Hollon, S., & Najavits, L. (1988). Review of empirical studies of cognitive therapy. In A. Frances & R. Hales (Eds.) *American Psychiatric Press review of psychiatry* (Vol. 7, pp. 643–666). Washington, DC: American Psychiatric Press.

Hollon, S., Shelton, R., & Loosen, P. (1991). Cognitive therapy and pharmacotherapy for depression. *Journal of Consulting and Clinical Psychology, 59*(1), 88–99.

Horney, K. (1936). *The neurotic personality.* New York: Norton.

Horowitz, M. (Ed.). (1991). *Person schemas and maladaptive interpersonal patterns.* Chicago, IL.: University of Chicago Press.

Ingram, R. (1984). Toward an information processing analysis of depression. *Cognitive Therapy and Research, 8,* 443–478.

Kanfer, F. (1971). The maintenance of behavior by self-generated stimuli and reinforcement. In A. Jacobs & L. Sachs (Eds.), *The psychology of private events: Perspectives on covert response systems.* New York: Academic Press.

Kegan, R. (1982). *The evolving self.* Cambridge, MA: Harvard University Press.

Kelly, G. (1955). *The psychology of personal constructs.* New York: Norton.

Kihlstrom, J. (1987). The cognitive unconscious. *Science, 237,* 1445–1452.

Kihlstrom, J. (1988). Cognition, unconscious processes. In G. Adelman (Ed.), *Neuroscience year: The yearbook of the encyclopedia of neuroscience* (pp. 34–36). Boston: Birkhauser.

Kovacs, M., & Beck, A. (1978). Maladaptive cognitive structures in depression. *American Journal of Psychiatry, 135*(5), 525–533.

Kovacs, M., Rush, A., Beck, A., & Hollon, S. (1981). Depressed outpatients treated with cognitive therapy or pharmacotherapy: A one year follow-up. *Archives of General Psychiatry, 38,* 33–39.

Layden, M., Newman, C. Freeman, A., & Byers, S. (1993). *Cognitive therapy of the borderline patient*. Boston: Allyn & Bacon.

Lazarus, A. (Ed.). (1976). *Multimodal behavior therapy*. New York: Springer.

Lazarus, A. (1981). *The practice of multimodal therapy*. New York: McGraw-Hill.

Lazarus, R. (1991). *Emotion and adaptation*. New York: Oxford University Press.

Lazarus, R., & Folkman, S. (1984). *Stress, appraisal, and coping*. New York: Springer.

Leventhal, H. (1984). A perceptual motor theory of emotions. In K. Scherer & P. Ekman (Eds.), *Approaches to emotion* (pp. 271–291). Hillsdale, NJ: Erlbaum.

Luria, A. (1961). *The role of speech in the regulation of normal and abnormal behavior*. New York: Liveright.

Mahoney, M. (1974). *Cognition and behavior modification*. Cambridge, MA: Ballinger.

Mahoney, M. (1977). Reflections on the cognitive-learning trend in psychotherapy. *American Psychologist, 32*, 5–13.

Mahoney, M. (1980). Psychotherapy and the structure of personal revolutions. In M. Mahoney (Ed.), *Psychotherapy process: Current issues and future directions* (pp. 157–180). New York: Plenum Press.

Mahoney, M. (1985). Psychotherapy and human change processes. In M. Mahoney & A. Freeman (Eds.), *Cognition and psychotherapy* (pp. 4–28). New York: Plenum Press.

Mahoney, M. (1991). *Human change processes*. New York: Basic Books.

Mann, J. (1973). *Time-limited psychotherapy*. Cambridge, MA: Harvard University Press.

Markus, H. (1977). Self-schemata and processing information about the self. *Journal of Personality and Social Psuychology, 35*, 63–78.

Markus, H., & Nurius, P. (1986). Possible selves. *American Psychologist, 41*, 954–969.

Maultsby, M. (1984). *Rational behavior therapy*. Englewood Cliffs, NJ: Prentice-Hall.

McMullin, R. (1986). *Handbook of cognitive therapy techniques*. New York: Norton.

Meichenbaum, D. (1977). *Cognitive-behavior modification*. New York: Plenum Press.

Meichenbaum, D., & Gilmore, J. (1984). The nature of unconscious processes: A cognitive-behavioral perspective. In K. Bowers & D. Meichenbaum (Eds.), *The unconscious reconsidered* (pp. 273–298). New York: Wiley.

Miller, R., & Berman, J. (1983). The efficacy of cognitive behavior therapies: A quantitative review of the research evidence. *Psychological Bulletin, 94*, 39–53.

Mischel, W. (1973). Toward a cognitive social learning reconceptualization of personality. *Psychological Review, 80*, 252–283.

Mizes, J., Landolf-Fritsche, B., & Grossman-McKee, D. (1987). Patterns of distorted cognitions in phobic disorders: An investigation of clinically severe simple phobics, social phobics, and agoraphobics. *Cognitive Therapy and Research, 11*, 583–592.

Murphy, G. E., Simons, A. D., Wetzel, R. D., & Lustman, P. J. (1984). Cognitive therapy versus tricyclic antidepressants in major depression. *Archives of General Psychiatry, 41*, 33–41.

Newell, A., & Simon, H. (1956). The logic theory machine: A complex information processing system. *IRE Transactions on Information Theory, 2*(3), 61–79.

Niemeyer, R. (1993). An appraisal of constructivist psychotherapies. *Journal of Consulting and Clinical Psychology, 61*(2), 221–234.

Ortony, A., Clore, G., & Collins, A. (1988). *The cognitive structure of emotions*. Cambridge: Cambridge University Press.

Persons, J. (1989). *Cognitive therapy in practice: A case conceptualization approach*. New York: Norton.

Peterson, C., & Seligman, M. (1984). Causal explanations as a risk factor for depression: Theory and evidence. *Psychological Review, 91*, 347–374.

Rehm, L. (1977). A self-control model of depression. *Behavior Therapy, 8*, 787–804.

Rosen, H. (1985). *Piagetian concepts of clinical relevance*. New York: Columbia University Press.

Rosen, H. (1989). Piagetian theory and cognitive therapy. In A. Freeman, K. Simon, L. Beutler, & H. Arkowitz

(Eds.), *Comprehensive handbook of cognitive therapy* (pp. 189–212). New York: Plenum Press.

Safran, J., & Segal, Z. (1990). *Interpersonal process in cognitive therapy.* New York: Basic Books.

Safran, J., & McMain, S. (1992). A cognitive-interpersonal approach to the treatment of personality disorders. *Journal of Cognitive Psychotherapy: An International Quarterly, 6*(1), 59–67.

Safran, J., Vallis, T., Segal, Z., & Shaw, B. (1986). Assessment of core cognitive processes in cognitive therapy. *Cognitive Therapy and Research, 10*(5), 509–526.

Segal, Z. (1988). Appraisal of the self-schema construct in cognitive models of depression. *Psychological Bulletin, 103,* 147–162.

Seligman, M. (1974). Depression and learned helplessness. In R. Friedman & M. Katz (Eds.), *The psychology of depression: Contemporary theory and research.* Washington, DC: Winston–Wiley.

Seligman, M. (1975). *Helplessness: On depression, development, and death.* San Fransisco: W. H. Freeman.

Shapiro, D., & Shapiro, D. (1982). Meta-analysis of comparative therapy outcome studies: A replication and refinement. *Psychological Bulletin, 92,* 581–604.

Simon, K., & Fleming, B. (1985). Beck's cognitive therapy of depression: Treatment and outcome. In R. Turner & L. Ascher (Eds.), *Evaluating behavior therapy outcome.* New York: Springer.

Simons, A., Garfield, S., & Murphy, G. (1984). The process of change in cognitive therapy and pharmacotherapy of depression: Changes in mood and cognition. *Archives of General Psychiatry, 41,* 45–51.

Smith, D. (1982). Trends in counseling and psychotherapy. *American Psychologist, 37,* 802–809.

Sokol, L., Beck, A., Greenberg, R., Berchick, R., & Wright, F. (1989). Cognitive therapy of panic disorder: A nonpharmacological alternative. *Journal of Nervous and Mental Disease, 177*(12), 711–716.

Stern, R., & Drummond, L. (1991). *The practice of behavioural and cognitive psychotherapy.* Cambridge: Cambridge University Press.

Sullivan, H. S. (1953). *The interpersonal theory of psychiatry.* New York: Norton.

Sweeney, P., Anderson, K., & Bailey, S. (1986). Attributional style in depression: A meta-analytic review. *Journal of Personality and Social Psychology, 50,* 974–991.

Tolman, E. (1949). *Purposive behavior in animals and men.* Berkeley: University of California Press.

Truax, C., & Carkhuff, R. (1964). Significant developments in psychotherapy research. In L. Abt & B. Reiss (Eds.), *Progress in clinical psychology* (Vol. 6, pp. 124–155). New York: Grune and Stratton.

Turk, D., & Salovey, P. (1985). Cognitive structures, cognitive processes, and cognitive-behavior modification: I. Client issues. *Cognitive Therapy and Research, 9,* 1–17.

Vygotsky, L. (1962). *Thought and language.* Cambridge, MA: MIT Press.

Whorf, B. (1956). *Language, thought, and reality.* Cambridge, MA: MIT Press.

Williams, J., & Moorey, S. (1989). The wider application of cognitive therapy: The end of the beginning. In J. Scott, J. Williams, & A. Beck (Eds.) *Cognitive therapy in clinical practice: An illustrative casebook* (pp. 227–250). London: Routledge.

Wright, J. (1987). Cognitive therapy and medication as combined treatment. In A. Freeman & V. Greenwood (Eds.), *Cognitive therapy: Applications in psychiatric and medical settings.* (pp. 36–50). New York: Human Sciences Press.

Wright, J. (1992). Combined cognitive therapy and pharmacotherapy of depression. In A. Freeman & F. Dattilio (Eds.), *Comprehensive casebook of cognitive therapy* (pp. 285–292). New York: Plenum Press.

Wright, J., & Schrodt, G. (1989). Combined cognitive therapy and pharmacotherapy. In A. Freeman, K. Simon, L. Beutler, & H. Arkowitz (Eds.), *Comprehensive handbook of cognitive therapy* (pp. 267–282). New York: Plenum Press.

Young, J. (1991). *Cognitive therapy for personality disorders: A schema-focused approach.* Sarasota, FL: Professional Resource Exchange.

Zwemer, W., & Deffenbacher, J. (1984). Irrational beliefs, anger, and anxiety. *Journal of Counselling Psychology, 31,* 391–393.

7

Existential–Humanistic Psychotherapy: New Perspectives

JAMES F. T. BUGENTAL
MOLLY M. STERLING

There is currently a variety of psychotherapeutic conceptions that claim some kinship to existential philosophy and/or humanistic values. No one conception can presume to speak for this entire remarkable range. Certainly the present authors are not so foolhardy. Instead we will offer our distillation of theory and practice in the hope that we will fairly—if perhaps incompletely—represent both antecedents and provide our readers with a useful overview of this wide-ranging and dynamic understanding of human experience.

BACKGROUND OF THE APPROACH

In simplest terms, the background of our existential–humanistic approach lies in all human thought about the miraculous fact of being and the supervening miracle of consciousness. Parsimoniously, we may identify more recent roots in the still ongoing shift from exclusive dependence on views that objectify human experi-

ence, typified by Aristotle, Newton, and Descartes, toward more balance with those giving significant place to human subjectivity—in our century, Husserl, Heidegger, Sartre, and Merleau-Ponty.

These existentialists, joined by the great seminal psychologists Gordon Allport, Buber, Freud, William James, Jung, and philosophers such as Ortega y Gasset and Pascal, have spoken for the crucial significance of the inner realm of human experience. They keep alive the continuing, if sometimes obscured, awareness of the importance of human consciousness, a task too frequently left only to artists, poets, and visionaries.

The humanistic perspective in psychology expressed by Anderson (1990), Bugental (1967), Arthur Deikman (1976), Erich Fromm (1941, 1947), George Kelly (1955), Sidney Jourard (1963, 1964), Abraham Maslow (1954, 1959, 1962), Carl Rogers (1951, 1961), and others has grown in the past four decades. Its concurrence with much that the existentialists urge (Boss, 1962, 1963; Havens, 1974, 1989; Heidegger,

1962; May, 1953, 1961; May, Angel, & Ellenberger, 1958; Wheelis, 1958) has produced a hardy and increasing therapeutic movement. This marriage brings professional attention back to the quintessential human issues: love, jealousy, fidelity, betrayal, courage, anger, sacrifice, creativity, cruelty, esthetic fulfillment, and the other rich and conflictful dimensions of our inner lives.

Part of the 1960s challenges to traditional patterns was the urge to break out of the stultifying formalism of classical psychoanalysis and to break up the conformity-reinforcing and limiting vision of the commonsense psychotherapy generally practiced by nonanalysts. This impulse led to excesses of "go with the flow," undisciplined reliance on impulsive therapist interventions, and blind faith in a light-sided view of human nature. The group dynamics movement, the discovery and promotion of poorly understood Eastern philosophies, and the general revival of an individualistic ethic (e.g., in the rock music festivals, draft card and bra burning, and student rebellions) supported wide and enthusiastic—but, not infrequently, ultimately damaging—experiments.

Today, it is the custom to look with pitying disdain on those patterns. Although we have drawn back from some of those excesses, we still need to recognize that we have gained from the new territory they illuminated. We know now that there is much awaiting our disciplined, inventive, and persistent efforts. Thus, our approach accepts the challenge of Alexander Pope's (updated) aphorism, "The proper study of [humans] is [humankind]." That enterprise inevitably gives central place to the subjective life (i.e., to awareness, intention, affectivity, cognition, and all the multifold dimensions at the heart of living).

This recognition has been forwarded by many of existential and/or humanistic persuasion (e,g., Buhler & Allen, 1972; Cantril, 1988; Friedman, 1964; Havens, 1989; Hoeller, 1986/1987; Koestenbaum, 1971, 1974, 1978; van Deurzen-Smith, 1988), each of whom gives it a unique spin, but all of whom share the underlying belief in the sanctity and potential of human life and especially of our inner living. This development has overlapped with the growing recognition of how phenomenological psychology opens experiencing itself to deeper perception (Bachelard, 1960; Levin, 1985; Merleau-Ponty, 1962, 1964; Phillips, 1980–1981; K. J. Shapiro, 1985).

Therapeutic Forerunners

So far our remarks have chiefly addressed the American or "humanistic" aspects of our allegiance. It is important to understand the European roots of the "existential" constituent as well, for it powerfully interacted with and influenced our outlook.

We are describing a river formed of three tributaries: existential psychology and philosophy, humanistic psychology and psychotherapy, and phenomenological research and perspectives. These have interacted to bring into being a stance that constitutes American existential–humanistic psychology and psychotherapy. Western cultural history of the mid-20th century fueled this development by its widespread assaults on the sources of meaning for human life.

In a Europe recovering from the massive traumata of World War II, all thinkers were confronted with the koan of human destructiveness. Some became strict mechanomorphs, seeing humans as machines directed solely by external influences. Some became blackly pessimistic, pronouncing the whole world absurd, and some sought to glean what hope could be salvaged from the devastation of war and economic failure.

This country was spared the full impact of many of these meaning-shattering experiences and so emerged with a more hopeful outlook. Perhaps that outlook contributed in some part to a fundamental change that occurred in our attitudes toward deliberate efforts to provide emotional help to individuals. In the 1930s and earlier, before World War II, few people except at the social extremes (wealthy and highly sophisticated or severely emotionally disturbed and likely to be on the public rolls) ever visited an "alienist" (as psychiatrists were then called), psychoanalyst, psychologist, or other psychotherapist. The family parson, rabbi, or priest was more apt to be the one called on for emotional upsets, and his (almost always *his* in those days) services were generally brief and didactic with no more fundamental impact expected. To "have to go to" someone because of emotional problems was a confession of personal failure and evidence of family shame.

World War II powerfully changed all of that. In this country, the "GI Bill of Rights" made available vocational and related counseling to literally hundreds of thousands of returning servicemen. Additionally many more who had suffered physical or emotional traumata were offered more thorough psychotherapy. No longer was this help stigmatizing; instead it suddenly was a *benefit* which could be claimed by those entitled and envied by others not so fortunate. The previous domination of the psychotherapy field by psychoanalysis was abruptly overthrown by the unprecedented demand for emotional aid to hundreds of thousands of servicemen and an increasing number of civilians.

Various proposals were hastily assembled to meet this exigency—and, realistically, to profit from this new and remunerative market. Group dynamics, encounter groups, and marathon ses-sions were such efforts. Short-term therapies were attempted: Rogers's *client-centered counseling* was one of the first of these (*Casebook of Non-Directive Counseling*, by Snyder, 1947, included a one-session successful therapy). Ellis's *rational psychotherapy* (the addition of the word "emotive" came later) and Frederick Thorne's *directive psychotherapy* were other early proposals, soon followed by a variety of behavior-shaping approaches (Lazarus, 1989; Wolpe, 1958, 1991; Wolpe & Lazarus, 1966). Many other "therapies" have been proposed, and these have varied from brief blips on the cultural screen to more lasting contributions to the praxis of the field.

In the meantime, many psychologists, psychiatrists, and social workers found that the traditional methods (largely based either on psychoanalysis or on practical commonsense advising) were not adequate. Contributing to this development were the changes in public attitude toward "being in therapy," and in lay expectations about what therapy should yield. Rather then rescue from major mental illnesses, the new clientele sought aid with the very real but more familiar exigencies of living. Divorce, depression, failed love, thwarted ambition, loneliness, jealousy, abuse, persistent worries and fears, and other issues of "normal" living (i.e., matters affecting existence) were brought to the consulting room. The impact was fundamental and is still shaking our field's basic beliefs and practices.

The established mental health professions were slow to recognize the change in what was required of them and in what needed to be taught. Consequently, many nonmedical professionals were enfranchised either de facto or de jure. Former teachers, psychological test administerers, social workers, employment interviewers, and well-meaning people, sometimes possessing master's degrees in related fields, began to respond to the newly aroused need and soon were caught up in this new calling.

A voluminous literature came into being and included works contributing significantly to the emerging existential–humanistic approach (e.g., Bugental, 1965, 1967, 1976, 1978; Burton, 1967; Keen, 1970; Mahrer, 1983, 1986; Ofman, 1976; D. Shapiro, 1965, 1989).

The existential–humanistic orientation we present in this chapter has roots of indebtedness in many directions. We will identify only some of the most influential: Sigmund Freud's demonstration of the importance of the resistance, transference and countertransference, and the extensity and richness of unconscious life. Carl Rogers's faith in the client's self-healing potential and the centrality of the self. Edmund Husserl's insistence on the central role of the subjective and on openness to our experience as it is freshly unfolding moment to moment within the context of daily human living. Rollo May's bringing the existential perspective with its emphasis on presence, confrontation with ultimate reality, and the central significance of intentionality. Additionally we need to acknowledge May's landmark studies of basic human experiences (e.g., anxiety, love, will, power, innocence).

There are, of course, others whose work is influential in the continuing evolution of this perspective: Allen Wheelis's repeated demand that we face the tragic, the distorting, and the bleak which are also part of life. Irvin Yalom's careful wedding of the implications for psychotherapeutic practice to the basic givens of being. Peter Koestenbaum's demonstration of the pertinence of basic philosophic thinking to the issues of daily life and his epochal study of the "vitality of death" (1971). And still the tally of indebtedness is incomplete, and we must at least mention Medard Boss, Ludwig Binswanger, Ernest Keen, and Emmy van Deurzen-Smith.

Evolution of Therapeutic Practice

As may be expected from the history we have just reviewed, practice under the banners of existentialism and humanism has varied widely indeed. For many, the perspective served chiefly to extend the horizon within which to adapt methods and conceptions brought from other backgrounds. Thus, today, the range extends from fairly traditional psychoanalysts to advocates of short-term, symptom-focused programs, to long-term, life-changing undertakings.

At this point in our presentation we depart from our roles as moderately neutral reporters and undertake to describe the conceptual stance, the clinical applications, and the value perspective with which we are particularly identified. In this effort we found not only our metaphysical stance but our practice itself on the existential view of the human condition. As will be evident, this occasions some significant contrasts with usual psychotherapeutic theory and practice. Even so, it also will be recognized that the approach we describe is indebted to the many predecessors already identified and to many more not so explicitly cited.

An Existential–Humanistic Perspective

We have described two shifts in psychological thought which are fundamental to our position: The first is the movement from objectification of human phenomena to a balance that gives significant—and thus more than is currently customary—recognition to the subjective. In starkest terms, we can say that much of the field of psychotherapy regards clients as objects to be understood, manipulated, and changed; as problems to be analyzed, accounted for, and solved; or as sufferers from pathology that must be treated and cured. The existential–humanistic view, as will become evident, regards the client as the primary subject in the therapeutic encounter, and the therapist is deemed a helper, consultant, or companion in the client's efforts to make life more fulfilling and less stressed.

The second shift is the broadening of the field of psychotherapy from a focus on classical psychopathology (of the major psychoses, psychoneuroses, and similar conditions) to a widened range of issues and distresses, significantly including those of usual living. These are importantly related developments, for so long as the field was chiefly concerned with more extreme and flagrant disorders, the focus of clients as well as the perspective of therapists supported objectification and manipulation, detached relations between professional and patient, and primary attention to symptoms.

This is a point of such importance to the understanding of the existential–humanistic approach that we will enlarge on it here: Formal diagnostic procedures require a distancing by the clinician (therapist) in order to determine the client's condition by looking at clusters of behaviors. This is an impersonal and objectifying stance. Subjectivity, on the other hand, grounds the attention of both client and therapist on the interior experience of felt sense, meaning, and affect occurring in the person from moment to moment and its manifestations in the lived relatedness of therapist and client during the actual encounters between them. This is a personal, interpersonal, and intrapsychic stance.

It needs to be recognized as well that these shifts—bringing the locus of concern to the subjective and the range of issues addressed to the more everyday living—amount to redefinitions of what it means to be human and the nature of human distress, and, thus, the mode of its amelioration. As a consequence, the way opens to recognize such distress as in some important part subjectively derived, rather than seeing it as a moral punishment, a medical disease "caught" by the patient, a failure of character, or a physical/chemical disorder.

These changes bring us to recognize that because the causation is in some part subjective, so must the alleviation be—at least in equal part. This is a point on which well-intentioned and well-informed people take quite contrasting postures. Those who advocate chemical remedies or behavioral routines are likely to insist that the subjective is the lesser element in either the complaints or the cures. They are opposed by those who maintain that much power resides in the person and that the power that has brought on the pain can be redirected toward relief. We number ourselves among those holding the latter position.

THE CONCEPT OF PERSONALITY

The term "personality" is not one we find useful in our technical discourse and writing. Personality is an inexact abstraction diversely employed in both scientific and popular writing and speaking. Most important from our perspective, personality is an abstraction; it is not phenomenological (i.e., one does not have a subjective experience of one's own personality). Rather than trying to assign it a special meaning here, we propose several linked concepts each identifying an important process aspect of the person.

BASIC PSYCHOLOGICAL PROCESSES IN UNDERSTANDING INDIVIDUALS

The key word here is "process." Rather than positing structures, we find it more helpful to recognize the continual dynamism of human life, the unending flow of our being in all its aspects. As Gordon Allport once phrased it, "Structure is the secretion of process" (personal communication, November 29, 1964).

Subjectivity

As already implied, the subjective perspective is fundamental to an existential–humanistic outlook (we prefer to reserve the term "phenomenological" for more formal research usages) (see Giorgi, 1970, 1986; Merleau-Ponty, 1962; Sterling, 1992). This calls for regarding the inner experiencing of both clients and therapists as the main scenes of our attention and efforts. Such a stance is in sharp contrast with much in current psychology and psychotherapy which seek to emulate the physical sciences.

To focus on the subjective is to attend to what is perceived, the affect that is present, the intentionality that informs the efforts, and the implicit wholeness of each person's (client's) experience. This is sometimes mistakenly seen as emphasizing emotions, and at times such a focus may be appropriate, but it is generally a distortion to view the subjective focus as elevating feelings to greater significance than the cognitive and intentional spheres.

Intersubjectivity

Two people intensely involved in their common enterprise, the psychotherapy of one of them, create a phenomenon which is greater than the sum of the two. This creation may be termed, the "intersubjective" (Levenson, 1983, 1991; Stolorow, Brandchaft, & Atwood, 1987). It is the product of conscious and subliminal awarenesses of what is said and what is left unsaid, of bodily and voice cues, of immediate memory and anticipations, of intentions of all levels of consciousness, and of much more that cannot be readily verbalized.

In more familiar existential terms we speak of the fundamental or "thrown" human condition of being at once apart from and a part of all others, and this has implications for the therapeutic contract and the analysis of both the resistance and the transference and countertransference (Bugental, 1987).

Presence

To be truly present is to be aware and participating as fully as one can be in the actuality of the moment, to let go of detachment, role playing, and self-objectification. Because our emotional states, intentionality, relation with other persons who are with us, and many other dimensions of our being are continually in flux (consciously or not), our degree of presence in any given situation is similarly continually changing. When we think of presence in the therapeutic situation, we recognize that as full presence as possible is desirable for both participants, but we recognize also that this is not a state to be once achieved and thereafter maintained. Rather, it is a goal continually sought, often ignored, and always important to the work of psychotherapy.

Wise therapists learn to monitor their own and their client's presence and to become aware of characteristic ways of avoiding it. Those ways, as we will see later, constitute the resistances that are so central to the work of therapy. So important is dealing with the issue of presence that it may be asserted that any depth therapy seeking lasting life changes must attend to it. For an existential therapy, it is absolutely central; thus European existential therapy is often called *daseinanalyse* (the analysis of being there—i.e., of presence).

The Self-and-World Construct System

From our earliest hours, literally, we are engaged in a task of discovery and invention—creating a world within which to live and an identity to give us a place within that world. Of course, much of this literally vital work is implicit, nonverbal, and beyond awareness. Nevertheless, our very lives depend on how we carry it out.

> Life means the inexorable necessity of realizing the design for an existence which each one of us is. . . . The sense of life . . . is nothing other than each one's acceptance of [this] inexorable circumstance and, on accepting it, converting it into [one's] own creation. (Ortega y Gasset, cited in May, 1981, p. 93)

Although we will not offer an extended description of the formation and functions of the self-and-world construct system, we will, however, sketch some of its main significances and point to other sources for elaboration (Bugental, 1987; Kelly, 1955; D. Shapiro, 1965, 1989).

In order to be in the world we need some grasp of what are the good things and the dangerous areas of life; of what will give us power, support, and protection; of what we must do to gain satisfactions and avoid pains and sorrows. As we form these views we are continually developing, revising, and living out our own notions of ourselves—of what are our strengths, our gifts, and our vulnerabilities; of how we handle certain recurring situations; and of what our deepest strivings seek. Of course, much of this system exists implicitly and, indeed, cannot be readily expressed in words.

Viewed from the outside, the products of the self-and-world construct system compose what we think of as a person's personality or character. From within, they seem "just the way things are and the way I am." This construct system is, itself, largely transparent and functions as a lens through which we view what is happening and what we are doing. Also like a lens, it screens out some things and focuses on others. And it distorts our perceptions as well.

The Existential "Givens"

It is useful to recognize that life presents all of us with certain conditions of our being and, though we vary widely in how we respond to these, respond we must. The self-and-world construct system is the persistent pattern of those responses. Or, viewed from a different angle, it is the chief way in which we cope with the anxieties, pursue the benefits, and limit the range of being itself.

Although other existentially oriented observers (e.g., Koestenbaum, 1971, 1978; Yalom, 1980) have compiled their own lists of the basic aspects of our lives, none can claim to have the one true list. The present authors find it useful to identify six "givens" of being human:

Awareness

Fundamental to all else in our lives is our capacity to attend to both the "out there" and the "in here." From this arises our consciousness, our awareness of being aware, which makes of human life a qualitatively different matter (so far as we know) from that of any other species on our planet. Because we know our own being, because we see our own impacts on that which is around us, because we can reflect on what we experience, human living is torn from the un-self-consciousness of objects or plant and animal existence. We can never be truly innocent; we leave our spoor wherever we pass.

Embodiedness

Our corporeal form attends all our days and nights, conditions and limits us, prompts and directs us. The arguments about dualism, monism, interactionism, and like matters are interesting, but they do not refute the constantly lived bodiliness of being.

Our bodies teach us that we are processes, not fixed structures. Their continual changefulness is metaphor, example, and fact, all of which we may try to ignore or deny but ultimately will be our reality. Ecstasy and pain are the voices of our bodiliness. And they are the polar references for all the abundant glossary of our emotions.

Finitude

In all our dimensions we know there are limits; although seldom do we actually come up against these in our subjective experiencing. Although it is manifest that we will die, that we cannot do whatever we choose, that the vast ocean of potential knowledge dwarfs the island of our knowing, still the inner impulse to completeness, to have it all, to know everything, is also intrinsic to our response to our finitude. Thus we turn our finitude into a stimulus to grow, enlarge, develop, invent, and create.

Actionable

We are players in the drama of being, not simply observers. We do and we withhold from doing, and it matters what we do and do not do; thus we have responsibility. From each such action (which includes nonaction) flows the widening ripples of consequences. Our limitedness prevents our foreseeing all that will ensue, but still we must place our bets. And what we wager is our life itself.

> So far as man stands for anything, and is productive, originative at all, his entire vital function may be said to deal with maybes. Not a victory is gained, not a deed of faithfulness or courage is done, except upon a maybe; not a service, not a sally of generosity, not a scientific exploration or experiment or textbook, that may not be a mistake. It is only by risking our persons from one hour to another that we live at all. And often enough our faith beforehand in an uncertified result is the only thing that makes the result come true. (James, 1897/1956, p. 59)

Autonomy

The quotation from James serves several purposes. Not only does it summarize the momentous implications of our capacity for action, it introduces the "given" of our choicefulness. Further it demonstrates the inextricable interrelatedness of these conditions of our being. It is necessary to describe each sequentially here, although we are actually but turning the ball in our hands and commenting on different facets of the same whole.

Confronting the emptiness of being, we ask for a sign, a portent, a superhuman clue as to how to play our maybes for the greatest possibility of success or, at least, less likelihood of failure and distress. And many are the candidates to fill that need: Persons, faiths, chemicals, rituals, philosophies, power merchants, popular entertainers, and all the commercial establishment eagerly grasp for our attention.

None proves its case to all; some come into ascendency overnight or for centuries, and then they are eclipsed. Still all of us must place our bets and do so, and there is never the ultimate sureness that all yearn after.

Yet therein lies our freedom. We would be but automatons of any universally acknowledged value, belief, or leader. In uncertainty there is anxiety, but it also is the cradle of our self-ownership, of our creativity, of our individuality, and of our emotional living. In the widest perspective, it is the wellspring of the ultimate contribution to existence made by each lived human life.

The "facts" or "laws" of the physical sciences approach such universality, at least for Western cultures. From their operations all manner of technological marvels have sprung. But to the extent those facts hold true and are observed, there is no choicefulness in the operations of those marvels. Efforts by some psychologists to copy the methods of the physical sciences in the hope of arriving at similar facts are, at root and unwittingly, endangering all that makes human life rich, innovative, and endlessly interesting.

Separate but Related

Each of us dwells in a separate subjective world. Try as they will, poets, lovers, composers, psychologists, salespeople, and many others can never fully know the innerness of another person. In that is a protection. In that is, also, a sense of ultimate aloneness.

The great world "macroproblems" of our time—pollution, the hole in the ozone layer, homelessness, AIDS, increasing disparities between the haves and the have-nots—all are threats not primarily because of lack of technical know how. We know enough already to remedy many of these situations (or, at the very least, to take beginning steps toward a solution, a beginning which very likely would lead to further steps). All of these are, ultimately, problems concerning the relationships among human beings. These macroproblems make the poverty of our self-knowledge dramatically evident.

The other facet of our separate-but-related condition is our capacity for relation, for bonding, joining with others. The richest experiences of life are, for most of us, those that celebrate our shared experiences with another or with others. Lovers, spouses, families, friends, companions, partners, comrades, and many other labels identify the abundance of forms these connections may take. It is likely that one can only know oneself with anything approaching completeness through having been deeply engaged with at least one other person.

Resistance and Defenses

A person's self-and-world construct system is that person's life—or at least the plan or pattern for that person's life. If that system has evolved over the years so that it brings reasonably dependable satisfactions and prevents excessive stresses, it is obvious that it will be strongly maintained and defended against any attempt to change it.

What may be less apparent is that even if the system is not working so well, the person is still likely to maintain and defend it. Therein lies the task of a depth psychotherapy that seeks to help the client make lasting life changes. Therein also lies a point that well-meaning therapists may incompletely grasp so that, unwittingly, they make their own work more difficult.

To change our ways of being ourselves and our views of the world is to undertake to examine and revise the very ground on which we stand. There is no neutral space into which we may retire to examine dispassionately what seems good or bad in life, to explore what influences are impacting us, or to reconsider how we view our own strengths and weaknesses. All such efforts require that the very subject matter to be explored also serve as the frame of reference for and the content of the examination all at the same time. It is rather similar to but not as simple as trying to take an X-ray of one's hands while using those hands to operate the X-ray camera. A clinical example may make this paradox clearer (Bugental, 1976, pp. 101–140; 1990c, various pages):

Frank grew up in circumstances that made it essential he always be on the alert against attack or mistreatment. He saved himself by being fast with his tongue, his feet, and—when needed— his fists. He learned early to trust no one to come too close. That learning had served him well. It also meant that he lived a lonely life, working much below his capacity, and continually feeling angry and aggrieved. So he came to psychotherapy.

What therapy asked of him, right from the start, was to be trusting, to allow himself to be open and vulnerable, and to delay expectations for immediate change or even for immediately understanding the process of therapy. In other words, the message to Frank was, "Give up all that you've learned to depend on, and risk much of what you've learned can hurt you deeply." And so Frank resisted the therapeutic work. Frank defended his own self-concept and his view of the world.

Of course, Frank was right to do so. So how can therapy solve this paradox?

Rational explanation of the problem was relatively futile. Frank was not rationally choosing to be oppositional. Emotional catharsis of the loneliness and frustration was useful but insufficient to bring about a change in Frank's whole way of being Frank.

The two terms familiar in psychotherapeutic usage, "resistance" and "defense" thus are seen as two aspects of a single process: the maintenance of the self-and-world construct system, the very life structure the client feels is essential to his being. There is, at first, no way for the person to get any fresh perspective on his self-and-world construct system.

Therapists who mistake the resistance to examining the client's only known way to be alive in the world for an opposition to them as persons or to the therapeutic process confuse the task of therapy and end up seeming to be the adversaries of their clients rather than their allies.

Searching

We will understand more about the work of therapy if we make an apparent detour now to discuss a human capacity too little recognized or appreciated but essential to life itself and central to existential–humanistic psychotherapy.

We humans have two "built-in," life-essential programs: One is what we call "searching"; the other is "learning." In simplest terms, learning is what we call on when we encounter situations to which we have practiced ways of responding (e.g., ordering a meal and eating it, driving a car, and speaking and listening when we understand the language and subject matter). Searching is the complementary process; it is what we do when we do not have a satisfactory preestablished path for dealing with a situation of importance to us.

Searching involves risking openness to the unknown, exploring possibilities, experimenting with some that seem likely, using alternative paths when blocked, and eventually resolving the situation. For an example we can return to Frank and his experience before he came to therapy. Finding himself in an anguish of loneliness, he made several abortive attempts to relate more congenially to people at work, but his seeming surliness foredoomed these attempts. Then he visited prostitutes for some physical relief but with increased emotional starvation. He set himself a rigorous reading schedule only to find he could not force himself to follow through on it. After several more unsuccessful attempts, he came for his first interview in psychotherapy. What he found there was evidently sufficiently encouraging that he chose to go further along this line.

What did Frank find?

He found someone who really made an effort to hear him beyond Frank's dismissing and argumentative words. He found an atmosphere that hinted at a different manner of relating. He found a challenge to look within himself in fresh ways. And, slowly but most important, he found that there was one person who, far from being unaffected by Frank's taunts, still hung in with him and called on him to be more than he had been.

What Frank also found—more subjectively and more important—was his own resistances to greater awareness of his inner life, needs, desires, and fears. The discoveries of these were subjective events of life-changing impact.

This searching capacity is not an invention or discovery of the present therapeutic orientation. It has been used throughout human history, but it is with the emergence of psychotherapy as a self-aware discipline that it has been given greater attention and named. "Searching" was the term used in American psychology for this process in the earlier years of this century. "Free association" in psychoanalysis, "unfolding" (Buber's term adopted by Welwood, 1982), and "focusing" (Gendlin, 1978) are other names for generally similar ways of tapping into the same human power.

What about Diagnosis and Personality Types?

From what has been described so far, it will be evident that the existential-humanistic perspective finds relatively little need for such conventions as formal diagnosis in terms of the fourth edition of *Diagnostic and Statistical Manual of Mental Disorders* (DSM-IV; American Psychiatric Association, 1994) or of personality types. In so much psychological and psychiatric usage the concepts of personality and the diagnostic categories are treated as though they referred to structures (such as the musculature of the body or the digestive system).

In contrast, we believe that a human being is a continually evolving process within which subprocesses that have a measure of gross continuity may be discerned. So phrasing it, we mean to convey that such an important constellation of processes as the self-and-world construct system is itself made up of a number of partial processes that persist in their main characteristics (e.g., Frank's mistrust of everyone he encountered), but that when any one aspect of these (e.g., Frank's attitude toward a new person) is followed for even a brief time, it will usually be found to be continually flowing, anything but unitary. Continual fluctuations in intensity, valence, impulse to action, and other dimensions are manifest, and these changes will interact with, among many influences, the circumstances of our meeting, Frank's mood prior to the meeting, and the therapist's gender, age, and other features.

We do not deny that patterns of behavior, emotionality, relationship, and similar dimensions may be observed. We believe, however, that the categories used to identify these patterns are so broad and ambiguous that they may do more to obscure than to clarify our understanding of a given individual. Concepts used to cluster disparate persons may be helpful shorthand for administrative purposes, but they often obscure the fundamental conditions of individual existences and thus hamper the work of depth psychotherapy.

It will be seen that such a perspective as ours gains nothing by assigning a single label or code number to a client. Each person must be encountered in his uniqueness, each encounter must be approached with an openness to discovery.

It will be obvious that this view gives rise to problems in bureaucratic settings. Third-party payers cannot readily accept unique individual characterizations; they demand seemingly objective clusters. Practicing therapists of this persuasion are, of course, subject to stress as a result.

THE PRACTICE OF THERAPY

Psychotherapy conducted from this existential–humanistic approach consists of fostering the client's greater awareness of how she has construed her own identity and the world in which that identity lives out its span. It is our conviction that what we call pathology is a system for thinking about awareness-constricting and awareness-distorting ways of defining oneself and one's world. Further we hold that as the client is helped to experience the ways in which she constricts her awareness, she thereby frees her perceptual capacity to some extent. As the range of capacity increases, the blocks and distortions afflicting it are revealed. This gain in perspective may make it possible for the client to modify those limiting and destructive patterns.

It will be evident from what has just been said that there is a clear division of tasks implied: The client alone has the power to make needed changes; the therapist's function is that of assisting (1) the client's discovery of what restricts her perceptual range and (2) the client's confrontation with what the effort to change that constriction may bring forth.

Amplifying this characterization, we can distinguish a series of therapeutic functions that generally need to be carried out in a thoroughgoing, life-changing therapeutic course. We will list these and then briefly discuss them.

- Developing a meaningful, realistic therapeutic contract.
- Introducing the mode of the therapeutic interview.
- Fostering the growth of a resilient alliance.
- Working through the situational resistances.
- Teaching the client higher-order searching skills.
- Working through some of the character resistances.
- Exploring client–therapist collusion (transference–countertransference issues).
- Working with residual transferential elements.
- Preparing for termination.

Not every client who enters this sort of psychotherapy goes through all these phases. Only those who stay with the process for some time and with a major commitment are apt to do so. Many follow this path productively for a while but find their needs adequately met short of the full sequence. Moreover, the sequence of steps may vary from this outline, and some steps may be combined and others omitted.

Developing a Meaningful, Realistic Therapeutic Contract

The term "contract" suggests an arrangement to which the parties both contribute and from which they both hope to gain. So it is with the therapeutic contract, which makes the understanding between client and therapist meaningful and realistic. Indeed, to satisfy those two criteria—meaningfulness and realism—may require some time and may overlap with the next several phases. Yet this is a cornerstone concern: If the basic understanding between the two participants is faulty, it is unlikely that they will accomplish what the client needs and the therapist intends.

Of course, this understanding is far more than a verbal matter. It is, rather, a meeting of intentions that encompasses both cognitive understandings that can be put in explicit terms and a more implicit agreement that inexorably extends beyond the reach of words. The latter is the more significant element.

Therapist and client alike must be ready to make major commitments to the undertaking—explicitly regularity of time, place, fees, and associated arrangements (e.g., policy about cancellations); implicitly dedication of concern, of willingness to let the work genuinely matter, of giving it emotional priority. There is, to be sure, a difference of degree in these commitments: For the client who seeks major life change, psychotherapy *must*, for a time, become the most important activity in her life. For the therapist, that same therapy must be genuinely important, but it *must not* become the *most* important activity of the therapist's life.

Many clients embarking on intensive psychotherapy have little notion of what that process will be, what it will demand, the emotions it will entail, or the inevitable ambiguities of its impacts on activities and current relations as well as of its outcomes. It is important to be clear about one point in this regard: These are not matters that can be spelled out in advance (as some who are naive about depth psychotherapy urge). The effort to do so is likely to prove frustrating to both participants and disruptive to the development of a genuinely therapeutic contract.

More important, the kind of information that can be given at the outset of therapy is only that based on past clients (diagnoses) or other persons in general (e.g., personality types or research subjects). What is needed for true understanding is always unique to the individuals entering this partnership and to the stage to which that partnership evolves.

The most responsible course is to make explicit what can be genuinely understood at whatever level of understanding is possible. Using this standard, it is often the case that some period of working together is needed by both therapist and client before either can genuinely commit for the long haul.

For example, typically, clients need to experience that although the therapist does not give advice or suggestions (as the client may expect or wish), what the therapist does do is meaningful and contributes to a client's developing feeling of power and purposefulness. Of course, this could be announced in so many words at the outset, but no amount of carefully crafted words can convey what is needed for a genuine understanding of this subtle point. It will require that the client gradually become aware of the expectations she is (often unwittingly) bringing to the work, of the frustration evoked by not having prompt answers to pressing questions, of the subtle support that the therapist does offer to the client's seeking within herself, and of the liberating effects of the client's discovery that she does have more inner resources than she realized on beginning this work.

To try to say all of this in the first few contacts would be to recite a therapist creed that the client could in no way truly grasp or appreciate. Indeed, it would very likely sidetrack those necessary beginning experiences that lead to a client's grasping what is offered in a more wholistic and ultimately more productive manner.

On the other hand, the fact that a client cannot yet understand a full account of what psychotherapy will involve is not warrant for the therapist's unconcern with the client's legitimate need for learning about how the work will go forward and what may be expected.

In sum, the therapeutic contract is not an abstraction but a living and evolving concurring, dynamic process. It begins with the first telephone call to make an appointment, goes through many evolutions, eventually extending to whatever posttherapy relationship may exist.

Introducing the Mode of the Therapeutic Interview

A client often brings to psychotherapy expectations carried over from visits to physicians: She will tell the "doctor" what troubles her; the doctor will ask questions to extend his understanding of the complaint; the doctor will then draw on training, experience, and professional resources to select and administer the healing modalities. In this pattern, the client is well named "patient," as the client's role is that of patiently providing information, patiently making herself available in any appropriate way the doctor indicates, and patiently waiting for the treatment (about which the patient must be patient while understanding very little) to be helpful.

This whole expectation system is a major initial obstacle or resistance to psychotherapy as we conceive it. While the term "client" has many defects, it has the merit of expelling patience, at least nominally, from the role of the person who seeks life change. Simplifying the matter, the client needs to learn as soon as possible that she is the only expert on the client's life in the consultation room. This means that *the therapeutic change agency resides in the client and not in the therapist* or in the therapist's training, knowledge, experience, or other resources.

The emphasized sentence contains the core of this orientation's view and expresses a point on which it contrasts significantly with many other perspectives. The next sentence amplifies this point. *The therapist needs to be an expert in how*

people may use their own powers most effectively in the conduct of their lives and not in what choices clients should make in carrying out that conduct.

To summarize, the client is responsible for the *what*, the *content*, the *applications*, and the *outcomes* of the psychotherapy. The therapist is responsible for the *how*, the *process*, and the *support* of the therapeutic work.

It is out of this perspective that early work in the therapeutic course usually must be devoted to teaching the client to explore inwardly (i.e., to search) for her own benefit rather than chiefly to inform the therapist. This teaching is best done a bit at a time because it often is threatening to the client.

Gradually the client is shown several key elements: When she listens to herself talk with genuine concern and at some length about what matters to her, "new material" comes into consciousness; the therapist's feedback is not fault finding but designed to highlight blocks to the client's awareness; having the therapist listen to and feed back how the client talks facilitates this emergence; and the client has developed habits or patterns in her way of perceiving her life, patterns that are limiting and contributing to the client's life distress.

Of course, all these learnings, and others, must be repeated over and over throughout the course of therapy, but a beginning needs to be made as early in the work as the client can tolerate. The therapist may begin this teaching by noting a time when the client seeks help in a way that fits the "doctor–patient" model. Then the therapist might say something such as,

"I hear you expecting that I'll ask you questions and guide our conversation now. This gives me the opportunity to point out that our work here will be most helpful to you if we have our talks along a different pattern than you may be used to. I'd like you to take the primary responsibility for telling me about what matters in your life, what troubles you and what you want, and anything else that comes into your awareness that is really meaningful for you. Meantime, I won't be talking so much from now on. I want to step back a bit and hear all that you tell me in a way that helps me get a somewhat different picture of how things are for you. Then I'll be able to comment from time to time. But for now, you must take over and tell me about your life just as the thoughts come to you."

Often this message will be given in segments while encouraging the client to comment and question concurrently. However it is given, though, one should not expect that the simple telling will take care of the matter once and for all. Repeated descriptions of the desirable working pattern, provided in the moment when they will be most pertinent both cognitively and emotionally, will be needed. In addition, at times it will be well simply to refer back to the prior structuring ("As you'll remember, it works best if you take the main responsibility to tell me about what matters to you").

The core mode of the therapeutic interview then becomes one in which the client is immersed in subjective search and reporting as clearly as possible what she is discovering while the therapist attends silently, occasionally commenting on points at which the client seems to have difficulty in carrying out this function, even more occasionally offering suggestions about patterns in client self-presentation and ways of relating.

Fostering the Growth of a Resilient Alliance

The therapeutic contract provides a foundation for therapy, but more is needed to establish a "container" that will hold the struggles, emotions, and relationship necessary to a major life undertaking. We can speak of this container as the "therapeutic alliance."

The therapeutic alliance is formed from the objective (business and administrative) arrangements that were part of the contract. It includes the mutual emotional investments already described. But it is grown most significantly from the shared experiences during the period of getting the work under way. This is, aside from the content exchanged, a time of preconscious testing of each other and of oneself. "Can I risk being fully with this person? What is aroused in me as we are together? Can I hang in through emotional storms? Will this person keep faith in a deep sense with our contract? What challenges about myself may this person evoke in me?"

It is to be noted that these questions are asked implicitly by client and therapist. This is no detached, objective operation; it is a living and lived engagement, and both will emerge from it changed in some ways. To say yes to the therapeutic alliance is an affirmation of oneself, the other, and life itself.

The therapeutic relationship when tested repeatedly and found to be durable (but not perfect or all accepting), when coupled with support when it is needed (but not necessarily when it is asked), when it shows the way toward a different experience of being alive (but promises only that the client can work toward that), and when it is at its deepest a genuine caring between two human beings, such a therapeutic relationship becomes a powerful alliance. That powerful alliance can support the client during the prolonged, anxious, and often agonizing work of confronting one's self and one's way of structuring the world.

Working through the Situational Resistances

In describing the mode of the therapeutic interview, we pointed out that this instruction for the client will have to be repeated and reinforced many times. This is apt to be needed, although with declining frequency, throughout even the most successful, long-term therapeutic effort. The reason is partly the contrast with the usual doctor–patient model, as we have seen, but more important, it is because for almost all clients the meanings attributed to being told that the client has to find her own answers and that these reside within her are confusing and frightening and portend life disruption. Clients protest in varying terms:

"You mean you can't help me?"
"If I had the answers inside of me, I'd have already found them."
"Then what do I need you for?"
"Just use will power and quit belly-aching, huh?"
"You're telling me I just have to think differently about my life. Is that it?"
"But then I'm left with just me! And that's not enough."
"I don't like to think that because if so, I've wasted an awful lot of time and missed a lot of good chances."

All of these people hear only discouraging news from the therapist. Most misunderstand the meaning of the instruction; only the last begins to get toward one of the big and actual threats in the message, though even that client hears only the remorseful aspect and overlooks the possibility of positive change.

It is the threat to familiar ways of being that underlies much of the difficulty people have in grasping and putting to use the message that they have within them the potential to deal with the life issues which have been so distressing heretofore. Remembering our earlier discussion of the importance to the self-and-world construct system to feelings of well-being and a sense of security in life,

it is apparent that these misunderstandings are, at least in part, motivated by the impulse to protect the construct systems of these clients.

These misunderstandings are "resistances" as we have already defined this term. Such resistances are not to be resolved by simple logical refutation or by vigorous argumentation. What is required is working through them in the moment in which they are manifest. Working through means identifying the frequency and pattern of the resistance, pointing out that it must be or seem to be useful in some way and that it has been learned or incorporated for that reason, and then exposing how the work of self-exploration is impeded by the pattern. Again, this is not a one-time matter; rather, repeated confrontations (coupled with appropriate support) adapted to each individual instance are what is called for. (See Bugental 1976, 1990 for examples.)

This work has to do with "situational resistances," obstacles to the work arising from the therapeutic situation itself. These are important, not only as they interfere with the development of a productive mode for the work but as "training" experiences for later facing and working through life patterns, "character resistances." Those patterns that are more centrally significant aspects of the client's self-and-world construct system must eventually be confronted if significant and lasting change is to result.

Teaching the Client Higher-Order Searching Skills

We have earlier described the vital human capacity to which we gave the name "searching." We all use this power when we are in a situation for which we do not have a well-practiced way of responding; however, few of us understand the nature of this power or how to realize the most from it.

Three conditions are essential to the client's use of searching: (1) as full a presence in the work as is possible, (2) an attempt to describe as fully as possible what really matters at this moment in one's life, and (3) maintaining an expectancy of discovery.

To be genuinely present in the work is to immerse oneself in one's concern about some life issue, mobilizing emotions, intelligence, and intentionality. Doing so requires an affirmative commitment in the moment to the task at hand (rather than a busyness about avoiding or excluding distraction), and it calls for risking going into the unknown and unknowing places within oneself.

The thorough account that is required means first of all a trust invested in the therapist. This seldom is complete until the pair have worked together for some time. To tell another person all that comes into one's awareness is an embarrassing, hazardous, and unfamiliar enterprise. In addition, so much comes into consciousness that there is inevitably the need to select. Early in the work, that selection is often guided by protecting one's image in front of the observer. Later, if the work goes well, it is guided by the client's growing sense of what is truly important to her life.

Finally, one of the most difficult elements for many clients is to learn how to maintain a genuine expectancy of discovery. As we have already observed, many of us initially expect to be reporting about ourselves to the doctor. A tremendous range of meanings reside in that expectation. Gradually we come to learn the so significant truth of how much more is available within ourselves than what has seemed the sum of consciousness. When that realization really strikes home, the world opens in fresh and exciting ways.

Working through Some of the Character Resistances

"Resistance" is a term we use for all client-derived influences that work to limit, slow, or mislead the client's inner searching and her bringing to awareness what searching discloses. The situation of psychotherapy itself engenders some resistances as we have already seen. As the therapeutic work deepens, another set of resistances arises due to the calling into question of the ways the client has defined himself and his world. This second layer of resistance is by far the more threatening for the client to confront.

Frank came to experience frustration that his relentless opposition was interfering with the progress of therapy, and he determined to change that pattern. However, when he actually attempted that change he discovered great waves of fear, resentment, and then remorse within himself. When he felt closeness with the therapist and that it was reciprocated, he panicked and quickly tried to start a verbal fight. For Frank, recognition of the need to reduce his antagonism in the therapy hour was relatively easy, but recognition of how much that antagonism was deeply embedded in his whole sense of himself and how he needed to be in order to survive in his world was a whole different matter (Bugental, 1976, pp. 101–140; 1990c, various pages).

The working-through process with character resistances is often more time-consuming and difficult because these are less easily circumscribed than situational issues. As described above, the process nature of the self-and-world construct system and its fluidity mean that defining percepts for one's own identity and for the perceptual world are significantly more implicit than explicit and that they frequently "bleed" into each other. Character structures/resistance arise from experience that actually began at the pre-verbal level and then are extended and modified by all the client's life and inner promptings. An analogy to a mixture of liquids is more accurate than one to a pile of building blocks.

Because of this fluid morphology, client and therapist must join in identifying patterns that are limiting and destructive and discovering them again and again in a variety of circumstances. It is doubtful whether all such influences can ever be spotted, but when a sufficient number and their unwanted consequences have been feelingfully recognized by the client, a lessening of their potency has already begun. As we will show next, valid perception of this kind is the change agency.

Exploring Client–Therapist Collusion (Transference–Countertransference Issues)

A potent route to discovery of the character resistance lies through investigating the evolution of the therapeutic alliance. A healthy bond between client and therapist is never a static linkage. This is obvious when we reflect again on the process nature of self-and-world construct systems, for the alliance is the engagement of two such systems, and both are in continual flux. When the work of therapy plateaus, it is often the case that there is an unconscious collusion between the participants, an unspoken and unrecognized accord not to open up areas that may be threatening for one or both.

Often the very qualities that have combined to facilitate the early therapeutic work—the forging of the original alliance, the overcoming of situational resistances, and the approach to characterological issues—these very bonding elements now are what stand in the way. They have served well, but their usefulness has been largely exhausted.

We will describe next a way of thinking about transference and countertransference. Suffice it to say, at this point, that the collusion demonstrates the presence of both of these distorting influences. Thus the resistance to recognizing what is happening comes from both sides. Here it is almost always the therapist's responsibility to recognize what has happened and to open the way for freeing awareness (and, often, the avoided material) to emerge.

Working with Residual Transferential Elements

It is important and realistic to recognize that all transference and countertransference projections are seldom if ever worked out. It is not necessary that they be. Much gain in life effectiveness and satisfaction is won from working through as much as time, money, and other circumstances warrant, giving at least nominal recognition that there is always more and then ending the engagement with mutual satisfaction.

The transference processes are not something gone wrong. They add dimension to all our relations and activities. If we were stranded on the barren shore of just what is actual and known to us at any point, we would be impoverished in our own experience and in our relations with each other. The myth of a perfect state free of all projections, distortions, and blind spots is indeed a myth. Indeed, it is itself a transference and a dangerous one. That danger is greater when the therapist unconsciously colludes with the client to strive for this chimera of perfection.

Preparing for Termination

It is likely that no phase of major psychotherapy is as elusive, as idiosyncratic, and as much the focus of debate as is the ending of the work. Textbook conclusions, including those written by the senior author (J.F.T.B.), are usually well structured, carefully worked out, and mutually satisfactory. Actual endings seldom match those ideals. What we can say, accordingly, will be incomplete and suggestive rather than prescriptive.

The therapeutic alliance is a professional arrangement, a love affair, a duel, a blood bond, a journey into unknown lands for untested companions, and an opportunity for both to grow. When the work goes well, it touches deeply into the psyche of both participants, it arouses a range of emotions, and it lives always under the threat of its ending.

Ideally, as the work progresses there come periods when the client begins to find her enthusiasm for the work fluctuating, when she feels more pull from other parts of her life than she knew when the exploration was at its height, and this change seems less a resistance than an expression of healthy interest expanding from the earlier necessary self-preoccupation.

The needed, but often difficult, transition is that of moving from being truly present to one's own inner living while in the sponsoring presence of a strong and supportive companion to trying to maintain this same inner attunement on one's own (or with others in one's life).

The client often experiences apprehension when the idea of no longer having the support of the therapist surfaces. This is, of course, a residual transference evoked by the thought of "going it alone" and seeking to make the therapist a continuing figure in the client's life (e.g., spouse, lover, or parent). It may also be an expression of appropriate regret at ending what for many is a fascinating chapter of their lives and at leaving a relationship of genuine and mutual caring.

Indeed, at the end of an extended, intimate, and productive course of depth psychotherapy, there is loss to both the client and the therapist. This is appropriate, and, if effectively recognized and worked with, working through this loss can be supportive of the gains that the client has made. Similarly, it can contribute to the therapist's maturing personally and professionally.

Posttherapy relations pose a problem. Many who speak on this matter pronounce any continuations an anathema, and much may be said for "once the therapist, always the therapist," with the flat proscription that implies. If a client needs to return to therapy after leaving it for some time, it is disruptive to have to work through any intervening connections the client and the therapist may have had. (Of course, there are many potential disruptions all along in therapy, and these must be incorporated into the work as they occur. This does not license posttherapy encounters, but it does put them in perspective.)

Probably the three most dependable guidelines for terminations are these: The client's expectations and the therapist's expectations should be open for mutual discussion. It is wisest to plan for no or minimal contact (e.g., occasional phone calls) at least at first until both parties have had a period of reflection. Third, in the event that the relation is resumed and especially if some intimacy occurs, it should be clearly understood that the client will seek other help if further therapy is required. The American Psychological Association's ethical code specifies that a 2-year hiatus is minimal before any sexual intimacy is acceptable.

This is a difficult area and one that is much discussed in the current literature. Unilateral and dogmatic pronouncements have only made rational exploration of the issues more difficult. It is hoped that further discussion will be relieved of this handicap.

THE STANCE OF THE THERAPIST

The notion of a *pou sto* (Greek phrase denoting a place from which to assert power or influence) is fundamental in this orientation. For example, in our perspective the therapist founds his participation on conceptions of the authentic situation of the client and the complementing authentic role of the therapist.

The authentic situation of the client: For example, this is a person in the midst of her life trying to make sense of what she experiences, trying to guide what she will do, trying to be more fulfilled and comfortable. She is talking to the therapist because she wants to be more able to be truly in her life and to accomplish her purposes in it more readily. When she is talking to the therapist, another person, she knows at some level that he is in a very similar situation and is neither all-knowing nor all-powerful.

The authentic therapist role: He is here to aid this person in her efforts to find greater fulfillment in her life. He can do this best if he confines the bulk of his efforts to noting how this person pursues fulfillment, how well the person uses all her resources, and how the person defeats herself. He does not know—nor can he ever know—all there is to know about this person; she will always know (at least latently) more about herself and her own life than he can or does. He does not know how she should live her life or guide her choices. He has his hands full just trying to manage his own life, so he cannot in conscience try to manage this person's life. He can, however, provide her with a trained awareness and a disciplined manner of intervening—both focused on how she uses her capacities for herself.

The moral of this stance is that therapists are not consultants in how to live. They can be consultants in how to use one's own capacities to better guide living (Bugental, 1984).

These conceptions make it possible to give a particular meaning to the familiar terms "transference" and "countertransference." Looking at the authentic client situation, we can ask, "How does she talk to the therapist?" "Does she talk in line with this reality, or is there implicit in what she says some distortion of this reality?" Obviously, if the latter is the case, transference is manifest.

Similarly, when we think about the authentic therapist's role, the questions are: "How does the therapist participate with the client?" "Does he become parental, advising, chiding, overly affectionate?" "Does he try to protect the client from the client's own actions?" "Does he get drawn into the client's extratherapy decisions?" Affirmative answers in such instances indicate countertransference.

The manner of the existential–humanistic therapist's carrying this *pou sto* into effect is distinctive in several ways:

1. Central attention is given to the presence (as this concept was described above) of both therapist and client.
2. The therapist chiefly attends to the process aspects of the patient's presentation, while the client is, of course, often occupied with the content.
3. Therapist interventions tend to direct attention to the ways the client is less than fully present and committed to the work (i.e., to the resistance).
4. The corrective effect of successful therapy is attained by the client's coming to recognize and reduce her self-imposed limits on and distortions of her own awareness and thus on her self-definition and her conception of the nature of world.

With process being so pivotal, the therapist must give particular attention to the quality of the client's presence in the work (e.g., earnest, flippant, troubled, dismissing, or defensive), to the client's readiness to attend to and be surprised by her own words and manner (in contrast to intending merely a report to the therapist), and to the recurrent ways in which the client disrupts or avoids subjective depth, emotionality, and unwelcome discoveries within himself. This last is, of course, the client's resistance.

The principle governing the bulk of the therapist's activity is that of assigning priority to whatever is likely to foster the client's own internal searching process and to help open for the client fresh vistas on her own life and the way in which she is conducting it.

Accordingly, therapists of this orientation vary markedly in the form and frequency of their interventions. Moreover, the same therapist may vary in these ways from client to client or even at various points with the same client. There is no standard procedure; there is only this overriding intent to foster the client's inner searching.

Therapists serving this purpose may be silent for long periods—especially early in the work when the client is relating history and complaining about his life or later when the client has learned the skill of inward searching and is carrying on her work without need of therapist intrusion.

At other times therapists may be active, reflecting back client attitudes and emotions, challenging habitual evasive patterns, calling for greater mobilization of client energies, sharing their own experiences or reactions to what is occurring, or supporting the client through pain and despair. These kinds of participation may be constant, even verging on being harassing; they may be occasional, seeking to highlight key points; or they may take other patterns depending on how the client is progressing in her task

of getting to know her own inner living patterns more fully and productively.

This searching process is the powerful human capacity to continually bring forward in consciousness fresh perceptions of matters of genuine life concern and all that is related to them. It is our conviction that the client's issues, in most cases, stem from truncated and distorted ways of seeing important life issues, ways brought about by earlier life experiences and now mistaken for the only way that life can be. Change comes when fresh perspectives open up possibilities that formerly were unseen.

We do not believe therapists can cause change; we do believe that therapists can throw light on life patterns that have brought about pain and frustration. When that occurs it is the client's responsibility to make whatever changes she feels possible and desirable.

In carrying out this program, therapists come to recognize that transference and countertransference (as we have identified these processes above) are always present in some degree. The task is to identify when such distortions interfere with the client's work of inner exploration. Early in the work the transference may actually further that work, while later in the therapy, countertransference is more likely to be at once helpful and distracting.

The skills required of therapists practicing in this way are varied, but all rest on a deep personal commitment to valuing human life and well-being. With that foundation, a next realm of highly refined sensitivity and articulateness in communication is called for. At a still higher level of development, the need is for the therapist to have the kind of self-knowledge and maturity that having one's own personal therapy should (but does not always) provide. Concurrently, a firm and continuous base of collegial support is so important as to approach being literally essential.

In one sense the foregoing constitutes a basis on which each therapist must develop a flexible but tough view of human nature, of the life confrontations with which we all must deal, and of the unique, subtle, powerful, and endlessly evolving relationships that are the therapeutic alliance.

CURATIVE FACTORS OR MECHANISMS OF CHANGE

Marcel Proust wrote, "The real voyage of discovery consists not in seeing new landscapes but in having new eyes." The fundamental change agency in all human experience is changed perception. When we see familiar situations freshly, we see possibilities previously invisible. The central task of existential–humanistic psychotherapy is to help the client discover the ways he has limited his perception of important life areas. As this recognition is being reached, change is already occurring. This is the startling reality: The process of coming to realize how we have blocked our awareness in any life area is at the same time the very process that begins to reduce that blockage.

To achieve this result, this freeing of the client's perception, the client must be helped to be as fully present in and to the work as possible. Presence, so conceived, is the quality of being fully accessible and unreservedly expressive in the moment. This is a dimension of experience without an ultimate point. We are always something less than fully present. The ways in which we limit our presence are the ways in which we limit our awareness, but—and this is the crucially important point—they are also the ways in which we give our lives form and meaning.

Thus, as therapist and client work to help the client reduce these restrictions (the "resistances"), that work is rightly experienced as threatening to the client's way of being. It is "rightly" experienced in that the way the client is in the world must be modified if she is to give her vision greater range, but not "rightly" in the sense that she is in genuine danger of being destroyed.

It will be evident from the foregoing that a very particular kind of "insight" is the key ingredient in therapeutic change. This is not the sort of insight that an interpretation from the therapist can offer or that a traditional psychoanalyst might advance or even that a client can express in a summarizing sentence or two.

"Inner vision" is a term that better conveys a broader grasp of subjective processes that is here intended and that is in contrast to a single perception ("you're angry with me because you see me as your father"). Inner vision is the multilevel, polymeaningful, affective–cognitive–conative, pre- or transverbal recognition that comes to us at times of authentic inner awareness. It is often so subtle and pervasive that it can only partially be grasped and reported in words. However, if truly experienced, the person will be changed in some measure thereafter.

Of course, one occurrence of such inner vision is neither the end point nor the "cure" the client seeks; nor is it sufficient in itself to bring about lasting changes. The working-through process in which a pattern of limitations on awareness is identified repeatedly and in a range of contexts is essential to any lasting changes.

From what has just been said, it will be apparent that the existential–humanistic therapist seldom, if ever, attempts interpretations that try to create inner vision directly. However, these therapists will often confront clients with the fact that they limit their awareness, with the manifested (if unconscious) need for so limiting themselves, and with the likelihood that they are paying a considerable price in their well-being to maintain these limitations.

This work centers around a focus on how the client is in her life. This rather ambiguous phrase summarizes the attitudes the client has toward the fact of her being alive, toward the direction her life is going, toward the degree to which the client feels able to bring about life changes, toward the relationships and activities with which her life is furnished, and toward her general outlook on being in both its broadest and its most immediate terms. The *how* of this *is* is a capacity to be open, allowing, and freshly appreciative of what lies as yet unknown within the client.

The main area of observation in attaining this focus is on the client's presence in therapy and on the client's use of the therapeutic opportunity. Presence is an experiential state known to everyone, at least implicitly, yet often overlooked. Perhaps it is most easily identified by what it is not. Presence is *not* "talking about" a client's issues, discussing the client's thoughts or patterns of behavior. It is *not* having a congenial relation or being responsive or discussing important matters in the client's life. Presence *is* an attitude of intention, commitment, and willingness to risk. When both client and therapist are present to the client's subjective experiencing, a powerful energy is evoked which may result in an increase in "aware being" for the client.

In the foregoing we have placed emphasis on the presence of both client and therapist. Therapy, as here conceived, is not something done to a client; it is an achievement of the partnership of the two so engaged.

The obvious implication of this recognition is that the mental–emotional well-being of the therapist is an essential variable in the process. This does not call for therapists to be "clear" or free of all emotional problems. It does mean that

to the extent that a therapist can be truly present in the engagement with the client, to that extent his contribution to the endeavor will be optimal.

Some therapeutic approaches have been characterized as "nothing but just being with the client." This is a naive and possibly dangerous oversimplification. To be genuinely with another person is the culmination of much individual and cooperative effort. As we have described above, some might regard presence as "just being with." When that dismissing attitude prevails, techniques often are of more concern to the therapist than is presence. The result is that limitations are introduced into the work without the therapist realizing it. To say it differently, preoccupation with techniques may be the therapist's resistance to genuinely being present with the client.

Successful therapy depends on the convergence of client and therapist presence. For this to occur, the client's concern for her life must be mobilized. It is useful to think of the client's concern as having four aspects: (1) pain, stress, anxiety, or some other form of distress; (2) hope, yearning for a different life experience; (3) readiness to commit fully—time, emotion, effort, money—to the task; and (4) acceptance of the need to attend inwardly to bring about the desired changes.

In the effective therapeutic alliance, the client's concern is met and supported by the therapist's matching concern which also can be characterized as having four facets: (1) the work must respond to some genuine *need* of the therapist; (2) the therapist comes to have a *vision* of the latent healthiness of the client; (3) the therapist is prepared to be *present* even before the client can attain that state; and (4) the therapist has learned to trust, protect, and use deep *sensitivity*.

This convergence of client and therapist concern—never total, but often growing—forges a force of great power which can contend with the weight of years of living out a cramped self-and-world view and, often, the pressures of others to keep the client from changing. When the therapeutic alliance does draw on this powerful energy, psychotherapy employs one of the most powerful forces in the world. If this characterization seems extreme, recall that all other energies—electrical, gravitational, mechanical, and others—have been harnessed and directed by human intention.

Toward Integration of Therapeutic Systems

Existential–humanistic psychotherapy shares many aspects with other depth approaches: emphasis on therapist emotional readiness, on the alliance with the client, on identifying resistances (although defining resistances somewhat differently by relating their significance to limiting one's life space and curtailing awareness of such limits), on the working-through process, and on respect for the client's autonomy and powers. In these regards, the contrasts are greatest with the directive, content-focused, and therapist-dominated modes of conducting psychotherapy.

We participate regularly in efforts to find bridges between therapeutic orientations, for we believe that important underlying regularities may be disclosed by comparisons among contrasting perspectives. Nevertheless, we are concerned that the urge for unification avoid leading to obscuring significant contrasts.

For us, there are three radical aspects of the existential–humanistic approach, aspects that must be taken into account in all such comparative studies:

1. The therapist does not seek to account for the client's complaint, symptoms, or condition in terms of the client's history. This kind of causal thinking is likely to result in objectifying the client and losing the genuine presence needed for productive searching. Instead, complaint, symptoms, and condition are recognized as manifestations of the way the client is in the world and of the client's efforts to make his life more satisfying and less painful.

2. The therapist's contribution is principally that of fostering greater client inner awareness, a task carried forward by identifying the constraining and distorting influences affecting that awareness.

3. The healing agency is identified as enlarging and changing the client's way of being alive in the world, and this is deemed to be an educative enterprise rather than a medical, curative, or healing one (in our usual conceptions of these terms).

TREATMENT APPLICABILITY

In estimating how widely the existential–humanistic approach is applicable, it is necessary to make a distinction between the existential–humanistic perspective on life and the ways in which that outlook may be applied in various settings and with contrasting client populations. The former is widely pertinent; the latter, as we are here describing it, is more limited.

The existential perspective regards the very fact of our being and our being conscious as the prime data on which all else rests—especially when we are concerned with human life. The humanistic value system posits a corresponding priority to the freeing and realizing (recognizing and making real) of latent human capacities for fuller, more creative, and more satisfying living. The combined perspective and value system has the potential to support and illuminate work with all human populations. At this point in the development of the view, we do not know with any certainty what may be the range of applicability of the therapeutic form we detailed above.

These application modes described here have been chiefly developed and applied to what are conventionally called the adjustment problems, character disorders, and psychoneuroses of adult clients. Moreover, they have been largely drawn from people within the broad span of the middle and upper socioeconomic levels. Some further extensions of the orientation have been informally reported in work with socially and economically deprived persons (e.g., homeless and vagrant), adolescent offenders, and noninstitutionalized psychotic persons. In most of these instances it is likely that the perspective and values have been the most effective ingredients, while the specifics of application have been modified to varying degrees. Published accounts of such efforts are lacking at this time.

A developing area is the extension of the perspective and some phases of the methodology to couples and families. In this work, the approach emphasizes that these clients are each living persons in the midst of a life situation that each seeks to make more satisfying and less painful and that their separate self-and-world systems include each other. Viewed this way, the relationships are explored to find where there is readiness for change and accommodation, how each person is "using" the others involved in efforts to be more fulfilled, and how the potential for growth may be mobilized.

When one examines the sorts of modifications that are usually made in applying this approach to other categories of persons, the key consideration is, once again, the readiness of the client to be genuinely present. When a potential client—individual, couple, or family—is considered, the questions are, can this

person (these persons) be helped to be significantly present in the work? If not, is the person (are the persons) sufficiently accessible to be helped toward greater (sufficient) presence?

This criterion means that the prognosis for the major psychoses, organic conditions, and sociopathic states is less hopeful for this approach. In such instances the existential–humanistic psychotherapist will usually refer to other resources. By the same token, when a potential client is unwilling to engage in the alliance and work toward greater presence and when a reasonable trial has demonstrated that that resistance is unlikely to change, referral for adjustment counseling may be appropriate.

Because of the emphasis on mutual presence, this form of therapeutic engagement may lead to greater risk of undue involvement of therapists and clients. It is scarcely an exaggeration to say that a long successful course of depth therapy is an intimacy not unlike a love affair. Like such an engagement, impulse and deep emotion can overwhelm judgment unless safeguards are in place. Very likely the best such protections come when therapists have intensive and extended personal psychotherapy and when they regularly share their experiences with peers and senior colleagues. These supports need to be reinforced by the value system of the perspective with its emphasis on respect for clients' autonomy and long-term needs.

CASE ILLUSTRATION

Scott is 32 years old, single, a college graduate, and successful in a creative field but unable to maintain employment in one firm. He was referred by his former lover who was concurrently entering therapy with me (M.M.S.). Because of this, I hesitated to accept him into treatment. I did, however, agree to see him once, anticipating that I would refer him to another therapist.

At our first meeting, Scott was tense, charged up, afraid. While not aggressive about it, he expressed extreme skepticism about the likely efficacy of therapy and the honesty and good will of therapists. He reported that as an unwilling teenager he was sent into therapy by his father. Thus, he asserted, he was suspicious about therapy now.

Desperate, confused, he wanted help he did not believe anyone could give. He knew he could not do what he needed for himself; yet he did not want to trust anyone, especially anyone who might employ an institutionalized way of doing things. From the beginning I could feel the challenge thrown down to me. Still, he was not hostile emotionally, just intellectually. Clearly, I was on trial.

Scott described being a mountain climber and motorcycle rider. He admitted to being unable to keep a job or a deep relationship. Candidly he told of being verbally abusive to the woman with whom he had been living, even though he considered her one of the "two loves of my life." This abuse pattern had also characterized the previous serious affair and was repeated to some extent in his work relations. Thus he was being forced to face the similarity between his conduct at work and at home.

Scott wanted answers. He wanted to figure himself out. He wanted me to know him and to tell him what I saw so that he could pick and choose whatever seemed accurate or reasonable or useful for him. He wanted to keep all the cards in his own hand.

My immediate concern was whether I could ethically and practically work with both Scott and his former lover, Bella. I explored this with my consultant and with both clients. Eventually we agreed that we would give it a trial, with the understanding that no information would pass through me in either direction.

As I outlined these matters to Scott, I also told him that I could help him find another therapist if that seemed best. At this point, there was a startling change in Scott: He became agitated, almost to the point of panic. The palpable fear he evinced surprised me. He gasped out, "I want to work with you. Please work with me. I don't know anyone else." The stark, lonely, bleak, emptiness in his soul and in his daily existence shocked me. Beneath his intellectual confidence and worldly success lived a very small and tender boy. I was taken aback. And with the caveat that when I saw her, I would have to ask Bella's agreement to this arrangement, I tentatively agreed to work with him.

As it worked out, I saw both Scott and Bella, each twice weekly for hour-long sessions. Therapy with Scott was often rocky but never distant. Looking back, I have not regretted working with both of these creative people simultaneously. In fact, it was a demanding and exciting learning process about the ways that one relationship, one incident, one topic could be seen and experienced dramatically differently by two people. While not a new recognition, seeing it vividly lived out in my consulting room revealed how shallow is our usual understanding of this fundamental reality: The self-and-world constructs of two people can drastically separate them despite their good intentions to the contrary.

Assessment

Beyond sensitive evaluation of the ego functioning of a prospective client, formal, objectified, and objectifying assessment is not in harmony with our perspective's emphasis on the subjective. Instead, we seek to be open to learn about, to know, and to enter a client's world. It is impossible fully to make explicit how a therapist knows the being-in-the-world of another while remaining separate and observant in a chair across the room. Yet that was precisely my task.

I attempted to empty myself of preconceptions in order to listen with as much presence as I could muster in any given moment. With Scott, the demand he placed on my presence was constant. He came with a creative mind, a vivid imagination, and a great deal of vitality and energy. What I said to him had to balance two sometimes conflicting necessities: to be as authentic in myself as possible while not providing grist for his continual, self-defeating intellectualizations and oppositional vigilance.

In time, this very interaction between his oppositional compulsion and my determination genuinely to stay with him led us to the way his transference was demonstrated in each hour. He would refute whatever I said to him. Although he was wearing me down, he needed to see he could not make me give up in rage, disapproval, or exhaustion. He appreciated that I never backed down, I could be delicate, and I named the unspeakable—accurate details of how I was experiencing the moment. For Scott, I was "real" instead of "professional" and therefore (somewhat) trustworthy, even when he felt distrust. Slowly, he became able to stay with the fear that underlay his quick verbal objections.

Not by direct history taking but by a gradual unfolding in the course of this work, we learned more of his background. Scott's gifted father had survived terrible war experiences, come to this country, and become very successful in his field—like his son's, a creative one. When he was in his midteens, Scott's mother, an artist, died at home after a long illness. As the eldest of three siblings, he became the protector of his sister (a year and a half younger) and brother (6 years younger) from his father's unreasonable demands and rages.

In one session, typical of the more constructive interviews, Scott vividly described feeling that he was on a rock alone battling for justice, completely misunderstood as a boy in need of love, his vitality seen as dangerous and his decency seen as rebellion. I confirmed his contrasting view, reinterpreted his seeming rebellion as a legitimate determination not to be stripped of his most needed character strength, and agreed that it was unfair for his father to beat and berate him and his younger brother. Scott's relief at being heard and having his actions affirmed as legitimate brought out a tender, fearful boy beneath the more familiar opposition. This contributed to his growing integration.

In this way he came to see that his vast energy fueled an urgent desire to overcome the loss of love and to protect himself and others. This force within him also at times took the form of a rage that was simultaneously righteous, patterned on his father, and expressive of grief for childhood losses. Now he began to "make sense" to himself and, with that, to develop some responsibility for the ways he expressed his passion.

Scott's characteristic intensity colored our work throughout. His emotional response to my insistence on his being truly present resulted in his feeling in a double bind of his own making: He hated my insistence on his presence, but he discovered that I would meet him in what he thought to be an unorthodox way (i.e., not with detached silence). That recognition reduced his initial concern that he would be treated in a routine manner.

Our work went forward marked by struggle, humor, seriousness, and sometimes tears, and by my repeatedly confronting him with his avoidance of his pain. The strength of our alliance was repeatedly tried, but it held. Once when he arrived in a panic, I insisted he not take refuge in his intellectual explanations or his objections to me and to therapy. Instead I kept him focused on his moment-to-moment experiencing. At one point, he cried out, "But why should I go directly into where I hurt?" Yet, his very intensity led him to do just that. And I watched in awe as a man who had been driven for years to avoid standing still and experiencing his own fear actually opened himself to that fear.

Scott was moving, in all probability, toward experiencing the pain of his mother's death and all the deprivations linked to that. As he neared a "yawning black pit" which he dreaded to enter, Scott left therapy prematurely. He announced that he wanted to be "on my own." He promised to contact me in a month, but his job took him away for a year. During this time he wrote to me occasionally, and I always answered.

He returned to therapy about 2 years later. Once again his rage was hurting his life. He had expected to be "cured" and was angry at me and this "artificial process" for not releasing him from the hell of recurrent fury. He listened to my explanations of the necessity for working through and the need for time. We struggled again, but with a difference. The change was typified by his letting himself really hear me when I told him that our joint commitment to his life was far more central to the work than his intellectualizing and figuring out on which he had largely relied. This was a direct challenge to his treasured defense of separateness, but now he did not reject it. For a year he puzzled over his continual difficulties in relationships, worked hard to understand situational battles, and, then, once again left to work in another city.

We both know there is more work to be done. This time, I have more confidence that he will return.

Commentary

I (J.F.T.B.) find this therapeutic course particularly interesting in that it clearly centered around the theme of presence. The client, an unusually intelligent, verbal, and manipulative man, relied on being apart, oppositional, and clever to feel safe in his world. However, this policy had resulted in his feeling isolated, incomplete, and rageful. Of course, he brought to the therapeutic engagement his unrecognized underlying fears, his well-practiced resistances to being really seen (in his view, "trapped"), and his pain and despair.

While the therapist (M.M.S.) used a range of responses, she maintained steady insistence on the client's facing his poverty of life and his great reliance on patterns that were futile. This stance might be typical of therapists representing a range of perspectives; what was distinctive was that putting prime emphasis on how the client was in the room (rather than working out a historic scenario to account for his problems) brought the whole process to immediate life.

Every client acts in terms of his own self-and-world construct system every moment (not just in the therapist's office). Yet for so long we have tried to objectify our clients, for so long sought to figure them out, and so frequently have overlooked the living reality of what is immediately present. Calling on the client to be truly present is calling for immediate display of the very patterns that cripple the client's life.

An intrinsic tenet of the existential–humanistic approach is that interpretations of the client's life and patterns are minimal except as these processes are immediately manifested in the room and as the client is ready to recognize their terrible cost. This therapist was drawn into interpreting and reframing some of Scott's experience (especially his defense of his brother from their father's brutality). As far as can be discerned, that intervention had desirable results. Taking a stance more strictly in keeping with our view, the therapist might have pondered the question, "Why did Scott, an extremely intelligent person, not see for himself this other way of viewing the matter?" What is suggested here is not a question to be actually voiced to Scott. It is a way the therapist might remind herself that there were important resistances preventing Scott's using that superior intelligence.

This approach might have had the advantage of bringing therapeutic attention to the more general resistance which limited Scott's readiness to use his own judgment. On the other hand, it may well have been that Scott was not yet ready to confront what was obviously a major resistance (and therefore central to his way of being in the world). It is evident that the reframing actually given expedited Scott's willingness to be more present in the work.

This contrasting of alternative interventions is illustrative of work in this vein: We always recognize there are many possible paths open for the therapeutic course and that therapist and client alike bear the continual responsibility to make the best choices they can at each moment. Also illustrated is our conviction that the modes we most emphasize (in this case attempting to bring the larger resistance to consciousness) are not absolute rules but helpful guides. Only the aware, present, and responsible judgment of the individual therapist is irreplaceable.

RESEARCH

Research and the further refinement of both the supporting conceptual structure and the clinical applications of our existential–humanistic approach are important to us. As will doubtlessly be evident from what has been described above, conventional research methods emphasizing objectification and statistical evaluations are fundamentally incompatible with this perspective. Thus our concern with research and development requires that we become a part of the growing movement loosely gathered under the name of "human sciences" (Giorgi, 1970, 1984, 1986; Packer & Addison, 1989; Polkinghorne, 1983).

Pertinent aspects of this fresh scientific mode include the emphasis on qualitative as opposed to quantitative data, the use of narrative (Howard, 1991; Polkinghorne, 1988), developing comparisons among views of the same subject (Kutash & Wolf, 1986; Saltzman & Norcross, 1990), and employment of the phenomenological approach (Giorgi, 1970, 1984, 1986; Merleau-Ponty, 1964).

Phenomenological investigations of various aspects of the therapy have been reported (Rahilly, 1993; Sterling, 1992; Sterling & Bugental, 1993, in press).

Authors identified with this perspective have contributed to the more extensive literature pertinent to the approach:

General comparative descriptions: Buber, 1965; Bugental, 1990b, 1991b; Bugental & Bracke, 1992; Bugental & Kleiner, 1993; Bugental & McBeath, 1994; Bugental & Sterling, 1991; Jourard, 1963, 1964; Koestenbaum, 1978; May, 1961; Mahoney, 1991; Schneider, 1990; Walsh, 1984; Yalom, 1980.

Discussions of issues in conducting such therapy: Boss, 1962, 1963; Bracke & Bugental, 1995; Bugental 1988; Bugental & Bradford, 1992; Bugental & Sapienza, 1992; Gendlin, 1962; Havens, 1989; Levenson, 1983, 1991; Mahrer, 1983, 1986; Phillips, 1980–1981; Sterling & Bugental, 1993; Stolorow, Brandchaft, & Atwood, 1987; van Deurzen-Smith, 1988.

Anecdotal case reports by therapists: Armstrong & Bugental, 1995; Bugental 1978, 1986, 1990a, 1990c; Schneider &

May, 1995; Yalom, 1990; Yalom & Elkin, 1974; and by former clients who have chosen to disclose their own identities (Cogswell, 1971; Walsh, 1984).

Teaching materials: Bugental, 1978, 1987, 1990d; Gendlin, 1978; Havens, 1974; Howard, 1991; Keen, 1970; May, Angel, & Ellenberger, 1958; Ofman, 1976; D. Shapiro, 1965, 1989; Sterling, 1990.

Observations about life: Bugental, 1991a, 1992; Bugental & Bugental, 1986, 1989; Bugental & Flannes, 1993; May, 1961; Schneider, 1993; Yalom, 1992.

It is beyond the scope of this presentation to survey the many forms in which creative research is being conducted using fresh modalities. Instead, we will select one and present a synoptic account of the phenomenological methods taught by Amadeo Giorgi (1984, 1986):

Lived ordinary experience is the subject matter of the phenomenological research tradition. This approach sets out to describe the phenomenon and to search for its essential structure and meaning. Psychological phenomenology does pursue a rigorous, disciplined analysis of the lived phenomenon, including acknowledging the encounter of the researcher with the data.

This method is congruent with existential thought in that it looks to the body as the source of experiencing. It attends to the gestalt of feeling and thought and to a sense of "fit" with being-in-the-world.

It is as though we are thrown into the world of the novelist and poet where the attempt is to capture and represent the deepest human experiences and the mystery of the human encounter. The interpenetration of our mutual living needs to be so rendered that the intrinsic spirit of the experience is transmitted as well as its form and function. This parallel to the arts suggests that psychology, deeming itself a science in this country, has

not yet found a way to remain true to its origin in the psyche while yet being a rigorous investigation into its own realm. (See Rahilly, 1993; K. J. Shapiro, 1985; Sterling, 1992.)

Just as we recognized in describing the concept of the self-and-world construct system, conventional language is too gross to handle the subtleties, the multiplicity, and the transverbal nature of the most significant and subjective human experiences. What is true of words is, of course, even truer of numbers. Treating any group—whether identified by diagnosis, personality type, presenting problem, or demographic variables—as though it were sufficiently homogeneous to be a stable "sample" of human experience is, to our way of thinking, an assured way of losing the most important variables affecting human life and that aspect of human life we call personal subjectivity (and thus the reach of depth psychotherapy).

Because there are major difficulties in developing adequate research methods is no reason to abandon the effort. Quite to the contrary, the task is so important (and has so much larger implications for human life generally) that we must accept the challenge, do what we can at this point, and persist in the effort to move toward more definitive research products.

NOTE

1. Sterling's case commented on by Bugental.

SUGGESTIONS FOR FURTHER READING

Case Reports

Bugental, J. F. T. (1976). *The search for existential identity*. San Francisco: Jossey-Bass.

Bugental, J. F. T. (1986). Existential-humanistic psychotherapy. In I. L. Kutash & A. Wolf (Eds.). *Psychotherapist's casebook* (pp. 222–236). San Francisco: Jossey-Bass.

Bugental, J. F. T. (1990). The envious lover. In N. Saltzman & J. C. Norcross (Eds.), *Therapy wars: Contention and convergence in differing clinical approaches* (pp. 92–112). San Francisco: Jossey-Bass.

Bugental, J. F. T. (1990). *Intimate journeys: Stories from life-changing psychotherapy.* San Francisco: Jossey-Bass.

Havens, L. L. (1989). *A safe place.* New York: Ballentine.

Yalom, I. D. (1990). *Love's executioner.* New York: Basic Books.

Yalom, I. D., & Elkin, G. (1974). *Every day gets a little closer: A twice-told therapy.* New York: Harper Books.

Research

Giorgi, A. (1986). Theoretical justifications for the use of descriptions in psychological research. In P. D. Ashworth, A. Giorgi, & A. J. J. deKonig (Eds.), *Qualitative research in psychology* (pp. 3–22). Pittsburgh: Duquesene University Press.

Mahoney, M. J. (1991). *Human change processes: The scientific foundations of psychotherapy: Basic processes.* New York: Brunner/Mazel.

Packer, M. J., & Addison, R. B. (Eds.) (1989). *Entering the circle: Hermeneutic investigation in psychology.* Albany: State University of New York Press.

Polkinghorne, D. E. (1988). *Narrative knowing and the human sciences.* Albany: State University of New York Press.

Polkinghorne, D. E. (1983). *Methodology for the human sciences: Systems of inquiry.* Albany: State University of New York Press.

Sterling, M. M. (1992). *The experience of role-playing during psychotherapeutic training: A phenomenological analysis with practicing therapists.* Unpublished doctoral dissertation, Saybrook Institute. (University Microfilms International No. 9225296)

Further Reading

Bugental, J. F. T. (1978). *Psychotherapy and process: The fundamentals of an existential–humanistic approach.* New York: McGraw-Hill.

Bugental, J. F. T. (1987). *The art of the psychotherapist.* New York: Norton.

Yalom, I. D. (1980). *Existential psychotherapy.* New York: Basic Books.

Yalom, I. D. (1992). *When Nietzsche wept.* New York: Basic Books.

REFERENCES

American Psychiatric Association. (1994). *Diagnostic and statistical manual of mental disorders* (4th ed.). Washington, DC: Author.

Anderson, W. T. (1990). *Reality isn't what it used to be: Theatrical politics, ready-to-wear religion, global myths, primitive chic, and other wonders of the postmodern world.* San Francisco: Harper & Row.

Armstrong, C. A., & Bugental, J. F. T. (1995). Attention must be paid. In K. Schneider & R. May (Eds.), *Existential–integrative psychology* (pp. 197–204). Boston: McGraw-Hill.

Bachelard, G. (1960). *The poetics of reverie: Childhood, language, and the cosmos* (D. Russell, Trans.). Boston: Beacon Press.

Boss, M. (1962). Anxiety, guilt, and psychotherapeutic liberation. *Review of Existential Psychology and Psychiatry, 2,* 173–207.

Boss, M. (1963). *Psychoanalysis and daseinsanalysis.* New York: Basic Books.

Bracke, P., & Bugental, J. F. T. (1995). Existential addiction: A model for treating Type-A behavior and workaholism. In T. C. Payuchant (Ed.), *In search of meaning: Managing for health of our organizations, our communities, and the natural world* (pp. 65–93). San Francisco: Jossey-Bass.

Buber, M. (1965). *Between man and man* (R. G. Smith, Trans.). New York: Macmillan.

Bugental, J. F. T. (1965). *The search for authenticity: An existential–analytic approach to psychotherapy.* New York: Holt, Rinehart & Winston.

Bugental, J. F. T. (Ed.). (1967). *Challenges of humanistic psychology.* New York: McGraw-Hill.

Bugental, J. F. T. (1976). *The search for existential identity: Patient–therapist dialogues in humanistic psychotherapy.* San Francisco: Jossey-Bass.

Bugental, J. F. T. (1978). *Psychotherapy and process: The fundamentals of an existential–humanistic approach.* New York: McGraw-Hill.

Bugental, J. F. T. (1984). *Processes of communication.* (Available from the author, 24 Elegant Tern Road, Novato, CA 94949)

Bugental, J. F. T. (1986). Existential–humanistic psychotherapy. In I. L. Kutash & A. Wolf (Eds.), *Psychotherapist's casebook* (pp. 222–236). San Francisco: Jossey-Bass.

Bugental, J. F. T. (1987). *The art of the psychotherapist.* New York: Norton.

Bugental, J. F. T. (1988). Testing the lows. *Journal of Integrative and Eclectic Psychotherapy, 7,* 462–465.

Bugental, J. F. T. (1990a). The envious lover. In N. Saltzman & J. C. Norcross (Eds.), *Therapy wars: Contention and convergence in differing clinical approaches* (pp. 92–112). San Francisco: Jossey-Bass.

Bugental, J. F. T. (1990b). Existential–humanistic psychotherapy. In J. K. Zeig & W. M. Munion (Eds.), *What is psychotherapy: Contemporary perspectives* (pp. 189–192). San Francisco: Jossey-Bass.

Bugental, J. F. T. (1990c). *Intimate journeys: Stories from life-changing therapy.* San Francisco: Jossey-Bass.

Bugental, J. F. T. (1990d). Ten commandments for therapists. *Psychotherapy, 27,* 143.

Bugental, J. F. T. (1991a). Lessons clients teach therapists. *Journal of Humanistic Psychology, 31,* 28–32.

Bugental, J. F. T. (1991b). Outcomes of an existential–humanistic psychotherapy: Tribute to Rollo May. *The Humanistic Psychologist, 19,* 2–9.

Bugental, J. F. T. (1992). The betrayal of the human: Psychotherapy's mission to reclaim our lost identity. In J. K. Zeig (Ed.), *The evolution of psychotherapy: The second conference* (pp. 155–164). New York: Bruner/Mazel.

Bugental, J. F. T., & Bracke, P. (1992). The future of existential–humanistic psychotherapy. *Psychotherapy, 29,* 28–33.

Bugental, J. F. T., & Bradford, G. K. (1992). What is betrayal in psychotherapy? *The Psychotherapy Patient, 8*(3/4), 1–9.

Bugental, J. F. T., & Bugental, E. K. (1986). Resistance to and fear of change. [Reprinted in F. Flach (Ed.). (1989). *Stress and its management* (Directions in Psychiatry Series No. 6) (Vol. 6, pp. 58–67). New York: Norton.]

Bugental, J. F. T., & Flannes, S. (1993, April). Is the "I" the "self"? If not, what are they? In Z. Gross (Chair), *The integrity of the self.* Symposium conducted at the meeting of the California Psychological Association, San Francisco.

Bugental, J. F. T., & Kleiner, R. I. (1993). Existential–humanistic psychotherapy. In F. Stricker & J. Gold (Eds.), *The comprehensive handbook of psychotherapy integration* (pp. 101–112). New York: Plenum Press.

Bugental, J. F. T., & McBeath, B. (1994). Depth existential therapy: Evolution since World War II. In B. Bongar & L. E. Beutler (Eds.), *Foundations of psychotherapy: Theory, research and practice.* Oxford University Press.

Bugental, J. F. T., & Sapienza, B. (1992). The three R's for psychology. *The Humanistic Psychologist, 20,* 273–284.

Buhler, C., & Allen, M. (1972). *Introduction to humanistic psychology.* Belmont, CA: Brooks/Cole.

Burton, A. (1967). *Modern humanistic psychotherapy.* San Francisco: Jossey-Bass.

Cantril, A. H. (Ed.). (1988). *Psychology, humanism, and scientific inquiry: The selected essays of Hadley Cantril.* New Brunswick, NJ: Transaction Books.

Cogswell, J. F. (1971). An experience in conflict between the self and technology. In B. Marshall (Ed.), *Experiences in being* (pp. 246–253). Belmont, CA: Brooks/Cole.

Deikman, A. J. (1976). *Personal freedom: On finding your way to the real world.* New York: Viking.

Friedman, M. (Ed.). (1964). *The worlds of existentialism: A critical reader.* Chicago: University of Chicago Press.

Fromm, E. (1941). *Escape from freedom.* New York: Holt, Rinehart & Winston.

Fromm, E. (1947). *Man for himself.* New York: Holt, Rinehart & Winston.

Gendlin, E. T. (1962). *Experiencing and the creation of meaning: A philosophical and psychological approach to the subjective.* Glencoe, IL: Free Press.

Gendlin, E. T. (1978). *Focusing.* New York: Everest House.

Giorgi, A. (1970). *Psychology as a human science: A phenomenologically based approach.* New York: Harper & Row.

Giorgi, A. (1984). Toward a phenomenologically based unified paradigm for psychology. In D. Kruger (Ed.), *The changing reality of modern man: Essays in honour of J. H. van den Berg* (pp. 20–34). Capetown, S.A.: Juta & Co., Ltd.

Giorgi, A. (1986). Theoretical justifications for the use of descriptions in psychological research. In P. D. Ashworth, A. Giorgi, & A. J. J. deKonig (Eds.), *Qualitative research in psychology* (pp. 3–22). Pittsburgh: Duquesene University Press.

Havens, L. L. (1974). The existential use of the self. *American Journal of Psychiatry, 131,* 1–10.

Havens, L. L. (1989). *A safe place.* New York: Ballentine.

Heidegger, M. (1962). *Being and time.* New York: Harper & Row.

Hoeller, K. (Ed.). (1986/1987). Readings in existential psychology and psychiatry [Special issue]. *Review of Existential Psychology and Psychiatry, 20*(1, 2, 3).

Howard, G. S.(1991). Culture tales: A narrative approach to thinking, cross-cultural psychology, and psychotherapy. *American Psychologist, 46,* 187–197.

James, W. (1897/1956). *The will to believe: Is life worth living?* New York: Dover.

Jourard, S. M. (1963). *Personal adjustment: An approach through the study of the healthy personality* (2nd ed.). New York: Macmillan.

Jourard, S. M. (1964). *The transparent self: Self-disclosure and well being.* Princeton, NJ: Van Nostrand.

Keen, E. (1970). *Three faces of being: Toward an existential clinical psychology.* New York: Irvington.

Kelly, G. A. (1955). *The psychology of personal constructs* (Vols. 1, 2). New York: Norton.

Koestenbaum, P. (1971). *The vitality of death: Essays in existential psychology and philosophy.* Westport, CT: Greenwood Press.

Koestenbaum, P. (1974). *Existential sexuality: Choosing to love.* Englewood Cliffs, NJ: Prentice Hall.

Koestenbaum, P. (1978). *The new image of the person.* Westport, CT: Greenwood Press.

Kutash, I. L., & Wolf, A. (Eds.). (1986). *Psychotherapist's casebook.* San Francisco: Jossey-Bass.

Lazarus, A. A. (1989). *The practice of multimodal therapy.* Baltimore: Johns Hopkins University Press.

Levin, D. M. (1985). *The body's recollection of being: Phenomenological psychology and the deconstruction of nihilism.* Boston: Routledge & Kegan Paul.

Levenson, E. A. (1983). *The ambiguity of change.* New York: Basic Books.

Levenson, E. (1991). *The purloined self.* New York: William Alanson White Institute.

Mahrer, A. R. (1983). *Experiential psychotherapy: Basic processes.* New York: Brunner/Mazel.

Mahrer, A. R. (1986). *Therapeutic experiencing: The process of change.* New York: Norton.

Mahoney, M. J. (1991). *Human change process: The scientific foundations of psychotherapy.* New York: Basic Books.

Maslow, A. H. (1954). *Motivation and personality.* New York: Harper & Row.

Maslow, A. H. (Ed.). (1959). *New knowledge in human values.* New York: Harper & Row.

Maslow, A. H. (1962). *Toward a psychology of being.* Princeton, NJ: Van Nostrand.

May, R. (1953). *Man's search for himself.* New York: Norton.

May, R. (Ed.). (1961). *Existential psychology.* New York: Random House.

May, R. (1981). *Freedom and destiny.* New York: Norton.

May, R., Angel, E., & Ellenberger, H. F. (Eds.). (1958). *Existence: A new dimension in psychiatry and psychology.* New York: Basic Books.

Merleau-Ponty, M. (1962). *Phenomenology of perception* (C. Smith, Trans.). Boston: Routledge & Kegan Paul.

Merleau-Ponty, M. (1964). *The primacy of perception and other essays on phenomenological psychology, the philosophy of art, history, and politics.* Evanston, IL: Northwestern University Press.

Ofman, W. (1976). *Affirmation and reality: Fundamentals of humanistic existential therapy and counseling.* Los Angeles: Western Psychological Services.

Packer, M. J., & Addison, R. B. (Eds.). (1989). *Entering the circle: Hermeneutic investigation in psychology.* Albany: State University of New York Press.

Phillips, J. (1980–1981). Transfer and encounter: The therapeutic relationship in psychoanalytic and existential psychotherapy. *Review of Existential Psychology and Psychiatry, 17,* 135–152.

Polkinghorne, D. E. (1983). *Methodology for the human sciences: Systems of inquiry.* Albany: State University of New York Press.

Polkinghorne, D. E. (1988). *Narrative knowing and the human sciences.* Albany: State University of New York Press.

Rahilly, D. A. (1993). A phenomenological analysis of authentic experience. *Journal of Humanistic Psychology, 33,* 49–71.

Rogers, C. R. (1951). *Client-centered therapy: Its current practice, implications, and theory.* Boston: Houghton Mifflin.

Rogers, C. R. (1961). *On becoming a person.* Boston: Houghton Mifflin.

Saltzman, N., & Norcross, J. C. (Eds.). (1990). *Therapy wars: Contention and convergence in differing clinical approaches.* San Francisco: Jossey-Bass.

Schneider, K. (1990). *The paradoxical self: Toward an understanding of our contradictory nature.* New York: Plenum Press.

Schneider, K. (1993). *Horror and the holy: Wisdom teachings of the monster tale.* Chicago and La Salle, IL: Open Court.

Schneider, K., & May, R. (Eds.). (1995). *The psychology of existence: An integrative clinical perspective.* Boston: McGraw-Hill.

Shapiro, D. (1965). *Neurotic styles.* New York: Basic Books.

Shapiro, D. (1989). *Psychotherapy of neurotic character.* New York: Basic Books.

Shapiro, K. J. (1985). *Bodily reflective modes: A phenomenological method for psychology.* Durham, NC: Duke University Press.

Snyder, W. U. (Ed.). (1947). *Casebook of nondirective counseling.* Boston: Houghton Mifflin.

Sterling, M. M. (1990). The use of role-play in psychotherapy training. In L. Cox, C. Phibbs, K. Wexler, & M. Riemersma (Eds.), *Practical applications in supervision* (pp. 73–84). San Diego: California Association of Marriage and Family Therapists.

Sterling, M. M. (1992). *The experience of role-playing during psychotherapeutic training: A phenomenological analysis with practicing therapists.* Unpublished doctoral dissertation, Saybrook Institute. (University Microfilms International No. 9225296)

Sterling, M. M., & Bugental, J. F. T. (1993). The *meld* experience in psychotherapy supervision. *Journal of Humanistic Psychology, 33*(2), 38–48.

Sterling, M. M., & Bugental, J. F. T. (in press). Jourard, Levinas, and intersubjectivity. In A. Richards (Ed.), [as yet untitled volume memorializing Sidney Jourard].

Stolorow, R. D., Brandchaft, B., & Atwood, G. E. (1987). *Psychoanalytic treatment: An intersubjective approach.* Hillsdale, NJ: Analytic Press.

Ulmer, J. M. (1991). *Men's experience of acceptance of therapy: A phenomenological analysis of male psychotherapy.* Unpublished doctored dissertation, Saybrook Institute. (University Microfilms International No. 9209543)

van Deurzen-Smith, E. (1988). *Existential counseling in practice.* London: Sage.

Walsh, R. N. (1984). Psychotherapy as perceptual training. *The American Theosophist, 72,* 171–175.

Welwood, J. (1982). The unfolding of experience: Psychotherapy and beyond. *Journal of Humanistic Psychology, 22,* 91–104.

Wheelis, A. (1958). *The quest for identity.* New York: Norton.

Wolpe. J. (1958). *Psychotherapy by reciprocal inhibition.* Stanford, CA: Stanford University Press.

Wolpe, J. (1991). *The practice of behavior therapy.* Needham Heights, MA: Allyn & Bacon.

Wolpe, J., & Lazarus, A. A. (1966). *Behavior therapy techniques: A guide to the treatment of neuroses.* Elkins Park, PA: Franklin Book Co.

Yalom, I. D. (1980). *Existential psychotherapy.* New York: Basic Books.

Yalom, I. D. (1990). *Love's executioner.* New York: Basic Books.

Yalom, I. D. (1992). *When Nietzsche wept.* New York: Basic Books.

Yalom, I. D., & Elkin, G. (1974). *Every day gets a little closer: A twice-told therapy.* New York: Harper Books.

8

Gestalt Therapy

GARY M. YONTEF

BACKGROUND OF THE APPROACH

When the Nazis came to power in Germany in 1933, a German couple, both psychoanalysts, fled to Holland and then to South Africa and together started a psychoanalytic institute. In 1942 they published the first book of what later came to be called Gestalt therapy (F. Perls, 1942/1992).

Frederick Saloman (Fritz) Perls, was a classically trained Freudian psychoanalyst who was influenced by the most progressive psychoanalysts of the day, including Theodore Ferenczi, Karen Horney, Otto Rank, Wilhelm Reich, and Harry Stack Sullivan (for an excellent biography see Clarkson & Mackewn, 1993). In his early days in Germany, he had been immersed in a field of progressive thinking, including the Bauhaus movement in art and architecture, existentialism, theater, and dance. Perls was influenced by Gestalt psychology and two closely related extensions: the organismic theory of Kurt Goldstein, with whom Perls studied briefly, and the field theory of Kurt Lewin.

Although Frederick Perls is usually credited with founding and popularizing

Gestalt therapy, his wife, Laura Posner Perls (1982/1992, 1992), is a cofounder and wrote parts of *Ego, Hunger and Aggression*. She deserves credit for much of the heart of Gestalt therapy and depth of understanding of the underlying philosophy. She studied in Germany with the Gestalt psychologists as well as the existential thinkers Martin Buber and Paul Tillich. The field–process theory of Gestalt psychology and the existential humanism of Buber and Tillich that are at the center of Gestalt therapy theory is due in large part to her influence.

When Frederick and Laura Perls perceived South Africa changing in the direction of apartheid and authoritarianism, they moved to the United States (1946). They quickly became part of the radical intellectual community of New York City. The ambience was one of political, philosophical, and intellectual debate and the desire to radically reform society. A group interested in establishing a psychotherapy system based on a radically new foundation formed around the Perls. They were influenced by the character analytic approach of Wilhelm Reich and the interpersonal approaches of Harry Stack Sullivan and Karen Horney.

Their work culminated in *Gestalt Therapy: Excitement and Growth in the Human Personality* (Perls, Hefferline, & Goodman, 1951), the second part of which presents the theoretical principles that remain the foundation of Gestalt therapy. Although the first draft of the manuscript was written by Frederick Perls, the final theoretical formulation was largely the work of Paul Goodman (1960, 1977/1991), the writer, teacher, and social commentator.

The founders of Gestalt therapy, along with many students of Sullivan, Horney, and Reich, reacted against classical Freudian psychoanalysis. Classical psychoanalysis at that time was very different from current progressive systems of psychoanalysis such as the relational and self psychological approaches. At that time, the analyst was to be a blank screen who did not reveal anything personal and upon which the patient would project and form a transference neurosis. The patient said whatever came to mind—free association—and the analyst interpreted the revealed transference according to a preset theory dominated by a belief in an inherent conflict between biological drives and society's perceived need for them to be repressed or sublimated.

Classic psychoanalytic theory promulgated the idea that conscious experience did not reveal most of the truth about why people do what they do. Therefore, conscious experience could not be trusted, but there was a reality underlying it that could be brought into consciousness only through the psychoanalytic process (see Wolitzky, Chapter 2, this volume). Thus the analyst was the authority, the expert who could discern the underlying reality, leaving the patient lacking self-regulation and self-responsibility.

The radical post-World War II intellectual community in New York out of which Gestalt therapy emerged had a particular antipathy to anything they regarded as authoritarian, mechanistic, or inflexible. Gestalt therapists regarded classic psychoanalysis as fostering a relationship that endowed the psychoanalyst with too much authority and the patient with too little, and that paid insufficient attention to what actually happened in the interaction between the person of the psychoanalyst and the person of the patient. They believed that psychoanalysis was insufficiently effective in promoting growth, due in large measure to a methodology that they perceived as lacking creativity and that was too restrictive and inflexible in the range of permissible interventions. They wanted to construct a system oriented to fostering growth more than to remediating pathology, to actual experience more than to interpretations of an unexperienced reality, and to the most authentic contact possible more than to a replaying of experience in the transference neurosis. The method that emerged was "awareness through dialogic contact."

As a *field theory*, Gestalt therapy theory orients to the whole field and contemporaneous relations in the field. Field theory accentuates process (i.e., development or action over time) rather than static structure.

As an *existential therapy*, Gestalt therapy emphasizes existence as people experience it and deemphasizes abstract explanatory schema. Gestalt therapists affirm the human capacity for organismic self-regulation, growth, and healing through interpersonal contact and insight. Although limited by biological inheritance, the self is seen as a process that develops in social interaction and not through the conflict of social repression and biological drives. The therapeutic relationship in Gestalt therapy is one of the active and authentic engagement (contact) of the person of the therapist with the person of the patient based on a model of existential dialogue and does not attempt to foster a transference neurosis by keeping a distant, neutral demeanor.

As a *phenomenological therapy*, Gestalt therapy replaces the free association of psychoanalysis with a methodology of "focused awareness." The phenomenological approach takes all that is given in immediate experience as valid data and does not take as valid data that which is merely inferred, theoretically derived, or carried over from the past. The phenomenological method attempts to "clean" awareness of therapist, patient and research subject much as one would clean a mirror by wiping off smears and fog. That which is obvious ("given" to the senses) is distinguished from assumptions and the latter are put aside ("put into brackets"). Guiding people into this enhanced usage of their own senses to gain insight makes the existential notion of personal agency and responsibility more realistic.

With phenomenologically enhanced awareness people have the tools for better understanding of themselves and others. Thus they learn to identify and accept their own needs, preferences, wants, emotions, observations, and values. In addition, by learning to be aware of their own awareness process, patients learn to regulate themselves with less distortion of their consciousness.

Gestalt therapy is an experimental phenomenology. Patients are encouraged and guided in experimenting with new behaviors for the purpose of gaining better understanding. By suggesting new behaviors as phenomenological experiments the therapist can use technical expertise to guide the patient in behavioral change through spontaneous awareness rather than through goal-directed behavior modification programs. (For more on experimental phenomenology, see Ihde, 1977; Spinelli, 1989.)

PERSONALITY THEORY

The Organism–Environment Field

Gestalt therapy theory is a radical ecological theory that starts from the interacting of the organism and its environment (the *organism–environment field*) and considers the individual and environment inseparable (F. Perls et al., 1951, p. 227). There is no meaningful way to consider a person psychologically apart from the organism–environment field, especially the interhuman aspects of the field, just as there is no way to perceive the environment except through someone's observational perspective. Even the need to be alone is defined in relation to others.

The field is differentiated by *boundaries*. Awareness and contact are active boundary processes that occur in the organism–environment field. The *contact boundary* has the dual functions of joining the individual with others and maintaining separation. Separation creates and preserves autonomy and protects against harmful elements. But only active exchange in the field enables life and growth. People grow by aware contact with that which is novel, especially meeting and acknowledging other people. Needs are met through contact.

People are defined by their boundaries. They establish their sense of "I" by I–thou or I–it contact, not by an isolated "I" (Hycner, 1985, 1991; Hycner & Jacobs, 1995; Jacobs, 1989, 1992). By distinguishing self and not-self, through the operation of the boundary processes of identification and alienation, people continually orient to their life space and construct a sense of who they are.

"All contact is creative adjustment of the organism and environment" (F. Perls et al., 1951, p. 230). All living creatures live in their environment and must adjust to the conditions of the field. But adjusting is not enough. People also need to shape the environment so that it conforms to their needs and values. This is the "creative" aspect.

Contact occurs with varying degrees of awareness. By necessity, most transactions are regulated at an habitual level in which there is minimal if any awareness. When the situation is complex, new, or conflicted, or when habitual modes of operation are not working, aware contact is needed. In health, awareness develops as needed.

"*Contact* is possible only to the extent that *support for* it is available. . . . *Support* is everything that facilitates the ongoing assimilation and integration of experience for a person, relationship or a society . . ." (L. Perls, 1992, p. 132). Support includes our physiology, language, customs, learning, intelligence, compassion, and so on. Identification with one's own experience is perhaps the most important aspect of self-support and central to the theory of change in Gestalt therapy.

Adequate support is a function of the total field, and optimal functioning of necessity requires both self-support and environmental support. One cannot breathe without air, but the individual needs to take the air in. A person needing a safe environment to talk about painful feelings must recognize the need, find a safe situation, let the need be known, and allow the interaction to have an effect.

Good contact is being mindful of current reality. Orientation and action occur in an actual present situation and can only be supported here and now. When talking about the past, the act of remembering and the feelings happen in the present. Similarly, in thinking about the future, the act of anticipating and the feelings happen in the present (L. Perls, 1992, p. 131).

To the degree that one is in touch with the past (old introjected beliefs, unfinished business) or the future (catastrophizing) without realizing it, to that degree one's awareness and functioning is compromised. For example, current contact is compromised when perception of another is confused with images of a person from the past. A pattern of self-support that once supported growth can become structural support for stagnation.

Gestalt

Gestalt is a German word that refers to configuration or pattern. A gestalt is organized by the relationship between a *figure* and *ground*. The figure is what stands out in one's experience and when regulation is organismic, the figure is regulated according to the needs of the person and the nature and needs of the situation. The ground is the entire context of phenomenologically relevant factors out of which the figure emerges. Ideally, the figure remains salient for as long as it is the dominant interest and then recedes to make way for the next figure.

"The spontaneous consciousness of the dominant need and its organization of the functions of contact is the psychological form of *organismic-self-regulation*" (F. Perls et al., 1951, p. 274). Gestalt formation is an ongoing process in which what is of greatest concern is in awareness so that it can be dealt with explicitly. Organismic energy goes into clarifying the figure and taking action to meet the need represented by the figure. (F. Perls et al., 1951; Polster & Polster, 1973; Zinker, 1977). When the figure of interest leads to successful action to meet the dominant need of the moment, the person's attention is released from that figure and organismic energy is free to go to the next figure. When the need is not met, the gestalt remains unfinished and makes claims on the person's attention.

For example, a child seeks love and does not get it and feels shame, yearning, and resentment. This gestalt may operate at varying levels of awareness. When kept out of awareness this unfinished gestalt constitutes unfinished business that may affect self-esteem, cohesive identity, and interpersonal contact for many years. One 60-year-old woman believed herself unlovable and expected abandonment based on unfinished business from childhood. She had been unconsciously waiting for the ultimate and inevitable rejection from her husband of 30 years, who disavowed any such intent and showed no signs of impending abandonment.

If the boundary functions are flexible and without interference, there is ongoing exchange and growth. To the degree that boundaries are fixed, the person becomes rigid and inflexible, as with the obsessive–compulsive character disorder. When the boundary processes are too porous, the person lacks clarity or consistency of self-definition, as for example, clinging and excessively accommodating people.

Meaning is the relation between figure and ground. Meaning is always contextual with regard to time, space, culture, and person. Without knowing the context, the "ground," a figure has no meaning; without a figure the background is not perceptually organized and hence is without meaning. For example, if Harry says to me, "I do not know what to say," what does he mean? Has there just been an argument and Harry is angry and sulking? Is Harry's mind blank as a form of self-protection? If so, is this common for Harry? Or perhaps Harry is overwhelmed by a trauma.

Of most relevance to therapy is a potent type of aware gestalt called insight. "Insight is a patterning of the perceptual field in such a way that the significant realities are apparent; it is the formation of a gestalt in which the relevant factors fall into place with respect to the whole" (Heidbreder, 1933, p. 355). Insight in Gestalt therapy is being aware of the structure of the organism–environment field being studied and that includes being in touch with self in the total field of one's life. It is precisely when this insightful awareness is needed and does not develop that psychotherapy is indicated.

Assimilation and Self-Formation

From birth to death, one's sense of self develops by creative adjustment. At birth, the biological organism interacts with the novel (i.e., the environment) and a self is created—a biosocial–psychological–spiritual being. The organism, an integration of all past interactions, continually interacts in the current organism–environment field, adjusting to the environment and adjusting the environment to it. Out of the interaction something new emerges at each moment, in a sense a new self.

Mental metabolism is a metaphor used in Gestalt therapy to describe the boundary processes by which people maintain themselves and grow. People become aware of a need, orient to the environment to ascertain resources to meet that need, make a selection, and take in and convert this foreign matter (the "novel") into the self. The process of taking the novel, that which is outside the organism, and making it part of self, is assimilation. Digesting food is a biological form of assimilation.

Once, while leading a group, there was a very upsetting crisis. During the break, my cotherapist put her hand on my shoulder to comfort me as she asked how I was doing. Although I needed the comforting, it could not benefit me until I recognized the touch and its meaning, breathed deeply, and savored her support. Her touch was outside novelty that I could experience within me as a warm, comforting sensation and a sense of being cared about. On other occasions, I have not benefited from such strokes because I did not take them in (assimilate them). Of course, that which is not needed, harmful, dangerous, and so forth must be rejected and only that which is nourishing or desired taken in.

That which is assimilated becomes part of the self; that which is taken in without assimilation (*introjection*) remains foreign. Automatic rejection of the viewpoint of another precludes dialogue or assimilation; automatic acceptance of the viewpoint of another without analysis is mere introjecting. Ideas taken into the mind without being examined (studied, broken into parts, thought about) are introjects. "Shoulds" (i.e., unassimilated moralisms) are often acquired during childhood and are a part of a self-alienation process in which one is not aware of what is really deemed appropriate by the whole self. Introjects detract from a clear sense of self, block openness to new experience, deplete one's harmony and vitality, and interfere with maximum functioning. Students taking a course might memorize facts or opinions to regurgitate on an exam, but without a full understanding or analyzing for themselves, they acquire memorized "fact" (introject) but not integrated knowledge.

In healthy personality organization, there is cohesion and stability of self-identification and a minimum of internal conflict and the self-support of identifying with one's ongoing nature and with the feelings and needs of each moment. This personality organization, along with the sense of self, is formed interactively. Children who are seen accurately usually learn to have an accurate sense of self—to identify with their actual states and traits. Children who are treated with love and respect usually develop a sense of self-esteem. Children who are encouraged to experiment, cope, and make mistakes; who are allowed to have an appropriate amount of disappointment and frustration; who learn from interacting with the world; and who are guided to deal with the contingencies of life in a manner consistent with their abilities and developmental level generally become competent.

During the course of living there are many moments of *impasse*. These are times when the external support is not forthcoming and the person does not know if he/she has the self-support to survive without it. The external support may be missing for various reasons: Because it is withdrawn, the situation changes, or the person has moved beyond his/her established, set modes of coping. This is an existentially anxious time, one in which there is a sense of both danger and opportunity. Rescue by others prevents people from finding out if they have sufficient self-support. Without rescue, the impasse situation becomes an opportunity to do something new and see what happens. This is an experiment and by experimenting people learn and grow.

PATHOLOGICAL OR DYSFUNCTIONAL PROCESS

People learn from experience. Dysfunction occurs when awareness does not develop as needed and patterns of behavior that inhibit growth, do not give personal satisfaction, or are socially destructive are repeated. The primary mechanism for awareness not developing is the interruption of the formation of the figure of interest so that the habitual does not become the subject of consciousness as needed. The process of the interruption of awareness can itself become figural and through this "awareness of awareness" the learning process is restored. When the awareness process is not restored, learning does not take place and more functional behavior is not instituted; then therapy is indicated.

Interruptive behaviors often begin in childhood when there is either insufficient support or children are overprotected and not allowed to experience and learn from the natural consequences of their behavior.

Interruptions occur at both the mental and somatic levels. For example, whenever Neil becomes frightened or embarrassed, he interrupts awareness of these feelings by becoming caustic and sarcastic. He thinks he is "just joking." At a somatic level awareness is avoided by interrupting the processes supporting emotional liveliness. For example, people interrupting awareness of feeling sad or the act of crying may do so by clamping down on the muscles of the jaw and eyes. The mechanisms of avoidant behavior often create new difficulties (e.g., tension headaches).

To the extent that individuals interrupt their self-functioning, self-support does not develop and these individuals need to get others to do for them what they could otherwise do for themselves. This often leads to mutually manipulative relationships, such as those between dependent people and people who need to have others dependent on them.

Those interrupting awareness in the present field are often in contact with introjects, memories, and unfinished business (unresolved affect and unmet needs) from earlier situations rather than being in fresh contact with the present. This explains a large part of the process of transference. For example, Joanne regards her therapist as warm and accepting, but she does not trust him because her alcoholic father's apparent warmth and acceptance would suddenly turn into unprovoked attacks.

Boundary Disturbances

When the cycle of figure formation is interrupted or distorted, there is a disturbance in awareness and in the contact boundary between the person and the rest of the field. Some people interrupt the figure formation cycle by quickly changing to a new figure before the old one can deepen. For example, Bonnie is effervescent and flirtatious and seems to be all over the room but does not stay in any one interaction long enough to deepen her sense of self or her connection with other people. She illustrates the pattern of changing figures too rapidly.

Tom illustrates staying too long with each figure: He stays with the phase of clarifying each figure so that it is continually being elaborated and he never moves into action. People experience him as a pedantic and obsessive person who gets lost in details.

Contact, Confluence, and Isolation

Good contact has the dual qualities of boundary discussed above: connection and separation. If the sense of connection with the environment is lost, people are isolated and neither in good contact with the environment nor in the best contact with themselves. Isolation can be healthy when it protects against toxicity. On the other hand, loss of the sense of separation is confluence, the polar opposite of isolation. Dependent people often operate in a confluent mode. Intimacy and group identification can be healthy forms of confluence. Optimally people move between healthy confluence and healthy withdrawal as needed.

Introjection and Projection

Although introjecting can be a healthy part of learning in new situations and necessary in childhood, introjects remaining out of awareness become a crucial part of the mechanism of pathology. For example, many children introject the idea, "If you can't say something nice, don't say anything at all." This interferes with being as assertive as life sometimes calls for.

Projection is the opposite of introjection. Whereas introjection is attributing to self that which is other, projection is attributing to other that which is self. It avoids experiencing a trait about self by attributing it to others. People sometimes avoid awareness of their own hate by thinking (projection) that others are hostile toward them. Projections vary in degree of accuracy, but all have the function of avoiding awareness.

Retroflection and Deflection

Retroflection and *deflection* occur later in the awareness cycle. Whereas in introjection and projection awareness is interrupted before people experience their feelings and impulses as their own, when someone retroflects or deflects they do accept the impulse as their own but change the direction or degree of impact. This blunting or misdirection can enable people to acknowledge their wishes while also modulating the response to meet the requirements of the situation.

In retroflection, the direction of the impulse or wish is changed from interpersonal to intrapsychic; that is, something that one wants to do to the other (or what one wants the other to do for self) is done to or for the self. A man who is angry might keep the situation safe by tensing to keep from striking out. A person wanting comfort might stroke him/herself.

Deflection is a blunting of the impact of interaction either to the self or from the self. Smiling to mitigate expression of criticism or anger is a prime example. Sloughing off a communication (e.g., by trivializing or ignoring it) is an example of deflecting incoming communication. Deflection can be important in protecting self and the situation. People who do not deflect outgoing aggression can make life difficult for others; those who do not deflect incoming aggression can be "thin-skinned."

The Gestalt Therapy Approach to Anxiety

True to the process orientation of its basic philosophy, the Gestalt therapy concept of anxiety emphasizes the process rather than the content of anxiety. The earliest definition of anxiety in Gestalt therapy is excitement minus support (F. Perls, 1942/1992; F. Perls et al., 1951). By this definition anxiety is the experience of interrupted or unsupported excitation (i.e., when the vitality of living is suppressed rather than supported). Excitement requires cognitive and physiological support. Anxiety can be created cognitively or with unsupportive breathing.

Cognitively anxiety is the experience of the gap between now and then, between now and the creative expression of the excitement (F. Perls, 1969/1992). It is created cognitively by losing present-centeredness ("futurizing"). This takes the form of negative predictions, misinterpretations, and irrational beliefs. When people "futurize," they center their awareness on something that is not yet present; hence they cannot support the energy that is aroused by taking action and completing the gestalt. Stage fright is a common example. Another example is faulty cognition of body sensations leading to panic attacks. Descriptively this is in agreement with the research of the cognitive theorists (Golden & Dryden, 1987; Weishaar & Beck, 1987). However, there is no agreement on or confirmation of the Gestalt therapy interpretation of the observations.

The Gestalt therapy view of anxiety from a physiological perspective refers to the organismic need for oxygen to support excitement. "A healthy, self-regulating individual will automatically breathe more deeply to meet the increased need for oxygen which accompanies mobilization and contact" (Clarkson & Mackewn, 1993, p. 81). When people breathe fully, tolerate increased mobilization of energy, are present-centered and reasonable in their cognitive processes, and put the energy into action, they will experience excitement rather than anxiety. Breath support means a full inhale and exhale, especially the latter, and also breathing at a rate that is neither too fast nor too slow.

One can create anxiety with faulty breathing. The rapid breathing that accompanies excitation increases oxygen metabolism, and increases the carbon dioxide in the residual air. When a person increases the rate of breathing in an effort to take in more oxygenated air without adequate exhaling, the fresh, oxygenated air cannot reach the alveolae. Then the person has the familiar sensations of anxiety, such as increased pulse rate, an inability to get enough air, hyperventilation, and so on. Research descriptively confirms the Gestalt therapy formulation, but there is no agreement on interpretation or causality (Acierno, Hersen, & Van Hasselt, 1993; Garssen, de Ruiter, & van Dyck, 1992; F. Perls, 1942/1992, 1973/1976, 1978; F. Perls et al., 1951). Gestalt therapy treats the anxiety directly and also relevant characterological issues. Patients learn to master the anxiety cognitively by staying present-centered and physically by breath retraining, meditation, relaxation exercises, and body-oriented awareness work. The theory of anxiety in Gestalt therapy indicates that when one is mindful of the present and breathes fully, anxiety is signficantly diminished. Going beyond control of the anxiety to characterological healing requires deeper awareness work to identify basic emotions, understanding forces of self-resistance (based on childhood introjects), and creating channels for acting in the world with the mobilized energy.

The Gestalt therapy theory and treatment of anxiety have been supported by clinical experience in Gestalt therapy with remarkable consistency since 1942. But it has never been scientifically validated as such and the exact parameters of practice and outcome are almost never specified. Fortunately, other research does support the major components of the theory and practice (Beck, Stanley, Baldwin, Deagle, & Averill, 1994, pp. 818–826; Garssen et al., 1992, pp. 149, 151).

Related reviews have recently found that the breathing and sensation aspects of anxiety are well described in the literature, and that while it is not clear that breathing retraining alone is enough, the effectiveness of breathing retraining for reducing anxiety is established (Garssen et al., 1992, pp. 149, 151); that the cognitive aspect of anxiety has been demonstrated, although exact causality has not been established (Acierno et al., 1993, p. 564; Logan & Goetsch, 1993, p. 557); that relaxation training and cognitive therapy are both effective (Beck et al., 1994); and that cognitive work that alters faulty cognitions is effective in long-term reduction of panic, although cognitive work has not been scientifically shown to be operating in isolation from other clinical interventions (Acierno et al., 1993, p. 576).

Impasse

When customary supports are lost and new supports are not yet mobilized, people do not know whether they will have enough support to survive existentially. An impasse results when outdated, rigid, or false self-images that have played important parts in constructing lives of safe repetititon and avoidance of the anxiety of authenticity become inoperative. When people who have supported the old persona no longer do so, an impasse results.

In the impasse people are stuck in the terrifying situation of not being able to go back and afraid they cannot survive if they go forward. They are paralyzed, with forward and backward energy fighting each other, as if one foot were on the gas pedal and the other on the brakes. This is often experienced in metaphorical terms, such as a void, hollow, blackness, going off a cliff, drowning, or being sucked into a whirlpool (F. Perls, 1969/1992, 1970). Will I drown or will I find support?

If one stays with the experience of the impasse, one may find support for authentic existence. This is existence with minimal illusion, good self-support, vitality, creativity, and good contact with the human and nonhuman environment. Authentic existence is existence with accurate perception and ability to put one's true self into the world and to see others accurately. It is marked by liveliness, a life of good gestalten, and knowing and maximizing what is important. When insufficient support is mobilized to complete this task, old habits prevail.

Paradoxical Theory of Change

It is a paradox that the more people try to be who they are not, the more they stay the same (Beisser, 1970). Fundamental growth does not occur out of self-hate and self-rejection but rather from identification with the reality of who one is. The more one identifies with oneself, with one's state and one's traits, the more one can grow. By accepting reality, energy that went into internal warfare can go into growth. By actively sensing (looking, hearing, smelling), sensing internally (body sense and affect), and taking action with one's whole self, one can experiment with new behavior, learn from the process, and not make one's sense of self-worth a function of outcome.

People commonly inhibit growth by identifying with a false sense of self (e.g., by identifying with a grandiose self-image) and/or by being ashamed of the self as is. Trying to actualize a false self keeps one from growing and being whole. Identifying with how one is includes regarding oneself as a human being worthy of love and respect even though flawed

and having more to learn. Self-respecting people can recognize behavior that is hurtful to others or inadequate without losing their sense of self-worth.

The feeling that accompanies the sense of being "not okay" and/or "not enough" is shame. Before shame-oriented persons can fully identify with themselves as they are, special work with the shame process is necessary (Yontef, 1993, pp. 489–523).

ASSESSMENT

Typically Gestalt therapists regard assessment and treatment as part of a unified process. Assessment starts from the very beginning of therapy and continues until termination. The therapist makes contact with the person or system being treated, clarifying the presenting request, needs, resources, history, characterological tendencies, and situation.

The unit of assessment depends on the unit of treatment. When families are treated, families are assessed. But even when an individual is being treated, assessment relates that individual to the total context of biology, society, ethnicity, family, community, work setting, and so forth. The Gestalt therapist is ready to assess all aspects of the field as relevant to the person and task at hand. When families are treated, the individuals composing the family must also be assessed as individuals.

Although Gestalt therapists have been working on creating a complete diagnostic personality system expressed in Gestalt therapy conceptual language, this has not been completed (see, e.g., Delisle, in press). In the meantime, Gestalt therapists work within the existing frameworks of personality diagnosis. (For an example of a discussion of character pathology and treatment of the borderline and narcissistic personality disorders in Gestalt therapy, see Yontef, 1993.)

Gestalt therapy assessment is phenomenological, emphasizing patterns of contact and awareness in the organism—environment field, including biological, intrapsychic, interpersonal, transpersonal, and societal factors as actually experienced by therapist and patient. Because it is believed that the figure–ground process organizes a person's awareness and self-regulation, therefore, "a careful phenomenological study of the process of a person's figure/ground meaning formation generates an understanding of the person's personality organization" (Yontef, 1993, pp. 400–401). A good phenomenological study puts aside assumptions of what constitutes personality strength and weakness (bracketing). It attempts to describe fully what the therapist observes, what the patient reports, and how the therapist is affected.

Gestalt therapists generally are more cautious than most clinicians in relying on standardized tests. However, when specific information is required, nothing in the theory precludes their use. For example, when treating a youngster with school problems, standardized tests of achievement, intelligence, organicity, or personality might well be used.

Because it is an experiential therapy, Gestalt therapists start with what is experienced. From the initial therapeutic contact, including initial telephone and waiting-room contact, the Gestalt therapist simultaneously observes the patient and notes his/her own subjective reaction to the patient. Of course, the therapist must separate that which is unfinished business in his/her own life and triggered by the patient (i.e., countertransference) and how the therapist is affected when present-centered.

The Gestalt therapist observes the fullest possible range of data and allows a clear figure to form. Observations include the person's body (posture, breathing, movement, tension), voice, behavior pattern in the session or on the phone (takes initiative, coherence, liveliness). The therapist tries to gain insight into how the patient functions in his/her life space and what in his/her background makes sense of immediate figures. Variables include level and type of patient self-support, available external support in the patient's life space, contactfulness, awareness, and cognitive style. Does the patient take initiative in life or in therapy, follow the lead of others, or show flexibility in leading or following? Of course, the person's social history, such as pattern of work and personal life, is crucial.

Gestalt therapy is based on here-and-now interactions, primarily on the relationship between therapist and patient. How the patient is affected by the therapist and how the therapist is affected by the patient give valuable clues to understanding and diagnosing. Assessment includes the coherence of the patient's story, the manner of storytelling, including the fit between story and the storyteller's affect, and the effect on the therapist (see Polster, 1987).

As a therapist makes observations, he/she asks: How do I make sense out of what I am observing in the patient? What would account for it? For example, a patient says that she is lonely and wants more social contact, yet she reports also keeping herself socially isolated. The therapist notices that she looks away shyly whenever he looks at her. How does that make sense? In one patient, it makes sense because any social contact brings on a feeling of shame at her longing, and that brings on an automatic, gut-level reaction of shame and hiding from exposure.

It is important to know the level and type of self-support and external support available to the patient. This knowledge dictates the range of interventions that are appropriate, effective, and safe. How well can the patient make contact? Express him/herself? Is the person psychotic, sociopathic, physically vulnerable, or in immediate crisis? Does the patient have a capacity for empathy, intimacy, and dialogue? What is the patient's capacity for joy, sexuality, and healthy assertion? How does the patient's consciousness work? Where does the patient interrupt him/herself, what are the preferred sense modalities, what is not allowed into awareness? We look at both the patient's intimate life (romantic, sexual, and friendships) and also the patient's work life.

Most frequently we ask: "What do you experience right now?" The content and the process of the answer provide information. Is the patient open to revealing him/herself? Does the patient know what he/she feels emotionally or what he/she wants? If the patient is in touch with sensations, does he/she know what the meaning is, what the affect is? Or, is the patient only in touch with thoughts and inferences that are labeled "feelings"—as in "I feel that she should treat me better"? If asked "What do you feel?" or "What do you need or wish right now?" can the patient answer that question? Is the patient in touch with his/her body, the sensations? Is the patient in touch with his/her thought processes (i.e., does the patient have some perspective on his/her thought processes)? Does he/she have the capacity and/or propensity toward reflection? If the patient does not feel safe, is he/she able to say so?

THE PRACTICE OF THERAPY

Basic Structure of Gestalt Therapy

Gestalt therapy is an integrative framework. It was designed to assimilate ideas, observations, and technology from a variety of sources into a methodology unified by philosophy but pluralistic in technique (F. Perls et al., 1951, p. viii). Gestalt therapists have been encouraged to understand the patient, the method, and the relationship and create or borrow any technique that will add to the felt sense of what is being explored (Zinker, 1977) and enable a patient to take the next step in his/her growth.

From the mid-1960s through the mid-1970s, some dramatic techniques used in Gestalt therapy demonstration workshops were widely publicized and became known as Gestalt therapy techniques. Some therapists mechanically used these set techniques when they lacked clinical understanding and experience, did not understand the philosophy or methodology of Gestalt therapy, or did not have enough personal support to intervene spontaneously and creatively. This has been widely criticized in the Gestalt therapy literature (L. Perls, 1992, pp. 133–134, 139, 155).

During the last decade, Gestalt therapy has continued in its path of being multi-technical and utilizing ideas, data, and interventions from multiple sources. The techniques that are noted to be Gestalt therapy techniques continue to be used, as they were with Barry (discussed later), but less frequently. In the last decade, Gestalt therapy practice has moved decidedly in the direction of techniques closely linked to the patient's experience (e.g., empathic reflection) and that explicate and strengthen the therapeutic relationship. This has given Gestalt therapy a markedly different appearance from the more dramatic and often bombastic appearance of 20 years ago (Yontef, 1987, 1988/1993, 1991/1993).

As a result of this eclectic attitude, Gestalt therapy is far from monolithic but rather a group of therapies with a common philosophy and methodology and a formidable range of variation on the dimensions of technique, choice of modalities, degree and type of structure of the therapy, and attitudes on most clinical issues. Because the path of Gestalt psychotherapy goes beyond symptom relief and medical necessity and into the realms of growth and even spiritual enhancement, it can be of indeterminate length. However, short-term treatment is one of the standard Gestalt therapy variations in the form of either a crisis model or an insight model. Frequently, open-ended Gestalt therapy spontaneously concludes successfully in a few sessions. Although the modal and average frequency is weekly, the range varies from several times per week to every other week or less.

Most patients start in individual or marital therapy, with group therapy often following as an accompanying modality and later as sole modality. Treatment frequently combines modalities and it is not unusual to have patients in combinations of individual, group, marital, or family therapy. Individual sessions average 45–50 minutes; marital and family sessions, 45–120 minutes; and weekly groups, 90–120 minutes. Workshops vary from 6–12 hours per day. Sessions are usually face to face with no desk or table between therapist and patient.

Sessions are structured by the interaction of therapist and patient and both take part in the structuring. A patient's perception of his/her own needs, preferences, and strengths are taken seriously and as the patient makes these known they become definite determinants of the structure of the therapy. Some patients come in and structure sessions by telling their story or establishing their own focus. The Gestalt therapist helps clarify patients' preferences and needs when they are not clear by sharing his/her observations, offering empathic reflections or information, and suggesting phenomenological experimentation that might clarify the patient's wishes. Sometimes the therapist has to struggle with pa-

tients to have them even consider new directions or new ways of working. But the structuring always emerges from the working together of patient and therapist.

The Gestalt therapist always has the responsibility of (1) identifying the themes that are central in the patient's self-organization; (2) the sequence, timing, and manner of the work; (3) establishing a safe and professional climate; and (4) inviting dialogic contact and facilitating dialogic interaction. Any structure in addition to these areas of therapist responsibility is configured by the interaction of therapist and patient regardless of the strength or weakness of the therapeutic relationship.

Goals and Strategies

Although Gestalt therapists are usually quite active, they do not structure a sequence of behavior change from the beginning of therapy to a preset end goal. The work of Gestalt therapy is through phenomenological exploration rather than by direct reconditioning of behavior or interpretation of the unconscious. Gestalt therapy operates by bringing awareness where blocked, by bringing awareness of the awareness process, by providing emotional support, and by teaching new methods of dealing with stress.

A pivotal feature of the philosophy of Gestalt therapy is that there are multiple, valid realities that need to be respected. There is a strong emphasis on the positive value of differences between people (e.g., in values, preferences, and beliefs). This is also true of differences between therapist and patient. Because Gestalt therapists show themselves personally (i.e., are relatively self-disclosing), patients are directly and indirectly exposed to different values, behaviors, skills, thoughts, and feelings. The patient is not encouraged to identify with the therapist's way of being, but rather to find his/her own unique way. The Gestalt therapist values assimilation and not introjection. Differences between therapist and patient become the focus of dialogue and phenomenological experimentation.

It is central in the philosophy of Gestalt therapy that patients learn to test what does and does not fit for them through their own awareness. It is particularly important that a therapy with an active therapist and a powerful method respect and foster patient resistance to introjection and it is the responsibility of the therapist to be vigilant in cases of patients' unaware accommodation to the therapist's influence.

The aim is autonomy and growth through awareness. The therapist guides this awareness by being actively present with caring, warmth, honesty, directness, perspective, liveliness, and creativity. Gestalt therapists share their observations and also feedback about how they are affected by the patient. Because Gestalt therapists are present as real persons, growth can occur by awareness work in the context of real contact between people.

Gestalt therapy's experimental phenomenology has featured guided experiments in sessions and homework assignments between sessions since its inception in 1942 (F. Perls, 1942/1992). A good Gestalt therapist has an overview of the therapy and makes suggestions guiding the exploration during and between sessions.

Max is a bright, affectionate man who is successful in a creative field and in a loving, long-term, live-in relationship. But he is usually agitated with his mind "going a thousand miles an hour." In one session he brought up the fact that he interrupts moments of happiness. The therapist asked him to focus on one such moment as if it were happening right now. He brought up a "sweet moment"

in which his girlfriend came up to him, touched him softly, and said she loved him. The therapist continued the phenomenological focusing by asking him to focus on the very moment of interruption. He became aware that immediately after the good feeling his mind started racing again and she suddenly became an intrusion.

Further description of the sense of intrusion brought up an association to his mother. His doting mother told him how loved he was but exuded depression and not joy when she was with him. The therapist used a fantasy experiment and asked Max to imagine himself as an infant, which he could do quite well. When he imagined being alone in his crib he was joyful, curious, and peaceful. When he did the experiment, his face softened, his eyes lit up, and he looked peaceful, happy, and vibrant. Then, in the fantasy, a dark, ominous presence came in the room and his good mood was definitely interrupted. Further focusing made clear that the presence was his mother. Although his mother was not abusive in any obvious way, there was the energy of depression and lack of joy when she looked at him and he reacted by his joy changing to tension and agitation.

A visualization experiment was used. Max was asked to imagine a mother—"metaphorical good mother" (MGM)—whose eyes lit up with joy when she looked at him. This was a very satisfying image for him and in the fantasy he could experience sustaining his joy *in her presence*. It was clear to Max that his difficulty staying with the sweet moment with his girlfriend was related to this old theme and not to a problem in the current relationship. He was given a homework assignment to spend a few minutes a couple of times a day visualizing himself as infant with the MGM.

Although the goals and the goal-setting process both vary with the stage of therapy, the therapeutic issues involved, the personality structure of the patient, and the setting, the basic Gestalt therapy framework of phenomenological exploration and the dialogue between therapist and patient operate from the very beginning of contact. The awareness and contact work form the process by which goals are clarified. Setting the goals of the therapy is one early area in which the self-support of the patient is strengthened by the two major aspects of Gestalt therapy: phenomenological explication of the patient's patterns of consciousness and behavior, and the ongoing therapeutic relationship between therapist and patient.

For example, a patient in the first session showed no initiative, waited for the therapist to provide all the leads, and could not respond to the question, "What do you want from therapy?" Something about the patient moved the therapist and he said warmly: "I would like to help! What would you like from me?" This particular patient was able to respond to a more explicitly personal communication.

The patient's level of support is always primary in choosing an intervention. Experiments and other therapeutic activities are informally graded in difficulty and enacted in a sequence that builds skills in earlier work so that the patient has more support and is not overwhelmed in later work. For example, patients who were abused in childhood can better work through emerging rage if they first learn to identify and safely express feelings, learn how to deliberately calm and relax themselves as needed, and have developed some sense of trust and safety with the therapist. The contact episode with the new patient just mentioned was a gentle step in building a working alliance. There followed a series of discussions about issues from the patient's life in which the patient did not know what he wanted, and the focus of the therapy was more on strengthening the ability of the patient to know what he wanted than

on the content of his "story of the week." In time the patient began to recognize how he interrupted his awareness of what he wanted; he began to like his growing sense of knowing what he wanted. He also started showing more initiative in the therapy sessions, and his relationship with the therapist became more important to him. At that point the patient had enough self-support for the therapist to make observations and interpretations that exposed intense affect and that dealt with the patient's role in dysfunctional interactions.

When practicing appropriately, the Gestalt therapist guides the sequence so that more intense, threatening, painful, riskier explorations do not exceed the self-support of the patient. The patient who is not guided in this way incurs increased risk of negative therapeutic effects.

The goal in Gestalt therapy is awareness. This includes microawareness (i.e., awareness of a particular content area) and awareness of the awareness process. Awareness of awareness strengthens the ability to choose to bring automatic habits into awareness as needed and to use focused awareness and phenomenological experimentation for clarification, centering, and trying out new behaviors. This awareness means knowing what one is choosing to do and therefore having the ability to meaningfully take responsibility for it. Centering is getting calm and aligned in time, space, context, and within one's self so that one is clearly oriented in the field, harmonious within oneself, breathing easily, and knowing one's preferences and boundaries.

Most beginning patients are interested primarily in solving problems or having symptoms relieved. Although Gestalt therapists value these goals, they are more concerned with the process of how patients support themselves or how they stand in their own way in the problem solving, symptom relief, and so forth.

The goal is not only problem solution and symptom alleviation *but that patients acquire tools* for problem solving and strengthening their overall self-organization. Gestalt therapy facilitates problem solving by increasing patient ability to self-regulate and self-support. As therapy goes on, the focus turns to more general personality issues. With the support of the skills learned in the earlier phases, patients can phenomenologically explore personality issues that run through all the concrete areas and achieve insight into how they function.

More specific goals emerge from a full appreciation of the particular character, history, and situation of each patient. When the situation in the organism–environment field is fully recognized, both the problems and solutions become clear (Wertheimer, 1945). For example, Barry is a 20-year-old man who complained to his female therapist that he is not successful at getting dates. In sessions with the therapist, he did not look at her. An obvious immediate goal was to have the patient explore the difficulty of looking at the therapist until he could do so comfortably. The therapist asked the patient to look at her and then worked with him on his breathing (relaxing) and introjected beliefs that inhibited good contact with her. It is often more effective to do this first in sessions and later work on generalizing to contact outside therapy than it is to start directly with the patient's general difficulty.

Two homework assignments emerged out of sessions with Barry. He was asked to look at women during the week and notice how that went. He noted that he liked looking at women but got very ashamed and guilty, especially when he was romantically interested. This opened a phase of work on his shame process, including feelings of shame, unfinished business with shaming interactions with his mother during childhood, and defenses against shame affect. Following

another session during this period he was asked to talk briefly with one woman every day, without thinking about dating—just to talk to her as a person.

Looking was not only important in its own right but also symbolic of a range of contact or contact-avoidant behaviors. Thus the intermediate goal in this particular case was to be able to establish greater contact throughout his day-to-day life, especially with women. A long-term focus emerged from this work by opening up an exploration of Barry's feelings of embarrassment, shame, wanting to shrink from view and hide, guilt at sexual impulses, and unfinished business with his mother.

As his memories of childhood events became clearer and he made linkages between episodes in childhood with each other and with his adult difficulties, Barry realized how angry he was at his mother. At this point, an "enactment technique" was used, "the empty-chair technique." Barry was asked to imagine that the mother of his childhood was sitting in an empty chair (which the therapist pulled up opposite him), and when he could imagine her in that chair, he was asked to talk to her. The method of direct expression resulted in a deeper level of experiencing and mobilized more affect than just talking about his feelings. Many different techniques besides this well-known Gestalt therapy technique are used to reach this same goal.

In one session Barry moved from talking to the mother in the empty chair to expressing his anger physically, expressing his rage (using a pillow as the mother symbol) by beating her up in a manner he would not and should not do in person. As he "stayed with" his feelings (a Gestalt therapy term for allowing the feeling to be the figure of awareness and to spontaneously transform itself without suppression or analysis), his feelings turned from rage to grief over the warmth, interest, affection, and soothing he so longed for from mother but did not get.

After that affective gestalt completed itself, he realized that mother's reaction was not due to his inadequacy but resulted from her own characterological difficulties, which stemmed from her own childhood. Then Barry was able to reexamine the beliefs he had acquired from her. He realized that she believed that men were aggressive beasts whose very interest in women violated them. As his anger toward mother waned and the experiments with talking and looking at women became more ego-syntonic, he experienced an increase in libido and enjoyment of his interactions with women.

Process of Therapy 1: I and Thou, Here and Now, What and How

Gestalt therapy is an experiential therapy and as such facilitates patients' growth by fostering a relationship based on dialogic contact and a methodology of discovery via patients' ongoing awareness. The slogan "I and Thou, Here and Now, What and How" captures the spirit of this process.

I and Thou

Gestalt therapy is based on direct, lively, emotionally engaged contact in which the therapist is both with the patient and also doing something with the patient (Greenberg, Elliott, & Lietaer, 1994). Dialogic Gestalt therapy (Hycner, 1985; Jacobs, 1989; Yontef, 1993), a trend in Gestalt therapy over the last decade, emphasizes not only actively facilitating patients' growth through phenomenological focusing and experimentation, which is necessary for maximum growth and healing, but also being with patients in a manner similar to that advocated by

Martin Buber, Carl Rogers, and the intersubjective self psychologists.

Techniques execute principles. Principles are important; particular techniques are not. Any techniques can be used in Gestalt therapy and no particular technique has special status. The cardinal principles in Gestalt therapy are the principles governing human relationships, especially the therapeutic relationship. This indispensable aspect of Gestalt therapy will be discussed in the section on the therapeutic relationship.

Techniques in Gestalt therapy are the flexible and creative application of the knowledge of the therapist to guide and enhance the experimental phenomenological learning situation and to facilitate the therapeutic interaction with a particular patient at a particular time. This attitude has resulted in novel and effective techniques that have been widely borrowed by other therapists (see examples given earlier of Max and Barry). Unfortunately, when techniques created in Gestalt therapy are borrowed or when researchers use single Gestalt therapy techniques or manualized procedures under the name of Gestalt therapy, the techniques are often emphasized but the process by which they are created and applied in Gestalt therapy are not mentioned. In Gestalt therapy theory, what therapists actually do and how they do it is important, but whether the technique is a Gestalt therapy technique is not.

Here and Now

Patients are neither viewed as determined by their past nor reduced to unconsciously repeating prior relationships. In field theory all factors that have influence are present here and now in the field. Kurt Lewin (1938) calls this the "Principle of Contemporaneity."

People have an omnipresent task: to make insightful gestalten out of material converging on the present from disparate time, space, and awareness dimensions. The influence of prior experience is explored in Gestalt therapy primarily using the data of the patient's experience rather than relying on interpretations based on abstractions derived from the therapist's favorite theoretical system. Staying close to the patient's direct experience keeps the therapist close to the patient's "truths," which are more valued in Gestalt therapy than the therapist's expert "truth."

Centering on the here and now enables an equality between therapist and patient, for in the present field all parties can use their senses, intuition, and creativity to explore the multiple influences that are always at work. Gestalt therapy does not assume that important data are not available to the patient's awareness (at least after the patient has learned some awareness skills) and does not assume any interpretation about the patient to be valid until confirmed by the patient's felt experience. The patient is assumed to be the expert on his/her awareness and existence and the therapist more of a consultant.

People can best be self-supportive by being present-centered. Present-centeredness means knowing with one's whole being what one is doing and what need is being addressed in the present organismic–environment field. Buddhists call this mindfulness. Being engaged vibrantly and with awareness of that which is most important at the moment facilitates the completion of gestalten (i.e., satisfaction) and the emergence of new gestalten (i.e., growth).

All activities take place contemporaneously, but frequently people do not have clear awareness about what they are doing and what is needed. Buddhists call this forgetfulness. If the patient is dealing with childhood memories and doing so in the present with feeling, the energy and memory activity is in the present. On the other hand, if the past is being recalled merely out of some theoretical belief in the past causing the present, or some deadening habitual repetition, what is of current interest is neglected in favor of this intellectualized activity.

So, too, planning for the future is a present activity in which the person is being systematic and mindful about the future and making preparations. Thinking about the future without present-centered awareness merely creates anxiety.

What and How

Both process theory and phenomenology favor use of descriptive rather than explanation-based methods. The prototypical question in Gestalt therapy is not *Why?* but *What?* What are you experiencing? What are you doing? What do you need? Description can be experience-near and sensed (observation and internal felt sense), whereas explanations are experience-far and speculative.

The companion question is *How?* "How?" is the heart of the process orientation of field theory: How exactly does this process in which the patient is engaged work? Asked what he is experiencing, a patient reports being frightened. Asked what he is doing, the patient might say, "I am scaring myself." The therapist might ask in response, "*How* are you doing that?" This brings attention to those aware and unaware acts of agency—cognitive, motoric, behavioral, social processes—that constitute what is being observed and worked with. "I scare myself by saying to myself that I will make a fool of myself and everyone will hate me."

Process of Therapy 2: Experimentation, Techniques, Strategies

Much of the power of Gestalt therapy comes from the combined emphasis on

(1) the relationship, which enables experimentation and deepens as a result of working together; and (2) insight into content and process acquired through actively focused awareness and experimentation. This power is enhanced by the wide range of techniques included within its purview. Although the techniques used in Gestalt therapy include all the ordinary therapeutic activities, such as empathic listening and reflecting, the repertoire available in Gestalt therapy extends well beyond this to include uniquely Gestalt therapy interventions, techniques assimilated from any available source, and interventions created on the spot. These techniques include cathartic experiments (as the enactment techniques used with Barry), visualization (as used with Max), cognitive monitoring, meditation and relaxation, and experiments with movement.

The focus of therapeutic awareness work ranges from discussion of concrete problems, through reflection on general themes and psychological skills training, to intensive insight work on patterns of personality functioning and developmental experience, and finally to integration and assimilation. (See discussion of levels of awareness, Yontef, 1976/1993.) Even when working at the content level, Gestalt therapists are very mindful of process, especially the process of the patient's interruption and support of contact and awareness. The ratio between explicit focus on these process variables and explicit focus on concrete problems varies. Sometimes the therapist observes the process but keeps the content themes in the foreground. Sometimes the content serves primarily as a concrete focus for the process work. Later in therapy pure process awareness can be a most powerful focus.

Particular interventions are the concrete behaviors of experimentation that arise out of the cooperative endeavors of therapist and patient. They are always experiments in that they are procedures to discover something and are not exercises to directly control behavior change. Experiments are suggestions for focusing awareness that patients can use to heighten the intensity, power, flexibility, and creativity of their therapy experience. Even simple centering exercises such as relaxation through breath control are treated with the same experimental attitude: "Slow your breathing, relax on the exhale, and see what happens."

Gestalt therapy encourages the therapist to be creative (Zinker, 1977). Therapeutic cookbooks (i.e., manualized therapies that prescribe interventions "by the numbers") are dissonant from Gestalt therapy's spirit. *What* is explored and in what sequence is partially determined by the therapist's training, experience, orientation, and scientific knowledge. *How* the exploration proceeds is mostly the art of therapy. Authenticity, creativity, and intuition are essential to the richness of contact and awareness that distinguishes Gestalt therapy from rigid, linear approaches.

In an experiential therapy, the therapist starts with what is experienced. The Gestalt therapist observes the fullest possible range of data (see discussion in assessment section) and allows a clear figure to form. From the initial therapeutic contact, the experiential therapist simultaneously observes and notes how he/she is subjectively affected by the patient. Of course, the therapist must separate that which is unfinished business in his/her own life and merely being triggered by the patient (i.e., countertransference) and present-centered effects.

Although Gestalt therapy experiments often appear to be aimed at a particular behavioral goal, in Gestalt therapy theory the experiments are true experiments: "Try it and learn." In that sense, the patient and therapist together experiment with their relationship, and out of this relationship comes the inspiration for particular experiments. To the degree that techniques do not come out of the dialogic relationship but rather are practiced mechanically or as a form of behavioral manipulation, they are not good Gestalt therapy practice.

The most basic and paradigmatic Gestalt therapy intervention is asking: "What are you experiencing right now?" This is frequently expanded to the experiment of the patient continuously reporting what he/she is experiencing (awareness continuum). This leads in many directions. For example, when a patient reports feelings toward someone not in the room, it may lead to the experiment of imagining the person sitting in the room in one of the empty chairs. Then, again, patients report what they experience. What follows may be more feeling, more clarity, wanting to escape, shame, relief, and so forth. Because direct expression usually brings sharper focus, more vivid experience, more clarity, and more resolution than "talking about," experiments such as the empty-chair experiments are used.

For example, Ellen talked about missing her deceased father. The therapist, remembering previous work with Ellen in which it became very clear that she was attached to her dead father to the point of its interfering with her desired relationship with men in her life, suggested, "Imagine he is here sitting in that chair and look at him and see what happens." She did so, and as soon as she did that visualization, tears filled her eyes. She turned to the therapist and said, "I miss him." The therapist noted that she broke off the contact with the visualized father, talked about him in the third person to the therapist, and the tears dried up. This keeps the gestalt of her emotions toward her father from completing itself. Because there was a good relationship between this patient and therapist and her primary self-interruption at that time was in completing emotional ex-

pressiveness, the therapist redirected Ellen away from telling him about her feelings and suggested, "Tell your father." The patient said, "I know, I know, I didn't want to feel how much I miss him and to accept the reality that he is not coming back." She turned to the empty chair, "I miss you, daddy." She sobbed deeply and later reported feeling relieved, centered, and more emotionally available to relate to another man.

This attitude or method of phenomenological experimentation and dialogic contact can be used in any modality and at any level. It is used in work with groups, families, couples, and institutions. It is most often practiced in a psychotherapy context, but with creativity, sensitive appreciation of limits, boundaries, and contracts, it has also been effective in "rap" groups, consulting groups in institutional settings, drop-in groups, and so on. The level of experimentation can be interpersonal or intrapsychic and ranges from introductory to very deep. The experiments are sometimes spiritual in nature, although many Gestalt therapists use a secular language even when it is a spiritual process, such as centering oneself in the universe and ascertaining what is central versus peripheral in importance. The techniques have the following general goals:

1. To clarify and sharpen what the patient is already aware of and to make new linkages between elements already in awareness.
2. To bring into focal awareness that which was previously only in peripheral awareness.
3. To bring into awareness what is needed but systematically kept out of awareness.
4. To bring into awareness the system of control of awareness, especially the mechanism of preventing thoughts or feelings from coming into focal awareness.

5. To experiment with new ways of thinking, behaving, and being aware, including proactive self-support such as meditation, relaxation, and breath control. It is often quite useful to experiment with new ways of exploring or framing old experiences. Therapy makes possible new action experiments (e.g., expanding social contacts after working through fear of intimacy). Many patients who have been abused find it healing to use their aggression against their abuser in role-playing or cathartic experiments (e.g., sexually abused patients sometimes make breakthrough progress by feeling and expressing power and movement in their pelvis).

The reader can get a sense of the Gestalt therapy method by considering a sample of material presented in first sessions and some Gestalt therapists' responses.

The initial session begins the experiment of getting acquainted. The therapist and patient must meet each other, define the issues, and feel each other out. This may be as simple as the patient saying why he/she is coming to the therapist, and it may include therapist-directed activities.

For example, a patient starts the first session talking about his life, but without any apparent focus. He does not say why he came to therapy, why he came to this therapist, or what he wants. He talks clearly about pieces of his story but is not clear about how they fit together and why he is talking about them. Of course, the therapist endeavors to clarify why the patient is there, what he wants, and what he feels. However, the therapist also focuses on the patient's contact process, especially his apparent failure to orient to the here-and-now therapy situation. The therapist needs to know whether this is typical of this patient, whether he knows this about his own process, and whether he is willing to explore and experiment.

The course of this kind of session might well develop into the therapist asking the patient the following question: "What are you feeling emotionally *right now*?" "And now?" "And now?" If the patient does not know, then experiments pointing the patient to how to know are in order. If the patient does know, it might lead to interventions such as: "You were talking about your roommate, and then you changed to talking about your history class. How did you get from one topic to the other (or what is the connection)?" Here the therapist is fairly active in directing the patient to a major concern, starting a process of exposing the patient to important self-support skills, and getting valuable diagnostic information about how the patient's awareness process works.

It is the therapist's responsibility to make good contact and intervene in a manner matching the individual patient—"to start where the patient is" and to know what is central for each patient rather than follow a set recipe. It is also the therapist's responsibility to care about, inquire into, and respect the patient's emotional response to the intervention. It is the therapist's responsibility to be sensitive to the patient's reactions and to take responsibility for his/her own demeanor and effect on the patient, and to do so nondefensively.

Another patient started by clearly identifying her need: "My husband died, I need to talk to someone." The patient was filled with grief and as soon as she sat down and identified the organizing figure, her eyes filled with tears. The patient explored her feelings; the therapist followed the patient's spontaneous expression of feeling and allowed himself to be affected.

The personal interaction between the grieving widow and the therapist is an important part of such situations. Regardless of the degree which this is explicit or implicit, the patient is affected by the therapist's openness. Sometimes merely allowing the process is just what the person needs; at other times a simple statement of the therapist's affect is very important. For example, sometimes the therapist is very touched emotionally by the grief and says so—with voice and eyes consistent with the words. This may be what the patient needs: Someone who listens, feels, and does not need to fix it.

Sometimes a grieving patient has difficulty finding a focus and needs direction from the therapist. Common interventions in such a situation are imagining the dead husband in an empty chair across from the patient, talking about the lost loved one, or role-playing the funeral or hospital scene and expressing what was not expressed at the time. It is important in such cases that neither the therapist nor the patient use technique to avoid being emotionally affected.

The point of experimentation is discovery and not catharsis. Frequently, what is discovered is fear of knowing, expressing, or letting go of affect. Often the surface feeling yields in awareness to a deeper feeling, such as when there is guilt or anger hidden beneath the sadness and preventing its completion or sadness and hurt beneath anger that prevents its completion. Sometimes what is discovered is a characterological armoring of thought and body that does not allow feelings to show or be expressed. Sometimes it is discovered that the initial feeling has the function of enabling the patient to avoid the fear of moving on ("What do I do now?"). When this mechanism is strong, it needs to be addressed before the grieving can be finished. Sometimes, such a patient needs to learn to make plans and sometimes to manage the anxiety and emptiness by relaxation, breath control, and cognitive self-

direction. Whatever is discovered, it becomes part of the ground that leads to new figures.

THE STANCE OF THE THERAPIST

The task of Gestalt therapy is the patient's growth through awareness; the operation of Gestalt therapy is through a dialogic relationship marked by an I–thou attitude. It is increasingly clear in psychotherapy that the single most important curative factor is the nature and quality of the relationship between therapist and patient. In Gestalt therapy, the relationship is horizontal; that is, neither the therapist nor the patient controls the other or the outcome and the therapist is not the arbiter of truth. The outcome emerges from working together.

Dialogue is meeting the other as an end in him/herself (I–thou) and not as a means to an end (I–it). Relating to a person in order to reach a goal is "aiming," an I–it activity. One cannot aim at a result and still be in dialogue. The purpose of dialogue is meeting the other, not self-actualization or cure. Although healing does result from dialogue, encountering the other person in order to reach that goal is an I–it encounter.

The dialogic relationship is marked by three I–thou characteristics: (1) inclusion and confirmation, (2) authentic presence and self-disclosure, and (3) a commitment to dialogue (Hycner, 1985, 1991; Hycner & Jacobs, 1995; Jacobs, 1989, 1992; Yontef, 1993).

1. *Inclusion* (Buber, 1965a, 1965b) is the process of projecting oneself as fully as possible into the experience or subjectivity of another, simultaneously maintaining awareness of oneself as a separate person. This is similar to empathy, but "inclusion includes moving further into the pole of feeling the other's viewpoint

than is sometimes meant by the term empathy, while simultaneously keeping a sharper awareness of one's separate existence than is sometimes implied in the term empathy" (Yontef, 1993, p. 37). Of course, the sense of the other person is only an approximation whose accuracy can be trusted only when confirmed by that person. The importance of inclusion or empathy has become clearer and more salient in Gestalt therapy in recent years, partially through the influence of the intersubjective self theorists (Jacobs, 1992).

One aspect of inclusion is that by speaking the experience of the other, "imagining the real," the therapist confirms the existence and experience of the patient. This *confirmation*, closely related to acceptance, is marked by confirming the entire existence of the other, including the other's potential (discussed in the Rogers–Buber debate, see Friedman, 1964). Inclusion in psychotherapy is not mutual. Therapists attend to the subjectivity of patients, but patients clarify their own.

2. *Presence*. The therapist also practices what Buber calls "genuine and unreserved communication" (Jacobs, 1989). The therapist does not try to appear or seem to be anything other than he/she is. Of course, this does require a relatively accurate self-picture by the therapist and a congruent style of doing therapy (L. Perls, 1992). In a discriminating way, the therapist shares his/her self as a regular part of the therapy. The therapist does not strive to present either an idealized picture or a blank screen for the patient's projections.

Self-disclosure by the therapist is at the service of and limited by the task at hand and the needs of the patient. It is strongly encouraged when withholding the communication would interfere with the emotional availability of the therapist (Jacobs, 1989). The degree and timing of self-disclosure are discretionary, the determining factors always being the therapeutic task and the welfare of the patient, including the support level of the patient, the immediate state of the patient, and the ethical and legal boundaries of the profession. If the therapist's own needs intrude on the therapy in the form of either excessive self-reference or excessive emotional isolation, further therapy or consultation for the therapist is indicated.

3. *Commitment to dialogue*. The therapist allows what emerges between therapist and patient to lead to an outcome not controlled or determined in advance. For this to happen, both parties must be willing to be affected by the interaction, to change as a result of the interaction, and to surrender to an outcome not of their choosing. This means the therapist must allow his/her self-picture, his/her subjectivity, to be affected by the dialogic interaction.

Dialogue is shared phenomenology and inherently experimental. People in dialogue spontaneously interact, the outcome is not predetermined, and learning and growth usually result. Gestalt therapy is explicit about its phenomenology and dialogue being experimental. In Gestalt therapy we enhance the learning and growth by giving permission to the therapist and patient to be creative in directing therapeutic activities. The dialogic philosophy is not imposed on the patient, but the patient is invited to experiment with it.

CURATIVE FACTORS OR MECHANISMS OF CHANGE

People maintain themselves and grow by contact in the field. With full awareness, they learn from the experience of that contact. When they do not identify with their experience, they interfere with their growth.

The change theory of Gestalt therapy is called the *paradoxical theory of change*:

Change occurs when one becomes what he is, not when he tries to become what he is not. Change does not take place through a coercive attempt by the individual or by another person to change him, but it does take place if one takes the time and effort to be what he is—to be fully invested in his current positions. By rejecting the role of change agent, we make meaningful and orderly change possible. (Beisser, 1970, p. 77)

Persuasion, interpretation, reconditioning, and so forth are not the primary means of change.

Rather, change can occur when the patient abandons, at least for the moment, what he would like to become and attempts to be what he is. The premise is that one must stand in one place in order to have firm footing to move and that it is difficult or impossible to move without that footing. (Beisser, 1970, p. 77)

Healing means to make whole, to bring conflicting aspects of a person's life into a meaningful and harmonious whole. To accept a change contract based on an idealized self-picture reinforces an inner dichotomy and fosters psychological discordance. Healing and growth from a Gestalt therapy perspective requires bringing warring sides into awareness, accepting all sides of the internal conflict, and ultimately integrating them into a more inclusive emerging whole self.

Relationship and Therapeutic Change

In Gestalt therapy theory, people cannot be meaningfully considered apart from their interpersonal field. Normal and pathological human development are social processes; health and pathology are both maintained by the interpersonal field. Psychotherapy is an interactive process, and the therapist–patient relationship accounts for the largest share of the variance.

People raised with the message of being worthless will incorporate this message into their self-structure and new learning will be assimilated into this structure. The girl who was told she was not loved because she was not pretty enough becomes and adult and often interprets contrary feedback in ways negating the new data and confirming the introject. For example, "If he loves me (and I am unlovable), there must be something wrong with him." Or, "He just doesn't know." Or, "He will realize the truth and regret being with me and leave me."

Fixed gestalten based on introjects and maintained by interrupted contact and awareness often form a closed system of self-fulfilling scripts that systematically fail to assimilate new experience. In order for the fixed gestalten to be broken down sufficiently for another and more effective gestalt to develop, outside input that addresses the structural issues is necessary. The therapist can make a difference in this structure by relating to the patient in ways that do not fit into old scripts, that make explicit comment on how the patient assimilates the new data, and directs experiential work that destructs the old Gestalt so that the new information can be effective and not just taken into an existing and unchanging, rigid self-belief system.

Change is facilitated when the therapist is dialogic in attitude, shows a clear understanding of the patient's subjective experience, is self-disclosing, and is warm and accepting.

Building Self-Support

The change process includes small changes and large changes. Early in therapy the activity may center around microawareness, skill acquisition, symptom relief, contact building, and the like. These are not yet changes in the system as a whole. In first-rate Gestalt therapy practice, these concrete improvements occur early in the therapy process and build a foundation for deeper changes that can only occur with long-term therapy. In Gestalt therapy a choice does not have to be made between short-term supportive therapy, skill acquisition, and insight therapy. Gestalt therapy starts where the patient is and works with an integrated method that flows from one level and focus to another, cumulatively building on prior work. At various points the patient faces the choice of terminating and enjoying the fruits of the therapy or moving to a higher level of work. It is not infrequent that a patient will stop therapy to enjoy the fruits of therapy, allowing time to digest and then return for higher-level work.

There are different views about the role of didactic instruction as a mechanism of change in Gestalt therapy. In some circles it is totally discouraged or devalued, although this has lessened considerably in the last decade. In other Gestalt therapy approaches, education is an important part of the process, especially in the beginning phase. While didactic talk does not in and of itself bring on significant changes, it can provide valuable preparation for and accompaniment of experiential work.

Insight

Particular behaviors, isolated aspects of the personality, can be changed in a number of ways: passage of time, ventilation of emotions, being in an accepting relationship, change of reinforcement contingencies, psychopharmaceuticals, and so on. But to change the structure of one's self-organization, to acquire tools for continued change and growth after therapy, and to maximize creative adjustment require insightful awareness that does not ordinarily develop without systematic work with a guide, usually an ongoing relationship with a psychotherapist.

Insight is the felt experience of the various background events of a person's life forming into a meaningful gestalt. In Gestalt therapy, the emphasis is on restoring or establishing an awareness process that leads to insight, including awareness of the still relevant past. The Gestalt therapy method of working stays in the present-centered interactional mode, but the awareness includes presently looking at the past. When the background influences are powerful, have been out of awareness, or stuck in rigid form and not amenable to learning and change of circumstances, exploration of the historical–genetic factors to the point of insight is absolutely necessary to destruct gestalten that are fixed and unresponsive to present need. Working only with the observable present without dealing with such background factors or working purely with "historical insight" would limit the effectiveness of the therapy.

One psychoanalyst comments on how insight develops in Gestalt therapy: "In Gestalt therapy the patient quickly learns to make the discrimination between . . . a statement of experience and a statement of a statement" (Appelbaum, 1976, p. 757). Believing that the chief tool of effective self-regulation is one's own felt sense (experience), Gestalt therapy prefers interventions close to the data of experience (i.e., sensing, describing, expressing, and experimenting) rather than verbal approximations. Interventions are preferred that teach patients to actively engage in sensing, experimenting, and self-discovery. Patients learn to look, hear, sense, feel, imagine, and discover what is important, true, and possible—for them.

While statements expressing direct experience are encouraged, explanations are statements about statements of primary experience and discouraged because they are distant from primary experience. Interpretations are often explanations (especially of causes or motives); hence they are usually statements about statements of experience (experience-far). Empathic interpretations are different in that they attempt to be experience-near statements about experience. In contrast to the Gestalt therapy view that interpretation per se is not as useful as descriptive, experiential, and experimental methods, in traditional psychoanalysis interpretation is *the* defining intervention. In fact, in some psychoanalytic circles interpretation is the only legitimate psychoanalytic intervention, and all other interventions are considered not psychoanalytic.

Gestalt therapy explores whatever processes are influencing the field with this same experiential attitude. Sometimes the process is palpable and observable here and now, such as being angry with the therapist. But Gestalt therapy uses this same experiential approach when exploring processes that operate in the background (e.g., themes of unfinished business from early childhood) and repetitive patterns (e.g., scripts and motivations). Abstract explanatory statements are eschewed in favor of the experiential techniques discussed earlier.

Insight can be pursued by focusing on various aspects of the field. One can intervene with the body (e.g., expressive movement exercises, breathing exercises, and medication) (for discussion of body work in Gestalt therapy, see Kepner, 1987), with cognitive processes (futurizing, depressing, and shaming attributions), by verbally expressing affect, and so on. Although changes by the patient influence systems of which he/she is a part (e.g., family, community, and corporation), sometimes the system

effects are so powerful that the system itself may have to be involved in a change process or the person may have to leave a system.

Factors of Success and Failure

In general, factors predicting success in therapy generically also predict success in Gestalt therapy. There are patient variables, therapist variables, and interaction variables.

Patient Variables

Gestalt therapy is particularly enhanced by patient openness to experience, modification of self-picture, novelty, and interpersonal contact. Patients who want to have their behavior changed without working on personal experience, reflecting on their self-picture, experimenting with anything new, or learning to be in authentic contact with the therapist would be better served in another type of therapy.

As in any therapy, the more strength and support the patient brings to the therapy, the more effective the therapy is likely to be. Support includes acknowledging the need for therapy, motivation to do the work of therapy, intelligence and education, financial support for carrying through on the therapy, and a history of commitment to completing tasks.

Therapist Factors

Gestalt therapy is enhanced by a therapist who cares for, accepts, and likes the patient. Gestalt therapy is enhanced by a therapist who is self-aware and able to be transparent, undefensive, authentic, and congruent. One might note that this covers the same ground as the Rogerian triad of congruence, warmth, and unconditional positive regard. With this foundation the therapist can practice the characteristics of dialogue (inclusion and confirmation, presence, and commitment to dialogue) and phenomenological exploration with minimal defensiveness or countertransferential distortion.

The demands of Gestalt therapy on the therapist are considerable and not limited to the factors in the last paragraph. They also include general psychotherapy knowledge (personality theory, developmental theory, diagnosis, therapeutic methodologies), knowledge of field theory, and the rest of the theory of Gestalt therapy, plus the ability to be creative in making links between patient and therapist, practice and theory, and specific Gestalt therapy methods (e.g., body work, expressive modalities, and use of experimentation) and general psychological knowledge.

Success also requires that the therapist fully understand the philosophy, methodology, and technology of the therapy being practiced. This is not unique to Gestalt therapy, although there is much that is unique in the particular therapeutic frame of Gestalt therapy. Moreover, the therapist must also understand the dynamics of various patient personality and social patterns and how they can be worked with.

The practice of Gestalt therapy requires the therapist to undergo personal therapy to the point of having enough self-regard, accuracy of self-perception, ability to be flexible in meeting otherness, and ability to be affected by the other, and even acknowledge error, to meet the needs of the patient. The therapist must get his/her own confirmation from sources other than the patient if the therapist is not to subtly convert the therapy into a process of therapist confirmation.

Interaction Variables

Beyond the factors of therapist and patient there are the factors of the "chemistry" between patient and therapist. Gestalt therapy theory emphasizes the importance of the relationship and clinical experience tends to support the general psychotherapy research showing the importance of the match between therapist and patient for good outcome.

TREATMENT APPLICABILITY

Range

Gestalt therapy can be used effectively with any patient population that the therapist understands and feels comfortable with. If the therapist can relate to the patient, the Gestalt therapy principles of dialogue and direct experiencing can be applied. With each patient, *general principles must be adapted to the particular clinical situation.* (Yontef, 1993, p. 163)

Individual, marital, family, and group Gestalt therapy have been used with almost all diagnostic populations. To do so successfully requires that the Gestalt therapist adopt his/her interventions and style to the personality of the patient, the diagnosis, the setting, the level of self-support, and the amount and type of available external support.

Gestalt therapy has a long history of application to overly restricted, intellectualized individuals and at one time was primarily known for treatment of that population (Shepherd, 1970, pp. 234–235; Yontef, 1993, pp. 164–165). The most widely known version of Gestalt therapy features Fritz Perls (in the 1960s) in a very confrontive, theatrical style. This was not the only style of Gestalt therapy even then and has steadily receded since the 1960s. The confrontive, dramatic style requires great caution and is most useful with constricted neurotic patients who do not have strong shame issues.

Gestalt therapy is most frequently practiced with patients with neuroses and character disorders. It is well suited for marital and sexual therapy. Yontef (1993) discusses psychoanalytically informed, intensive Gestalt therapy treatment of borderline and narcissistic personality disorders, although cautioning that this has not been scientifically tested (Yontef, 1993).

Similarly, Gestalt therapy has been applied to the treatment of alcoholic and psychotic patients but with little empirical evidence (Carlock, Glaus, & Shaw, 1992; Dublin, 1973, 1978/1992; Harris, 1992; Paige, 1975/1992). Obviously, work with psychotic or other severely disturbed patients requires caution, support, patience, long-term commitment, and the persistent building of relationship. It requires precise knowledge of the nature of the particular psychopathology and stages of its development and treatment so that the internal support mechanisms of the patient can be augmented to deal with the overwhelming pain, rage, shame, and despair that surface. This enables the creation of the safest possible treatment process given the psychopathology. Treatment of these patients also requires appropriate institutional and pharmacotherapeutic supports.

Gestalt therapy is considered to be effective with patients of all ages. It has been widely used with children in therapy (Oaklander, 1969/1988) and also in school settings (Brown, 1971/1990; Lederman, 1969, 1970).

Dangers of Gestalt Therapy

The safe and effective practice of psychotherapy requires that the therapist be clear in defining the therapeutic framework, firm about professional boundaries, and sensitive to the patient's experience. This is especially true in Gestalt therapy with the wide range of interventions and therapeutic styles that are allowed and created, the degree of therapist self-disclosure that is encouraged, the intensity of activity and personal interaction by the Gestalt therapist, the intensity of expression of feelings, and the lack of rule-based restrictions on allowable therapeutic procedures. Without therapist sensitivity these activities can lead to the patient's feeling overwhelmed, intruded upon, in danger, used, seduced, shamed, and so forth.

Expressive and confrontive techniques that break down defenses require personal humility and diagnostic caution. In recent years, dialogical Gestalt therapy has emphasized the relationship and understanding personality structure more than catharsis or confrontation (Hycner, 1985; Jacobs, 1989; Yontef, 1993). Therapists with a weak professional background or who are poorly trained in Gestalt therapy pose a danger that techniques and emotional involvement will proceed without clarity about goals, what is central to each patient, alternative methods, and so on.

Referral to another therapist is indicated if the chemistry between patient and therapist suggests that a better therapeutic relationship could develop with a different therapist, if the therapist is not trained and skilled in working with a particular type of patient, or if the therapist does not like the patient. If the patient does not want, or cannot support, awareness-oriented therapy, then referral to another type of therapy is indicated— usually to a behavior therapist or for medication.

Group therapists must attend to many such issues of boundaries and relationship (e.g., envy, jealousy, competition, and shame induction by suspected favoritism).

Issues of boundaries, limits, and meanings are especially pertinent to the area of touch. Touching between patient and therapist is allowed in Gestalt therapy, but sexual activity between therapist and patient is not. Touch might include handshake, hugging, therapeutic touch in working with breathing, massage, and other body work. The therapist must be mindful of the effects of any interactions, such as fantasies that might be stirred up, dangers aroused, and false expectations stimulated.

CLINICAL EVALUATION

The process of clinical evaluation of outcome is an integral part of the therapeutic work and is carried out on an ongoing basis. It is done by the therapist and the patient, and, when it is foreground, by the therapist and patient working together.

The primary sources of information for therapist and patient are (1) what they observe, (2) their felt bodily and affective sense, and (3) feedback from others who observe the patient (e.g., others in a group, family, friends, teachers, and bosses). Data from separate sources (i.e., patient, therapist, and others) increase confidence in the validity of the observed improvement.

One of the most significant changes that can take place is in the patient's subjective sense of self. Successful therapy can be measured by a heightened sense of self-esteem and accuracy of self-picture. The patient who can be routinely accurate and honest in self-appraisal and feel, "I like me, with my flaws," is a patient who has benefited from therapy. Such a patient shows clarity of self-definition, cohesive self-identity across situations and time, and dependable self-esteem.

The improved patient looks more lively, makes better contact with other people and with life tasks, and has more clarity in self-definition and self-regulation. Patients with improved self-regulation can state accurately what they want in a particular situation at a particular time and can go about getting it to whatever extent it is possible in the situation. Physically the improved patient looks more graceful, is better supported by gravity, and is literally and figuratively better grounded and able to move with more fluidity. A particularly accurate domain of observation is the quality of breathing and general physiological support (Kepner, 1987). The improved patient is less tense and inhales and exhales smoothly.

Patients showing these changes also show a concomitant change in awareness. They develop insight; that is, they experience and express "aha!" reactions. They are more aware of their feelings, impulses, wishes, and behavior and take responsibility for them. They are aware of what motivates their current behavior and experience and how this links with their past history. They are aware of themes that run through work, social relationships, intimacy, and childhood. They also manifest a decrease in boundary disturbances.

Because Gestalt therapy is based on an ecological theory, another measure of success of Gestalt therapy is that the patient not only takes more responsibility for self but also is in good contact with the environment in which he/she lives and takes an appropriate share of responsibility for it.

There is also a change in patients' awareness process, one that is observed during sessions by patient and therapist. Patients will be observed to report spontaneously what they feel and what they need, as well as making reflexive observations on what they are doing right now. They are more aware of differences between people, and more aware of the validity of conflicting views of reality. They are more aware of the difference between what they observe and what they infer. At the highest level of improvement not only do these insights occur in therapy, but the phenomenological attitude becomes a regular and ingrained part of ongoing functioning (phenomenological ascent).

Objective measures of improvement are also considered, but their meaning has to be defined on a case-by-case basis. Evidence of work and school functioning, patterns of relationship, decrease in addictive behavior, and so on, can be more or less objectively obtained. The difficulty is knowing the meaning of the changes. For example, regular work attendance is usually considered a sign of therapeutic success. However, sometimes leaving work is a sign of success. A young woman who had finished high school and college, started working, but never took time to enjoy life or explore alternatives quit her job and started traveling across the country. At her age (early 20s), with her history, this taking leave of conformity and ambition was a real step in growth. It was followed by her being clearer about what she wanted, what was important to her, and a feeling of autonomy, self-direction, and choice. In another patient who left his job to do the same thing, it was a sign of the lack of success of the therapy. The second patient had problems finishing anything, and leaving his job and therapy to travel was not novel and experimental for him but a repetition of old behavior that did not lead to growth, satisfaction, or productivity.

RESEARCH

What the therapist does and the qualities of therapist–patient relatedness are more important than the therapy system designation or the emotional strength of the patient (Lafferty, Beutler, & Crago, 1989; Luborksy et al., 1986; Tellgen, Frassa, & Höniger, 1979). "There is theoretically no reason why Gestalt therapy should be more generally effective than therapies under other names that follow the principles of good psychotherapy" (Simkin & Yontef, 1984/1993, p. 167). The importance of relationship factors is supported by research on the working alliance, empathy in the Rogerian and self psychology traditions, and directive experiential research (Harman, 1984; Jacobs, 1992; Norcross & Rossi, 1994).

One of the central principles in Gestalt therapy theory is that the therapist intervene creatively and flexibly in accordance with patient need. Although there is evidence that clients differentially benefit from different methods (Beutler, Engle, Mohr, Daldrup, & Bergan, 1991; Grawe, Caspar, & Ambül, 1990; Greenberg et al., 1994; Meyer, 1981; Tscheulin, 1990), this is usually approached in the research literature by comparing different systems of therapy rather than what therapists do. Whether therapy is more effective when therapists creatively adapt to the needs of each particular patient and moment rather than follow a set procedure has not been scientifically proven.

The classic Lieberman, Yalom, and Miles (1973) study of encounter groups confirms that what therapists do is more important than therapeutic labels. There were two Gestalt groups, both with very active Gestalt therapists. One followed the principles of good therapy discussed in this article, and his group was among those with the most gain and least negative results. The other Gestalt therapist did not follow these guidlines but was abrasive, insensitive, and charismatic rather than dialogic and experimental. This group showed little gain and the most negative results. What therapists do counts; labels do not.

The best Gestalt therapy research is a program of Leslie Greenberg and associates. Greenberg (1986) explicates the connection between the use of specific Gestalt therapy techniques and immediate, intermediate, and final outcomes. He has conducted a number of studies in what he calls process-directive experiential therapy. He considers this form of active experiential therapy a combination of a Rogerian client-centered relationship and Gestalt therapy techniques. For purposes of research, we can consider modern, dialogic Gestalt therapy equivalent to process-directive experiential therapy, with the exception that Gestalt therapy practice uses a wider range of techniques than have so far been measured in Greenberg's program.

Gestalt therapy as a form of process-directive experiential therapy postulates that growth occurs as a result of new awareness and acceptance of self-in-the-world through focused phenomenological exploration in a horizontal therapeutic relationship. The ideal research confirming this mechanism of change would measure the covariance of self-awareness, self-acceptance, active phenomenological experimentation, and a particular type of therapeutic relationship. There is some support for this mechanism of change from the Greenberg program (discussed later).

Gestalt therapy is based on the relationship plus a methodology of very actively focused phenomenological experimentation. This has been precisely the focus in many of Greenberg's studies. Greenberg et al. (1994) reviewed 13 studies comparing experiential therapies with cognitive and behavioral treatments. Using meta-psychological statistics they found the latter slightly more effective. However, when reviewing the seven studies that compared directive experiential treatments with cognitive or behavioral treatments, there was a small (not statistically significant) difference in favor of the directive experiential. This is an indication that more active experiential therapies are more effective than the classic client-centered approach in which the therapist does not direct phenomenological experimentation.

In a significant series of experiments, Greenberg and colleagues have shown

that the Gestalt therapy two-chair technique resulted in a greater depth of experiencing than did empathic reflection alone (Greenberg, 1982; Greenberg & Clarke, 1979; Greenberg & Dompierre, 1981; Greenberg & Higgins, 1980; Greenberg & Rice, 1981). Paivio and Greenberg (1992) showed the empty-chair dialogue effective for resolving unfinished emotional issues with significant others. Pre–posttesting showed reduction in general distress as well as in unfinished business. The two-chair technique has also been shown to be effective in healing internal splits (Greenberg, 1979; Greenberg & Higgins, 1989).

According to the Gestalt therapy change theory, self-knowledge and self-acceptance are necessary for healing and growth. A "harsh internal critic" is an introjection-based rejection of self that prevents self-acknowledgment, healing, and growth. The two-chair technique has been shown to be effective in softening the "harsh internal critic" (Greenberg, 1980). Greenberg (1982) also showed that conflict resolution in the two-chair dialogue occurred by deeper experience of previously rejected aspects of the self. This provides some confirmation of the Gestalt therapy methodology and theory of change.

Greenberg and Webster (1982) showed that softening the critic of patients with intrapsychic conflicts that interfere with decision making resulted in an improvement in conflict resolution, less discomfort, greater mood change, and greater goal attainment compared with patients who did not experience "softening." Along the same lines, Rice and Greenberg's (1984) discussion supports the important role of softening of introjected self-criticism in resolving intrapersonal conflicts, thereby supporting the Gestalt therapy change theory.

The Gestalt therapy method emphasizing focused phenomenological experiments and factors of relationship rather than either emphasis alone is corroborated by this research combining Gestalt therapy techniques and client-centered relationship.

Discussion

Research that does not account for the importance of the therapeutic relationship or that limits the therapist's interventions to set procedures is of reduced value in process or validation research on Gestalt therapy.

For example, the empty-chair and two-chair work lend themselves to manualized research. These interventions are effective and easy to specify but are neither the only effective techniques in Gestalt therapy nor in any way essential. Some people need expressive work on unfinished business but have difficulties with the empty-chair technique. For example, some are too inhibited or cannot imagine the other person in the empty chair clearly enough to use the technique effectively. Gestalt therapy stands on the belief that therapists are more effective who can use either the empty-chair technique or one of the alternatives such as role-playing, pounding pillows, poetry writing, journal writing, artistic expression, mental experimentation, and so forth.

Clinicians work with unique individuals and nomothetic research works with quantified group data that produces probability statements. Norcross and Rossi (1994) state that "psychotherapy is more fruitfully conceived and researched as a human relationship than as a technical, manualized treatment. The outcomes of particular therapist–patient dyads are probably more illuminating than the group means . . ." (p. 537). Most Gestalt therapists have some healthy skepticism about how valid or useful nomothetic data are in actual clinical situations. "No statistical approach can tell the individual patient or therapist what works for him or her. What is shown to work for most does not always work for a particular individual" (Yontef, 1993, p. 165). Gestalt therapy has emphasized ideographic observation and experimentation with each patient more than scientific verification (F. Perls et al., 1951, p. 7; Yontef, 1969/1993, p. 27; Yontef, 1993, p. 166). Each session is considered an experimental encounter in which the next step is suggested by the results of the previous exploration and verification is phenomenological.

Gestalt therapists do take nomothetic data seriously in the sense of utilizing the information to sharpen their sensitivity as they observe individual patients. For example, the empirical findings of the cognitive-behavioral therapists have resulted in clarifying and strengthening the cognitive awareness work already a part of Gestalt therapy in treating depression. Whereas in former years depression was treated in Gestalt therapy mostly with expressive work, which still is effective for some patients, other depressives benefit greatly from work on irrational cognitions. Cognitive work now plays a larger role in Gestalt therapy.

Data from controlled research in which the complexities of clinical practice are eliminated have only limited relevance for daily practice (Goldfried, Greenberg, & Marmar, 1990). Subjects who are eliminated from research programs because of various complications constitute the bulk of patients treated by Gestalt therapists. Testing effectiveness of a procedure with depression and eliminating patients with personality disorders, psychoses, addictions, legal difficulties, and medical difficulties and those who do not complete the study, and so on, give scientific data but data of limited value for those dealing with the "impurities" of practice.

CASE ILLUSTRATION

The Presenting Situation

Rachel is an attractive 41-year-old woman who came to therapy a month after her mother died of cancer. Her mother had been abusive to Rachel during childhood and in adulthood continued to be self-absorbed, narcissistic, and perhaps psychotic. When Rachel tried talking with her mother before she died, her mother made real contact impossible by maintaining her usual paranoid accusatory attitude—now exacerbated by the cancer and medication.

Rachel also had marital problems of crisis proportions, an ulcer, dangerously severe vaginal bleeding, and a frightening precancerous colon condition that warranted close medical supervision in light of a strong family history of cancer. The pattern of multiple crises and medical problems continued long into her therapy. She was depressed, which was partially defended against by productive hypomanic activity. She had just begun taking an antidepressant and medication for her ulcers.

The weekend before her first contact with me she had cut her wrists—not for the first time. These were not cuts designed to kill herself, as the cuts were purposely superficial. She thought that perhaps with "a little death" she could get some relief from the pain, despair, and shame. The cuts were a way of letting out affective energy, feeling alive, defending against more intense emotional pain, and containing more dangerous impulses.

Rachel is a successful artist and author with a backbreaking schedule of writing, lecturing, teaching, and so forth. She has an advanced degree in classics and combines first-rate scholarship and art in her books. Although she has a wide range of skills and interests—she fences, plays the cello, loves opera, and learned self-hypnosis from a high school therapist—she does not consistently allow herself to enjoy these activities. She is a very competent and devoted mother.

Rachel spoke rapidly, frequently interrupting herself by abruptly changing subjects at lightning speed. She would then return to previously interrupted subjects and could maintain a sense of continuity with all of them. She was very dramatic and her emotions were at a fever pitch, but she interrupted each thought and feeling before its coming to completion. Her face clearly showed the building emotion and the interruption.

Her fund of information and rapidity of access to it had as great a range and depth as any person I have known. Her speed of thinking and ability to keep several themes going without losing her place, as well as the speed with which she digested and worked with my comments, indicated that she was clearly exceptionally intelligent.

The combination of speed, frequent change of topics, emotional intensity, multiple presenting difficulties and crises, and chronic posttraumatic difficulties going back to childhood made it a real challenge to keep in contact with her at each moment and also to keep a clear thematic focus.

From the beginning I shared with her what I observed as it occurred. For example, I shared with her my observation of her process of self-interruption and her nonverbal expressions, such as her seeming to reach out and pull me with her eyes. I made centering suggestions such as, "taking three long slow breaths." I also made suggestions for guiding her phenomenological focus, for example, "Say that again, slowly." I was generally self-disclosing about how I was affected by her; for example, when she talked about being abused as a child I said, "That was an outrageous way to treat a child. It makes me angry and I want to go back and protect the little girl."

Obviously, I needed to learn about her true self, the self that lay underneath the turbulence and that manifested itself through the behavioral patterns that transcended the immediate moments in therapy. As I reached out to understand these larger patterns, I kept grounding both of us by staying as present-centered as possible, especially exploring what was immediately emotionally present for her. Frequently I would ask, "What are you experiencing right now?" or, "What are you feeling right now."

She appreciated that I was able to follow, understand, and facilitate her process, especially in telling her what I observed. This contrasted with her previous therapist, who had interrupted her process by trying to tell her what she felt. That had been like a repetition of her family history in which her experience did not count. Her reaching out to me with her eyes appeared to have been, in part, trying to ascertain whether I was overwhelmed with her as her last therapist had been or whether I found her disgusting, as she found herself.

In exploring processes as they occurred during early sessions with me, she also gained some clarity about her relationship with her previous therapist. She had had several sessions with him at her health maintenance organization (HMO), terminating with him when she started Gestalt therapy with me. One of the messages she gets from people, especially family members and her two husbands, is that she is "too much." She also got this message from her previous therapist. This activates a sense of primary shame in which she reacts to hurtful interpersonal interactions by feeling there is something wrong with her.

From a Gestalt therapy perspective, it is the therapist's responsibility to have enough self-support so that the patient's emotional state is not too much for him/her. Rachel's previous therapist was not able to support himself so that he could help her with her immediate emotional state, to cope better with her current life crises, or to establish a working alliance in order to work through her long-standing patterns. He was not helping her with the grief work or her spiral of depression and emotional flight. Unfortunately, his direct and nonverbal messages left her with the shame-inducing message that he was not able to work with her because she was "too much."

Rachel's History

Rachel's pretherapy history was filled with people who violated her and abandoned her but did not make good contact. Rachel has been married twice, and her husbands were both prime examples. Her first marriage, at age 20, was a short-lived one with a professional athlete who was physically abusive and also had an affair with her mother while married to Rachel. When Rachel began Gestalt therapy she had been married to her alcoholic second husband for 14 years. His mental picture was of 14 years of a good marriage; her picture was of 14 years of depression. He said she wanted too much, she said he gave too little. There were two children at home, ages 11 and 7, and also a 20-year-old stepdaughter from her second husband's first marriage who was away at college.

At the beginning of our second session she said she wanted a divorce. The marital therapist they had been seeing concurrently at the HMO had recommended an alcohol abuse clinic for her husband. He refused this recommendation and came to the following session with a hangover. The marital therapist was intent on saving the marriage rather than conducting a more open, focused psychotherapy. Rachel told her husband at the following marital session of her intention to get a divorce.

Rachel clearly needed to be literally and figuratively touched by him and also needed the boundary between them to be clearer. He would talk about topics such as politics and archeology but was pathologically unmindful of the present, did not really talk to her, and demonstrated no interest in or capacity for intimacy. He had a history of doing such things as abandoning her with two young children in a foreign city when she was ill with a 104° fever. In recent times he had been known to take the children somewhere, forget them, and leave without them or forget to feed them. He drank a lot and constantly. Although he would say that he loved Rachel, he did not really know or express his feelings or want to touch her or to be touched; she was filled with loathing, disgust, and rage and did not want him near.

When Rachel's mind was not compulsively racing, a rare occurrence, "gremlins" (i.e., posttraumatic stress disorder flashbacks) got to her. This generated insomnia and difficulty being still or meditating and interfered with enjoying herself. As a child, she was sexually molested by her grandfather and severely punished by her grandmother, as well as by her grandfather and mother. Her grandmother was the only adult who was any source of affection. She was also raped by a stranger when she was 5.

Her mother varied between overtly abandoning Rachel and intrusively and sadistically punishing her. Punishments included being beaten, bound, and locked in a closet; her hair being punitively cut off; being forced to sit in a room without objects to work on or play with for hours at a very young age; having her clothes cut up in a maternal pique; punitive enemas; being dragged by one leg while her head bounced on the ground; and so forth. Amazingly, in spite of this, Rachel was quite successful

in her art even as a child. Her mother publicly attacked and humiliated her, even while Rachel was receiving awards or having a showing of her art.

The abuse continued during the beatings of her first marriage. When she was 21 she spent some time in Guatemala with her first husband and witnessed several brutal and callused murders of women. In one of them she was in her hotel room and men in the street below bet on how quickly they could kill two women. During the same period she was in a car and witnessed men forcing two women to fight to the death with knives, betting on the winner. At the end of that period her husband beat and raped her so badly that she returned to the United States for follow-up medical treatment. The combination of these adult traumas resulted in flashbacks that also triggered flashbacks of the childhood abuse.

There was a bizarre contrast between the family's abusive treatment and their aristocratic, socialite, upper-class status and facade. This was a white, Anglo-Saxon, Protestant family that lived anachronistically as if in the Victorian age, replete with white gloves, correct fork, never touching dirt, always polite, with no one good enough for the family. The family imposed a dress and manner code incongruous with that of her peers.

Rachel's mother told her that she was conceived by her father raping her mother at gunpoint, pulling her hair, and then falling asleep with a gun in his hand. Her mother then divorced her father. Rachel only had contact with her father a few times, all very unsatisfactory, with his showing no genuine interest in meeting her. Her mother remarried when Rachel was 7 years old. The stepfather made sexual advances toward Rachel on several occasions.

In those early weeks of treatment, and later during times of stress, she called between sessions. The calls were brief, and no demands or threats of suicide were made. She needed to touch some-one on an emotional level and could maintain herself if she heard the thera-pist's voice or talked briefly.

Rachel survived a childhood filled with abuse and neglect in part by being totally absorbed in art and school and by isolating herself from the family. She was filled with shame, fear, rage, guilt, and grief. She developed a keen interest in other cultures and improving the human condition. She is a speaker in demand internationally. Nevertheless, she often accepts invitations to schools where there are neglected or abused children, touch-ing and inspiring them, when her own interests would dictate declining in order to have more time to repair her own life and accept more lucrative assignments.

Process of Therapy with Rachel

The first stage of therapy was establish-ing contact, thematic awareness, and es-tablishing and solidifying necessary skills of self-regulation. In this stage Rachel re-membered incidents from her past, ob-served current events in her psychic life, and started to make linkages between them. Experiments focused around fin-ishing old business (anger, fear, and shame) and letting go, grieving what had occurred in her life.

A typical piece of work on finishing old business started with an intruding memory. One time Rachel remembered something vaguely disturbing about the basement in the city library as a child of 5. She was upset and did not remember why. I asked her to describe the scene more fully. As she started to do so, the picture became more vivid for her and she could feel the wood, smell the books, and see the lighting. Then she remem-bered that her mother had left her there, it was close to closing, and she loved libraries. Then she felt herself blocking the scene. We continued and she became

aware of fright and then a memory of a man suddenly looming over her. She could smell him as he cornered her and groped her. We continued until her memory of the scene was clear and vivid, then we went over it again feeling the emotions (fear, disgust, rage, shame). Then we imagined the man present in the empty chair and she pushed him away and used her adult strength to con-front him as she could not do as a child. I felt touched and protective of the little girl and told Rachel that. By the end of the hour we both felt a warm bond be-tween us.

After that session Rachel felt seering shame. In the next session we explored the shame. Back to memory: She was afraid to tell her mother about the viola-tion because her previous experience was that mother would blame her. Rachel was also worried that mother would be upset that the sweater she was wearing, borrowed from her sister, had gotten dirty. At that point I asked her to be her current age and picture the 5-year-old girl. She did so and was filled with love and comfort and wanted to protect the little girl. After that second session the shame diminished and some of the emo-tional energy was freed up. Of course, this did not completely finish the work on healing this trauma.

The letting go occurred when the anger and shame diminished and Rachel felt sad. The grief work, accepting the reality of what had happended and could not be changed, resulted in crying and letting go of the tension and ultimately to some modicum of peace.

The ongoing contact followed the characteristics of dialogue discussed above. As the therapist I regularly put myself in Rachel's subjective position, confirming her experience by "imagin-ing the real" and accepting her. But more than that, I have been genuinely moved by Rachel, felt love and warmth toward her and respect for her. This was expressed both directly and through the practice of inclusion. I sat with her and felt her pain (as I imagined it) and my own pain in response—not minimizing the pain while affirming my positive picture of her survival and productivity in the face of great odds and also my belief that her prospects for future happiness were positive.

She interrupted awareness of memories or strong affect early in the awareness cycle, often by changing from subject to subject. When she experimented in therapy with not interrupting herself and stayed with her feelings, she was flooded by intense and overwhelming affect. Her rage was usually retroflected (i.e., turned against herself) in the form of punitive demands, judgments, self-loathing, and subjugating herself to work. Direct expression of affect, either in person or in cathartic work in sessions, was very difficult for Rachel. One line of exploration has been reversing the retroflection and using her healthy aggression to create better boundaries. For example, when talking of an incident of abuse Rachel would frequently physically tighten and pull herself in, sometimes hitting her thigh with her fist, and verbally started attacking herself. One technique was to ask her to imagine that the offender was in the empty chair and to express her anger (verbally and physically) at the offender.

Early in the therapy I had to bring to Rachel's attention polarities that she split asunder and direct the work of integrating them. In addition to the simple interruption of the awareness cycle, she showed a more complicated pattern called splitting. Splitting is a pattern in which she allowed awareness of half of a polarity, suppressing awareness of the other half. Although this sounds like simple repression or unawareness, the complication is that on other occasions this would reverse: The pole that had formerly been kept out of awareness would

now be in awareness. Thus two polar feelings that, if brought together, would mean integration were kept separated, never the twain to meet. This is a more disruptive pattern than ambivalence, which is a pattern of simultaneously holding contradictory feelings and not resolving them.

One central split is between competence and nurturance. Rachel assumed that in order to be nurtured one has to give up competence and independence. For Rachel, the price of nurturance was total accommodation and seeing herself as begging pathetically. Concomitantly, if one is competent and autonomous one must be self-sufficient and then others would withhold nurturance—a position of emotional starvation. Within the family of her childhood, her only alternative to begging was emotional starvation. She would be taken care of if she begged, accommodated, and apologized for her existence. With independence of any sort came withdrawal of any aid, attack, and abandonment. Her grandmother stated it explicitly: If she became an artist (i.e., independent and competent), she would inevitably wind up alone in a gutter. Her only alternative was to marry a society man who would take care of her, even if she would be miserable.

To much of the world Rachel showed only her competent side, taking very little from anyone, acting as if she could do it all and needing no one. In therapy she allowed the needy side to show, reassuring me several times with profuse apologies and self-contempt that no one else saw this side of her. But at first it was very hard for her to access her competence when she was in her "hungry infant" mode.

In fact, Rachel's friends have seen the need under the self-sufficient facade and they invite, encourage, and cajole her into letting herself be taken care of, at least a little. Usually they are unsuccessful in this effort. For Rachel, surrendering to their loving efforts feels very dangerous. Being taken care of means a regressive slide into a fused position as the object of scorn and ridicule. Being taken care of means being dominated, tortured, and humiliated. It has taken a lot of support and confrontation in therapy sessions to get her to even protect her health and acknowledge basic needs in planning her daily life schedule.

Over time Rachel has been able to work directly on the process of splitting and has recognized that she is both interdependent and competent. At first this work was done by my simultaneously making an empathic reflection of her current feeling together with reminding Rachel of the opposite polarity. "Today you seem to insist on doing everything yourself—and not remembering how lonely and wanting of help you were last week." I also told her about splitting so she would understand how I was intervening and what she was doing. At first when she brought in both sides of the polarity, she did so with "or" statements ("I either feel self-sufficient or feel like a needy infant"). I had her experiment with changing these to "and" statements ("Sometimes I feel self-sufficient and sometimes I feel like a needy infant"). I also had her use the two-chair technique for developing a dialogue between these two subselves).

As a result, Rachel has shown increasing ability to regulate herself competently, simultaneously acknowledging her limitations, needs, and vulnerability. She has made moves toward adjusting the environment to her, although there is still a lot of work to do on this score.

Healthy self-regulation for Rachel required that she interrupt the interruption of her awareness cycle. Doing this required two kinds of work: (1) being able to tolerate moments of silence, to still her obsessing mind, and (2) finishing old business. She has had to work through enduring reactions to the childhood abuse, including resultant affect and pictures of self and the world that still color her perception. For example, based on the attitude of her family toward even a minimal expression of feelings or needs, Rachel introjected the notion that wanting or crying were disgusting acts of a pitiful person, a bother deserving ridicule. She often projects this judgmental attitude on others (i.e., fearing that they have this attitude toward her).

Currently she continues integrating. Now when she has a need she can recognize it and considers plans to have it met. Now, when she is in her productive, competent mode, not only can she remember that she is a person who helps others, but she also shares with the rest of humanity the fact that she has wants and needs that are ignored only at great cost.

Although the work with Rachel was contemporaneously grounded as specified by the Gestalt therapy methodology, her therapy required extensive focus on bringing half-forgotten childhood experiences back into awareness. This was necessary in order to complete unfinished affective gestalten, explicate introjects and shame reactions, and bring new awareness and flexibility into repetitive behavioral patterns stemming from the childhood experience. In Gestalt therapy language, the old gestalten needed to be recognized and broken up, preparing the ground for the emergence of new gestalten.

Rachel's Outcome

In the middle phase of her therapy Rachel began to acknowledge her interruption of her awareness process and expanded her active repertoire of centering activities.

As a result of expressing her anger, structuralizing an internal good parent, and having increased good feelings about herself, she was able to spend less time being bitter at her family of origin. She continues to be a good mother and her children continue to be emotionally and intellectually quite competent and even deal very maturely with their alcoholic father.

She completed her divorce, agreeing to minimal child support from her husband in return for his finally agreeing to a settlement and signing the divorce papers. She has been quite relieved since the separation, although not without some feelings of abandonment, resentment, regret, shame, and self-recrimination.

Since childhood she has pictured relief from tension, stress, anxiety, attack, and so on through images of death. One of her favorites was imagining being hit by a Mac truck. Her use of such images has drastically decreased as the therapeutic relationship continued to deepen, her self-processes strengthened, her needs became more recognized, and unfinished business completed. At moments of being flooded by flashbacks, she does occasionally revert to these forms of relief.

She continues to retroflect as a main coping mechanism, thus creating body tension, especially around the eyes; sleep difficulties; pain in her upper stomach; and breathing difficulties. Work proceeds on undoing the retroflection by relaxation and enactments of emotional expression and boundary assertiveness. Her assertiveness is much improved, but she is still very reluctant to contactfully and powerfully express her anger or to be "mean." Activities along these lines include role-playing of pushing back against her mother and grandparents, pushing to get space for herself, and cathartic release of anger. Relaxation exercises are still difficult for Rachel because of the danger of the intrusion of flashbacks. As these posttraumatic symptoms decrease, the support for a more relaxed posture continues to grow.

She still protects herself against the dangers of contact by isolating and deflecting. The dangers are polar: total isolation from others (preventing anything good or bad from entering her space) or total vulnerability to intrusion (attack followed by either rejection or being trapped, smothered, or captured). Rachel still has not reached a point where she feels safe to enter into intimacy with a lover, although she continues her therapy work. Based on her steady and consistent therapeutic movement, her prognosis is excellent.

She has started to construct a sense of self that encompasses both needs and achievement/autonomy. She is taking better care of herself, sometimes getting enough sleep, and so forth. Further changes in lifestyle and centering require continued work to master the hardest and most enduring area of her work: working through the childhood trauma. She has uncovered and discussed numerous memories of abuse and worked extensively with the affect, mental attitudes, and pictures resulting from this trauma.

Therapeutic work continues to focus on strengthening the self-function of bringing her maternal, adult mode to bear in healing the wounds of childhood and protecting and nourishing her child ego mode. (See discussion on treating patients with character disorders in Yontef, 1993, pp. 419–488.) Rachel has begun to spontaneously incorporate the steps she takes in therapy sessions into her everyday functioning, and it is anticipated that this will continue.

SUGGESTIONS FOR FURTHER READING

Alexander, R., Brickman, B., Jacobs, L., Trop, J., & Yontef, G. (1992). Transference meets dialogue. *The Gestalt Journal*, *15*(2), 61–108. This article is a discussion of the case in Hycner and Jacobs (1995) by a panel of two Gestalt therapists, including myself and the therapist, and two self psychologists.

Hycner, R. (1985). Dialogical Gestalt therapy: An initial proposal. *The Gestalt Journal, 8*(1), 23–49.

Hycner, R. (1991). *Between person and person: Toward and dialogical psychotherapy.* New York: Gestalt Journal Press. This book expands the material in Hycner's 1985 article.

Hycner, R., & Jacobs, L. (1995). *The healing relationship in Gestalt therapy: A dialogic self psychology.* New York: Gestalt Journal Press. This is a useful and readable volume which includes verbatim case material. For example, an interesting case report by a psychoanalytically oriented Gestalt therapist includes verbatim recordings of three sessions with the patient. The case is discussed in Alexander, Brickman, Jacobs, Trop, and Yontef (1992).

Jacobs, L. (1989). Dialogue in Gestalt theory and therapy. *The Gestalt Journal, 12*(6), 25–67. These are excellent articles for readings on dialogue and relationship in Gestalt therapy.

Perls, F. (1942/1992). *Ego, hunger and aggression.* New York: Gestalt Journal Press. This first Gestalt therapy book was originally published in 1942 and has been reprinted several times.

Perls, F. (1969/1992). *Gestalt therapy verbatim.* New York: Gestalt Journal Press. The most effortless introduction to Gestalt therapy, this work contains four lectures and verbatim material from a Perls workshop. Unfortunately, this is also the most untechnical and sketchy of Perls's works. The 1992 edition is improved by an excellent new introduction by Michael Vincent Miller.

Perls, F., Hefferline, R., & Goodman, P. (1951). *Gestalt therapy: Excitement and growth in the human personality.* New York: Julian Press. The second volume on Gestalt therapy is the most complete theoretical work in Gestalt therapy, although diligence is required to read and understand it. No thorough understanding of Gestalt therapy is possible without digesting this book.

Polster, E., & Polster, M. (1973). *Gestalt therapy integrated.* New York: Brunner/Mazel. This volume is a complete and readable introduction to Gestalt therapy.

Yontef, G. (1993). *Awareness, dialogue, and process: Essays on Gestalt therapy.* New York: Gestalt Journal Press. Readings on the history, theory, and clinical practice of Gestalt therapy.

Other verbatim accounts of Gestalt therapy sessions or research reviews:

Aylward, J., Bauer, R., Freedman, H., Harman, R., & Perls, L. (1986). A case presentation in Gestalt therapy. *The Gestalt Journal, 9*(1), 16–35. Other case presentations can be found in the pages of this journal.

Greenberg, L., Elliott, R., & Lietaer, G. (1994). Research on Experiential psychotherapies. In A. Bergin & S. Garfield (Eds.), *Handbook of psychotherapy and behavior change.* New York: Wiley. This is the best relevant research review on experiential therapies.

Harman, R. (1984). Gestalt therapy research. *The Gestalt Journal, 7*(2), 61–69. This is an earlier review of research developments in Gestalt therapy.

Harman, R. (1989). *Gestalt therapy with groups, couples, sexually dysfunctional men, and dreams.* Springfield, IL: Charles C. Thomas. This volume also includes several case examples.

REFERENCES

Acierno, R., Hersen, M., & Van Hasselt, V. (1993). Interventions for panic disorder: A critical review of the literature. *Clinical Psychology Review, 13*, 561–578.

Alexander, R., Brickman, B., Jacobs, L., Trop, J., & Yontef, G. (1992). Transference meets dialogue. *The Gestalt Journal, 15*(2), 61–108.

Appelbaum, S. (1976). A psychoanalyst looks at Gestalt therapy. In C. Hatcher & P. Himelstein (Eds.), *The handbook of Gestalt therapy* (pp. 755–778). New York: Jason Aronson.

Aylward, J., Bauer, R., Freedman, H., Harman, R., & Perls, L. (1986). A case presentation in Gestalt therapy. *The Gestalt Journal, 9*(1), 16–35.

Beck, J., Stanley, M., Baldwin, L., Deagle, E. III, & Averill, P. (1994). Comparison of cognitive therapy and relaxation training for panic disorder. *Journal of Consulting and Clinical Psychology, 42,* 818–826.

Beisser, A. (1970). The paradoxical theory of change. In J. Fagan & I. Shepherd (Eds.), *Gestalt therapy now* (pp. 77–80). Palo Alto, CA: Science & Behavior Books.

Beutler, L., Engle, D., Mohr, D., Daldrup, R., & Bergan, J. (1991). Differential response to cognitive, experiential, and self-directed psychotherapeutic procedures. *Journal of Consulting and Clinical Psychology, 59,* 333–340.

Brown, G. (1990). *Human teaching for human learning: An introduction to confluent education.* New York: Gestalt Journal Press. (Original work published 1971)

Buber, M. (1965a). *Between man and man.* New York: Macmillan.

Buber, M. (1965b). *The knowledge of man.* New York: Harper & Row.

Carlock, C., Glaus, K., & Shaw, C. (1992). The alcoholic: A Gestalt view. In E. Nevis (Ed.), *Gestalt therapy: Perspectives and applications* (pp. 191–238). New York: Gardner Press.

Clarkson, P., & Mackewn, J. (1993). *Fritz Perls.* London: Sage.

Delisle, G. (in press). *Personality disorders: A Gestalt perspective.* New York: Gestalt Journal Press.

Dublin, J. (1973). Gestalting psychotic persons. *Psychotherapy: Theory, Research, and Practice, 10,* 149–152.

Dublin, J. (1992). The power of the Gestalt dialog in dreamwork: Integration of a "multiple personality." In E. W. L. Smith (Ed.), *Gestalt voices* (pp. 164–169). Norwood, NJ: Ablex. (Original work published 1978)

Friedman, M. (1964). Dialogue between Martin Buber and Carl Rogers. In M. Friedman (Ed.), *The worlds of existentialism: A critical reader* (pp. 485–497). New York: Random House.

Garssen, B., de Ruiter, C., & van Dyck, R. (1992). Breathing retraining: A rational placebo? *Clinical Psychology Review, 12,* 141–153.

Golden, W., & Dryden, W. (1987). Cognitive-behavioral therapies: Commonalities, divergences and future developments. In W. Dryden & W. Golden (Eds.), *Cognitive behavioral approaches to psychotherapy* (pp. 356–378). New York: Harper & Row.

Goldfried, M., Greenberg, L., & Marmar, C. (1990). Individual psychotherapy: Process and outcome. *Annual Review of Psychology, 41,* 659–688.

Goodman, P. (1960). *Growing up absurd.* New York: Gestalt Journal Press.

Goodman, P. (1991). *Nature heals: The psychological essays of Paul Goodman* (Taylor Stoehr, Ed.). New York: Gestalt Journal Press. (Original work published 1977)

Grawe, K., Caspar, F., & Ambül, H. (1990). Differentielle psychotherapieforschung: Vier therapieformen im vergleich. *Zeitschrift für Klinische Psychologie, 19,* 287–376.

Greenberg, L. S. (1979). Resolving splits: The two-chair technique. *Psychotherapy: Theory, Research and Practice, 16,* 310–318.

Greenberg, L. S. (1980). The intensive analysis of recurring events from the practice of Gestalt therapy. *Psychotherapy: Theory, Research and Practice, 17,* 143–152.

Greenberg, L. S. (1982). Toward a task analysis of conflict resolution in Gestalt therapy. *Psychotherapy: Theory, Research and Practice, 20,* 190–201.

Greenberg, L. S. (1986). Change process research. *Journal of Consulting and Clinical Psychology, 54,* 4–9.

Greenberg, L. S. (1991). Research in the process of change. *Psychotherapy Research, 1,* 14–24.

Greenberg, L. S., & Clarke, K. (1979). Differential effects of the two-chair experiment and empathic reflections at a conflict maker. *Journal of Counseling Psychology, 26,* 1–9.

Greenberg, L. S., & Dompierre, L. (1981). Specific effects of Gestalt two-chair dialogue on trapsychic conflict in counseling. *Journal of Counseling Psychology, 28,* 288–295.

Greenberg, L. S., Elliott, R., & Lietaer, G. (1994). Research on experiential psychotherapies. In A. Bergin & S. Garfield (Eds.), *Handbook of psychotherapy and behavior change* (pp. 509–539). New York: Wiley.

Greenberg, L. S., & Higgins, H. (1980). The differential effects of two-chair dialogue and focusing on conflict resolution. *Journal of Counseling Psychology, 27,* 221–225.

Greenberg, L. S., & Rice. L. N. (1981). The specific effects of Gestalt therapy intervention. *Psychotherapy: Theory, Research and Practice, 18,* 31–38.

Greenberg, L. S., & Webster, M. (1982). Resolving decisional conflict by Gestalt two-chair dialogue: Relating process to outcome. *Journal of Counseling Psychology, 29,* 468–477.

Harman, R. (1984). Gestalt therapy research. *The Gestalt Journal, 7*(2), 61–69.

Harman, R. (1989). *Gestalt therapy with groups, couples, sexually dysfunctional men, and dreams.* Springfield, IL: Charles C. Thomas.

Harris, C. (1992). Gestalt work with psychotics. In E. Nevis (Ed.), *Gestalt therapy: Perspectives and applications* (pp. 239–262). New York: Gardner Press.

Heidbreder, E. (1933). *Seven psychologies.* New York: Century.

Hycner, R. (1985). Dialogical Gestalt therapy: An initial proposal. *Gestalt Journal, 8*(1), 23–49.

Hycner, R. (1991). *Between person and person: Toward a dialogical psychotherapy.* New York: Gestalt Journal Press.

Hycner, R., & Jacobs, L. (1995). *The healing relationship in Gestalt therapy: A dialogic self psychology.* New York: Gestalt Journal Press.

Ihde, I. (1977). *Experimental phenomenology: An introduction.* Albany: State University of New York Press.

Jacobs, L. (1989). Dialogue in Gestalt theory and therapy. *The Gestalt Journal, 12*(6), 25–67.

Jacobs, L. (1992). Insights from psychoanalytic self-psychology and intersubjectivity theory for gestalt therapists. *The Gestalt Journal, 15*(2), 25–60.

Kepner, J. (1987). *Body process: A Gestalt approach to working with the body in psychotherapy.* New York: Gestalt Institute of Cleveland Press.

Lafferty, P., Beutler, L., & Crago, M. (1989). Differences between more and less effective psychotherapists: A study of select therapist variables. *Journal of Consuling Clinical Psychology, 57,* 76–80.

Lederman, J. (1969). *Anger and the rocking chair.* New York: McGraw-Hill.

Lederman, J. (1970). Anger and the rocking chair. In J. Fagan & I. Shepherd (Eds.), *Gestalt therapy now* (pp. 285–294). Palo Alto, CA: Science & Behavior Books.

Lewin, K. (1938). The conflict between Aristotelian and Galilean modes of thought in contemporary psychology. In *A dynamic theory of personality* (pp. 1–42). London: Routledge & Kegan Paul.

Lieberman, M., Yalom, I., & Miles, M. (1973). *Encounter groups: First facts.* New York: Basic Books.

Logan, A., & Goetsch, V. (1993). Attention to external threat cues in anxiety states. *Clinical Psychology Review, 13,* 501–540.

Luborksy, L., Crits-Christoph, P., McLellan, A., Woody, G., Piper, W., et al. (1986). Do therapists vary much in their success? *American Journal of Orthopsychiatry, 56,* 501–512.

Meyer, A. E. (Ed.). (1981). The Hamburg Short Psychotherapy Comparison Experiment. *Psychotherapy and Psychosomatics, 35,* 81–207.

Norcross, J., & Rossi, J. (1994). Looking weakly in all the wrong places? *Journal of Consulting and Clinical Psychology, 62*(3), 535–538.

Oaklander, V. (1988). *Windows to our children: A Gestalt therapy approach to children and adolescents.* New York: Gestalt Journal Press. (Original work published 1969)

Paige, P. (1992). A gestalt awareness process for working with problem drinkers who do not want to stop drinking. In E. W. L. Smith (Ed.), *Gestalt voices* (pp. 170–177). Norwood, NJ: Ablex. (Original work published 1975)

Paivio, S., & Greenberg, L. (1992). *Resolving unfinished business: A study of effects.* Paper presented at the annual meeting of the Society for Psychotherapy Research, Berkeley, CA.

Perls, F. (1970). Four lectures. In J. Fagan & I. Shepherd (Eds.), *Gestalt therapy now* (pp. 14–38). Palo Alto, CA: Science & Behavior Books.

Perls, F. (1976). *The Gestalt approach and eye witness to therapy.* New York: Bantam. (Original work published 1973)

Perls, F. (1978). Finding self through Gestalt therapy, *The Gestalt Journal, 1*(1), 54–73.

Perls, F. (1992). *Ego, hunger and aggression.* New York: Gestalt Journal Press. (Original work published 1942)

Perls, F. (1992). *Gestalt therapy verbatim.* New York: Gestalt Journal Press. (Original work published 1969)

Perls, F., Hefferline, R., & Goodman, P. (1951). *Gestalt therapy: Excitement and growth in the human personality.* New York: Julian Press. [Also (1965). New York: Dell (Delta Book).]

Perls, L. (1992). A workshop with Laura Perls. In E. W. L. Smith (Ed.), *Gestalt voices.* Norwood, NJ: Ablex. (Original work published 1982)

Perls, L. (1992). *Living at the boundary.* New York: Gestalt Therapy Press.

Polster, E. (1987). *Every person's life is worth a novel.* New York: Norton.

Polster, E., & Polster, M. (1973). *Gestalt therapy integrated.* New York: Brunner/Mazel.

Rice, L. N., & Greenberg, L. S. (Eds.), (1984). *Patterns of change: Intensive analysis of psychotherapy process.* New York: Guilford Press.

Shepherd, I. (1970). Limitations and cautions in the Gestalt approach. In J. Fagan & I. Shepherd (Eds.), *Gestalt therapy now* (pp. 234–238). Palo Alto, CA: Science & Behavior Books.

Simkin, J., & Yontef, G. (1984). Gestalt therapy. In R. Corsini (Ed.), *Current psychotherapies* (3rd ed., pp. 279–319). Ithasca, IL: Peacock. [Reprinted in Yontef (1993)]

Spinelli, E. (1989). *The interpreted world.* Newbury Park, CA: Sage.

Tellgen, F., Frassa, M., & Höniger, S. (1979). Characteristics of therapists and client behavior in Gestalt therapy sessions. *Zeitschrift für Klinische Psychologie Forschung und Praxis, 8,* 148–155.

Tscheulin, D. (1990). Confrontation and non-confrontation as differential techniques in differential client-centered therapy. In G. Lietaer, J. Rombauts, & R. Van Balen (Eds.), *Client-centered and experiential psychotherapy in the nineties* (pp. 327–336). Leuven, Belgium: Leuven University Press.

Weishaar, M., & Beck, A. (1987). Cognitive therapy. In W. Dryden & W. Golden (Eds.), *Cognitive behavioural approaches to psychotherapy.* New York: Harper & Row.

Wertheimer, M. (1945). *Productive thinking.* New York: Harper & Bros.

Yontef, G. (1976). Gestalt therapy: Clinical phenomenology. In V. Binder, A. Binder, & B. Rimland (Eds.), *Modern therapies* (pp. 65–79). New York: Prentice Hall. [Reprinted in Yontef (1993)]

Yontef, G. (1987). Gestalt therapy 1986: A polemic. *The Gestalt Journal, 10*(1), 41–68. [Reprinted in Yontef (1993)]

Yontef, G. (1988). Assimilating diagnostic and psychoanalytic perspectives into Gestalt therapy. *The Gestalt Journal, 11*(1), 5–32. [Reprinted in Yontef (1993)]

Yontef, G. (1991). Recent trends in Gestalt therapy in the U.S. and what we need to learn from them. *British Gestalt Journal, 1*(1), 5–20. [Reprinted in Yontef (1993)]

Yontef, G. (1993). *Awareness, dialogue and process: Essays on Gestalt therapy.* New York: Gestalt Journal Press.

Zinker, J. (1977). *Creative process in Gestalt therapy.* New York: Brunner/Mazel.

9

Transactional Analysis

MURIEL JAMES

BACKGROUND OF THE APPROACH

Transactional Analysis began when psychiatrist Eric Berne noticed that his patients were not getting well as fast as he hoped they would. Practicing in Carmel, California, he often treated people on an individual basis as an analyst, 1 hour a day, 5 days a week, for 3 years. Obviously, many people were unable, or unwilling, to invest that amount of time and money in treatment. This led him to search for a new theory and method that would be more effective than traditional psychoanalysis.

Eric Berne, born Eric Lennard Bernstein in Montreal in 1910, was the son of David Hillel Bernstein, a physician, and Sarah Gordon Bernstein, a professional writer and editor. Eric's father, a general practitioner, often took Eric on his medical rounds but died suddenly when Eric was 9 years old. After that, his mother supported the family by her writing.

When Eric was 11, he too began to write and continued to do so until his death. His witty, brilliant style was sometimes a bit difficult to decipher.

Like a child who has been traumatized by a parent's sudden death, that part of Eric's personality seems to have been fixated at age 9, and the result of this was sometimes evident in his writing, as if he were trying to impress his father or entertain his mother.

After receiving his M.D. in 1935 from McGill University, Eric changed his name by dropping the Lennard and shortening Bernstein to Berne, came to the United States, and became an American citizen. He did his psychiatric residency at Yale University, became a clinical assistant at Mt. Sinai Hospital in New York City, and entered the Army Medical Corps as a psychiatrist in 1941. His task at an army induction center was to assess, in 2 minutes, whether an inductee had the psychological ability to be a soldier. Because of the brief time he was allotted with each interview, Berne began to depend greatly on his intuitive ability.

The development of his early ideas in Transactional Analysis can be observed in his articles on intuition written between 1949 and 1962 (Berne, 1977). Using references to Paul Federn, Eugene

Khan, and H. Silberer, in his first article, Berne indicated how he arrived at the concept of ego states and where he got the idea of separating "adult" from "child." The greatest influence was Federn (1952). Thoroughly grounded in psychoanalysis (one of his analysts was Eric Erikson), Berne (1961) disagreed with some basic psychoanalytic tenets. For example, he differentiated between the Id and the phenomenon of the Child ego state, "The Child means an organized state of mind which exists or once actually existed, while Freud describes the Id as 'a chaos, a cauldron of seething excitement . . . it has no organization and no unified will" (p. 61). In addition, like Harry Stack Sullivan and Karen Horney, Berne (1961) also emphasized the interpersonal component of personality and behavior.

In his second article, Berne developed the tripartite schema for the personality used today, namely, *Parent, Adult,* and *Child* ego states. (When capital letters are used for these three parts of the personality, they refer to ego states; when not used, they refer to actual people.) He also introduced the three-circle method of diagramming ego states and named this part of his system, structural analysis. This, he said, was "a new psychotherapeutic approach." And, indeed, it was.

He sometimes used the words "exteropsyche" for the Parent ego state and "neopsyche" for the Adult and "archaeopsyche" for the Child, but he preferred the more colloquial terms because a client's Child could understand them easily, thus leaving the client's Adult more freedom and energy to think about the concepts without being confused or feeling stupid for not understanding "big" words. Berne (1966) frequently advised other clinicians to write and speak as though to an 8-year-old child, not paternally but clearly, simply, and directly. In fact, his first book, *The Mind in Action,*

published in 1947, when revised and enlarged, was given a new title, *A Layman's Guide to Psychiatry and Psychoanalysis* (Berne, 1968).

His third article, presented at the Western Regional Meeting of the American Group Psychotherapy Association in 1957 by invitation, was titled "Transactional Analysis: A New and Effective Method of Group Therapy." With the subsequent publication of this paper in the *American Journal of Psychotherapy*, in October 1958, Transactional Analysis, a new theory of diagnosis and treatment, became a permanent part of the psychotherapeutic literature. It is often considered to be one form of humanistic psychology because those who use it believe that individuals are responsible for their actions and interactions and can change many of their attitudes and behaviors through insight and decision.

THE FIRST CASE

The case of Mr. Segundo was an early stimulus to Eric Berne in developing his personality theory of structural analysis on which his entire therapeutic system is based. Berne (1961) tells the following story:

> An eight year old boy, vacationing at a ranch in his cowboy suit, helped the hired man unsaddle a horse. When they were finished, the hired man said: "Thanks, cowpoke!", to which his assistant answered: "I'm not really a cowpoke, I'm just a little boy."
>
> The patient then remarked: "That's just the way I feel. I'm not really a lawyer, I'm just a little boy." Mr. Segundo was a successful courtroom lawyer of high repute, who raised his family decently, did useful community work, and was popular socially. But, in treatment, he often did have an attitude of a little boy. Sometimes during the hour he would ask: "Are you

talking to the lawyer or to the little boy?" When he was away from his office or the courtroom, the little boy was very apt to take over. He would retire to a cabin in the mountains away from his family, where he kept a supply of whiskey, morphine, lewd pictures, and guns. There he would indulge in childlike fantasies, fantasies he had as a little boy, and the kinds of sexual activity which are commonly labeled "infantile."

At a later date, after he had clarified to some extent what in him was Adult and what was Child (for he really was a lawyer sometimes and not always a little boy), Mr. Segundo introduced his Parent into the situation. That is, after his activities and feelings had been sorted out into the first two categories, there were certain residual states which fitted neither. These had a special quality which was reminiscent of the way his parents had seemed to him. This necessitated the institution of a third category which, on further testing, was found to have sound clinical validity. These ego states lacked the autonomous quality of both Adult and Child. They seemed to have been introduced from without, and to have an imitative flavor.

Specifically, there were three different aspects apparent in his handling of money. The Child was penurious to the penny and had miserly ways of ensuring penny-wise prosperity; in spite of the risk for a man in his position, in this state he would gleefully steal chewing gum and other small items out of drugstores, just as he had done as a child. The Adult handled large sums with a banker's shrewdness, foresight, and success, and was willing to spend money to make money. But another side of him had fantasies of giving it all away for the good of the community. He came of pious philanthropic people, and he actually did donate large sums to charity with the same sentimental benevolence as his father. As the philanthropic glow wore off, the Child would take over with vindictive resentfulness toward his beneficiaries, followed by the Adult who would wonder why on earth he wanted to risk his solvency for such sentimental reasons. (pp. 33–34)

These three parts of Mr. Segundo's personality were subsequently labeled the Parent, Adult, and Child ego states, and the theory of ego states became the rock-bottom foundation of Transactional Analysis. Ego state theory assumes that whatever happens to people is recorded in their brain and nervous tissue. This includes everything they experience in their childhood, all they incorporate from their parent figures, their perceptions of events, feelings associated with these events, and distortions they bring to their memories. These experiences are like tape recordings that can be replayed and, when they are, can be recalled and reexperienced. However, memories are often distorted or embellished. They are like tapes that have been altered, and sometimes altered several times, as perceptions change.

It was the findings of the neurosurgeon Wilder Penfield that stimulated Berne to use the tape recorder as a metaphor. Penfield (1952a) found that an electrode applied to different parts of a person's brain evoked memories and feelings long forgotten by that person. Berne (1966) responded, "In this respect the brain functions like a tape recorder to preserve complete experiences in serial sequence, in a form recognizable as "ego states" indicating that 'ego states' comprise the natural way of experiencing and of recording experiences in their totality. Simultaneously, of course, experiences are recorded in fragmented forms" (p. 281).

Throughout his career, Berne was open to modifying his early discoveries. University students, as well as experienced professionals, were welcomed at his seminars. I joined the weekly San Francisco seminar group in 1958 and continued with it until his death in 1970. For about 2 years, he was my supervisor, and a very demanding one indeed. Each week, I was required to take a tape of working with an individual client or leading a group therapy session. I was expected to know exactly what was on the tape and be able to identify the moment that either a client or I would switch ego states or get hooked into a "script" or "game." I was also expected to be able to identify the transactions that occurred and reasons behind such transactions, the script themes and other script elements, and the psychological games that were played. To do this sometimes required listening to my tape several times before the supervision hour. I did not always like what I heard, yet what I got from this supervision has been of enormous value.

In this chapter, I stress primary sources, the writings of Eric Berne, and encourage wider reading because the theory and applications of Transactional Analysis continue to expand. Currently, in over 80 countries there are psychotherapists who are certified, or seeking certification, at an advanced level of Transactional Analysis expertise. Such work is coordinated by the International Transactional Analysis Association through its offices in San Francisco.

Transactional Analysis is firmly based on a concept of personality manifested through ego states and experienced both structurally and functionally. Structure refers to *parts* of the personality; function refers to *how* a person uses the parts to function. The concept of ego states is the foundation of Transactional Analysis. Ego states are defined as "consistent patterns of feeling and experience which are directly related to corresponding consistent patterns of behavior" (Berne, 1966, p. 364).

THE CONCEPT OF PERSONALITY

Berne (1966), with his preference for simple words, writes that Parent ego states are "borrowed from parental fig-ures and reproduce the feelings, behavior, and responses of these figures" (p. 220). People's parent figures are not necessarily their natural parents. A person reared by grandparents, older siblings, adopted parents, and so forth, will have these people in his/her Parent ego state. Outwardly, the Parent is often expressed toward others in prejudicial, critical and nurturing behavior. Inwardly, it is experienced as old parental messages which continue to influence the inner Child.

The Adult ego state is not related to a person's age. It is oriented to current reality and the objective gathering of information. It is capable of organizing, testing reality, and estimating probabilities. The Adult is not merely a computer; the Adult is also concerned with social issues and has feelings about involvement in them. Consequently, an autonomous integrated person, client or therapist, will, according to Berne (1969), "crusade against The Four Horsemen—War, Pestilence, Famine, and Death" (pp. 7–8). This integration has been stressed in *Born to Win* by James and Jongeward (1971).

The Child ego state contains the genetic inheritance and all the natural feelings, needs, impulses, and loving potentialities of infants. It also contains creative, manipulative, and intuitive capacities as well as the adapted feelings and behavior learned during childhood, such as compliance, withdrawal, rebellion, and procrastination. (See Figure 9.1.)

As first noted in the case of Mr. Segundo, there are four basic ways to diagnose the Parent, Adult, and Child ego states: behaviorally, socially, historically, and phenomenologically. M. James (1986) expands Berne's concept to show how diagnosis, using this model, is effective in developing treatment plans.

Behavioral diagnosis involves recognition of how ego states *function* including posture, voice, facial expressions, gestures, words, and actions (Dusay, 1977).

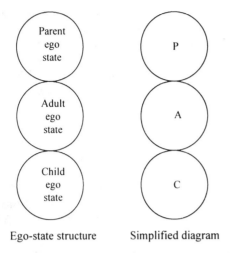

Ego-state structure   Simplified diagram

FIGURE 9.1. Personality structure in Transactional Analysis.

Often behavior that comes from the Parent ego state may be expressed with critical words, voice, and gestures or brutality. It may be more nurturing behavior, affectionate and protective, smiling indulgently, or giving unsolicited but well-meaning advice. Or, it may be withdrawal behavior, which others interpret as dislike or disinterest. When people are in their Parent ego state, they often act out the preferences of their parent figures for or against people of a different race, religion, educational background, and so forth.

Behavior that is likely to reflect the Adult ego state is straightforward and focused on reality, as when working efficiently, asking direct questions, and looking up information.

Behavior that may emerge from the Child ego state is like typical behavior of a young child: withdrawing, complying, and rebelling, as when pouting, having temper tantrums, withdrawing, or laughing. Children have natural desires to explore, create, and develop some measure of autonomy. When these qualities are observable, the behavior may be coming from the Child ego state or from an integrated Adult who allows the Child

a measure of freedom. Childlike behavior can even come from the Parent ego state. The incorporation of parent figures often includes incorporating parts of their Child behavior.

Few transactional analysts limit themselves to *behavioral* data. According to Berne (1961), what appears to be Parent may, on further investigation, be coming from a different ego state. He comments that a therapist, *playing a supportive Parent role*, may really be in the Child ego state, "very much like a little boy playing doctor" (pp. 233–234). To lessen this possibility, I find it useful to ask clients for three or four adjectives to describe each of the parent figures they had in childhood and work with these specific adjectives instead of using only the words "critical" and "nurturing." For example, people who have incorporated indifferent parents may, when their energy is in their Parent ego state, be indifferent to the needs of others. The words "critical" and "nurturing" do not apply to that part of their personalities.

Historical diagnosis involves discovering how past events have contributed to a client's unique personality and patterns of interpersonal relations. For example, a man who comes to treatment resentful of his children's bids for his attention, may discover that he has incorporated parts of his father into his personality and is acting exactly as his father once did by being too busy for his family. Or, the same man could be responding from his Child ego state if his parents claimed too much of his attention so that he had no time left for himself. As a consequence, he may avoid family ties with his own children. Recalling these facts, and discovering which ego state is actually involved, is the aim of historical analysis.

Social diagnosis does not focus on what the person does or did, but on the current responses elicited from others. People who attract others who continually ask them for help or advice are likely to be using the Parent ego state more than they realize. People who feel competent themselves, who seek others who are also competent, and who exchange information on the basis of mutual respect, are likely to be in the Adult ego state most often. Those who continually seek others to be the voices of authority or act as caretakers, and thus avoid taking responsibility for their own lives, are likely to be in the Child ego state more than they know.

Phenomenological diagnosis occurs when clients reexperience childhood traumas and feelings in therapy, or when they report doing so outside therapy. For example, a client sexually abused in childhood may feel panic if touched in any way by a therapist or even if the therapist moves his/her chair "too close for comfort." Someone constantly criticized in childhood may reexperience rage in later life when this occurs. Conversely, pleasant experiences from the past can also be relived. Developing new pleasant experiences that can be remembered when times get tough help fill the vacuum left when negative memories are worked through.

In Transactional Analysis, clients discover that feelings can come from any ego state. Those that are copied from significant others, usually as parental attitudes of beliefs, are likely to be in the Parent ego state. Feelings that were originally experienced in infancy and childhood, and reappear in later life, are likely to be in the Child ego state. Feelings that are a genuine response to an actual situation happening now are likely to have some Adult involvement. Either the Adult informs the Child of the situation so that the response is authentic or certain feelings have been integrated into the Adult. Genuine respect of others which is based on objective observations is also Adult. Temper tantrums and crying jags are more likely to be *rackets* of the Child.

Rackets have also been defined as substitutes for other feelings (Zalcman, 1990). Berne (1966) defines rackets as "self-indulgence in feelings of guilt, inadequacy, hurt, fear, and resentment" (p. 308). In contrast, trust and admiration are authentic feelings of a Child who believes in the basic goodness of people.

A Wholistic Approach

Opinions about what should be included in psychotherapy vary greatly. Generally speaking, physicians have been expected to deal with the body, psychologists with the mind, and the clergy with the spirit or "soul." Historically, these "specialists" have often been critical of each other. Some, especially in the Western world, have considered the concept of the spiritual part of a person to be archaic and "not scientific." The concept of the human spirit has usually been ignored in most psychological and medical training programs. This is changing. The interacting effects of mind and body are now more accepted. There is an increasing openness to the possibility of comprehensive, holistic approaches, which includes recognizing the power of the human spirit as well. In the past this has remained outside of the realm of many psychotherapists, due no doubt to the fact that many equate spirit or spirituality with religion. Freud was strongly against religion, epecially Jewish religion (Jones, 1953). Religion, to Freud (1927), was rooted in the Oedipus complex and although deeply interested in the origin of religion, he believed it to be based on illusion (Freud, 1927). As far as I know, he did not deal with the nonreligious spiritual dimension but was mostly opposed to ritual and dogma.

There have been, however, some notable exceptions that can be found in the writings of several other parent figures of modern psychology. Jung (1963) wrote,

"Like every other being, I am a splinter of the infinite deity" (p. 4). Adler (1954) believed that the soul is a psychic organ and that a person is a unity struggling for wholeness (p. 29). Wholeness, according to Frankl (1975), comes when the somatic, psychic, and spiritual are integrated (p. 28). And, according to Allport (1950), "A mature personality always has some unifying philosophy of life, although not necessarily religious in type, nor articulated in words, nor entirely complete" (p. 60).

Each of these theorists believed in a spiritual dimension of life, yet none of them developed a comprehensive theory about the human spirit, what it is, and how it interacts with mind and body. My colleague, John James, and I have attempted to do this. Based on 20 years of intensive research in many cultures, we have developed a theory and process that can be used in conjunction with Transactional Analysis or alone for both diagnosis and treatment (M. James, 1973a, 1981b; M. James & Savary, 1977; M. James & J. James, 1991). Central to the theory is the concept that everyone has a human spirit which is the inner core of the self. This inner-core self is different from the psychological or physiological selves yet interacts with both. Whereas most psychological theories are based on models that focus on people's blocks, impasses, and pathologies, this new paradigm of the human spirit demonstrates that all people of all times and places have seven basic inner urges which do not fit traditional biological or psychological categories. They are motivating forces that sometimes moves a person beyond the everyday confines of this world into transcendent moments when wholeness is experienced.

When this theory is integrated with Transactional Analysis, the ego states are shown with a core drawn down the center, much like an apple core in an apple (see Figure 9.2). The boundaries of the core can be closed or open. When open, the energies from the human spirit become passions for life and are used to increase the health of mind and body.

Within the inner core of self are seven universal *urges of the human spirit*. Any of them can flow freely or be restricted. Each one is directed toward a specific goal. To reach the goal, a specific strength is needed. Like the urges, these strengths are universal and, if blocked, can be released. First is the *urge to live* which is not only concerned with survival and comfort but also the search for meaning. To reach this goal, hope is required. The *urge for freedom*, whether physical, emotional, or intellectual freedom, is directed toward the goal of self-determination. To reach that goal often requires courage to break free of painful psychological impasses, inappropriate social expectations, and unreasonable cultural scripts. The *urge to enjoy*, with the goal of happiness, requires enthusiasm and involvement and sometimes looking through rose-colored glasses when the day seems gray. The *urge to understand* leads to the search for knowledge and what is needed to reach the goal is the recovery of basic curiosity. The *urge to create* motivates people to be innovative and, for this, imagination is needed. The *urge for authentic connections* is

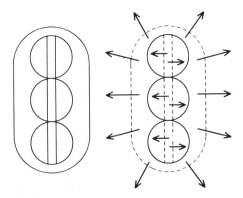

FIGURE 9.2. The inner core of the self.

directed toward giving and receiving love which is achieved when genuine caring, often altruistic caring, is released. Finally, there is the *urge to transcend* the routine boundaries of everyday life and find unity in a greater dimension of life. Being open to what is and what might be allows this to happen. The whole person evolves in new ways—the despairing ones become happy, the unknowing ones become well informed, the lonely souls find love. They reach out to life.

Development and Autonomy

A major Transactional Analysis concept is that people can be autonomous. Yet autonomy is a rare possession. According to Berne, most people have the illusion that they are autonomously making their own decisions when actually they are more like persons sitting down to a player piano, playing notes that have been previously programmed. They are not autonomous; they are "scripted" to feel, think, and act in certain ways. People do not have to be enslaved by their past. They can decide who to be and who not to be, what to do and what not to do, how to feel and how not to feel. With the use of Transactional Analysis, they can "work through" and transcend past influences, plan creatively for the future, and learn to respond in freedom to the here and now of daily existence.

To become autonomous, most people need to rethink the decisions they made in early childhood about themselves and about other people, about being OK or not OK. Many of these decisions are the result of parental programming. Yet, claims Berne (1970), "Parental programming is not the 'fault' of parents—since they are only passing on the programming they got from their parents—any more than the physical appearance of their offspring is their 'fault,' since they

are only passing on the genes they got from their ancestors" (p. 198). Parental programming is a fact of life and is both negative and positive. Forgiving one's parents for being who they were is sometimes a final step in a client's treatment program.

It is increasingly evident, in both popular and professional literature, that in the United States such a strong emphasis is placed on independence and autonomy that some people equate it with breaking away from families and blaming their parents for whatever goes wrong. Encouraging such separation may be necessary in some cases and it can be a gross error in others. Many cultures in the world believe in maintaining close family ties even if the family is far from perfect. To discount this value may be counter-therapeutic and increase personal alienation instead of potential harmony.

Many children receive positive messages from their parents. The messages are given verbally and nonverbally—messages to think, to feel, to be healthy, to succeed, to enjoy people, and to respect the environment. These children, when grown, are likely to be more autonomous than others. They are not likely to seek therapy except for an unexpected crisis such as a serious accident or illness.

Other children pick up negative messages, given verbally or nonverbally, from their parent figures. These messages are often prohibitive injunctions. According to Goulding and Goulding (1979), common injunctions are, "Don't be," "Don't be you," "Don't be a child," "Don't be grownup," "Don't be close," "Don't make it," "Don't be sane," "Don't be important," and "Don't belong."

In response to these kinds of parental injunctions, symptoms develop as children make decisions such as "I won't grow up," "I won't be close," and "I can't make it." These decisions can become part of negative or banal scripts that tend to be acted out in later life through patterns of rebelling, withdrawing, and procrastinating.

Effecting changes at both cognitive and emotional levels is an important focus of therapy and is accomplished in many ways. People can and do change; they can become integrated instead of being fragmented or with disowned or dissociated parts. People who are integrated have their Adult ego states as the executive of their personalities and are able to process data rationally. They also exhibit certain childlike characteristics, parental affection, and caring, as well as ethical concerns. Seemingly, these qualities are filtered from the Parent and Child into the Adult ego state. With an integrated Adult, people take responsibility. They also have the natural Child capacity for pleasure. Berne (1961) described the integrated Adult as one who has responsible feelings toward the rest of humanity. This "integrated" person is charming, courageous, and so forth, in the Adult state, whatever qualities he/she has or does not have in the Child and Parent ego states. In contrast, the "unintegrated" person may *revert* to being charming, and may feel that he/she *should* be courageous.

PERSPECTIVE ON MENTAL HEALTH

The definition of mental health is ambiguous. It differs from one culture to another and from one subculture to another. Therefore, this section will not deal with standardized clinical diagnoses which most therapists are able to use, and are sometimes required to use, for insurance purposes or hospitalization or communicating with other professionals. Instead, it will describe specific ways of diagnosing clients by using a Transactional Analysis model.

Necessary as clinical diagnosis is, Berne claimed that a label applied to an illness could become almost as damaging as the illness itself. In Transactional Analysis, words such as "pathology" and "dysfunctional" are avoided if possible. "Disorder" is more acceptable as it implies that basic mental health can occur when certain parts of a person's personality and life are put in order.

Transactional analysts usually diagnose personal and interpersonal problems or difficulties in terms of (1) ego state boundary problems, to be discussed in this section; (2) destructive or banal life scripts; (3) faulty patterns of transacting with others; and (4) psychological games that are played—internally or externally. This section will focus on identifying ego state boundary problems that create personality problems and interfere with mental health. The other categories will be dealt with later in the chapter.

Diagnosing Personality Problems

Ego states can be thought of as having boundaries that are like permeable membranes through which a person's psychic energy can flow (Berne, 1961). Occasionally, personality problems, as well as physical problems, are genetic. More often, they are due to something wrong with ego state boundaries. Like a car out of alignment, the boundaries need straightening out. The mentally healthy person is able to switch from one ego state to another, spontaneously and by cognitive choice, in response to current situations. This person can solve problems or redefine them so that they are manageable; is interested in and able to care for others in appropriate ways; and is autonomous, aware, and capable of intimacy. Effective treatment is not likely to occur, or it may be delayed unduly, unless ego state boundary problems are diagnosed and corrected. Basic to Transactional Analysis is an understanding of four ego state boundary problems: rigidity, contamination, laxness, and lesions. These need to be corrected.

Rigid Ego State Boundaries

At any time, one ego state can be cathected and have executive power over the others. In some people, however, the boundaries are so rigid that the energy is locked in and unable to flow easily from one ego state to another (M. James & Jongeward, 1971, p. 228). This problem is due to rigid ego state boundaries and is often called *exclusion* because some parts of the personality are unconsciously repressed or consciously suppressed (see Figure 9.3).

Some people, instead of staying primarily in one ego state and excluding two others, favor the use of two and exclude only one. In a couple relationship, for example, one person may be quite rigid and exclude his/her own inner Child or not be willing to show it. Whereas the other person may be primarily in his/her Child ego state, feeling angry or sad, and exclude his/her thinking Adult capacities. A person who tries to exclude the Child is often one who cannot tolerate not being the authority or feels the need to defend against the pain of recalling childhood experiences, yet the inner Child may not like to be excluded and may try to break open a door into awareness.

Contamination of the Adult

The most common problem of ego state boundaries is contamination of the Adult. It occurs when the clear thinking of the Adult is interfered with by childhood experiences and decisions or by parental injunctions, or both.

All people have some contamination. Much is due to family or cultural prejudices in the Parent ego state that seep through the ego state boundary into the Adult so that the person is judgmental without sufficient cause. Prejudices about gender roles are common Parental contaminations.

Contaminations from the Child ego state into the Adult are also common and due to childhood training and experiences. Children who are ridiculed due to race, ethnicity, religion, gender, or appearance may retain some anxiety which

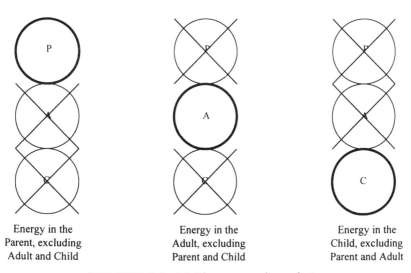

| Energy in the Parent, excluding Adult and Child | Energy in the Adult, excluding Parent and Child | Energy in the Child, excluding Parent and Adult |

FIGURE 9.3. Rigid ego state boundaries.

can seep up through the Adult ego state boundary. In such cases, a person may avoid others to avoid potential ridicule or may become unduly aggressive. Contamination is diagrammed in Figure 9.4.

Currently, expected gender roles are undergoing radical changes. Instead of compliance, there is often rebellion against what is expected. This leads many couples to therapy. In addition, in both work and in academic situations, perceptions of gender roles are also changing. Decontamination is a lifelong task that needs to be recognized and worked through, by therapists as well as by clients.

Lax Inner Boundaries

Clients who have lax ego state boundaries appear to lack identity and are very confused in their thinking and their behavior. When speaking, they may be almost impossible to understand. As their ego state boundaries are not firm enough, the psychic energy is not directed. It is somewhat like an overcooked stew that has turned into soup. The result of lax boundaries is easily observable in back wards of some state hospitals where patients who have little or

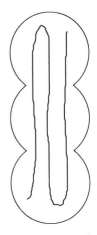

FIGURE 9.5. Lax ego state boundaries. Energy is labile, person is confused and unstable.

no Adult control are heavily medicated. However, anyone may have this problem in times of crisis, may feel like "falling apart," and may need a vacation to alleviate stress. This person may or may not need intensive psychotherapy. Lax ego state boundaries are diagrammed in Figure 9.5.

Lesions in the Child or Parent

Boundary lesions are another serious problem. However, the symptoms may

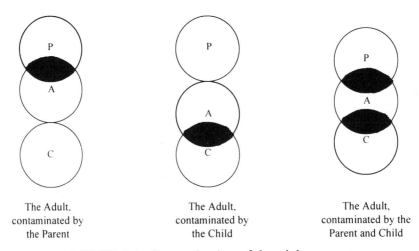

The Adult, contaminated by the Parent

The Adult, contaminated by the Child

The Adult, contaminated by the Parent and Child

FIGURE 9.4. Contamination of the adult ego states.

not be observable until something nega-tive happens. Then lesions are mani-fested by a gross overreaction to the real-ity of the stimulus. Irrational explosions into rage or grief are often due to earlier injuries which have not healed. A shout, "I can't take it anymore," often accom-panies the explosive behavior. Occasion-ally, lesions are displayed as coming from the Parent ego state. When clients' psychic energy is in the Parent they may explode as their parents once did; this is especially true in child brutality. Most often, lesions are in the Child and can be diagrammed with a dotted line on one part of the circle to represent a particular vulnerable spot in the Child which, if touched, results in uncontrollable, irra-tional behavior, that is not uncommon, even among so called "successful" people who have suffered severe emotional trauma and tried to block it off (see Fig-ure 9.6). Then, if something rubs their sore spot, the old injury breaks open and can lead to a psychotic break, a homicide, or a suicide. The eruption of a lesion oc-curs when feelings have been denied or repressed for so long that they erupt like a volcano. This is different from people who erupt out of a self-indulgent habit; which is not a lesion but a game that may be part of a script.

Causes of Ego State Boundary Problems

Causes of any of these ego state bound-ary problems are multiple. The cause can be a genetic component, childhood con-ditioning by others, or a situational cri-sis. Furthermore, a person may have more than one boundary problem. For example, someone who senses a danger-ous lesion in his/her Child may develop a rigid personality in an attempt to con-trol the lesion being activated.

People who are not symptomatic often come from emotionally healthy environ-ments in childhood, where, although they may not have received "perfect" parenting, they have had their needs suf-ficiently met so that they develop a sound foundation for problem solving in healthy ways (Mahler, Pine, & Bergman, 1975). However, even people without those advantages in childhood may not develop symptoms of mental illness be-cause they decide to get out of a sick situation as soon as possible, or to be strong enough not to be overwhelmed by it. Later, this "be strong" inner driver may not always be useful; it, too, can be modified (Kahler & Capers, 1974).

The absence of disorders are some-times due to a "significant other" such as a teacher or therapist who enters a per-son's life at a crucial time and reinforces his/her positive characteristics. A woman who lost her mother in early childhood, was sexually molested, and whose father and two brothers were in prison several times made the decision in Transactional Analysis that past was past and she could live in the present because of her personal power and her therapist's encouragement.

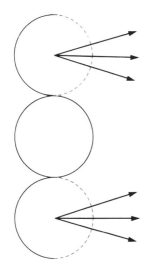

FIGURE 9.6. Lesion in the Child ego state. The broken line represents the lesion that leads to an explosion.

THE ASSESSMENT OF DYSFUNCTION

Assessment of dysfunction begins formally or informally during the first session. Whether it is an individual problem, a problem in a couple relationship, a family or a group, script issues are quickly apparent. To be or not to be, to speak or not to speak, is sometimes the question.

Some clients enter therapy not knowing what to expect and need a bit of encouragement to begin speaking. If information is not volunteered by the client, one of the beginning questions from a therapist may be something like, "Why did you decide to seek therapy at this time?" Answers to this question often point to particular areas of life that concern clients and the problems that they are willing to discuss. While listening to the answer, the therapist is likely to be assessing whether the problem being presented is due to a current situational crisis, to a long-standing or newly emerging personality problem, or to an interpersonal situation at home or at work.

Standardized tests, such as the Minnesota Multiphasic Personality Inventory (MMPI), are seldom used unless required by a referring agency or when they are necessary to clarify diagnosis. When they are used, the testing procedure is often separate from the treatment although the interpretation of such tests to clients may be an integrated part of therapy. Assessment using categories under the fourth edition of the *Diagnostic and Statistical Manual of Mental Disorders* (DSM-IV; American Psychiatric Association, 1994) is fairly frequent, especially if payment is to be made through insurance sources, and it is usually integrated into diagnosis and treatment.

Regardless of what problem is presented, many people who seek professional help do so because they feel hopeless, depressed, unloved, unable to get through a routine day, unable to find a friend, hold a job, earn enough money, or please a boss or spouse. Many others come in with quite different feelings. They feel angry that they may not be able to control their world, that other people do not appreciate them or obey them or recognize their value. Regardless of the feelings being expressed or hidden, at this point therapists are assessing whether this person can be helped, if so, by whom, and what kind of treatment would be most useful.

Clients may feel unable to take control of their self-destructive behavior or may claim to be inadequately educated, spiritually bereft, or incapable of functioning independently due to accident, illness, or aging. That may be true or partly true. Yet early in the therapeutic process, the assessment of strengths to deal with life is also a necessary aid for the recovery and building of strong mental health. "What are the strengths you have that you have sometimes been able to use, either in your childhood or your current life?" is a question that helps in the assessment. Other questions to get to the same point are, "What do you like about yourself that you are not willing to give up, no matter what?" or, "What are some strengths that you sense you have and would like to release, or that are new and you would like to develop further?"

From Script to Autonomy

Individual, family, and cultural scripts frequently interfere with healthy functioning, so transactional analysts help clients analyze their scripts as part of the assessment process and use the assessment to develop treatment plans. A *script* can be defined as an *unconscious life plan*, very much like that of a dramatic stage production, which an individual feels compelled to play out. Psychological life plans are based on the early decisions children make about themselves and others. Berne (1972) says they are "reinforced by the parents, justified by subsequent events, and culminating in a chosen alternative" (p. 446).

Scripts people live by are adaptations of stories, fairy tales, and myths that children hear in childhood or create for themselves because of their hopes and fears. "That's me," or, "That's the way my life is going to turn out," they might conclude when they hear folk tales and fairy tales, myths of famous or infamous people. There are an unlimited number of historical or imagined figures available to children to use as role models in developing their own life scripts, and they usually do this without awareness of doing so. When clients say something like, "Why does this always happen to me?" they are getting ready for script analysis.

The roles of *Victim*, *Persecutor*, and *Rescuer* advance the script. Although people are not aware of doing so, each one compulsively plays out the parts in a drama that is a true adventure, a comedy, a farce, or a tragedy. Like theatrical plays, psychological life dramas have themes of success and failure. These are constructive, destructive, or banal and going nowhere. A question such as "What would be the logical conclusions if you go on as you now are?" may elicit important information on the script theme and how the curtain will go down at the end of the client's next act, or at the end of one's life.

One of the issues getting increasing attention today is how women have often been "scripted" to perceive themselves as less important and less powerful than men. Now they are "rewriting" their personal and cultural scripts and frequently bringing issues into the therapist's office that were much less frequently talked about than in the past (M. James, 1977).

People with *constructive scripts* seldom seek therapy except for a situational crises, and even then they may not. Factors that contribute to having constructive scripts include receiving love and protection in childhood, being encouraged to feel and to think, not only about oneself but also about others. However, some people who do not have these kinds of positive childhood experiences live out constructive lives regardless of the past. They learn from their negative experiences and decide to succeed in life rather than let themselves get beaten down by it. Their multiple strengths are apparent if they have a problem and seek help and the length of treatment is relatively brief.

People with *destructive scripts* act like losers. Sooner or later, they injure themselves and/or others. They may do so gradually, over an extended period, or suddenly in a dramatic fashion. Some people with destructive scripts act them out in a series of crimes. Others may get involved in substance abuse; get addicted to eating, spending, or gambling; or get into situations in which they will be physically or psychologically abused at a serious level or will abuse others.

People with *banal scripts* are quite harmless, yet they are "going nowhere." They restrict their own growth, limit their own opportunities, and avoid the full realization of their potentialities. On the surface, they may appear successful; however, they inevitably undermine themselves in some way so they do not quite succeed. This is the script of many who do not set realistic goals or realistic plans of action or who procrastinate on making important changes they need to make and do not follow through on their plans. They keep on doing the same things instead of risking change (Allen & Allen, 1968).

Individual scripts are, to a large degree, strongly determined by cultural scripts. As noted in *Born to Win*:

> Cultural scripts are the accepted and expected dramatic patterns that occur within a society. They are determined by the spoken and unspoken assumptions believed by the majority of the people within that group. Like theatrical scripts, cultural scripts have themes, characters, expected roles, stage directions, costumes, settings, scenes, and final curtains. Cultural scripts reflect what is thought of as the "national character." The same drama may be repeated generation after generation. (M. James & Jongeward, 1971, p. 70)

Cultural scripts need to be assessed. So do the subcultures to which clients belong and which are defined by geography, language, religion, age, sex, race, and ethnic grouping or in some other general way. Subcultures are so influential that many adolescents, desiring peer approval, allow their teen subculture to function as a strong parent, making demands and withdrawing favors. With the escalating use of illegal drugs, and pressures of gang membership, the Peer Parent is an increasing problem.

The family as a small subculture often has the greatest influence. Some families are angry and punitive. Some are cold and indifferent. Others are warm and loving. Furthermore, each family lives by traditions they believe to be true and often related to gender roles and expectations, academic and vocational achievements, how to rear children, and treat friends, how to work, and how to play (M. James, 1977). Each family also perpetuates a kind of family history with its lifestyles and myths. Even stories of famous or infamous family members can script children to conform or rebel against what is implied (M. James, 1977).

Assessing which ego state is used most often can show whether a client is living the same script as one of his/her parents or living a different script chosen in childhood. However, scripts can also be chosen in later years. For example, a physician may have learned a surgical procedure as an adult in medical school but unless the procedure is updated, the surgeon is script-bound. Or, a person may have learned to drive on country roads, and unless the skills are updated for freeway driving, the person is script-bound in the Adult and also is dangerous. Or, therapists may learn specific theories and techniques in graduate school and not expand their knowledge and, thus, be script-bound. Most people have several stages on which to act out their lives. The most common are home, work, academic, and social situations. Problems related to what goes on at work are reported in therapy almost as often as are problems at home. The scripts played out on various stages may or may not coincide. One client's scripting when "on stage" at home can call for "acting" in nonproductive ways and for the work stage may call for competency and success. A growing interest among transactional analysts is multiculturalism and the diversity of personal as well as cultural scripts (M. James, 1991). The *Journal of the International Transactional Analysis Association* frequently publishes articles on this subject. Script checklists or questionnaires are sometimes given as homework to aid clients in clarifying individual problems and interpersonal conflicts due to unresolved script issues and how they are related to their scripts (M. James, 1983).

Scripts can be "rewritten" or changed when people, using the educated Adult and the tenacious Child, make psychological redecisions from an emotional as well as a cognitive level. The use of a deathbed fantasy is one way. In doing this, clients relax deeply and visualize themselves on their deathbed while looking at a movie of their life as though on television. Then the therapist asks,

"What are people around your deathbed saying and what would your epitaph be?" When I first got in touch with my own epitaph, I was surprised. I imagined the words "She was responsible" would be on my tombstone and decided that was not enough. Therefore, I made a contract with myself to be in such a way that the words "and fun" would be added to my epitaph. "Fun," I said to myself, "What's that?" For so many years, I had been so busy being responsible from my Adult and Parent that I had almost shut off this part of my Child. It took time to release it, time to find new fun-loving friends, and time to experiment with and practice new behavior. However, it worked. I am convinced that if I died today my epitaph would read, "She was responsible and fun," and that pleases me greatly. Transactional analysts believe that change can happen at any old age and now, at 78, I continue to change and have fun in the process.

THE PRACTICE OF THERAPY

Transactional Analysis, as originally designed by Berne, was intended to be a brief form of therapy. He recommended that the transactional analyst say, "Get better first, and we can analyze later," then added, "Surprisingly enough, in most cases the patient will oblige." The intent of his statement was to encourage the therapists to help clients take control of their lives—their feelings, behaviors, and value systems—and to do so in the early stages of therapy. Therefore, the amount of time, and the way time is used, is an important consideration in Transactional Analysis.

In private practice with individuals, therapy is usually 1 hour a week except in critical periods when it may be more frequent. Groups are more likely to meet for 1½ or 2 hours weekly, and the length

of time people choose to be in therapy varies widely. Family therapy usually has a similar schedule and it is not unusual for clients in family therapy to also be in individual therapy (McClendon & Kadis, 1983). Psychological games, discussed later in this section, can be played in any of these situations.

Weekend marathons or weeklong intensive therapy and training groups are also common. In hospitals, institutions, rehabilitation centers, and halfway houses, therapy is more likely to be scheduled on a daily basis. For people who travel great distances, especially when they come from other countries, I sometimes schedule concentrated sessions, seeing one client for 5 hours a day for 3 consecutive days. Perhaps, because time is limited, and motivation is high, therapy is effective and game playing is minimal, although reporting games, and recognizing how pervasive they are, may be a necessary step to reach the desired goal. To clarify and reach goals, there are basically three phases of treatment. The first is primarily that of establishing a working relationship between the therapist and client so that healing and problem solving can occur. The middle phase is often called the working-through phase because the causes and dynamics of the problems are identified and worked on. During this phase clients take increasing responsibility for establishing contracts for solving problems. The third phase is the termination process, which, hopefully, both client and therapist agree to.

Early Stages of Therapy

Establishing a climate of trust is the first and perhaps the most important task of any therapist. There are multiple ways this can be done. Respecting the dignity and potential growth of a client is crucial. Recognizing the person's strengths, listening with empathy, and giving honest feedback when asked for are a few general ways transactional analysts develop a nourishing climate for growth. Then there are specifics that are applicable to some. For example, clients who had parents who frequently did not keep their promises to meet them at school or be home on time, or clients whose parents left them by death or desertion, need therapists who are on time and do not go away without careful explanations and arrangement for clients to see other therapists if necessary.

Regardless of who the transactional analyst is, how time is structured, or what other systems are used in conjunction with Transactional Analysis, there is wide agreement on the necessity for goal setting. Most agree on the need for a clear statement of the presenting problem or major complaint, the history of when it began, and the efforts, if any, previously made to solve the problem. The client's personal history is also taken, briefly or in detail, and sometimes a very brief introduction about Transactional Analysis and how it can be used with the presenting problem is made during the initial session. In this way, the therapist and client get the chance to look each other over and decide whether their relationship will be conducive to growth. With some clients, it is clear from the beginning that a therapeutic relationship can be established (M. James, 1977; Cornell, 1986).

Goal Setting in the Early Phase

Goal setting is essential in Transactional Analysis. Reaching a goal is accelerated through the use of contracts. The sooner the client is able to establish and maintain a contract, the sooner the problem is solved, especially if clients know what they want for themselves, what they need to change, and what they are willing to do to make the changes.

According to James and Jongeward (1971), a contract is a bilateral, not a unilateral, agreement between the therapist and client. It is one they both agree to and is a clear statement in operational form of the individual or interpersonal problems to be solved and the action required to solve them. It is absolutely essential that the statement be clear, concise, and direct. Therefore, treatment goals must be realistic, achievable, and measurable. A contract such as "cutting down on smoking" does not fit this criteria. To "stop smoking entirely," is measurable and achievable. "Losing weight" is not a contract; losing 20 pounds is measurable and achievable and may be life saving. Clients who are unsure about their goals are given "permission" to think about it for a few sessions. Or, they can start learning Transactional Analysis through reading and recognizing their own ego states. *Born to Win* has been useful for this purpose because exercises are given at the end of each chapter to accelerate the therapeutic process (M. James & Jongeward, 1971). One very shy, withdrawn woman who found it difficult to talk was able to do so after reading an exercise and doing homework. She drew a stick figure and colored the places she had been touched in childhood and discovered that her mouth had been frequently slapped as her mother shouted at her, "Shut up." One professional man who did not understand why he went into sheer panic at the sound of a woman's loud voice discovered, when asked to sit on the floor of a therapist's office and draw a scene from early childhood, that, at age 3, he had rolled his toy truck in the wrong direction and tripped his grandmother who then exploded in anger.

Some transactional analysts who prefer to use only a verbal and cognitive approach do not use techniques such as role-playing or drawing to access the Child ego state. I occasionally use them, not as techniques adapted from other therapeutic systems (Transactional Analysis precedes many contemporary systems) but because they are natural ways for children to act and useful ways to understand developmental stages that may have been missed and the unresolved traumas in a client's Child, which can then be worked through. Of course, any technique that releases the Child needs to be part of a treatment plan, not an impulsive suggestion of the therapist.

Although it is sometimes believed that Transactional Analysis is eclectic and borrows from many other modern therapies, the reverse is more often true. Transactional Analysis, which was developed in 1958, precedes many of the newer psychotherapies. Yet, it is worthy of noting again that Berne was strongly influenced by psychoanalysis, which he respected and challenged. He claimed that the original formulations of Freud (1949) were best used in formal discussions and then went to some length to explain how his theory differed from Freud's (Berne, 1961).

A successful research physicist sought therapy out of feelings of despair because he had suddenly become so unhappy on his job. He stated that he did not know what was wrong with him or what he wanted because he had just received a prestigious title and raise. His despair had begun when his new job required management skills and his complaint was, "Although I understand physics, I have no understanding of people." This statement became the basis of his contract, "To learn basic Transactional Analysis theory in order to understand people and communicate more effectively, and do it in 10 weeks." Although this was an ambitious contract, he was so highly motivated that he studied Transactional Analysis theory on his own, entered a Transactional Analysis group, and also had a private session weekly to clarify his goals and progress.

It is not surprising that he achieved the goal he set for himself.

The emphasis of a contract is on personal change, not on changing others, although the two are often related, especially in family therapy. Goals can be made around the relief of (1) physical symptoms, such as ulcers or excessive fatigue; (2) psychological symptoms, such as phobias or obsessions; or (3) a change in behavior, such as exercising regularly, stopping the use of illegal drugs, or even studying systematically instead of just before exams. Contracts can also be made for increasing self-esteem by going back to school and learning a new career, repairing an important relationship, refusing to be sexually harassed, completing an important project, and so on. In other words, there are unlimited numbers of goals that can appeal to clients.

After the goal is established, it is necessary to develop a treatment plan based on a contract. Clients often know what would make them happier, so the therapist can ask, " What do you want that would *enhance* your life?" The word "enhance" is important because some people want what is inhibiting of life rather than enhancing, or know what they want to stop but not what they want to start doing instead. Goals can be personal, such as learning something new "for fun." They can be interpersonal, for example, learning how to give and take compliments.

The next question a therapist can ask is, "What would *you* need to do or to change to get what you want?" Whining does not change many things, as most children discover. Therefore, if a client starts complaining about a spouse, a child, a business associate, and so on, a possible Transactional Analysis response is, "Are there any changes *you* need to make that would enhance your life and move you closer to your goal?" The answer to this may not be immediately clear. Assessing the strength of the desire for a particular goal, and the strength of the client to reach it, is part of the therapeutic process.

After this point is clarified, the harder question comes, "What would you be *willing to do* to effect the change?" Many clients know what they need to do, or believe they should do, but are not willing to do it. This question encourages them to take responsibility and take responsibility now. Some clients enter therapy with the expectation that the therapists have magical wands and will "do me something," and this question begins to challenge the fantasy of "being done to."

Clients benefit from knowing that when they change, they are likely to feel, look, and act in more positive ways. Hence, the next question is, "How would you or other people know when the change has been completed?" Answers could be, "I will have lost 20 pounds and that will show." Or, "I will have made three new friends and will be going out at least once a week."

The final question is, "How might you sabotage yourself?" The answer to this reveals the behavior and games that clients might engage in to undermine themselves. For example, getting too tired is often used as an excuse for overeating and drinking. When this happens, the initial contract may need to be revised to include getting more rest and exercise or planning an activity that will be more interesting than addictive reactions to stress. After clients make these decisions, it helps to discuss details of when, where, and how. Sometimes clients work on several contracts simultaneously, for example, to lose weight, to restructure a budget, and to find a new friend.

In addition to individual contracts, contracts in groups may also be established. An exceedingly shy person who wants to stop withdrawing from people may make a contract to say something every 15 minutes during group sessions.

This is realistic, achievable, and measurable. Another group member, who may drive people away by talking too much, may set a goal of developing closer friendships and may contract to speak no longer than 5 minutes within a 30-minute period so that others have a chance to talk.

Therapists, and sometimes clients, keep a record of contracts, the dates they are established, and when they are completed. This record serves as a focal point during group and individual sessions and as a tool for review. Reviewing contracts that have been completed, or reviewing them with the intention of modifying the goals or the action needed, increases contract-setting skills and self-esteem. A client who says, "I'm not getting anywhere," may become aware of having made considerable progress when reviewing previous contracts and thus have confidence for the next step.

The Middle Phase of Therapy

The middle phase of treatment begins when a working relationship has been established between the client and therapist, when the client has initial information about Transactional Analysis, feels accepted and understood, has established a temporary or initial contract, and is willing to talk about his/her feelings and behaviors. The way Transactional Analysis is used during the middle phase depends on the contract as well as on the therapist's knowledge, skills, and style of treatment. Authenticity is usually more important than techniques, and transactional analysts use different techniques with different clients. In a grief-filled session, some therapists may say little to allow time for emotions to be freely expressed. Some may comfort clients who are overcome by similar feelings of despair. At other times, these same therapists may take a very active role and interrupt those who oververbalize, rationalize, justify, and blame others to avoid solving their own problems. Or, they may encourage those who act fearful or tongue-tied to speak out. Such clients grow in strength if they contract to say something every 15 minutes during group. Smiles, brief positive statements, even applause, may follow a major piece of work, and this reinforces new behavior.

Giving active feedback in a relaxed fashion about how ego states show in the group, or the kind of behavior that elicits predictable responses, helps free people from understandable resistances they have built up over many years. Reduced resistance also comes with empathetic listening and patience on the part of the therapist. The impatient one is often met with higher resistance than one who will adjust to the client's timetable. After all, people who come for therapy usually have unsatisfactory patterns of behavior that are so long-standing that suggestions of change may be threatening and elicit procrastination or outright rejection. It is during the middle phase that the analysis of psychological games becomes an important focus.

Game Analysis

Games, often played outside awareness, are a series of transactions that on the surface may appear to be straightforward but actually have ulterior, manipulative purposes (Berne, 1964; Stewart & Joines, 1987). When the series of transactions are over, the players feel self-righteous, angry, or depressed and also feel entitled to act out their feelings in some way. For example, after a typical family fight, one may feel entitled to sulk and be silent for a few days and the other may feel entitled to go spend money as a way to feel better. In either case, both of them believe their responses to the other person are justifiable.

After games are defined, there are numerous ways to analyze them. One, often used in marital and family therapy, is the "Game Plan" (J. James, 1973). As in a football game where certain plays are planned, families act out patterns of behavior without other family members being consciously aware of the repetitive patterns. These can be illuminated by asking the following questions in this order. What keeps happening over and over again? What happens first? What happens next? What happens next? How does it end? How does each person feel in the end? What does each one do?

One family came to therapy because the parents could not get along with their 16-year-old son. They learned to identify their game plan:

SON: (*Asks to borrow the car.*)

MA: No.

SON: Why not?

MA: Because . . .

SON: (*Argues each point and begins yelling.*)

MA: (*Yells back, bringing up past errors of the son.*)

SON: (*Leaves the house, slamming the door as he goes.*)

MA: (*Goes and complains to Pa.*)

Son ends up feeling misunderstood; Ma ends up feeling inadequate.

When the parents recognized this pattern, they decided that they would not raise their voices when talking to their son. Later they decided to give their reasons only once and not bring up past misdeeds each time he asked for something. Within a short time, the son began to stop yelling and, instead, talked reasonably. Eventually the family set mutually agreeable standards for his behavior that would allow him to use the car.

People play psychological games as indirect ways to get what they need or want (J. James, 1976). They beat around

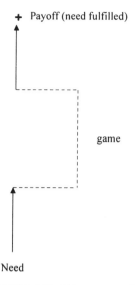

FIGURE 9.7. The game plan.

the bush instead of asking for what they want directly (see Figure 9.7).

A son may need or want his father's attention. If Dad spends time with the boy, all is well. But if Dad is "too tired" from a busy day, Son may do something to evoke Dad's attention, such as fight with his sister, stub his toe, or make an obvious mistake of some sort. The attention he gets for doing this is a payoff that temporarily satisfies an underlying psychological need. To discover payoffs, the question is, "After things go wrong, what do you do next?" Common payoffs are getting time alone, receiving attention from someone, and avoiding some unwanted activity. In families, if games are played at a more serious level, the payoffs can be critical emotional explosions or dangerously bizarre behavior (M. James & J. James, 1978).

Termination as the Third Phase

Termination is an important part of therapy. Preferably, it is a cooperative decision between client and therapist. It is sometimes a decision made by the client alone and is acceptable if the client is at no danger to self or others. In some instances, clients are encouraged to continue therapy and set new goals. However, because contracts are bilateral and allow for individual choice and decision, termination can be accepted.

Sometimes termination is a game if a client enters therapy not to get cured but only to learn how to play games more cleverly. According to Berne (1972):

> [If someone is playing the game of *Alcoholic*] he will *quit* if the therapist declines to play entirely, and also if the therapist is a pigeon and can be too easily conned. In this respect, transactional games are like chess: an enthusiastic chess player is not interested in people who do not want to play at all, nor in people who do not offer any real opposition. In a treatment group, a confirmed *Alcoholic* player will get angry of no one offers to rescue or persecute him, or play the patsy or the connection, and will soon leave. He will also leave if the rescuers are too sentimental, or the persecutors too vehement, because there is no fun if he hooks them too easily. Like other game players, he prefers a little finesse and some reticence on the part of his partners or opponents. (p. 350)

When clients reduce the intensity of their games their symptoms are lessened, and there is a potential for premature termination. As termination is inevitable, it is the therapist's responsibility to see it coming and plan that it goes well. In some cases, suggesting a new contract is effective.

Group Therapy Strategies

Some clients are sophisticated regarding group therapy. Others are skeptical and unreceptive, reluctant, and fearful of the group. Each person's participation in the group needs to be considered individually so that the group work can be effective.

Some groups are open-ended, meaning that they continue indefinitely; some are established for a specified number of weeks. Both types have advantages and disadvantages. Advantages of the open-ended group include the convenience to the therapist of having a regular schedule, the convenience of being able to add new members whenever space becomes available, and the feeling that there will be enough time to work things through so that no one needs to be pressured to hurry. When a group is open-ended, new members may be encouraged by the progress reports of others. Old members may be educated by the problems and solutions new members bring up. A disadvantage of open-ended groups is that clients and therapists may settle in for an indefinite period of time, become passive, and depend on group energy instead of taking personal initiative for rapid change.

Advantages of groups that meet for a specified number of sessions include the willingness of clients to commit themselves to brief therapy when they would not agree to an indefinite time commitment, the challenge to the therapist to be effective quickly, and the challenge to groups members to fulfill their contracts during the allotted period of time. For new therapists just opening a private practice, this is a useful way to begin. The major disadvantage is that the specified number of sessions may not be enough for the clients to complete their contracts and another series may be in order. In a couples therapy group I led many years ago, the four women were very verbal and goal-oriented, and the four men were very passive and only came because they were "brought." The group was a challenge, and I was glad when the 8 weeks were over so that they could transfer into my other groups in which the personalities and ways of transacting were more heterogeneous.

When groups begin, there is often a brief period of rituals and pastimes while the members get settled. As transactional analysts are generally in the business of curing people, not making them feel "comfortable," they seldom introduce group members to each other. Instead, they carefully observe what goes on, who transacts with whom, and in what ways. Information is given about the group time schedule, the way fees will be paid, permission for anyone to say what they want to say, and the fact that no physical violence is allowed. Although it is not enforceable, I also suggest the members respect each other by keeping confidential everything that is disclosed in the group.

As the therapist sits down, hopefully with a clear mind and fresh perspective, the meeting begins. Clients may look around using their intuitive powers to psych out others so that they can guess at what might happen next, or they use projections to do the same. New therapists sometimes feel the need "to do something" to get things going. When this is the case, the therapist may need more experience or supervision in group process work.

During the first group session, after the usual brief rituals, members may state their contracts and how they are going to work on them outside and inside the setting. In weeklong workshops or weekend marathons, goals and contracts may be written out by group members on large sheets of paper and fastened to the walls. These sheets become referral points that focus clients' energies.

In ongoing groups, contract review usually occurs whenever a new member joins. Reviewing is not done by going around the circle asking each member to speak up. This can establish a teacher–student or Parent–Child relationship and activate games that are inherent in both. Instead, a suggestion is casually made for members to introduce themselves by first name only and restate their contracts. In these brief moments, the therapist observes the content, style, and order in which group members speak and the ego state boundary problems that may be showing and considers the possible significance of statements that sound like scripts, as well as the invitations given, either overtly or covertly, to enter psychological games.

Therapists' Errors

Therapists, as well as patients, are motivated by the Parent and Child aspects of their personalities, and these ego states can influence them more pervasively than they may realize. It may take months to perceive that the interventions they are using are not effective. It may take even longer to become clear that much of what they say has a controlling or exploitative quality that is characteristic of a game and arises from a masked ulterior goal. Berne says that to reduce these therapeutic errors, the productive question is not, "Am I playing a game?" but rather, "What game am I playing?"

Therapists can diagnose their own games by discovering how they get into the roles of Victim, Persecutor, and Rescuer and how they switch from one role to another (Karpman, 1968; M. James, 1977) (see Figure 9.8). In therapy clients can learn to identify when, where, and with whom, they switch roles in life dramas.

These roles, seldom played with Adult ego state awareness, can be played externally with others, or internally between the Parent and Child ego states. Usually, but not always, the Victim role comes from the Child ego state and the Rescuer and Persecutor from the Parent. When these three words are capitalized, they refer to the game roles. When they are not, they refer to legitimate behavior. Examples of legitimate roles are the *persecutor*, someone who sets necessary limits on behavior or is charged with enforcing a rule; the *victim*, someone who qualifies for a job but is denied it because of race, sex, religion, or national origin; the *rescuer*, someone who helps nonfunctioning or poorly functioning persons to rehabilitate themselves, to stand on their own two feet and take responsibility for their feelings and behavior.

Therapists may find themselves in each of these roles for legitimate reasons. Legitimately, therapists need to rescue children from homes where they are being abused. As legitimate persecutors, they criticize the one who is doing the abusing. However, the one criticized may try to "get even" by withholding payment or in some more aggressive way. Thus, the therapist becomes a victim. When Transactional Analysis therapists are legitimately rescuing, persecuting, or being victimized, they are dealing with the here and now, aware of the current situation, and data processing the potentials for getting into game roles. Games are like short scenes in dramas and meant to manipulate other charac-

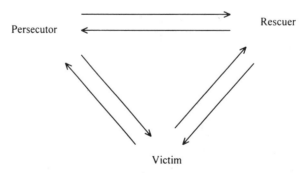

FIGURE 9.8. The drama triangle.

ters. In game roles, *Persecutors* are people who are overly critical, who set unnecessarily strict limits on other people's behavior, or who enforce rules sadistically. *Rescuers* are people who, in the guise of being helpful, are often very controlling and give a lot of unwanted advice. *Victims* find themselves injured psychologically or physically. In couple relationships, games and roles are often interlocking. As in drama scripts, it takes one kind of "character" to attract another (J. James & Schlesinger, 1987).

When therapists are into game roles, the Adult is contaminated by parental prejudices, behaviors, and opinions from the past or contaminated by Child experiences of the past, or by expectations, hopes, or fears of the future. People are seldom aware of the games they play because the games feel familiar, having been learned in childhood. They are so programmed into people's personalities that people often have great difficulty recognizing them as learned feelings and behavior. Consequently, they tend to intellectualize and justify themselves and find it difficult to give up the roles and the particular games played to fulfill the roles.

Therapists, as well as clients, may have learned how to be Persecutors in childhood if they were given heavy parental responsibility over younger siblings when they were too young to handle it, or if they were allowed to bully others to get their own way, or if they had a parent figure as a model who persecuted others and implied that it was acceptable for the child to do likewise. Therapists, as well as clients, learn how to be Rescuers in childhood if they were often encouraged to rescue their parent figures, who may have been feeling unhappy, or nurture younger siblings who were feeling likewise, or if they strongly identified with a parent figure who was a big Rescuer. Therapists, as well as clients, also learn how to be Victims in childhood if they are victimized physically or verbally by those with more power, including

parents and grandparents, siblings and neighbors, teachers, baby sitters, and so forth.

Common Persecutor games, sometimes played by therapists, are *Blemish*, and *Now I've Got You, You S.O.B.* In the game of *Blemish*, the therapist acts as a nitpicker, finding small things wrong with clients and verbally stating or inferring that these small things need changing, much like parents who demand perfection from their children. Such therapists do not teach others to know the difference between trivial and important problems. In the game of *Now I've Got You, You S.O.B.*, the therapist waits for the client to make an error and, when it happens, pounces strongly on the person with a sense of inner relish, much like parents who justify their abusive behavior in the guise of, "Now I'll teach you a lesson."

Common Rescuer games, sometimes played by therapists, are *I'm Only Trying to Help You* and *Why Don't You?* Both games look the same from the therapist's "helping" position, but the end of each game is quite different because of different responses. In *I'm Only Trying to Help You*, the therapist gives some "well-meaning" advice and the client seemingly takes the suggestions. Later the client messes up in some way and then returns to blame the therapist for things not going right, playing a complementary game of *Look What You Made Me Do*.

Common Victim games, sometimes played by therapists, are *Look How Hard I'm Trying*, *Harried*, and *Poor Me*. Therapists who give more of themselves than appropriate are playing games. One way they do this is by not paying attention to the clock and letting sessions run over their allotted time.

Another way is if a pattern develops of having private conversations with some group members while others are leaving.

Hard-working therapists may also play *Harried*, overscheduling themselves by taking on new clients or always being available to old clients and not saving time for their own personal and social lives. In such cases they may begin to get forgetful, make mistakes, or feel sad and burnt out. Their reasons for overscheduling may be valid if clients are in crisis and no one else is available to work with them, or if a the client is too upset to consider seeing someone else. Or they may be playing "good" games such as *Busman's Holiday, Happy to Help,* or *They'll Be Glad They Knew Me.* Whereas these games may be useful to clients, they are still games (Berne, 1964).

Poor Me is another common game that can be played by the therapist who allows clients to be slow in paying their bills or lets too many clients come for reduced fees. Then, when it comes time for therapists to pay their own bills, they may have barely enough money to get by and end up feeling discouraged and depressed and imagining that nobody really cares about "poor me." Reducing game playing in favor of other activities and genuine intimacy is a major step toward autonomy for therapists as well as for clients.

THE STANCE
OF THE THERAPIST

Therapists are made, not born. A therapist who has received good training, and treatment, who stays involved in continuing education, and who has integrity as a person is likely to be effective. Unless it is a crisis, few transactional analysts control one-to-one therapy sessions overtly. The level at which they are active depends on their training, experience, preferred style of being and doing, and the contracts made with the client. Responsibility is shared. Those who are certified in Transactional Analysis must also comply with the professional practices and strict code of ethics of the International Transactional Analysis Associa-

tion as well as to the ethics, laws, and expectancies in the jurisdictions in which they work.

In the process of doing therapy, healthy and unhealthy transference occurs. Transference refers to the ideas and feelings that the client has displaced from previous figures and projected onto the therapist with anticipatory, fantasy expectations. Everyone who enters groups, including the therapist, does so with a personal agenda, which may or may not be a part of a contract, and, knowingly or unknowingly, also brings what Berne called a "provisional group imago." The group imago is the image or fantasy of what the group will be like and how the members will transact with each other. It is likely to be different in the mind of each client as well as in the mind of the therapist. Whether working with an individual or with a group, the transactional analyst does not act as a "mirror," as in psychoanalysis. Some actively invite transference; some seek to minimize it. Countertransference involves therapists' responses that are unhealthy if they initiate transactions or respond to those initiated by others on the basis of their own "unfinished business." However, some transactions that could be interpreted that way can be useful. Brief moments of self-disclosure often facilitate the therapeutic process. As Clarkson (1992) writes, "It is natural to feel affection for a lovable patient, appreciative of a creative client and respect for a humble person" (p. 155).

Potency, Permission,
and Protection

Authenticity, integrity, creativity, and the ability to listen are most essential qualities for therapists. With these qualities therapists are potent when faced with treatment challenges. They give people permission to change and get well and are able to protect them, if necessary, during the process.

Potency in Transactional Analysis therapists refers to having a personal sense of authenticity, credibility, trustworthiness, and responsiveness. These therapists do not use waste or energy in putting on performances. Instead, using their own unique styles, they respond appropriately to therapeutic challenges and work to protect and increase the well-being of their clients. Potent therapists may not know all the answers, yet they have solid knowledge about how clients can discover their own answers by understanding their own ego states, transactions, games, and scripts and how they are interrelated. As for themselves, potent therapists are continually in the learning process. They are able to analyze their own ego states and transactions, change them when appropriate, decrease the frequency and intensity of their games, and rewrite their own scripts.

Permission to grow and change is given to clients to encourage them to act in life-enhancing ways and experience positive feelings and thoughts based on living in the real world, not tied to some fantasized utopia or to a tragic script. Permission may be given with remarks such as, "It's OK to think for yourself and make your own decisions," or, "I think it would be great if you decide to look for a better job where you get less hassling." Permission is also given nonverbally with a smile, nod, and clap on the back, a handshake, or some other sign of caring or goodwill (Crossman, 1963, pp. 152–153). A playful laugh from the Child ego state often gives as potent a permission to enjoy life as can be given by a nurturing Parent remark or rational Adult feedback.

Potent permission-giving therapists often need to provide *protection* simultaneously because a client's Child can be very vulnerable when experimenting with new behavior. As a rule of thumb,

if a person is genuinely hurting—physically or emotionally—therapists are both tender and strong, thus protective. In a crisis, they are available or have dependable referral sources. To establish what is a crisis and what is not, a Transactional Analysis therapist may say something like, "Phone me immediately if you think you might hurt yourself or anyone else. Otherwise, only phone me for appointments." This kind of statement not only provides the client with needed protection, it also provides some for the therapist.

Potency, permission, and protection—everyone wants them, everyone needs them, and everyone can have them—therapists as well as clients. Effective Transactional Analysis therapists use these three "Ps" of treatment and do it with humility knowing that power is in clients and they can recognize and take responsibility for their own potency, can give themselves permission to change, and can establish ways to protect themselves.

From Pain to Joy

Some therapists believe all therapy should be taken seriously; this is seldom the case with transactional analysts. One of the important skills to be learned by a transactional analyst is when and how to deliberately use laughter. As Berne (1970) wrote, "The road to freedom is laughter" (p. 194).

Laughter is a sign of cure and a way of curing. It is used as part of the growing awareness of the need for a holistic approach in therapy. Laughter releases the capacity to laugh *at* oneself, at one's self-deception, and at the absurdity of the world. It also releases the capacity to laugh *with* others. There is a universal human urge to laugh. It activates the chemistry for the will to live, reflects insight, attracts friends, breaks tension in work and social situations, and increases the capacity to fight against disease. By expanding the chest, increasing respiration, and forcing poisoned air from lung cells, laughter relaxes the body and helps stimulate the balance which is called health (M. James, 1979).

Learning to laugh in spite of pain is a life-saving skill that can be learned. One of the most dramatic cases of the curative effects of laughter is that of Norman Cousins, editor and senior lecturer who recently taught courses in laughter at the Medical School of the University of California, Los Angeles. He had laughed his way out of the hospital and out of a very serious, crippling collagen illness which doctors believed to be irreversible. With the cooperation of his attending physician to use nontraditional techniques for cure, Cousins (1976), hospitalized with excruciating pain, developed a hypothesis, "If negative emotions produce negative chemical changes in the body, wouldn't the positive emotions produce positive chemical changes? Is it possible that love, hope, faith, laughter, confidence, and the will to live have therapeutic value?" (pp. 1458–1463)

It is not easy to laugh when hurting, so Cousins secured a movie projector and watched humorous films from the television series *Candid Camera*. He also read books of humor and made the discovery that 10 minutes of genuine belly laughter had an anesthetic effect that gave him at least 2 hours of pain-free sleep. Then, when the painkilling effect of laughter wore off, the movie projector was turned on again, and it often would lead to another pain-free sleep interval. Cousins' high sedimentation rate began to drop a little after each laughter session. It stayed down; the effect was cumulative. Laughter, he decided, was good medicine and essential for health.

Granted, not all things are laughable; sometimes laughter is a "gallows transaction" or a symptom of disease in which laughter becomes uncontrollable. Yet the stance of many transactional analysts is in favor of laughter as one way that pain can be replaced with joy, whether the pain is caused by problems that might be solved or problems that cannot be solved and need to be accepted. The case at the end of this chapter shows how laughter can be part of Transactional Analysis treatment plan.

CURATIVE FACTORS AND MECHANISMS OF CHANGE

Although Transactional Analysis is a sophisticated theory and process, one of its most important curative factors is that it appears simple to those who have not studied it in depth. It can be explained, in abbreviated form, with everyday words that anyone can understand. It is so vital and comprehensive a system that using Transactional Analysis theory is often sufficient for any client. Techniques that are preferred differ from therapist to therapist in relation to different clients. However, regardless of the techniques or process used, both phenomenological insight and cognitive understanding are expected to occur outside the therapy room as well as inside it, and new interpersonal skills are learned in the process rather than didactically.

Because people learn visually as well as auditorially and experientially, it is common for transactional analysts to draw and explain three stacked circles to represent personality structure, or triangles to represent how people switch roles in the psychological games they play, or lines between two sets of stacked circles to demonstrate communication between the ego states of two or more persons and accelerate change. I have a small chalkboard beside my chair that I may pick up and use comfortably without seeming like a teacher.

Transactional Analysis Proper

When someone in Transactional Analysis therapy wants to improve communication, the focus of the therapy can be cognitively directed to the kinds of transactions that people commonly use with each other. Berne called this part of his system *Transactional Analysis (Proper)*, to distinguish it from the theory as a whole. There are three kinds of transactions: complementary, crossed, and ulterior.

A *complementary transaction* occurs when the stimulus by one person gets the expected response from the other. It is not the same as a compliment, although it may be one. With complementary transactions, the lines between the ego states are open and parallel. They may be Child to Child, as when two people are having fun together, or Adult to Adult, as in the straightforward exchange of information, or Parent to Parent, as when sharing common prejudices, or Parent to Child, when one asks for nurturing and receives it from another. The main value of complementary transactions is that communication remains open, although it may become static instead of dynamic.

A *crossed transaction* is an interpersonal problem when one person initiates a conversation and receives an unexpected response. "Let's go out and have some fun," could be the stimulus. The unexpected response might be, "You always want to go out." If in a group someone asks the time, and the response is, "Why don't you wear a watch of your own?" this is also a crossed transaction. Therapists sometimes cross transactions deliberately to change the subject or interrupt a game. This technique is sometimes used with clients who, without awareness, antagonize others and set themselves up for psychological "kicks" (Karpman, 1971, pp. 79–87). Some clients almost "ask for it." But, instead of responding critically, a transactional analyst might intervene with, "What kind of response do you expect when you look and talk as you're now doing?" This question is designed to hook the client's Adult and give the person permission to think. "What is the worse thing that could happen if you did or didn't do or say . . . ?" This question is meant to clarify the catastrophic expectations in the Child. To get to the archaic Child in another way the question might be, "How were you punished when you were young and what brought on the punishment? Go back to that scene and see it in the present moment."

Ulterior transactions are more complex. The verbal and the nonverbal messages are not congruent. "It's not what you say it's the way that you say it," usually refers to an ulterior transaction that has carried a critical message. Not all ulterior transactions are critical. During courtship, hinting often occurs and the hint given with a light touch or smile may develop into intimacy (Berne, 1970). Currently in many workplaces, light touches are not taken lightly but as sexual overtures or abuses. All psychological games involve ulterior transactions.

Mechanics of Change

The curative factors in Transactional Analysis are related to correcting ego state boundary problems, discovering old scripts and rewriting them, decreasing the intensity and frequency of games, and improving ways of transacting with others. According to Berne (1966), catalysts that therapists use to accelerate cures fall into eight categories. As a general rule, they are used in logical sequence. The first four are called *interventions*. Using these, the therapist decontaminates the Adult. The second four are *interpositions*. With these, the therapist interposes something between the patient's Adult and his/her other ego states in order to stabilize the patient's Adult and make it more difficult for him/her to slide into Parent or Child activity. All eight are used in certain situations, but not in others.

1. *Interrogate:* To ask questions to clarify points that will be of clinical value. Interrogation is used when something needs to be documented and the client's Adult is likely to respond, not the Parent or Child, or when the therapist needs to find out which ego state would respond to a particular question.

2. *Specify:* A statement made by the therapist to "fix" information in the client's mind that might be referred to later. It is used when the therapist believes the client might later deny that he/she said or meant something, or as preparation for an explanation that will follow.

3. *Confront:* The use of previous information to disconcert and point out inconsistencies for the purpose of cathecting the uncontaminated part of the client's Adult. It is well used when the client is playing *Stupid* and the therapist is not playing Persecuting games such as *Blemish* or *Now I've Got You,* or Rescuing games such as, *Why Don't You?*

4. *Explain:* To strengthen and decontaminate the client's Adult. Explanation is used when the Adult is listening and sometimes if the client is wavering between game playing and authenticity.

5. *Illustrate:* Used to stabilize the Adult. It may follow a successful confrontation if the Expressive Child, as well as the Adult, is likely to hear. It may also soften undesirable effects of confrontation as the Adult is likely to hear.

6. *Confirm:* Is used if the Adult is strong enough so that new information will not be used by the client's Parent against his/her inner Child or used by the Child against the therapist. It continues the process of reinforcing ego state boundaries.

7. *Interpret:* Is what the therapist may do when the client's Adult has joined forces and become cotherapist. Interpretation is related to the pathway of the Child. It is not used if it directly opposes the Parent or asks too much sacrifice from the Child or arouses too much fear of parental retaliation or desertion.

8. *Crystallize:* Is only used when each ego state is prepared for it. It is a statement from the therapist's Adult to the client's Adult that summarizes the client's positions and the available choices.

Common to All

Many therapists who do not use Transactional Analysis as their basic modality incorporate it successfully into other systems. Regardless of what theory is used, there are three categories of doing treatment that are basic to the mechanisms of change and are not unique to Transactional Analysis. Wolberg (1967) calls these categories supportive therapy, reeducative therapy, and reconstructive therapy (p. 617).

Supportive therapy is not to be confused with therapy coming from the Parent ego state, which may be patronizing. Supportive therapy can come from the transactional analyst's Adult who decides that support is necessary at a particular time and decides what kind of support to give. Sometimes just "being" with a client is more important than "doing." Supportive therapy can be countertherapeutic if it reinforces passive behavior and encourages avoidance of responsibility in clients. Berne was against supportive therapy except with particular cases, such as with schizophrenics orphaned in childhood (Berne, 1966). In these cases or in a sudden tragedy, the focus turns to reduction of pain and relief from debilitating anxiety. The current and sudden increase in AIDS calls for supportive therapy.

Reeducative therapy shows clients how to think, feel, and act in new ways. There are literally hundreds of techniques that can be used in reeducation, including assigned homework. Sometimes, I suggest that clients observe parents with children in a supermarket or on a playground, observe the ego state behavior of people waiting on customers in restaurants, and observe their own ego states when they attend a course, a party, or a meeting. Some clients are helped by taking a course in logic at a nearby adult center or community college; others by doing specific exercises in Transactional Analysis books and keeping a journal. Depending on the person and the problem, I might suggest reading a specific myth, fairy tale, children's story, novel, self-help book, or academic material that is related to the problem. However, before giving reading assignments I check to see whether clients enjoy reading. People with a history of dyslexia may prefer to observe situations instead of struggling with the printed page.

Reconstructive therapy often focuses on curing personality disorders caused by ego state boundary problems, destructive transactions with others, and erroneous belief systems. These problems, previously described, are treated in specific ways (M. James, 1974). In brief, lax ego state boundaries occur when energy is scattered and thinking highly confused. New boundaries are reconstructed if clients receive lots of positive attention for thinking and acting with the Adult and are not criticized when in confusion but encouraged to think clearly. The theory is based on the idea that what you "stroke" is what you get. A stroke is any form of recognition—a word, a smile, a gesture—and can be positive or negative. If clients receive positive strokes for their actual and potential strengths, they begin to think in more realistic terms and respond in healthier ways.

Rigid ego state boundaries are loosened up, not with aggressive confrontation but with empathetic listening in a non-threatening environment. Clients with rigid boundaries sometimes elicit confrontation from the therapist who wants them to "express feelings." The confrontation seldom works. More effective is saying something like, "Hmm," or, "That's a different point of view you're expressing"; then, without further conversation, switching the subject. When this procedure is used, clients do not feel the need to defend themselves. They have been listened to, instead of being argued with, as is often the case. Sometimes humor is used to poke holes in rigid boundaries that have excluded some parts of the personality, as will be seen in a case study at the end of this chapter. (I have a few Transactional Analysis books lying around my office, including one I wrote that pokes fun at me [M. James, 1973b].)

Lesions in the Child ego state are healed with awareness of the historical event that created the problem. Being kind, not confrontative, yet keeping clients aware of their sore spots and how they may need to be exposed so that healing can happen helps the reconstructive process until confrontation is no longer feared. For *decontamination*, the therapist using the Adult asks, "Do you have some data for your statement?" A client might answer, "I *feel*. . . ." The therapist then responds, "Feelings are OK and what do you *think*, what's your data for your statement?" And so it goes; decontamination of thinking and feeling is a lifelong task.

Research on Redecision and Self-Reparenting

There have been many developments in Transactional Analysis since it was first designed. Some of these developments have been tested, some only described. Readers are strongly encouraged to seek information on them from the International Transactional Analysis Association in San Francisco and from the database of the American Psychological Association.

One Transactional Analysis theory that has been carefully researched with experimental studies and control groups is Self-Reparenting. Self-Reparenting is so-called because clients decide for themselves what they need to restructure in their Parent ego states to supplement or override negative parent attributes that they incorporated during childhood at home and in school. This theory is based on the concept that many people who are mentally healthy, as well as those with serious psychological problems due to childhood abuse or other traumatic experiences, need encouragement and or limit setting that automatically comes from a healthy, internal parent. Muriel James (1974, 1981a, 1983, 1985) developed the theory with a very specific design and methodology for doing this. It uses both cognitive Adult and regressive Child work.

Research on its effectiveness involved four experimental groups, with four different leaders; all used the same process outline. There were also four matched control groups that did not go through the Self-Reparenting process. All eight groups were tested four times with pre- and midtesting and post- and follow-up testing to measure their self-concept and if and how it changed. A standardized test, the Interpersonal Checklist, was used. Results showed that in the Self-Reparenting groups, participants' perceptions of themselves came closer to their concepts of an ideal self and thus their perceptions of their parent figures changed and remained changed (Franklin, 1988).

Currently, Self-Reparenting is used in intensive group workshops and in private practice with clients who know they have Adult ego states and who want to understand and improve the quality of their lives by breaking free of negative pasts. It is also used in correctional institutions (Noriega, 1990), rehabilitation hospitals, and day treatment centers for people with personality disorders who need specific methods for self-growth and self-esteem.

A different theory incorporates Gestalt techniques into Transactional Analysis and is called redecision therapy. Redecision therapy is designed to release the Child from being script-bound because of negative experiences and injunctions. Developed by Mary and Robert Goulding (1979), it is an innovative theory and method blending Transactional Analysis with gestalt. It is primarily used in groups or during weekend marathons or longer workshops. Briefly, the therapist invites clients to give an example of something they want to change. Then, taking a strong leading role, the therapist takes a client back to an original scene to experience it emotionally and work through the stuck points.

One research project by McNeel (1982) on redecision therapy that was developed for a Ph.D. program focused on an intensive 3-day weekend workshop in which change in the participants was measured using with the standardized Personal Orientation Inventory and the Personal Growth checklist (a nonstandardized instrument designed by the researcher). Each participant was interviewed by skilled professionals who had been trained by the Gouldings and also served as observers during the workshop to keep track of contract work, impasse clarification, and completed redecisions. Although the researcher states that the theory was not proven, because control groups with other leaders were not used, follow-up with clients pointed to the effectiveness of the therapists.

Another project on redecision therapy involved a weeklong multiple family program with an experimental group of five families that used redecision work, and a control group of five families that did not. All participants were tested with the Family Environment Scale, the California Psychological Inventory, and the

Personal Orientation Inventory. These tests were given before, at the end of the program, and 2 months later. Families gained in cohesion, expressiveness, and independence. Individuals in the families increased in constructive dominance (Bader, 1976).

TREATMENT APPLICABILITY

An important point about treatment applicability is that Transactional Analysis is culturally relevant because it recognizes the importance of cultural scripts and historical analysis to work with the unique qualities in each person's ego states (J. James, 1983). It is applied universally as evidenced by the many Transactional Analysis training centers throughout the world. For example, in Kerala on the southern tip of India, as well as in New Delhi in the north, there are strong training and treatment programs. In Africa and the Middle East and South and Central America, programs are well established, as well as in New Zealand and Australia. China, Singapore, and Japan have professional Transactional Analysis organizations and almost every country in Europe has a number of highly trained transactional analysts. So do Canada and most states in the United States. Furthermore, an increasing number of Transactional Analysis books and journals are being written in different languages and translated into others.

In the United States, with its highly mobile and diverse population with different racial, ethnic, and religious backgrounds and languages, lifestyles, and values, transactional analysts are expanding their ways of thinking so that what they have to offer is relevant to a very diverse population.

Therapy at Any Age

In the past, psychotherapy was commonly thought of as only for the mentally ill and somewhat of a disgrace. People who have grown up with such a negative view of psychotherapy or counseling may not voluntarily seek this kind of help. The popularity of Transactional Analysis with relatively healthy people who wish to solve professional and personal problems, as well as its use with those who have severe emotional problems, has helped to change negative views. The elderly, in particular, are often fearful that a symtom of normal aging may carry a psychiatric label (Spar & LaRue, 1990). Consequently, they go only if a family member, caretaker, or physician insists.

Those who do seek therapy on their own usually do so because of an overwhelming sense of loneliness or fear of illness or death. One may come for grief work, another because a spouse abuses alcohol, and still another hoping to understand a grown child with a serious problem (Knight, 1992).

One woman, aged 82, lived many miles from me but was referred to me for a one-time phone consultation. Her husband had been murdered in front of her when their house was being robbed 4 months before her call to me. She had understandably fallen apart and was placed in a residential treatment center for seniors. She was very unhappy and fearful of the inadequate care she was getting. However, when she phoned she spoke with clarity that did not disguise the grief as she told me about her husband's muder and her situation. Then she asked, "Do I sound crazy to you?" "No," I answered, "you sound as if you have posttraumatic stress syndrome," and I explained what this meant. "Oh," she immediately responded, "Now I know what to tell people. I can get over that eventually, now that I know I'm not crazy."

Brief therapy using Transactional Analysis is often very effective for learning how to accept what cannot be changed. The therapeutic search for seniors is not to find "a new me" but to discover the meaning of life in general and of their own lives in particular. For this, supportive therapy is often needed, reeducation can be very useful, and restructuring personality may be much less appropriate.

Instead of seeking therapy, it is much more common for people over the age of 60 to seek educational opportunities related to specific problems such as memory loss. Under skilled leadership, class members may respond to each other much as they would in group therapy—giving advice or criticism, information and data, sympathy and empathy. The difference is that the focus of such classes is to provide information that can be therapeutic, whereas the focus of therapy groups is to provide psychotherapy, which can also be educational (Fielding, 1977).

At the other end of the age spectrum are children. Very few children who enter therapy are psychotic. Their problems are more often developmental disorders that are misunderstood (Silvers, 1984). They enter therapy because their parents or teachers are worried about their learning skills, or their lack of attention or other kinds of behavior, which can range from normal mischief to serious delinquency. Complaints about eating disorders, tics, stuttering, enuresis, anxiety, and night terrors are less frequent. Recurrent abdominal pain in some children prods some parents to seek medical treatment for them. Along with physical pain there are often psychological problems due to stressful events, such as the loss of a parent, unhappy incidents in school, and physical and sexual abuse. Transactional analysts who work with children and adolescents look for symptoms as well as listen to complaints (M. James, 1977). They look for potential family dysfunction and take appropriate steps to provide protection if there is brutality in the home or school. If personal-ity and behavioral disorders become more apparent and impulsive and aggressive behavior increases, the possibility of crisis is intensified. Strong intervention with hospitalization may be required (Jemerin & Philips, 1988).

CASE ILLUSTRATION

Following is a case of Lee, a man who had been hospitalized intermittently and for extended periods of time for about half of his 30 years. Lee was brought to me by a desperate, well-intentioned family who had exhausted traditional treatment opportunities and so were going to try Transactional Analysis as a last chance before another hospitalization, which, according to his psychiatrists (he had several simultaneously), might be permanent. His family could no longer afford private hospitals and did not want to put him in a state institution. They selected me because a family member had read *Born to Win* (M. James & Jongeward, 1971), and told Lee's parents about it, suggesting maybe I could help. Given his history, I told them I did not know if I could or not and would need to see him twice weekly for a month before deciding.

Fortunately, Lee's thinking during the first session was clear. He had been told a number of times that he was a paranoid schizophrenic. In addition to this clinical diagnosis, he described himself as a "marginal man that nobody liked," and one "who often suffered from severe anxiety attacks." This seemed like a clear statement and I respected it, as well as his rather formal-acting parents who had emigrated from another country where psychotherapy was not common. They had learned English when living in this country as graduate students, then returned to their homeland until Lee was 7 years old. At that time, they immigrated to the United States permanently.

The parents, much older than most, remained for half of the first session and seemed to genuinely care for Lee in spite of their very reserved and formal manner. They rejected the possibility of coming again as it did not fit their cultural background and family values. He was clearly the "identified patient" and, understandably, they were worried.

When not in the hospital, Lee lived with his parents. He had three older siblings whom he saw only occasionally. Lee reported that he had never had a friend, had been dropped from several community colleges, and was not able to hold a job for more than 1 day. His first psychotic break occurred at age 14 and for the next 15 years he had recurrent episodes that required long-term hospitalization as he deteriorated into chronic schizophrenia with severe disability and paranoid thinking. He frequently believed others were talking about him and ridiculing him. That was probably true as he did not know how to control his behavior or words in socially acceptable ways.

Lee said he was regularly taking 100 mg Thorazine (chlorpromazine), 50 mg of Stelazine (trifluoperazine hydrochloride), and 30 mg of Dalmane (flurazepam hydrochloride). I suggested that he limit himself to only one psychiatrist for medication and see his general practitioner, if needed, for other medical concerns. He was willing to do this and, later, was also willing to learn biofeedback and meditation to reduce his anxiety.

His difficulties had actually started long before adolescence and were probably directly related to his early school experience. When he first attended school in this country at age 7, no one spoke his native language, nor did they speak it in the neighborhood in which he lived. Although he eventually learned English, he was often called "crazy" in childhood because he did not understand it well. When I asked him what

might trigger an episode that could require hospitalization he replied immediately, "If somebody calls me crazy, I might go crazy." "What might you do?" I asked. "I don't know what I'd do, I've never done anything destructive, but I might try to break down a wall in a room."

His comment about the word "crazy" was an important clue to a serious lesion in his Child ego state. Clearly, the lesion would need to be protected for a while and healed later. First, his extremely lax ego state boundaries needed to be strengthened as they were only partially controlled with medication. This could help him avoid further hospitalization, protect his inner Child if he felt like exploding, and help to reduce his severe anxiety. After all, we would work directly on his personal disorders and interpersonal problems.

I decided that from the beginning I would treat him Adult to Adult and give him any information he wanted about theory, techniques, and the process we would be using and why we would be using them. By ignoring his inappropriate behavior in the first stage of treatment and treating him as a person capable of thinking and taking responsibility, I was certain his lax ego state boundaries would become stronger. In addition, I planned to use specific verbal and nonverbal encouraging transactions from my Adult to his Child that he might experience as coming from a nurturing parent.

As an educator as well as a therapist, I often assess the age and manner in which a client may be developmentally stuck by trauma or conditioning. I then design positive transactions, nonverbal as well as verbal, to reach that person's inner child at the age just *preceding* the time when things went wrong. I did this with Lee. He did not have any psychotic breaks while in treatment, although at times his symptoms were occasionally severe with agitated excitement, conceptual disorganization, and incoherent speech. Sometimes he gave absurd or irrelevant answers to questions and intermingled his ideas in ways that made them impossible to understand. When this occurred, the use of the blackboard and three circles to show how he was not controlling his ego state boundaries was effective.

During his third therapy session Lee complained about being mentally "sick." I asked how sick he thought he was. He responded, "About 90%." I suggested that as he increased his percentage of mental health, his 90% illness would decrease. He liked my responding with an answer that included percentages. Eight months later Lee had cut out Thorazine and greatly reduced Stelazine and announced that he was 50% well. When he finally terminated, he evaluated himself as "almost 90% well."

Another time percentages came up was when Lee complained that he was "born unlucky." I asked him, "What percent 'born unlucky?' What were you 'born' with?" After a few complaints, he began to speak of his positive inherited characteristics, including physical health, pleasing appearance, and intelligence and claimed that tests showed he had an IQ of 130. This fit my intuitive assessment. Next, after expressing pleasure with his genetic inheritance, he took personal credit for his strong determination to get well. After this, Lee permanently dropped the "I was born unlucky" self-assessment.

Within 3 months he had established some long-range goals and during the next 3 years, seldom lost sight of them These goals were: to sleep without pills, be able to hold a good job, make friends, and get married. Many contracts were necessary so that he could reach his goals, and they were designed with the contract questions discussed earlier in this chapter. "What would you need to do to achieve your goal?" and "What are you willing to do?"

Lee had always lived with his parents when not in the hospital and all was not smooth at home. He spent most of his time sleeping and in delusional thinking. However, in 8 months he was able to move into his own apartment, which his parents paid for, and occasionally used a housekeeping service as he had no knowledge about how to care for his physical environment. He then contracted to do one thing different each weekend that might lead to developing some friends. One of his first so-called "friends" wanted to borrow a large sum of money from him to establish a business. He recognized what was going on and began to learn about games.

He also wanted to work but was fired from his first job for asking too many questions inappropriately. I recommended he start with a volunteer job to get some work experience and also sign up for some vocational training classes. He agreed with both suggestions. Then he became discouraged and very anxious and considered dropping out but did not. Like many, he sometimes "forgot" his contracts and needed encouragement. I explained how therapy is like learning a new language, or learning how to walk. When learning a new language, people often become frustrated and impatient and want to quit. If their motivation is high enough, they continue to study in spite of their negative feelings and eventually master their new skills. Children also become frustrated when learning to walk. They revert to lying down and screaming or sucking their thumbs passively. Then they get up and try walking again. This same process, I told Lee, often occurs when learning something new. Although resistance to change is normal, so is the desire to change and grow.

One night, Lee went out for dinner with his family and was confronted about his silly laughter. This was very upsetting to him so I explained how children laugh, sometimes just to be silly and for the joy of life, and how grown-ups sometimes disapprove of, or lose, this kind of spontaneity. He said he wanted a contract to be able to laugh at the right time and in the right way and not be ridiculed. This was a good social contract so I explained laughter and demonstrated how it could come from any ego state. I also explained how people of different cultures laughed at different things. This interested him greatly and occasionally he would bring in a joke or story to therapy for us to laugh about.

Lee strengthened his ego state boundaries in many ways so that he could usually cathect his Adult at will. The Adult-leveling position (Ernst, 1968) was an important technique that he learned. It can be used by anyone who fears losing control over his/her behavior, or whose feelings are so overwhelming that he/she cannot think, and who wishes to have the Adult as executive of the personality for problem-solving purposes. When learning the Adult-leveling position, a client is instructed to sit in a relatively straight chair with back straight but not rigid, with both feet flat on the floor, arms uncrossed and hands resting on one's legs with palms up, and head straight, not tipped to the side. The chin must be parallel to the floor, neither up nor down. No matter what the stress of the moment is, this technique inevitably decathects the Child and puts the Adult in the executive position. Lee learned to use this technique and it was very effective for him.

To increase his social skills, a 15-minute "conversation time" was structured into the therapy session once or twice a month. In preparation, for this we would both read the same news article in a current magazine and talk about it. Sometimes I would role-play various kinds of people in various situations so that he could experiment with various ways of transacting. Then, drawing two sets of stacked circles on the blackboard, he or I would draw lines between them to illustrate the transactions that had just occurred.

After 1 year, Lee was able to participate in several 1-day workshops with specific themes such as learning how to overcome procrastination. After 2 years, he was able to participate successfully in a 5-day workshop designed for increasing self-esteem through decontamination of the Adult.

I asked him once whether he thought our style of teamwork was effective for him. He immediately responded, "Oh, yes. You're honest, you work hard and you like me." I thanked him and pointed out that these qualities he saw in me also described him very well. By this time, he was comfortable in therapy discussing masturbation, contraceptives, dating, and other intimate sexual matters. His medication was greatly reduced. Progress was further demonstrated when he was called "crazy" in his adult vocational school by another student who had done the same years earlier when he was in Lee's third-grade class. Although Lee resented this, he did not lose control as he might have in the past. Instead he replied very strongly, "Maybe I was at one time; not any more! Go get lost." As he told me about this, he realized that his lesion about being defined as "crazy" was healed. It was one of those special moments.

A different kind of episode that throws light onto Lee's treatment had occurred about 4 months earlier when he was stressed out at school with examinations and not getting enough sleep. One day when he came to therapy he said suspiciously, "I think you threw rocks on the roof of my house last night to wake me up, and you pinched the dog's tail to make it bark." I decided to confront him by joining him in his delusioned thinking. Exaggerating my tone of voice and gestures I agreed, "Yes, I got up in the middle of the night and drove 30 miles to where you live and found some rocks to throw and pinched the dog so it would bark." With that, he exploded with a healthy belly laugh. That was the beginning. It became important for us to laugh each session. Sometimes the laughter would be in response to something funny, sometimes just for the fun of laughing.

Lee terminated after 4 years. He had reached his goals and had developed several strong friendships, was dating, and had a job and few overt symptoms. Since then, he comes in once a year for "mental health checkup." At one such checkup, I asked him why he thought he had made so much progress. "Learning to laugh," he said, "that was *the* most important. Now, for the first time in my life I have friends, even a girlfriend, and even a job. Now isn't that funny!" And we both laughed with joy. Silly, hebephrenic laughter? I say not, merely relaxed and human.

Berne (1966) once said, "Psychotherapists are parapeople but they are entitled to laugh occasionally just like real people—only for a few seconds, however, and then they must get back to work" (p. 338). For me, a few seconds is not enough. I prefer the words of the philosopher, Martin Buber, which are on a poster that hangs over my sewing machine: "There are those who suffer greatly and they go their way full of suffering. But if they meet someone whose face is bright with laughter he can quicken them with gladness. And it is no small thing to quicken a human being." Courageously, Lee had found his natural urge to enjoy life that came from the inner core of the self and also learned how to connect with others in appropriate ways so that they too enjoyed him. No small task!

SUGGESTIONS FOR FURTHER READING

Berne, E. (1961). *Transactional Analysis in psychotherapy.* New York: Grove. The seminal work of the founder of Transactional Analysis.

Berne, E. (1966). *Principles of group treatment.* New York: Grove. A survey of the procedures for establishing group therapy and a comparison of four commonly used methods.

Cartman, S. (1968). Fairy tales and script drama analysis. *Transactional Analysis Bulletin, VII* (26). How drama triangles lead to erroneous views of life.

James, J. (1973). The game plan. *Transactional Analysis Journal, 3*(4), 14–17. Demonstrates how ulterior transactions lead to psychological games and primary or secondary payoffs.

James, M. (1983). Cultural scripts: Historical events versus historical interpretation. *Transactional Analysis Journal, 13*(4), 217–223. Understanding cultural and subcultural scripts of families and organizations facilitates psychotherapy.

James, M. (1986). Diagnosis and treatment of ego state boundaries. *Transactional Analysis Journal, 16,* 188–196. A Transactional Analyst's approach to the diagnosis and treatment of personality and behavioral problems.

James, M., & Jongeward, D. (1971). *Born to win: Transactional Analysis with Gestalt exercises.* Reading, MA: Addison-Wesley. The classic overview of theory and practice with brief case illustrations and exercises.

Zalcman, M. (1990). Game analysis and racket analysis: Overview, critique, and future developments. *Transactional Analysis Journal, 20*(1), 4–19. Psychological games become habitaul patterns which in turn become rackets to exploit others.

For further information: Contact the International Transactional Analysis Association, 450 Pacific Avenue, Suite 250, San Francisco, California 94133-4640.

REFERENCES

Adler, A. (1954). *Understanding human nature.* New York: Fawcett Premier.

Allen, J., & Allen, B. (1968). Conflict and desynchronization. *Transactional Analysis Journal, 8,* 127–129.

Allport, G. (1950). *The individual and his religion.* New York: Macmillan.

American Psychiatric Association. (1994). *Diagnostic and statistical manual of mental disorders* (4th ed.). Washington, DC: Author.

Bader, E. (1976). *Redecisions in family therapy: A study of change in an intensive family therapy workshop.* Unpublished doctoral thesis, California School of Professional Psychology, Alameda.

Berne, E. (1961). *Transactional Analysis in psychotherapy.* New York: Grove.

Berne, E. (1964). *Games people play.* New York: Grove.

Berne, E. (1966). *Principles of group treatment.* New York: Grove.

Berne, E. (1968). *A layman's guide to psychiatry and psychoanalysis* (3rd ed.). New York: Simon & Schuster.

Berne, E. (1969). The basic value standard. *Transactional Analysis Bulletin, 8,* 7–8.

Berne, E. (1970). *Sex in human loving.* New York: Simon & Schuster.

Berne, E. (1972). *What do you say after you say hello?* New York: Grove.

Berne, E. (1977). *Intuition and ego states: The origins of Transactional Analysis* (Paul McCormick, Ed.). New York: Harper & Row.

Clarkson, P. (1992). *Transactional Analysis psychotherapy.* London and New York: Tavistock/Routledge.

Cornell, W. (1986). Setting the therapeutic stage: The initial sessions. *Transactional Analysis Journal, 16,* 4–10.

Cousins, N. (1976). Anatomy of an illness (as perceived by the patient). *New England Journal of Medicine,* 1458–1463.

Crossman, P. (1963). Permission and protection. *Transactional Analysis Bulletin, 5,* 152–153.

Dusay, J. (1977). *Egograms.* New York: Harper & Row.

Ernst, F. (1968). *Activity of listening* (1st ed.). Vallejo, CA: Golden Gate Foundation for Group Treatment.

Federn, P. (1952). *Ego psychology and the psychoses.* New York: Basic Books.

Fielding, E. (1977). Therapeutic education for older adults. In *Techniques in Transactional Analysis for psychotherapists and counselors* (pp. 420–430). Reading, MA: Addison-Wesley.

Frankl, V. (1975). *The unconscious god.* New York: Simon & Schuster.

Franklin, M. (1988). *Changes in concepts of self and parent figures in self-reparenting groups.* Unpublished doctoral thesis, California School of Professional Psychology, Alameda.

Freud, S. (1927). The future of an illusion. In *Standard edition of the complete works of Sigmund Freud* (Vol. 21). London: Hogarth.

Freud, S. (1949). *An outline of psychoanalysis.* New York: W. W. Norton.

Goulding, R., & Goulding, M. (1979). *Changing lives through redecision therapy.* New York: Brunner/Mazel.

James, J. (1973). The game plan. *Transactional Analysis Journal, 3,* 14–17.

James, J. (1976). Positive payoffs after games. *Transactional Analysis Journal, 6,* 259–262.

James, J. (1983). Cultural consciousness: the challenge to TA. *Transactional Analysis Journal, 13,* 207–216.

James, J., & Schlesinger, I. (1987). *Are you the one for me?* Reading, MA: Addison-Wesley.

James, M. (1973a). *Born to love.* Reading, MA: Addison-Wesley.

James, M. (1973b). *Transactional Analysis for moms and dads.* Reading, MA: Addison-Wesley.

James, M. (1974). Self-reparenting theory and practice. *Transactional Analysis Journal, 4,* 32–39.

James, M. (1977). *Techniques in Transactional Analysis for physiotherapists and counselors.* Reading, MA: Addison-Wesley.

James, M. (1979). Therapy doesn't always hurt: Laugh therapy. *Transactional Analysis Journal, 9,* 244–250.

James, M. (1981a). *Breaking free: Self-reparenting for a new life.* Reading, MA: Addison-Wesley.

James, M. (1981b). TA in the 80's: The inner core and the human spirit. *Transactional Analysis Journal, 11,* 54–64.

James, M. (1983). Cultural scripts: Historical events versus historical interpretation. *Transactional Analysis Journal, 13,* 217–223.

James, M. (1985). *It's never too late to be happy: The psychology of self-reparenting.* Reading, MA: Addison-Wesley.

James, M. (1986). Diagnosis and treatment of ego state boundaries. *Transactional Analysis Journal, 16,* 188–196.

James, M., & James, J. (1978). Games parents play. In L. E. Arnold (Ed.), *Helping parents help their children* (pp. 65–82). New York: Brunner/Mazel.

James, M., & James, J. (1991). *Passion for life: Psychology and the human spirit.* New York: Penguin/NAL.

James, M., & Jongeward, D. (1971). *Born to win: Transactional Analysis with Gestalt exercises.* Reading, MA: Addison-Wesley.

James, M., & Savary, L. (1977). *A new self: Self therapy with Transactional Analysis.* Reading, MA: Addison-Wesley.

Jemerin, J., & Philips I. (1988). Changes in in-patient child psychiatry: Consequences and recommendations. *Journal of American Academy of Child and Adolescent Psychiatry, 27,* 397–403.

Jones, E. (1953). *The life and work of Sigmund Freud: Vol. 1, 1856–1900, the formative years and the great discoveries.* New York: Basic Books.

Jung, C. (1963). *Memories, dreams, reflections.* New York: Pantheon.

Kahler, T., & Capers, H. (1974). The miniscript. *Transactional Analysis Journal, 4,* 26–42.

Karpman, S. (1968). Fairy tales and script drama analysis. *Transactional Analysis Bulletin, 7,* 39–43.

Karpman, S. (1971). Options. *Transactional Analysis Journal, 1,* 79–87.

Knight, B. (1992). *Older adults in psychotherapy: Case histories.* Newbury Park, CA: Sage.

Mahler, M., Pine, F., & Bergman, A. (1975). *The psychological birth of an infant.* New York: Basic Books.

McClendon, R., & Kadis, L. (1983). *Chocolate pudding and other approaches to intensive multiple family therapy.* Palo Alto, CA: Science & Behavior Books.

McNeel, J. (1982). *Redecisions in psychotherapy: A study of the results of an intensive weekend group workshop.* Unpublished doctoral thesis, California School of Professional Psychology, Alameda.

Noriega, G. (1990). *What can you expect from me if you think I am "incorrigible"? Self-reparenting: A technique of TA used with female delinquents in jail.* Unpublished master's thesis, Universidad Nacional Autonoma de Mexico, Mexico City.

Penfield, W. (1952a). Memory mechanisms. *Archives of Neurology and Psychiatry, 67,* 178–198.

Silvers, L. (1984). *The misunderstood child: A guide to parents of learning disabled children.* New York: McGraw-Hill.

Spar, J., & LaRue, A. (1990). *A concise guide to geriatric psychiatry.* Washington DC. American Psychiatric Press.

Stewart, I., & Joines, V. (1987). *TA today: A new introduction to Transactional Analysis.* Chapel Hill, NC: Life Space.

Wolberg, L. (1967). *The technique of psychotherapy* (2nd ed.). New York: Grune & Stratton.

Zalcman, M. (1990). Game analysis and racket analysis: Overview, critique, and future developments. *Transactional Analysis Journal, 20,* 4–19.

10

The Family Therapies

NADINE J. KASLOW
MARIANNE P. CELANO

BACKGROUND OF
THE APPROACH

Historians, anthropologists, sociologists, and religious scholars have acknowledged the centrality of the family unit since the beginning of civilization. There is a historical precedent for community leaders to aid a family when an individual member is distressed. However, only during the past century has there been documented use of education, counseling, or therapy to help the family unit. This section traces influential activities in the development of family therapy during the past century.

The roots of family therapy date to the late 1800s and early 1900s and are found in the social work, marriage and family life education, and marriage counseling movements (Broderick & Schrader, 1991; Thomas, 1992). From its inception, social work has considered the family the unit of concern, and social workers have played key roles in the practice of family therapy. The marriage and family life education movement provided preventive classes for individuals, typically women, interested in learning about marriage, parenting, and family life. These students often discussed their own relationships and were offered guidance, prompting the family life approach to change its didactic focus to a more practical approach. These early efforts at informal counseling paved the way for more formal marital counseling, conducted by professionals trained in marital counseling. Many leaders in the marriage and family life education movement later served as pioneers of marital counseling.

Marriage counseling centers were established in the 1930s, the most notable being the Marriage Council of Philadelphia headed by Emily Mudd. Similar developments were afoot in Europe, including the establishment of the Marriage Guidance Council in Great Britain under David and Vera Mace. During the 1930s and 1940s, the field became increasingly professionalized, as evidenced by the emergence of two organizations, the National Council of Family Relations (NCFR) for family life educators and the American Association of Marriage Counselors (AAMC) for marital counselors. Both organizations remain active today, although the AAMC, renamed the American Association of Marriage and Family Therapy (AAMFT) in the 1970s, expanded its goals and redefined its membership criteria. Family therapy also has origins in clinical psychiatry, a field historically devoted to treating individuals' psychopathology from a psychodynamic perspective. Many early family theorists, who had extensive psychoanalytic training, began including family members in the treatment. This change reflected their concern that the patient's symptoms partially were maintained by dysfunctional family interactional patterns and that individual therapy was insufficient to change these patterns.

The evolution of family theory also can be traced to the application of general systems and communication theories to understanding human interactions (e.g., Bateson, 1972; Parsons & Bales, 1955). Many family therapy models are systemic and underscore the interrelatedness and reciprocal influences of the individual, the family, and the social system.

Early research undergirding family theories and therapy was conducted with schizophrenic adults and their families (Guerin, 1976). This research stemmed from clinicians' observations of the relation between family interactional patterns and the behaviors of schizophrenic individuals. The seminal paper linking family communication patterns to the development of psychopathology in a family member was titled "Toward a Theory of Schizophrenia" (Bateson, Jackson, Haley, & Weakland, 1956). Using anthropological methods and social systems theory, these authors asserted that the essential family determinant in the development of schizophrenia was "double bind" communications, two or more contradictory messages from the same person in which a response is required by the recipient and failure to please the presenter is guaranteed. The double-bind concept has been reworked and now is considered more pertinent to the maintenance, rather than the etiol-

ogy, of schizophrenic symptoms. In addition to the aforementioned researchers and their colleague Virginia Satir, at the Mental Research Institute (MRI) in Palo Alto, other family therapy founders studied schizophrenics and their families: (1) Theodore Lidz, at Johns Hopkins and then at Yale, and his coworkers Stephen Fleck, Alice Cornelison, and Ruth Lidz; (2) Murray Bowen, at the Menninger Clinic in Topeka and with Lyman Wynne at the National Institute of Mental Health (NIMH) in Washington, DC; (3) Ivan Boszormenyi-Nagy, at Eastern Pennsylvania Psychiatric Institute in Philadelphia; and (4) Carl Whitaker, at Emory in Atlanta and later in Madison, Wisconsin, and his colleagues in Atlanta, Thomas Malone and John Warkentin. Other leaders at this time were John Bell, one of the first to conduct sessions with all family members, and Christian Midelfort, who authored the first book solely devoted to family therapy, *The Family in Psychotherapy* (1957).

Simultaneous with the above developments, clinicians feeling frustrated in their individual contacts with children turned their focus to the family. Nathan Ackerman, a child psychiatrist and psychoanalyst, asserted that the family is the proper unit of diagnosis and treatment. His paper, "Family Diagnosis: An Approach to the Preschool Child" (Ackerman & Sobel, 1950), has been considered by some to be the founding document of the family therapy movement (F. W. Kaslow, 1982). Some early family research was conducted in child guidance clinics. For example, Salvador Minuchin and colleagues at the Philadelphia Child Guidance Center studied family therapy with delinquents and low-socioeconomic-status families (Minuchin, Montalvo, Guerney, Rosman, & Schumer, 1967) and psychosomatic families (Minuchin, Rosman, & Baker, 1978).

The second wave of the family therapy movement (1962–1977) (Broderick & Schrader, 1991) began with the publication of *Family Process*, the first family therapy journal. Training centers were established throughout the country. Emphasis was placed on certification and licensure, with AAMFT recognized as the official accrediting agency for training programs. This decade witnessed the development of competing schools of thought and training models and an increasing focus on outcome studies and interactional research. The end of the second wave was marked by the establishment of the American Family Therapy Academy (AFTA) in 1977, under the leadership of Bowen. Unlike its multidisciplinary predecessors, AFTA initially was composed primarily of psychiatrist family therapists; it has evolved into a more multidisciplinary organization. There remains today a mercurial relationship between AAMFT and AFTA. At times, the relationship is collaborative; at other times, there is tension between the two organizations.

The most recent chapter in the history of family therapy (post-1977) encompasses a number of significant changes. First, in addition to the development of a broader range of models of family theory and therapy (for review, see Gurman & Kniskern, 1991), integrative models borrowing from various family theories and other schools of therapy have been developed (e.g., Duhl & Duhl, 1981; Feldman, 1992; Gurman, 1981; F. W. Kaslow, 1981; Kirschner & Kirschner, 1986; Pinsof, 1983). Second, there has been increased empirical verification of family therapy tenets and the efficacy of family interventions, made possible by the development of reliable and valid assessment measures and interactional coding schemas, and by the increased collaboration between scientists and practitioners. The family psychology movement, a division of the American Psychological Association, has played a pivotal role in the refinement of family research. Most relevant to the present chapter is the empirical support for the effectiveness of family therapy compared to control and alternative conditions in enhancing family interactions and decreasing symptoms (for review, see Hazelrigg, Cooper, & Borduin, 1987). Third, recent years have witnessed the internationalization of the field, with the development of the International Family Therapy Association and the publication of materials on international family therapy (e.g., F. W. Kaslow, 1982). Family therapy in the United States has been influenced increasingly by the clinical and theoretical developments throughout the world, most notably the Milan School (e.g., Selvini-Palazzoli, Boscolo, Cecchin, & Prata, 1978). Fourth, ethical guidelines specifically for conducting family therapy (American Association for Marriage and Family Therapy, 1988; Doherty & Boss, 1991) and family research (e.g., N. J. Kaslow & Gurman, 1985) have been developed. Emphasis on consumer protection also is evidenced by the passage of state licensure and certification bills for the practice of marital and family therapy. Fifth, increased attention has been paid to specialization in such areas as sex therapy and divorce mediation, which require additional credentials. Sixth, the field has become more sensitive to diversity in families, with particular emphasis on ethnicity (e.g., McGoldrick, Pearce, & Giordano, 1982), race (e.g., Boyd-Franklin, 1989), and gender (e.g., Goodrich, Rampage, Ellman, & Halstead, 1988; Walters, Carter, Papp, & Silverstein, 1988). Finally, the field has undergone a shift in emphasis regarding the role of psychotropic medication in treatment, with an increased acceptance of adjunctive psychopharmacological treatments for alleviating symptoms associated with psychiatric disorders.

THE CONCEPT OF THE FAMILY

Family theory has viewed the family as the primary unit of focus, departing from the traditional view that dysfunctional behavior primarily is influenced by individual characteristics, such as personality. Recently, attempts have been made to integrate individual personality development, family development, and the sociocultural context within which the individual and family are embedded (Feldman, 1992).

The nuclear family traditionally was defined as a group of people, connected by blood or legal bonds, who share a residence. This definition has evolved to include groups of people perceived to be a family, united by marriage, blood, residence sharing, and/or adoption. Stepfamilies, cohabitating heterosexual or gay couples, foster families, and commuter marriages represent variations of the modern family. Despite changes in the structure of family systems, the family's primary function continues to be mutual exchange among family members to meet the physical and emotional needs of each individual.

General systems theory, which emerged from the biological sciences, provides the theoretical underpinnings for major family therapy models. A *system* is a group of elements interacting with one another (von Bertalanffy, 1968). Paradoxically, family units continually change and advance toward greater levels of organization and functioning (anamorphosis), simultaneously self-regulating to maintain equilibrium, or *homeostasis*. The balance between change and stability enables the family to function adaptively throughout the family's and individual's life cycle.

Family systems continuously exchange information via *feedback loops*, circular patterns of responses in which there is a return flow of information within the system. *Positive feedback* increases deviation from the steady state, enabling the family to evolve to a new state. However, too much amplification of the deviation may destroy the system. For exam-

ple, a fight between marital partners simultaneously may increase intimacy and self-definition, or the fight may escalate out of control. *Negative feedback* counteracts deviations in the system to restore homeostasis. For example, a child may become symptomatic after his/her sibling becomes less overinvolved in the marital relationship.

As these examples suggest, family interactions reflect *circular causality*, in which single events are viewed as both cause and effect, and reciprocally related with no beginning or end to the causal sequence of events. According to the structural functionalism that dominated American social science during the 1950s and 1960s (Parsons & Bales, 1955), families are viewed in terms of *structure* and function. Structure refers to the family organization, the way in which the subsystems are arranged, and the power hierarchy or chain of command. The key structural property of the family unit is its *wholeness*; namely, the whole is greater than the sum of its parts. The family unit comprises interdependent *subsystems* that carry out distinctive functions to maintain themselves and sustain the system as a whole. Each individual is his/her own subsystem. Each family member belongs to several subsystems simultaneously, providing the basis for differential relationships with other family members. Subsystems can be formed by generation (parental or sibling subsystem), gender (mother–daughter dyad), interest (shared hobbies), and/or function (caretakers). The family unit also is a subsystem, as it interacts with the extended family, larger community, and outside world.

Subsystems are delineated and separated by *boundaries*, which protect the subsystem's integrity while allowing interaction between subsystems. Boundaries can be more or less permeable and adapt to the changing needs of the family system. Impairments in adaptive functioning arise if boundaries are too *rigid*, not allowing adequate communication between subsystems, or too *diffuse*, allowing too much communication with other subsystems. In an extreme form, rigid boundaries lead to *disengagement*, where family members are isolated from one another and function autonomously. Diffuse boundaries are associated with *enmeshment*, where family members are overinvolved in each others' lives. Family systems also have boundaries that regulate transactions with the outside world. An *open system* has relatively permeable boundaries, permitting interaction with the outside community without compromising the integrity of the family system. Conversely, a *closed system* has relatively rigid boundaries, minimizing contact with the outside world.

To maintain their structure, family systems have *rules*, operating principles enabling them to perform the tasks of daily living. Some rules are negotiated openly and overt, whereas others are unspoken and covert. Healthy families have rules that are consistent, clearly stated, and fairly enforced over time yet can be adapted to the changing developmental needs of the family.

Each family member plays a number of *roles*, exhibiting a predictable set of behaviors associated with their social position. Role behavior may be influenced by one's family of origin, gender, and generation within the nuclear family. Roles may include that of spouse, parent, child, sibling, victim, caretaker, martyr, scapegoat, and hero. Optimally, family members' roles are negotiated to accommodate the developmental stages of the participants and to eliminate dysfunctional roles (e.g., victim). According to the structural functionalist view, all behavior (e.g., roles, symptoms, and communication patterns) serves a purpose. For example, an individual's maladaptive behavior may return the family to homeostasis. Specifically, an adolescent with an eating disorder increasingly may become symptomatic following graduation, leading to increased family involvement and concern about his/her transition to college. The eating disorder may slow down the separation–individuation process, which the family perceives as threatening to their integrity. While this symptom may return the family to a homeostatic state, it impedes the adolescent's individual development. However, the symptom may enable the family to receive psychotherapeutic help to cope with the family developmental crisis associated with launching a child.

Family Development

Family development refers to the growth of individual family members; changes in the structure, tasks, and interactional process of the family unit over time; and the reciprocally related subcycles involving the marital–parental couple, the sibship, and the extended family. Passage through family life cycle stages includes continuous and discontinuous change. Each stage qualitatively is different; developmental tasks are negotiated in new ways. Successful passage through these stages depends on the effectiveness of developmentally appropriate negotiations of tasks and stressors. A family member's symptom may reflect the family's difficulty moving from one developmental stage to the next (Haley, 1973). Interactions at any family life cycle stage are influenced by interactions at earlier stages, and thus dysfunctional resolution at one stage increases the likelihood of further impairments in the family's functioning.

Carter and McGoldrick (1988) delineated six stages of the American *family life cycle*, a model that acknowledges the confluence of situational, developmental, and family-of-origin (historical) stressors. The first stage, between families, encompasses the unattached young adult's tasks of separation– individuation, the development of close relationships, and the establishment of an identity linked to one's educational pursuits, job, or career. The second stage, the joining of families through marriage, describes the development of the new marital dyad and the realignment of relationships with one's family of origin and social support system to include the spouse. In the third stage, the family with young children adjusts the marital bond to include children, incorporate parenting roles, and redefine relationships with extended family to include grandparents. In the fourth stage, the family with adolescents flexibly supports the adolescents' drive for autonomy and self-definition. The adults redirect their attention to their own personal and professional development and often become caretakers for their parents. The fifth stage is characterized by the parents launching children and moving on. Parents support their young adult children's physical separation from the family, renegotiate the marital system as a more intimate dyad, develop more egalitarian relationships with their adult children, reorganize the family system to include in-laws and grandchildren, and cope with failing health and death of parents. In the sixth stage, the family in later life, the couple explores new family and social role options and addresses loss and mortality, and the adult children express their respect for their parents' wisdom and experience. Carter and McGoldrick (1988) underscore the variability in the family life cycle associated with different sociocultural contexts, characterizing distinctive features of the life cycles of low-income and professional families, and families of various ethnic, racial, and religious backgrounds. Others have described the life cycle of single-parent families (Hill, 1986), remarried and stepfamilies (Visher & Visher, 1987), and the roles of children and adolescents in the family life cycle (e.g., Combrinck-Graham, 1988).

Normal Family Functioning

What is a normal or healthy family? The answer to this question is complex and depends on the theoretical perspective utilized. Family theorists differ in their views of the applicability of the construct of normality to individual family members, family units, or a combination of the two. As Wamboldt and Reiss (1991) have asked: Can families be described as normal if one member is symptomatic? Conversely, can an individual be viewed as normal if he/she grows up in a severely dysfunctional family yet functions adaptively? Normal families may evidence (1) asymptomatic family functioning (absence of symptoms of dysfunction), (2) optimal family functioning (successful according to the values of a given conceptual paradigm), (3) average family functioning (fits a typical or prevalent pattern and falls in the normal range), and/or (4) transactional family processes (adaptation over the course of the family life cycle to a particular socioecological context) (Walsh, 1982).

Some authors (e.g., Satir & Baldwin, 1983) depict healthy families as those composed of healthy individuals. According to these authors, human beings basically are good and strive for growth. Health may be evident in several functional domains: physical, spiritual, contextual, nutritional, interactional, sensual, emotional, and intellectual. Just as the various components of each individual's functioning contribute to his/her overall sense of self, each family member's sense of self contributes to the overall level of health in the family system.

Utilizing a systemic perspective, clinical researchers have developed schemata (e.g., Epstein, Bishop, & Baldwin, 1982;

Beavers, 1977; Olson, Sprenkle, & Russell, 1979; Reiss, 1981) and portraits (e.g., Whitaker & Bumberry, 1988) of healthy family functioning. The pattern of characteristics indicative of healthy functioning changes across the family life cycle (Olson et al., 1983) and depends on the family's sociocultural context. Cohesion, change, and communication are the key dimensions along which family functioning is characterized. Family cohesion refers to the level of emotional bonding among family members and the commitment family members have to the unit. Optimal families are cohesive, with a clear, yet flexible structure. Generational and individual boundaries are mutually understood, allowing a sense of closeness and belonging to coexist with respect for the privacy of the individual and the subsystems. Healthy families encourage age-appropriate autonomy for all members, express a range of well-modulated positive and negative emotions, are supportive of and empathically attuned to one another, maintain a sense of humor even in the face of adversity, and are open to receiving feedback from each other. Family members share beliefs, enabling them to transcend their immediate reality and address existential concerns such as meaning/purpose of life, self-definition, and mortality. These transcendent values are transmitted across generations, thus connecting a nuclear family with its past and future and with the larger social environment. Finally, these families have a world view that is optimistic and they are cognizant of their place in the world.

Change refers to the degree of flexibility within the family system. Healthy families adapt their power structure, role relationships, and rules in response to situational and developmental demands and new information from the environment. Relatively equal power is the norm for the marital dyad. A clear power hierarchy exists between the parental subsystem and the children, and control and authority dynamics are clear to all family members. The power dynamics change throughout the family life cycle, with power becoming more shared as the children mature. Standards for controlling behavior are reasonable, and there is ample opportunity for modification of these standards utilizing skilled negotiation and effective problem solving. All family functions are filled such that members are not overburdened with too many roles, and there is flexibility in roles played. These families recognize when they need community assistance.

In the communication domain, healthy families communicate clearly and effectively about their feelings, as well as about practical matters. There is congruence between the content and process of the communications (*contextual clarity*), such that few double-binding messages occur. For example, a verbal expression of loving feelings is communicated in a caring tone, with physical gestures consistent with the positive feeling being expressed. This is in contrast to a double-bind communication in which a family member verbalizes his/her loving feelings in a hostile tone of voice, with minimal eye contact, and a physical distancing.

THE PATHOLOGICAL OR DYSFUNCTIONAL FAMILY

Historically, psychiatric diagnoses indicating pathology have been applied to individuals. Many family theorists argue that psychiatric nomenclature is less relevant in understanding family pathology than are family interaction patterns. The gap between the psychiatric viewpoint and family systems theories is evidenced by the lack of a family classification system in the fourth edition of the *Diagnostic and Statistical Manual of Mental Disorders* (DSM-IV; American Psychiatric Association, 1994). Despite this lack, an individual's family situation and background have bearing on all five axes of clinical diagnoses (Fleck, 1982). Some argue for including a classification of family functioning in future revisions of the DSM (e.g., Frances, Clarkin, & Perry, 1984). Unfortunately, no comprehensive system of family diagnoses and associated recommended treatments has been accepted widely and only recently have efforts been made to develop a classification of family diagnosis (e.g., Beavers & Hampson, 1990). Further, debate continues in the family therapy community regarding the value of developing a family diagnostic schema and of incorporating such a schema within the DSM.

Family theorists' conceptualizations of dysfunction emphasize either the development of family classification schemata or the linking of family interaction patterns to individual psychopathology. Family researchers have developed classification schemata describing the functioning of family units from healthy/adaptive to severely dysfunctional/extreme along the previously discussed dimensions of cohesion, change, and communication (Beavers, 1982; Olson et al., 1983). Severely dysfunctional families are inflexible and not adaptable; they fail to change in response to environmental or situational demands or developmental changes. These families tend to be undifferentiated, have poor boundaries, and fail to provide an environment conducive to the healthy development of each individual and the establishment of trusting relationships. Severely dysfunctional families have a poorly defined power structure, impaired communication (e.g., inconsistent communications), difficulties with problem solving and negotiation, and a pervasively negative affective quality with minimal expressions of caring and warmth. There is, however, heterogeneity in the expression of the family pathology dependent on the

family's characterization on such dimensions as cohesion, adaptability, and communication style.

Olson and colleagues (1983) developed a circumplex model of family functioning, describing the family's level of adaptability and cohesion. Family adaptability describes a continuum of functioning related to the extent to which the family system is flexible and able to change its power structure, role relationships, and rules in response to situational and developmental demands. A healthy family is flexible or structured in its approach to change, whereas unhealthy families either are chaotic at one extreme of the continuum or rigid at the other extreme of the continuum in their approach to dealing with change. Family cohesion, also a continuous variable, refers to the degree of emotional bonding (separate vs. connected) family members have toward one another. An adaptive level of family cohesion is one in which family members either are separated or connected, as opposed to the extremes of the continuum (disengaged or enmeshed). A balance between adaptability and cohesion is associated with optimal family functioning and healthy individual development, whereas extreme functioning on both dimensions characterizes dysfunctional families. Four types of dysfunctional families emerge in this classification schema: chaotically disengaged, chaotically enmeshed, rigidly disengaged, and rigidly enmeshed. Chaotically disengaged families feel disconnected from one another. Unrestricted external influences are allowed, blurred boundaries predominate, and the family's interaction is unpredictable, marked by limited and/or erratic leadership and discipline, endless negotiations, and dramatic role shifts and rule changes. Similar to chaotically disengaged families, rigidly disengaged families experience a sense of isolation within the family, with their primary bonds being with individuals outside the family system. However, rigidly disengaged families also are characterized by an authoritarian leadership style, with strict and rigidly enforced rules, limited negotiations, and stereotyped roles. Chaotically enmeshed families present as extremely close, with high loyalty demands and little tolerance for privacy, separateness, or external influences. This family overinvolvement prevails in an unpredictable and volatile family environment. Conversely, rigidly enmeshed families legislate their intense family closeness through strict rules, rigid roles, and an authoritarian leadership style. Research reveals that family type is associated with individual pathology. For example, many low-socioeconomic-status African American families with a juvenile delinquent member are chaotically enmeshed (Rodick, Henggeler, & Hanson, 1986).

Another schema useful in characterizing healthy, midrange, and severely dysfunctional families is that of Beavers (1982), based on research conducted at the Timberlawn Psychiatric Research Foundation in Dallas. Beavers depicts family functioning according to level of adaptability and stylistic presentation, noting that stylistic differences are primarily relevant to dysfunctional families. Family adaptability is defined as the family's capacity to function competently in effecting change and tolerating individual differentiation. Families high on adaptability tend to be healthy and are characterized by adequate negotiation, a lack of intimidation, a respect for individual choice, and open and clear communication. Families low on adaptability are more likely to be dysfunctional as they are inflexible and manifest poor boundaries and confused communication. Severely dysfunctional families, low on adaptability, may exhibit either a centrifugal or a centripetal stylistic presentation. Centrifugal families, similar to disengaged families, expect gratification

from outside the family, predominantly trust nonfamily members, and experience premature demands for separation. Centripetal families seek gratification from within the family, have difficulties with separating and individuating, and are less trustful of the external environment, similar to enmeshed families. Centrifugal families low on adaptability often have an antisocial member; centripetal families low on adaptability often have a schizophrenic member.

Others have linked individual psychopathology with specific family interaction patterns (for review, see Jacob, 1987). This research initially addressed the etiological role of aberrant family patterns (e.g., distorted communication) in the development of individual psychopathology, particularly schizophrenia (e.g., Bateson et al., 1956; Lidz, Cornelison, Fleck, & Terry, 1957; Wynne, Ryckoff, Day, & Hirsch, 1958).

During the past 15 years, research on family variables associated with the pathogenesis of psychopathology has addressed the temporal ordering and reciprocal influences of family process and psychopathology, and the differential contributions of environment and heredity. For example, schizophrenic individuals are most vulnerable to relapse if they reside in a family in which high levels of expressed emotion are reported (Vaughn & Leff, 1976) or a comparable dysfunctional affective style is observed (e.g., Doane, West, Goldstein, Rodnick, & Jones, 1981). High expressed emotion refers to critically and emotionally overinvolved verbal attitudes, revealed during an interview, toward the schizophrenic individual by his/her relatives; a dysfunctional affective style refers to similar patterns of behavior observed in the context of a laboratory-based interaction task. Individuals with depression (Hooley & Teasdale, 1989) and bipolar disorder (Miklowitz, Goldstein, Nuechterlein, Snyder, & Doane, 1987) in critical and emotionally overinvolved families also have a poorer prognosis than their counterparts in families characterized by low levels of expressed emotion and adaptive affective styles. These findings question the specificity of the association between high expressed emotion, negative affective style, and schizophrenia. However, the combination of a negative affective style and high levels of communication deviance (i.e., situations in which the listener is unable to glean a consistent image from the speaker's words) may be specific to schizophrenia spectrum disorders (Goldstein, 1987). Although the bulk of research has focused on families of schizophrenics, investigators have examined family interaction patterns and depression (for review, see Coyne, Kahn, & Gotlib, 1987), eating disorders (Minuchin et al., 1978), child aggression (Patterson, 1990), alcoholism (for review, see Jacob & Seilhamer, 1987), and borderline personality disorders (Everett, Halperin, Volgy, & Wissler, 1989).

Investigators are struggling to answer the question: Why are only some family members symptomatic? An individual's symptomatology depends on characteristics of the individual (e.g., biological predisposition, temperament, intelligence, personality), interactive effects (e.g., parent–child attachment, marital satisfaction, and sibling position), and extrafamilial influences (e.g., social support, economic status, and external stressors). Thus, an individual with considerable personal strengths and external resources can reside in a dysfunctional family yet function adaptively over time, whereas, another family member may have fewer strengths and/or resources and thus may be more vulnerable to developing psychopathology. Each family member's personal characteristics influence how other family members interact with him/her. These interaction patterns in turn affect the individual's level of functioning.

THE ASSESSMENT OF DYSFUNCTION

Multisystem, Multimethod Approach

A multisystem, multimethod approach, evaluating the individual, various dyads, and the family system as a whole using multiple assessment methods, is useful for assessing family dysfunction. Several family constructs are evaluated: structure, adaptability, emotions and needs, interaction and communication patterns, developmental stage of the individual and family, family of origin, sociocultural factors, and strengths and resources. Despite a growing consensus about the value of family assessment and the constructs to be examined, there is divergence regarding the significance, interrelationships, and underlying processes of these constructs. Various schools of thought place differential emphasis on assessing intrapsychic variables, behavioral functioning, and systemic patterns. Ideally, assessment is integrated into the therapeutic process, as it is cost-effective and yields a relatively rapid overview of marital/family dynamics, useful in problem identification, treatment selection, evaluation of ongoing therapy, and determination of treatment efficacy (Filsinger, 1983). When assessing a family, the clinician may use measures examining individual family members' cognitive or emotional functioning, and marital and family functioning. Marital and family functioning measurement tools can be divided into self-report measures and interactional coding schemata (for review, see Jacob, 1987).

Self-Report Measures

Self-report measures are easy and inexpensive to administer and score, and useful in assessing marital/family satisfaction. However, they do not adequately assess several key variables (e.g., family power), and they measure individual differences rather than a system and its interrelationships. The most commonly used, reliable, and valid self-report measures of marital functioning include the Locke–Wallace (Locke & Wallace, 1959) and the Dyadic Adjustment Scale (DAS; Spanier, 1976), both of which assess general marital adjustment. The DAS also includes measures of dyadic satisfaction, consensus, cohesion, and affectional expression. Among the enumerable self-report measures of family adjustment, the most frequently used and psychometrically sound instruments include the Family Environment Scale (FES; Moos & Moos, 1981), the Family Adaptability and Cohesion Evaluation Scales (FACES; Olson et al., 1983), the McMaster Family Assessment Device (FAD; Epstein, Baldwin, & Bishop, 1983), and the Family Assessment Measure (FAM; Skinner, Steinhauer, & Santa-Barbara, 1983). The FES assesses three dimensions characterizing the family's social environment: relationship, system maintenance, and personal growth. The FACES, based on the circumplex model, addresses family cohesion and adaptability. The FAD assesses families according to the McMaster Model of Family Functioning along the dimensions of problem solving, communication, roles, affective responsiveness, affective involvement, and behavior control. The FAM provides a quantitative index of family strengths and weaknesses. There are also numerous self-report measures of marital communication and intimacy, family life events, and the quality of family life (for review, see Fredman & Sherman, 1987).

Observational Methods

Direct observation provides information regarding the complexities of the interac-

tional processes of which family members may or may not be conscious. Observational measurements are obtained by rating specified nonverbal and verbal interactions of given subsystems in response to a structured task completed in a standard setting. The resulting data are then reduced via a coding schema to glean meaning from the complex set of behaviors exchanged among family members. Most coding schemata assess six dimensions that hypothetically discriminate between normal and dysfunctional families: dominance, affect, communication, information exchange, conflict, and support/validation (Markman & Notarius, 1987).

There are enumerable coding schemata to assess marital or family interactions from a microanalytic or macroanalytic perspective (Markman & Notarius, 1987). A microanalytic coding schema is one that focuses on specific behaviors emitted by individuals in interactional sequences providing a detailed behavioral analyses, whereas a macroanalytic perspective focuses on larger units of behavior and offers a more global perspective. The Family Interaction Coding System (FICS; Patterson, Ray, Shaw, & Cobb, 1969), the most widely used family microanalytic coding system, provides a sequential analysis of aversive and prosocial behaviors in family interactions during a semistructured task to obtain a summary of the family's level of coerciveness. The Marital Interaction Coding System (MICS; Hops, Wills, Patterson, & Weiss, 1972), based on the FICS, is the most commonly used marital observation system and has influenced the development of similar coding systems. The MICS has been used to compare interactions of distressed and nondistressed couples and to evaluate the efficacy of marital therapy. The recent revision of the MICS (MICS III) evaluates marital interaction according to the dimensions of problem description, blame, proposal for change, validation, invalidation, facilitation, irrelevant, and nonverbal affect. As microanalytic coding systems, the FICS and the MICS allow for careful analysis of complex interactions and the discrete behaviors of which these interactions are comprised. Despite the richness and ecological validity of the resultant data, the attainment, coding, and analysis of such data are labor intensive and costly. In a nonresearch environment, the process of family observation to inform treatment typically is informal and not standardized.

Macroanalytic coding schemata frequently are applied to observational data collected in a relatively unstructured situation. For example, the Beavers–Timberlawn Family Evaluation Scale is a clinician's global rating, on a 10-point Likert-type scale, of five dimensions (structure of the family, mythology, goal-directed negotiation, autonomy, family affect) based on the clinician's observations of the family's discussion of desired changes (Beavers, 1985). Macroanalytic coding schemata are easier to use than are microanalytic schemata and capture the interactional gestalt, rather than each individual's discrete behaviors.

THE PRACTICE OF THERAPY, THE STANCE OF THE THERAPIST, CURATIVE FACTORS, AND TREATMENT APPLICABILITY

There is not one brand of family therapy. Thus, we would do a disservice to depict the practice of family therapy as homogenous. This section of the chapter focuses on nine of the most widely practiced and influential schools of family therapy. There is inconsistency regarding how to categorize the various approaches; our presentation reflects one possible division. These schools are presented in a sequence organized by the extent to which they emphasize the past versus the present and intrapsychic versus interpersonal dimensions (F. W. Kaslow, 1987). The psychoanalytic, intergenerational, and family-of-origin approaches emphasize primarily the past. However, the psychoanalytic perspective also primarily focuses on intrapsychic issues, whereas the intergenerational and family-of-origin models address both intrapsychic and interpersonal dimensions equally. The experiential–humanistic brands of family therapy occupy the middle of both spectrums, placing relatively equal emphasis on past and present, and on intrapsychic and interpersonal dimensions. Strategic, systemic, structural, cognitive-behavioral, and psychoeducational approaches focus on the present and on interpersonal factors. To facilitate comparison of the various schools of thought, our presentation of each model will consider the basic structure of the therapy, goals, therapeutic techniques and strategies, therapeutic process, role of the therapist, curative factors, and treatment applicability. Table 10.1 presents the nine major models of family therapy articulated below in detail.

For purposes of clarity, the models are delineated separately. However, because the schools of family therapy are relatively consistent in conceptualizing the role of psychotropic medications in the therapeutic process, a general comment here will suffice. Early in the family therapy movement, an individual's symptoms were viewed solely as reflections of dysfunction in the family system, and thus the use of medication for a symptomatic member was eschewed. As the field of family therapy has become more integrated into the mainstream of psychiatric practice and as more evidence has accumulated supporting the interaction of biological and environmental etiological factors for severe psychopathology, psychotropic medications have come to be viewed as a useful adjunct to family treatment. However, medication is offered to alleviate a family member's distressing symptoms rather than to make fundamental changes in either the individual or the family. The exception to this practice is found in the family psychoeducational approach, which stresses the importance of compliance with medication regimens for individuals with severe psychiatric disorders (McFarlane, 1991).

Many family therapists have integrated the various perspectives delineated below in a thoughtful and well-informed manner, to address individual families and their unique problems (e.g., Duhl & Duhl, 1981; Feldman, 1992; Gurman, 1981; F. W. Kaslow, 1981; Kirschner & Kirschner, 1986; Pinsof, 1983). We share with other integrationists the view that while the beginning of the family therapy field demanded explication of relatively distinct and diverse theoretical approaches, the current state of the field is served best by an integrative perspective. We also believe that it is essential that family therapy be gender sensitive (Goodrich et al., 1988; Luepnitz, 1988; McGoldrick, Anderson, & Walsh, 1989; Walters et al., 1988) and culturally informed (Boyd-Franklin, 1989; F. W. Kaslow, 1982; McGoldrick et al., 1982). In this vein, new perspectives are being articulated that build on current intervention approaches, and that respect the diversity of human experience across gender, race, ethnicity, and sociocultural and socioeconomic contexts.

Psychoanalytic Family Therapy

As many family therapy pioneers were trained in the psychoanalytic tradition, psychoanalytic concepts have been integral in the development of several family therapy models. However, given family therapists' rebellion against the psychoanalytic tradition, continuities between psychoanalytic and family theory have been minimized. Psychoanalytic family therapy is one of the only family models that acknowledges its ties to psychoanalytic thinking, valuing the role of the unconscious and past history in determining behavior and motivations, the necessity of insight for behavior change, and the importance of transference and countertransference dynamics.

Nathan Ackerman, the "grandfather of family therapy," is the most noted early psychoanalytically oriented family therapist. Other key figures include James Framo, Ivan Boszormenyi-Nagy, Robin Skynner, Norman Paul, and John Bell. Recently, a number of writers have integrated current psychoanalytic theory (i.e., object relations theory) with family systems models, referring to their work as *object relations family therapy* (Scharff & Scharff, 1987; Scharff, 1989; Slipp, 1988). Object relations theory, with its basic assumption that the need for satisfying interpersonal relationships is a fundamental human motive, lends itself more readily to the understanding of family dynamics than does classical analytic theory, which emphasizes intrapsychic dynamics. In bridging psychoanalytic tenets and systems theory, psychoanalytically oriented family therapists attend to the individual's unique personality and background, family interactional processes, and the association between the family and the sociocultural context.

Experience in one's family of origin (i.e., parents, grandparents, and siblings) provides the foundation for sense of self, internalized images of significant others (*introjects*), and expectations for intimate relationships. Symptomatic behavior represents unresolved conflicts stemming from one's family of origin, which are reenacted with one's family of cre-

TABLE 10.1. Models of Family Therapy

Theory	Key proponents	Temporal focus	Focus of therapeutic change	Structure	Goals	Techniques	Stance of therapist
Psychoanalytic	Ackerman, Framo, Slipp, the Scharffs	Past	Intrapsychic issues	Long-term weekly treatment with unstructured sessions; membership varies depending on goals being addressed	Increase insight; strengthen ego functioning; develop more mature self representation and more satisfying interpersonal relationships; increase access to "true self"; and develop a balance between strivings for autonomy and intimacy	Provision of "holding environment"; develop interpretations linking past and present; address resistances, transference, and countertransference dynamics; termination	Provides a "holding environment" in which the therapist serves as a good-enough parent and reparents the family
Intergenerational–contextual	Boszormenyi-Nagy	Primary focus on past; some focus on present	Equal attention to intrapsychic and interpersonal dynamics	Therapy is conducted by cotherapy team, usually on a long-term basis; participants are individuals, nuclear families, and/or multigenerational families	Identify and address invisible loyalties; repair strained family relationships	Facilitation of each family member's perspective (multidirected partiality); acknowledgment of defenses and resistances; encouragement to face ethical issues from which resistances derive; homework	Catalyst for change who aligns with healthy aspects of the family; therapists communicate empathy, flexibility, creativity and compassion
Family of origin	Bowen	Past	Relatively equal attention to intrapsychic and interpersonal	A relatively structured therapy typically conducted with the marital dyad, by a single therapist, on a long- or short-term basis, either weekly or more sporadically; may include multigenerational family sessions	Differentiation of self within one's own family of origin	Using the genogram the therapist provides theoretically based feedback regarding historical patterns of family behavior; the therapist remains a neutral participant and works on his/her own self-differentiation	A "coach" who develops a person-to-person relationship with each member, without becoming emotionally entangled in family relationships (detriangulation)
Experiential and humanistic	Whitaker, Satir	Equal focus on past and present	Equal attention to intrapsychic and interpersonal dynamics	Relatively unstructured time unlimited therapy of intermediate duration, conducted by cotherapy team or therapist and consultant; sessions include family and may include index person's social support network	Increase family members' cohesion; help family facilitate members' individuation; increase creativity and spontaneity of family as a unit and individual members	"Joining" with family; battles for structure and initiative; management (not interpretation) of resistance; definition of symptoms as efforts toward growth; explication of covert conflict; therapist's use of self (e.g., absurdity and "acting in")	Coaches or surrogate grandparents who suggest but do not direct change; therapists share their internal processes with the family without losing their differentiated sense of self

Approach	Theorists	Temporal orientation	Emphasis	Structure	Goals	Techniques	Role of therapist
Strategic	Haley, Madanes, Bateson	Present	Interpersonal	Structured, brief intervention conducted by a single therapist; sessions may include whole family or one or more family members	Solve family's presenting problem by altering the interactional sequences maintaining the problem	Straight or paradoxical directives to change interactional sequences; reframing problem behaviors; homework	Powerful, authoritative, and often charismatic figure who persuades family to follow directives
Systemic	Selvini-Palazzoli, Prata, Boscolo, Cecchin, Hoffman, Papp	Present	Interpersonal	Relatively structured intervention consisting of 3–20 monthly sessions, conducted by a single therapist or cotherapy pair and observed/supervised by other members of therapy term	Goals are defined by family unless family's choices are harmful to one or more members	Circular questioning; positive connotation; rituals; counterparadoxical interventions	Neutral and nonreactive; family is responsible for change
Structural	Minuchin	Present	Interpersonal	Brief intervention typically conducted by a single therapist; sessions include family members who interact daily	Resolution of presenting problem by restructuring the family unit to facilitate more adaptive interactional patterns; change family's construction of reality regarding their presenting problem	Joining process; assessment of six domains of family functioning; restructuring techniques—enactments, boundary marking, unbalancing family alignments; homework	"Distant relative," often a colorful and dramatic figure who actively and authoritatively directs the treatment
Cognitive-behavioral	Jacobson & Margolin, Alexander & Parsons, Epstein, L'Abate	Present	Interpersonal	Relatively structured, brief timed-limited intervention conducted by a single therapist; session membership depends on goals of treatment, but typically includes marital dyad or family	Enhance marital or family satisfaction by changing members' cognitive processing of their own and one another's behavior	Formal assessment of family members' beliefs, causal attributions and expectancies regarding the present problem; cognitive restructuring technique (e.g., logical analysis of distorted automatic thoughts); self-instructional training; homework; communication skill building	Teacher/consultant who teaches family members about cognitive and behavioral processes and supervises their rehearsal of new behaviors
Psychoeducational	Anderson, Hogarty, Reiss	Present	Interpersonal	Structured intervention conducted with individual families or with multiple family groups; frequency of sessions and duration of treatment depends on status of patient's psychiatric illness; treatment is typically conducted by two therapists	Integrate patient with psychiatric illness into the community; prevent relapse	Parallel meetings with patient and family to establish rapport, allay anxiety and discuss treatment philosophy; assessment culminating in development of treatment contract; educational workshops for family and friends of patient; homework; build problem-solving and communication skills of family members	Therapists work collaboratively with patient, family and other members of treatment team; they are active in treatment process, providing advice, information, and support

357

ation (i.e., spouse and children) (Framo, 1982). Reenactment occurs via individuals' use of projection of introjected "bad objects" (negative internalized image of one's parent[s]) onto significant others in their adult life (Framo, 1982). Interpersonal interactions unconsciously are interpreted in a fashion consistent with each member's inner object world of positive and negative introjects. Further, each individual unconsciously seeks a mate who will be a willing recipient of his/her lost and split-off introjects, resulting in a collusive partnership (Framo, 1982).

A family member's symptom becomes part of a recurring, predictable, interactional pattern that ensures equilibrium for the individual but impairs the family's ability to adapt to change due to rigid, stereotypical, or rapidly shifting family roles (Ackerman, 1958). Such role distortions and the breakdown of role complementarity is associated with intrapsychic and interpersonal conflicts, often occurring simultaneously and exacerbating each other. Unresolved conflicts often result in the unconscious placement of a family member in a role in which he/she is consistently exposed to criticism and blamed for the family tension (scapegoating). Scapegoating further validates negative introjects, thus exacerbating individual symptomatology and family dysfunction.

Object relations family therapy is the dominant psychoanalytically oriented family therapy approach practiced today and thus the following comments are devoted to this approach.

Basic Structure of Therapy

Object relations family therapy is typically a long-term family treatment conducted on a weekly basis. The work is long term to address unresolved intrapsychic conflicts that are reenacted in one's current life and causing interpersonal and intrapsychic difficulties. Membership in the sessions may vary, depending on the presenting problem and the goals of each phase of the work. Membership may include one's family of origin, family of creation, marital dyad, and/or the individual person, and concurrent treatments may be conducted. Therapy hours are relatively unstructured. While the therapist is responsible for providing the external structure, the family's interactions and comments provide the internal structure.

Goal Setting

The goals of object relations family therapy are relatively similar across families with a variety of presenting problems and are implicit in the therapy rather than overtly discussed and negotiated. Goals are not specifically differentiated into intermediate- and long-term goals. These therapies attempt to help family members achieve increased insight; strengthen ego functioning; acknowledge and rework defensive projective identifications; attain more mature internal self and object representations; develop more satisfying interpersonal relationships supporting their needs for attachment, individuation, and psychological growth; and reduce interlocking pathologies among family members. The desired therapeutic outcome is for individual family members to have more access to their true selves, become more intimate with the true selves of significant others, and view others realistically rather than as projected parts of themselves. This enables the family to achieve a developmental level consistent with the needs of its members and the tasks to be addressed.

Techniques and Process of Therapy

In the initial phase of object relations family therapy, the therapist provides a frame, a *holding environment*, consisting of a specified time, space, and structure for the therapy. The therapist observes family interactions during an open-ended interview to ascertain family members' level of object relations, predominant defense mechanisms, and the relation between current interactional patterns and family of origin dynamics. A comprehensive history of each family member is conducted with all members present, with attention paid to family-of-origin dynamics, early experiences, presenting problems, and treatment history.

The importance of establishing a *therapeutic alliance* is underscored. Once an alliance is established, the therapist interprets conflicts, defenses, and patterns of interaction. Interpretations may address individual family member's dynamics and/or various family subsystems. Effective interpretations link an individual or family's history with current feelings, thoughts, behaviors, and interactions, permitting more adaptive family interactional patterns and intrapsychic changes. In making empathic interpretations, the therapist relies on theoretical knowledge and affective responses to each individual and the family unit.

The Fine family, an upper-middle-class Jewish family, sought treatment for their adolescent daughter's anorexic symptoms. During the therapy, it was discovered that the adolescent's eating disorder symptoms escalated when her father, a commercial pilot, would be away from the family on lengthy trips. The therapist's own affective reactions to Mrs. Fine led the therapist to question whether she was depressed. It was revealed that although Mrs. Fine appeared to manage effectively, she became sad and hopeless during her husband's absences. The separations reactivated her unresolved grief regarding her father's death during her adolescence. The therapist conceptualized the daughter's symp-

toms as efforts to distract her mother from her depression, just as Mrs. Fine needed to care for her mother upon her father's death. This conceptualization led the therapist to empathically comment on how painful the separations were for each family member and to help the family develop ways for Mr. Fine to provide more object constancy for his wife (e.g., more frequent telephone calls and love notes left behind). This collaboratively designed intervention took into account Mr. Fine's employment, which necessitated separations; Mrs. Fine's vulnerability to separations; and the daughter's need to care for her mother in order for her mother to be emotionally available to her regardless of whether her father was present.

Technical errors occur when a safe holding environment has not been established, interpretations are poorly timed and do not attend to significant intrapsychic and interpersonal dynamics, and comments reflect unresolved countertransference issues rather than being empathically attuned to the family's affective experience. The primary treatment techniques are interpretations of resistance, defenses, negative transference, and family interactional patterns indicative of unresolved family-of-origin and intrapsychic conflicts. Out-of-session tasks and homework assignments are not utilized routinely.

Psychoanalytically oriented therapists assume that individuals and families are resistant to change. To facilitate change, external and internal resistances are addressed. For example, when a family member refuses to attend sessions, the therapist may interpret this individual's behavior as an expression of the family's shared reluctance to participate in the change process. Object relations family therapists address transference and countertransference dynamics to facilitate the therapeutic endeavor. Therapists use their own reactions to the family's behavior and interaction patterns (*objective countertransference*) to understand empathically the shared, yet unspoken experiences of each family member regarding family interactional patterns (*unconscious family system of object relations*). Therapists employ their objective countertransference reactions to interpret interpersonal patterns in which one family member is induced to behave in a circumscribed and maladaptive fashion (*projective identification*).

Termination is attended to during each session and toward the end of the treatment process both covertly and overtly by the therapist. Time boundaries for ending sessions and for ending the therapy course are respected, communicating the therapist's commitment to the family as a consultant to, rather than conductor of, their change process. The ending of each session raises issues of loss and separation, which need to be worked through in preparation for treatment termination. When appropriate, the therapist addresses how the family's history and present system of object relationships interfere with healthy, autonomous functioning. Overt discussions and interpretations regarding conflicts and feelings of separation and mourning precipitated by the finite nature of sessions help the family prepare for the ultimate termination of the family therapy. During the termination phase, salient conflicts are reviewed and unresolved family transferences in modified forms are reworked. There is an opportunity for mourning the loss of the therapist, who has become an important attachment figure.

Mr. Williams, a 52-year-old African American accountant, remains unaware of his anger toward his mother for her overinvolvement in his marriage. He frequently spends time with his mother in a way that perpetuates her involvement. Rather than acknowledging his anger at his mother, Mr. Williams projects this anger onto his wife, a pediatrician, who accepts the projected anger and continually feels enraged at her mother-in-law. Thus, even when Dr. Williams and her mother-in-law have potentially enjoyable interactions, Dr. Williams creates conflict in the relationship to justify her anger. Dr. Williams continuously is disappointed in his wife for her conflictual and hostile relationship with his mother. One goal of the therapy was to enable Mr. Williams to become more cognizant of his negative feelings toward his mother. Working through these feelings helped him more appropriately separate from his mother and develop a more intimate relationship with his wife. Additionally, Dr. Williams was freed to engage in more gratifying interactions with her mother-in-law. This work entailed understanding Mr. Williams's resistance to experiencing simultaneously positive and negative feelings toward his mother, the couple's reluctance to have a more intimate relationship, and Dr. Williams's propensity to engage in negative interactions with older women. This in turn, led Dr. Williams to examine unresolved negative feelings toward maternal objects, including her mother and overprotective grandmother. The termination phase of the work entailed repeated efforts at addressing and integrating both partners' negative and positive feelings toward the therapist, who had come to represent a maternal figure for each of them.

Stance of the Therapist

Of utmost importance in conducting object relations family therapy is the provision of a "good enough" holding environment, where the therapist enables family members to feel safe and secure so that they can express openly their feelings and beliefs and feel more intimate with one another while maintaining a sense of self. The therapist functions as a "good enough" parent, reparenting the family by providing consistent nurturance and structure (e.g., limit setting) to enhance the development of individual members and the family unit.

Curative Factors

Therapy focuses on individuals' early family experiences, feelings about one another, and relationships. Primary mechanisms of change are interpretations of interpersonal patterns, including transference and countertransference dynamics, offered in the context of a positive working alliance and a safe holding environment. Interpretations help family members gain both historic–genetic and interactional insights into their psychological realities. Although the therapy does not directly teach more adaptive interpersonal skills, the development of these skills is believed to be an outgrowth of increased insight. Finally, effective management of affects elicited during the termination process is considered crucial to a successful outcome, as it provides an opportunity to rework unresolved separation issues related to one's family of origin. Although the curative factors of object relations family therapy have been articulated, there is minimal empirical validation of their efficacy. The research conducted takes the form of intensive, descriptive case studies with the family session being the unit of focus (e.g., Shapiro, 1989).

There are specific techniques associated with object relations family therapy. Techniques, however, are considered secondary to the relationship between therapist and family and thus do not define the practice of object relations family therapy. Rather, the defining characteristic is the therapist's joining with the family and creating a safe holding environment within which family members rediscover each other and the lost parts of the self projected onto one another. While most family therapies emphasize the therapeutic relationship, it is psychoanalytically oriented family therapists who focus on the relationship as a curative factor and who use transference interpretations as a cornerstone of the treatment.

Given the importance of addressing countertransference dynamics, the therapist's psychological health and his/her family-of-origin dynamics influence the work between therapist and family. The therapist needs to address unresolved intrapsychic and interpersonal conflicts in supervision and personal treatment.

Treatment Applicability

Clinicians typically use object relations family therapy with high-functioning families in which none of the members is severely disturbed. These families tend to be psychologically minded, educated, and interested in gaining insight, and they possess the resources necessary to engage in long-term treatment. Some clinicians also have advocated its use with families with a schizophrenic, borderline, or narcissistic family member (for review, see Scharff, 1989). Additionally, this therapeutic approach has been practiced with families with young children, school-age children, and adolescents; families of divorce and remarriage; and families coping with trauma, loss, or death (e.g., Scharff & Scharff, 1987).

Intergenerational–Contextual Family Therapy

Intergenerational–contextual family therapy, associated with Ivan Boszormenyi-Nagy (Boszormenyi-Nagy & Spark, 1973; Boszormenyi-Nagy, Grunebaum, & Ulrich, 1991), is an outgrowth of psychoanalytically oriented family therapy. Intergenerational–contextual family therapy emphasizes intrapsychic and interpersonal dynamics and while emphasizing the past, also focuses on the present.

Intergenerational–contextual family therapy, which is conceived within an ethical–existential framework, views the family of origin as central. Nagy and Geraldine Spark's classic work, *Invisible Loyalties* (1973), stresses concepts of legacy, loyalty, indebtedness to one's family of origin, and the profound influence of one's biological roots. *Loyalties* are structured expectations to which family members are committed. One's fundamental loyalty is to the maintenance of the family, not to self-differentiation. Family members maintain a *ledger of merits* (investments into relationships) and *debts* (obligations) for each relationship. This ledger changes according to family members' investments (e.g., supporting others) and withdrawals (e.g., exploiting others). When perceived injustices occur, repayment of psychological debts is expected. Additionally, every family maintains a family ledger, a multigenerational accounting system of who owes what to whom. Obligations rooted in past generations covertly influence the behavior of family members in the present (*invisible loyalties*). Dysfunction results when individuals or families feel they have chronically imbalanced ledgers which are not resolved. This diminishes the level of trust among family members, resulting in destructive entitlement or overindebtedness in family members who feel deprived, or the presence of an identified patient scapegoated by the family. Thus, to understand the etiology, function, and maintenance of this individual's symptomatology, one must consider the history of the problem, the family ledger, and unsettled individual accounts.

Michael Pasadeno and his second wife, Judy Brown, sought couple therapy shortly after the birth of their first child together (Jonathan). Michael had two older daughters from his prior marriage. He paid significant sums of child support to his former wife, adhered to visitation requirements, and sought additional opportunities for contact with his daughters. Although Judy developed a positive relationship with her stepdaughters, she was resentful of the financial compromises the newly formed stepfamily needed to make to meet Michael's child support obligations. Judy supported her husband's relationship with his daughters; however, she felt it diminished his developing relationship with his son and the intimacy in the marriage. In other words, Judy was angry about her husband's financial and emotional debts. She perceived she was investing more in the marriage than she was receiving. An examination of Judy's family of origin revealed that she had unresolved feelings of resentment toward her parents for paying more attention to her handicapped older brother than to her. This, in turn, heightened her dissatisfaction with her marriage, as she so desperately needed her husband to shower her with attention, to make up for the attention she lacked in her family of origin. Although Michael was committed to his blended family, he remained loyal to his promises to be a good provider for his first wife (invisible loyalty) and their children.

Basic Structure of Therapy

Intergenerational–contextual therapy is intensive long-term therapy for individuals and families, and may include multigenerational family sessions. This work is most effectively conducted by a cotherapy team, as they provide a balanced model to the family unit, complementing one another (Boszormenyi-Nagy & Spark, 1973). The therapist maintains control of the sessions, encouraging members to openly express themselves and validating each individual's worth.

Goal Setting

The goals of intergenerational–contextual family therapy are universal and not dependent on specific family characteristics. The therapy aims to identify and address invisible or hidden loyalties within the family; recognize unsettled individual and family accounts; rebalance in actuality one's obligations (*rejunction process*) to repair ruptured or strained relationships and develop adaptive ways of relating, more trusting relationships, and an equitable balance of give and take among family members; and develop a preventive plan for current and future generations. Although symptom alleviation and the amelioration of distress are important intermediate goals, developing self-object delineation and responsible engagement within relationships (*self-validation*) are the overriding aims.

Techniques and Process of Therapy

In intergenerational–contextual family therapy, the assessment process involves creating a trusting atmosphere so that family members feel safe to express their sense of entitlement and indebtedness. One method used to develop a trusting therapeutic environment, *multidirected partiality*, refers to the therapist's acknowledgment of each individual's perspective on an issue. Having one's views acknowledged leads to an increased capacity to communicate and listen to others.

A comprehensive history is taken focusing on facts, psychology, interactional patterns, and relational ethics. The use of a three-or-more-generation genogram (described later in the section "Family-of-Origin Therapy") enables the therapist(s) to help the family ascertain the fairness and violations of fairness between family members and generations. In contrast to the other family therapists who have some of their roots in psychoanalytic theory, intergenerational–contextual family therapists conceptualize the assessment process as integral to the development of a trusting relationship with the family and the ongoing therapeutic process.

Following the assessment phase and the establishment of a treatment contract, intergenerational–contextual family therapy enters the working-through phase, where defenses and resistances are acknowledged. Transactions occurring during the family session are discussed in light of each individual's object relations. Major therapeutic techniques enhancing the working-through process include the therapists' siding with each family member to maintain multidirectional partiality, crediting each family member for his/her efforts to help the family, encouraging mutual accountability to replace mutual blame, and using the rejunction process. Issues of loss, separation, and abandonment are discussed during the termination phase. Successful termination occurs when individuals are able to face invisible loyalties within the family system and rebalance unsettled accounts.

Throughout the entire treatment process, the use of the cotherapy relationship enhances the work via empathic involvement in the family, acknowledgment of each family member's contribution, and investment in the trustworthiness of familial relationships. Although the cotherapists are catalysts for the change process, family meetings held at home, family rituals, and occurrences among family members between sessions serve as the actual work. Homework may be assigned, including writing letters, making telephone calls, and visiting one's family of origin, to help family members develop more positive and trusting relationships. The most common resistances occur when the family remains fixated in symbiotic or distanced relationships and the regressive forces of therapy are experienced as intolerable. In such instances, therapy is rejected.

Less serious resistance is evident in families whose members find the in-depth reworking of relationships too painful and thus desire only the alleviation of the presenting problem. Although this goal is acceptable to the therapists, they do communicate their perspective that lasting change requires successful rebalancing of individual and family ledgers. As is the case with all insight-oriented therapies, common resistances that impede the exploration of relational balances include the mobilization of a variety of defense mechanisms, failure to develop new insights, and an unwillingness to be accountable. These resistances are not interpreted or bypassed. Rather, family members are encouraged to face in their real relationships the ethical issues from which their resistances derive, define their positions regarding these issues, and move toward multilateral consideration of one another's interests.

Stance of the Therapist

Intergenerational–contextual family therapy typically is conducted by cotherapists who align with the healthy aspects of the family. The cotherapy team communicates empathy, compassion, flexibility, complementarity, creativity, and a concern for family members' capacities for individuation and relatedness. The therapists are the catalysts for the work, take an active role in the process, and communicate that family members can help heal one another. They encourage the family to rebalance accounts and suggest alternative interactional patterns. However, from the outset, the therapeutic task belongs to the family and family members are held accountable for their actions. Thus, the therapist–family relationship is a mutual one.

Curative Factors

The primary curative mechanism is the development of a trusting alliance between the family and the therapists, a process that may be enhanced by pertinent self-disclosures on the part of the therapists. Reframing the presenting problem as reflecting unbalanced family ledgers and family loyalty conflicts and making invisible loyalties overt are additional mechanisms for change. Reframing paves the way to the redressing of the imbalances in the nuclear and extended family.

Family members are helped to face their distortions about significant family members by learning more about their histories. This enables them to have more compassion for other family members and thus to exonerate their parents and rebalance their relational account of debts and merits. This work frequently includes the parental and grandparental generation to rebalance in reality one's accounts. In these multigenerational sessions, feelings are openly expressed to develop a more meaningful dialogue and more positive interactions. This relieves the grandchildren of the burden of unsettled accounts passed down through the generations.

Insight into one's family-of-origin dynamics is crucial to the change and healing process in intergenerational–contextual family therapy. Insight is achieved through the process of dialogic relating induced by the therapist, not by classical interpretations. Insight is not sufficient for change; rather, lasting change entails efforts at rejunction. Enhanced relational capacities, a vital outcome of the work, are not conceived to be instrumental skills and thus are not taught by the therapist. Rather, it is assumed that individuals benefit from rewarding interpersonal interactions which are an outgrowth of the rejunction process, and which enable them to relate in a healthier fashion.

Intergenerational–contextual family therapists assert that the most important transference distortions are between family members. Transference reactions may, however, occur between family members and therapists, with the therapists frequently seen as the parents. The therapists manage this transferential parentification process by helping family members understand and modify their relationships and underscoring the importance of family roles (e.g., parents are responsible for parenting their children). This occurs within a context of nurturance in which the therapist provides the necessary reparenting to support the rejunction process.

Sam, a 43-year-old competent health care professional, became emotionally overwhelmed when his therapist informed him of an upcoming hiatus in the treatment for medical reasons. The patient's strong reaction harkened back to his early adolescence when his older sister was in a car accident and became comatose and his parents were preoccupied with her extended recovery and subsequent impairments. Although rationally he understood his parents' need to attend primarily to his sister, he felt emotionally abandoned and that his needs were not important. The therapist and patient realized that this particular event provided an opportunity for reparenting the patient regarding feelings of neglect and sense of isolation in dealing with the myriad affects associated with the physical problems of a loved one. Working through the therapist's absence, by discussing openly and in a supportive relationship the feelings associated with the therapist's illness and providing additional supports to the patient during this time, led Sam to feel more able to discuss with his parents that traumatic time in the life of the family. Not only was he able to more openly share his feelings and needs, but he also experienced more empathy for each of his family members' plights. This led them to develop more mutual and trusting relationships and enabled them to rebalance their relational "need" accounts.

The therapist's personal maturity and the degree to which he/she has worked through a sense of entitlement and is conscious of family loyalties influences his/her capacity for multidirectional partiality, which in turn, impacts the effectiveness of the rejunction process and thus the therapeutic endeavor. Countertransference reactions are construed as resources for deepening one's engagement in the multilateral process and thus, if well-understood, can enhance the rejunction process.

Treatment Applicability

Intergenerational–contextual family therapy is applicable to most human problems (Boszormenyi-Nagy et al., 1991). However, it may be most efficacious in conjunction with other established treatments for individual symptoms (e.g., medications for an individual's depression or substance abuse treatment). It is important to note, however, that minimal empirical validation of the efficacy of this approach exists.

Family-of-Origin Therapy

Family-of-origin family therapy, also referred to as *multigenerational or Bowenian therapy*, has Bowen as its primary proponent. This perspective also is an outgrowth of psychoanalytically oriented family therapy. Similar to intergenerational–contextual family therapy, family-of-origin therapy emphasizes both intrapsychic and interpersonal dynamics. However, unlike intergenerational–contextual family therapy, family-of-origin therapy focuses primarily on past family dynamics. The family of origin is the central unit of focus in this approach.

According to Bowen (1978; for review, see Friedman, 1991), the family is an emotional relationship system. Dysfunction arises when individuals are enmeshed in their families of origin and thus unable to assert their feelings and thoughts and/or when efforts to cope with chronic and inevitable anxiety are maladaptive. Bowen offers eight interlocking constructs to elucidate his theory.

Differentiation of self, the cornerstone of the theory, refers to the degree to which individuals differentiate between emotional and intellectual functioning. The self-differentiation continuum ranges from fusion of emotions and intellect or an "undifferentiated family ego mass" (the emotional stuck togetherness in families) at the low end to differentiation at the high end, in which intellectual and emotional functioning are relatively independent. Well-differentiated individuals have satisfying interpersonal relationships and can pursue their chosen life goals. These individuals are neither overly invested in the emotional climate of their family of origin nor totally withdrawn from them and negating their importance (*emotionally cut off*).

John is a 35-year-old individual who evidences symptoms consistent with a schizophrenia spectrum disorder. When queried about his opinions regarding an issue at hand, John looks to other family members for guidance. He answers questions tentatively, expressing his feelings rather than his thoughts. The process and content of his communications are dominated by the affective state of his family. For example, if a family member feels anxious about a job-related concern, John manifests that anxiety. His parents frequently speak for him and criticize his contributions to the sessions and his functioning in the community, thus maintaining John's low level of self-differentiation and keeping John dependent on the family.

The *family emotional system* refers to emotionally interdependent people comprising a system with its own organizational principles and including feelings and thoughts of all members. A nuclear family emotional system is formed by marital partners, typically similar in their level of self-differentiation. Their emotional interactional patterns are based on their level of differentiation from their families of origin. When two well-differentiated individuals marry, they usually form a stable marital dyad.

A marital dyad is vulnerable to experiencing anxiety when both partners manifest low levels of self-differentiation. To reduce this anxiety, couples may emotionally distance from one another or evidence marital conflict, a symptomatic spouse, or *triangulation* of another person (e.g., offspring, friend, lover, parent, or therapist) to stabilize the marital tension. When triangulation fails to stabilize a situation, additional individuals are recruited to form interlocking triangles. Patterns of triangulation are repeated and become dysfunctional when individuals develop fixed or stereotypical roles (e.g., depressed parent, acting-out child, high-functioning sibling). A symptom also may serve as the third point in the triangle. For example, a family member may abuse alcohol to escape the pain associated with unresolved marital discord. Excessive alcohol consumption, in turn, exacerbates the marital discord.

The most common triangle in an intact family includes mother, father, and child. The most vulnerable child is triangulated in response to marital dysfunction (*family projection process*). Projection in this context refers to the parents' transmission to the child of their own lack of self-differentiation from their family of origin. The intensity of the family projection process is a function of the degree of undifferentiation of the parent(s) and the level of anxiety and stress within the nuclear family. This family projection process may lead to impairment in the child and possibly his/her siblings. The child chosen to be triangulated is typically the most fusion-prone offspring and this often depends on the *sibling position* of the parents.

The *multigenerational transmission process*, the recapitulation of the family projection process and the reenactment of conflictual family issues across multiple generations, has been associated with the development of severe psychopathology in a family member. Psychiatric disorders are considered a product of history and develop over the course of successive generations.

Mrs. Campisi, the third of six children from an Italian Catholic family, was furious at her parents for refusing to pay for her college education and thus chose to have virtually no contact with her family of origin from that point forward (emotional cutoff). She married Mr. Campisi shortly after graduating high school. Mr. Campisi's father abandoned the family when he was young, and his mother died shortly after his marriage. The Campisis had three children and the family functioned adequately until the middle child, Anna Maria, entered kindergarten. Anna Maria became electively mute, refusing to speak to anyone outside her nuclear family. The teacher referred the child for an evaluation. The therapist, in evaluating the child and the family, determined that Anna Maria's elective mutism reflected her parent's inability to communicate with their families of origin. It was difficult for Anna Maria to develop age-appropriate interpersonal relationships outside her immediate family and become a well-differentiated individual until her parents addressed their unresolved anger at their parents for abandoning them.

In extending his theory to society at large, Bowen asserted that chronic anxiety, external pressures, and stresses lower the society's functional differentiation, resulting in *societal regression*. This societal regression, indicative of periods of societal disorganization and social unrest, impacts negatively on the family as it places added external stress on family units.

Basic Structure of Therapy

Bowenian family therapy is conducted with the marital dyad or individual adults, by a single therapist, on a long- or short-term basis, and may occur weekly or more sporadically. The marital dyad is the primary focus, as the theory posits that increased self-differentiation within the marital dyad leads to amelioration of symptoms in other family members. The therapy is relatively structured, as the therapist takes responsibility for alternately asking each partner questions about themselves and their responses to their partner's comments.

Goal Setting

The central goal of all family–of–origin work is achieving a greater level of differentiation of self within the family of origin. This long-term goal is implicit in the therapeutic contract, although it is rarely discussed overtly between therapist and family members. All the work is geared toward attaining this long-term goal.

Techniques and Process of Therapy

The primary technique in family-of-origin therapy is the therapist organizing the session such that each spouse speaks rationally about personal and emotional issues directly to the therapist rather than to his/her spouse. To facilitate this, Bowenian therapists ask questions about the presenting problem and the nuclear and extended family, provide a didactic presentation of Bowenian theory, utilize genograms, and recommend visits to one's family of origin.

Family *genograms* are visual representations or maps of the process and structure of at least three generations of a family (McGoldrick & Gerson, 1985). Information in a complete genogram includes family members' names and ages, dates of significant life events (e.g., births and marriages), psychiatric and medical history, key personality characteristics, and description of the nature of relationships (e.g., disengaged, enmeshed, or highly conflictual). Genograms graphically depict complex family patterns, are useful in engaging with the family, and offer a rich source of hypotheses regarding family patterns associated with the presenting problem. Genograms enable the therapist to use a systemic perspective in conceptualizing the current and past family situation to unblock the system, clarify family patterns, and reframe and detoxify family issues (McGoldrick & Gerson, 1985). Family members are often encouraged to make trips home and meet with their family of origin to obtain information and work through unresolved emotional attachments, in an effort to achieve increased self-differentiation.

Figure 10.1 presents a partial genogram of the Michael Pasadeno–Judy Brown family described earlier who sought marital therapy shortly after the birth of their first child. The genogram was used by the therapist to help the couple identify family dynamics contributing to their marital difficulties. As seen on the genogram, Michael's father abandoned him at a young age, putting the burden on his mother to be the sole provider. Michael made a commitment to himself that he would never abandon his own children, as he had suffered emotional and financial hardship as a result of his father's lack of involvement in his life. Although Michael had found his mother to be a good caretaker and provider, he was sensitive to the disadvantages of being raised in a single-parent home. Thus, he felt it essential to have frequent contact with his daughters from his first marriage and to support them financially in the manner to which they had become accustomed, to protect them from the feelings of abandonment and deprivation which had clouded his own childhood.

Additionally, he had no model for being a father to a son. His difficulty attaching to his son may have been complicated further by the similarity between his father's and son's names. As can be seen on the genogram, there are a number of factors that contributed to Judy's sensitivity to feeling neglected by a family member: her mother's overinvolvement with Judy's physically impaired older brother (Roger), Judy's distant relationship with her father, and the recent loss of her father to cancer. Her father had been ill for a number of years prior to his death, and thus Judy's mother had been overburdened with the caretaking demands placed on her by her husband and her son. She was thus emotionally unavailable when her first grandchild, Jonathan, was born. Examination of the genogram helped the couple to identify those unresolved family-of-origin issues complicating their marital relationship.

In family-of-origin therapy, a couple is considered ready for termination when each partner is capable of staying detriangled in his/her family of origin and creation, and when each spouse remains objective and is no longer pulled into the family emotional system. According to Bowen's theoretical formulations, issues regarding resistance and technical errors are not considered important variables impeding the change process and thus are not discussed in detail (Friedman, 1991).

Stance of the Therapist

The Bowenian therapist is responsible for the tone and structure of the sessions, modulating the emotional intensity and directing questions to each spouse. The therapist helps the family achieve cognitive understanding by relating meaningfully to each family member (person-to-person relationship) while remaining curious, relatively objective, and calm in response to the couple's emotional reactivity. The therapist becomes a part of the couple's triangle without becoming

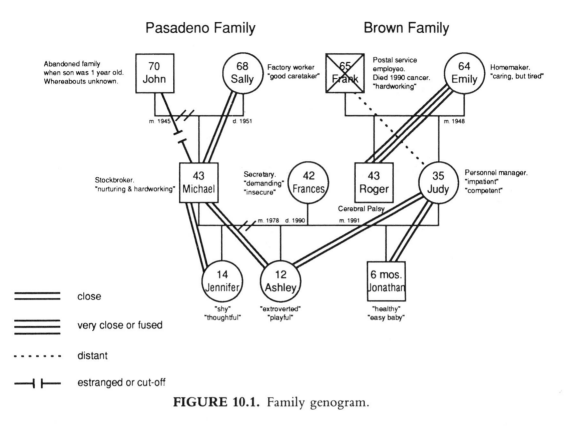

FIGURE 10.1. Family genogram.

emotionally entangled in or reactive to their relationship, a process termed "detriangulation." The therapist encourages each spouse to detriangle by developing a meaningful and well-differentiated relationship with the therapist in the presence of the spouse. The Bowenian therapist's role is that of "coach" rather than healer or therapist. Transference, interpretations, and self-disclosure are avoided as much as possible.

Curative Factors

Both techniques and the person-to-person relationship are important in the practice of Bowenian therapy. Family-of-origin therapy has many similarities to psychoanalytically oriented family approaches, particularly those of Framo (1982). The curative factor in family-of-origin therapy is increased cognitive awareness, resulting in increased self-differentiation. This is attained through a comprehensive examination of family-of-origin dynamics and the process of detriangulation from one's family of origin, one's family of creation, and the therapist. Although interpretations per se are rarely offered and interpersonal skills are not directly taught, the Bowenian therapist offers theoretically based feedback and observations regarding historical patterns of family behavior, using the genogram as a primary data source. Family-of-origin therapists value the therapist's lifelong process of self-differentiation from his/her own family of origin to enhance objectivity and neutrality in his/her work with couples and families (Titelman, 1987). Thus, the therapist's degree of self-differentiation plays an important role in the outcome of the treatment. If the therapist is unable to remain calm and objective and/or if the family's emotional reactivity is too high, treatment is unlikely to be successful. Treatment is most effective when the therapist is a neutral participant and well differentiated and when family members are capable of rational thinking.

The second author of this chapter (M.P.C.), supervised a female clinician's marital therapy with Mr. and Mrs. Davis, both professionals in education. This Protestant, Caucasian couple's presenting complaint was their dissatisfaction with their sexual relationship. Specifically, although the couple had no difficulty expressing affection toward one another and "cuddling," Mrs. Davis felt disappointed, and at times resentful, that she and her husband did not have more frequent and passionate sexual contact. Mr. Davis experienced the couple's sexual relationship as acceptable but felt badly that his wife was unhappy with the situation. He, however, was not interested in changing their sexual relationship. The therapist helped the couple understand the family-of-origin dynamics contributing to their current difficulty. For example, Mr. Davis became aware that similar to his mother, he perceived his wife as controlling. He felt that sex was the only arena in which he could exercise control in his marriage. Mrs. Davis realized that their initial, unspoken marital contract was to have a more affectional than a sexual relationship. However, through her own individual therapy, she became more accepting of her emotional and physical needs and she forged a sexual identity. Thus, she wanted a redefinition of the marital contract regarding the sexual relationship, a renegotiation her husband experienced as undesirable.

Although initially the therapy proceeded well, the supervisor recognized in the middle phase of treatment that a therapeutic impasse had occurred. Specifically, the therapist and the couple had become hopeless about the couple's ability to improve their sexual relationship, despite accumulated insight into the family-of-origin dynamics contributing to their difficulties. During supervision it became clear that the therapist's unresolved family-of-origin dynamics, namely, her history of sexual abuse by her stepfather, led to discomfort with her own sexuality and uncertainty about negotiating power and intimacy dynamics in her relationships with men. Thus, the therapist had difficulty maintaining a relatively neutral and objective stance in the face of the couple's struggles. She overidentified with the husband's lack of interest in sex and the wife's hopelessness and felt emotionally overwhelmed by the tension in the marriage. Until the therapist became more differentiated from her family of origin vis-à-vis sexual dynamics, she remained triangulated in the couple's struggle and too emotionally entangled with them to help them resolve their difficulties.

Treatment Applicability

Family-of-origin therapy is particularly applicable to marital dyads in which self-differentiation is relatively high, anxiety levels are low, and objective processing of emotions is possible. Bowenian therapists tend to work with the healthiest family members, based on the view that these individuals are most capable of change. The efficacy of family-of-origin work has not been examined in detail. However, it evolved from early research endeavors with schizophrenic individuals and their families.

Experiential and Humanistic Family Therapies

Experiential and humanistic family therapies conceptualize dysfunctional behavior as a failure to fulfill one's potential for personal growth. An experiential–humanistic perspective, a philosophy of growth, assumes that growth is a natural and spontaneous process and that pain is a natural component of such growth. These schools emphasize present experiences and affects and associated meanings attributed to these experiences. A number of theorists have been identified with the experiential–humanistic school of family therapy, including Whitaker (Whitaker & Keith, 1981), Satir (1967, 1972), Duhl and Duhl (1981), Kempler (1981), and Kantor and Lehr (1975). Due to space limitations, only Whitaker's approach is presented in detail. Incorporated in this presentation is a discussion of Satir's key experiential therapeutic techniques useful in family therapy and the training of psychotherapists.

Experiential Symbolic Family Therapy

Experiential symbolic family therapy was developed by Whitaker and associates, at Emory University in Atlanta, and later at the University of Wisconsin–Madison. Whitaker's approach is atheoretical; theory is viewed as a hindrance to clinical practice (Whitaker, 1976). His views, however, on the healthy or well-functioning marriage and family and on pathological or dysfunctional marriage and family have been articulated, particularly as they influence the therapy process (Roberto, 1991).

Basic Structure of Therapy

Symbolic experiential family therapy is time-unlimited and of intermediate duration. It is conducted at a variable frequency, usually weekly or biweekly, with monthly sessions in the latter phases. Sessions optimally include the symptomatic family member, the nuclear family residing with the symptomatic person, the extended families, and the index person's social support network. Therapy usually is conducted by a cotherapy team or may include a therapist and a consultant.

Goal Setting

The ultimate goals of experiential symbolic family therapy apply to all dysfunctional marital and family units. The specific operationalization of these goals is developed between a couple/family and the cotherapy team, based on the unique family system and its relational patterns. Ultimate goals are to (1) increase family members' perceptions of belongingness and cohesion, (2) help the couple or family facilitate each family member's individuation and completion of developmental tasks, and (3) foster the creativity ("craziness") and spontaneity of the family unit and individual members. Mediating goals include disorganizing rigid recycling of interaction to allow for more adaptive responses, activating and allowing constructive anxieties by positively reframing symptoms as efforts toward competence, expanding the presenting problem to include each members' role in the dysfunction, encouraging and supporting new decisions, creating transgenerational boundaries, and creating a therapeutic suprasystem in which the family and cotherapy team develop a shared meaning system and intermember alliances (Roberto, 1991).

Techniques and Process of Therapy

Similar to most therapies, experiential symbolic family therapy includes beginning, middle, and end phases. The therapy becomes less structured as treatment progresses. Out-of-session homework assignments are not typically given, with the exception of preparation for the extended family reunion. Resistances are considered inevitable in the change process and are not interpreted. Rather, they are managed with a combination of challenge, support, and humor.

During the beginning phase, the therapists establish personal contact with the family (joining), using metaphors, reframing, and humor to engage the family in a relatively nonthreatening fashion (Satir, 1967, 1972). The *battle for structure* and the *battle for initiative* must be fought before the family trusts the cotherapy dyad enough to allow them to help the family reorganize to cure the scapegoated member and develop greater differentiation (Whitaker & Keith, 1981). The battle for structure, which begins at the initial contact, refers to a battle over ground rules regarding treatment structure, session membership, scheduling, and fees. This battle is completed when a minimum of a two-generational structure to the therapy is established, with the therapist(s) in charge and having maximal freedom to move in and out of the family system and "call the shots." The battle for structure, if successfully won, induces regression in the family, engenders an intense transference relationship, and communicates that therapy is "serious business." The battle for initiative occurs after the therapeutic structure is established, the therapeutic relationships are formed, and the family situation is delineated. The cotherapy team encourages the family to take initiative for their own growth and responsibility for life decisions. This battle is resolved when the cotherapy team establishes an existential adult-to-adult relationship with each family member, with mutual involvement in the therapeutic exchange from all participants. During this phase, information is gleaned regarding the presenting problem, families of origin, and family interactions. Symptoms are reframed as attempts to grow and the mutual responsibility of multiple parties are emphasized, thus decreasing scapegoating.

Virginia, a 27-year-old office manager, presented for therapy complaining that she had developed symptoms of bulimia nervosa after becoming involved with Cindy, her first lesbian lover. Virginia and Cindy had been living together for the past 3½ years, and reportedly had a satisfactory relationship. However, Virginia acknowledged that she became more symptomatic whenever she was angry at Cindy. The couple had never overtly discussed Virginia's bulimic symptoms and Virginia had sought help without Cindy's knowledge. After the initial evaluation session, the therapist recommended couple therapy, and Virginia adamantly refused. They agreed to meet a second time and discuss the situation. During the second session, the therapist was aware that the battle for structure had begun and must be won by the therapist if meaningful change was to occur. The therapist, therefore, articulated clearly to Virginia her view that change would not occur unless Cindy was included in the treatment. Couple sessions were begun reluctantly by both partners and a second therapist joined the treatment. Although the therapist(s) had won the battle for structure, it became clear that the battle for initiative was now the central focus. Specifically, although both Virginia and Cindy attended sessions promptly and regularly and were responsible about paying the bill, Virginia refused to discuss her bulimia in Cindy's presence, and Cindy denied any awareness of difficulties in their relationship. The couple was not taking any responsibility for the content and process of the therapeutic encounters. The therapists attempted to make overt the covert undertones in the couple's communication. For example, one of the therapists provided the following personal anecdote: "You know, I just had the following recollection and I don't know why. I remember when I was a young child and I would become angry at my mother for trying to boss me around, I would go in my bedroom, cover my face with a pillow, and scream so that no one could hear me. When my mother would try to talk with me, I said that nothing was the matter." Such personal vignettes were coupled with other metaphors about how unexpressed anger inhibits healthy communication and efforts to grow. During the seventh session, Virginia and Cindy reported a recent fight about "something stupid" and then slowly began exploring their disappointments in their relationship, their difficulties expressing their anger directly toward one another for fear of being rejected, and their desire for more closeness and communication. The battle for initiative was therefore under way.

In the middle phase, the family defines and actively addresses its life difficulties with the help of the cotherapists, who have become personally involved with the family. Throughout this phase, Whitaker and Keith (1981) advocate implementing techniques to facilitate change and create alternative interactional patterns that reduce scapegoating and blame of the caretaking parent. Some specific techniques utilized include redefining symptoms as efforts toward growth; explicating covert conflict; separating interpersonal and internal stress and modeling fantasized alternatives to stress; the therapists' use of self, including unconscious material, absurdity, and "acting-in" (affective confrontation of family members by the therapist); involving grandparents and other extended family members in treatment; and reversing roles (for review, see Roberto, 1991). Satir (1967, 1972) advocates a number of techniques which also may be implemented during this phase of the work. Satir values touch as a means of expressing nonverbal support in a respectful manner. Family members may be asked to act out scenes in their lives (drama, family reconstruction) and/or demonstrate interrelationships using bodily positions and nonverbal gestures in a static (family sculpture) or dynamic (stress ballet) fashion. This phase of the work may yield positive results such that the family continues to work effectively

in the therapy or chooses to leave therapy feeling competent to handle problems effectively. However, this process may lead to an *impotence impasse* in which the therapists feel that despite their best efforts, the family does not change or take responsibility for their own problems (Whitaker & Keith, 1981). This impasse is successfully negotiated when decisions about treatment are mutually agreed on between the family and the cotherapy team.

In the end phase, the cotherapy team disentangles itself from the family system and takes a more peripheral role, intervening only when necessary (e.g., when new symptoms emerge). The family observes its own functioning and takes responsibility for making decisions and solving problems. Thus, the cotherapy team and the family work as equal partners rather than as consultant and patient. This relational shift is facilitated by several techniques used by the cotherapists, including spontaneous self-disclosure, expression of grief regarding termination, and requests for feedback about the therapy. The family and the cotherapy team part with the recognition of mutual interdependence and loss. Termination is indicated when family members appear self-confident and the family demonstrates that it possesses the requisite resources to resolve problems and tolerate life stress.

Stance of the Therapist

Experiential symbolic family therapists are actively engaged in the family's interactional processes yet do not direct the therapy. They listen, observe, attend to their own affective reactions, and intervene actively to change the family's functioning without focusing on the etiology of the difficulties. These therapists openly express warmth and caring for the family and use their personalities (true self) in sharing their internal processes with the family without losing their differentiated sense of self. They are like "coaches" (who observe and suggest but do not direct or change) or surrogate grandparents, roles that require structure and discipline as well as caring and personal availability. Emphasis on participant observation underscores the family's responsibility for change, even though the therapists are responsible for the interventions.

Experiential symbolic family therapy is typically conducted by a cotherapy team, which enables each therapist to perform unique functions and to interchange these functions when indicated. The cotherapy team models adaptive interpersonal relationships and provides experiential alternatives for family interactions.

Curative Factors

The basic assumption of experiential symbolic family therapy is that families change as a result of experiences, not through education or interpretation (Whitaker & Keith, 1981). Chief mechanisms for change are the experience of new relational stances with family members, the expression of strong emotions, and the challenging of current interactional patterns, all of which lead to interactional insights. Interactional insights are considered more prominent and effective than are historical insights. The therapists' own roles within their families of origin and creation impact their interactions with the family and the cotherapist. Therefore, family therapy for the therapist is strongly encouraged.

Treatment Applicability

Experiential symbolic family therapy has been used with families in which the identified patient presents with a range of problems, including severe forms of psychopathology (i.e., schizophrenia). However, it is particularly difficult to use this approach with families in which an individual member presents with severe personality disorders, notably antisocial or narcissistic personality disorders. Additionally, in families coping with a trauma, such as divorce or abuse, this treatment may be emotionally overwhelming and thus contraindicated. No treatment may be recommended when the family is dissatisfied with treatment elsewhere and when a marital dyad has completed a successful course of therapy and experiences acute difficulties. Although the proliferation of writings on symbolic experiential family therapy and individual family's subjective attestations of improvement are suggestive of this model's efficacy, empirical studies have not been presented in the literature.

Strategic Family Therapy

A number of groups of family therapists can be classified as strategic family therapists: (1) the *communicational school* of the MRI group and later the Brief Therapy Center in Palo Alto, which initially included Gregory Bateson, Donald Jackson, John Weakland, Jay Haley, and Virginia Satir and later added Paul Watzlawick, Richard Fisch, and Arthur Bodin (Bateson et al., 1956; Watzlawick, Weakland, & Fisch, 1974); and (2) Jay Haley (Haley, 1976) and Cloe Madanes's (Madanes, 1981) *problem-solving therapy*. Strategic therapy approaches were influenced heavily by Bateson's focus on communication processes and the strategic therapy of Milton Erickson.

Strategic approaches, which are change- rather than growth-oriented, view problems as maintained by maladaptive family interactional sequences, including faulty and incongruent hierarchies and malfunctioning triangles. The behavioral sequences observed in the family's attempts to solve the problem are assumed to perpetuate the presenting problem (Haley, 1976). These sequences of behavior are viewed as complex and circular, rather than linear, and therefore change within the family system is a necessary prerequisite for individual change. Problems are also conceptualized as resulting from prior unsuccessful attempts to solve a given difficulty (Watzlawick et al., 1974).

These approaches are ahistorical, emphasizing present interactions and communications rather than the past. These models attend to *metacommunications* (communications about communications) among family members, focusing on the covert, nonverbal messages that amplify the meaning of overt, verbal messages. The presenting problem is an *analogical message*, a metaphor for underlying dysfunction. For example, a couple's fighting over trivial matters may reflect their power and/or intimacy struggles.

The following discussion focuses on Haley and Madanes's brand of strategic therapy, as illustrative of strategic approaches.

Basic Structure of Therapy

Strategic therapies are brief interventions, which may include the whole family or only one or two members of a family system. Sessions occur weekly or biweekly and are conducted by a single therapist. The approach is structured, as the therapist directs the questioning, gives directives, and intervenes actively.

Goal Setting

The primary goal is solving the family's presenting problem within the social context. This is accomplished by the therapist and family setting small, concrete goals related to the presenting problem. Goals are formulated as increases in positive behaviors rather than reduction of problematic behaviors. This helps the

family feel motivated, as success seems possible. Additional and more long-term goals include altering the interactional sequences maintaining the problem and helping family members resolve a crisis and progress to the next stage of the family and individual life cycle.

Thus, successful strategic therapy achieves *second-order change* (Watzlawick et al., 1974), fundamental changes in the family system's structure and functioning, rather than *first-order change* in which superficial modifications are made that do not affect the structure of the system itself. For example, in a family with an oppositional adolescent who repeatedly demands to borrow the family car, first-order change may be evident when the parents become more lenient about allowing their son to borrow the car and the son becomes more willing to comply with parental requests. This improved state of affairs is considered first-order change when no other changes in the family structure or interactional patterns are noted. Second-order change becomes apparent when the adolescent evidences more compliant behavior in the context of age-appropriate separation from his parents, and his parents becomes closer to each other and thus no longer need to triangulate their son in their relationship. In such cases, the executive power hierarchy is strengthened concurrent with an increased level of intimacy within the marital subsystem. Additionally, the adolescent forms more age-appropriate peer relationships and his oppositional behavior serves to define identity without engaging in self- or other-destructive behavior.

Techniques and Process of Therapy

Problem-solving therapy is a process that occurs in stages until the presenting problem is resolved and other treatment goals are achieved. The first stage encompasses the initial interview, in which the family problem and the context within which it is embedded are ascertained. This interview is divided into five stages: (1) social stage—therapist makes direct contact with each family member, makes initial hypotheses about the family, and matches the family's mood; (2) problem stage—therapist asks formal questions regarding the problem; (3) interaction stage—therapist asks family members to talk with one another about the problem and observes communication patterns; (4) goal-setting stage—therapist ascertains changes desired by the family and specifies these in behavioral terms; and (5) task-setting stage—therapist gives the family a directive, typically a homework assignment, designed to alter dysfunctional interactional sequences.

Once a family diagnosis is determined and the problem is defined, the therapist formulates a therapeutic approach consisting of an overall plan for a series of tactical interventions, labeled directives. These directives serve several functions: change the underlying interactional sequences maintaining the problem; intensify the therapeutic relationship; and gather information about the family, particularly their resistance to change. Directives may be straight or paradoxical. Straight directives, designed to elicit the family's cooperation with the therapist's request, are useful in crisis situations. Paradoxical directives are useful when the family is resistant to change, as they encourage the family to oppose the therapist.

Strategic family therapists assess and track the cycle of family interactional sequences by asking questions, break the cycle through straightforward and/or paradoxical directives, and support termination when the presenting problem has been alleviated. Techniques are relatively indirect and nonconfrontive and retrospectively focus on out-of-session behavioral sequences and emphasize out-of-session directives.

Positive feedback cycles are emphasized such that the family's homeostasis is challenged in order to change the family's behavioral patterns. Key techniques to alter existing behavioral sequences include paradox; *reframing*, or relabeling (use language to provide new meaning to the situation such as *positive connotation* in which problem behaviors are relabeled in a positive light); *ordeals* (recommending that a family member engage in a behavior he/she dislikes but one that would improve his/her relationship with significant others); *pretending* (prescribing that a symptomatic person pretend to exhibit his/her symptom which reclassifies the symptom as voluntary and thus alters family members reactions); *unbalancing* through creating alternative coalitions; and prescribing homework. There are many forms of paradoxical interventions, including (1) therapeutic use of *double-bind* communication; (2) *positioning*, where the therapist accepts and exaggerates what the family members are saying, underscoring the absurdity of the situation and therefore forcing them to take a different position; (3) *restraining*, where the therapist discourages change by enumerating the dangers associated with positive change; and (4) *symptom prescription*, where the therapist directs the family member to practice his/her symptom and provides a compelling rationale for the prescription.

In strategic therapies, the time-limited nature and problem-solving focus make termination a natural process (Segal, 1991). Families are ready to terminate when significant and durable improvements in the presenting problem have occurred and the family reports handling their problems without the therapist (Segal, 1991). During the termination phase, the family is given credit for their improvements yet cautioned against developing a sense of false optimism that family problems will not return. For families hesitant about terminating, termination may be framed as a break from therapy in which gains are consolidated.

Stance of the Therapist

Strategic therapists are active and present in a powerful, authoritative, and charismatic fashion and use their powers of persuasion to convince a family to follow a precise directive, whether straightforward or paradoxical. These therapists have been considered to be highly manipulative in implementing their interventions, as is the case when they recommend that a marital couple chronically in conflict fight at planned times during the day for a specified period. The therapist intervenes when he/she chooses rather than when the family requests participation. Strategic therapists avoid being aligned with one family faction; however, they will voluntarily take sides to overcome an impasse.

Curative Factors

Techniques are of paramount importance in effecting change. Curative factors include correcting the hierarchy by encouraging the parental subsystem to effectively and appropriately utilize its power, helping family members negotiate and reach agreements, and reuniting family members in an effort to heal old wounds (Madanes, 1991). Insight is not valued and interpretations, in the classical sense, are rare. Family members are not educated directly in interpersonal skills, yet the directives offered typically require the development of a more adaptive interpersonal style. Change in the identified patient's problem behavior is inextricably interwoven with systemic changes. Therapists who discuss strategic family therapy approaches pay little attention to the therapist's psychological health or personality.

Treatment Applicability

While strategic therapy has been applied to couples and families presenting with a wide variety of problems, specific applications are noteworthy. Haley's problem-solving therapy and the MRI group's strategic therapy approaches have documented efficacy in case studies and treatment outcome and follow-up research for schizophrenia, anorexia, substance abuse, violence, anxiety disorders (e.g., phobias and obsessive–compulsive disorder), and child and adolescent behavior problems (Stanton, 1981). Madanes (1990) adapted strategic family therapy for incestuous families and developed a 16-step intervention for reparation. There is, however, minimal methodologically sophisticated treatment process and outcome research addressing the efficacy of strategic approaches to family intervention.

Systemic Family Therapy

Systemic family therapy was pioneered in Italy by the Milan group, originally consisting of Mara Selvini Palazzoli and colleagues, Luigi Boscolo, Gianfranco Cecchin, and Giuiana Prata (Selvini-Palazzoli et al., 1978). In 1980, the group divided, with Selvini-Palazzoli and Prata focusing on research and clinical endeavors and finding a universal, invariant prescription relevant to all families. In 1985, Selvini-Palazzoli, with a separate group of research collaborators, delineated a systemic model of psychotic processes in families (Selvini-Palazzoli, Cirillo, Selvini, & Sorrentino, 1989). Boscolo and Cecchin emphasized training new generations of systemic family therapists. They asserted that interventions should remain flexible, with alternative interventions tailored to the family being viewed as optimal. Systemic family therapy has been popularized in the United

States by Lynn Hoffman at the Ackerman Institute and in Amherst, Massachusetts (Hoffman, 1981) and by Peggy Papp, Olga Silverstein, and their colleagues at the Ackerman Institute in New York. The development of systemic family therapy has been a complex and dynamic process, the evolution of which has been detailed (Campbell, Draper, & Crutchley, 1991).

Like strategic approaches, systemic family therapists were influenced by Bateson. The systemic model is the purest application of Bateson's circular epistemology. The Milan model focuses on process rather than structure. Consistent with the beliefs posited by the MRI group, the systemic approach views the family and therapist as an *ecosystem* in which each member affects the health of all other members over time. Thus, symptomatic behavior is perpetuated by *rule-governed transactional patterns*. The symptom keeps the family system in a homeostatic state. In accord with Bateson's cybernetic model, systemic therapists view the family as a nonlinear and complex *cybernetic system*, with interlocking feedback mechanisms and repetitive patterns of behavior sequences. Systemic family therapists are unified in their efforts to comprehend the meaning of *second-order cybernetics* (the cybernetics of cybernetics) and to use these understandings as a basis for practicing family therapy.

Basic Structure of Therapy

Systemic therapy is a long brief intervention conducted with all family members present. Specifically, sessions frequently are spaced at monthly intervals, allowing time for the intervention to take effect and elicit change throughout the system. Typical courses of therapy are between 3 and 20 sessions, with 10 sessions being modal. The number of sessions is agreed on in advance and adhered to rigidly. Sessions are conducted by a single therapist or a cotherapy pair, with other members of the therapy team providing live supervision through a one-way mirror. These observers enhance the objectivity of the therapist(s) working directly with the family. The therapists are responsible for structuring the process of the sessions.

Goal Setting

The therapist's goals are to create a context within which the family's belief system can be explored and change can occur. This is accomplished by the therapist maintaining a systemic view of the family and offering a new conceptualization (cognitive map) of family problems. However, the specific goals are determined by the family members and how the family changes is considered their responsibility. If the therapist does not agree with the family's goals, he/she respects the family's wishes unless the family's choices may be harmful to one or more family members (e.g., abusive behavior toward a child).

Techniques and Process of Therapy

Systemic family therapists, who incorporate a more evolutionary perspective than do their strategic counterparts, assert that problematic behaviors emerge when the family's *epistemology* (rules and conceptual framework for understanding reality) is no longer adaptive. Thus, they attempt to create an environment in which new information inviting spontaneous change is introduced to foster the family's development of an alternative epistemology. Utilizing this framework, sessions follow a relatively standard format, including (1) the presession during which the therapists gather information for the session; (2) the session during which information is given and discussions occur allowing observation of the family's transactional patterns; (3) discussion of the session in a separate room by the therapist/cotherapy pair and behind-the-mirror observers, during which suggestions, opinions, and observations are shared, culminating in a systemic hypothesis and associated intervention; (4) rejoining the family by the therapist or cotherapy pair to offer a comment and a prescription (typically a paradoxical directive which may be offered in a form of a letter) for an outside the session task; and (5) postsession therapy team discussion of the family's reaction to the intervention and a written formulation summarizing the session.

Systemic family therapists use many techniques described in the strategic therapy section. They combine the basic principles of paradoxical intervention (Watzlawick et al., 1974) with systemic hypotheses (hypotheses to explain behavior that create a framework from which to ask questions and devise interventions) and rituals (individualized prescription of an action or series of actions designed to alter the family's roles).

A number of techniques are associated particularly with the Milan school of systemic family therapy. *Circular questioning*, in which one member is asked to comment on the interactional behaviors of two other members, is an effective diagnostic and therapeutic technique. Circular questioning addresses family members' differential perceptions and experiences of events and relationships. This enables the therapist and the family to perceive differences nonjudgmentally, conceptualize problems systemically (e.g., what is the function of the symptom), and intervene accordingly.

Positive connotation is a form of reframing in which the therapist labels all behavior as positive because it maintains family homeostasis and cohesion. Positive connotation fosters the family' acceptance of the therapists' interventions and leads the family to question why symptomatic behavior is essential for family cohesion. Interventions, based on the hypothesized systemic formulations of family games, are made to all family members through paradoxes and the use of rituals or counterparadoxical prescriptions.

Rituals, designed to address the conflict between unspoken (analogic) and spoken family rules, are prescriptions directing the family to change its behavior leading to modification of associated cognitive maps.

Counterparadoxical interventions occur when the therapist places the family in a therapeutic double bind to counteract the family members' pattern of paradoxical communications. The use of counterparadoxical interventions, in which the overt communication is for the family not to change, is based on the assumption that symptomatic behavior maintains the homeostasis and thus a prescription of no change supports the homeostatic tendency of the family.

Thus, rather than issuing prescriptions designed to elicit resistance, systemic therapists offer prescriptions designed to provide information about family connectedness. Taken together, these interventions uncover family games, introduce a new cognitive map, and engender the family to discover the solution to its problems via a transformation in family rules and relationships.

Because behavioral goals are not specified, it is often unclear when the therapy should be terminated. Termination typically occurs when the problem behavior is alleviated or when the family no longer perceives the behavior to be a problem. Therapist and family usually mutually agree that they have no reason to continue to meet and thus a decision to terminate is made. The therapist may recommend to the family members that they return for a review session at a later point in time.

Stance of the Therapist

Unlike strategic therapists, systemic therapists historically have taken a relatively neutral, objective, and nonreactive stance as they avoid becoming part of any family alliance or coalition. This position of neutrality, in which the therapist avoids issues of hierarchy, power, and alignments, typically allows for maximum leverage for achieving change. The therapist is free to attend to the system in its entirety and is not pulled into the *family games* (Selvini-Palazzoli et al., 1989), specific repetitive patterns of family interaction. More recently, Selvini-Palazzoli and colleagues (Selvini-Palazzoli et al., 1989) have advocated that the therapist develop a relationship with each spouse, openly share his/her hypotheses for what is occurring in the family system, and minimize the use of paradoxical techniques. Consistent with the cybernetics of cybernetics, the referring source and the therapy team are considered integral parts of the coevolving ecosystem, affecting each other in circular feedback loops.

Curative Factors

Systemic family therapy shares with other approaches respect and empathy for the family, a value on joining with the family, an acknowledgment of interlocking family behaviors, an awareness of the importance of offering alternative cognitive maps, and a recognition of providing an appropriate context within which to conduct the work. Mechanisms of change associated specifically with systemic family therapy include interviewing the family in a manner that permits individuals to develop new connections between events and their meanings and creating a new family meaning system that leads to the development of alternative behaviors and interactional patterns. This work does not require insight

and the value of insight is minimized. Interpretations are not incorporated in this approach.

The therapist's personality is considered important in the endeavor insofar as it enables the therapist to relate attentively while simultaneously entertaining systemic hypotheses. Although it is acknowledged that the therapist's personality influences the family and the work, it is not considered central to the change process. Therapy is most efficacious when there is a good fit between therapist and family such that the family permits the therapist to explore and challenge its belief system and the therapist can provide feedback in a challenging, yet respectful manner.

Treatment Applicability

The Milan group's systemic approach has been used with families with a variety of severe emotional problems, most notably psychosomatic (Selvini-Palazzoli, 1974) and psychotic symptoms (Selvini-Palazzoli et al., 1978). Campbell and colleagues (1991) assert that the Milan approach is appropriate for any family whose solution to their problems has become interwoven with the family's meaning system such that alternative solutions for problem solving are limited.

Evaluations of treatment efficacy are sparse and typically consist of self-report data. However, one systematic outcome study comparing problem solving versus systemic family therapies found that while both interventions yielded significant symptom reduction, families completing the systemic treatment evidenced a broader systemic perspective regarding their family's functioning (Bennun, 1986).

Structural Family Therapy

Salvador Minuchin and colleagues (e.g., Auerswald, Montalvo, Aponte, Haley,

Hoffman, and Rosman) founded the structural model of family therapy (Minuchin et al., 1967, 1978; Minuchin, 1974), which serves as the basis for much of the family therapy conceptualized and practiced today. The model was an outgrowth of the authors' work at the Philadelphia Child Guidance Clinic, where they worked with delinquent youth and their families from a low socioeconomic status who were predominantly African American. The model continues to be utilized and expanded for the African American population as it incorporates a more ecostructural perspective in which the family's transactions with outside agencies and systems are the focus of concern (Boyd-Franklin, 1989).

Structural family therapy is a theoretically based approach for intervening with identified patient children/adolescents and their families, which incorporates structuralist conceptualizations. Adaptive and maladaptive functioning are described in terms of the organized patterns of interactions among individuals, their families, and the environment. Individual functioning is understood in light of the individual's interaction with the social context. The structural model identifies a number of basic concepts relating to the structure, communication patterns, and expression of affect, which are useful in explaining the family's organization, coping patterns, and adaptation to developmental transitions (for review, see the aforementioned books written by Minuchin and colleagues; Aponte & Van Deusen, 1981; Colapinto, 1991). *Structural organization* refers to relational patterns common to all families, influenced by the personal idiosyncracies of each family, adapted for addressing social tasks in a developmentally sensitive fashion within the context in which the family is embedded.

Family transactional patterns provide information about *boundaries* and *hierarchy*, *alignments*, and *power*. Boundaries demarcate subsystems and "are the rules defining who participates and how" (Minuchin, 1974, p. 53) in various tasks and activities. Families are hierarchically organized, with parents in the executive subsystem positioned above their children. Alignment refers to the "joining or opposition of one member of a system to another in carrying out an operation" (Aponte, 1976, p. 434). Under the rubric of alignment are the concepts of *coalition* (a covert alliance between two family members against a third) and *alliance* (two individuals share a common interest not held by a third person). Power, also referred to as force, has been defined as "the relative influence of each [family] member on the outcome of an activity" (Aponte, 1976, p. 434). The structural dimensions of boundaries and alignments depend on power for action and outcome (Aponte & Van Deusen, 1981).

Dysfunctional families have impairments in boundaries, alignments, and/or power balance evidenced by the failure to adapt to stressors in a developmentally appropriate manner. Families evidence maladjustment when they rigidly and tenaciously cling to familiar interactional patterns. The nature of the family dysfunction associated with the manifestation of symptoms or problems may be categorized according to the structural dimensions of boundary, alignment, and power which are most salient. The terms "enmeshment" and "disengagement" refer to maladaptive expressions of family boundaries and reflect extreme points on a continuum of family contact. Another family pattern indicative of impairments in family boundaries has been termed the "violation of function boundaries." The classic example of this inappropriate intrusion of one family member into the domain of other family members is the case of the parental child, where the child assumes the power, authority, and responsibilities that more appropriately belong to someone in the executive subsystem.

Common dysfunctional family alignments include stable coalitions, detouring coalitions, and triangulation and require at least three participants. *Stable coalitions* are those in which two family members are consistently in agreement against a third person. When the two allies agree that the third person is the source of their problem (i.e., our son's bad behavior causes our marital problems), a *detouring coalition* is formed to reduce the stress in the dyad, giving the impression of harmony.

Triangulation occurs when an opposing family member (frequently one of the parents) demands that a third person (typically a child) side with him/her against the opposing party. The third person consequently feels a split alliance, necessitating siding with one party and then the other. This process emotionally paralyzes the triangulated individual, resulting in symptomatic behavior. Dysfunctional family patterns relevant to the power dimension often are indicative of a lack of functional power, which reflects the inability of family members to utilize their authority to implement their assigned roles. The classic example is that of weak executive subsystem functioning, in which the parental subsystem fails to exert the force required to guide the children.

Additional structural problems that incorporate more than one of the key structural dimensions are worthy of note. *Cross-generational stable coalitions*, in which spouses argue their conflict through their child, reflect problems with boundaries and alignments. Chronic cross-generational stable coalitions are commonly evident in families in which a member presents with a psychosomatic illness (e.g., anorexia nervosa) or a substance abuse problem (Colapinto, 1991). Families deficient on all three structural domains are underorganized, having limited coping strategies and structure that they employ rigidly yet inconsistently. In contrast, healthy families have "well-defined, elaborated, flexible, and cohesive" (Aponte & Van Deusen, 1981, p. 315) family structures that accommodate the changing functions and roles of individual family members, the various family subsystems, and the sociocultural environment.

Basic Structure of Therapy

The structure of this intervention approach is flexible in terms of number of therapists, which family members participate in an interview, and location, length, and frequency of interviews. Typically, however, structural family therapy is a brief intervention (5 to 7 months on average) whose primary participants are family members who interact daily. Rather than focusing predominantly on the content (what is said) of family communication, the primary focus is on verbal and nonverbal interactional processes as they reflect the family structure. Structural family therapy is most often conducted by a single therapist because the therapeutic techniques employed are more difficult to carry out when coordination between two therapists is required. The presence of a cotherapy dyad also makes it technically more difficult to exert maximal control over the family's transactional patterns. Although a one-way mirror may be used for purposes of family restructuring (e.g., removing the children to have them observe the parents interact), there rarely is a consultant behind the mirror. However, when more than one therapist is involved in a case, it is optimal for these extra therapists to serve as observers behind the mirror.

Goal Setting

Typically, the primary goal negotiated between the therapist and the family is the resolution of the presenting problem. The therapist helps the family identify common goals when possible and acknowledge conflicting goals when they exist. The family may desire resolution of the presenting problem with a focus on the identified patient and a lack of attention to underlying structural patterns. However, the therapist asserts that this goal can only be attained by restructuring the family unit so that more adaptive interactional patterns prevail. A second important aim of the work is to change the family's construction of reality (Minuchin & Fishman, 1981). In other words, the therapist helps the family to develop alternative explantory schemata for viewing the problem, which enables them to develop more adaptive family transactions.

Techniques and Process of Therapy

The structural family therapy approach entails three cyclical and overlapping stages: joining, assessing, and restructuring. Similar to other family therapists, structural family therapists join the family rapidly and in a position of leadership. This enables the therapist to develop an understanding of the family's construction of reality and structure. To facilitate the *joining process*, the therapist utilizes three procedures: *maintenance* (supporting the existing structure of the family or subsystem), *tracking* (following the content of the family's communication with minimal intervention), and *mimesis* (adopting the style and affective experience of the family). The therapist initially accepts the family's view of the presenting problem as the real problem and designs interventions to ameliorate the problem by changing the structure of the

family system. As symptom reduction proceeds, the family may gain more confidence in the therapist's expertise and thus be more inclined to address underlying structural issues.

The *assessment* stage focuses on six domains of family functioning: (1) structure, boundary quality, and resonance (sensitivity to the actions of individual members and tolerance for deviation from the family norm); (2) flexibility and capacity for change; (3) interactional patterns of the spousal, parental, and sibling subsystems; (4) role of identified patient and how his/her symptom maintains family homeostasis; (5) ecological context within which the presenting problem develops and is maintained; and (6) developmental stage of the family and its individual members. This assessment enables the therapist to develop a family map and diagnosis in which relationships between structural problems and current symptoms are delineated.

Cassandra, a 15-year-old Caucasian female, was referred for an evaluation after she was suspended from school for "doing crack" in the school bathroom. An evaluation was conducted with Cassandra; her older brother, George, who had recently moved into a dormitory at the local state college; and their mother, Ms. Sutton, a single parent who was employed as a salesperson. Mr. and Mrs. Sutton had divorced when the children were young, and Mr. Sutton had infrequent contact with his children. George and Ms. Sutton had been extremely close, and Ms. Sutton had often sought George's advice on how to handle Cassandra. George often took on a paternal role toward his younger sister, taking responsibility for both protecting and disciplining her. Cassandra had many friends, unlike her older brother, spending considerable time outside of the family. Since her brother had left home, Cassandra's schoolwork had deteriorated, and she and her mother had become more withdrawn from one another. A structural assessment revealed the following: The Sutton family was having difficulty negotiating the developmental transition of "launching children and moving on." This difficulty was compounded by a preexisting family structure characterized by a parental child, lack of appropriate generational boundaries, a stable coalition between the mother and the son against the daughter, and a restricted capacity for change as evidenced by the mother's resistance to developing intimate relationships with adults outside the family. Cassandra's substance use in the school served a protective function for the family as it distracted Ms. Sutton from her own dysphoric affects associated with her son's departure, an experience that had reactivated her pain about her earlier marital separation and subsequent divorce.

The third phase, *restructuring*, redresses the structural difficulties noted during the assessment. For example, with enmeshed families, the goal is to increase age-appropriate separation–individuation; with disengaged families, the restructuring process entails enhancing family attachments. A number of techniques have been associated with the restructuring process. *Enactments*, in which the therapist promotes the family's acting out of dysfunctional and habitual transactional patterns of relating during the session, enables the therapist to observe dysfunctional patterns and intervene to facilitate structural change. Additional techniques include escalating stress, boundary marking, unbalancing the family alignments, assigning homework tasks, and providing support, education, and guidance (for review, see Colapinto, 1991).

According to Minuchin, a family member's symptom is indicative of dysfunctional family patterns for managing stress. He recommends escalating stress within the family system to develop more effective interactional patterns. Strategies for escalating stress include in-creasing the intensity of the enactment by prolonging its occurrence, introducing new variables (e.g., new family members), blocking typical patterns of relating by challenging the communication rules and structure of the family, emphasizing differences, or suggesting alternative transactions during the session that may provide a useful model for changing interactions outside the session. Spatial interventions, including rearranging the seating and removing members from the room temporarily and having them observe the interactions from behind a one-way mirror, alter the perspectives of family members regarding the interrelationships in an effort to improve interpersonal boundaries. Minuchin advocates assigning tasks to the family, both inside and outside (homework) the session. Tasks are diagnostic probes that yield valuable information about the family's openness to change and serve to change maladaptive family communication patterns and structure. Tasks may be assigned in a direct fashion, paradoxically, or in a combination of the two.

Stance of the Therapist

Minuchin (1974) describes the role of the therapist as that of a distant and friendly relative who takes an active and authoritative stance by asking probing and open-ended questions and giving directions and homework assignments. Consistent with Minuchin's persona, the structural family therapist is often colorful and dramatic, demands that family members accommodate to the therapist to facilitate therapeutic progress, and communicates his/her expertise in assisting the family members to mobilize their adaptive resources to facilitate change. The structural family therapist is, thus, the stage director or producer of the family drama.

Curative Factors

Emphasis is on interactions occurring in the present and the therapeutic task is one of behavior change as opposed to insight. The structural approach is more symptom-oriented than are the psychoanalytic schools, yet less symptom-focused than are strategic therapies. Further, the structural approach is very technique oriented, incorporates a developmental perspective in understanding the relationship between individual/ family life-stage transitions and dysfunction, conceptualizes communicational sequences or transactional patterns in terms of both cybernetic properties *and* organizational structure of the family, and views the family assessment process in a holistic framework taking into account the therapist's impact on the family in the data gathering process.

Resistance to change is either circumvented through the use of enactments or directly challenged by escalating the stress within the family system. However, resistances to change are not typically interpreted by the therapist. Genuine change in the identified patient occurs only when the family structure is transformed.

The effective use of structural family therapy techniques requires a "clarity of purpose and a difficult balancing of commitment to change and sensitivity to corrective feedback from the family" (Colapinto, 1991, p. 439) on the part of the therapist. Other aspects of the therapist's psychological health and personality are not specifically highlighted. This is not surprising given that transference and countertransference dynamics are not considered integral to the curative process.

Treatment Applicability

Although designed initially for low socioeconomic status families, the structural approach has been applied successfully, according to results from empirically based treatment outcome studies, to a range of families evidencing a wide variety of problems and symptoms (e.g., psychosomatic illnesses, externalizing behavior disorders, and substance abuse). Additionally, this intervention approach has been applied effectively to work with multiproblem, disorganized families and with families in the process of divorce or rebuilding a remarried, blended, or stepfamily. The structural model has not developed an independent set of techniques for working with couples. Rather, the couple is a subsystem of the family, which may become a focus of the treatment process.

Cognitive and Behavioral Family Therapy

Behavioral family therapy, predicated on social learning theory and behavior exchange principles, includes a diverse array of family and marital therapy techniques (for review, see Holtzworth-Munroe & Jacobson, 1991). Behavioral approaches to family/marital treatment began with Richard Stuart's (1980) behavioral marital therapy and Robert Liberman's (1970) conjoint behavioral family and couples therapy. More recent behavioral family therapy approaches include Jacobson and Margolin's behavioral marital therapy (1979), Alexander and Parsons's *functional family therapy* (1982), L'Abate and Weinstein's *marital enrichment* (1987), and the *McMaster problem-solving model* of Epstein, Bishop, and Levin (1978). Behavioral techniques also have been applied to *parent training* (for review, see Gordon & Davidson, 1981) and the treatment of sexual dysfunction (for review, see Heiman, LoPiccolo, & LoPiccolo, 1981). A number of authors have devised methods of cognitive-behavioral family therapy (Epstein,

Schlesinger, & Dryden, 1988) and cognitive therapy for couples (e.g., Beck, 1988).

With its emphasis on environmental, situational, and social determinants of behavior, the behavioral perspective is well suited to addressing problematic behavior in a family context. Maladaptive behavior is generated and maintained by environmental contingencies, including one's learning history. Interactions reflect reciprocal patterns of behavior in which one person's behavior reinforces the other's behavior, and circular and potentially escalating patterns of interaction emerge. Like all behavioral therapists, behavioral marital and family therapists attend to environmental events that precede and follow problem behaviors to determine how the behaviors have been learned and reinforced. In addition, these therapists underscore the family as a system, emphasizing the interdependent behavior patterns between family members (Jacobson & Margolin, 1979).

Cognitive-behavioral approaches to marital and family therapy, outgrowths of individual cognitive therapy (Beck, 1976) and rational–emotive therapy (Ellis, 1962), assume that one's cognitive processing (e.g., perceptions, interpretations, evaluations, attributions, and expectancies) influences family members' behaviors, transactions, and emotional and behavioral reactions. Each family member experiences a number of external events, including other family member's behaviors, the combined effects of several members' behaviors toward him/her, and their observations of interactions among family members. As family members cognitively appraise these events, they develop cognitions regarding self, the relationship between self and family members, and interrelationships among family subsystems. In healthy families, these perceptions are positive, realistic, and open to change via direct verbal communication. In dysfunctional families, perceptions tend to be distorted. According to Epstein and coworkers' (1988) model of cognitive-behavioral marital therapy, marital distress is indicative of both dysfunctional behavioral exchanges and distorted and rigid cognitive appraisals of one another. Behavioral and cognitive-behavioral marital therapies will be discussed as illustrative depictions of the application of behavioral and cognitive techniques to work with couples and families.

Basic Structure of Therapy

Behavioral and cognitive-behavioral marital therapies are brief, time-limited, and typically conducted by a single therapist. Membership is usually limited to the marital dyad. The therapy is relatively structured, with the structure provided by the therapist.

Goal Setting

A hallmark of behavioral marital therapy approaches is the process of developing specific and measurable treatment goals. Goal setting follows a functional analysis that assesses (1) maladaptive affective and instrumental behaviors and the environmental contingencies supporting these behaviors and (2) the ways in which the spouses' reciprocal interactions affect their marital satisfaction. Based on the functional analysis, the therapist and couple together delineate specific treatment goals. The intervention is discussed, and the therapist obtains a commitment from both partners to participate in a specified treatment plan. This commitment is formalized in a treatment contract.

Although treatment goals are tailored to the specific problems of the couple, general goals of behaviorally oriented marital therapy include changing maladaptive behaviors by modifying environmental contingencies, facilitating flexible behavior control, increasing positive interactions between spouses, altering environmental conditions that interfere with positive interactions, teaching more adaptive behaviors, and facilitating the maintenance and generalization of newly acquired behavioral changes. In addition, cognitive-behavioral marital therapy aims to change both partners' cognitive processing of their own and one another's behavior such that marital satisfaction is improved.

Techniques and Process of Therapy

The following incorporates the work of Stuart (1980), Liberman (1970), Jacobson and Margolin (1979), and Epstein and colleagues (1978). In the first phase, the therapist and couple develop a collaborative relationship and an assessment of the presenting problem is conducted. The assessment incorporates self-report measures of marital functioning and marital satisfaction questionnaires which detail daily activities, general targets for change, and marital commitment. Behavioral marital therapists use assessment throughout therapy, at termination, and at follow-up.

The second stage is that of formalizing the treatment contract. The therapist proposes an intervention to attain the goals identified during the assessment, and the therapist and couple agrees on a treatment plan. This plan may be in written or spoken form and can be modified when new treatment goals emerge.

During the third stage, the therapist helps the couple restructure their interpersonal environments to enhance their marital satisfaction. Spouses are helped to develop the expectation that they can reinforce each other in a positive and collaborative fashion. Several techniques are used, tailored to the unique needs, problems, and resources of each dyad. Like other family therapists, behavioral marital therapists model behavior and provide education to facilitate the attainment, maintenance, and generalizability of behavior changes. However, behavioral marital therapists also emphasize the use of structured tasks during and outside the session. For example, they may encourage the couple to devise written contracts stipulating specific desired behavioral changes in an effort to resolve persistent problems plaguing the couple. Another structured task is the "caring days" exercises (Stuart, 1980) in which the spouse explicitly states the behaviors he/she perceives as loving, carries out agreed-upon caring behaviors to demonstrate his/her commitment to the relationship, and documents the frequency and feelings of pleasure when caring behaviors are implemented. Caring days enable each partner to increase his/her initiation and acknowledgment of positive interactions and to better utilize reinforcers with one another.

Most behavioral marital therapists teach couples communication skills, including (1) active and effective listening, (2) thoughtfully timed and constructive requests using self-statements for which the speaker takes responsibility ("I" statements), (3) appropriate use of positive feedback, and (4) clarification of verbal and nonverbal messages to develop a consensus about their meaning. Behavioral marital therapy typically includes segments focusing on enhancing the couple's decision-making, problem-solving, and conflict resolution skills.

Behavioral marital therapists facilitate maintenance of treatment gains by assuring that the couple has learned how to engage in the requisite activities to improve dysfunctional interactions, teaching the couple to expect and predict relapses and ways to cope with them effectively, identifying interpersonal support systems, and equipping the couple with a written description of successful techniques that helped them improve their relationship. Generalization of treatment gains is facilitated by the therapist's gradual withdrawal of cues and initiation of an intermittent reinforcement schedule for adaptive behaviors. Treatment is terminated when the couple has attained the specified treatment goals and learned ways to cope with potential relapse.

Cognitive-behavioral marital therapists begin by assessing cognitive and behavioral processes associated with marital dysfunction. Only cognitive processes will be discussed, as the behavioral processes are noted above. Formal instruments or informal clinical interview techniques and observation are used to assess three cognitive processes: (1) beliefs about marital/family relationships and individual functioning, (2) causal attributions regarding the marital/family problems, and (3) expectancies about the likelihood of the occurrence of specified behaviors under particular conditions. Cognitive restructuring procedures are the dominant techniques used to help couples ascertain the accuracy of their cognitions regarding marital interaction. Spouses are encouraged to become perceptive observers of their own automatic thoughts and basic beliefs related to marital interactions and to evaluate the validity of these cognitions. Distorted automatic thoughts are modified via logical analysis, the collection of relevant data about their own interactional patterns, and the couple's gathering of information regarding normal marital/family functioning. Additionally, partners are instructed to identify the advantages and disadvantages of believing and adhering to their basic beliefs. Based on this evaluation of beliefs, the couple is guided in revising their basic beliefs to be more realistic and adaptive. A final form of cognitive restructuring is self-instructional training in which spouses are taught to give themselves covert directions for controlling their reactions to and perceptions of their partner. Self-instructional training can be used to diminish aversive transactions and disrupt escalating spirals of negative behavior. Because individuals' basic beliefs are relatively enduring, integrated in their *weltanschauung*, and reinforced by feedback from family members, considerable effort is needed to modify one's basic beliefs.

Robert and Gloria Williams, an African American couple in their mid-30s, sought couple therapy because Robert had been feeling increasingly depressed and hopeless during the past 3 months. His depression had been interfering with his work as an attorney and with their marital satisfaction. During the first few therapy sessions, it became clear that Robert had a negative view of himself, the world, and the future, and perceived events through these negative cognitive filters. He blamed himself for negative interactions with his wife, viewing the cause of these interactions as stable over time and generalizable across situations. Thus, when Gloria was attending to the children, Robert concluded, "She doesn't love me because I'm such a failure." His profoundly low self-esteem led him to feel more helpless, which in turn led him to function less effectively. His more passive and self-deprecating stance angered Gloria, who in turn would become more critical of her husband and less patient with him. This led him to feel more unloved and unworthy of being loved. The therapist helped Robert to explore the assumptions underlying his faulty attributions, reality-test these assumptions with Gloria to ascertain their validity, and develop alternative and more adaptive attributions for the couple's interactions. This shift in cognitive approach led to an amelioration of Robert's depressive mood, a process facilitated by Gloria's increased awareness of how Robert's faulty cognitions interfered with his functioning in their relationship, with the children, and at work.

Stance of the Therapist

Behavioral marital therapists function as scientists, educators, and role models.

They direct the treatment process, taking responsibility for setting the agenda, reviewing homework, and enforcing the treatment contract. Although a collaborative working alliance is considered essential for behavior change, transference is not addressed specifically nor considered important.

The role of the cognitive-behavioral marital therapist is that of a teacher, typically in the Socratic tradition. Therapists provide didactic information to teach the couple about cognitive and behavioral processes associated with marital dysfunction and improved marital satisfaction. The therapist functions as a consultant to the couple, as they test their perceptions and generate and rationally assess alternative hypotheses regarding individual functioning and marital interactions. Because the cognitive-behavioral approach is geared to the building of more adaptive skills (e.g., communication, assertiveness, problem solving, conflict resolution, and negotiation), the therapist serves as a teacher who supervises the couple's rehearsal of new behaviors.

Curative Factors

The mechanisms of change in behavioral marital therapy are related to the specific techniques used to attain treatment goals. For most couples, learning new interpersonal skills (e.g., communication and conflict resolution) is curative. Cognitive-behavioral marital therapists also view reality testing as essential for behavior change. In both behavioral and cognitive-behavioral marital therapies, the focus is on the present, insight is not viewed as necessary for accomplishing behavioral change, and interpretations are not utilized. The therapist's personality or psychological health does not play a direct role in bringing about change. However, a therapist who has difficulty structuring the sessions (e.g., does not stop a couple's arguing) or helping the couple to challenge their distorted cognitions is unlikely to be successful in effecting behavior change or improving marital satisfaction.

Treatment Applicability

Behavioral and cognitive-behavioral marital and family therapies have been applied to a broad range of problems (e.g., marital discord, child behavior problems, sexual dysfunction, and affective disorders). Behavioral marital therapy, the most extensively researched marital/family treatment approach, consistently has been shown to be superior to control groups in alleviating marital discord and enhancing marital satisfaction (e.g., for review, see Holzworth-Munroe & Jacobson, 1991). This therapy is most successful with families that actively engage in the treatment process, form a collaborative partnership with the therapist, and comply with homework assignments. Cognitive-behavioral marital and family interventions are most efficacious with couples/families in which all members are at least of average intellectual functioning and have the capacity for abstract thought, the children are school age or older, and family members are relatively accepting of one another (Epstein et al., 1988).

Other forms of behavioral marital or family therapy have been found efficacious. Behavioral parent training is effective for managing disruptive behavior disorders, elimination disorders, and anxiety disorders. Functional family therapy (Alexander & Parsons, 1982) yields an extremely low recidivism rate for juvenile delinquents whose families comply with treatment. The outcome research on sexual dysfunction reveals good success rates for behavioral treatment of premature ejaculation, female primary orgasmic dysfunction, and paraphillias (e.g., Heiman et al., 1981). Cognitive-behavioral family therapy has proven effective for remarried families,

families with older adults, addicted individuals, suicidal and depressed persons, and adults with sexual dysfunctions (for review, see Thomas, 1992).

Psychoeducational Family Therapy

Psychoeducational family therapy is a relatively new family therapy model. Because this approach has been used primarily with schizophrenic patients and their families (e.g., Anderson, Reiss, & Hogarty, 1986), it is only beginning to enter the mainstream family therapy field (for a review, see McFarlane, 1991).

Basic Structure of Therapy

Family psychoeducation, a structured treatment approach, can be conducted with an individual family or in a multiple family group format. The frequency of the sessions depends on the stage of the work and the status of the patient's psychiatric illness. The treatment may take a few years, with longer intervals between sessions during the latter phases. Some have argued that the psychoeducational family approach is not a form of family therapy but rather an approach to working with families with an individual with a biologically based illness.

Goal Setting

The intermediate goals are to stabilize the patient's condition, involve all family members in the psychoeducation process, educate the family about psychotic illnesses and antipsychotic medications, establish a treatment team that includes family members and emphasizes continuity of care, encourage the use and development of the social support network, help the family cope with the complex burdens associated with a prolonged psychiatric disorder in a family member, and teach more adaptive family stress management. The long-term goals are the prevention of relapse and the integration of the patient into the community. These goals are explicit and openly negotiated with all participants, a process that continues throughout the therapy. The underlying assumption of the model is that family members can be educated to create an optimal environment for their disabled loved ones, an environment that minimizes stresses exacerbating the patient's illness and enhances the patient's capacity for adaptive functioning.

Techniques and Process of Therapy

Both single family and multiple family psychoeducation approaches consist of four phases. The first phase begins at the time of the schizophrenic family member's first psychotic episode or subsequent relapse, typically an acute psychotic episode necessitating hospitalization or day treatment. The therapists (typically two clinicians) join with the family rapidly, forming an alliance with all relevant family members. Family meetings occur frequently and often are held without the patient to allay the family's anxiety and decrease distressing family–patient interactions. Separate meetings between the therapist and patient foster a supportive, working relationship and help the patient understand the philosophy of the approach. An assessment is undertaken entailing an evaluation of the present crisis, elicitation of family members' reactions to the patient's psychiatric disorder and the treatment system, and an examination of the family's structure, coping resources, and social support network. This phase culminates with the development of a contract, specifying conditions for the patient's discharge and the structure of the intervention.

The second phase consists of an educational workshop, which often occurs over the course of a day or weekend. However, some psychoeducational approaches utilize briefer, more ongoing educational workshops to communicate the information. Educational workshops are designed for family members and friends of the patient. Many advocate concurrent presentation of the educational material to the patient in a patient psychoeducational group format. Educational workshops are didactic, with a lecture and discussion format. Audiovisual aides are used to illustrate brain morphology, biochemistry of the disorder, medication effects and side effects, common symptoms and signs of the disorder, and guidelines for more effective management of the disorder. These guidelines presume that the patient's disability is caused by biological factors and that interpersonal and environmental stresses are key risk factors for relapse. The therapists educate the family to reduce expectations for rapid progress; use a relaxed manner of relating to the patient; reduce external stimulation in the patient's environment; set limits on the patient's disruptive, bizarre, or violent behavior; ignore symptoms that cannot be changed; use clear and simple communications; comply with the recommended treatment plan; maintain routine daily activities; avoid substance use; and ascertain warning signs suggestive of relapse.

The third phase is the reentry period, during which time the patient leaves the hospital and returns to the community. The goal is to stabilize the patient out of the hospital. Sessions are held less frequently, typically biweekly, and continue for at least 12 months. The clinician(s) meets with a single family, including the patient, or with the multiple families that attended the workshop together.

In the last phase, rehabilitation, the clinician and the family work together to increase the patient's level of adaptive functioning. Decisions to reduce the frequency of the sessions and, eventually, to terminate treatment are based on the patient's improvement, the family's preference, and, in the case of multiple family psychoeducation, the group members' need for continued social support. Social support is crucial in helping families and patients maintain treatment gains.

Clinicians adhere to the following steps when conducting family psychoeducation sessions: (1) socialize with family and patient; (2) review the outcome of the task assigned in the previous meeting; (3) review the week's events, particularly those that may be characterized as stressors; (4) reframe the family's reported stressors in the context of the realities of the patient's illness, and integrate this with the guidelines presented during the educational component of the intervention; (5) educate the family in adaptive problem-solving and communication skills; and (6) underscore the importance of medication compliance in the rehabilitation process.

Stance of the Therapist

The therapist creates a collaborative relationship with the patient, the family, and the other members of the treatment team. Psychoeducational family therapists are active during the sessions, providing direct advice, guidance, and information. They communicate their expertise in managing psychiatric disorders while recognizing the patient's and family's knowledge about the patient's unique psychiatric presentation and their resources to creatively solve family problems. The clinician's role differs depending on the phase of the work. During the joining phase, the therapist actively works to establish rapport with the family. In the educational phase, the therapists present themselves as teachers and experts in methods for managing psychiatric disorders and may facilitate the development of a social support network among families in the multiple family group. During the reentry and rehabilitation phases, the therapists help the family to utilize problem-solving and communication techniques to monitor the patient for relapse and help the patient to increase independent functioning.

Curative Factors

Because the psychoeducational family therapy approach is a relatively new form of treatment, there is limited information regarding the mechanisms of change (McFarlane, 1991), including such variables as the role of the therapist's mental health or personality in affecting change. Change is believed to be most durable when it occurs in the patient, the family, and the larger social support network. Change is not viewed as brought about by insight or interpretation but rather by increased knowledge, skills, and use of social support. Given the chronicity of the psychiatric disorders for which this approach was developed, continuity of care is considered important and termination is not particularly stressed. Many of these families, particularly those in multiple family groups, choose to participate indefinitely.

Treatment Applicability

Psychoeducational approaches have been used most frequently with schizophrenic patients and their families. However, more recently this approach has been used with families with a member with a mood disorder (e.g., Anderson, Griffin, et al., 1986). McFarlane (1991) asserts that the psychoeducational approach, similar in many respects to a behavioral approach, may be applicable to other problems, including sexual dysfunction, attention deficit disorder, and physical ailments.

CASE ILLUSTRATION

The following case illustration highlights assessment and treatment techniques reflective of an integrative approach to family therapy. Specifically, the family therapy incorporated techniques associated with the object relational, structural, systemic, and cognitive-behavioral approaches. The use of an integrative approach represents our own theoretical orientation. In addition, integrative approaches are the most widely practiced forms of family therapy used today in the United States.

Case Background

Mrs. Shaw, a 37-year-old, divorced, Caucasian computer programmer was referred to psychotherapy by her children's pediatrician due to the apparent "withdrawal and sadness" of her 9-year-old son, Frank. The family also included a 12-year-old daughter, Kristie, and the children's father, Mr. Shaw, a 37-year-old, Caucasian, mechanical engineer. The parents were divorced, with joint legal custody of the children. Mrs. Shaw had physical custody and the children had frequent visitation with their father. None of the family members had received prior psychological treatment. Family therapy was recommended due to the presence of a specific family stressor, and parents' and children's availability and motivation for treatment. To intervene with all appropriate subsystems, a cotherapy model was utilized, with the coauthors of this chapter serving as the cotherapists.

Assessment

Initial sessions were devoted to assessment, feedback, and treatment planning. During the initial contacts with the family, the cotherapy team focused on creating a safe, secure "holding environment," by specifying a regular time and location for the work and providing relevant rules governing behavior during the sessions (e.g., no violence) in an empathic and nurturing style. Clinical assessment of the Shaw family took place over several sessions and was based on interviews, self-report, and observational data. To facilitate a systemic understanding of the presenting problem, the therapists met with the nuclear family as a unit as well as with its subsystems (i.e., sibling subsystem, parental subsystem, mother and children, and father and children) during the assessment phase.

Interview data revealed the following history: Frank's depressive symptoms emerged following his parents' unexpected separation that resulted in divorce. In the ensuing 6 months, he continued to do well in school but withdrew from peers, felt negatively about himself, gave up Little League Baseball, and felt low in energy despite increased sleep. Frank acknowledged feelings of helplessness and a sense that there was no point in living; however, he denied a plan for suicide. He felt rejected by his father, despite regular contact. Kristie denied psychological distress, though her mother reported oppositional behavior at home. Kristie admitted feeling angry toward both parents for disrupting her life. Mrs. Shaw was preoccupied with her children's adjustment and unaware of any personal difficulties, aside from financial strain. Mr. Shaw reported deep concern about his children; however, he felt the marriage was untenable. All family members evidenced feeling negatively about themselves, experienced activities as less pleasurable, and reported more interpersonal conflicts. However, all family members had good social skills and were able to articulate their thoughts and concerns.

A family genogram was used to elicit information about the parents' families of origin. Both parents reported experiences of feeling rejected or abandoned in their families of origin. Both families viewed the expression of negative affects (sadness, anger) as unacceptable. Mrs. Shaw's father was an alcoholic who was in and out of psychiatric hospitals and her mother was "kind, but ineffectual." Mr. Shaw's adoptive mother died when he was 10 years old, and following her death, his father began drinking excessively and became depressed. Neither parent had regular, meaningful contact with members of his/her family of origin.

Administration of self-report measures indicated that Frank was depressed. Kristie was rated as significantly aggressive and inattentive by her mother but not by her father. All family members' responses to the FACES suggested that the family was chaotically enmeshed. In other words, they acknowledged considerable family closeness without clear rules and roles. Consistent with an enmeshed family presentation, all family members concurred in their reports that the family was very cohesive, but lacked clear leadership and an appropriate power hierarchy.

Circular questioning revealed the children's perception that Frank's depressive symptoms caused both mother and father to "act worried" and "stop fighting with each other," and that Kristie's oppositional behavior caused mother to "act bossy," an indirect way of expressing her anger at her ex-husband for leaving. Mrs. Shaw believed that Kristie acted out to "get attention," whereas Frank withdrew "because he's upset about the divorce and doesn't know how to talk about it." Mr. Shaw believed that the divorce, which he initiated, caused all the family problems and he felt guilty about this. But, he also felt that his own needs and sense of self would have been compromised had he remained married.

Family members' responses to the circular questioning process led to the following systemic hypothesis: Frank's depressive behavior served to maintain the family homeostasis and cohesion threatened by the parents' divorce. Additionally, observation of family interaction patterns revealed a weak executive subsystem, with poor boundaries between parents and children. For example, neither Mr. nor Mrs. Shaw was able to set limits on Kristie's disruptive behavior during the session. Therefore, Kristie's oppositional behavior was hypothesized to be an attempt to reestablish the parental hierarchy in the family system. Finally, Mr. and Mrs. Shaw's experiences in their families of origin raised the possibility that their marriage had deteriorated in part because they had projected onto one another their internalized images of rejecting parents. That is, Mr. Shaw experienced his former wife as similar to his mother, perceiving her to be emotionally unavailable as she did not meet his needs for romance, and Mrs. Shaw perceived her ex-husband as unreliable, distant, and rejecting, like her father.

Goal Setting

Responsibility for goal setting was shared between the cotherapy team and the family. The process was interactive and collaborative, facilitating family members' perceptions of the therapists as partners, as well as experts in facilitating change. The cotherapy team was respectful of the family members' wishes, hopes, and fears; where wishes conflicted (e.g., parental reunification vs. divorce), therapists helped family members find an overarching goal that all members could endorse (e.g., reduce parental discord).

Goals for treatment initially articulated by the family included (1) decrease Frank's depression, (2) improve relationships between Mrs. Shaw and Kristie, and between Mr. Shaw and Frank, and (3) help the family deal with the divorce. To facilitate evaluation of goal attainment, we worked together with the family to operationalize these goals in behavioral terms. For example, "decreased depression" was redefined in terms of Frank's return to Little League, increased peer interaction, and an absence of negative statements about himself. After delineating specific treatment goals in behavioral terms, we proposed a time-limited family therapy intervention, obtaining a commitment from all family members to participate in the treatment. A treatment contract specifying the goals, proposed duration, and parameters (e.g., time and location) of treatment was negotiated and formalized. This contract included an acknowledgment that the session membership may vary depending on the issues being addressed.

Although we accepted the family's goals of change in individual members and in two key relationships, we conceptualized these goals in the context of a broader transformation in the family system's structure and functioning (second-order change). Our conceptualization of Frank's depression as reflecting family dysfunction was indicated by our recommendation for a family intervention rather than individual therapy for Frank. Specifically, we felt it important to support the parents in effectively coparenting the children, despite their divorced status. Given that Frank's depressive symptoms did not meet diagnostic criteria for a major depressive episode, as well as the fact that the onset of symptoms occurred following a discrete family stressor, an evaluation for medication did not seem warranted.

Treatment

The family therapy was conducted over a course of 22 weekly sessions. We continued to nourish a holding environment such that each family member could safely express concerns and risk the vulnerability associated with making changes. Additionally, throughout the work, we attended to our own emotional responses to the family and shared these reactions with one another. In instances in which we felt that sharing our countertransference responses with the family would be therapeutic, we communicated our affective reactions. For example, Dr. Celano often found herself overidentifying with Kristie and felt inclined to interact with the parents in a passive–aggressive fashion similar to Kristie's style. She shared with the parents her own frustration at them for appearing too self-involved to attend adequately to the children. Dr. Kaslow noted that although Mrs. Shaw denied feeling sad herself, Dr. Kaslow felt depressed when interacting with her. Dr. Kaslow wondered aloud whether this depression might mirror underlying despair in Mrs. Shaw, which she had projected onto both Frank and Dr. Kaslow.

Throughout the course of the work, we encouraged family members to articulate their emotional reactions to our interactions with them, thereby highlighting transference dynamics. Not surprisingly, Mrs. Shaw experienced Dr. Celano as unpredictable, similar to how she had perceived her alcoholic father. Although she found Dr. Kaslow to be "a good listener," she felt Dr. Kaslow was powerless to help her or her family, a reaction not unlike the one she felt toward her ineffectual and depressed mother.

The major structural intervention consisted of boundary marking. Specifically, the family was informed that subsequent family sessions would not routinely include all four family members, in recognition of the two distinct and overlapping family subsystems. That is, the majority of sessions would be held with the mother and the children or the father and the children. Additional sessions with the parent and sibling subsystems separately also would be conducted. This structural shift highlighted the two separate but overlapping family units and clarified the reality and permanence of the divorce and the need for each triad to learn to function effectively as a family unit. A series of sessions were held with Mr. and Mrs. Shaw to help them work through the emotional separation associated with the divorce and enable them to work cooperatively in their coparenting roles. Sessions with the sibling subsystem provided an opportunity for both Frank and Kristie to share their myriad feelings about the divorce. This work with the children was complicated by the implicit family prohibition against experiencing and sharing negative affects (sadness, anger, guilt, hopelessness), a prohibition stemming from both parents' experiences in their respective families of origin. Thus, to facilitate this work, sessions were held with the mother and the children and the father and the children to identify and share emotional reactions to the divorce and to understand that individuals express affective distress differently. Family members were supported and reinforced by the therapists for the expression of feelings of rejection, hopelessness, and anger. The parents were helped to appropriately respond to and accept their children's expressions of affective distress. As the family struggled to acknowledge these feelings, Frank's depression and Kristie's anger were interpreted as reflecting the pain experienced by all family members in the wake of the divorce. The parents were encouraged to receive comfort and support from adults outside the nuclear family, enabling them to work through their own feelings of loss and anger without inappropriately seeking support from their children or one another. Additionally, this receipt of support enabled Mr. and Mrs. Shaw to be emotionally available to both nurture and discipline their children.

The discussion of family members' feelings about the divorce revealed that each member blamed him/herself for family problems. Mrs. Shaw felt her involvement with the children contributed to the marital dissolution, and Mr. Shaw felt guilty about the negative impact on the children of the separation he had initiated. Kristie did not take credit for her contributions to positive family events, and Frank believed that he was the cause of his parents' divorce. During sessions emphasizing interpersonal problem solving and affective education, family members began to recognize the influence of maladaptive attributions on mood states and behaviors. Attribution retraining helped family members to make realistic self and other attributions for positive and negative events. For example, Frank was offered an alternative explanation for his parents' divorce, attributing the decision to divorce to their incompatibility rather than to his mistakes.

Although these family interventions led to significant symptom relief for Frank as he became more engaged in previously pleasurable activities and more able to enjoy these endeavors, Kristie's oppositional behavior increased and generalized to the school setting, prompting multiple teacher–parent conferences attended by both parents. The therapists reframed Kristie's oppositional behavior as a final and valiant attempt to "keep the family together" due to the children's continuing concerns that neither Mr. nor Mrs. Shaw was ready to discipline adequately without the other present. This reframe was accompanied by a homework assignment to be implemented at both homes. The children were instructed to "practice" acting in an oppositional manner, but only in the home and during specified times, to give each parent the opportunity to learn how to manage their behavior without the other parent present. This intervention initially resulted in an increase of reported oppositional behavior from both children at each parent's home, with a gradual return to more adaptive (premorbid) levels of functioning as it became apparent that each parent separately could appropriately manage the behavior.

Although the children became less symptomatic, there continued to be tension between Mrs. Shaw and Kristie, and between Mr. Shaw and Frank. Thus, each of these dyads was encouraged to engage in mutually chosen pleasurable activities. The strengthening of these within gender parent–child relationships not only was gratifying but also served to reduce the overinvolvement in the mother–son dyad.

As the children became less involved in their parents' relationship, as boundaries between parents and children and between the two separate families became clear, Mrs. Shaw acknowledged symptoms of depression and loneliness and Mr. Shaw reported his abuse of alcohol. Mrs. Shaw's depression was interpreted in light of her history of significant losses, and Mr. Shaw's alcohol abuse was interpreted as an attempt to escape from pain associated with perceived guilt and early losses.

Family therapy was terminated when Frank's depression diminished, Kristie's oppositionality decreased, and the specified parent–child relationships improved according to the terms in the treatment contract. However, we recommended continued individual therapy for both parents and an alcohol rehabilitation program for Mr. Shaw. Several sessions were devoted to discussing feelings related to the termination of family treatment. Family members' conflicts regarding loss and abandonment were reworked without significant increases in maladaptive behaviors. Feelings regarding termination of the intact family system, as well as of the therapy, were tied to each parent's unresolved struggles with his/her family of origin. This working through was facilitated by the use of the previously completed genogram. The process of addressing family-of-origin conflicts would continue in the parents' separate individual therapy endeavors.

SUGGESTIONS FOR FURTHER READING

Clinical Case Studies

Gurman, A. S. (Ed.). (1985). *Casebook of marital therapy.* New York: Guilford Press.
Napier, A. Y., & Whitaker, C. (1978). *The family crucible.* New York: Harper & Row.

Research Articles

Gurman, A. S., Kniskern, D. P., & Pinsof, W. M. (1986). Research on the process and outcome of marital and family therapy. In S. L. Garfield & A. E. Bergin (Eds.), *Handbook of psychotherapy and behavior change* (pp. 565–624). New York: Wiley.
Hazelrigg, M. D., Cooper, H. M., & Borduin, C. M. (1987). Evaluating the effectiveness of family therapies: An integrative review and analysis. *Psychological Bulletin, 101,* 428–442.

Reference Books

Gurman, A. S., & Kniskern, D. P. (Eds.). (1981). *Handbook of family therapy.* New York: Brunner/Mazel.

Gurman, A. S., & Kniskern, D. P. (Eds.). (1991). *Handbook of family therapy* (Vol. 2). New York: Brunner/Mazel.

REFERENCES

Ackerman, N. (1958). *The psychodynamics of family life.* New York: Basic Books.
Ackerman, N., & Sobel, R. (1950). Family diagnosis: An approach to the preschool child. *American Journal of Orthopsychiatry, 20,* 744–753.
Alexander, J., & Parsons, B. V. (1982). *Functional family therapy.* Monterey, CA: Brooks/Cole.
American Association for Marriage and Family Therapy. (1982, rev. 1988). *AAMFT code of ethical principles for marriage and family therapists.* Washington, DC: Author.
American Psychiatric Association. (1994). *Diagnostic and statistical manual of mental disorders* (4th ed.). Washington, DC: Author.
Anderson, C. M., Griffin, S., Rossi, A., Pagonis, I., Holder, D. P., & Treiber, R. (1986). A comparative study of the impact of education versus process groups for families of patients with affective disorders. *Family Process, 25,* 185–206.
Anderson, C. M., Reiss, D. J., & Hogarty, G. E. (1986). *Schizophrenia and the family: A practitioner's guide to psychoeducation and management.* New York: Guilford Press.
Aponte, H. J. (1976). Underorganization in the poor family. In P. J. Guerin (Ed.), *Family therapy: Theory and practice* (pp. 432–448). New York: Gardner.
Aponte, H. J., & Van Deusen, J. M. (1981). Structural family therapy. In A. S. Gurman & D. P. Kniskern (Eds.), *Handbook of family therapy* (pp. 310–360). New York: Brunner/Mazel.
Bateson, G. (1972). *Toward an ecology of mind.* New York: Ballantine Books.
Bateson, G., Jackson, D. D., Haley, J. E., & Weakland J. (1956). Toward a theory of schizophrenia. *Behavioral Science, 1,* 251–264.
Beavers, W. R. (1977). *Psychotherapy and growth: Family systems perspective.* New York: Brunner/Mazel.

Beavers, W. R. (1982). Healthy, midrange, and severely dysfunctional families. In F. Walsh (Ed.), *Normal family processes* (1st ed., pp. 45– 66). New York: Guilford Press.

Beavers, W. R. (1985). *Manual of Beavers– Timberlawn Family Evaluation Scale and Family Style Evaluation.* Dallas, TX: Southwest Family Institute.

Beavers, W. R., & Hampson, B. B. (1990). *Successful families: Assessment and intervention.* New York: Norton.

Beck, A. T. (1976). *Cognitive therapy and emotional disorders.* New York: International Universities Press.

Beck, A. T. (1988). *Love is never enough.* New York: Harper & Row.

Bennun, I. (1986). Evaluating family therapy: A comparison of the Milan and problem solving approaches. *Journal of Family Therapy, 8,* 235–242.

Boszormenyi-Nagy, I., Grunebaum, J., & Ulrich, D. (1991). Contextual therapy. In A. S. Gurman & D. P. Kniskern (Eds.), *Handbook of family therapy* (Vol. 2, pp. 200–238). New York: Brunner/ Mazel.

Boszormenyi-Nagy, I., & Spark, G. (1973). *Invisible loyalties.* New York: Harper & Row.

Bowen, M. (1978). *Family therapy in clinical practice.* Northvale, NJ: Jason Aronson.

Boyd-Franklin, N. (1989). *Black families in therapy: A multisystems approach.* New York: Guilford Press.

Broderick, C. B., & Schrader, S. S. (1991). The history of professional marriage and family therapy. In A. S. Gurman & D. P. Kniskern (Eds.), *Handbook of family therapy* (Vol. 2, pp. 3–40). New York: Brunner/Mazel.

Campbell, D., Draper, R., & Crutchley, E. (1991). The Milan systemic approach to family therapy. In A. S. Gurman & D. P. Kniskern (Eds.), *Handbook of family therapy* (Vol. 2, pp. 325–362). New York: Brunner/Mazel.

Carter, E., & McGoldrick, M. (1988). *The changing family life cycle: A framework* (2nd ed.). New York: Gardner.

Colapinto, J. (1991). Structural family therapy. In A. S. Gurman & D. P. Kniskern (Eds.), *Handbook of family therapy* (Vol.

2, pp. 417–443). New York: Brunner/ Mazel.

Combrinck-Graham, L. (Ed). (1988). *Children in family contexts: Perspectives on treatment.* New York: Guilford Press.

Coyne, J. C., Kahn, J., & Gotlib, I. H. (1987). Depression. In T. Jacob (Ed.), *Family interaction and psychopathology: Theories, methods, and findings* (pp. 509–534). New York: Plenum Press.

Doane, J. A., West, K. L., Goldstein, M. J., Rodnick, E. H., & Jones, J. E. (1981). Parental communication deviance and affective style: Predictors of subsequent schizophrenia spectrum disorders in vulnerable adolescents. *Archives of General Psychiatry, 38,* 679–685.

Doherty, W. J., & Boss, P. G. (1991). Values and ethics in family therapy. In A. S. Gurman & D. P. Kniskern (Eds.), *Handbook of family therapy* (Vol. 2, pp. 606–637). New York: Brunner/Mazel.

Duhl, B. S., & Duhl, F. J. (1981). Integrative family therapy. In A. S. Gurman & D. P. Kniskern (Eds.), *Handbook of family therapy* (pp. 483–516). New York: Brunner/Mazel.

Ellis, A. (1962). *Reason and emotion in psychotherapy.* New York: Stuart.

Epstein, N., Baldwin, L., & Bishop, S. (1983). The McMaster Family Assessment Device. *Journal of Marital and Family Therapy, 9,* 171–180.

Epstein, N., Bishop, D. S., & Baldwin, L. M. (1982). McMaster model of family functioning: A view of the normal family. In F. Walsh (Ed.), *Normal family processes* (1st ed., pp. 115–141). New York: Guilford Press.

Epstein, N. B., Bishop, D. S., & Levin, S. (1978). The McMaster model of family functioning. *Journal of Marital and Family Counseling, 4,* 19–31.

Epstein, N., Schlesinger, S. E., & Dryden, W. (Eds.). (1988). *Cognitive-behavioral therapy with families.* New York: Brunner/Mazel.

Everett, C., Halperin, S., Volgy, S., & Wissler, A. (1989). *Treating the borderline family: A systemic approach.* Boston: Allyn & Bacon.

Feldman, L. B. (1992). *Integrating individual and family therapy.* New York: Brunner/Mazel.

Filsinger, E. E. (1983). *Marriage and family assessment: A sourcebook for family therapy.* Beverly Hills, CA: Sage.

Fleck, S. (1982). The family and psychiatric diagnosis. *American Journal of Social Psychiatry, 2,* 19–23.

Framo, J. L. (1982). *Explorations in marital and family therapy: Selected papers of James L. Framo.* New York: Springer.

Frances, A., Clarkin, J. F., & Perry, S. (1984). DSM-III and family therapy. *American Journal of Psychiatry, 141,* 406–409.

Fredman, N., & Sherman, R. (1987). *Handbook of measurements for marriage and family therapy.* New York: Brunner/Mazel.

Friedman, E. H. (1991). Bowen theory and therapy. In A. S. Gurman & D. P. Kniskern (Eds.), *Handbook of family therapy* (Vol. 2, pp. 134–170). New York: Brunner/Mazel.

Goldstein, M. J. (1987). Family interaction patterns that antedate the onset of schizophrenia and related disorders: A further analysis of data from a longitudinal prospective study. In K. Hahlweg & M. J. Goldstein (Eds.), *Understanding major mental disorder: The contribution of family interaction research* (pp. 11–32). New York: Family Process Press.

Goodrich, T. J., Rampage, C., Ellman, B., & Halstead, K. (1988). *Feminist family therapy: A casebook.* New York: Norton.

Gordon, S. B., & Davidson, N. (1981). Behavioral parent training. In A. S. Gurman & D. P. Kniskern (Eds.), *Handbook of family therapy* (pp. 517–555). New York: Brunner/Mazel.

Guerin, P. J. (1976). Family therapy: The first twenty-five years. In *Family therapy: Theory and practice* (pp. 2–39). New York: Gardner.

Gurman, A. S. (1981). Integrative marital therapy: Toward the development of an interpersonal approach. In S. H. Budman (Ed.), *Forms of brief therapy* (pp. 415–457). New York: Guilford Press.

Gurman, A. S., & Kniskern, D. P. (Eds.). (1991). *Handbook of family therapy* (Vol. 2). New York: Brunner/Mazel.

Haley, J. (1973). *Uncommon therapy: The psychiatric techniques of Milton H. Erickson, M.D.* New York: Norton.

Haley, J. (1976). *Problem-solving therapy.* San Francisco: Jossey-Bass.

Hazelrigg, M. D., Cooper, H. M., & Borduin, C. M. (1987). Evaluating the effectiveness of family therapies: An integrative review and analysis. *Psychological Bulletin, 101,* 428–442.

Heiman, J. R., LoPiccolo, L., & LoPiccolo, J. (1981). The treatment of sexual dysfunction. In A. S. Gurman & D. P. Kniskern (Eds.), *Handbook of family therapy* (pp. 592–630). New York: Brunner/Mazel.

Hill, R. (1986). Life cycle stages for types of single-parent families: On family development theory. *Family Relations, 35,* 19–29.

Hoffman, L. (1981). *Foundations of family therapy.* New York: Basic Books.

Holtzworth-Munroe, A., & Jacobson, N. S. (1991). Behavioral marital therapy. In A. S. Gurman & D. P. Kniskern (Eds.), *Handbook of family therapy* (Vol. 2, pp. 96–133). New York: Brunner/Mazel.

Hooley, J. M., & Teasdale, J. D. (1989). Predictors of relapse in unipolar depressives: Expressed emotion, marital distress, and perceived criticism. *Journal of Abnormal Psychology, 89,* 229–235.

Hops, H., Wills, T. A., Patterson, G. R., & Weiss, R. L. (1972). *Marital interaction coding system.* Eugene: University of Oregon Research Institute.

Jacob, T. (Ed.). (1987). *Family interaction and psychopathology: Theories, methods, and findings.* New York: Plenum Press.

Jacob, T., & Seilhamer, R. A. (1987). Alcoholism and family interaction. In T. Jacob (Ed.), *Family interaction and psychopathology: Theories, methods, and findings* (pp. 535–580). New York: Plenum Press.

Jacobson, N. S., & Margolin, G. (1979). *Marital therapy: Strategies based on social learning and behavior exchange principles.* New York: Brunner/Mazel.

Kantor, D., & Lehr, W. (1975). *Inside the family: Toward a theory of family process.* San Francisco: Jossey-Bass.

Kaslow, F. W. (1981). A dialectic approach to family therapy and practice: Selectivity and synthesis. *Journal of Marital and Family Therapy, 7,* 345–351.

Kaslow, F. W. (Ed.). (1982). *The international book of family therapy.* New York: Brunner/Mazel.

Kaslow, F. W. (1987). Marital and family therapy. In M. B. Sussman & S. K. Steinmetz (Eds.), *Handbook of marriage and the family* (pp. 835–859). New York: Plenum Press.

Kaslow, N. J., & Gurman, A. S. (1985). Ethical considerations in family therapy research. *Counseling and Values, 30*, 47–61.

Kempler, W. (1981). *Experiential psychotherapy within families.* New York: Brunner/Mazel.

Kirschner, D. A., & Kirschner, S. (1986). *Comprehensive family therapy: An integration of systemic and psychodynamic treatment models.* New York: Brunner/Mazel.

L'Abate, L., & Weinstein, S. E. (1987). *Structured enrichment programs for couples and families.* New York: Brunner/Mazel.

Liberman, R. (1970). Behavioral approaches to family and couple therapy. *American Journal of Orthopsychiatry, 40*, 106–118.

Lidz, T., Cornelison, A. R., Fleck, S., & Terry, D. (1957). The intrafamilial environment of the schizophrenic patient: I. The father. *Psychiatry, 20*, 329–342.

Locke, H. J., & Wallace, K. M. (1959). Short marital adjustment and prediction tests: Their reliability and validity. *Marriage and Family Living, 21*, 251–255.

Luepnitz, D. A. (1988). *The family interpreted: Feminist theory in clinical practice.* New York: Basic Books.

Madanes, C. (1981). *Strategic family therapy.* San Francisco: Jossey-Bass.

Madanes, C. (1990). *Sex, love, and violence.* New York: Norton.

Madanes, C. (1991). Strategic family therapy. In A. S. Gurman & D. P. Kniskern (Eds.), *Handbook of family therapy* (Vol. 2, pp. 396–416). New York: Brunner/Mazel.

Markman, H. J., & Notarius, C. I. (1987). Coding marital and family interaction: Current status. In T. Jacob (Ed.), *Family interaction and psychopathology: Theories, methods, and findings* (pp. 329–390). New York: Plenum.

McFarlane, W. R. (1991). Family psychoeducational treatment. In A. S. Gurman & D. P. Kniskern (Eds.), *Handbook of family therapy* (Vol. 2, pp. 363–395). New York: Brunner/Mazel.

McGoldrick, M., Anderson, C. M., & Walsh, F. (Eds.) (1989). *Women in families: A framework for family therapy.* New York: Norton.

McGoldrick, M., & Gerson, R. (1985). *Genograms in family assessment.* New York: W.W. Norton.

McGoldrick, M., Pearce, J. K., & Giordano, J. (Eds.). (1982). *Ethnicity and family therapy.* New York: Guilford Press.

Midelfort, C. F. (1957). *The family in psychotherapy.* New York: McGraw-Hill.

Miklowitz, D. J., Goldstein, M. J., Nuechterlein, K. H., Snyder, K. S., & Doane, J. A. (1987). The family and the course of recent-onset mania. In K. Hahlweg & M. J. Goldstein (Eds.), *Understanding major mental disorder: The contribution of family interaction research* (pp. 195–211). New York: Family Process Press.

Minuchin, S. (1974). *Families and family therapy.* Cambridge, MA: Harvard University Press.

Minuchin, S., & Fishman, H. C. (1981). *Family therapy techniques.* Cambridge, MA: Harvard University Press.

Minuchin, S., Montalvo, B., Guerney, B., Rosman, B., & Schumer, F. (1967). *Families of the slums.* New York: Basic Books.

Minuchin, S., Rosman, B. L., & Baker, L. (1978). *Psychosomatic families: Anorexia nervosa in context.* Cambridge, MA: Harvard University Press.

Moos, R. H., & Moos, B. S. (1981). *Family Environment Scale manual.* Palo Alto, CA: Consulting Psychologists Press.

Olson, D. H., McCubbin, H. I., Barnes, H., Larsen, A., Muxen, M., & Wilson, M. (1983). *Families: What makes them work.* Beverly Hills, CA: Sage.

Olson, D., Sprenkle, D., & Russell, C. (1979). Circumplex model of marital and family systems: Cohesion and adaptability dimensions, family types, and clinical applications. *Family Process, 18*, 3–28.

Patterson, G. R., Ray, R. S., Shaw, D. A., & Cobb, J. A. (1969). *Manual for coding of family interactions* (rev. ed.). New York: Microfiche Publications.

Parsons, T., & Bales, R. F. (1955). *Family, socialization and interaction process.* Glencoe, IL: Free Press.

Patterson, G. R. (Ed.). (1990). *Depression and aggression in family interaction.* Hillsdale, NJ: Erlbaum.

Pinsof, W. M. (1983). Integrative problem-centered therapy: Toward the synthesis of family and individual psychotherapies. *Journal of Marital and Family Therapy, 9,* 19–35.

Reiss, D. (1981). *The family's construction of reality.* Cambridge, MA: Harvard University Press.

Roberto, L. G. (1991). Symbolic–experiential family therapy. In A. S. Gurman & D. P. Kniskern (Eds.), *Handbook of family therapy* (Vol. 2, pp. 444–476). New York: Brunner/Mazel.

Rodick, J. D., Henggeler, S. W., & Hanson, C. L. (1986). An evaluation of the Family Adaptability and Cohesion Evaluation Scales of the Circumplex Model. *Journal of Abnormal Child Psychology, 14,* 77– 87.

Satir, V. (1967). *Conjoint family therapy.* Palo Alto, CA: Science & Behavior Books.

Satir, V. (1972). *Peoplemaking.* Palo Alto, CA: Science & Behavior Books.

Satir, V., & Baldwin, M. (1983). *Satir step by step: A guide to creating change in families.* Palo Alto, CA: Science & Behavior Books.

Scharff, J. S. (Ed.). (1989). *Foundations of object relations family therapy.* Northvale, NJ: Jason Aronson.

Scharff, D. E., & Scharff, J. S. (1987). *Object relations family therapy.* Northvale, NJ: Jason Aronson.

Segal, L. (1991). Brief therapy: The MRI approach. In A. S. Gurman & D. P. Kniskern (Eds.), *Handbook of family therapy* (Vol. 2, pp. 171–199). New York: Brunner/Mazel.

Selvini-Palazzoli, M. (1974). *Self starvation.* London: Human Context Books.

Selvini-Palazzoli, M., Boscolo, L., Cecchin, G., & Prata, G. (1978). *Paradox and counterparadox.* Northvale, NJ: Jason Aronson.

Selvini-Palazzoli, M., Cirillo, S., Selvini, M., & Sorrentino, A. M. (1989). *Family games: General models of psychotic processes in the family.* New York: Norton.

Shapiro, R. L. (1989). The origination of adolescent disturbances in the family: Some considerations in theory and im-

plications for therapy. In J. S. Scharff (Ed.), *Foundations of object relations family therapy* (pp. 53–76). Northvale, NJ: Jason Aronson.

Skinner, H. A., Steinhauer, P. D., & Santa-Barbara, J. (1983). The family assessment measure. *Canadian Journal of Community Mental Health, 2,* 91–105.

Slipp, S. (1988). *The technique and practice of object relations family therapy.* Northvale, NJ: Jason Aronson.

Spanier, G. B. (1976). Measuring dyadic adjustment: New Scales for assessing the quality of marriage and similar dyads. *Journal of Marriage and the Family, 38,* 15–28.

Stanton, M. D. (1981). Strategic approaches to family therapy. In A. S. Gurman & D. P. Kniskern (Eds.), *Handbook of family therapy* (pp. 361–402). New York: Brunner/Mazel.

Stuart, R. B. (1980). *Helping couples change: A social learning approach to marital therapy.* New York: Guilford Press.

Thomas, M. B. (1992). *An introduction to marital and family therapy: Counseling toward healthier family systems across the lifespan.* New York: MacMillan.

Titelman, P. (Ed.). (1987). *The therapist's own family: Toward the differentiation of self.* Northvale, NJ: Jason Aronson.

Vaughn, C. E., & Leff, J. P. (1976). The influence of family and social factors on the course of psychiatric illness. *British Journal of Psychiatry, 129,* 125–137.

Visher, E., & Visher, J. (1987). *Old loyalties, new ties: Therapeutic strategies with stepfamilies.* New York: Brunner/Mazel.

von Bertalanffy, L. (1968). *General systems theory: Foundations, development, applications* (rev. ed.). New York: George Braziller.

Walsh, F. (1982). *Normal family processes* (1st ed.). New York: Guilford Press.

Walters, M., Carter, B., Papp, P., & Silverstein, O. (1988). *The invisible web: Gender patterns in family relationships.* New York: Guilford Press.

Wamboldt, F. S., & Reiss, D. (1991). Task performance and the social construction of meaning: Juxtaposing normality with contemporary family research. In D. Offer & M. Sabshin (Eds.), *The diversity of normal behavior: Further contributions to normatology* (pp. 164–206). New York: Basic Books.

Watzlawick, P., Weakland, J., & Fisch, R. (1974). *Change: Principles of problem formation and problem resolution.* New York: Norton.

Whitaker, C. (1976). The hindrance of theory in clinical work. In P. J. Guerin Jr. (Ed.), *Family therapy: Theory and practice* (pp. 154–164). New York: Gardner Press.

Whitaker, C. A., & Bumberry, W. M. (1988). *Dancing with the family: A sym-bolic–experiential approach.* New York: Brunner/Mazel.

Whitaker, C. A., & Keith, D. V. (1981). Symbolic–experiential family therapy. In A. S. Gurman & D. P. Kniskern (Eds.), *Handbook of family therapy* (pp. 187–225). New York: Brunner/Mazel.

Wynne, L. C., Ryckoff, I. M., Day, J., & Hirsch, S. I. (1958). Pseudomutuality in the family relationships of schizophrenics. *Psychiatry, 21,* 205–220.

11

An Eclectic and Integrative Approach: Transtheoretical Therapy

JAMES O. PROCHASKA

BACKGROUND OF THE APPROACH

Transtheoretical therapy began with a comparative analysis of the major systems of psychotherapy (Prochaska, 1979). This analysis was initiated with the eclectic spirit of seeking the best that each system had to offer. Each of the major systems was found to have brilliant insights into the human condition. Each system provided a logical, coherent and convincing construction for understanding human function and dysfunction, once the core assumptions of the theory were accepted. Applying each system to the same complex clinical case indicated how differently and yet convincingly each system could explain and treat the same troubled individual. All the systems provided practical insights and ideas that could be useful within an eclectic approach to therapy. Most of the systems were inspiring and encouraged

deeper exploration about the theory and its methods.

There were also shortcomings with the major systems. Most were much more rational than empirical in construction. None could demonstrate empirically greater ability to predict how people would respond in therapy or greater ability to help people change as a result of psychotherapy. Most systems focused more on theories of personality and psychopathology, which are usually theories of why people do not change, than on constructing theories of how people do change. And, of course, none of the major systems provided models for how profound insights and helpful ideas from diverse therapies might be integrated in a more coherent and comprehensive approach to change. In an integrative spirit, we set out consciously and intentionally to construct a model of therapy and change that would draw from across the major theories of therapy; hence the name "transtheoretical therapy."

We set out certain criteria for constructing a new model. First and foremost it had to be empirical; that is, each of the fundamental variables had to be able to be measured and validated. If this model could not outpredict and/or outperform previous approaches, why should anyone pay the price of struggling to understand a new system of psychotherapy?

There were other demands placed on the model. It must be able to account for how people change without therapy as well as within therapy. The facts show that the vast majority of people with disorders listed in the fourth edition of the *Diagnostic and Statistical Manual of Mental Disorders* (DSM-IV; American Psychiatric Association, 1994) do not seek professional assistance (Veroff, Douvan, & Kulka, 1981a, 1981b). How do these people proceed in attempts to overcome disabling disorders? The facts also show that clients in therapy spend more than 99% of their waking time outside therapy. How do these people proceed in their attempts to overcome disorders between therapy sessions? The facts also show that, in general, clients spend very brief periods of their lives in therapy. How did these people attempt to change prior to entering therapy and how will they proceed to change after they leave therapy? Therefore, we set out to develop a model that included therapy as part of the change process, but only a part, and, unfortunately, often only a small part. However, being realistic about what part psychotherapy plays in the change process can help us to be more realistic about what can be accomplished in our often brief encounters with clients.

We also wanted to develop a model that could generalize to a broad range of human problems. Psychopathology is only part of the multitude of problems that can disrupt people's lives. We wanted to be able to help with problems that diminished the length of people's lives as well as the quality. Consider one startling statistic. Of the people alive in the world today, 500 million will die from one behavior—the use of tobacco (Peto & Lopez, 1990). Half of these people will die before their time, losing an average of 20 years of their lives. This means that one behavior problem will destroy 5 billion years of human life. Ironically, that is as many years as the world has existed. Smoking will produce a plague like none other in the history of humanity. Yet smoking is not taken seriously by most theorists or practitioners of therapy. Therefore, we wanted to develop a model that could be useful for solving the major killers of our time, the lifestyle killers, as well as the problems of psychopathology that diminish the quality of people's lives. We wanted a model relevant to health behavior problems as well as to mental health problems (Prochaska, DiClemente, & Norcross, 1993; Prochaska, Norcross, & DiClemente, 1994).

Finally, we wished to create a model that could enable eclectic and integrative therapists to become innovators and not just followers. The eclectic tradition usually meant that therapists begged, borrowed, and stole from the leading systems of psychotherapy. Rarely did eclectic therapists create new theoretical constructs or therapeutic interventions. If they were creative at all it was in the way they put together their techniques rather than in creating new concepts that others could borrow.

Transtheoretical therapy did not develop in a vacuum, but it was part of the *spirit* of the 1980s. The spirit of the times was the integrationist movement which has been the most rapidly growing approach to psychotherapy. This movement was heralded by Goldfried's (1980) classic call for a rapprochement across systems of therapy.

Psychotherapy was approaching a crisis that had the potential to lead to a new wave of creativity. The potential for crisis came in part from the unprecedented pace at which new therapies were placed on the market. In 1975, Parloff reported that there were 130 therapies in the therapeutic marketplace (or jungleplace as he more aptly described it), and by 1979, *Time* magazine was reporting that there were over 200 therapies.

Divergence had dominated the past decade of development within the field of psychotherapy. Yet, divergent thinking has been characterized by Guilford (1956), among others, as a necessary part of creativity. Divergent thinking allows for an unlimited creation of options and hypotheses. The increased divergence in psychotherapy thus provides the potential for a new wave of creativity. What was needed to prevent the increasing divergence from leading to fragmentation, confusion, and chaos and how could it be the foundation for a more creative future?

Heinz Werner's (1948) theory of development served as a guide in this regard. Development, as opposed to other forms of change, such as regression or chaos, is characterized by a combination of increasing differentiation and hierarchic integration. The increasing production of new forms of psychotherapy could be seen as an expression of the increasing differentiation of a growing discipline such as psychotherapy. Increasing differentiation alone, however, can become like a cancer of uncontrolled growth that threatens to destroy the very body of knowledge in which it is growing. Unless increasing differentiation is matched by more effective forms of integration, crisis, rather than creativity, is the result. In Guilford's (1956) terms, an increase in divergent thinking needs to be followed by higher levels of convergent thinking.

The identification of converging themes in psychotherapy (Goldfried, 1982) was seen as the most important new trend in psychotherapy (Bergin, 1982). An increasing number of leaders in the field recognized the need for a systematic eclecticism based on what is common to all forms of effective therapy. Experts such as Bergin (1981), Garfield (1981), Goldfried (1980, 1982), and Strupp (1981) cited the need for integrative models of change which could help to synthesize the increasingly diverse and disordered discipline of psychotherapy.

The transtheoretical approach developed within the spirit of a search for a synthesis (Prochaska & DiClemente, 1982), of trying to identify and integrate the best of what different therapy systems had to offer. Both eclectic and many noneclectic therapists agreed that eclecticism offered the best hope for a comprehensive approach to psychotherapy (Smith, 1982). The problem, as Goldfried (1982) pointed out in his provocative book, *Converging Themes in Psychotherapy*, is that adequate integrative models of psychotherapy were not available for a more systematic eclecticism. As a result, both eclectics and noneclectics criticized eclecticism for being fragmented and superficial (Smith, 1982). Frank (1973), for example, criticized eclecticism for contributing to the therapeutic confusion because eclecticism provides no model for doing systematic practice or research. The lack of integrative models has been interpreted as the major reason for the decline of eclecticism as an orientation which was favored by 55% of clinical psychologists in 1973 (Garfield & Kurtz, 1977) but only by 30% of clinical psychologists in 1981 (Norcross & Prochaska, 1983).

Besides growing fragmentation, there were other forces fostering the integrative movement. In the early 1970s, reviews of comparative outcome research consistently concluded that one legitimate form of therapy rarely outperformed another. It seemed to be, as

Luborsky, Singer, and Luborsky (1975) had dared to suggest, that "all had won and all must be given prizes" (p. 95).

The late 1970s witnessed the emergence of the statistical procedure called meta-analysis (Smith & Glass, 1977), and these more sophisticated analyses continued to support the conclusion that the outcomes of therapies A, B, and C were comparable. How could it be that therapies differing so dramatically in their assumptions about human personality, psychopathology, and change could result in common outcomes? One conclusion was that there are common factors across these different therapies that could account for common outcomes. These common factors could serve as the basis for constructing a more systematic eclecticism. Garfield (1992) and Beitman (1992) are two leading examples of theorists applying *a common factors approach to integration*. Garfield (1992) cites the relationship, emotional release or catharsis, explanation and interpretation, reinforcement, desensitization and confrontation as effective factors that are commonly used across a diversity of therapies. From Garfield's perspective, finding effective methods for integrating these common factors is the major challenge for more integrative therapists.

Beutler (1983; Beutler & Consoli, 1992) and Lazarus (1992) prefer a *technically eclectic approach*. This is the more traditional approach that searches the literature for specific techniques that are most effective for specific types of patients with specific types of problems. The foundation of this approach is actuarial rather than theoretical: Applying what the research literature predicts will work best under specific conditions. Technical eclectics use techniques drawn from different sources without necessarily accepting the theories that generated the procedures even if the assumptions underlying the therapies conflict. For example, Lazarus's (1992) multimodal therapy applies the most promising techniques across a range of modalities: behavior, affect, sensation, imagery, cognition, interpersonal relationships, and drugs (captured by the acronym, BASIC I.D.).

A third approach, *theoretical integration*, involves the synthesis of two or more therapies in the hope that the emergent integration will surpass the separate therapies. The emphasis here is on integrating the underlying theories of psychotherapy. Wachtel (1977, 1987) produced one of the most promising approaches to integrating psychoanalytic and behavioral theories of therapy. The integrative movement is especially strong in the field of marital and family therapy. Excellent examples of such integration can be found in the works of Feldman (1989), Gurman (1981), Lebow (1984), and Pinsof (1983).

Theoretical integration is based on a commitment to a conceptual creation that progresses beyond an eclectic mixture of common factors or empirical techniques. The goal is to create a conceptual framework that can synthesize the best elements of two or more approaches to therapy. This is clearly the goal of transtheoretical therapy—not a simple combination or mixture but an emergent theory that is more than the sum of its parts and that leads to new directions for research and practice.

In Table 11.1, Norcross and Newman (1992) list the differences between the terms "eclecticism" and "integration."

As appealing as theoretical integration might appear, it is not without its critics. Messer (1992) provides profound criticisms about the philosophical belief structures underlying integrationism. First, integrationists believe in a unity–discovery model of science which posits that underlying the appearance of diversity and contradiction in the world is a basic unity. When data are organized at a superordinate level, apparent contra-

TABLE 11.1. Eclecticism versus Integration

Eclecticism	Integration
Technical	Theoretical
Divergent (differences)	Convergent (commonalities)
Choosing from many	Combining many
Applying what is	Creating something new
Collection	Blend
Applying the parts	Unifying the parts
Atheoretical but empirical	More theoretical than empirical
Sum of parts	More than sum of parts
Realistic	Idealistic

dictions disappear and the integrated fabric of knowledge emerges. This is exactly what transtheoretical therapy is striving to discover and create.

Messer's key criticism hinges on the fact that this organic world view is only one of four world hypotheses identified by Pepper (1942). Most of the major systems of psychotherapy are not based on this organicist view. Furthermore, there is no way at this time to tell which, if any, of Pepper's four world views is superior. Integrationists lose sight of this fact and proceed as if only the unity view has validity.

As an eclectic, I am all too aware of the pluralistic and relativistic nature of knowledge. I know that no one theory of therapy has a monopoly on the truth. I appreciate that different therapists can make ethical commitments to very different approaches to helping people. My own commitment is to try to help the field and help others by searching for a synthesis in a discipline that could deteriorate into chaos. I recognize that working to discover unity amongst diversity is not always politically correct or popular. I also recognize that seeking such a synthesis could result in failure and frustration rather than integration. But let me share with you what we have discovered to date and allow you to decide whether it can be a source for constructive change.

DIMENSIONS OF CHANGE

As already indicated, one of the dissatisfactions with most systems of psychotherapy is that they rely more on theories about personality and psychopathology—that is, theories about why people do not change—rather than how people can change. Psychotherapy should be based on an adequate theory of change because most people enter therapy seeking help in changing patterns or problems that are threatening to the quality and/or length of their lives. So, our search is for fundamental dimensions of change and to date we have discovered three: processes, stages, and levels of change.

The Processes of Change

We began with the assumption that integration across a diversity of therapy systems most likely would occur at an intermediate level of analysis between the basic abstract assumptions of theories and the concrete techniques applied in therapy, namely, at the level of processes of change. Coincidentally, Goldfried (1980, 1982), in his call for a rapprochement among the psychotherapies, independently suggested that principles of change were the appropriate starting point at which rapprochement could begin.

Processes are the covert or overt activities that people engage in to alter affect, thinking, behavior, or relationships related to particular problems or patterns of living. Initially, the processes were theoretically derived from a comparative analysis of the leading systems of psychotherapy (Prochaska, 1979). They were then modified, based on research on how people attempt to change addictive behaviors on their own or within a professional treatment program (DiClemente & Prochaska, 1982; Prochaska & DiClemente, 1983).

The following is a list of the 10 processes of self-change that have received the most empirical support to date.

1. Consciousness raising
2. Dramatic relief
3. Self-reevaluation
4. Environmental reevaluation
5. Self-liberation
6. Social liberation
7. Counterconditioning
8. Stimulus control
9. Reinforcement management
10. Helping relationship

This is clearly an eclectic set of processes with consciousness raising having roots in the psychoanalytic tradition, dramatic relief or catharsis having roots in the Gestalt therapy tradition, self-reevaluation and environmental reevaluation having roots in the cognitive and experiential traditions, self-liberation and social liberation having roots in the existential tradition, counterconditioning, stimulus control, and reinforcement management having roots in the behavioral tradition, and the helping relationship having roots in the client-centered tradition.

Our studies indicate that people in the natural environment generally use these 10 different processes of change to over-come problems (Prochaska, Velicer, DiClemente, & Fava, 1988). Most major systems of therapy, however, emphasize only two or three of these processes. One of the positions of the transtheoretical approach is that therapists should be at least as cognitively complex as their clients. They should be able to think in terms of a more comprehensive set of processes and be able to apply techniques to engage each process when appropriate.

The Stages of Change

The appropriate use of change processes involves understanding the stages of change through which people progress (Prochaska & DiClemente, 1982). When we tried to assess how frequently people applied each of the 10 processes in self-change and change through therapy, people kept saying that this depended on what stage in the course of change we were talking about. At different points, they used different processes. In their own words, our research participants were describing the phenomenon we now call stages of change.

We discovered that change unfolds over a series of six stages: precontemplation, contemplation, preparation, action, maintenance, and termination. Stages of change had not been identified in any of the major systems of psychotherapy and are a unique contribution from the eclectic and integrative tradition.

Stages are fundamental to understanding change for a number of reasons. First, the concept of stages provides a temporal dimension, and change is a phenomenon that unfolds over time. Second, stages are at a middle level of abstraction between personality traits and psychological states. Stages have a stable quality like traits in that they tend to endure over relatively long periods. But traits are usually construed as not being particularly open to change. Stages are dynamic in nature and thus are open to change, but unlike states they do not change so easily and thus require special efforts or interventions. Stages then are relatively stable as well as dynamic in nature. The types of chronic problems that we see in therapy also have a dual nature of being both stable over time and yet open to change.

The concept of stages has also proven to be a remarkably fruitful dimension for integrating core constructs from across diverse systems of psychotherapy and competing theories of behavior change. Empirically, the stages of change have been useful in integrating processes of change from seven different systems of psychotherapy (Prochaska & DiClemente, 1983, 1984, 1985), the self-efficacy construct from Bandura's (1977, 1982) social–cognitive theory, and the decisional balance concept from Janis and Mann's (1977) theory of decision making, conflict, and commitment. To appreciate these integrative discoveries, we need first to describe in more detail each of the stages of change.

Precontemplation is the stage at which a person has no intention of changing behavior in the foreseeable future. Many individuals in this stage are unaware or underaware of their problems. As G. K. Chesterton once said, "It isn't that they can't see the solution. It is that they can't see the problem." Families, friends, neighbors, or employees, however, are often well aware that the precontemplators have problems. When precontemplators come for psychotherapy, they often do so because of pressure from others. Usually they feel coerced into changing by a spouse who threatens to leave, an employer who threatens to dismiss them, parents who threaten to disown them, or courts that threaten to punish them. They may even demonstrate change as long as the pressure is on. Once the pressure is off, however, they may quickly return to their old ways.

Even precontemplators can *wish* to change, but this is quite different than intending or seriously considering change in the foreseeable future. Typical statements used to identify precontemplation on a continuous stage-of-change measure include: "As far as I'm concerned, I don't have any problems that need changing," and, "I guess I have faults but there's nothing that I really need to change" (McConnaughy, Prochaska, & Velicer, 1983). Resistance to recognizing or modifying a problem is the hallmark of precontemplation.

Contemplation is the stage at which people are aware that a problem exists and are seriously thinking about overcoming it but have not yet made a commitment to take action. People can remain stuck in the contemplation stage for long periods. In one study of self-changers, we followed a group of 200 smokers in the contemplation stage for 2 years. The modal response of this group was to remain in the contemplation stage for the entire 2 years of the project without ever moving to significant action (Prochaska & DiClemente, 1984; DiClemente & Prochaska, 1985).

The essence of the contemplation stage is communicated in an incident related by Benjamin (1987). He was walking home one evening when a stranger approached him and inquired about the location of a certain street. Benjamin pointed it out to the stranger and provided specific instructions. After readily understanding and accepting the instructions, the stranger began to walk in the opposite direction. Benjamin said, "You are headed in the wrong direction." The stranger replied, "Yes, I know. I am not quite ready yet." This is contemplation: knowing where you want to go but not being quite ready yet to go there.

Preparation is a stage that combines intention and some attempt at behavior change. Individuals in this stage are intending to take action immediately and have unsuccessfully taken action in the past year. As a group, individuals who are prepared for action report some small behavior changes, such as smoking five cigarettes less or delaying their first cigarette of the day for 30 minutes longer than do precontemplators or contemplators (DiClemente et al., 1991). Although they have made some reductions in their problem behaviors, individuals in the preparation stage have not yet reached a criterion for effective action, such as abstinence from smoking, alcohol abuse, or heroin use. They are intending, however, to take such action in the very near future. On a continuous measure they score high on both the contemplation and action scales.

Action is the stage at which individuals modify their behavior, experiences, and/or environment in order to overcome their problems. Action involves the most overt behavior changes and requires a considerable commitment of time and energy. Modifications of a problem behavior made in the action stage tend to be most visible and receive the greatest external recognition. Many people, including professionals, often erroneously equate action with change. As a consequence, they overlook the requisite work that prepares changers for action and the important efforts necessary to maintain the changes following action.

Individuals are classified as being in the action stage if they have successfully altered a problem behavior for a period from 1 day to 6 months. Successfully altering a problem behavior means reaching a particular criterion, such as abstinence. With smoking, for example, cutting down by 50% or changing to lower tar and nicotine cigarettes are behavior changes that can better prepare people for action but do not satisfy the field's criteria for successful action. On a continuous measure, individuals in the action stage endorse statements such as, "I am really working hard to change," and, "Anyone can talk about changing; I am actually doing something about it." They score high on the action scale and lower on the scales assessing the other stages of change. Modification of the target behavior to an acceptable criterion and significant overt efforts to change are the hallmarks of action.

Maintenance is the stage in which people work to prevent relapse and consolidate the gains attained during action. Traditionally, maintenance was viewed as a static stage. However, maintenance is a continuation, not an absence, of change. For chronic problem behaviors, this stage extends from 6 months to an indeterminate period past the initial action. For some behaviors maintenance can be considered to last a lifetime. Being able to remain free of the chronic problem and/or to consistently engage in a new, incompatible behavior for more than 6 months is the criterion for considering someone to be in the maintenance stage. On a continuous measure of maintenance, representative items are, "I may need a boost right now to help me maintain the changes I've already made," and, "I'm here to prevent myself from having a relapse of my problem." Stabilizing behavior change and avoiding relapse are the hallmarks of maintenance.

As is now well-known, most people taking action to modify addictions do not successfully maintain their gains on their first attempt. With smoking, for example, successful self-changers make an average of three to four action attempts before they become long-term maintainers (Schachter, 1982). Many New Year's resolvers report 5 or more years of consecutive pledges before maintaining the behavioral goal for at least 6 months (Norcross & Vangarelli, 1989). Relapse and recycling through the stages occur quite frequently as individuals attempt to modify or cease addictive behaviors. Variations of the stage model are being used increasingly by behavior change specialists to investigate the dynamics of relapse (e.g., Brownell, Marlatt, Lichtenstein, & Wilson, 1986; Donovan & Marlatt, 1988).

Because relapse is the rule rather than the exception with problems such as the addictions, we found that we needed to modify our original stage model. Initially we conceptualized change as a linear progression through the stages; people were supposed to progress simply and discretely through each step. Linear progression is a possible but relatively rare phenomenon with many chronic problems such as the addictions.

Figure 11.1 presents a spiral pattern that illustrates how many people actually move through the stages of change. In this spiral pattern, people can progress from contemplation to preparation to action to maintenance, but many individuals will relapse. During relapse, individuals regress to an earlier stage. Some relapsers feel like failures—embarrassed, ashamed, and guilty. These individuals become demoralized and resist thinking about behavior change. As a result, they return to the precontemplation stage and can remain there for various periods. Ap-proximately 15% of smokers who relapsed in our self-change research regressed back to the precontemplation stage (Prochaska & DiClemente, 1984).

Fortunately, this research indicates that the vast majority of relapsers—85% of smokers, for example—recycle back to the contemplation or preparation stages (Prochaska & DiClemente, 1984). They begin to consider plans for their next action attempt while trying to learn from their recent efforts. To take another example, fully 60% of unsuccessful New Year's resolvers make the same pledge the next year (Norcross, Ratzin, & Payne, 1989; Norcross & Vangarelli, 1989). The spiral model suggests that most relapsers do not revolve endlessly in circles and that they do not regress all the way back to where they began. Instead, each time relapsers recycle through the stages, they potentially learn from their mistakes and try something different the next time around (DiClemente et al., 1991).

On any one trial, successful behavior change is limited in the absolute numbers of individuals who are able to achieve maintenance (Cohen et al., 1989;

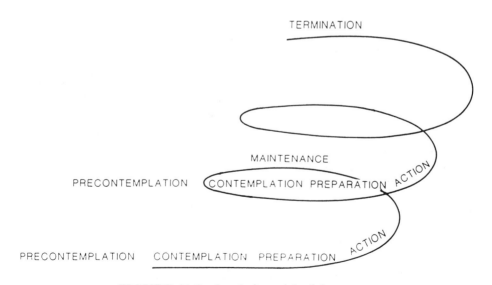

FIGURE 11.1. A spiral model of the stages.

Schacter, 1982). Nevertheless, looking at a cohort of individuals, the number of successes continues to increase gradually over time. However, a large number of individuals remain in contemplation and precontemplation stages. Ordinarily, the more action taken, the better the prognosis. We need much more research to better distinguish between those who benefit from recycling and those who end up spinning their wheels.

Termination is the stage in which people have 100% confidence or self-efficacy across all previous problem situations that they will never engage in the old pattern or behavior again. Also, they have no urges to engage in the old pattern or problem. These people are no longer recovering—they are recovered. It is as if they never had the chronic problem in the first place. In a group of recovering alcoholics who had progressed to the maintenance stage, 17% met the criterion for termination, and in a group of former smokers 16% met the criterion (Snow, Prochaska, & Rossi, 1992). The former alcoholics had no urges to drink whether they were angry, anxious, bored, depressed, lonely, socializing, or in any situation previously associated with drinking. The time criterion we use for termination is 5 years of being symptom free. People can recover but it takes a long time, and even then not all of them are free from risks of relapse.

Table 11.2 presents a diagram showing the integration of the stages and processes of change based on our research (Prochaska & DiClemente, 1983, 1992). During precontemplation, individuals use change processes significantly less than do people in any other stage. It was found that precontemplators process less information about their problems, spend less time and energy reevaluating themselves, experience fewer emotional reactions to the negative aspects of their problems, are less open with significant others about their problems, and do little

to shift their attention or their environment in the direction of overcoming their problems. In therapy these are clients who are labeled "resistant."

What can help assist people to move from precontemplation to contemplation? As Table 11.2 suggests, there are several change processes that are most helpful. First, *consciousness-raising* interventions by the therapist, such as observations, confrontations, and interpretations, can help clients become more aware of the causes, consequences, and cures of their problems. For example, to move to the contemplation stage, clients have to become more aware of the negative consequences of their behavior. Often we first have to help clients become more aware of their defenses before they can become more conscious of what they are defending against. Second, the process of *dramatic relief* provides clients with helpful affective experiences using techniques from psychodrama or Gestalt therapy. These experiences can release emotions related to problem behaviors. Life events can also move precontemplators emotionally, such as the disease or death of a friend or lover, especially if such events are related to the client's problem.

Clients in the contemplation stage are most open to consciousness-raising interventions and are much more likely to use bibliotherapy and other educational interventions than are precontemplators. As clients become increasingly more aware of themselves and the nature of their problems, they are freer to reevaluate themselves both affectively and cognitively. The *self-reevaluation* process includes an assessment of which values clients will try to actualize, act upon, and make real and which they will let die. The more central the problem behaviors are to their core values, the more will their reevaluation involve changes in their sense of self. Contemplators also reevaluate the effects their behaviors

TABLE 11.2. Processes of Change Emphasized at Particular Stages of Change

Precontemplation	Contemplation	Preparation	Action	Maintenance
Consciousness raising				
Dramatic relief				
Environmental reevaluation				
	Self-reevaluation			
	Self-liberation			
			Contingency management	
			Helping relationship	
			Counterconditioning	
			Stimulus control	

have on their environments, especially the people they care most about. Addicted individuals may ask, "How do I think and feel about living in a deteriorating environment that places me and my family at increasing risk of disease, death, poverty and/or imprisonment?" For some addictive behaviors, such as heroin addiction, the immediate effects on the environment are much more real. For other addictions, such as smoking, the emphasis may need to be on longer-term effects.

Movement from precontemplation to contemplation and movement through the contemplation stage involve increased use of cognitive, affective, and evaluative processes of change. To better prepare individuals for action, changes are required in how they think and feel about their problem behaviors and how they value their problematic lifestyles.

The preparation stage indicates clients' readiness to change in the near future and the acquisition of valuable lessons from past change attempts and failures. They are on the verge of taking action and need to set goals and priorities accordingly. They often develop an action plan for how they are going to proceed. In addition, they need to make firm commitments to follow through on the action

option they choose. In fact, they are often already engaged in processes that would increase self-regulation and initiate behavior change (DiClemente et al., 1991). Individuals typically begin by taking some small steps toward action. They may use *counterconditioning* and *stimulus control* processes to begin reducing their problem behaviors. Counterconditioning involves learning to substitute healthier alternatives in conditions that normally elicit problems, such as learning to relax instead of smoking in certain stressful situations. Stimulus control involves managing the presence or absence of situations or cues that can elicit problems, such as not stopping at a bar after work. Addicted individuals may delay their use of substances each day or may control the number of situations in which they rely on the addictive substances.

During the action stage it is important that clients act from a sense of *self-liberation*. They need to believe that they have the autonomy to change their life in key ways. Yet they also need to accept that coercive forces are as much a part of life as is autonomy. Self-liberation is based in part on a sense of self-efficacy (Bandura, 1977, 1982), the belief that one's own efforts play a critical role in succeeding in the face of difficult situations.

Self-liberation, however, requires more than just an affective and cognitive foundation. Clients must also be effective enough with behavioral processes, such as counterconditioning and stimulus control, to cope with those conditions that can coerce them into relapsing. Therapists can provide training, if necessary, in behavioral processes to increase the probability that clients will be successful when they do take action. As action proceeds, therapists provide a *helping relationship* in which they serve as consultants to the clients as self-changers, to help clients identify any errors they may be making in their attempts to change their behavior and environment in healthier directions. Because action is a particularly stressful stage of change that involves considerable opportunities for experiencing coercion, guilt, failure, rejection, and the limits of personal freedom, clients are also particularly in need of support and understanding. Knowing that there is at least one person who cares and is committed to helping eases some of the distress and dread of taking life-changing risks.

Just as preparation for action is essential for success, so too is preparation for maintenance. Successful maintenance builds on each of the processes that has come before and also involves an open assessment of the conditions under which a person is likely to be coerced into relapsing. Clients need to assess the alternatives they have for coping with such coercive conditions without resorting to self-defeating defenses and pathological responses. Perhaps most important is the sense that one is becoming more of the kind of person one wants to be. Continuing to apply counterconditioning and stimulus control is most effective when it is based on the conviction that maintaining change preserves a sense of self that is highly valued by oneself and at least one significant other.

The Levels of Change

Until this point, I have focused only on how to approach a single, well-defined problem. However, as we all realize, reality is not so accommodating and human behavior change is not so simple and straightforward. Although we can isolate certain symptoms and syndromes, these occur in the context of complex, interrelated levels of human functioning. The third basic element of the transtheoretical approach addresses this issue. The "levels of change" represents a hierarchical organization of five distinct but interrelated levels of psychological problems that can be addressed in psychotherapy. These levels are:

1. Symptom/situational problems
2. Maladaptive cognitions
3. Current interpersonal conflicts
4. Family/systems conflicts
5. Intrapersonal conflicts

Historically, systems of psychotherapy have attributed psychological problems primarily to one or two of these levels and focused their interventions on them. Behavior therapists have focused on the symptom and situational determinants, cognitive therapists on maladaptive cognitions, family therapists on the family/systems level, and analytic therapists on intrapersonal conflicts. It appears to us to be critical in the process of change that eventually therapists and clients agree as to which level they attribute the problem and at which level or levels they are willing to mutually engage in as they work to change the problem behavior.

In the transtheoretical approach we prefer to intervene initially at the symptom/situational level. Change tends to occur more quickly at this level as it often represents the primary reason for which the individual entered therapy. The further down the hierarchy we focus, the further removed from awareness are the determinants of the problem, and the more historically remote and more interrelated the problem is with the sense of self. Thus, we predict that the "deeper" the level that needs to be changed, the longer and more complex therapy is likely to be and the greater the resistance of the client (Prochaska & DiClemente, 1984). The decision to intervene at level 1 is similar to Pinsof's (1983) assessment and decision making model which was developed independently for family therapists.

These levels, it should be emphasized, are not completely isolated from one another; change at any one level is likely to produce change at other levels. Symptoms often involve intrapersonal conflicts, and maladaptive cognitions often reflect family/system beliefs or rules. In the transtheoretical approach, therapists are prepared to intervene at any of the five levels of change, though the preference is to begin at the highest (closest to level 1) and most contemporary level that clinical assessment and judgment can justify.

In summary, the transtheoretical approach views therapeutic integration as the differential application of the processes of change at specific stages of change according to the identified problem level. Integrating the levels with the stages and processes of change provides a model for intervening hierarchically and systematically across a broad range of therapeutic content. Table 11.3 presents an overview of the integration of levels, stages, and processes of change.

Table 11.3 indicates that as therapy progresses through the stages at the symptom/situational level, particular processes are applied at each stage. The arrows indicate a shifting to a deeper level, if necessary, and a progression through the stages of change by applying each of the particular processes relevant to each stage.

This shifting levels approach is one strategy for applying transtheoretical therapy. Another is the *key level strategy* in which one particular level is assessed as relevant for a particular patient with a particular problem. With this strategy, therapy focuses only on one key level and progress involves movement though the stages by applying appropriate processes at each stage.

A third approach is the *maximum impact* strategy, which involves impacting

TABLE 11.3. Interaction of Levels, Stages, and Processes of Change

Levels	Stages				
	Precontemplation	Contemplation	Preparation	Action	Maintenance
Symptom/situational	Consciousness raising				
	Dramatic relief				
	Environmental reevaluation				
			Self-reevaluation		
			Self-liberation		
				Contingency management	
				Helping relationship	
				Counterconditioning	
				Stimulus control	
Maladaptive cognitions					
Interpersonal conflicts					
Family systems conflicts					
Intrapersonal conflicts					

on all the relevant levels at once, such as consciousness raising for the situational, cognitive, interpersonal, family-of-origin, and intrapersonal determinants of the problem. Interventions can be created to affect clients at multiple levels of a problem in order to produce a maximum impact for change in a synergistic rather than sequential manner.

THE ASSESSMENT OF DYSFUNCTION

Transtheoretical therapy's innovative contribution to assessment is the development of dynamic measures for assessing clients' readiness for therapy and for change, their use of change processes within and between therapy sessions, and the levels of change to which clients attribute their problems. The *stages of change* can be assessed with a 32-item questionnaire that yields profiles on four scales. The profiles can be readily interpreted for assessing the stage clients are in at the beginning of therapy and how they are progressing through the stages over the course of therapy (DiClemente & Hughes, 1990; McConnaughy, DiClemente, Prochaska, & Velicer, 1989; McConnaughy et al., 1983; Prochaska, Rossi, & Wilcox, 1991). In the health psychology area, we have found a five-item questionnaire to be a remarkably reliable and valid assessment of stage for such behaviors as smoking cessation, quitting cocaine, weight control, safer sex, condom use, changing high fat diets, exercise acquisition, and stopping adolescent delinquent behaviors (DiClemente et al., 1991; Prochaska & DiClemente, 1983; Prochaska et al., 1994).

The *processes of change* can be assessed with a 40-item questionnaire that contains 4 items for each of the processes (Prochaska & DiClemente, 1985; Prochaska, DiClemente, Velicer, & Rossi, 1993; Prochaska, Velicer, DiClemente, & Fava, 1988). The processes can be interpreted both normatively, comparing the client's use of processes to those by peers who have progressed the most through particular stages, and ipsatively, comparing the client to his/her own previous assessment scores (Prochaska, et al., 1993). The processes also can be assessed between therapy sessions to determine whether clients are making the types of efforts between sessions that are most appropriate for progressing to the next stage (Prochaska, Norcross, Fowler, Follick, & Abrams, 1992; Prochaska et al., 1991). Shorter forms of the process measures can be used to assess both the client's and the therapist's perceptions of their use of process of change within sessions (Prochaska et al., 1991).

The levels of change can be assessed with a 50-item questionnaire that contains 5 items for each of 10 problem levels (Norcross, Prochaska, Guadagnoli, & DiClemente, 1984; Norcross, Prochaska, & Hambrecht, 1985). The categories that are assessed most often are the five levels emphasized in transtheoretical therapy. While clients usually perceive their problems as being caused or controlled by variables at one or more of these psychosocial levels, they, at times rely on other attributions, such as religious causes, bad luck, and biological determinants which constitute three of the remaining five levels. The levels of change can be assessed from the perspective of the client, the therapist, and/or a significant other (Begin, 1988).

As eclectic therapists, we are open to using assessments from a wide range of traditions, usually depending on the level of change being assessed. As empirical therapists, we try to select the instruments that have the best psychometric properties and are most valid for particular problems. Instruments that are used include situational assessments such as the behaviorally based Fear Inventory (Wolpe, 1973) or cognitive assessments like rational–emotive measures of irrational beliefs (Ellis & Dryden, 1987); interpersonal measures such as the Locke–Wallace (Locke & Wallace, 1959) marital satisfaction instrument; family systems measures such as Grebstein's (Tavinian, Lubiner, Green, Grebstein, & Velicer, 1987) family atmosphere scales, and intrapersonal measures such as the Rorschach, which is often interpreted psychoanalytically.

Because about 80% of clients prefer individual therapy, most of our assessments are done with individuals. However, when working with couples or families, stages of change are assessed for each client. One of the complications of working with dyads or triads is that individuals can be in quite different stages of change. With couples, for example, the woman is often prepared to take action to improve the relationship while the man may be denying that there are any problems. The therapist can be in a dilemma of being seen as proceeding too quickly by one spouse or too slowly by the other. The transtheoretical therapist clarifies to the clients the dilemma of the spouses being in different stages and then indicates that the spouse who is furthest along will be encouraged to slow down somewhat while the other spouse is encouraged to speed up somewhat.

Even in our most controlled research projects, assessments are integrally linked with treatment. Clients are systematically given feedback on their stages of change, the processes they are underutilizing, overutilizing, or utilizing adequately between treatment sessions. They are also given feedback on other dynamic variables such as *decisional balance*, which involves the patient's assessment of the pros and cons of changing a particular problem, and *self-efficacy*, which involves confidence that changes can be continued across problem situations. Clinically it is usually helpful to share with clients the levels that will be the focus of therapy.

THE PRACTICE OF THERAPY

Basic Structure

Therapists once had the illusion that they could determine the structure of therapy, including the frequency, duration, and number of sessions. The fact that 30% to 60% of clients typically dropped out of therapy was generally ignored and was attributed to the client's resistance rather than to the client's wish to determine how long therapy would last (Medeiros & Prochaska, 1994). Therapists today are well aware that they have much less ability than formerly to structure how therapy will proceed as managed care organizations, insurance companies, employers, and clients take much more active roles.

Many therapists are faced with trying to have a significant impact on clients who will be in therapy for 12 sessions or less. In transtheoretical therapy, clients who are at risk of dropping out early are informed that therapy can make a significant difference if it lasts at least six sessions. Some clients are informed that therapy can make a substantial difference if it lasts 26 sessions (Howard, Kopta, Drause, & Orlinsky, 1986). All clients are informed that how quickly they progress is a function of what stage of change they are in, how much they use appropriate change processes within and between therapy sessions, and which levels of problems need to be changed.

The frequency of sessions varies according to the client's stage of change. For clients in precontemplation or contemplation, sessions are typically scheduled weekly. For clients who are taking effective action, sessions can be scheduled biweekly. Clients who are progressing toward maintenance can be seen monthly, and once in maintenance, they can be seen on an as-needed basis. Therapy sessions are 50 minutes in length.

The number of sessions required varies both according to the stage and level of change and according to how hard and smart clients work between sessions. Clients who enter therapy prepared to take action can have a successful experience in therapy in 6 to 10 sessions. The more defenses clients have to work through and the less successful work they have been able to do prior to entering therapy, the longer the course of therapy, typically ranging from 6 to 24 months.

For clients with problems at the situational and cognitive levels, therapy typically can be shorter. For clients with problems that are more deeply embedded in the context of a dysfunctional family history or a dysfunctional intrapersonal history, therapy will need to be of longer duration. Problems that develop in a current interpersonal relationship usually average about 12 months. The more problems are multilevel in origin, the longer therapy will need to be.

The amount of structure that the therapist needs to provide also varies with the client's stage of change. Precontemplators need much more help in getting started and dealing with defenses. Contemplators love to engage in consciousness-raising and self-reevaluation processes and can typically do much of the within-session work with minimal structure. Once it comes to taking action, clients vary in how much direction they seek from therapy. Those who have become demoralized about their abilities to maintain change usually look to the therapist for guidance on how they can be more effective in their next action attempt. Other clients can be quite creative in how they can best apply behavioral processes to modify their situations, cognitions, interpersonal relationships or family systems.

Goal Setting

Given that the majority of clients stay in therapy for less than 10 sessions, realistic goals must be set. For clients at high risk for dropping out before 3 sessions, the immediate goal is to help them continue for 6 sessions. In five different studies the stage-of-change measures were the best predictors of drop-out, with precontemplators making up the vast majority of premature terminators (e.g., Medeiros & Prochaska, 1994). For clients who are likely to stay in therapy for just a few sessions, an appropriate goal is to help them progress just one stage. Our research suggests that clients whom we help progress just one stage in 1 month of therapy are twice as likely to take effective action on their own over the next 6 months than those who stay in the same stage during the first month. Given that many clients enter therapy having been stuck in the same stage of change for years, therapy will make a major difference if it helps them progress to the next stage in a relatively brief period of time.

For example, one client in the precontemplation stage entered therapy as an angry and abusive alcoholic whose marriage and business were deteriorating. Six sessions later, he left therapy as an angry and abusive alcoholic who proceeded to lose his marriage and his company. For years, I could not understand why he was one of my best sources of referrals. I thought I had failed him. Later, I contacted him and he told me that he was convinced that through my confrontations and interpretations I had helped him progress to the contemplation stage. Two years later, he quit drinking on his own; he has remained sober for 9 years; he raised four successful children on his own; he has remarried and re-created a gratifying career.

It is not a realistic goal to expect patients in precontemplation to progress to maintenance in 28 days of inpatient care or 6 months of outpatient therapy. People rarely change that quickly. However, it is a realistic goal to help people become more effective self-changers. For some clients, this will mean helping them to get unstuck from a long-lasting stage so that they can progress more freely on their own. For others, it will mean helping them to have greater awareness and understanding of the level or levels that are causing or controlling a particular problem. Clients who are trying situational cures such as changing jobs, moving to California, or buying a new house, when their problem is embedded in how they relate to people at work or at home, can best be helped to direct their change efforts at the interpersonal level.

Other clients misapply particular processes of change and, in spite of themselves, make things worse. This is well known to happen in clients with depression who try to counter their moods with central nervous system depressants such as alcohol. Less well known are clients with sexual impotence who try to rely exclusively on self-liberation or willpower to will erections but who end up feeling helpless and impotent. Just as people need expert guidance when applying powerful psychotropic medications, so, too, do many people need expert guidance in applying the most powerful psychological processes of change.

In the health psychology area we often hear people say that they have tried every treatment or technique available. Therapists can feel intimidated if clients have already tried the most promising procedures and failed. But rarely do therapists inquire as to how long or how frequently the clients used the processes. If depressed clients reported that they tried the most promising antidepressant medication, we would not say that there is no sense in trying that again. We would assess whether clients used enough of the medication for a long enough duration to give it a fair trial. Similarly, with psychological processes we need to be able to assess more systematically how frequently and for how long clients used them to determine whether the processes were given a fair trial. We also need to assess how skillfully therapists helped them to apply the processes.

Strategies of Change

We first teach clients our model of how people change and have them apply it to a particular problem. The principles of the stages and processes have been found to be valid for a broad range of problems. Thus, if clients can use the model to be more effective at changing one chronic problem, they can also generalize the model to solving problems outside therapy.

Usually, we recommend starting on a problem on which the client is prepared to take action. This is often a problem the client has been working on prior to therapy. We can assess how well the client has used processes such as consciousness raising, dramatic relief, and self-re-evaluation. We can assess the client's plan for action and the techniques that will be used to counter the problem conditions, to alter the environment, and to reinforce small steps in the right direction. We can also assess how well the client is learning based on his/her previous attempts to change that resulted in relapse. Clients need to learn that changing a long-standing pattern requires an existential commitment based on a belief in personal freedom and the ability to use that freedom to determine a better future.

As indicated earlier, three basic strategies can be employed for intervening across multiple levels of change. The first is a *shifting levels* strategy. Therapy would typically focus first on the client's symptoms and the situations supporting the symptoms. If the processes could be applied effectively at the first level and the client progressed through each stage of change, therapy could be completed without shifting to a more complex level of analysis. If this approach were not effective, therapy would necessarily shift to other levels in sequence in order to achieve the desired change. The strategy of shifting from a higher to a deeper level was illustrated in Table 11.3 by the arrows moving first across one level and then down to the next level. The second is the *key level* strategy. If the available evidence points to one key level of causality of a problem and the client can be effectively engaged at that level, the therapist would work almost exclusively at this key level.

The third alternative is the *maximum impact strategy*. With many complex cases, it is evident that multiple levels (e.g., interpersonal and familial) are involved as a cause, an effect, or a maintainer of the client's problems. Interventions can be created to affect clients at multiple levels of a problem in order to establish a maximum impact for change in a synergistic rather than a sequential manner.

Theoretical complementarity and integration are the keys to synthesizing the major systems of psychotherapy. Table 11.4 illustrates where leading systems of therapy fit best within the integrative

framework of the transtheoretical approach. The therapy systems included in Table 11.4 have been the most prominent contributors to the transtheoretical approach. Depending on which level and at which stage we are working, different therapy systems will play a more or less prominent role. Behavior therapy, for example, has developed specific interventions at the symptom/situational level for clients who are ready for action. At the maladaptive cognition level, however, Ellis's rational–emotive therapy and Beck's cognitive therapy are most prominent for clients in the preparation and action stages.

Hypothetically, we do not exclude any therapy system from the transtheoretical approach. Ours is an open framework that allows for inclusion of new and innovative interventions, as well as the inclusion of existing therapy systems that research or clinical experience suggest are most helpful for clients in particular stages at particular levels of change.

A major therapy system that is not included in Table 11.4 is Rogers's (1951, 1959) client-centered therapy (see Bohart, Chapter 4, this volume). Rogers's system has been most prominent in articulating and demonstrating the importance of the therapeutic relationship as a critical process of change. Our own thinking and research on the helping rela-

TABLE 11.4. Integration of Major Therapy Systems within the Transtheoretical Framework

Levels	Stages				
	Precontemplation	Contemplation	Preparation	Action	Maintenance
Symptom/situational				Behavior therapy	
Maladaptive cognitions	Adlerian therapy		Rational–emotive therapy Cognitive therapy		
Interpersonal conflicts	Sullivanian therapy		Couples communication Transactional Analysis		
Family systems conflicts	Strategic therapy		Bowenian therapy	Structural therapy	
Intrapersonal conflicts	Psychoanalytic therapies		Existential therapy	Gestalt therapy	

tionship as a major process of change has been most influenced by client-centered therapy even though we do not rely only on client-centered techniques for developing a helping relationship. Thus, Rogers's influence on the transtheoretical approach cuts across the levels of change.

Process of Therapy

Matching therapy to the client's stage and level of change is one of the most important strategies for creating a therapeutic alliance. A client and therapist each working at different stages is one of the most common sources of resistance. If the therapist is an action-oriented therapist and the client is in the precontemplation stage, the client will experience the therapist as insensitive and coercive, like a parent pressuring change when the client is not convinced that change is needed. Conversely, if the client is prepared to take action and the therapist relies almost exclusively on consciousness-raising and self-reevaluation processes, the client will experience therapy as moving much too slowly while the therapist might believe the client is being resistant.

Similarly, clients who believe that immediate situational changes will improve their symptoms are likely to be resistant to spending much time becoming more conscious of their childhood. Conversely, therapists who rely heavily on situationally focused techniques such as desensitization can experience resistance from clients who are convinced that their phobias are rooted in much deeper levels which they want to understand. A client who was being treated with systematic desensitization for a social phobia by one of our graduate students complained, "It seems to me that the therapy you are using is like treating a cancer with aspirin."

The most resistant clients are those in the precontemplation stage, particularly those who have been pressured into therapy by spouses who are threatening to leave them, employers who are threatening to fire them, schools that are threatening to expel them, or judges who are threatening to imprison them. To help such clients accept therapy, we need to be able to empathize with their situation—to let them know we have a sense of how it must feel to be in therapy when they are not convinced that they need to change or when they are convinced that other people are the problem. At times, we engage such resistant clients by helping them learn how they can change someone else. In the process, they will have to change their ways as well, but at least they are less defensive about learning how people change.

One of the most serious technical errors is to fail to match treatment to the client's stage of change. Clients are likely to have enough sources of resistance to change and do not need therapeutically produced resistance. Traditionally, too many clients have dropped out of therapy, only to be blamed for not being motivated rather than being provided with processes appropriate to the stage at which they are motivated to work.

Similarly, failing to match the client's preferred level of change is another serious error. If therapists can only work effectively at one level of change, then they had better have the luxury of selecting clients who match that level. In choosing a therapist, clients are often implicitly seeking someone who works at a level that they believe is most relevant to their problems. This is a major reason why some clients prefer behavior therapists while others seek psychoanalytic therapists and still others seek interpersonal or family therapists. Potentially a transtheoretical therapist can be trained to match the needs of a much broader range of clients. Such therapists would need to have adequate training in the theories and techniques appropriate to each level. What we do not know at this point is what constitutes adequate training to facilitate change at each level.

Therapists who are well matched to clients' stage and level of change are likely to experience the therapeutic process as progressing more smoothly. Of course, clients can become stuck in a stage, but at least the therapist is aware of not contributing to such stuckness. Clients who have been stuck in the contemplation stage tend to substitute thinking and reflecting for acting. At times, we refer to these individuals as chronic contemplators. They can be very comfortable with therapists who prefer to rely on more contemplation-oriented processes such as consciousness raising and self-reevaluation. But encouraging such clients to go deeper and deeper into more levels of their problems can be iatrogenic (i.e., the therapy can produce difficulties, such as feeding into clients' problems of being "chronic contemplators"). At some point, action must be taken. But if the therapist has not been trained to use action-oriented processes effectively, the therapist might prefer to avoid action in the same way that chronic contemplators can avoid action. After years and years of archaeological expeditions into the deepest levels of problems, such clients may yell out like the character on a *New York* magazine cover: "Help, I'm being held captive in psychotherapy!"

At some point, therapy must terminate. These days, therapy often terminates before the clients' problems are terminated, especially with managed cases. This is one of the reasons why there can be a fair amount of anxiety around the termination process. Intuitively all parties know that the client is not yet home free. Even with our most effective techniques for agoraphobia, for example, by the end of treatment fewer than 30% of clients have recovered or reached normal levels of functioning (Jacobson, Wilson, & Tupper, 1988). Many more have improved but they are not symptom free. Similarly, with addictive problems fewer than 30% of clients will be free from their addictions a year after they have terminated the best therapies available (Hunt, Barnett, & Branch, 1971). Unfortunately, most clients are not willing or able to cover the costs of continuing therapy until they have reached the termination stage.

Three criteria are usually used to decide on when termination should occur. Perhaps the most common is the client's criterion of feeling good enough to go back to coping on his/her own. Clients may communicate this directly or they may use indirect methods such as missing some weekly sessions or asking to have sessions less frequently. The worst case is when clients terminate therapy unilaterally without even discussing it with the therapist. I find that clients are often ready to terminate therapy before the therapist is ready, especially the student therapist.

One of the themes of transtheoretical therapy is to work in harmony with how people change naturally. One of the natural termination processes is to gradually fade out therapy once effective action is being taken. Thus, once the action criterion is reached and continued for a month or two, termination begins with biweekly sessions in place of weekly ones. Then we progress to monthly meetings. Most clients experience such changes in scheduling as rewarding, as signs of both the excellent progress they have been making as well as saving time, money, and effort.

A particularly good sign that clients are ready to terminate is when they function so effectively as self-changers that they solve some problems that have not been the focus of therapy. We know that our clients are not going to be problem free, but we also know that we have truly helped clients when they are free to overcome their most pressing problems on their own.

THE STANCE OF THE THERAPIST

The stance of the therapist varies with the stage clients are in. With clients in the *precontemplation stage*, therapists need to be more active in keeping them from dropping out of therapy and to help them to begin to explore problems in the face of considerable resistance and defensiveness. Therapists may need to be more active in asking questions to help precontemplators to participate; they may need to inform clients about the many pros of therapy, such as the salaries of clients increasing faster than control comparisons, because these clients seriously underestimate the benefits of therapy; and they need to teach clients about how people change and where the clients' current experiences fall within the cycle of change. Therapists need to be able to identify with the precontemplators' defensiveness rather than react to it, and in this sense to join with clients and their uncomfortable place in therapy. Reflecting clients' resentments or reservations about being in therapy, their doubts and indecision can all help such resistant clients to feel that this therapist can be on their side rather than joining with the forces who were pressuring them to enter therapy in the first place.

With clients in the *contemplation stage*, the therapist's work is easier. The therapist can be more passive and leave much of the contemplative work to these clients who are eager to explore and to understand but slow to act. Therapists may need to be more active at times in helping clients remain more focused on the levels of change that are most appropriate to their problems. As actors, clients can

often shift to *situational* attributions, while therapists as observers tend to be biased toward *dispositional* attributions such as those at the intrapersonal level (Jones & Nisbett, 1972). According to attribution research, actors tend to attribute negative behaviors, such as excessive drinking, to situational determinants ("I was unemployed"). Observers tend to attribute the same behaviors to the actor's disposition or personality ("The client has an addictive or dependent personality"). As more objective observers, therapists can help shift the focus of sessions to the levels that have been assessed to be most crucial in causing or controlling clients' particular problems.

Therapists will also have to be prepared to become more active with clients who relate like chronic contemplators. If prior to and during therapy clients have spent many months and even years analyzing their issues, the therapists will need to become more directive and help clients start to take at least some small steps toward action.

With clients who are prepared to take *action*, therapists have a number of useful alternatives. The first is to review the client's plan of action to see if it has a high probability of success. If so, the therapist can sit back and let the client run with it. If therapists know that there are particularly effective action plans available for particular problems, such as sensate focusing for sexual dysfunctions (Masters & Johnson, 1970) or *in vivo* desensitization for phobias (Wolpe, 1973), these should be shared and encouraged. Typically, we try to provide clients with a couple of choices for action including their own creative plans, so that they can maximize their commitments to plans rather than feel that their only choices are to follow their therapist's directions or resist.

If clients are not adequately prepared to take action, they are encouraged to engage in further contemplation or preparation processes. Clients, for example, who are tempted to use situational-level actions (e.g., moving to a warm climate) to solve interpersonal-level problems (e.g., marital conflicts) are likely to discover that such "travel therapy" is ineffective. Such ineffective action would be analogous to what psychodynamic therapists view as "acting out."

The amount of responsibility that therapists assume varies with the stage clients are in. The greatest burden of responsibility is with precontemplators because they are least able to change themselves and most likely to resist therapy. But the therapist's responsibility is to help clients become less defensive and more open to exploration and understanding, to help them progress to the contemplation stage and not to pressure for premature changes such as taking action. With clients who are prepared to take action, much more of the burden will fall on the client for carrying out an action plan, as most of this activity will occur between therapy sessions. The therapists' responsibilities include adequately reviewing an action plan to make sure it is realistic and potentially effective and to revise the plan in aspects that are not working well.

The therapist's stance at different stages can be characterized as follows. With precontemplators, often the role is like that of a *nurturing parent* who can join with the resistant and defensive youngster who is both drawn to and repelled by the prospects of becoming more independent. With contemplators, the role is more like that of a *Socratic teacher* who encourages clients to achieve their own insights into and ideas about their condition. With clients who are in the preparation stage, the stance is more like that of *an experienced coach* who has been through many important matches and can provide a fine game plan or can review the person's own plan. With clients who are progressing into action and *maintenance*, the therapist becomes more

of *a consultant* who is available to provide expert advice and support when action is not progressing as smoothly as expected. As *termination* approaches in longer-term therapy, the therapist is consulted less and less often as the client experiences greater autonomy and ability to live a life freer from past patterns and problems that were disabling. In some ways, this sequence of stances parallels the changing roles that effective parents play as their children grow through stages of personal development. In this sense, the therapeutic relationship changes and evolves as clients progress through stages of intentional change. In long-term therapy, the therapist can be experienced by the client first as a nurturing parent, then as a favoriate teacher, next as a caring coach, and finally as a concerned consultant relating to a more self-directed client. Like parents, therapists should not strive to be perfect role models but "good enough" guides who can help clients through the complexities of changing.

MECHANISMS OF CHANGE AND TREATMENT APPLICABILITY

Transtheoretical therapy has generated more data about how people change than have most systems of psychotherapy. We know, for example, that how much people change following a brief course of therapy is directly related to the stage they are in prior to therapy. This is true whether we are talking about brain-impaired patients in rehabilitation programs (Lam, McMahon, Priddy, & Gehred-Schultz, 1989); anxiety patients with panic receiving one of the most promising chemotherapies (Beitman, in press), cardiac patients receiving counseling for smoking (Ockene et al., 1992), or Mexican Americans in community-based communication programs for smoking cessation (Gottleib, Galarotti, McCuan, & McAlister, 1991). There is a strong stage effect both immediately following intervention as well as 12 and 18 months afterwards (Gottleib, 1991; Ockene et al., 1992; Prochaska et al., 1992).

Research is also clarifying where in the stages of change people are when we offer interventions to populations with a broad range of problems. Across a set of 15 health and mental health related problems, fewer than 20% of a representative sample of people with problems are in the preparation stage; 40% to 60% are in the precontemplation stage, and the rest (about 30%) are in the contemplation stage (Rossi, 1992). These data suggest that if we offer action-oriented interventions to entire populations, we are likely to misserve or not serve the vast majority. Other research clearly indicates that of people with health behavior problems, fewer than 10% seek professional help (Shapiro et al., 1984). Of people with DSM-IV disorders, only about 25% ever seek professional help (Veroff et al., 1981a, 1981b). In controlled research testing three different methods for marketing free home-based interventions for smoking, only 1% to 5% of the eligible smokers participated. Similarly, in a health maintenance organization (HMO) study offering state-of-the-art action-oriented, home-based services for smokers, fewer than 5% participated. In our stage-matched transtheoretical programs that use outreach recruitment procedures, we are having 75% of a representative sample of smokers participate and 80% of an HMO population (Laforge, Prochaska, Velicer, & Fava, 1992). These data strongly suggest that if we are going to draw or recruit much higher percentages of populations with problems to our therapeutic programs, we may need to combine more proactive social marketing strategies and offer programs that match the stages people are in.

Research is also clarifying who remains in therapy once a client makes the effort to participate. It has been well-known for some time that approximately 40% of patients terminate therapy prematurely, dropping out of treatment after a few sessions against the therapist's advice (Medeiros & Prochaska, 1994). What has not been known are the characteristics of who drops out of therapy. We tried to predict dropouts from a variety of therapies by using the variables that have traditionally been among the best predictors of therapy outcome. These include client characteristics such as demographics, and problem characteristics such as duration, intensity, and type of problems. We were unable to predict therapy dropouts. When we used transtheoretical variables, such as the stage and processes of change and the pros and cons of therapy, we were able to correctly classify 93% of the premature terminators compared to the therapy continuers and the early but appropriate terminators. The stage profile of the entire group of the 40% who dropped out of therapy was the profile of precontemplators. The stage profile of the 20% who terminated quickly but appropriately as judged by the therapists was the profile of people in the action stage. The therapy continuers had a stage profile that was similar to the individual profile of contemplators (Medeiros & Prochaska, 1994).

If we are going to attract to our therapies a much higher percentage of people in need, we must learn how to reach the large proportion of people who are in the precontemplation stage. Similarly, if we are going to do justice to the important portion of patients who terminate therapy prematurely, we will also need to know how to relate to and help people in the precontemplation stage of change.

Fortunately, we are learning much more about how people progress from precontemplation to action. We can predict which variables differentiate people in the action stage from those in the precontemplation stage. Fortunately, static variables that are not very open to change, such as demographics and problem history, are not important differentiators. Dynamic variables that are open to change are much better differentiators. The balance of pros and cons in the client's mind for changing their problem behaviors are examples of the best predictors of stages both cross-sectionally and longitudinally (DiClemente et al., 1991; Prochaska, DiClemente, Velicer, Ginpil, & Norcross, 1985; Prochaska, Velicer, et al., 1994; Velicer, DiClemente, Prochaska, & Brandenberg, 1985; Wilcox, Prochaska, Velicer, & DiClemente, 1985). Across 12 different problem behaviors, we find common patterns of relationships between people's decisional balance about changing and the stages they are in. For all problems, the cons of changing outweigh the pros for people in the precontemplation stage; the opposite is true for people in the action stage (Prochaska, Velicer, et al., 1994). For all problems, the pros of changing increase from precontemplation to contemplation. For all problems, the cons of changing decrease from contemplation to action. The pros of changing begin to outweigh the cons for people in the contemplation stage for 7 of the 12 problems and in the preparation stage for the other problems.

What is even more important, we can predict the magnitude of the differences that must occur in the pros and cons if people are to progress from precontemplation to action. The pros of changing must increase approximately one standard deviation while the cons decrease one-half of a standard deviation (Prochaska, 1994). To put this magnitude in perspective, it would take a 15-point increase to improve one standard deviation on an intelligence test. We have tested these principles from precontemplation

to action for progress in four new studies with four problem behaviors and the magnitude of the changes all support the principles. That makes 16 out of 16 studies supporting these principles for progressing from precontemplation to action. We know of no other theoretical principles in the therapy or behavior change field that have successfully predicted the magnitude of the differences on key variables even though such predictions are routine in the physical sciences (Meehl, 1978). For the first time, the field may have lawful principles of how people change problem behaviors.

If we are to help people progress from precontemplation to action, we must help them to change their mind. Of course, in a very real sense, this is the historic mission of psychotherapy— helping people to change their mind. We must help them to change their mind about how they evaluate the pros and cons of how they have been living and how they evaluate the pros and cons of healthier ways of being and behaving. The magnitude of the change necessary is remarkable. To facilitate a change of one standard deviation in the pros of a new way of living means that our therapies would have to account for 20% of the variance on this dynamic measure (Cohen, 1977). But the best estimate we have is that therapeutic processes used within therapy sessions account for less than 10% of the therapeutic outcome variance (Lambert, 1986).

So what is a scientific therapist to do? First, we can reject science; second, we can reject therapy; or, third, we can seek methods that impact on more of the variance. One of the domains in which transtheoretical therapists seek to have greater impact is the 99% of the waking week that clients spend between therapy sessions. We need to find methods to help clients make use of our most powerful processes of change when they are not in therapy sessions. There is growing evidence that it is these change processes that alter people's minds and the way they evaluate the pros and cons of changing (Velicer, Hughes, Fava, Prochaska, & DiClemente, 1992). These processes are eclectic in nature and are aimed at altering people's rational selves (consciousness raising), affective selves (dramatic relief), evaluative selves (self and environmental reevaluation), existential selves (self- and social liberation), conditional selves (counterconditioning, stimulus control, and reinforcement management), and social selves (helping relationships). If people are going to become prepared to take action on such core parts of themselves, they are going to have to work at change outside the treatment hour.

One of the special missions of our research is to create home-based interventions that permit people to work as wisely on their problems at home as they do when they are under the expert guidance of therapists (Prochaska, Norcross, & DiClemente, 1994). In the health psychology area, we have created computer-driven expert systems that provide people feedback about which stage they are in, how they are evaluating the pros and cons of changing, and which of the processes of change they are underutilizing, overutilizing, or utilizing appropriately. Such an expert system that is theory-based and computer-driven has been found to produce two-and-a-half times as much success as the best home-based program for smoking cessation (Prochaska et al., 1993). Furthermore, this expert system program was producing more progress at 18-month follow-up than was a program that included talking with a counselor. The effects of the counselor condition reached a plateau at 12 months, while the computer condition was continuing to be effective at 18 months. It is possible that the participants in this study had become more dependent on their counselors and once

treatment was terminated they were less able to progress on their own than was the group whose members only received feedback on how they could best direct their own self-change processes and procedures.

These results suggest that people need expert feedback in order to change more effectively. Most people need increased awareness about how people change and about the personal mistakes and gains they are making in their own efforts to change. People whose problems are rooted in the context of family and intrapersonal conflicts are also likely to need more historic–genetic awareness while those whose problems are rooted in current interpersonal conflicts need more interactional insight. There are others who need the type of situational and environmental analysis that behaviorists can best provide through functional analysis. And there are those who would benefit from cognitive insights such as those evoked through Ellis's ABCD approach, with A being the activating situations, B the person's beliefs about those situations, C the emotional consequences of those beliefs, and D the rational beliefs that can be used to dispute the irrational thoughts that are causing or controlling the person's problems.

Interpretation is one of the most commonly used techniques for activating consciousness and it is a very useful technique. Therapists' observations and confrontations are techniques that also can increase awareness and understanding. Bibliotherapy techniques are particularly effective for enhancing consciousness-raising and self-reevaluation processes between sessions, especially when the books and articles are matched to the stage and level of change for a particular client (Prochaska, Norcross, & DiClemente, 1994). The book *Feeling Good*, by David Burns (1980), for example, provides excellent self-assessments and exercises to help people understand and modify their maladaptive cognitions that may cause them to be depressed.

Consciousness-raising techniques such as interpretations, observations, and confrontations are effective in producing progress from precontemplation to action. But, once people are adequately prepared to take action, continued reliance on such techniques may become counterproductive. We have published empirical case studies that demonstrated how a therapist failed to help a client progress because of an excessive reliance on experiential processes within sessions. The client showed an increased reliance on consciousness-raising techniques between sessions but no progress out of the contemplation stage and no improvement over the course of therapy (Prochaska et al., 1991). The same therapist utilized more action-oriented processes with a comparable client. That client showed an increased reliance on five action-oriented processes between sessions, progressed to the action stage, and showed marked improvement on symptoms over the course of therapy.

In a cognitive-behavioral therapy program for obesity, the program employed action-oriented processes within therapy sessions. The clients who were most likely to remain in therapy and progress the most were those who showed the greatest increase in use of the same five action-oriented processes between sessions.

These results suggest that the processes of change that therapists emphasize within therapy sessions have an impact on the processes of change that clients use between therapy sessions. This combination of within- and between-session use of appropriate change processes is what will produce the greatest progress through the stages of change and the greatest freedom from disabling patterns and problems. For clients in the early stages of change the appropriate processes are more experiential in nature

and are designed to change people's minds, including how they evaluate the prospects of being free from historic patterns of being and behaving. For clients in later stages, the processes are more behavioral in nature and are designed to change the person's environment—the physical and social contexts in which chronic problems have occurred.

The process that is used most across the stages of change is the helping relationship (Prochaska & DiClemente, 1983, 1985). To facilitate a helping relationship therapists need to have a healthy enough personality. Caring, understanding, and commitment to the well-being of clients are values that should be essential elements in the identity of a therapist. Therapists feel most free as therapists when they are able to care about their clients, understand their clients, and be committed to their well-being. There are times, of course, when therapists can be affected by countertransference or other problems so that they are not really caring about the client in the session but rather about their own needs. Or they are not really understanding this client but rather are responding to their projections onto the client. Therapists, however, are committed to putting their own needs and problematic projections aside so that they can be free to focus on client needs.

Ironically, clients need first to feel that the therapist is free to identify with them before the client is free to identify with the therapist. Identifying with a client involves a combination of focusing, empathizing, and understanding. If the client feels that the therapist cannot identify with the client's predicament in life because the therapist does not care, does not understand, or is not committed, the client is likely to terminate therapy before it begins. Clients need to believe that therapists can identify with them as if they were friends and family, not foreigners who are alien to them. If clients believe the therapist cannot identify with them because the therapist is of the wrong gender, ethnic background, social class, or sexual orientation, clients will not feel free in therapy. Clients are likely to avoid such therapists lest they risk coercion to change according to stereotypes of gender, ethnicity, social class, or sexual orientation.

As clients and therapists begin to develop a shared identity that is the essence of a therapeutic relationship, clients become much more open to influence from therapists. Clients are much freer to respond to feedback and education about the alienated aspects of their lives. They are particularly free to process information from therapists or others with whom they have a helping relationship. Therapists also become more open to influence from their clients, such as having a favored formulation invalidated by further information from the client. But our focus shall remain centered on how clients change in therapy rather than on how therapists change over the course of therapy.

A helping relationship, such as a therapeutic relationship, provides people with the freedom to process developmental or environmental events in a friendly rather than coercive atmosphere. Easing up on their defenses, they can begin to see themselves more clearly. They can begin to contemplate making intentional changes in their lives without feeling that they are entirely coerced by developmental or environmental events. Movement into the contemplation stage, like many changes in life, is usually experienced as a combination of coercion and personal freedom.

Once clients begin to move into the contemplation stage, their insight and understanding are critical for further progress. Whether the insight is historic–genetic, interactive, cognitive, or situational depends on the level of change that is needed. For clients working at the symptom/situational level, a functional analysis of the immediate antecedents and consequences of troubled behavior may be all the understanding that is needed. Clients attempting to change troubled relationships, however, will need insight into the interactive nature of their problems. Clients who are not free enough from their family of origin or who are plagued by internalized intrapersonal conflicts are more likely to need insight into the nature of the relationship they form with the therapist (transference) and into the historic–genetic causes of their conflicts.

Affectively experienced insight into the causes of conflicts can be the most important source of progress from contemplation to preparation. This is a change of no small magnitude. While insight helps prepare clients to take action, insight alone will not guide individuals through the complexities of action and maintenance. Different processes are needed at these stages, processes that have been advocated more by existentialists, client-centered therapists, and behaviorists.

Insight and understanding can become an endless process of consciousness raising, however, when clients wish to have a complete grasp of all that influences them. Some personalities have a propensity to become bogged down in prolonged contemplation of a problem. Obsessive personalities in particular prefer to believe that if they keep thinking enough about an issue, eventually the problem will go away or enough understanding will be gained that points to a perfect solution to a complex problem. The obsessive does not like to admit that there are serious limits to thinking and that many personal problems can only be resolved by commitments that go beyond contemplation. The fear of facing the irrational can keep obsessives seeking for years sufficient insights, moving from one book to another or from one therapist to another. Of course, some therapists are also afraid of making commitments to action without an obsessive understanding of their client's problems.

Just as many traditional therapists can prolong chronic contemplation, so, too, can many contemporary therapists rush to premature action. Especially when pressures are on to keep therapy as brief as possible, therapists can pressure clients to take action before clients have an adequate awareness of the source of their problems or before they are adequately prepared for action. In therapies that are just action oriented, clients who are in the precontemplation or contemplation stages can feel pressured or coerced into taking action that may or may not be aimed at resolving their core conflicts. These clients are likely not to feel at home in action-oriented therapies and the result can be premature termination, resistance, or premature action that may provide temporary relief but may soon be followed by relapse. Therapy can be damaging if it moves too quickly through the stages, just as it can be demoralizing if it moves too slowly.

The number one factor that limits the probability of successful therapy is the lack of basic knowledge of how people change and of applied knowledge on how to facilitate progress at each stage and level of change. In particular, the greatest increase in our probability of success is likely to emerge from research on how to help clients maximize their efforts to change when they are in the context of their everyday lives with all the demands, conflicts, temptations, and turmoil of contemporary life, rather than in the safe and accepting context of the therapy session.

In practice, perhaps the greatest limit to success is the relatively brief amount of time that clients are able or willing to commit to change generally and therapy specifically. Our research clearly demonstrates that change of chronic problems does not occur quickly. Nevertheless, third-party payers and the public alike are looking for fast change. The most successful we can expect to be in a relatively brief course of therapy is to help clients become unstuck from a particular stage and to help them become freer and more able to use appropriate processes over the entire course of change.[1]

All therapies are heavily dependent on the client's potential for self-change. Imagine modern medicine trying to keep people healthy if their self-healing processes were not working. Most of the powers of contemporary physicians seem insignificant in the face of immune systems that are not functioning effectively, as in the case of patients with AIDS. If patients are so damaged by conditions such as paranoid schizophrenia that prevent them from participating in self-change, psychotherapists will also feel impotent.

One of the unique features of transtheoretical therapy is that it is based on research on self-change. If the transtheoretical approach has any special powers to outpredict or outperform other systems, it is precisely because it is built on the experiences of thousands of people who have taught us how they progress from one stage of change to the next and how they frequently become stuck in a stage or relapse and regress to an earlier stage of change. We try to work in harmony with how people change naturally. And we try to work in harmony with what we have learned scientifically.

CASE ILLUSTRATION

By its very nature, an integrative and eclectic approach to therapy cannot be illustrated adequately by a single case. Rather, it would take an extended series of cases to reflect the full range of stages, levels, and processes of change used with a diversity of clients. One of the essential values of a transtheoretical orientation is that it encourages therapists to be rich, diverse, and creative in their choices of interventions with individual clients.

If the reader were to observe over time a transtheoretical therapist, the therapist's interventions would be seen to vary tremendously depending on the needs of particular clients. With a phobic client who is prepared to take action at the symptom and situational level, the therapist might appear to be a behavior therapist who is prescribing cue exposure or *in vivo* desensitization in order to counter the client's chronic anxiety and avoidance. With a depressed client who is in the contemplation stage, the therapist may use a rational–emotive method to analyze the ABCs of irrational thinking at the cognitive level. With a person with a narcissistic character disorder who is in the precontemplation stage with little insight into the intrapersonal nature of a cluster of problems, the therapist might appear to be a psychodynamic therapist who is using consciousness-raising methods to help the client become aware of defense mechanisms and the inner conflicts that are being defended against.

Given that no case can comprehensively reflect a multilevel, multistage, and multiprocess approach to change, I will present a case of mine that ended recently.

David was the identified client who was pressured to come to therapy lest his wife, Diane, leave him. Diane was convinced that David was an alcoholic and her preference was to have him sent to an inpatient treatment facility followed by intensive psychoanalysis. Diane's mother was a psychoanalytically oriented therapist in Boston who was convinced that David was a psychopath with impulse disorders. She was convinced that David would never cooperate in therapy and that Diane should just leave him now. David was convinced

that Diane was paranoid about his drinking and that she had a compulsive need to be in control of everything and everyone in her environment. He resented having been pressured to enter therapy for a problem that was a figment of Diane's fears.

DAVID: Her father was an alcoholic; her grandfather was an alcoholic. Her father died from drunk driving. She puts all of that stuff on to me and insists my drinking is out of control. It's her obsessiveness that's out of control.

DIANE: David, you're out of control. You come home every night slurring your speech, unable to stay awake. You've been in a whole series of fights and accidents. You're insulting important associates of yours. You've had valuable employees quit because they can't put up with your angry tirades. You made a fool out of yourself at your last press conference.

DAVID: Diane, you know I have to live on the edge. I'm an author: My work is at the cutting edge. People expect authors to act out. What do you want me to be—some highly inhibited choir boy with no vitality and no creativity?

And so it went, with Diane trying to convince David and me that he had to take action on his alcoholism and related impulse disorders. David was in the precontemplation stage in regard to his drinking but he was prepared to take action to help Diane with her obsessions about alcohol.

The therapist faces a dilemma when faced with one spouse who is already taking action on her spouse's alcohol problem while the other does not believe there is a problem. If the therapist attends to the alcohol problem, the wife will be pleased but the husband may feel that the therapist is colluding with his controlling wife to coerce him into changing a problem that does not exist. If the therapist does not attend to the alcohol problem, the husband will be pleased but the wife may feel that the therapist is colluding with her uncontrolled husband to enable him to continue in self-defeating and self-destructive patterns of drinking and disorder.

One therapeutic starting point is to help the partners become aware of the dynamics of change and how conflict occurs when spouses are in different stages of change. With David in the precontemplation stage and Diane taking action, interpersonal conflict is certain to occur. I could share my dilemma with the couple to see if they would agree that if I supported Diane's action, David would feel coerced and want to leave. Conversely, if David's perspective was supported, Diane might feel like the odd one out and would want to leave. They both could appreciate the situation.

THERAPIST: Let's first try to understand each other more fully before we try to change each other. Let's first see if each of you can step back from a more defensive place so that you can communicate with less conflict and less struggle for control. Have there been any important problems that the two of you have been able to pull together on?

Immediately, we shifted from the current interpersonal level, plagued by conflicts of communication and control over who was going to define whose reality, to the level of their families of origin and the struggles each of these 30-something-year-olds have had in establishing their autonomy.

Diane first shared her efforts to become freer from being controlled on one side of the family by her maternal grandparents and the other side by her father. First, it had been her parents who fought for her loyalty, during a difficult divorce. Then, her grandparents took up the battle, trying to hold on to Diane the way they had held on to her mother. David

had fought some of her battles and was seen as the heavy by both sides of Diane's families.

Diane, in return, had helped David to deal with the guilt generated by his Catholic mother—guilt for not visiting more, for not socializing more with his family, and for not having a better relationship with his famous father who was now threatened by a serious cancer condition.

What was most evident was the pattern of so many triangles in the relationships of both extended families. Diane and David both appreciated the triangulating interpretation of their historical family conflicts (see Kaslow & Celano, Chapter 10, this volume). Diane had been in intensive therapy for over a year but had not become aware of her historical triangles as inherently troubling patterns of relating. On her own, she had the insight that even her previous therapy was triangulated—with David threatened by her therapist. David said, "Why wouldn't I be threatened? She was encouraging you to leave me." "That's true," said Diane. "As good as Carol was, that was the one thing I didn't like. I'm not sure she has worked out her own relationships with men." We quickly became aware that the present therapy was also at risk of being triangulated. However, we were working together, using consciousness raising and reevaluation to appreciate the patterns of our initial interactions.

But that did not solve all of the problems. How were we going to proceed with David's drinking and Diane's controlling? At the interpersonal level, I used interpretations from Transactional Analysis to understand the dynamics of this couple's dance (see James, Chapter 9, this volume). Who was the parent and who was the child in this drama? That was obvious to both of them. If Diane acts like a controlling parent, she should not be surprised if David reacts like a rebellious child. "Look, Diane, you're not going to control me" ("like my mother did," I added). "David, I don't want to control you. I want you to control yourself" ("like my father didn't," I added).

"Imagine how it would be, Diane, if you didn't feel responsible for David's drinking," I suggested. "I would feel so relieved, so free from this constant worry. Will you adopt him?" she joked, "Well, I like him, but I don't think David needs a new dad. I think he needs a chance to work out some issues with his own dad," I guessed.

A lucky guess or good intuition, but it turned out that David's drinking was a way of masking and medicating an underlying depression over the prospect of his father dying. His father had been a source of inspiration and a powerful protection from his domineering mother. Besides, if his father died, David would be the oldest man in the family and would be responsible for his mother (his brother could take care of himself). But David was not ready to be fully adult. He dreaded the thought. He believed he would lose touch with the "creative child" in him. He also wanted to hang on to his image as a combination of Ernest Hemingway and James Dean. A rebel with a cause.

Getting through David's defensiveness about his drinking was not as difficult as I had expected. It helped to meet alone because his defenses were even more interpersonal than intrapersonal, designed to protect himself from being overwhelmed by his wife and other women in his life. Part of the process was to help David become more conscious of how much he consumed and the consequences of such consumption. He only drank three or four gin and tonics he said, though they turned out to be doubles or triples. He had no idea what amount of alcohol was considered to be high-risk drinking. He was shocked to learn that he consumed four to five times a safe level daily.

When asked whether there was anyone whose drinking concerned him, he said Peter, his best friend. When asked how he might help Peter, he smiled—"You mean quit myself." But David was not prepared to quit. He was contemplating his drinking more clearly. He was beginning to appreciate the many dynamics surrounding his drinking—from rebellious fun to angry acting out, from countering his wife's control to drowning his depression with a depressant, from fulfilling his artistic image of Hemingway to becoming anesthetized to the pain of critics and the anxiety of creating at the cutting edge.

Early in therapy, David's father called and urged me to have him hospitalized. He was still being the protective parent. I understood his feeling and reaction. I, too, felt anxiety at times that David might destroy himself before he got his drinking under control. But I did not want to be locked into becoming the rescuing parent if I could help it. Besides, there was no way David would consider entering a hospital. He would not even consider Alcoholics Anonymous, let alone inpatient care.

We both knew that David had drawn on his self-change powers in the past to liberate himself from a serious cocaine addiction. The challenge became to help him use these powers to free himself from his destructive drinking and other patterns of acting out. First he began to cut back some as he became more conscious of the amounts he drank. He announced publicly to Peter that it was time to control his drinking. "I'll drink to that," said Peter. He elicited Peter's support as much to help Peter as to help himself.

David also elicited the help of the bartender at his favorite restaurant to switch his drinks to straight tonic after two drinks. When people bought David a drink the bartender omitted the gin and kept as a tip the cost of the alcohol. David was less confident that he could control his drinking in some situations, such as a party celebrating his publishing a book. So, he worked on not being defensive about his art, reevaluating his self-image as the literary world's bad boy, and asked his agent to arrange to have his drinks be alcohol free after the first or second cocktail.

Diane was delighted. She slipped several times by looking over David's shoulder to monitor his drinks. But she had already become aware of how she had progressed from rescuer to persecutor to victim. She had learned to counter her urges to control David by telling herself things like: "I'm not his parent; he's got Jim to help him; he got free from cocaine on his own, he can get free from alcohol; he's not my dad; and I need to focus on my own issues."

As David progressed through the stages of changing his destructive drinking, Diane progressed through stages of changing her compulsive controlling. Over the course of about 8 months they did some excellent work together at multiple levels, including the symptom and situational level for David's drinking, the cognitive level for Diane's obsessing about David's drinking, the interpersonal level for their shared tendency to triangulate, and the family-of-origin level for their shared struggle to become more independent and autonomous adults.

After a 6-month break from therapy, David and Diane returned concerned about a lapse in their progress. In spite of a serious economic recession, they had pulled together to free themselves from the threat of bankruptcy; David was creating his best work ever, including a written piece that received rave reviews; Diane had gained control of a trust fund and was using it to create a new home for themselves and their newborn daughter; David was drinking, but within low-risk levels; and instead of being divorced as

they both had expected when they first entered therapy, they were sharing more intimacy than they had ever known before.

In spite of these gains, Diane was struggling with anxiety and depression about leaving her old town. It was the prominent town in which she had grown up and the place her parents and grandparents had all lived. For her, it was like a safe village within a scary environment. Diane was surprised that she was still having conflicts over separating from her extended family. Certainly, her family was having trouble letting her go. It was against the rules to move away. While David was impatient at times with Diane's childlike distress, he was able to provide more of a helping relationship in which she could continue to change and grow. Diane did some nice work on her own, networking with other couples and women to develop a support system in her new community to substitute in part for her extended family.

Diane and David knew from their own efforts that change was rarely a straightforward experience. They knew they were not home free, but they were not overwhelmed by occasional lapses or relapse. Instead, they struggled to learn from their falls and failures so that they could pick themselves up and move ahead.

The case of David and Diane illustrates a common conflict in couple therapy—one spouse prepared to take action on a problem such as alcohol abuse while the other is in the precontemplation stage. Consciousness raising was used to clarify the dilemma for David, Diane, and the therapist. At the interpersonal level, the spouses were too far apart initially to cooperate on making constructive changes.

At the family-of-origin level, however, the two were more prepared to cooperate to help free each other from patterns of being controlled by parents and grandparents. Insights into the patterns of triangulation in their families of origin allowed the couple to appreciate how their current therapy was at risk of being triangulated.

Pulling together to take some constructive action with their overcontrolling parents permitted the partners to focus next on their own interpersonal control problems. Further consciousness raising and self-reevaluation allowed the couple to progress toward action on their own parent–child conflicts over control of David's drinking.

As the control and communication conflicts improved at the interpersonal level, David felt freer to take constructive actions on his own to bring his alcohol abuse under control. While David and Diane had made significant progress separately and together, therapy terminated before many of the chronic problems had terminated. One of the anxieties of terminating therapy under these conditions is the awareness that given significant stress or distress relapse could still occur. But at least therapy had helped this couple discover more about the levels of their chronic patterns and problems and the processes for progressing through the stages of change at different levels of change.

NOTE

1. Editors' note: See Hoyt (Chapter 12, this volume) for a different view of the efficacy of brief therapy.

SUGGESTIONS FOR FURTHER READING

Reference Books

Norcross, J. C., & Goldfried, M. R. (Eds.). (1992). *Handbook of integrative psychotherapy.* New York: Basic Books.

Prochaska, J. O., & Norcross, J. C. (1994). *Systems of psychotherapy: A transtheoretical analysis.* Pacific Grove, CA: Brooks/Cole.

Prochaska, J. O., Norcross, J. C., & DiClemente, C. C. (1994). *Changing for good,* New York: William Morrow.

Research Articles

Prochaska, J. O., DiClemente, C. C., & Norcross, J. C. (1993). In search of how people change. *American Psychologist, 47,* 1102–1114.

Prochaska, J. O., DiClemente, C. C., Velicer, W. F., & Rossi, J. S. (1993). Standardized, individualized, interactive, and personalized self-help programs for smoking cessation. *Health Psychology, 12,* 399–405.

Case Studies

Prochaska, J. O., & DiClemente, C. C. (1984). Charles the computer client. In *The transtheoretical approach: Crossing traditional boundaries of therapy.* Pacific Grove, CA: Brooks/Cole.

Prochaska, J. O., Rossi, J. S., & Wilcox, N. S. (1991). Change processes and psychotherapy outcome in integrative case research. *Journal of Integrative Psychotherapy, 1,* 103–120.

REFERENCES

American Psychiatric Association. (1994). *Diagnostic and statistical manual of mental disorders* (4th ed.). Washington, DC: Author.

Bandura, A. (1977). Self-efficacy: Toward a unifying theory of behavior change. *Psychological Review, 84,* 191–215.

Bandura, A. (1982). Self-efficacy mechanism in human agency. *American Psychologist, 37,* 122–147.

Begin, A. (1988). *Levels of change attribution in alcoholics, their spouses and therapists.* Unpublished dissertation.

Beitman, B. D. (1992). Integration through fundamental similarities and useful differences among the schools. In J. C. Norcross & M. R. Goldfried (Eds.), *Handbook of psychotherapy integration*. New York: Basic Books.

Beitman, B. D. (in press). Pharmacotherapy and the stages of psychotherapeutic change. In *Annual Review of Psychiatry* (Vol. 12). Washington, DC: American Psychiatric Press.

Bergin, A. (1981, August). *Toward a systematic eclecticism*. Symposium chaired at the 89th annual meeting of the American Psychological Association, Los Angeles.

Bergin, A. (1982). Comment on *Converging themes in psychotherapy*. In M. Goldfried (Ed.), *Converging themes in psychotherapy*. New York: Springer.

Benjamin, A. (1987). *The helping interview*. Boston: Houghton Mifflin.

Beutler, L. E. (1983). *Eclectic psychotherapy: A systematic approach*. Elmsford, NY: Pergamon Press.

Beutler, L. E., & Consoli, A. J. (1992). Systematic eclectic psychotherapy. In J. C. Norcross & M. R. Goldfried (Eds.), *Handbook of psychotherapy integration*. New York: Basic Books.

Brownell, K. D., Marlatt, G. A., Lichtenstein, E., & Wilson G. T. (1986). Understanding and preventing relapse. *American Psychologist, 41,* 765–782.

Burns, D. D. (1980). *Feeling good: The new mood therapy*. New York: William Morrow.

Cohen, J. (1977). *Statistical power analysis for the behavioral sciences* (rev. ed.). New York: Academic Press.

Cohen, S., Lichtenstein, E., Prochaska, J. O., Rossi, J. S., Gritz, E. R., Carr, C. R., Orleans, C. T., Schoenbach, V. J., Biener, L., Abrams, D., DiClemente, C. C., Curry, S., Marlatt, G. A., Cummings, K. M., Emont, S. L., Giovino, G., & Ossip-Klein, D. (1989). Debunking myths about self-quitting: Evidence from ten prospective studies of persons quitting smoking by themselves. *American Psychologist, 44,* 1355–1365.

DiClemente, C. C., & Hughes, S. (1990). Stages of change profiles in outpatient alcoholism treatment. *Journal of Substance Abuse, 2,* 217–235.

DiClemente, C. C., & Prochaska, J. O. (1982). Self-change and therapy change of smoking behavior: A comparison of processes of change in cessation and maintenance. *Addictive Behavior, 7,* 133–142.

DiClemente, C. C., & Prochaska, J. O. (1985). Processes and stages of change: Coping and competence in smoking behavior change. In S. Shiffman & T. A. Wills (Eds.), *Coping and substance abuse*. New York: Academic Press.

DiClemente, C. C., Prochaska, J. O., Fairhurst, S. K., Velicer, W. F., Valesquez, M. M., & Rossi, J. S. (1991). The processes of smoking cessation: An analysis of precontemplation, contemplation, and preparation stages of change. *Journal of Consulting and Clinical Psychology, 59,* 295–304.

Donovan, D. M., & Marlatt, G. A. (Eds.). (1988). *Assessment of addictive behaviors*. New York: Guilford Press.

Ellis, A., & Dryden, W. (1987). *The practice of rational–emotive therapy*. New York: Springer.

Feldman, L. B. (1989). Integrating individual and family therapy. *Journal of Integrative and Eclectic Psychotherapy, 8,* 41–52.

Frank, J. D. (1973). *Persuasion and healing* (rev. ed.). Baltimore: Johns Hopkins University Press.

Garfield, S. L. (1981, August). *Toward an empirically based eclecticism*. Paper presented at symposium entitled "Toward a systematic eclecticism," 89th annual meeting of the American Psychological Association, Los Angeles.

Garfield, S. L. (1992). Eclectic psychotherapy: A common factors approach. In J. C. Norcross & M. R. Goldfried (Eds.), *Handbook of psychotherapy integration*. New York: Basic Books.

Garfield, S. L., & Kurtz, R. (1977). A study of eclectic views. *Journal of Clinical and Consulting Psychology, 45,* 78–83.

Goldfried, M. R. (1980). Toward the delineation of therapeutic change principles. *American Psychologist, 35,* 991–999.

Goldfried, M. R. (1982). (Ed.). *Converging themes in psychotherapy*. New York: Springer.

Gottlieb, N. H., Galavotti, C., McCuan, R. S., & McAlister, A. L. (1991). Specification of a social cognitive model predicting smoking cessation in a Mexican-American population: A prospective study. *Cognitive Therapy and Research, 14,* 529–542.

Guilford, J. (1956). The structure of intellect. *Psychological Bulletin, 53,* 267–293.

Gurman, A. S. (1981). Integrative marital therapy: Toward the development of an interpersonal approach. In S. H. Budman (Ed.), *Forms of brief therapy.* New York: Guilford Press.

Howard, K. I., Kopta, S. M., Drause, M. S., & Orlinsky, D. E. (1986). The dose–effect relationship in psychotherapy. *American Psychologist, 41,* 159–165.

Hunt, W., Barnett, L., & Branch, L. (1971). Relapse rates in addiction programs. *Journal of Clinical Psychology, 27,* 455–456.

Jacobson, N. S., Wilson, L., & Tupper, C. (1988). The clinical significance of treatment gains resulting from exposure-based interventions for agoraphobia: A reanalysis of outcome data. *Behavior Therapy, 19,* 539–559.

Janis, I. L., & Mann, L. (1977). *Decision making: A psychological analysis of conflict, choice and commitment.* New York: Free Press.

Jones, E., & Nisbett, R. (1972). The actor and the observer: Divergent perceptions of the causes of behavior. In E. Jones, D. Kanouse, H. Kelley, R. Nisbett, S. Violins, & B. Weiner (Eds.), *Attribution, perceiving and the causes of behavior.* Morristown, NJ: General Learning Press.

Laforge, R., Prochaska, J. O., Velicer, W. F., & Fava, J. (1992). [Recruitment rates for home-based smoking cessation programs for a random digit dialing sample and an HMO population of smokers]. Unpublished raw data.

Lam, C. S., McMahon, B. T., Priddy, D. A., & Gehred-Schultz, A. (1989). Deficit awareness and treatment performance among traumatic head injury adults. *Brain Injury, 2,* 235–242.

Lambert, M. J. (1986). Some implications of psychotherapy outcome research for eclectic psychotherapy. *International Journal of Eclectic Psychotherapy, 5,* 16–45.

Lazarus, A. A. (1992). Multimodal therapy: Technical eclecticism with minimal integration. In J. C. Norcross & M. R. Goldfried (Eds.), *Handbook of psychotherapy integration.* New York: Basic Books.

Lebow, J. L. (1984). On the value of integrating approaches to family therapy. *Journal of Marital and Family Therapy, 10,* 127–138.

Locke, H., & Wallace, K. (1959). Short marital adjustment and prediction test: Reliability and validity. *Marriage and Family Living, 21,* 251–295.

Luborsky, L., Singer, B., & Luborsky, L. (1975). Comparative studies of psychotherapy: "Is it true that everyone has won and all must have prizes?" *Archives of General Psychiatry, 32,* 995–1008.

Masters, W., & Johnson, V. (1970). *Human sexual inadequacy.* Boston: Little, Brown.

McConnaughy, E. A., DiClemente, C. C., Prochaska, J. O., & Velicer, W. F. (1989). Stages of change in psychotherapy: A follow-up report. *Psychotherapy, 26,* 494–503.

McConnaughy, E. A., Prochaska, J. O., & Velicer, W. F. (1983). Stages of change in psychotherapy: Measurement and sample profiles. *Psychotherapy, 20,* 368–375.

Medeiros, M., & Prochaska, J. O. (1994). *Predicting premature termination from psychotherapy.* Manuscript submitted for publication.

Meehl, P. E. (1978). Theoretical risks and tabular asterisks: Sir Karl, Sir Ronald, and the slow progress of soft psychology. *Journal of Clinical and Consulting Psychology, 46,* 806–834.

Messer, S. B. (1992). A critical examination of belief structures in integrative and eclectic psychotherapy. In J. C. Norcross & M. R. Goldfried (Eds.), *Handbook of psychotherapy integration.* New York: Basic Books.

Norcross, J. C., & Newman, C. F. (1992). Psychotherapy integration: Setting the context. In J. C. Norcross & M. R. Goldfried (Eds.), *Handbook of psychotherapy integration.* New York: Basic Books.

Norcross, J. C., & Prochaska, J. O. (1983). Clinicians theoretical orientations: Selection, utilization and efficacy. *Professional Psychology*, *14*, 197–208.

Norcross, J., Prochaska, J., Guadagnoli, E., & DiClemente, C. (1984). Factor structure of the Levels of Attribution and Change (LAC) Scale in samples of psychotherapists and smokers. *Journal of Clinical Psychology*, *40*, 519–528.

Norcross, J., Prochaska, J., & Hambrecht, M. (1985). The Levels of attribution and Change (LAC) Scale: Development and measurement. *Cognitive Therapy and Research*, *9*, 631–649.

Norcross, J. C., Ratzin, A. C., & Payne, D. (1989). Ringing in the New Year: The change processes and reported outcomes of resolutions. *Addictive Behaviors*, *14*, 205–212.

Norcross, J. C., & Vangarelli, D. J. (1989). The resolution solution: Longitudinal examination of New Year's change attempts. *Journal of Substance Abuse*, *1*, 127–134.

Ockene, J., Kristeller, J. L., Goldberg, R., Ockene, I., Merriam, P., Barrett, S., Pekow, P., Hosmer, D., & Gianelly, R. (1992). Smoking cessation and severity of disease: The Coronary Artery Smoking Intervention Study. *Health Psychology*, *11*, 119–126.

Pepper, S. P. (1942). *World hypotheses: A study in evidence*. Berkeley: University of California Press.

Peto, R., & Lopez, A. (1990). World-wide mortality from current smoking patterns. In B. Durstone & K. Jamrogik (Eds.), *The global war: Proceedings of the 7th World Conference on Tobacco and Health* (pp. 62–68). East Perth, Western Australia: Organizing Committee of Seventh World Conference on Tobacco and Health.

Pinsof, W. M. (1983). Integrative problem-centered therapy: Toward the synthesis of family and individual psychotherapies. *Journal of Marital and Family Therpay*, *9*, 19–35.

Prochaska, J. O. (1979). *Systems of psychotherapy: A transtheoretical analysis*. Chicago: Dorsey.

Prochaska, J. O. (1994). Strong and weak principles of progress from precontemplation to action for twelve problem behaviors. *Health Psychology*, *13*, 47–51.

Prochaska, J. O., & DiClemente, C. C. (1982). Transtheoretical therapy: Toward a more integrative model of change. *Psychotherapy: Theory, Research and Practice*, *19*, 276–278.

Prochaska, J. O., & DiClemente, C. C. (1983). Stages and processes of self-change in smoking: Toward an integrative model of change. *Journal of Consulting and Clinical Psychology*, *5*, 390–395.

Prochaska, J. O., & DiClemente, C. C. (1984). *The transtheoretical approach: Crossing traditional boundaries of change*. Homewood, IL: Dow Jones/Irwin.

Prochaska, J. O., & DiClemente, C. C. (1985). Common processes of change in smoking, weight control, and psychological distress. In S. Shiffman & T. Wills (Eds.), *Coping and substance abuse*. New York: Academic Press.

Prochaska, J. O., & DiClemente, C. C. (1992). Stages of change in the modification of problem behaviors. In M. Hersen, R. M. Eisler, & P. M. Miller (Eds.), *Progress in behavior modification*. Sycamore, IL: Sycamore Press.

Prochaska, J. O., DiClemente, C. C., & Norcross, J. C. (1992). In search of how people change: Applications to addictive behaviors. *American Psychologist*, *47*, 1102–1114.

Prochaska, J. O., DiClemente, C. C., & Velicer, W. F. (1988). Comparative analysis of self-help programs for four stages of smoking cessation. In T. Glynn (Chair), *Four National Cancer Institute-funded self-help smoking cessation trials: Interim results and emerging patterns*. Symposium conducted at the annual meeting of the Association for the Advancement of Behavior Therapy, New York.

Prochaska, J. O., DiClemente, C. C., Velicer, W. F., Ginpil, S., & Norcross, J. C. (1985). Predicting change in smoking status for self-changers. *Addictive Behaviors*, *10*, 407–412.

Prochaska, J. O., DiClemente, C. C., Velicer, W. F., & Rossi, J. S. (1993). Standardized, individualized, interactive, and personalized self-help programs for smoking cessation. *Health Psychology, 12,* 399–405.

Prochaska, J. O., Norcross, J. C., & DiClemente, C. C. (1994). *Changing for good.* New York: William Morrow.

Prochaska, J. O., Norcross, J. C., Fowler, J. Follick, M., & Abrams, D. B. (1992). Attendance and outcome in a work-site weight control program: Processes and stages of change as process and predictor variables. *Addictive Behavior, 17,* 35–45.

Prochaska, J. O., Rossi, J. S., & Wilcox, N. S. (1991). Change processes and psychotherapy outcome in integrative case research. *Journal of Integrative Psychotherapy, 1,* 103–120.

Prochaska, J. O., Velicer, W. F., DiClemente, C. C., & Fava, J. (1988). Measuring processes of change: Applications to the cessation of smoking. *Journal of Consulting and Clinical Psychology, 56,* 520–528.

Prochaska, J. O., Velicer, W. F., Rossi, J. S., Goldstein, M. G., Marcus, B. H., Rakowski, W., Fiore, C., Harlow, L. L., Redding, C. A., Rosenbloom, D., & Rossi, S. R. (1994). Stages of change and decisional balance for twelve problem behaviors. *Health Psychology, 13,* 39–46.

Rogers, C. (1951). *Client-centered therapy.* Boston: Houghton Mifflin.

Rogers, C. (1959). A theory of therapy, personality, and interpersonal relationships as developed in the client-centered framework. In S. Koch (Ed.), *Psychology: A study of a science: Vol. III. Formulations of the person and the social context.* New York: McGraw-Hill.

Rossi, J. S. (1992). *Stages for change for 15 health risk behaviors in a HMO population.* Paper presented at 13th meeting of the Society for Behavior Medicine, New York, New York.

Schacter, S. (1982). Recidivism and self cure of smoking and obesity. *American Psychologist, 37,* 436–444.

Shapiro, S., Skinner, E., Kessler, L., Van Korff, M., German, P., Tischler, G., Leon, P., Bendham, L., Cottler, L., & Regier, D. (1984). Utilization of health and mental health services. *Archives of General Psychiatry, 41,* 971–978.

Smith, D. S. (1982). Trends in counseling and psychotherapy. *American Psychologist, 37,* 802–809.

Smith, M. L., & Glass, G. V. (1977). Meta-analysis of psychotherapy outcome studies. *American Psychologist, 36,* 1546–1547.

Snow, M. G., Prochaska, J. O., & Rossi, J. S. (1992.) Stages of change for smoking cessation among former problem drinkers. *Journal of Substance Abuse, 4,* 107–116.

Tavinian, M., Lubiner, J., Green, L., Grebstein, L. C., & Velicer, W. (1987). The development of the Family Functioning Scale. *Journal of Social Behavior and Personality, 2,* 191–204.

Strupp, H. (1981, August). *Some implications of psychotherapy research for training.* Paper presented at sympoisum entitled "Toward a systematic eclecticism," 89th annual meeting of the American Psychological Association, Los Angeles.

Velicer, W. F., Hughes, S. L., Fava, J., Prochaska, J. O., & DiClemente, C. C. (1992). *An empirical typology of subjects within the stages of change.* Manuscript submitted for publication.

Velicer, W. F., DiClemente, C. C., Prochaska, J. O., & Brandenberg, N. (1985). A decisional balance measure for assessing and predicting smoking status. *Journal of Personality and Social Psychology, 48,* 1279–1289.

Veroff, J., Douvan, E., & Kulka, R. A. (1981a). *The inner America.* New York: Basic Books.

Veroff, J., Donovan, E., & Kulka, R. A. (1981b). *Mental health in America.* New York: Basic Books.

Wachtel, P. L. (1977). *Psychoanalysis and behavior therapy: Toward an integration.* New York: Basic Books.

Wachtel, P. L. (1987). *Action and insight.* New York: Guilford Press.

Werner, H. (1948). *Comparative psychology of mental development*. Chicago: Follett.

Wilcox, N., Prochaska, J. O., Velicer, W. F., & DiClemente, C. C. (1985). Client characteristics as predictors of self-change in smoking cessation. *Addictive Behaviors, 40*, 407–412.

Wolpe, J. (1973). *The practice of behavior therapy*. Elmsford, NY: Pergamon Press.

12

Brief Psychotherapies

MICHAEL F. HOYT

When a therapist and patient endeavor to get from Point A (the problem that led to therapy) to Point B (the resolution that ends therapy) via a direct, parsimonious, and efficient route, we say that they are deliberately engaging in *brief therapy*. The approach is intended to be quick and helpful, nothing extraneous, no beating around the bush. Another closely related term is "time-limited therapy," which explicitly emphasizes the temporal boundedness of the treatment. Synonymous with *brief therapy* is the phrase "planned short-term therapy," meaning literally a "deliberately concise remedy/restoration/improvement." As Bloom (1992a) has written:

> The word planned is important; these works describe short-term treatment that is intended to accomplish a set of therapeutic objectives within a sharply limited time frame. (p. 3)

This is how de Shazer (1991a) describes it:

> "Brief therapy" simply means therapy that takes as few sessions as possible, not even one more than is necessary. . . . "Brief therapy" is a relative term, typically meaning: (a) fewer sessions than standard, and/or (b) a shorter period of time from intake to termination, and/or (c) a lower number of sessions and a lower frequency of sessions from start to finish. (pp. ix–x)

"Brevity" and "shortness" are watchwords signaling efficiency, the contrast being the more intentionally protracted course of traditional long-term (usually psychodynamic) therapy. Actually, most therapy is de facto brief, by default or design, meaning a few sessions, weeks to months. As Budman and Gurman (1988) and others (Bloom, 1992a; Garfield, 1986; Koss & Butcher, 1986) have noted, numerous studies have reported the average length of treatment to be three to eight sessions, the period of time in which most change occurs even in treatments that are not planned as brief therapy (Howard, Kopta, Kraus, & Orlinsky, 1986; Hoyt & Austad, 1992). The modal or most common length of treatment is actually only one session—even with this "briefest of brief" duration, many successful outcomes are reported (Bloom, 1992b; Hoyt, 1994b; Hoyt, Rosenbaum, &

Talmon, 1992; Rosenbaum, Hoyt, & Talmon, 1990; Talmon, 1990). Various authors have given different definitions of what constitutes brief therapy. Some have emphasized a number of sessions, such as "5–10," "12," or "up to 20"; some have emphasized certain types of problems they attempt to address, while others have focused more on the idea of the passage of time being a contextual pressure (Hoyt, 1990). Budman and Gurman (1988), for example, eschew a specific number of sessions in their definition, instead referring to deliberate or planned brief therapy as "time sensitive" treatment.[1] Focused intentionality is the key. Make everything count; don't be wasteful. Get to it. Sullivan (1954) put it well:

> I think the development of psychiatric skill consists in very considerable measure of doing a lot with very little—making a rather precise move which has a high probability of achieving what you're attempting to achieve, with a minimum of time and words. (p. 224)

Planned or intentional brief therapy is predicated on the belief and expectation that change can occur *in the moment*, particularly if theoretical ability, practical skill, and efficacious interest are brought to bear (M. Goulding & R. Goulding, 1979; Hoyt, 1990). The work is not superficial or simply technique oriented; it is precise and beneficial, often yielding enduring long-term benefits as well as more immediate gains.

Indeed, as Koss and Butcher (1986) have concluded from their major review of the research literature on psychotherapy outcome:

> Those studies that have directly compared brief and long-term methods have found equal effectiveness. Since brief therapy requires less time (both therapist and patient) and therefore less social cost, it has been suggested that brief methods are equally effective and more cost efficient than long-term psychotherapy. (p. 658)

These findings may actually underestimate the effectiveness of planned brief therapy, because so few of the therapists in the original studies were specifically oriented or trained in brief therapy methods (Hoyt & Austad, 1992; Koss, Butcher, & Strupp, 1986). While one can ignore these findings or argue that brief therapy and long-term therapy have different goals, the equivalence of outcomes is compelling. As Bloom (1992a) has concluded:

> Virtually without exception, these empirical studies of short-term outpatient psychotherapy, or inpatient psychiatric care . . . have found that planned short-term psychotherapies are essentially equally effective and are, in general, as effective as time-unlimited psychotherapy, virtually regardless of diagnosis or duration of treatment (Koss & Butcher, 1986). Indeed, perhaps no other finding has been reported with greater regularity in the mental health literature than the equivalence of effect of time-limited and time-unlimited psychotherapy. (p. 9)

Given the social and professional imperative to provide psychological services to the wide range of persons who might need and benefit from mental health care, the thrust of the accumulated data seems clear. However, before we turn to some of the specific ways that effective brief psychotherapies endeavor to translate complicated understanding into methods likely to yield results sooner rather than later, let us consider some of the overarching principles that guide the practice of brief therapy.

THE CONCEPT OF BRIEF THERAPY

The fundamental assumption of all forms of deliberate brief therapy is an attitude and expectation—supported by various theories, methodologies, and findings—that significant and beneficial changes can be brought about relatively quickly. The brief therapist recognizes that there is no time but the present. Historical review may yield some clues about how the patient is "stuck" and what may be needed to get "unstuck" (Hoyt, 1990), but whatever the therapist's particular theoretical orientation, primary effort is directed to help the patient recognize options in the present that can result in enhanced coping, new learning, growth, beneficial changes, and improvements. Yapko (1990) has noted three factors that determine whether a patient will benefit from brief therapy interventions: (1) the person's primary temporal orientation (toward past, present, or future); (2) the general value given to "change," whether he or she is more invested in maintaining tradition or seeking change; and (3) the patient's belief system about what constitutes a complete therapeutic experience.

It is this fundamental assumption—that with skillful facilitation useful changes can be set into motion relatively quickly and that patients can then maintain and often expand the benefits on their own—that underlies the "universal elements" or "common ingredients" of brief treatment that have been synthesized by various authors (Bloom, 1992a; Budman & Gurman, 1988; Friedman & Fanger, 1991; Hoyt & Austad, 1992; Koss & Butcher, 1986; Wells & Phelps, 1990). As Budman, Friedman, and Hoyt (1992) have written, the most frequently cited generic components of brief treatment are:

1. Rapid and generally positive working alliance between therapist and patient.
2. Focality, the clear specification of achievable treatment results and goals.

3. Clear definition of patient and therapist responsibilities, with a relatively high level of therapist activity and patient participation.
4. Emphasis on the patient's strengths, competencies, and adaptive capacities.
5. Expectation of change, the belief that improvement is within the patient's (immediate) grasp.
6. Here-and-now (and next) orientation, the primary focus being on current functioning and patterns in thinking, feeling, and behaving—and their alternatives.
7. Time sensitivity.

This set of defining characteristics is reflected in the comparison of the dominant values of long-term and short-term treatment presented in Table 12.1.

Many of these same value differences can also be detected in many of the "resistances" or contrary attitudes some therapists hold about brief or short-term therapy (Hoyt, 1985a, 1990, 1991):

1. *The belief that "more is better,"* often held despite the lack of any evidence justifying the greater expense of long-term or open-ended treatment (Bloom 1992a; Budman & Gurman, 1988; Koss & Butcher, 1986).

2. *The myth of the "pure gold" of analysis* (to use Freud's [1919] term for idealized insight) and the faulty assumption that change and growth necessarily require "deep" examination and anything else is dismissable as "superficial" or "merely palliative." While making clear his preference for orthodox analysis, Freud (1919) acknowledged the value of combining techniques to produce a more effective therapeutic instrument: "It is very probable, too, that the large-scale application of our therapy will compel us to alloy the pure gold of analysis freely with the copper of direct suggestion; and hypnotic influence, too, might find a place

TABLE 12.1. Comparative Dominant Values of the Long-Term and Short-Term Therapist

Long-term therapist	Short-term therapist
1. Seeks change in basic character.	Prefers pragmatism, parsimony, and least radical intervention; does not believe in the notion of "cure."
2. Believes that significant change is unlikely in everyday life.	Maintains an adult developmental perspective from which significant psychological change is viewed as inevitable.
3. Sees presenting problems as reflecting more basic pathology.	Emphasizes patients strengths and resources.
4. Wants to "be there" as patient makes significant changes.	Accepts that many changes will occur "after therapy."
5. Sees therapy as having a "timeless" quality.	Does not accept the timelessness of some models of therapy.
6. Unconsciously recognizes the fiscal convenience of long-term patients.	Fiscal issues often muted, either by the nature of the practice or the organizational structure.
7. Views therapy as almost always benign and useful.	Views therapy as sometimes useful and sometimes harmful.
8. Sees therapy as being the most important part of the patient's life.	Sees being in the world as more important than being in therapy.
9. Views therapist as responsible only for treating a given patient.	Views therapist as having responsibility for treatment of a population.

Note. From Budman and Gurman (1988, p. 11). Copyright 1988 by The Guilford Press. Reprinted by permission.

in it again . . ." (pp. 167–168). It should also be noted that in 1937, Freud seemed to regret the "interminable" nature of pure analysis.

3. *Belief in the inappropriateness of greater therapist activity*, including the need to be selectively focused, confrontative, directive, and risk taking.

4. *The confusion of patients' and therapists' interests*, the tendency of therapists to seek and treat perfectionistically putative "complexes" and "underlying personality issues" rather than attend directly to patients' complaints and stated treatment goals. Most patients seek therapy because of a specific problem and want the most succinct help available.

5. *Financial pressures*, the temptation to hold on to that which is profitable and dependable, as well as other incentives

such as the pleasures of intimate conversation and the lure of vicariously living through an extended relationship (Whitaker, 1989).

6. *Countertransference and termination problems*, including the need to be needed and difficulties saying good-bye. The term "countertransference" is used here in the very specific sense, following Freud (1910, 1915), of meaning a reaction or counter to the patient's transference (e.g., the therapist has difficulty letting go because the patient presents as needy and guilt evoking). In other instances it may be more the *therapist's* own transference (unconscious agenda), not the patient's "pull," that is the source of termination difficulties.

7. *Psychological reactance*, the interesting response of valuing something more

if you cannot have it (Brehm, 1966). Being told that one has to treat a patient with brief therapy (e.g., because of insurance restrictions or simply because that is what the patient wants) may trigger resentment and the thought, "No one is going to tell me what to do. I'm a professional." The fact is, however, that restrictions such as insurance limits and clinic policies regarding possible length of treatment do get imposed. There is also the social responsibility to provide needed services to the many rather than many services to the privileged few (Hoyt 1985a; Hoyt & Austad, 1992). Given these necessities, we may have to treat people briefly, even if it helps them!

The foregoing notwithstanding, there are certainly times when short-term therapy will not be adequate and appropriate—including instances when a longer process is required for the patient to make desired changes or when ongoing support is required to maintain a tenuous psychosocial adjustment—although the basic attitudes of making the most of each session, accessing strengths and resources, and taking as few sessions as possible will still be valuable. Indeed, if the needs of more than a handful of patients are to be served, the skillful application of brief therapy methods whenever possible will be necessary to make longer-term treatments available for those who truly need them.[2]

To summarize this section, it appears that there are essentially three factors that tend to determine the length of treatment:

1. The theoretical orientation of the therapist, whether his or her beliefs and working assumptions align the therapist more with the list of dominant values in the left- or right-hand column in Table 12.1.
2. Money—how much and for how long the patient can afford to pay.[3]

3. The patient's problems, situation, personality, psychopathology, and capacities.

WHY DO PATIENTS COME TO THERAPY?

Most patients come to therapy because they hope that working with a psychotherapist will soon relieve some state of unhappiness, distress, or dysfunction that has become so troublesome that professional consultation appears preferable to continuing the status quo.[4] The person feels that something timely has to be done since, as the old adage has it, "If you don't change directions, you'll wind up where you're heading." As Budman and Gurman (1988) have articulated it, there are five common answers to the question, "Why now does a patient come for treatment?"—five interrelated themes or foci that can often be addressed productively in brief therapy:

1. *Loss*, including bereavement and divorce, as well as other losses such as certain changes in social status, health problems, and betrayals of trust and confidence.
2. *Developmental dysynchronies*, life-cycle transitions or passages for which the patient is not well prepared and which thus present problems of adjustment (e.g., adolescent emancipation, marriage, starting a family, the empty-nest syndrome, retirement).
3. *Interpersonal conflicts*, problems with significant others such as spouse, children, authority figures, coworkers and friends.
4. *Specific symptoms*, such as depression, anxiety, or sexual dysfunctions.
5. *Personality issues*, characterological issues that come to the fore if the patient makes them the focus of

therapy and/or if they impede within- or between-session work to the extent that they require direct attention for therapy to be successful.

Brief therapists generally do not consider assessment to be a separate process to be completed before beginning treatment but, rather, see the two as inextricably intertwined. The questions one asks help to cocreate the reality in which therapist and patient work, and the patient's responses to trial interventions provide useful information about what is likely to be beneficial. It is helpful to keep in mind the idea that the word "diagnosis" comes from Greek and Latin words (*via gnossis*) meaning "the way of knowing," and this is just what a good functional diagnosis should do: provide information that illuminates a path (Hoyt, 1989). Pathology-oriented nosology may contain some important information, but it is seldom enough. Consider, for example, the five axes of the fourth edition of the *Diagnostic and Statistic Manual of Mental Disorders* (DSM-IV; American Psychiatric Association, 1994):

I. Clincial Disorders and Other Conditions That May Be a Focus of Clinical Attention
II. Personality Disorders and Mental Retardation
III. General Medical Conditions
IV. Psychosocial and Environmental Problems
V. Global Assessment of Functioning, usually expressed by a numerical index.

Important data may be summarized in the DSM-IV (and may be especially useful for communicating with insurance companies and clinical researchers as well as for differentially diagnosing whether medication is likely to be of help), but

reviewing the axes also reveals a potentially discouraging orientation toward "disease" and "sickness." As Barten (1971) noted, "Our training predisposes us to describe areas of illness rather than areas of health, and this illness orientation can make the prognosis of a great many people appear rather bleak" (p. 8). Consider what the five DSM-IV axes tell us about a person:

I. What's wrong with the patient now
II. What's been wrong with the patient for a long time
III. What's wrong with the patient's body
IV. What's wrong with the patient's social situation
V. How well has he or she adapted

Data such as these, including information about potential suicidality and alcohol and substance abuse, can be vital, but we also need to focus on the patient's strengths and capacities, his or her resources and motivations that will be needed for treatment to proceed successfully.

A therapist wishing to do effective brief treatment will need to accomplish a number of tasks early on with a patient:

1. Make contact and establish rapport.
2. Define the purpose of the meeting.
3. Orient and instruct the patient on how to use therapy.
4. Create an opportunity for the patient to express thoughts, feelings, and behavior.
5. Assess patient's problems, strengths, motivations, goals, and expectations.
6. Establish realistic (specific and obtainable) treatment goals.
7. Make initial treatment interventions, assess effects, and adjust accordingly.

8. Assign tasks or "homework" as appropriate.
9. Attend to such business matters as future appointments and fees.

It is important in the first session to engage the patient and to introduce some novelty. As will be seen in the cases presented here, as well as those reported in *The First Session in Brief Therapy* (Budman, Hoyt, & Friedman, 1992), in virtually all successful brief therapies something new happens in the first meeting. More of the same (behavior, outlook, defense, etc.) does not produce change. A *symptom* is an attempted solution to a problem that does not work or that engenders unwanted results (Edelstien, 1990; Fisch, Weakland, & Segal, 1982; Yapko, 1992). Effective therapy involves breaking such a pattern, doing something different. The novelty may come by seeing oneself differently, by practicing a new way of transacting with others, by experiencing unacknowledged feelings, by utilizing strengths and abilities that were overlooked previously. Whatever the means, the brief therapist looks for ways to start or amplify the patient's movement in the desired direction as soon as possible.

Attending carefully to the early identification of specific, achievable goals promotes effective brief work (Cade & O'Hanlon, 1993; de Shazer, 1985, 1988; Goulding & Goulding, 1979; Haley, 1977, 1989, 1990; O'Hanlon & Weiner-Davis, 1989).[5] Operational definitions contribute to treatment accountability, counter the temptation to diffuse/confuse/refuse focality, and help to assure that genuinely obtainable results are not replaced with vague or unrealistic "missions impossible" or "therapeutic perfectionism" (Malan, 1976). Questions such as the following help to focus treatment and involve the patient:

- What problem are you here to solve?
- If you work hard and make some changes, how will you be functioning differently?
- What are the smallest changes you could make that would tell that you are heading in the right direction?
- At those times when the problem is not so bad or is absent, what are you doing?
- What will tell us we're done?
- How will we know when to stop meeting like this?
- How might therapy help, and how long do you expect it to take?

Treatment revolves around what the patient wants to accomplish plus the answers to three interrelated transtechnical heuristic questions (Hoyt, 1990): (1) How is the patient "stuck" (what is the problem or pathology)? (2) What does the patient need to get "unstuck?" and (3) How can I, as therapist, facilitate or provide what is needed? The good brief (or any) therapist needs to be multitheoretical, able to reckon from a variety of perspectives lest patients be forced into the Procrustean bed of a pet theory or technique or be dismissed and blamed for being resistant, unmotivated, or ego deficient. As the saying goes, "If all one has is a hammer, everything begins to look like a nail." How you look determines what you will see (Hoyt, 1994c). The importance of having "an array of observing positions" has been well described by Gustafson (1986; also see White & Epston, 1990), who identifies four key paradigms in tracing the history of attempts to answer the question of how patients get stuck and unstuck:

Psychoanalysis sees the hidden demands of the animal in us. The analysis of character sees the "constant attitude" which protects the animal from without. Interpersonal interviewing sees the interactions which tie us into trouble with other people. Systemic interviewing sees these interactions in the service of stable social relations. (p. 6)

The therapist wishing to be parsimonious (brief and effective) may need to choose which conceptualization(s) will allow for the best chance of a change-producing intervention. Should the approach be toward revealing the intrapsychic domain of warded-off feelings, modifying the patient's typical way of viewing and meeting the world, altering the social skills with which the patient interacts, or changing the rules of the labyrinthine games that ensnare patients into maintaining the status quo? Or what else? And how to do so? Educational instruction? Cognitive-behavioral techniques? Psychodynamic interpretations? Systemic interviewing and strategic interventions? Hypnosis? Commonsense appeals or wise exhortations? The brief therapist asks: *What would be likely to work with this patient and this therapist at this time?*

INTERLUDE: A BRIEF HISTORY OF BRIEF THERAPY

People have been having problems and getting help since time immemorial, although the history of psychotherapy as a practice and a profession is considered to have begun in earnest only about 100 years ago (Zeig, 1987; Freedheim, 1992). Sigmund Freud, usually thought of as the founder of psychoanalysis, was also the father of brief therapy. Reading his early cases (Breuer & Freud, 1893–1895), one finds him interacting actively with patients and treating them in days, weeks, and months. Psychoanalysis was also a research instrument, however, and treatment became longer and longer as the early pioneers became fascinated with

the psychological phenomena that would emerge (such as Oedipal fantasies and transference neuroses) if the therapist remained a relatively inactive and a neutral "blank" screen while the patient freely associated. An early effort to experiment with more active methods in treatment was made by Ferenczi and Rank (1925), but some of their methods were questionable and the time for revisionism was not right since psychoanalysis was still struggling to establish itself. At the end of his life, Freud (1937) wrote his last great clinical paper, "Analysis Terminable and Interminable," in which he expressed his frustration about the limited therapeutic benefits of psychoanalysis and called for the development of new methods based on the psychoanalytic understanding of transference, resistance, and unconscious material.

World War II intervened, with many consequences for the practice of brief (and other) psychotherapy. Prior to the war, psychological treatment usually had been a long-term luxury of the privileged and had fallen under the purview of the psychoanalytic and psychiatric–medical establishment. There were so many soldiers needing services, however, that (1) psychologists and clinical social workers were finally recognized as bonafide psychotherapy providers rather than being relegated to their respective "auxiliary" roles as psychometric testers and home visitors; (2) group therapy was greatly expanded as a treatment of choice (and necessity) rather than being an isolated and rare specialty; (3) the Veterans Administration (VA) medical system emerged as a training ground for mental health professionals; and, most salient to our present topic, (4) interest was spurred in treatment methods that would help soldiers quickly reduce symptoms and return to function either in the combat zones or back in civilian life. Psychoanalytic theory continued to predominate, but "reality factors" were becoming increasingly influential—harbingers of what is today called "accountability" (Johnson, 1995).

In 1946, Alexander and French published *Psychoanalytic Therapy: Principles and Applications*. The book was (and is) extraordinary, revisiting and updating many of the ideas of Ferenczi and Rank (1925) regarding the use of greater therapist activity and suggesting that the length and frequency of sessions might be varied, both from case to case and within the same patient's treatment, to avoid excessive dependency in the patient which prolonged therapy and to bring about what Alexander and French referred to as a "corrective emotional experience." Many successful brief therapies were reported. Still, the politics of psychoanalysis were not quite ripe for change and it remained for two leading psychoanalytic figures of the time, Bibring (1954) and Gill (1954), to publish their seminal papers about modifying the parameters of treatment and calling it psychoanalytically *oriented* therapy (and not psychoanalysis) before attempts at psychodynamic modifications were recognized as legitimate by the mainstream.

By the early 1950s, a number of workers were exploring what could be done using psychodynamic principles in more active and shorter treatment. In London, Balint, Ornstein, and Balint (1972) and Malan (1963, 1976) were developing "focal psychotherapy"; in Boston, Sifneos (1972) was beginning to experiment with "short-term anxiety-provoking psychotherapy"; and in New York, Wolberg (1965) was investigating various ways of shortening the length of treatment, including using hypnotherapy to work through patients' resistance more quickly. At the same time, several other important figures were becoming disenchanted with psychoanalytic methods and began to originate other, more active methods for bringing about psychological change more rapidly. Perls, Heffer-line, and Goodman (1951) began to develop the theory and techniques of Gestalt therapy; Wolpe (1958) and Wolpe and Lazarus (1966) were developing behavior therapy; Ellis (1962, 1992) began to develop rational–emotive therapy, the first systematic form of what is now called "cognitive therapy"; and Berne (1961, 1972) began to develop Transactional Analysis. A number of publications started calling professional attention to the expanding field of brief therapy, including important books by Malan (1963), Wolberg (1965), Bellak and Small (1965), Parad (1965), Barten (1971), and Lewin (1970). Concurrently, the psychiatrist Milton Erickson (1980) was still working in relative obscurity in Phoenix, Arizona, but his uniquely creative uses of hypnosis and strategic interventions to capitalize on patients' existing capacities would soon be recognized (especially with the 1973 publication of Haley's *Uncommon Therapy*) and contributed greatly to both the emerging family therapy movement and various schools of strategic and systemic therapy.

Writing about the expanding spectrum of the brief therapies, Barten (1971) underscored the convergence of a number of historical developments, including a growing professional commitment to providing appropriate mental health services to all segments of the community, an increasing shift from psychoanalysis to more ego-oriented techniques and a recognition of the value of limited therapeutic goals, a diversifying of the roles of mental health professionals, long overdue recognition of the special needs of the disadvantaged,[6] and increased consumer demand for economically feasible services. The community mental health movement of the 1960s and the federal Health Maintenance Organization (HMO) Act of 1973 gave further mandate to brief treatment. Strategic therapists were guided by Haley (1963, 1969, 1973, 1977,

1984), Madanes (1981, 1984), and the work of the Mental Research Institute of Palo Alto (Watzlawick, Beavin, & Jackson, 1967; Watzlawick, Weakland, & Fisch, 1974; Fisch et al., 1982) and the Brief Family Therapy Center of Milwaukee (de Shazer, 1982, 1985, 1988), while psychodynamicists wanting to work more concisely drew special inspiration from the work of Sifneos (1972), Mann (1973), Malan (1963, 1976), and Davanloo (1978, 1980). In 1988, a conference entitled "Brief Therapy: Myths, Methods and Metaphors," sponsored by the Erickson Foundation, was held in San Francisco, with several thousand mental health professionals attending (Zeig & Gilligan, 1990). The recent enormous acceleration in various forms of managed health (Austad & Berman, 1991; Austad & Hoyt, 1992; Feldman & Fitzpatrick, 1992; VandenBos, Cummings, & DeLeon, 1992; Hoyt, 1995b), which by 1992 covered approximately 100 million Americans, has given further impetus to the development and expansion of various forms of brief therapy.

THE STRUCTURE OF BRIEF THERAPY

While we have already emphasized the importance of the first session in brief therapy as a prelude to considering some specific approaches, it will be helpful to gain an orienting perspective on the overall structure of treatment, the issues and tasks associated with the early, middle, and later stages of psychotherapeutic work. Brief psychotherapy (as well as other, more prolonged or open-ended treatments) can be conceptualized as having a structure of five sequenced phases. In actual practice, of course, the phases blend into one another rather than being so discretely organized. The structure tends to be epigenetic or pyramidal; that is, each phase builds on the prior phase,

so that successful work in one is a precondition for the next (e.g., the patient electing treatment and the therapist applying selection criteria and accepting the patient precedes forming a working alliance, which precedes focusing and making a contract, which precedes termination, which precedes continuing work and following through).

As noted elsewhere (Gustafson, 1986; Hoyt, 1990), there is often an interesting parallel between the process of each individual session and the structure of the overall course of treatment: Like the idea of ontogeny recapitulating phylogeny, each session and each therapy involves connecting, working, and closing.[7] Often, there is also a parallel process wherein brief therapy students/trainees repeat in sequence with their supervisors some of the same issues that are concurrently occurring between the students and their patients (Dasberg & Winokur, 1984; Frances & Clarkin, 1981a; Hoyt, 1991).

Each phase of treatment has its special issues:

1. *Election and selection.* Even before the first session occurs, change often begins with the recognition of a problem and the decision to seek therapy (Weiner-Davis, de Shazer, & Gingerich, 1987). Can the therapist capitalize on this? How? What may need to happen before change is possible? Is the patient ready, and what will circumstances permit? Is the patient a willing customer, an unwilling complainant, or simply a visitor (de Shazer, 1988)? Looked at from a somewhat different perspective, we can recognize the importance of the patient's stage of change: Is the patient in the precontemplation, contemplation, planning, action, or maintenance stage (Prochaska, DiClemente, & Norcross, 1992)? It is also good to remember that there are some patients—spontaneous improvers, nonresponders, and negative therapeutic

reactors—for whom "no treatment" may be the prescription of choice (Frances & Clarkin, 1981b).

2. *Beginning.* As already discussed, key issues involve forming a working alliance; assessing patients' strengths, weaknesses, and motivations; finding a psychological focus, establishing achievable goals and forming a treatment plan and contract; introducing novelty and getting the patient actively involved in treatment; and attending to business matters. No mean feat![8]

3. *Middle phase.* This is the "working through" stage, meaning staying on task, doing homework, and applying the lessons of therapy in real life, as well as possibly increasing insight into the original and present-day sources of problems. Maintenance and possible refinement of a central theme/focus/goal occur here.

4. *End phase.* This includes termination and possible mourning: possible arousal of underlying separation–individuation issues in both patient and therapist, with possible return of symptoms and temptations to avoid ending; the need to subtract the therapist from the successful equation (Gustafson, 1986); maintaining gains, continuing change, and avoiding possible backsliding or "self-sabotage" (Hoyt, 1986); relapse prevention; inviting a follow-up or "check-in" appointment with the possibility of later return to treatment.

5. *Follow-through.* This includes continuation of psychological work and change beyond the formal ending of therapist–patient contact. Internalization of favorable aspects of the treatment occur here. In short-term therapy, much more than in longer treatments, change processes may be started or amplified without being completely worked through during the course of formal treatment. This is consistent with the distinction between treatment goals and life goals (Ticho, 1972), the former involving getting "unstuck" and better

equipped to deal with whatever life presents down the road. There is also, of course, the possibility of intermittent, episodic, serial, or distributed therapy (Bennett, 1983, 1984; Budman, 1990; Cummings & Sayama, 1995; Hoyt, 1990; Kreilkamp, 1989; Siddall, Haffey, & Feinman, 1988)—the patient can return later for additional treatment as needed.

MODELS OF BRIEF THERAPY

There are various models or "schools" of brief therapy (see Bloom, 1992a; Budman, 1981; Budman, Hoyt, & Friedman, 1992; Gustafson, 1986; Wells & Giannetti, 1990, 1993; Zeig & Gilligan, 1990). While each case is different and the skillful application of psychological principles is part of what makes therapy an interesting and artful endeavor, there are broad general guidelines in theory and practice that distinguish different forms of brief treatment. We highlight and illustrate a few of them here,[9] but the reader should keep in mind three important caveats: (1) no summary or case presentation can do more than suggest a few broad brushstrokes—by necessity, more has been omitted than included under each rubric, and therefore in each section there are basic references cited to guide those wishing to get started on a fuller study of a particular approach; (2) most therapy is eclectic and integrative, drawing ideas and methods from a range of sources rather than adhering to one particular theory; and (3) as Milton Erickson said, "each person is a unique individual. Hence, psychotherapy should be formulated to meet the uniqueness of the individual's needs, rather than tailoring the person to fit the Procrustean bed of a hypothetical theory of human behavior" (quoted in Zeig & Gilligan, 1990, p. xix).

Short-Term Psychodynamic Psychotherapies

Beginning with Freud, numerous theoreticians and clinicians have applied the psychoanalytic concepts of the unconscious, resistance, and transference to brief forms of treatment. Building on the principles described in Freud's (1914) paper, "Remembering, Repeating, and Working Through," various short-term dynamic methods have been developed to bring the patient to a greater awareness of his or her maladaptive defenses, warded-off feelings, and counterproductive relationship patterns.[10] As many reviewers have noted (Bauer & Kobos, 1987; Crits-Cristoph & Barber, 1991; Donovan, 1987; Horner, 1985; Horowitz et al., 1984; Levenson & Butler, 1994; Malan, 1976; Marmor, 1979; Peak, Borduin, & Archer, 1988; Rasmussen & Messer, 1986), the emphasis in all of the various short-term dynamic psychotherapies has been on increased therapist activity within a limited, central focus. There has been a general recognition that relative inactivity on the part of the therapist in the face of increasing resistance leads to prolonged and diffuse treatment. Hence, Malan (1980), in an allusion to Freud's (1919) paper "Turnings in the Way of Psychoanalysis," refers to Freud's technique of free association as "a wrong turning" that lead to "doubtful therapeutic effectiveness" (pp. 13–14). Brief dynamic therapists endeavor to promote change within a focalized area of conflict via an admixture of de-repression and affective release, corrective emotional experience, relearning, and application of the patient's will. Let us sketch a few of the main short-term psychodynamic approaches in terms of their central characteristics of focus, primary techniques, and length of treatment.

1. *Short-term anxiety-provoking psychotherapy* (Sifneos, 1987, 1992). Primarily for carefully selected patients with Oedipal conflicts, anxiety-provoking confrontations and transference interpretations are made by a teacher/therapist endeavoring to produce emotional relearning. Length of treatment varies but is typically about 6 to 15 sessions.

2. *Short-term dynamic psychotherapy* (Malan, 1963, 1976). This method also focuses on issues of Oedipal conflict and loss, with the therapist emphasizing interpretive links between transference, past, and present issues. Treatment is typically 30 to 40 sessions.

3. *Time-limited psychotherapy* (Mann, 1973; Mann & Goldman, 1982). A firm 12-session treatment framework is established with an emphasis on the patient's sense of self and his or her present and "chronically endured pain." The empathic therapist helps the patient master underlying separation issues that become manifest in terms of themes of unresolved mourning, activity versus passivity, independence versus dependence, and adequate versus diminished self-esteem.

4. *Stress response therapy and microanalysis* (Horowitz, 1976; Horowitz et al., 1984). The focus is on the patient's "states of mind" (images of self and other and information-processing styles) to help the patient rework and emotionally master a recent stress event, usually over the course of 12 sessions.

5. *Short-term intensive dynamic psychotherapy* (Davanloo, 1978, 1980, 1991; Worchel, 1990). The therapist functions as a "relentless healer," vigorously confronting and interpreting defenses until there is an "unlocking of the unconscious" and a breakthrough into true feelings. The focus is broad, with strong emphasis on characterological defenses as they are manifested within the basic psychoanalytic "Triangle of Conflict" (impulse feeling/anxiety/defense) and "Triangle of Person" (transference/current significant persons/past significant per-

sons), with special attention directed toward an experience in the transference. Treatment length generally varies from 5 to 40 sessions, with progress expected to be evident early on.

6. *Time-limited dynamic psychotherapy* (Strupp & Binder, 1984; Butler, Strupp & Binder, 1992). A "cyclical maladaptive pattern" is identified and interpreted, involving acts of self, expectations of others, acts of others, and self-introjects. The therapist is empathic, appreciating the pull of countertransference as an opportunity to provide a corrective emotional experience. Treatment is usually 25 sessions.

There have been many reports of how coming to grips with warded-off conflicts has helped people achieve greater happiness in relationships, success at work, and the ability to say good-bye. Although the data are not without complication, the overall direction of the findings has been summarized by Hoyt (1985a):

There has been controversy in the short-term therapy literature about patient selection, therapeutic techniques, and expected outcomes. . . . Simply stated, the "conservative" position has been that brief treatment generally is appropriate only for the mildly and recently distressed, that techniques should be supportive rather than uncovering or anxiety-producing, and that expected results are basically superficial and symptom suppressive. The "radical" position, on the other hand, is just what the name literally implies: "going to the root"; the radical view is that the skillful clinician working within an explicitly short-term treatment framework can use a full range of psychodynamic methods with a variety of neurotic patients, often achieving some genuine and lasting personality modifications as well as symptomatic relief. While there is more research to be done, the general thrust of the evidence is clear: Many patients benefit from brief, focused, psychodynamic therapy. (p. 95)

Short-term dynamic psychotherapy, of course, is not for everyone. It requires a reasonably functional patient with a grip on reality and an ability to tolerate painful emotional material. It is also not a panacea, since there are many biological, social, situational, and existential factors besides intrapsychic dynamics that may require clinical attention. It is also important to remember that for psychodynamic psychotherapy to be effective, regardless of whether it is short-term or more extended, insight must serve as a vehicle and not as a final destination. That is, the real question is not how far back does a problem go but how much farther will it be carried forward? As one enthusiast for intensive short-term dynamic therapy has put it:

Intrinsic in short-term therapy's technique is the appeal to the individual to take action. How to change? The answer is part and parcel of the therapy's technique: the challenge to the defenses and the focus on your buried feelings exhort you to go from a passive to an active stance, to take charge of the way you look at life and deal with your emotions. (Zois, 1992, p. 212)

The following case fragment illustrates some aspects of a short-term psychodynamic approach.

The Case of the Forlorn Lover

David was a 52-year-old man who sought therapy a few months after his lover died of AIDS. On the telephone, he tensely asked whether I was prejudiced against working with homosexuals. When I answered that I was not, he said he would see me at the appointment time I had offered.

He arrived a few minutes early, neatly dressed in tie and coat, coming from his job as an office manager where he had worked for many years. He spoke slowly with great control—formal, severe, constricted—as he described his dilemma.

He had never been close to anyone, he reported. He had grown up in an emotionally cold European household and had then spent many years as a monk in a religious order. Finally, he had left and eventually made his way to San Francisco. He was accepting of his sexual orientation and spent most of his offwork time among gays and lesbians because of greater compatibility and to avoid discrimination. He had adopted a lifestyle of occasional brief sexual encounters until he met Richard. It was difficult for him even to speak his late friend's name, the loss was so painful. Several times he start to choke up, would put his hand over his face, and recompose himself.

Near the end of our first session, I asked him why he had come to therapy, what did he want to accomplish? "The pain is so great I can't stand it, but damn him, he made me feel and now I don't want to go back to that cold life I had before. I'm lost." He cried a bit, then pulled himself together. He remarked that he found me kind and easy to talk with, and that he was relieved that I had directly answered his question about possible antigay prejudice because his insurance restricted whom he might be able to see. He asked if he could have an appointment to come back. When I agreed and asked when he would like to return, he indicated that his work schedule would require a 2-week interval between sessions. We set an appointment. (This time frame would also allow him to better regulate the intensity of whatever might transpire in our meetings, I thought, but did not share with him.)

Over the next three sessions, David gradually told me more about his relationship with Richard. The telling was slow and painful. Several times, when he felt a wave of emotion, he would either close his eyes and tremble until it passed, or he would set his jaw and actively suppress his feelings. He was grieving at a pace that seemed tolerable for him while I mostly listened and occasionally asked leading questions. His level of tension and control was remarkable. He would make sure that the sessions stopped exactly on time. When I was a few minutes late to begin, he became especially cold and distant. When I commented that he seemed "somewhat tense," he paused until he was composed and then told me that he was "furious inside." I said I was sorry for the lateness and added:

THERAPIST: It is remarkable how you are able to keep your feelings in.

PATIENT: Yes, I can eliminate someone from my emotions. I am well trained not to feel.

THERAPIST: Yes, but to do that would render me useless to you. And that wouldn't be good for you.

He looked at me and palpably reconnected.

In the next two sessions, David hesitantly revealed more details about Richard, including various complaints about his drinking and bouts of irritability. David then became increasingly unforthcoming. I asked why.

PATIENT: If I talk more about him and let myself grieve then the images and memories might fade and I will have nothing left. . . . (Silence)

THERAPIST: You're trying to hold on to him in your mind the way some people keep a room exactly like it was the day someone died. It's like a museum, as though time can be frozen. . . . But it can't.

PATIENT: Oh, God, yes, that's it. (He cries and then recomposes himself.)

THERAPIST: So, what are you going to do?

PATIENT: I want to go forward, but I don't know how. Oh, I do, there are other people, but I'm scared.

THERAPIST: Of what?

PATIENT: Of getting hurt again.

THERAPIST: Then go slow, when you're ready. But life is in front of you.

He continued his mourning process. He also began to experiment over the next several weeks, attending a dance club, having supper with someone, even asserting himself at his workplace and refusing to acquiesce to things he felt were unfair. He was well aware of his pattern of "stuffing" his feelings and still often did so when threatened or hurt, but with increased cognizance he also sometimes expressed himself more. He even occasionally smiled, and told stories that revealed a growing tenderness in his relations with others, including a new willingness to forgive and to remain involved with people rather than "eliminating" them if they were sometimes inconsiderate or annoying. He began to exercise and lost a few "extra" pounds that he had been carrying, all in preparation for the possibility of finding a new mate.

Follow-Up and Comment. This case might best be described as "eclectic–integrated" and falling within the "expressive–supportive" range of brief dynamic therapies (Pinsker, Rosenthal, & McCullough, 1991). Attention was paid to exploring the patient's warded-off feelings, his images of self and others, and ways his defenses and relationship patterns were repeated with the therapist. As one might expect, therapy termination was not easy for David. Relinquishing the therapist reminded him of losing Richard and also meant giving up a person that he had learned to trust and felt at ease talking with, but by the 12th therapy session he felt strong enough to go forward and so stopped treatment as planned. Consistent with Mann's (1973; also see Hoyt, 1979a) model, themes of unresolved mourning, activity versus passiv-

ity, and independence versus dependence were prominent throughout the therapy and especially during the explicit termination phase. Indeed, there was a countertransference "pull" to extend treatment (Hoyt & Farrell, 1984), but this was not done and we ended our meeting. David's goals for treatment—to get through the pain and to resume moving toward people rather than retreating into isolation—were largely accomplished. He was encouraged to return to therapy as needed, and agreed to do so.

Transactional Analysis and Redecision Therapy

The Transactional Analysis (TA) school of therapy was developed by Eric Berne (1961, 1972) out of his desire to help patients more quickly see their autonomous role in their personal difficulties. While TA involves a complicated and comprehensive model of human development, intrapsychic organization, and interpersonal dynamics (see Stewart & Joines, 1987; James, Chapter 9, this volume), there are three popular and readily accessible ideas from TA with which Berne is most identified: (1) the "I'm OK, You're OK" matrix of existential positions pertaining to how one regards self and others[11]; (2) the Parent–Adult–Child conceptualization of personality ego states (the progenitor of various "Inner Child" theories); and (3) the "Games People Play" (Berne, 1964) idea of recognizing many of the ulterior motivations behind dysfunctional relationship patterns.

Combining some of the theory of TA with Gestalt techniques plus many of their own innovations, Robert and Mary Goulding (1978, 1979) developed what they call redecision therapy. Their approach is built on the theory that, as children, people often make key life deci-

456 ESSENTIAL PSYCHOTHERAPIES: THEORY AND PRACTICE

sions (such as "Don't feel," "Don't think," "Don't be a child," "Don't grow up," "Don't be close," "Don't be important," "Don't enjoy," "Don't be") in order to survive or adapt to perceived and often veridical parental pressures. In therapy, the patient reenters and reexperiences the pathogenic scene as a child, via imagery and Gestalt work, and with the encouragement and support of the therapist makes a *redecision* that frees the patient from the pernicious injunction that he or she had earlier accepted and internalized. Rather than working within a psychodynamic transference model, in which the therapist becomes a participant–observer "object," the patient is encouraged to do two-chair Gestalt work in which he or she "becomes" the pathogenic parent (extrojecting the introject, so to speak) and then engages in a powerful dialogue in which he or she experiences and reclaims a sense of power, self-determination, and well-being. "I'm OK and will take care of myself even if you don't think I'm OK." There is implicit the idea of state-dependent learning (and relearning), the work being conducted in the voice of the present tense in order to bring to life how the patient is carrying the conflict. A powerful combination of affect and insight is involved, with support and behavioral anchors maintaining the gains achieved.

Robert Goulding (1989; M. Goulding & R. Goulding, 1979) describes a thinking structure to guide work in redecision therapy. While many of the important details go beyond the scope of the present discussion, it should be noted that each of the following main headings is an essential feature for making this approach brief and effective:

1. *Contact*, forming an alliance with the patient;
2. *Contract*, constructing the focus or goal of treatment in a way that can be specified and achieved;
3. *Con*, emphasizing patients' power and responsibility by confronting their efforts to disown autonomy through various ways they attempt to fool ("con") themselves and therapists into believing that others control their thoughts, feelings, and behavior or with disingenuous claims of "trying" to make changes;
4. *Chief bad feelings, thinkings, behaviors, and psychosomatics*, identifying the painful or problematic counterproductive symptoms;
5. *Chronic games, belief systems, and fantasies*, clarifying the interpersonal and intrapsychic ways symptoms are maintained;
6. *Childhood early decisions*, bringing to vivid awareness a reexperience of childhood feelings via the imaginal reliving of an early pathogenic scene, including recognition of the chief parental messages (injunctions and counterinjunctions), childhood script formation, and stroking (reinforcement) patterns;
7. *Impasse resolution*, including redecisions, ego state decontamination and reconstruction (involving the strengthening of distinctions between Parent–Adult–Child functions), reparenting, and other techniques; and
8. *Maintaining the victory*, including anchoring the patient's new and healthier ways of responding, making changes in stroke (reinforcement) patterns, and forming plans for how to use the redecision in the future.

Since this presentation is necessarily brief and schematic, the reader is referred to the Gouldings' work already cited, as well as Mary Goulding (1985, 1992), Goulding and Goulding (1989), Hoyt (in press-a) Hoyt and Goulding (1989), Kadis (1985), McClendon & Kadis (1983), and Phillips (1988) for numerous clinical applications and examples.

Consistent with the question Eric Berne would ask himself before each session, "What can I do to cure this patient today?" (reported in Goulding & Goulding, 1979), the Gouldings have developed Berne's concept of *contractual therapy* and ask patients, as they begin each treatment session, "*What are you willing to change today?*" In this one pithy sentence, the key elements of brief therapy all occur! Here they are, spelled out (from Hoyt, 1990, pp. 125–126):

What [specificity, target, focus]
are [active verb, present tense]
you [self as agent, intrapsychic, personal functioning]
willing [choice, responsibility, initiative]
to change [alter or be different, not just "work on" or "explore"]
today [now, in the moment]
? [inquiry, open field, therapist receptive but not insistent]

The question focuses the therapist and the patient on making rapid changes. As the following vignette illustrates, this approach, which combines the theory of injunctions with Gestalt techniques "so that the patient does a great deal of experiential work *and* has a good understanding of his place in his life script, is more likely to change both his behavior and his feelings" (R. Goulding, 1983, p. 634). As M. Goulding (1990) has written, attention to contract plus redecision helps get the important work done fast.

The Case of the Woman Who Stood Up for Herself

Maria, who was 25 years old, came to therapy complaining of "insecurity" and "low self-esteem" in her relationships with men as well as in her work performance. She needed to gather her confidence to move on in her adult life. She already had some understanding that many of her insecurities stemmed from her relationship with her verbally abusive, highly critical father. "I know he did this to me," she said, "but what can I do about it?" It appeared that she needed an experience that would separate her from her past, that would "empower" her, a shift out of the "victim" position. She "knew" her father was still living in her head ("It's an old tape"), but so what?

By the end of our first meeting she had achieved several important steps:

1. Good contact with the therapist, establishing a sense of safety and working alliance.
2. Increased awareness that her pattern of low self-esteem was a carryover from how her father had treated her.
3. A greater sense of her present role or personal autonomy; that is, she could see more clearly that she did the putdowns to herself, that the origin of her problem may have been in childhood with her father but that he was not "making" her feel bad now—she was.

As the session drew near an end, the therapist remarked: "So what you want to do, so to speak, is to get his critical voice out of your head, right?" She agreed, and the contract was made specific: to stop putting herself down and, instead, to give herself due credit and not let others demean her.

Conditions were ripe for redecision work. At the second meeting, the therapist reiterated the contract to make sure it was still what she wanted. Maria was then asked to give an example of a recent time when she felt lacking in confidence and self-esteem. She did, and was then asked how she felt in that situation and what she had said in her head about herself and the other person. She had felt scared, she had said to herself, "I can't do anything right," and she had said about the other person, "He is mad and doesn't like you." The therapist then said: "You feel scared, you think you can't do anything right, and he is mad at you. How does that fit in with your childhood? What do you think of?"

Maria recalled a time when she was about 6 years old. She had spilled juice in the living room, and her father was chastising her for it. The therapist asked her to stay with the scene, to imagine it vividly, to really get into it. "Let yourself be six years old again and go back there, see the room and the juice on the rug and all the details, and let yourself feel yourself being that scared six-year-old girl." Maria paused and as she recalled and "got into" the scene, one could see her get smaller and shrink into herself.

The therapist then said to her, "Now sit in this other chair over here [Maria changed seats], and in this chair be your father, looking at the juice on the rug and being furious." With a little prompting, Maria got into the role. The therapist then proceeded to conduct a brief "Parent interview" (McNeel, 1976), asking the "Father" his name and occupation and asking questions to evoke "his" feelings and thoughts about the little girl who in the scene would be cowering in front of him. "He" was angry and did not like to have to clean up the mess, but as he talked more it became clear that he was not all that ferocious and that he actually did love the girl, too.

The therapist had Maria switch back to the 6-year-old seat and from there tell her father that she was scared and that she did not like it when he yelled at her. "I'm only a little kid and I make mistakes, but I'm not bad and you shouldn't yell at me," she spontaneously added. "Yeah," said the therapist, "Good. That's right. Stand up and tell him again. Let him know that he's not going to hurt you, and that you're OK even if you sometimes make mistakes." The little girl stood up for herself.

When she seemed done, the therapist said, "Good job. Notice how strong you feel. Now, as you come back to yourself in the present you'll remember whenever you need to, how it feels to stand up."

Follow-Up and Comment. The role playing had a powerful effect. Using the three questions, "How do you feel? What do you say about yourself? What do you say about the other person?" as a kind of affect bridge back to an early scene often works to rapidly access a pathogenic (perhaps screen) memory, taking a different and quicker route than waiting for a transference neurosis to fully bloom. The two-chair work then allows a reworking or redecision, a new and healthier resolution of the impasse (cf. Blackstone, 1987). For this patient, this was a turning point, a casting off of the "Don't Be a Child" and "Don't Be Important" injunctions she had earlier internalized. Therapy continued for another three visits, the first two occurring weekly and the last one occurring a month later, as the patient made plans and applied (worked through) her "breakthrough" in a variety of current life situations. With support, reminders, and practice, she learned to discount herself less and less. Her treatment goals of enhanced confidence and self-esteem were well met and demonstrated in a variety of contexts.

Cognitive-Behavioral Approaches to Brief Therapy

Cognitive-behavioral approaches to treatment (see Freeman & Reinecke, Chapter 6, this volume) tend, by their very nature, to be brief therapy (Wilson, 1981). They are highly goal-directed, offering direct and specific remedies for specific problems. As a group, they are characterized by careful and thorough assessment of particular problems and complaints and the active recruitment of the patient's participation and cooperation in treatment. Then, following the basic conception that psychopathology results from and is maintained by dysfunctional cognition and conation, various techniques are applied to alter maladaptive thoughts and behaviors as they are occurring in the present and to prevent their recurrence in the future (Burbach, Borduin, & Peake, 1988).

Cognitive approaches (which typically include behavioral aspects as well) have been categorized by Mahoney and Arnkoff (1978) into three main groups: (1) *cognitive restructuring*, such as Ellis's (1962, 1992) rational–emotive therapy and Beck's (1976, 1988) cognitive therapy; (2) *coping skills*, such as Wolpe's (1958) systematic desensitization and Meichenbaum's (1977, 1993) stress inoculation training; and (3) *problem solving*, such as D'Zurilla and Goldfried's (1973) behavioral problem-solving therapy and Mahoney's (1974, 1977) "personal science" approach. Faulty learning is revised as distortions in cognitive schemata are corrected, relaxation skills and relapse prevention methods are taught, and constructive decision making is increased. In addition to the sources already cited, useful descriptions of cognitive therapy techniques have been provided by Beck, Rush, Shaw, and Emery (1979), Beck, Freeman, and Associates (1990), McMullin (1986), Meichenbaum (1994), Persons (1989), and Schuyler (1991); the books, *Feeling Good: The New Mood Therapy* (Burns, 1980) and *The Feeling Good Handbook* (Burns, 1989) are valuable references for the lay public. Some cognitive-behavioral methods (such as assertiveness training and relaxation programs) are semistructured and thus can be adapted nicely to cost-effective, short-term psychoeducational group therapy formats (Hoyt, 1993a).

Clear operationalism is one of the hallmarks and advantages of cognitive-behavioral treatments. As Lazarus and Fay (1990) have written:

> Some long-term therapy is not only inefficient (taking longer than necessary because it was insufficiently focused or precise), but even detrimental because of the reinforcement of pathological self-concepts. One of the great advantages of the short-term focus is that if the therapy doesn't work, it will be apparent much sooner. . . . In this regard, to paraphrase an old saying, effective treatment depends far less on the hours you put in, than on what you put into those hours. (pp. 39–40)

They go on:

> We also believe that there are three major impediments to the development and clinical implementation of rapidly effective therapies: (1) the lack of a sufficiently broad technical armamentarium—largely a result of factionalism within our profession; (2) ignorance of, or inadequate attention to, the biological aspects of "psychological" problems; and (3) the concept of resistance and its elaboration, particularly the notion that the locus of resistance is within the patient. . . . Our position is that "resistance" does not rest with the patient, but hinges on the methodology of the therapy as well as the skill and personal qualities of the therapist (cf. de Shazer, 1985).[12] It is *our* responsibility to find the keys to the puzzle. (p. 41)

What is needed, they suggest, is a schema for systematically, comprehensively, and exhaustively assessing a patient's psychological and psychiatric problems as a preparation for the selection of specific effective interventions. They recommend "multimodal therapy" (Lazarus, 1976, 1989). This approach, which they sometimes prefer to call "limited goal therapy," is not so much a "school" of therapy as a way of organizing information obtained from the client and then selecting treatments in terms of seven interactive modalities of human personality expressed in the acronym BASIC I.D.—for *B*ehavior, *A*ffect, *S*ensation, *I*magery, *C*ognition, *I*nterpersonal, and *D*rugs (a euphonic choice to complete the acronym, referring more broadly to the biological sector). The Modality Profile displayed in Table 12.2, composed for a 33-year-old woman who sought therapy for "depression and anxiety," illustrates how the multimodal framework can be used to identify problems and plan treatments.

Cognitive-behavioral approaches are often useful for the brief therapy of both emotional disorders (anxiety and depres-sion) and marital discord. Although there is a complicated range of possible interrelationships between individual and conjoint problems that highlight the need for careful idiographic case concep-tualization (see Addis & Jacobson, 1991), the appropriate integration of cognitive and behavioral treatment technologies makes great sense if progress is to be made and maintained without undue de-lay. Important source material to guide practitioners has been provided by Beach, Sandeen, and O'Leary (1990), Beck (1988), Fay (1990), Jacobson and Gurman (1995), Jacobson and Margolin (1979), and Stuart (1981). A useful over-

TABLE 12.2. Modality Profile

Modality	Problem	Proposed treatment
B	"Disorganized/sloppy"	Contingency contracting
	Phobic avoidance	Systematic desensitization
	Leaves things to the last minute	Time management
A	Guilt	Explore antecedents and irrational ideas
	Anxiety related to criticism and rejection	Coping imagery and rational disputation
	Sadness/despondency	Explore faulty thinking and encourage her to seek out positive events
S	Fatigue/lower back pain/tension headaches	Relaxation training/physiotherapy exercises
I	Loneliness images/poor self-image/ images of failing	Coping imagery exercises
C	Dichotomous reasoning/too many "shoulds"/overgeneralizes	Cognitive restructuring
I.	Nontrusting	Risk taking
	Overly competitive	Cooperation training
	Unassertive	Assertiveness training
	Avoids social gatherings	Social skills training
D.	Uses alprazolam p.r.n.	Monitor to avoid dependency
	Overweight	Weight control methods (e.g., contingency contracting, self-monitoring, support group)
	Insufficient exercise	Physical fitness program

(A thorough medical examination replete with laboratory tests revealed no diagnosable contributing organic pathology.)

Note. From Lazarus and Fay (1990, p. 46). Copyright 1990 by Brunner/Mazel, Inc. Reprinted by permission of the publisher.

view is also provided by Robinson (1991), who has summarized typical objectives, techniques, and patient assignments for early, middle, and late phases of treating couples within the parameters of prepaid health care (see Table 12.3).

Brief cognitive-behavioral treatment of the confluence of depression and mari-

tal discord is described in the following case report.

The Case of the Martyred Mother

Jackie, a 53-year-old nurse, was referred for therapy after being discharged from a psychiatric hospital where she had been

TABLE 12.3. A Cognitive-Behavioral Model for Treating Couples in Prepaid Health Care

Objectives	Techniques	Patient assignments
	Initial phase	
Assessment of problem	Formal assessment Objectification Reframing	Relationship Belief Inventory Written statements of their part in problem
Assessment of satisfaction	Formal assessment Long- and short-term focusing	Marital Happiness Scale Dyadic Adjustment Scale
Assessment of communication skills	Observations	Communication practice sessions: Objectification, expressing appreciation
Increase in positive exchange	Refocusing attention Noting strengths Increasing rate of caring behaviors Defining collaboration	Sharing romantic or humorous memories "Caring Days" Recalling examples of collaboration

Planning and obtainment of commitment
  to treatment
	"As if" participation
	Discussing model
	Pros and cons of participation
	Treatment contract
		Listing questions or concerns
		Discussing beliefs about treatment
		Planning ways to deal with obstacles to
		  completing treatment

	Middle phase	

Problem solving	Generating solutions
	Discussing pros and cons of possible
	  solutions
	Discovering obstacles
		Listing advantages and disadvantages of
		  present solution

Increase of positive exchange	Discussing and identifying Shared Recreational Activities (SRAs)	Scheduling, doing, and evaluating SRAs

Increasing communication skills:
  validating, listening, making specific
  positive requests
	Instructions, modeling, behavioral
	  rehearsal, feedback
	Practice sessions
		Reading written instructions

Introduction of role of self-talk and self- reinforcement	Instructions, examples	Thought identification
	Later phase	

Increasing communication skills:
  expressing feelings directly,
  negotiating, problem solving
	Instructions, modeling, behavioral
	  rehearsal, feedback
		Holding a practice session
		Keeping a problem-solving notebook

Problem solving and revising	Discussing "good faith" and "quid pro
	  quo" contracts
		Writing, implementing, and evaluating
		  contracts

Increasing abilities to monitor self-talk	Practicing in problem-solving and conflict deescalation situations	Listing thoughts Writing cognitive scripts

Relapse prevention planning	Discussing effective strategies
	Planning ways to maintain positive
	  exchange rates
	Planning method to help maintain
	  interaction skill usage
	Fading treatment
		Making individual lists
		Choosing a monitoring method
		Deciding on cue to signal the need for a
		  tune-up
		Planning a booster

Note. From Robinson (1991, pp. 176, 179–180). Copyright 1991 by the American Psychological Association. Reprinted by permission of the publisher.

briefly committed following a threat to kill herself. The patient and her husband, a pleasant and mild-mannered school teacher, were seen together. When asked by the therapist, "What problem were you trying to solve?" and what each was hoping to get from therapy, Jackie said that she was tired of working all day and then coming home and having to cook and clean and do everything else as well. She and her husband had six children, "all supposedly adults," and three of the children were still living at home and did little to nothing to help. "They ignore me and laugh at me when I want something," she complained. The day of her hospitalization had been her birthday. When 10 P.M. came without a card or birthday greeting from anyone in the house, the identified patient became even more unhappy than usual. An overweight and diabetic woman, she had pulled out a syringe and had threatened to kill herself with a lethal overdose of insulin. Now she admitted that she probably would not have actually injected herself but that she was desperate and had just wanted them to pay attention to her.

Charles, the husband, said that he loved his wife and was greatly concerned, and admitted, "Yes, maybe I don't do enough." He then began to complain about the children still living at home, particularly one son who was lazy, borrowed money and never returned it, and generally acted the part of a ne'er-do-well. Jackie quickly began to protect the children. She would like the kids out, too, especially the troublesome son, but she was not willing to push him or "do any of that toughlove stuff" because it had taken a great deal of effort to get him off drugs and if he went back to the street he would probably quickly resume using and dealing. She reiterated her complaint that the family used her and ignored her and that her depression and suicidal threat were the result of frustration and isolation. When asked, "What's your goal for therapy, how will we know when to stop meeting like this?" Jackie responded: "I'd be happy if they would listen to me and treat me like a person and if I could sometimes get someone to do something for me without having to threaten to kill myself." When Charles then said, "I just want to have peace at home, and I try to do what I can," Jackie quickly became passive and acquiesced. She got quiet and looked obviously more unhappy. The husband tried to comfort her but she said "It's okay" and withdrew. Charles then averred, "This is what always happens. I know it's my fault, too, but I just can't stand any conflict, with Jackie or the kids."

Assessment at the hospital and in the office revealed no evidence for biological depression. (Jackie was overweight but her diabetes was well managed and stable.) Her unhappy mental status was a product of intertwined interactional and characterological factors. There was obviously poor communication and a lack of satisfying exchanges, conditions that were promoted by and in turn reinforcing of the patient's schemata of self and others and of future expectations. Her husband was fully part of the equation, too. Evaluation along the lines described in Tables 12.3 and 12.4 revealed a variety of problems that might be amenable to improvement with treatments designed to restructure thought processes, enhance coping skills, promote constructive problem solving, and increase satisfying marital interaction. The therapist remarked that improvement was possible but that hard work would be required and that progress might be slow, "but we won't meet any longer than we need to." To enhance motivation and promote cooperation, he added, "It's up to you, of course, but you know what they say—'If you don't change directions you'll wind up where you're heading.'" The couple knew they both needed help and agreed to participate in therapy together.

A series of weekly sessions was held. Careful attention was paid to helping each of them see how they thought and acted in ways that did (or did not) promote progress. Assertiveness training was provided. The focus was on helping the couple improve their skills in listening, validating, and making positive requests effectively, with both in-session practice and between-sessions "homework." Shared enjoyable activities were encouraged and prescribed, including an evening out together, a visit with friends, and a daily "report" time where each person talked for a few minutes (sometimes while going for a recommended walk together) about his or her day and feelings while the other listened actively. Progress was achieved, although not always smoothly, with both partners at times needing much encouragement not to give up or return too long to the counterproductive patterns that led to the crisis that had precipitated therapy.

Follow-Up and Comment. After 10 therapy sessions the couple was functioning with much more cooperation and mutual enjoyment. Jackie was not feeling depressed or suicidal and both partners began to express readiness to "take off the training wheels," as they put it. Two more weekly sessions were held to discuss ways to continue progress and to prevent relapse. We reviewed what they had learned and discussed strategies regarding how to recognize and respond to "warning signals" of emerging problems. Two follow-up sessions were then held, a month apart, to monitor progress. The couple was encouraged to continue what they had found effective and to recontact the therapist as needed.

The emphasis in this therapy was on the identification and modification of observable behaviors. The wife already had some awareness of her feelings and the use of suicidality as a way of solving her problems. She and her husband needed to learn more effective and healthy ways of getting their needs met. Informed by cognitive-behavioral and systemic perspectives (see Coyne, 1986; Shoham, Rohrbaugh, & Patterson, 1995), an integrated combination of techniques was employed.

At one point in the third session, the therapist made a mistake that could have had major deleterious effects for the therapy. He requested that the difficult son be brought to the next session. A week later Charles and Jackie came without the son. He had refused to attend but had suggested that his mother ask whether her "symptoms" could be manic–depressive illness. A few quick questions and answers ruled out the diagnosis. The therapist then quipped: "What you have is hereditary, though—if you don't work together you can get it from your kids!" The couple appreciated the humor and the message that emphasized family structure and the importance of the marital bond. The therapist also recognized that if the son had come in and if the therapist had tried to get the son out of the house, he probably would have failed, lost his power, and maybe lost his patients, as well. (Recall the husband's initial complaint about the son at home and the wife's refusal to put him out: The therapist might have appeared to be siding with the husband against the wife, who characteristically then might have withdrawn when feeling ganged up on and unappreciated.) One could approach the situation in many different ways, of course, but it was helpful to remember the primary agenda of the patients: greater marital harmony.[13] What might be called "resistance" could also be seen as the system providing feedback to the therapist about what was ready to happen. Interestingly, several sessions later—after the marital relationship was clearly improved—Jackie began a meeting by announcing that she and Charles had given the at-home children notice that they had to move out within 6 weeks, a decision the couple (and kids) followed through successfully. To be effective in brief therapy one sometimes needs to go slow and, to avoid stumbling, to take small steps in the right order.

Ericksonian Strategic–Systemic Approaches to Brief Therapy

The term "Ericksonian" is applied to a broad field of creative methods that derive their inspiration from the life and work of the remarkably innovative psychiatrist Milton H. Erickson. He overcame great personal adversities (such as paralytic polio) to develop a hypnosis-based approach oriented toward growth and problem solving via utilization of whatever assets the patient might bring to therapy. See Erickson's (1980) four-volume *Collected Papers* as well as several excellent books about his concepts and techniques, such as those by Haley (1973), Havens (1989), Lankton & Lankton (1983), O'Hanlon (1987), O'Hanlon & Hexum (1990), Zeig (1982), and Zeig & Lankton (1988). His work has directly or indirectly had a tremendous influence on many schools of therapy, including hypnotherapy, family therapy, and interactional approaches.

It is especially difficult to summarize Ericksonian strategic therapy because it is so individualistically based on the talents of particular patients and therapists—a situation that also makes systematic research quite problematic. Still, some broad outlines are possible. As Rosenbaum (1990) has described it:

> Strategic therapy is not a particular approach or theory. . . . It rather refers, in its broadest sense, to any therapy in which

the therapist is willing to take on the responsibility for influencing people and takes an active role in planning a strategy for promoting change. (p. 354)

Haley (1973) elaborates:

> Therapy can be called strategic if the clinician initiates what happens during therapy and designs a particular approach for each problem. When a therapist and a person with a problem encounter each other, the action that takes place is determined by both of them, but in strategic therapy the initiative is largely taken by the therapist. He must identify solvable problems, set goals, design interventions to achieve those goals, examine the responses he receives to correct his approach, and ultimately examine the outcome of his therapy to see if it has been effective. (p. 17)

What characterizes Ericksonian work? Lankton (1990) explains:

> The Ericksonian strategic approach is a method of working with clients emphasizing common, even unconscious natural abilities and talents. Therapy goals are built upon the intelligence and health of individuals. It works to frame change in ways that reduce resistance, reduce dependency upon therapy, bypass the need for insight, and allow clients to take full credit for changes. Most problems are not viewed as internal pathologies but as the natural result of solving developmental demands in ways that do not fully work for the people involved. The Ericksonian strategic approach is distinctive in that it is associated with certain interventions upon which it relies heavily during extramural assignments and therapy sessions. These include skill building homework, paradoxical directives, ambiguous function assignments, indirect suggestions, hypnosis, reframing, metaphors, and therapeutic binds. These are not so much interventions as characteristic parts of the therapist's interactions with clients. As such they are used to motivate clients to actively

participate in changing the way they live with themselves and others. (p. 364)

Lankton goes on to underscore that the Ericksonian approach emphasizes creative reorganization of relationships rather than a resistance-stimulating focus on diagnosing pathology. Noting that clients tend to follow suggestions that are most relevant to them, he also emphasizes that strategic therapy is interested in getting patients to take action outside the therapist's office:

It is from the learning brought by new actions and not from insight or understanding that change develops. Consequently, a client's understanding or insight about a problem is not of central importance. The matter of central importance is the client's participation in new experiences and transactions that congeal developmentally appropriate relational patterns. (Lankton, 1990, p. 365)[14]

For Lankton, Erickson's work has seven defining characteristics:

1. *Nonpathology-based model.* Problems are seen as part of, and a result of, attempts at adaptation; symptoms are essentially natural (but limiting) responses of unique individuals.
2. *Indirection.* This concerns itself with helping an individual or members of a family discover talents and resources, options, and answers, seemingly without the aid of the therapist.
3. *Utilization.* Whatever the patient brings to the office (understandings, behaviors, motivations) is used as part of the treatment.
4. *Action.* Clients are expected and encouraged to quickly get into actions related to desired goals—a basic ingredient of most successful brief therapies regardless of theoretical orientation (Budman, Friedman, & Hoyt, 1992).

5. *Strategic.* The therapist takes responsibility for influencing the patient and is active in setting or initiating the stages of therapy.
6. *Future orientation.* The focus is on action and experience in the present and future rather than the past.
7. *Enchantment.* Treatment engages the mind, appeals to the patient, and captures the ear of the listener.

Ericksonian interventions require careful attention to the three principles of proper evaluation and creative planning, cultivating and assuring patient commitment, and emphasizing on patient strengths and tailoring treatment to the individual (K. Erickson, 1988). The importance of *how* rather than *why* is also emphasized by Zeig (1990, p. 376), who stresses the utility of building on positive change and the accessing of the unconscious mind as a health-seeking source of solutions. He, too, values hypnosis and the tailoring and sequencing of treatment to fit the particular patient:

The job of the therapist in Ericksonian psychotherapy can be summarized as a five-step procedure that is conducted more simultaneously than sequentially:

1. Decide what to communicate to the patient.
2. Decide how to communicate it. Usually this entails being indirect, but it could be the presentation of any therapeutic maneuver.
3. Ascertain what the patient values; that is, the position the patient takes.
4. Divide the solution into manageable steps. Each step may be initiated by a therapeutic intervention.
5. Present the intervention within a therapeutic sequence, tailoring the intervention to fit the patient's values. This usually entails a three-step procedure: moving in small, directed Steps; Intervening; and Following Through. This procedure has been tabbed "SIFT." (Zeig, 1990, p. 373)

An "Ericksonian" perspective can be appreciated in a wide range of interventions:

1. The indirection of a police-officer asking for a cup of coffee as a way of separating a domestically disputing couple (Everstine & Everstine, 1983), or the charming Japanese folktale (retold by de Shazer, 1991b) of a villager who, unable to warn his neighbors of an impending tidal wave, sets their hillside terraces on fire so that they will rush up the mountain to battle the flames and thus inadvertently be saved from drowning.
2. The use of imagery and hypnosis to construct more useful realities (Andreas & Andreas, 1989; Bandler & Grinder, 1982; Erickson, Rossi, & Rossi, 1976; Lankton & Lankton, 1983; Yapko, 1990).
3. Instructing and motivating with teaching stories and metaphoric communications (Gordon, 1978; Rosen, 1982).
4. The use of provocation to challenge and motivate patients (Farrelly & Brandsma, 1974), including a last-ditch (and successful) effort to motivate a prideful patient out of a deep funk with humiliating taunts (Haley, 1973).
5. Prescribing ordeals, symptoms, and other paradoxical maneuvers (Weeks, 1991; Haley, 1984; Selvini-Palazzolli, Cecchin, Prata, & Boscolo, 1978) to get patients to abandon undesirable behaviors.
6. Assigning ambiguous tasks (such as having an unhappy couple climb a nearby peak) to structure a decision-making experience or elicit an unconscious understanding (Furman & Ahola, 1992; Lankton & Lankton, 1986).
7. Providing directives to alter the conflict-generating rules that govern relationships, as seen in various strategic–systemic therapies such as those developed at the Mental Research Institute of Palo Alto (Watzlawick et al., 1974; Fisch et al., 1982), the Family Therapy Institute of Washington, DC (Haley, 1977; Madanes, 1981), and the Brief Family Therapy Center of Milwaukee (de Shazer, 1982).

The basic principle underlying all these techniques and methods is *utilization*. The essential paradigmatic shift is from deficits to strengths, from problems to solutions, from past to future (Fisch, 1990, 1994), utilizing whatever the patient brings in the service of healthful change (de Shazer, 1988). For Erickson, the basic problem was not so much one of pathology or defect but *rigidity*, the idea that people get "stuck" by failing to use a range of skills, competencies, and learnings that they have but are not applying. Various interventions are thus designed to get people to have experiences that put them in touch with their latent or overlooked abilities. As Erickson said: "Patients have problems because their conscious programming has too severely limited their capacities. The solution is to help them break through the limitations of their conscious attitudes to free their unconscious potential for problem solving" (Erickson et al., 1976, p. 18).

Even a simple and relatively direct approach can have Ericksonian elements. Remembering how little can actually be conveyed through a single case presentation (including tone, timing, and nonverbal communication), consider the following report (adapted from Hoyt, 1993b; see also Hoyt, 1995a).

The Case of the Baseball Fan

Sam was a 67-year-old man when I met him sitting in a wheelchair next to his wife in the waiting room of the HMO psychiatry department. He had been referred by his internist: "Post-stroke. Fear of falling." When I introduced myself and shook hands I could see that he was a pleasant and engaging man. He had not shaved in a few days, was casually dressed, and was wearing an Oakland A's baseball cap. His wife immediately began to talk (a lot) and quickly told me that Sam could walk but was afraid to. He had come into the building on his own, then gotten into the wheelchair. She was nice and trying to be helpful, but I sensed that it would be useful to have some time with the patient alone, so I asked: "Do you want to walk or ride to my office?" He replied: "I'll take a ride, at least this time."

As I pushed him around the corner and down the corridor, we talked base-ball—about a recent trade and how the game had gone that day. His remarks showed a good knowledge of the game and an alert, up-to-date interest. I asked questions, and we connected as we talked.

At my office door I stopped and asked him to take a few steps into my office and use a regular chair, so that I would not have to move the furniture around—an indirect approach that used his natural courtesy to bypass discussion of his need for the wheelchair. He obliged. When we sat down I asked, "So, what's up?" I learned that he was a retired mechanic and printing pressman. He had suffered a stroke 3 years earlier, with a residual partial paralysis of one arm and leg. He had grown "too damn depen-dent" on his wife, he said, but could no longer drive and had considerable diffi-culty walking. "I sure miss Dr. Jarrett," he interjected, referring to his former in-ternist who had himself retired a few years earlier. When he told me what Dr. Jarrett would have said to get him mov-ing, I "borrowed" the good doctor's mantle of authority and replied: "Took the words right out of my mouth."

Sam went on to tell me that he wanted to go to an upcoming A's game his sons had invited him to, but he had to first overcome his great fear of falling because "I get so worried and down that I freeze up." He knew how to fall safely (pro-tecting his head and softening the fall) but was fearful because "I'm not sure what would happen to me if I fell and no one was around. I might not be able to get back up."

He was a practical man with a predica-ment. (By coincidence, I had the night before read my 4-year-old son a story about a series of animals that each gets stranded, culminating with an elephant stuck on his back until an ant he be-friended rescues him with the help of an ant hoard.) After ascertaining that he was not worried about safety or embar-rassment, I suggested: "I'll tell you what. Let's do a little experiment. I'll be you, you be the coach, and teach me how to get up." I then proceeded to sort of throw myself on the floor in front of him. He got right into it, advising me, "No, turn the other way, get up first on three points," etc. I said, "Let's try it with my arm not working," and held it limply against my side. For the next 8 to 10 minutes I repeatedly got down on the floor and Sam instructed me on how to get myself up again.

Back in my chair, I asked him if he wanted to "try it" there in my office or wait until he got home — an "illusion of alternatives" (Lankton & Lankton, 1983) with the underlying implication that he would perform the action. He chose to wait until he was home but offered to show me "some exercises I can still do." I watched and then asked him to "stand and do a little walking just so I can see how you do." I opened the office door and we proceeded into the corridor. We slowly made our way up and down the hallway, with my remarking a couple of times "Good," and "Nice, better than I expected." As we went up and down the hallway I switched back to baseball, ask-ing him about the game he was planning to attend with his sons. "Where are you going to park? Which ramp will you take?" I painted aloud a vivid picture of father and sons entering the baseball stadium as we made our way up and down the hallway a couple of times.

Back in my office he expressed concern about his wife. She was trying to be helpful but was wearing out both herself and Sam with her watchfulness. "Maybe you could talk to her, too," he asked. I said I would be glad to "when you begin to do more walking on your own so that I'll really be able to convince her to back off." He understood and agreed to practice his falling and getting up, and we playfully bargained about how many times he would do it a day, settling on twice a day to start and then three times a day until I saw him in 2 weeks.

Before leaving my office I added, "You know, I think it's really important that you go to that game with your sons if you can. I know you want to, but I think it will be even more important for them. Someday they will look back and remember going to the game with you, you know what I mean?" Sam did not know exactly how baseball was in my blood, my history of going to games with my father, but he knew I was saying something heartfelt and important.[15] It spoke to him: "I'm sure going to give it my best."

Follow-Up and Comment. When next I saw Sam he proudly walked into my office, slowly. He had been practicing and was eagerly anticipating going to the game the next week with his sons. I then brought his wife into the session and we talked about ways she could help by doing things and ways she could help by not doing things. Two weeks later, he told me about going to the game and his plans to go to another one. He also expressed the desire for more activity, and I suggested attending an older adults therapy group (see Hoyt, 1993a) as well as some other outings with neighbors and former coworkers. He followed through on these suggestions, and I re-main available if and when he may again request to meet with me.

Sam's worries about falling were taken seriously. The approach here was highly pragmatic, strategies being directed toward quickly getting the patient walking. It was helpful and felt natural to temporarily reverse roles, Sam becoming the teacher/coach rather than the humbled stroke patient. This was morale restoring and opened possibilities for change. The hallway walk into the ballpark was hypnotic and future oriented. His desire for assistance in managing his wife was used to further promote treatment compliance. Part of effective brief therapy is deciding what paths *not* to take. Exploring Sam's concerns about failing powers and limited mortality were issues that might be worthwhile (and would be addressed in the older adults group), but first helping Sam to regain his confidence in walking and being able to get up when he fell enhanced the quality of his life and put him in a stronger position to realistically appraise his future options. This is what Sam and his wife wanted. Being alert to and using whatever resources are available in the service of the patient's therapeutic needs—including the therapist's own personal experiences with baseball, inverted elephants, and father–son relations—is what I take Erickson and Rossi (1979) to mean when they suggest: "To initiate this type of therapy you have to be yourself as a person. You cannot imitate somebody else, but you have to do it in your own way" (p. 276).

An aspect of Ericksonian work that has received considerable attention recently is called *solution-focused* (de Shazer, 1985, 1988, 1991) or *solution-oriented* therapy (O'Hanlon & Martin, 1992; O'Hanlon & Weiner-Davis, 1989; O'Hanlon & Wilks, 1987). The basic premise is deceptively simple: Increase what works; decrease what doesn't work. What are the "exceptions" to the problem? What is the patient doing differently at those times when he/she/they are not anxious, depressed, quarreling, and so on? What has worked before? What strengths can the patient apply? What would be a useful solution? How to construct it? Behind these apparently simple questions is a profound paradigmatic shift: Competencies, not dysfunctions, are the focus; the quest is to access latent capacities, not latent conflicts. The orientation is toward the future and toward the full appreciation and utilization of human abilities. Some aspects of this shift are delineated in Table 12.4. The approach is not just technical, but when taken to heart epitomizes what is best about the Ericksonian perspective: the belief that with skillful facilitation, people have within themselves the resources necessary to achieve their goals.

One of the leading solution-focused therapists, Steve de Shazer (1985, 1988, 1991b), prefers minimalist interventions. He sometimes "fast-forwards" to a solution by asking the "Miracle Question": "Suppose tonight while you're sleeping a miracle happens and the problem that brought you here is resolved. . . . How will you know, in the morning, that a miracle has happened?" Patients get enchanted by the question and, with or without prompting, draw on their own wisdom and experience to create answers that are uniquely theirs and thus more hopeful and likely to occur. Various methods can then be used to promote continued changes (Adams, Piercy, Jurich, 1991; Kral & Kowalski, 1989). As the title of a number of useful books have it: *In Search of Solutions* (O'Hanlon & Weiner-Davis, 1989), we welcome *Clues* (de Shazer, 1988) and *Keys to Solutions in Brief Therapy* (de Shazer, 1985) since *Becoming Solution-Focused in Brief Therapy* (Walter & Peller, 1992) leads to *Constructive Therapies* (Hoyt, 1994a, in press-b), *Putting Difference to Work* (de Shazer, 1991b), *Solution Talk* (Furman & Ahola, 1992b), *Therapeutic Conversations* (Gilligan & Price, 1993), and *The New Language of Change* (Friedman, 1993), which may yield *Expanding Therapeutic Possibilities* (Friedman & Fanger, 1991), perhaps even in *Single Session Therapy* (Talmon, 1990), that will help in *Rewriting Love Stories* (Hudson & O'Hanlon, 1992), *Resolving Sexual Abuse* (Dolan, 1991), *Di-*

TABLE 12.4. Solution-Building Vocabulary

In	Out	In	Out
Respect	Judge	Forward	Backward
Empower	Fix	Future	Past
Nurture	Control	Collaborate	Manipulate
Facilitate	Treat	Options	Conflicts
Augment	Reduce	Partner	Expert
Invite	Insist	Horizontal	Hierarchical
Appreciate	Diagnose	Possibility	Limitation
Hope	Fear	Growth	Cure
Latent	Missing	Access	Defense
Assets	Defects	Utilize	Resist
Strength	Weakness	Create	Repair
Health	Pathology	Exception	Rule
Not Yet	Never	Difference	Sameness
Expand	Shrink	Solution	Problem

Note. From Hoyt (1994d, p. 4). Copyright 1994 by The Guilford Press. Reprinted by permission of the publisher.

vorce Busting (Weiner-Davis, 1992), *Making Friends with Your Unconscious Mind* (Hudson, 1993), pursuing *Narrative Means to Therapeutic Ends* (White & Epston, 1990), and *Working with the Problem Drinker* (Berg & Miller, 1992)!

EVEN ONE SESSION (OR LESS) MAY BE ENOUGH (FOR NOW)

Therapy should not be "long term" or "short term." It should be sufficient, adequate, and appropriate, "measured not by its brevity or length, but whether it is efficient and effective in aiding people with their complaints or whether it wastes time" (Fisch, 1982, p. 156). Many people solve psychological problems without professional consultation. For some others, the "light touch" of a single visit may be enough, providing experience, skills, and encouragement to help them get "unstuck" and continue in their life journey. If used appropriately, such "ultra brief" treatments can promote patients' sense of self-empowerment and autonomy (versus dependency) as well as conserve limited resources for those truly requiring longer treatments.

Considerable evidence has accumulated (see Bloom, 1992b; Rosenbaum et al., 1990; Talmon, 1990) that single-session therapy—one visit without further contacts—is de facto the modal or most common length of treatment, generally occurring 20–50% of the time. While most traditional psychotherapy training suggests that stopping after one visit is "dropping out" or "premature termination," there exists scattered through the literature anecdotal reports by leading practitioners of varying theoretical perspectives suggesting the utility of single-session therapy (SST) with selected patients. The list of authorities reporting successful one-session treatments, beginning with Freud, reads like a *Who's Who* in the psychotherapy field: Berne, Davanloo, Erickson, Goulding and Goulding, Haley, Lazarus, Mahrer, Malan, Sifneos, Sullivan, Whitaker, Winnicott, Wolberg, and others (see Bloom, 1981, 1992b; Hoyt et al., 1992; Rosenbaum et al., 1990). There are also three more systematic studies of the effectiveness of single-session therapy.

1. Medical utilization was found to be reduced 60% over 5-year follow-up after a single session of psychotherapy in a study done at the Kaiser Permanente Health Plan (the nation's largest health maintenance organization) by Follette and Cummings (1967). A second study (Cummings & Follette, 1976) found the benefits of SST still in effect after 8 years and concluded that decreased medical utilization was due to a reduction in physical symptoms related to emotional stress.

2. Significant symptom improvements years later were noted by Malan, Heath, Bacal, and Balfour (1975) in 51% of "untreated" patients who had only an intake interview (which served to increase their insight and sense of personal responsibility) conducted at the Tavistock Clinic in London, and half of those patients were also judged to have made important personality modifications.[16]

3. Patients and therapists agreed that a single treatment visit had been sufficient in 58.6% (34 of 58) of attempted SSTs in another study conducted at Kaiser Permanente by Hoyt, Rosenbaum, and Talmon (reported in Talmon, 1990). The other patients continued meeting with their therapists. On 3- to 12-month follow-ups, 88% of the SST-only patients reported either "much improvement" or "improvement" in their presenting symptoms since the session, and 65% also reported other positive "ripple" effects, figures that were slightly (and

statistically insignificantly) higher than those for the 24 patients seen more than once.

There is no single method or goal for attempting SST other than being with patients and using the skills that patient and therapist bring to the endeavor. Treatments may be as varied as the patients (and therapists) and what they come to accomplish. Single-session therapies, like all forms of psychotherapy, can occur either by default (usually when the patient stops unilaterally) or by design (when patient and therapist mutually agree that additional sessions are not then indicated). The choice of a single session (or more, or less) should, whenever possible, be left to the patient. "Let's see what we can get done today," is much more "user friendly" and likely to succeed than the resistance-stimulating, "We're only going to meet one time." Most effective SST is thus *not* time-limited therapy—it is open-ended and the patient elects to stop after one visit.

A single therapy session will not be sufficient or appropriate for many patients, of course, although the following brief examples may suggest some of the instances in which a single visit promoted new learnings, enhanced coping, and growth, a chance for the patient to make a productive shift or pivot. In each case, the patient made the choice (with the therapist's assent) to complete treatment with the one session and agreed to return for additional treatment when desired.

Case 1. An elderly gentleman made an appointment in our HMO psychiatry clinic, indicating to the receptionist that his reason for seeking services was "guilt." It turned out that his wife had died in surgery the year before. He missed her. His mourning and adjustment were disrupted by his gnawing sense of guilt. He had advocated that she

undergo the high-risk surgery, he said, to help her but also "for my own selfish reasons. I wanted her well so we could travel and do the things I enjoy. If I hadn't pushed her, she'd be alive today." We had a long and poignant talk. Reviewing the facts, her medical situation and prognosis (with or without surgery), the distinction between grief and guilt, her willingness to have the surgery, and "What else do you feel guilty about?" ("I wasn't always the best husband") left him feeling relieved. We discussed some practical steps he would be taking. He had a good network of support from friends and family. He was grateful for our talk ("I really see things differently now") and felt no need to return.

Case 2. Chronic nightmares in 23 patients were successfully treated with one session of desensitization or rehearsal instruction, with 7-month follow-up, according to a recent report by Kellner, Neidhardt, Krakow, and Pathak (1992). Half the patients were instructed to practice progressive relaxation while imagining the nightmare; the other patients were instructed to write down a recent nightmare, change it and write down the modified version, and rehearse the changed nightmare in imagery while in a relaxed state. In both conditions, patients were seen once and were to practice at home. On follow-up, the two methods were both successful and no one had worsened, whereas in a quasi-control group (consisting of seven persons who were not treated after initial evaluation because of illness or declining to participate) less change had occurred and two patients had actually worsened.

Case 3. A ceremony was used as part of an elaborate production to help a woman "emotionally divorce" her abusive father (see Talmon, Hoyt, & Rosenbaum, 1990, pp. 45–47, for a truncated report of the case). To help consolidate her gains and demarcate a before-and-after change of status (cf. White & Epston, 1990), the patient (with her husband attending) read an extraordinary auto-biographical plaint, played carefully selected music, and burned her father's photograph in my office. Hypnotherapeutic "inner child" work was also done. At the end of the session and on follow-up the patient felt considerable relief in regard to her relationship with her father, but she also continued to have other psychological problems that might have benefited from additional therapy.

Case 4. Parents brought their teenage son to therapy because of difficulties they were having setting limits and maintaining what they felt to be an appropriate level of control and discipline over him. In our meeting a variety of techniques were used, including family sculpting (in which silent poses are held to nonverbally accentuate relationship patterns), behavioral skill training, and some exploration of the parents' own families-of-origin experiences with parenting. By the end of the session, which lasted 75 minutes, they had the hang of it and felt they could carry on successfully at home. A follow-up phone call a month later confirmed that they were managing and maintaining what they had come to accomplish.

Many additional clinical examples of successful single-session therapies can be found in the work of Bloom (1981, 1992b), Hoyt (1990, 1993b, 1994b, 1994c), Hoyt and Talmon (1990), Hoyt et al. (1992), Rosenbaum (1990, 1993, 1994), Rosenbaum et al. (1990), Spoerl (1975), and Talmon (1990, 1993). These reports also contain important information about productive attitudes and orientations, clinical guidelines and technical methods, plus various cautions and contraindications such as inappropriately stopping treatment with suicidal or psychotic patients. Although SST is obviously not a panacea nor even appropriate for everyone, clinical experience and some preliminary supporting data suggest that when given the choice many patients elect a single treatment session

and find it useful, especially if the therapist is open to this possibility and oriented toward maximizing the impact of the session.

A LONG FUTURE FOR BRIEF THERAPY

Brief therapy has a long history, beginning with Freud, and it appears that it will have a long future as well. The convergence of market forces, the desire of most persons for rapid relief from psychological distress, and the development of new treatment technologies augur well for the continued ascendancy of short-term therapy. HMOs, the emergence of managed care, and the continuing debate about some form of national health care reform as responses to the runaway costs of health services all suggest the further expansion of brief treatment. What is clear is that consumers, insurers, and health care professionals are all increasingly recognizing the importance of providing psychotherapeutic services that are as efficient as possible. As Shectman (1986) has said, necessity sometimes proves to be the mother of intervention. Brief therapy methods are becoming increasingly attractive, both as treatments of choice and for their value in resource conservation.

Managed care—which may be defined as arrangements to regulate the costs, site, and/or utilization of services (Austad & Hoyt, 1992)—has been estimated as covering 100 million Americans in 1992, with numbers growing rapidly each year. Short-term therapy is the backbone of managed care mental health services. Cutting across various administrative systems and specific brief therapy approaches are a series of principles that characterize what Austad and Berman (1991), Hoyt and Austad (1992), and Hoyt (1995b) have called *HMO therapy*. These principles summarize much of what constitutes effective brief psychotherapy:

1. *Rapid setting of clearly defined goals*, with an orientation toward specific problem solving. A rapid, accurate assessment leads to an effective and comprehensive treatment plan. In many cases, assessment and intervention are intertwined, with trial interventions being used to refine the working diagnosis.

2. *Rapid response and crisis intervention preparedness*, so that problems are dealt with before they get entrenched or produce secondary problems.

3. *Clear definition of patient and therapist responsibilities*, including a clear understanding (sometimes called a "contract") of the purpose, schedule, and duration of treatment. The patient is encouraged to assume much of the initiative and responsibility for the work of therapy, including carrying out "homework" tasks and implementing behavioral changes outside therapy sessions.

4. *Flexible and creative use of time*, varying the frequency, length, and timing of treatment sessions according to patient needs.

5. *Interdisciplinary cooperation*, including the use of psychopharmacology when needed.

6. *Use of multiple formats and modalities*, with treatments sometimes involving concurrent or sequential combinations of individual, group, and/or family therapy. Referrals to appropriate community resources are also frequent, including various 12-step, self-help, and support groups.

7. *Intermittent treatment* and a "family practitioner" model that replaces the notion of a definitive once-and-for-all "cure" with the idea that the patient can return for "serial" or "distributed" treatment through the life cycle (Cummings & Sayama, 1995). The therapist–patient relationship may be long term although frequently abeyant; as soon as the therapist is not needed, he or she recedes into the background of the patient's life until needed again. The brief therapist operates like a road service to help people who have gotten "stuck" (Bergman, 1985) get back "on track" (Walter & Peller, 1994). But would it not be strange if, after repairing your tire, the service person jumped into your car and rode along with you or insisted that you pass by the shop every week to make sure you are still going okay?

8. *Accountability and results orientation*, the evaluation of services to see if work is being accomplished in an efficient manner. *Utilization review* monitors that services are not being offered wastefully; *quality assurance* makes sure treatment goals are being met.

We can expect training in brief therapy to expand dramatically in the coming years, stimulated by both the demands of consumers for more efficient mental health services and the fiscal pressures of managed care (Butler, 1992; Goode, 1992). While there has been some attention paid to aspects of brief therapy teaching and learning—such as potential parallel processes between therapy and training (Dasberg & Winokur, 1984; Frances & Clarkin, 1981a; Hoyt, 1991), the use of manuals (Levenson & Butler, 1994), and the impact of training on skills and attitudes (Burlingame & Behrman, 1987; Burlingame, Fuhriman, Paul, & Ogles, 1989; Henry, Schacht, Strupp, Binder, & Butler, 1993; Levenson & Bolter, 1988)—there has been a dearth of high-quality training for most clinicians. A recent study by Levenson, Speed, and Budman (1992) of psychologists in California and Massachusetts, for example, found that while most therapists report a sizable portion of their clinical work to be short-term treatment, one-third of those doing brief therapy reported having minimal training in brief therapy techniques, and more than 25%

of all brief treatment hours were being conducted by clinicians with little or no formal training in the special orientation and skills of time-sensitive therapy! Even in managed care settings such as HMOs, preferred provider organizations (PPOs), and employee assistance programs (EAPs), there has been up to now surprisingly little attention to systematic training in brief therapy (Budman & Armstrong, 1992; Hoyt, 1991). Combining the fiscal imperative of the managed care movement with the fact that brief therapy is the treatment of choice for many patients, serving their needs as well as providing the socioeconomic advantage of allowing patients who would otherwise go without to receive the benefits of professional mental health care, we can expect increasing attention to the practice and study of brief psychotherapy in the years ahead.

CODA

The goal of brief psychotherapy, regardless of the specific theoretical approach or technical method, is to help the patient resolve a problem, to get "unstuck" and to move on. Techniques are specific, integrated, and as eclectic as needed. Treatment is focused, the therapist appropriately active, and the patient responsible for making changes. Each session is valuable, and therapy ends as soon as possible. Good outcome, not good process, is most valued. More is not better; *better* is better. The patient carries on and can return to treatment as needed. The simple truth is that most therapy *is* brief therapy and will be increasingly so; for the sake of our patients and our profession, we should learn to practice it well.

NOTES

1. Setting a specific number of sessions may at times be helpful, for example, to provide structuring (Wells, 1982) or to deliberately stimulate a termination process (Mann, 1973; Hoyt, 1979, 1990). Attention to temporal parameters is important since Parkinson's law ("Work expands or contracts to fit the allotted time") may operate in psychotherapy (Appelbaum, 1975). Generally, however, the focus should not be on the limit but on the present. If one makes the most of each session, treatment will be efficient and as brief as possible.

2. One can also question whether brief therapy is a "resistance" to doing long-term work (e.g., if there is sometimes operating in brief therapists a countertherapeutic desire to avoid extended intimacy, the demands of a prolonged nurturing-dependent relationship, and possible discomfort with "deeper" levels of psychological material). These could all be true in certain instances, of course, although good brief therapists do not turn away from painful subjects if they need to be addressed for useful change to occur. The brief therapist's quest, however, is to help people change in ways that will make the therapist unnecessary as soon as possible; mirroring the finitude of life itself, the goal is termination rather than proliferation (Goldberg, 1975). To point out the strange logic that suspects those who help quickly, Duncan, Drewry, Hubble, Rusek, and Bruening (1992; also see Haley, 1969) have written a spoof titled "Brief Therapy Addiction: The Secret Compulsion," in which Duncan confesses in a tongue-in-cheek way his weakness for efficient treatment, so typical of those with "pragmatic personality disorder," and reports that he and his Inner Child are "in recovery" and attending daily Brief Therapy Anonymous meetings!

3. In this regard, Haley (1990, pp. 14–15) has observed: "When we look at the history of therapy, the most important decision ever made was to charge for therapy by the hour. The ideology and practice of therapy was largely determined when therapists chose to sit with a client and be paid for durations of time rather than by results." Recognizing that "therapy will become briefer as insurance companies limit the length of therapy" (p. 14), he foresees changes in the basic financing of therapy and recommends charging a flat fee for relief of a symptom since such an arrangement would require thera-

pists to hone skills and increase efficiency. Actually, similar arrangements already do exist, in managed health-care plans such as closed-panel HMOs where the company is "at risk" to provide all needed services in exchange for a set payment (Broskowski, 1991), and in preferred provider networks where continued referrals will depend upon demonstrated efficacy. Such situations necessitate that treatment be efficient and thus mostly brief. Wells and Phelps (1990) characterize this emerging trend as "Survival of the Shortest."

4. Throughout this chapter the terms "patient" and "client" are used interchangeably, as they tend to be in the literature. The former term may carry more connotation of distress and a quest for relief (not necessarily in a medical model, although the implication is that of a relatively passive supplicant), while the latter term may seem more "egalitarian" or "businesslike" (but may deny the special quality of suffering that leads people to seek mental health services). It is important to recognize what the choice of either term may imply regarding the model of helping relationship being coconstructed by the patient/client and therapist and how these implications may impact on their subsequent work together (Hoyt, 1979b, 1985b).

5. de Shazer (1991b, p. 112) has described the general characteristics of well-formed goals: (1) small rather than large; (2) salient to clients; (3) described in specific, concrete behavioral terms; (4) achievable within the practical contexts of clients' lives; (5) perceived by the clients as involving their "hard work"; (6) described as the "start of something" and not as the "end of something"; and (7) treated as involving new behavior(s) rather than the absence or cessation of existing behavior(s).

6. Barten (1971) went on to say:

> Once we redefine our task as the provision of treatment services to patients in all classes with all kinds of problems, traditional, slow-paced techniques become obviously insufficient. . . . Poor and uneducated patients in particular seemed unreached by sophisticated techniques which they found alien and esoteric, assuming they were even available. As a rule these pa-

tients want therapists who are warmly supportive and who provide concrete help rather than an opportunity to examine feelings, though some of them can be taught how to utilize the latter approach. (p. 7)

While this statement—like any about an entire group or social class—may be an oversimplification, it is true that much psychotherapy is primarily oriented toward the lifestyles, values, and problems of the middle and upper classes. The complicated issues of culture, class, ethnicity, and race go far beyond the scope of this discussion, of course, and the reader is referred to Kupers (1981), McGoldrick, Pearce, and Giordano (1982), Lorion and Felner (1986), Sue (1990), Mays and Albee (1992), and Gonzalez, Biever, and Gardner (1994) for useful overviews. One needs to appreciate cultural differences and work respectfully, especially if one hopes to form a rapid working alliance and mobilize patients' resources for their therapeutic benefit in brief therapy. It should also be recognized that while psychotherapy can play a valuable role—and especially brief therapy with its emphasis on efficiency and specific goals—problems that fundamentally result from pernicious social and economic conditions may require redress at political and socioeconomic levels.

7. The questions one asks, beginning with the first, do much to set the theme and temporal orientation of each session and the overall treatment (Goulding & Goulding, 1979; Hoyt, 1990; Kaiser, 1965; Melges, 1982; Yapko, 1989). If one asks, for example, "How have things gone?" the direction is largely toward reviewing the *past*. If one instead asks, "What are you experiencing? or "What are you willing to change today?" the direction is more *present* centered. Asking "What do you need to discuss to do well next week?" or "How will you be different when the problem is solved?" points to the *future*.

8. Alexander and French (1946), probably influenced by the geopolitical *Zeitgeist*, used an important military metaphor: They likened the therapist at the beginning of treatment to a general overlooking the battlefield, deciding where to deploy the troops. Once the fray is joined, the overall perspective changes as one becomes more of a participant-ob-

server. Where best to focus, to expend one's energies?

9. I (M.F.H.) was the therapist in each case reported, and all treatments occurred within the context of a staff-model HMO (Hoyt, 1995b).

10. Freud was not opposed to such developments, although he made it abundantly clear that one should not confuse such alloys with the "pure gold of analysis." In 1910 he wrote:

> In practice, it is true, there is nothing to be said against a psychotherapist combining a certain amount of analysis with some suggestive influence in order to achieve a perceptible result in a shorter time. . . . But one has a right to insist that he himself should be in no doubt about what he is doing and should know that his method is not that of true psychoanalysis. (pp. 111–120)

In his later paper, "Analysis Terminable and Interminable," Freud (1937) further cautioned that the introduction of nonanalytic elements would interfere with or even eliminate the possibility of completing a formal psychoanalysis in a given case.

11. The famous "I'm OK, You're OK" phrase was actually coined by Robert Goulding in a discussion with Berne (Hoyt, in press-a).

12. Also see de Shazer's (1984) discussion of "The Death of Resistance." In this regard, another interesting perspective is provided by Furman and Ahola (1992a):

> In our view, therapists are like pickpockets on a nudist camp. Some of them see front pockets and some see back pockets, depending on their particular specialisation. The therapist has to actually sew pockets on to the clients in order to start stealing. Fortunately, clients are very generous and they will let the therapist sew almost any type of pocket on them in order to let the therapist do the job. If, however, the client shows signs of discomfort in the process of sewing, this is aptly called resistance. (p. 8)

13. While a cognitive-behavioral model is particularly useful in brief couples therapy because it lends itself readily to specifying particular actions to be changed (thus avoiding broad generalizations that can easily lead to conflict escalation), it is also important to have an overarching integrated view that includes interpersonal, developmental, and existential perspectives (Budman & Gurman, 1988). As Gurman (1992) has written:

> We detail the areas of assessment that we find important to be aware of in most, if not all, couples therapy: presenting problems, attempted solutions, and the consequences of change; individual and couple assets and strengths; communication and problem-solving skills and styles; styles of influence; relational boundaries; life-cycle status and accomplishment; affection and attachment; marital (couple) relationship history; sexuality and sexual functioning; relationship commitment; spousal and substance abuse. . . . keep in mind that "assessment" does not end at the end of the first session. (p. 199)

14. Since the strategic therapist assumes responsibility for using the treatment session to "make something happen," key significance is not placed on the session *per se* but on what results *from* the session. Whereas traditional psychodynamic therapists largely judge the "good session" (Hoyt, 1980; Hoyt, Xenakis, Marmar, & Horowitz, 1983) by the depth of feeling and meaningfulness of what occurs in the consulting room, strategic therapists are more directly concerned about what happens after the session and thus will need to see its impact (outcome: change and durability) before assessing the "goodness" of a session.

15. I love the story my father told me (recounted in Hoyt, 1993a) about the time he was at a baseball game at Wrigley Field in Chicago, and a drunken and belligerent fan in the bleachers was verbally abusing one of the players. The man let it be known that he was packing a gun, and it became alarmingly possible that he might use it. My father, who was a salesman by trade and something of a strategic therapist, got involved. Dad was also a gun fancier, and he got the irate fan engaged in a discussion about the type of gun, showed some interest, and wound up bargaining and buying the gun on the spot. (The police never came.) When I asked my father what he had done with the weapon,

he said he had taken it to a shop and sold it—for a profit. When I asked why he had done that, he replied, "Hey, you've got to get paid for this kind of work!"

16. A similar study by Jacobson (1968) at the Beth Israel Hospital in Boston examined the effects of two hour-long evaluation interviews and also found many patients to have benefited significantly from such a brief psychiatric encounter.

SUGGESTIONS FOR FURTHER READING

Among the many outstanding resources available, the following books are especially recommended to continue learning about brief therapy:

Bloom, B. L. (1992). *Planned short-term psychotherapy.* Boston: Allyn & Bacon. An encyclopedia of brief therapy approaches, each summarized and concisely illustrated in a few pages.

Budman, S. H., & Gurman, A. S. (1988). *Theory and practice of brief therapy.* New York: Guilford Press. Excellent overview of various methods integrated into an interpersonal–developmental-existential framework.

Budman, S. H., Hoyt, M. F., & Friedman, S. (Eds.). (1992). *The first session in brief therapy.* New York: Guilford Press. A unique collection of essays by various master practitioners of brief therapy in which, after short theoretical descriptions, the reader gets to look over each therapist's shoulder and see how he or she works in ways that characterize the beginning steps of effective treatment within each particular approach.

Cummings, N., & Sayama, M. (1995). *Focused psychotherapy: A casevook of brief, intermittent psychotherapy throughout the life cycle.* New York: Brunner/Mazel. Highly original and savvy treatment in case after case of real-life therapy.

de Shazer, S. (1988). *Clues: Investigating solutions in brief therapy.* New York: Norton. Elegantly precise examination of the things that therapist and client do during

a session that lead to discovering "what works" and a solution.

Fisch, R., Weakland, J. H., & Segal, L. (1982). *The tactics of change: Doing therapy briefly.* San Francisco: Jossey-Bass. The major exposition of the highly influential strategic–interactional approach developed at the Mental Research Institute of Palo Alto, California.

Haley, J. (1973). *Uncommon therapy: The psychiatric techniques of Milton Erickson, M.D.* New York: Norton. A fascinating introduction to the work of the genius who spawned many schools of strategic interventions, family therapy, and hypnotherapy.

Hoyt, M. F. (Ed.) (1994). *Constructive therapies.* New York: Guilford Press. Experts illustrate a variety of "user-friendly" collaborative and future-oriented treatment approaches based on the facilitation of patients' existing strengths and competencies. (Volume 2 is in press.)

Hoyt, M. F. (1995). *Brief therapy and managed care: Readings for contemporary practice.* San Francisco: Jossey-Bass. Key information on methods and models of brief therapy, especially as they pertain to the evolving requirements of insurance coverage and possible health care reform.

Johnson, L. D. (1995). *Psychotherapy is the age of accountability.* New York: Norton. Very thoughtful and integrated view promoting well-focused, quality-oriented treatment to meet the challenge of managed care.

O'Hanlon, W. H., & Weiner-Davis, M. (1989). *In search of solutions: A new direction in psychotherapy.* New York: Norton. A major statement, with illuminating discussions of assumptions and strategies, of the trend toward emphasizing strengths and solutions rather than problems and pathology.

Strupp, H. H., & Binder, J. L. (1984). *Psychotherapy in a new key: A guide to time-limited dynamic psychotherapy.* New York: Basic Books. Valuable description of an approach that combines contemporary psychodynamic and interpersonal formulations to help patients resolve maladaptive interpersonal patterns via both increased self-awareness and the achievement of corrective emotional experiences within the therapeutic relationship.

Zeig, J. K., & Gilligan, S. G. (Eds.) (1990). *Brief therapy: Myths, methods, and metaphors.* New York: Brunner/Mazel. The proceedings of the historic 1988 San Francisco conference, containing the keynote addresses and major papers given by many presenters of various theoretical persuasions.

REFERENCES

References marked with (*) have been reprinted in M. F. Hoyt (1995). *Brief therapy and managed care: Readings for contemporary practice.* San Francisco: Jossey-Bass.

Adams, J. F., Piercy, F. P., & Jurich, J. A. (1991). Effects of solution focused therapy's "formula first session task" on compliance and outcome in family therapy. *Journal of Marital and Family Therapy, 17,* 277–290.

Addis, M. E., & Jacobson, N. S. (1991). Integration of cognitive therapy and behavioral marital therapy for depression. *Journal of Psychotherapy Integration, 4,* 249–264.

Alexander, F., & French, T. M. (1946). *Psychoanalytic therapy: Principles and applications.* New York: Ronald Press.

American Psychiatric Association. (1994). *Diagnostic and statistical manual of mental disorders* (4th ed.). Washington, DC: Author.

Andreas, C., & Andreas, S. (1989). *Heart of the mind.* Moab, UT: Real People Press.

Appelbaum, S. A. (1975). Parkinson's law in psychotherapy. *International Journal of Psychoanalytic Psychotherapy, 4,* 426–436.

Austad, C. S., & Berman, W. H. (Eds.). (1991). *Psychotherapy in managed health care.* Washington, DC: American Psychological Association.

Austad, C. S., & Hoyt, M. F. (1992). The managed care movement and the future of psychotherapy. *Psychotherapy, 29,* 109–118.

Balint, M., Ornstein, P. H., & Balint, E. (1972). *Focal psychotherapy.* London: Tavistock.

Bandler, R., & Grinder, J. (1982). *Reframing.* Moab, UT: Real People Press.

Barten, H. H. (Ed.). (1971). *Brief therapies.* New York: Behavioral Publications.

Bauer, G. P., & Kobos, J. C. (1987). *Brief therapy: Short-term psychodynamic intervention.* New York: Jason Aronson.

Beach, S. R. H., Sandeen, E. E., & O'Leary, K. D. (1990). *Depression in marriage: A model for etiology and treatment.* New York: Guilford Press.

Beck, A. T. (1976). *Cognitive therapy and the emotional disorders.* New York: International University Press.

Beck, A. T. (1988). *Love is never enough.* New York: Harper & Row.

Beck, A. T., Freeman, A., & Associates. (1990). *Cognitive therapy of personality disorders.* New York: Guilford Press.

Beck, A. T., Rush, A. J., Shaw, B. F., & Emery, G. (1979). *Cognitive therapy of depression.* New York: Guilford Press.

Bellak, L., & Small, L. (1965). *Emergency therapy and brief psychotherapy.* New York: Grune & Stratton.

Bennett, M. J. (1983). Focal psychotherapy—terminable and interminable. *American Journal of Psychotherapy, 37,* 365–375.

Bennett, M. J. (1984). Brief psychotherapy and adult development. *Psychotherapy, 21,* 171–177.

Berg, I. K., & Miller, S. D. (1992). *Working with the problem drinker.* New York: Norton.

Bergman, J. S. (1985). *Fishing for barracuda: Pragmatics of brief systemic therapy.* New York: Norton.

Berne, E. (1961). *Transactional Analysis in psychotherapy.* New York: Grove Press.

Berne, E. (1964). *Games people play.* New York: Grove Press.

Berne, E. (1972). *What do you say after you say hello?* New York: Grove Press.

Bibring, E. (1954), Psychoanalysis and the dynamic psychotherapies. *Journal of the American Psychoanalytic Association, 2,* 745–770.

Blackstone, P. (1987). Loving too much—disease or decision? *Transactional Analysis Journal, 17,* 185–190.

Bloom, B. L. (1981). Focused single-session therapy: Initial development and evaluation. In S. H. Budman (Ed.), *Forms of brief therapy* (pp. 167–216). New York: Guilford Press.

Bloom, B. L. (1992a). *Planned short-term psychotherapy.* Boston: Allyn & Bacon.

Bloom, B. L. (1992b). Bloom's focused single-session therapy. In *Planned short-term psychotherapy* (pp. 97–121). Boston: Allyn & Bacon.

Brehm, J. (1966). *A psychological theory of reactance.* New York: Appleton-Century-Crofts.

Breuer, J., & Freud, S. (1893–1895). Studies in hysteria. *Standard Edition, 2,* 1–319. London: Hogarth Press, 1955.

Broskowski, A. (1991). Current mental health care environments: Why managed care is necessary. *Professional Psychology: Research and Practice, 22,* 6–14.

Budman, S. H. (Ed.). (1981). *Forms of brief therapy.* New York: Guilford Press.

Budman, S. H., & Armstrong, E. (1992). Training for managed care setting: How to make it happen. *Psychotherapy, 29,* 416–421.

Budman, S. H. (1990). The myth of termination in brief therapy: Or, it ain't over till it's over. In J. K. Zeig & S. G. Gilligan (Eds.), *Brief therapy: Myths, methods, and metaphors* (pp. 206–218). New York: Brunner/Mazel.

Budman, S. H., Friedman, S., & Hoyt, M. F. (1992). Last words on first sessions. In S. H. Budman, M. F. Hoyt, & S. Friedman (Eds.), *The first session in brief therapy* (pp. 345–358). New York: Guilford Press.

Budman, S. H., & Gurman, A. S. (1988). *Theory and practice of brief therapy.* New York: Guilford Press.

Budman, S. H., Hoyt, M. F., & Friedman, S. H. (Eds.). (1992). *The first session in brief therapy.* New York: Guilford Press.

Burbach, D. J., Borduin, C. M., & Peake, T. H. (1988). Cognitive approaches to brief psychotherapy. In T. H. Peake, C. M. Borduin, & R. P. Archer, *Brief psychotherapies* (pp. 57–86). Newbury Park, CA: Sage.

Burlingame, G. M., & Behrman, J. A. (1987). Clinician attitudes toward time-limited and time-unlimited therapy. *Professional Psychology: Research and Practice, 18,* 61–65.

Burlingame, G. M., Fuhriman, A., Paul, S., & Ogles, B. M. (1989). Implementing a time-limited therapy program: Differential effects of training and experience. *Psychotherapy, 26,* 303–312.

Burns, D. D. (1980). *Feeling good: The new mood therapy.* New York: Signet.

Burns, D. D. (1989) *The feeling good handbook.* New York: Plume.

Butler, K. (1992, April 15). Hard times shrink psychotherapy. *San Francisco Chronicle,* pp. 1, A6.

Butler, S. F., Strupp, H. H., & Binder, J. L. (1992). Time-limited dynamic psychotherapy. In S. H. Budman, M. F. Hoyt, & S. Friedman (Eds.), *The first session in brief therapy* (pp. 87–110). New York: Guilford Press.

Cade, B., & O'Hanlon, W. H. (1993). *A brief guide to brief therapy.* New York: Norton.

Coyne, J. C. (1986). Strategic marital therapy for depression. In N. S. Jacobson & A. S. Gurman (Eds.), *Clinical handbook of marital therapy* (pp. 495–511). New York: Guilford Press.

Crits-Cristoph, P., & Barber, J. P. (Eds.). (1991). *Handbook of short-term dynamic psychotherapy.* New York: Basic Books.

Cummings, N. A., & Follette, W. T. (1976). Brief therapy and medical utilization. In H. Dorken (Ed.), *The professional psychologist today.* San Francisco: Jossey-Bass.

Cummings, N. A., & Sayama, M. (1995). *Focused psychotherapy: A casebook of brief, intermittent psychotherapy throughout the life cycle.* New York: Brunner/Mazel.

Dasberg, H., & Winokur, M. (1984). Teaching and learning short-term dynamic psychotherapy: Parallel processes. *Psychotherapy, 21,* 184–188.

Davanloo, H. (Ed.). (1978). *Basic principles and techniques in short-term dynamic psychotherapy.* New York: Spectrum.

Davanloo, H. (Ed.). (1980). *Short-term dynamic psychotherapy.* New York: Jason Aronson.

Davanloo, H. (1991). *Unlocking the unconscious: Selected papers.* West Sussex, England: Wiley.

de Shazer, S. (1982). *Patterns of brief family therapy.* New York: Guilford Press.

de Shazer, S. (1984). The death of resistance. *Family Process, 23,* 79–83.

de Shazer, S. (1985). *Keys to solution in brief therapy.* New York: Norton.

de Shazer, S. (1988). *Clues: Investigating solutions in brief therapy.* New York: Norton.

de Shazer, S. (1991a). Foreword. In Y. M. Dolan, *Resolving sexual abuse.* New York: Norton.

de Shazer, S. (1991b). *Putting difference to work.* New York: Norton.

Dolan, Y. M. (1991). *Resolving sexual abuse.* New York: Norton.

Donovan, J. (1987). Brief dynamic psychotherapy: Toward a more comprehensive model. *Psychiatry, 50,* 167–183.

Duncan, B., Drewry, S., Hubble, M., Rusck, G., & Bruening, P. (1992). Brief therapyism: A neglected addiction. *Journal of Strategic and Systemic Therapies, 10,* 32–42.

D'Zurilla, T. J., & Goldfried, M. R. (1973). Cognitive processes, problem solving, and effective behavior. In M. R. Goldfried & M. Merbaum (Eds.), *Behavior change through self-control* (pp. 267–312). New York: Holt, Rinehart, & Winston.

Edelstien, M. G. (1990). *Symptom analysis: A method of brief therapy.* New York: Norton.

Ellis, A. (1962). *Reason and emotion in psychotherapy.* New York: Stuart.

Ellis, A. (1992). Brief therapy: The rational–emotive method. In S. H. Budman, M. F. Hoyt, & S. Friedman (Eds.), *The first session in brief therapy* (pp. 36–58). New York: Guilford Press.

Erickson, K. K. (1988). One method for designing short-term intervention-oriented Ericksonian therapy. In J. K. Zeig & S. R. Lankton (Eds.), *Developing Ericksonian therapy: State of the art* (pp. 379–396). New York: Brunner/Mazel.

Erickson, M. H. (1980). *Collected papers* (Vols. 1–4). (E. Rossi, Ed.). New York: Irvington.

Erickson, M. H., & Rossi, E. (1979). *Hypnotherapy: An exploratory casebook.* New York: Irvington.

Erickson, M. H., Rossi, E., & Rossi, S. (1976). *Hypnotic realities.* New York: Irvington.

Everstine, D. S., & Everstine, L. (1983). *People in crisis: Strategic therapeutic interventions.* New York: Brunner/ Mazel.

Farrelly, F., & Brandsma, J. (1974). *Provocative therapy.* Cupertino, CA: Meta-Publications.

Fay, A. (1990). *PQR: Prescription for a quality relationship.* New York: Simon & Schuster.

Feldman, J. L., & Fitzpatrick, R. J. (Eds.). (1992). *Managed mental health care.* Washington, DC: American Psychiatric Press.

Ferenczi, S., & Rank, O. (1925). *The development of psychoanalysis.* New York: Nervous and Mental Disease Publication Co.

Fisch, R. (1982). Erickson's impact on brief psychotherapy. In J. K. Zeig (Ed.), *Ericksonian approaches to hypnosis and psychotherapy* (pp. 155–162). New York: Brunner/Mazel.

Fisch, R. (1990). The broader implications of Milton H. Erickson's work. *Ericksonian Monographs, 7,* 1–5.

Fisch, R. (1994). Basic elements in the brief therapies. In M. F. Hoyt (Ed.), *Constructive therapies* (pp. 126–139). New York: Guilford Press.

Fisch, R., Weakland, J. H., & Segal, L. (1982). *The tactics of change: Doing therapy briefly.* San Francisco: Jossey-Bass.

Follette, W. T., & Cummings, N. A. (1967). Psychiatric services and medical utilization in a prepaid health care setting. *Medical Care, 5,* 25–35.

Frances, A., & Clarkin, J. (1981a). Parallel techniques in supervision and treatment. *Psychiatric Quarterly, 53,* 242–248.

Frances, A., & Clarkin, J. F. (1981b). No treatment as the prescription of choice. *Archives of General Psychiatry, 38,* 542–545.

Freedheim, D. K. (Ed.). (1992). *History of psychotherapy: A century of change.* Washington, DC: American Psychological Association.

Freud, S. (1910). The future prospects of psychoanalytic therapy. *Standard Edition, 11,* 139–151. London: Hogarth Press, 1953.

Freud, S. (1914). Remembering, repeating and working through. *Standard Edition, 12,* 145–156. London: Hogarth Press, 1953.

Freud, S. (1915). Observations on transference–love. *Standard Edition, 12,* 157–171. London: Hogarth Press, 1953.

Freud, S. (1919). Turnings in the ways of psychoanalytic therapy. *Standard Edition, 17,* 157–168. London: Hogarth Press, 1953.

Freud, S. (1937). Analysis terminable and interminable. *Standard Edition, 23,* 209–254. London: Hogarth Press, 1953.

Friedman, S. (Ed.). (1993). *The new language of change: Constructive collaboration in psychotherapy.* New York: Guilford Press.

Friedman, S., & Fanger, M. T. (1991). *Expanding therapeutic possibilities: Getting results in brief psychotherapy.* New York: Lexington Books/Macmillan.

Furman, B., & Ahola, T. (1992a). *Pickpockets on a nudist camp: The systemic revolution in psychotherapy.* Adelaide, Australia: Dulwich Centre Publications.

Furman, B., & Ahola, T. (1992b). *Solution talk.* New York: Norton.

Garfield, S. L. (1986). Research on client variables in psychotherapy. In S. L. Garfield & A. E. Bergin (Eds.), *Handbook on psychotherapy and behavior change* (3rd ed., pp. 213–256). New York: Wiley.

Gill, M. M. (1954). Psychoanalysis and exploratory psychotherapy. *Journal of the American Psychoanalytic Association, 2,* 771–797.

Gilligan, S., & Price, R. (Eds.). (1993). *Therapeutic conversations.* New York: Norton.

Goldberg, C. (1975). Termination—A meaningful pseudodilemma in psychotherapy. *Psychotherapy: Theory, Research and Practice, 12,* 341–343.

Gonzales, R. C., Biever, J. L., & Gardner, G. T. (1994). The multicultural perspective in therapy: A social constructionist approach. *Psychotherapy, 31,* 515–524.

Goode, E. E. (1992, January 13). Therapy for the '90s. *U.S. News & World Report,* pp. 55–56.

Gordon, D. (1978). *Therapeutic metaphors.* Cupertino, CA: MetaPublications.

Goulding, M. M. (1985). *Who's been living in your head?* (rev. ed.). Watsonville, CA: WIGFT Press.

Goulding, M. M. (1990). Getting the important work done fast: Contract plus redecision. In J. K. Zeig & S. G. Gilligan (Eds.), *Brief therapy: Myths, methods, and metaphors* (pp. 303–317). New York: Brunner/Mazel.

Goulding, M. M. (1992). *Sweet love remembered: Bob Goulding and redecision therapy.* San Francisco: TA Press.

Goulding, M. M., & Goulding, R. L. (1979). *Changing lives through redecision therapy.* New York: Grove Press.

Goulding, M. M., & Goulding, R. L. (1989). *Not to worry!* New York: William Morrow.

Goulding, R. L. (1983). Gestalt therapy and transactional analysis. In C. Hatcher & P. Himelstein (Eds.), *Handbook of Gestalt therapy* (pp. 615–634). New York: Jason Aronson.

Goulding, R. L. (1989). Teaching transactional analysis and redecision therapy. *Journal of Independent Social Work, 3,* 71–86.

Goulding, R. L., & Goulding, M. M. (1978). *The power is in the patient.* San Francisco: TA Press.

Gurman, A. S. (1992). Integrative marital therapy: A time-sensitive model for working with couples. In S. H. Budman, M. F. Hoyt, & S. Friedman (Eds.), *The first session in brief therapy* (pp. 186–203). New York: Guilford Press.

Gustafson, J. P. (1986). *The complex secret of brief psychotherapy.* New York: Norton.

Haley, J. (1963). *Strategies of psychotherapy.* New York: Grune & Stratton.

Haley, J. (1969). The art of psychoanalysis. In *The power tactics of Jesus Christ and other essays* (pp. 11–26). New York: Avon.

Haley, J. (1973). *Uncommon therapy: The psychiatric techniques of Milton H. Erickson, M.D.* New York: Norton.

Haley, J. (1977). *Problem-solving therapy.* San Francisco: Jossey-Bass.

Haley, J. (1984). *Ordeal therapy.* San Francisco: Jossey-Bass.

Haley, J. (1989). *The first therapy session: How to interview clients and identify problems successfully.* San Francisco: Jossey-Bass. [Audiotape]

Haley, J. (1990). Why not long-term therapy? In J. K. Zeig & S. G. Gilligan (Eds.), *Brief therapy: Myths, methods, and metaphors* (pp. 3–17). New York: Brunner/Mazel.

Havens, R. A. (Ed.). (1989). *The wisdom of Milton H. Erickson* (Vols. 1 & 2). New York: Paragon House.

Henry, W. P., Schacht, T. E., Strupp, H. H., Binder, J. L., & Butler, S. F. (1993). The effects of training in time-limited dynamic psychotherapy. III. Mediators of therapists' response to training. *Journal of Consulting and Clinical Psychology*, *61*, 441–447.

Horner, A. J. (Ed.). (1985). *Treating the Oedipal patient in brief psychotherapy*. New York: Jason Aronson.

Horowitz, M. J. (1976). *Stress response syndromes*. New York: Jason Aronson.

Horowitz, M. J., Marmar, C., Krupnick, J., Wilner, N., Kaltreider, N., & Wallerstein, R. (1984). *Personality styles and brief psychotherapy*. New York: Basic Books.

Howard, K. I., Kopta, S. M., Kraus, M. S., & Orlinsky, D. E. (1986). The dose–effect relationship in psychotherapy. *American Psychologist*, *41*, 159–164.

Hoyt, M. F. (1979a). Aspects of termination in a time-limited brief psychotherapy. *Psychiatry*, *42*, 208–219. (*)

Hoyt, M. F. (1979b). "Patient" or "client": What's in a name? *Psychotherapy: Theory, Research and Practice*, *16*, 16–17. (*)

Hoyt, M. F. (1980). Therapist and patient actions in "good" psychotherapy sessions. *Archives of General Psychiatry*, *37*, 159–161.

Hoyt, M. F. (1985a). Therapist resistances to short-term dynamic psychotherapy. *Journal of the American Academy of Psychoanalysis*, *13*, 93–112. (*)

Hoyt, M. F. (1985b). "Shrink" or "expander": An issue in forming a therapeutic alliance. *Psychotherapy*, *22*, 813–814.

Hoyt, M. F. (1986). Mental-imagery methods in short-term dynamic psychotherapy. In M. Wolpin, J. Shorr, & L. Krueger (Eds.), *Imagery*, *4* (pp. 89–97. New York: Plenum Press.

Hoyt, M. F. (1989). Psychodiagnosis of personality disorders. *Transactional Analysis Journal*, *19*, 101–113. (*)

Hoyt, M. F. (1990). On time in brief therapy. In R. A. Wells & V. J. Giannetti (Eds.),

Handbook of the brief psychotherapies (pp. 115–143). New York: Plenum Press. (*)

Hoyt, M. F. (1991). Teaching and learning short-term psychotherapy within an HMO. In C. S. Austad & W. H. Berman (Eds.), *Psychotherapy in managed health care* (pp. 98–108). Washington, DC: American Psychological Association. (*)

Hoyt, M. F. (1993a). Group psychotherapy in an HMO. *HMO Practice*, *7*, 129–132. (*)

Hoyt, M. F. (1993b). Two cases of brief therapy in an HMO. In R. A. Wells & V. J. Giannetti (Eds.), *Casebook of the brief psychotherapies* (pp. 235–248). New York: Plenum Press.

Hoyt, M. F. (Ed.). (1994a). *Constructive therapies*. New York: Guilford Press.

Hoyt, M. F. (1994b). Single session solutions. In M. F. Hoyt (Ed.), *Constructive therapies*. New York: Guilford Press.

Hoyt, M. F. (1994c). Introduction: Competency-based future-oriented psychotherapy. In M. F. Hoyt (Ed.) *Constructive therapies* (pp. 1–10). New York: Guilford Press.

Hoyt, M. F. (1995a, December). *Managed care, HMOs, and the Ericksonian perspective. Managed care, HMOs, and the Ericksonian perspective.* Paper presented at the Fifth International Congress on Ericksonian Approaches to Psychotherapy and Hypnosis, Phoenix, Arizona. (*)

Hoyt, M. F. (1995b). *Brief therapy and managed care: Readings for contemporary practice*. San Francisco: Jossey-Bass.

Hoyt, M. F. (in press-a). Contact, contract, change, encore: A conversation with Bob Goulding. *Transactional Analysis Journal*.

Hoyt, M. F. (Ed.). (in press-b). *Constructive therapies*. New York: Guilford Press.

Hoyt, M. F., & Austad, C. S. (1992). Psychotherapy in a staff-model health maintenance organization: Providing and assuring quality care in the future. *Psychotherapy*, *29*, 119–129. (*)

Hoyt, M. F., & Farrell, D. (1984). Countertransference difficulties in a time-limited psychotherapy. *International Journal of Psychoanalytic Psychotherapy*, *10*, 191–203.

Hoyt, M. F., & Goulding, R. L. (1989). Resolution of a transference–countertransference impasse using Gestalt techniques in supervision. *Transactional Analysis Journal, 19*, 201–211. (★)

Hoyt, M. F., Rosenbaum, R. L., & Talmon, M. (1992). Planned single-session psychotherapy. In S. H. Budman, M. F. Hoyt, & S. Friedman (Eds.), *The first session in brief therapy* (pp. 59–86). New York: Guilford Press.

Hoyt, M. F., & Talmon, M. (1990). Single-session therapy in action: A case example. In M. Talmon, *Single-session therapy* (pp. 78–96). San Francisco: Jossey-Bass.

Hoyt, M. F., Xenakis, S. N., Marmar, C. R., & Horowitz, M. J. (1983). Therapists' actions that influence their perceptions of "good" psychotherapy sessions. *Journal of Nervous and Mental Disease, 171*, 400–404.

Hudson, P. (1993). *Making friends with your unconscious mind: The user friendly guide.* Omaha, NE: Center Press.

Hudson, P., & O'Hanlon, W. H. (1992). *Rewriting love stories: Brief marital therapy.* New York: Norton.

Jacobson, G. (1968). The briefest psychiatric encounter: Acute effects of evaluation. *Archives of General Psychiatry, 18*, 718–724.

Jacobson, N. S., & Gurman, A. S. (Eds.). (1995). *Clinical handbook of couple therapy.* New York: Guilford Press.

Jacobson, N. S. & Margolin, G. (1979). *Marital therapy: Strategies based on social learning and behavior exchange principles.* New York: Brunner/Mazel.

Johnson, L. D. (1995). *Psychotherapy in the age of accountability.* New York: Norton.

Kadis, L. B. (Ed.). (1985). *Redecision therapy: Expanded perspectives.* Watsonville, CA: WIGFT Press.

Kaiser, H. (1965). The problem of responsibility in psychotherapy. In L. B. Fierman (Ed.), *Effective psychotherapy: The contribution of Hellmuth Kaiser* (pp. 1–13). New York: Free Press.

Kellner, R., Neidhardt, J., Krakow, B., & Pathak, D. (1992). Changes in chronic nightmares after one session of desensitization or rehearsal instructions.

American Journal of Psychiatry, 149, 659–663.

Koss, M. P., & Butcher, J. N. (1986). Research on brief psychotherapy. In A. E. Bergin & S. L. Garfield (Eds.) *Handbook of psychotherapy and behavior change: An empirical analysis* (3rd ed., pp. 627–670). New York: Wiley.

Koss, M. P., Butcher, J. N., & Strupp, H. H. (1986). Brief psychotherapy methods in clinical research. *Journal of Clinical and Consulting Psychology, 54*, 60–67.

Kral, R., & Kowalski, K. (1989). After the miracle: The second stage in solution-focused brief therapy. *Journal of Strategic and Systemic Therapies, 8*, 73–76.

Kreilkamp, T. (1989). *Time-limited intermittent therapy with children and families.* New York: Brunner/Mazel.

Kupers, T. (1981). *Public therapy.* New York: Free Press/ Macmillan.

Lankton, S. R. (1990). Ericksonian strategic therapy. In J. K. Zeig & W. M. Munion (Eds.), *What is psychotherapy? Contemporary perspectives* (pp. 363–371). San Francisco: Jossey-Bass.

Lankton, S. R., & Lankton, C. (1983). *The answer within: A clinical framework for Ericksonian hypnotherapy.* New York: Brunner/Mazel.

Lankton, S. R., & Lankton, C. (1986). *Enchantment and intervention in family therapy.* New York: Brunner/Mazel.

Lazarus, A. A. (1976). *Multimodal behavior therapy.* New York: Springer.

Lazarus, A. A. (1989). *The practice of multimodal therapy.* Baltimore: Johns Hopkins University Press.

Lazurus, A. A., & Fay, A. (1990). Brief psychotherapy: Tautology or oxymoron? In J. K. Zeig & S. G. Gilligan (Eds.), *Brief therapy: Myths, methods, and metaphors.* (pp. 36–51). New York: Brunner/Mazel.

Levenson, H., & Bolter, K. (1988). *Short-term psychotherapy values and attitudes: Changes with training.* Paper presented at annual convention of the American Psychological Association, Atlanta.

Levenson, H., & Butler, S. F. (1994). Brief dynamic individual psychotherapy. *Textbook of psychiatry* (2nd ed.). Washington, DC: American Psychiatric Press.

Levenson, H., Speed, J., & Budman, S. H. (1992). *Therapists' training and skill in brief therapy: A survey.* Paper presented at the annual meeting of the Society for Psychotherapy Research, Berkeley.

Lewin, K. K. (1970). *Brief psychotherapy: Brief encounters,* St. Louis, MO: Warren H. Green.

Lorion, R. P., & Felner, R.D. (1986). Research on psychotherapy with the disadvantaged. In S. L. Garfield & A. E. Bergin (Eds.), *Handbook of psychotherapy and behavior change* (3rd ed., pp. 739–776). New York: Wiley.

Madanes, C. (1981). *Strategic family therapy.* San Francisco: Jossey-Bass.

Madanes, C. (1984). *Behind the one-way mirror.* San Francisco: Jossey-Bass.

Mahoney, M. J. (1974). *Cognition and behavior modification.* Cambridge, MA: Ballinger.

Mahoney, M. J. (1977). Personal science: A cognitive learning therapy. In A. Ellis & R. Grieger (Eds.), *Handbook of rationale–emotive therapy* (pp. 352–366). New York: Springer.

Mahoney, M. J., & Arnkoff, D. (1978). Cognitive and self-control therapies. In S. L. Garfield & A. E. Bergin (Eds.), *Handbook of psychotherapy and behavior change* (2nd ed., pp. 689–722). New York: Wiley.

Malan, D. H. (1963). *A study of brief psychotherapy.* Tavistock, London.

Malan, D. H. (1976). *The frontier of brief psychotherapy.* New York: Plenum Press.

Malan, D. H. (1980). The most important development in psychotherapy since the discovery of the unconscious. In H. Davanloo (Ed.), *Short-term dynamic psychotherapy* (pp. 13–23). New York: Jason Aronson.

Malan, D. H., Heath, E. S., Bacal, H. A., & Balfour, H. G. (1975). Psychodynamic changes in untreated neurotic patients. II. Apparently genuine improvements. *Archives of General Psychiatry, 32,* 110–126.

Mann, J. (1973). *Time-limited psychotherapy.* Cambridge, MA: Harvard University Press.

Mann, J., & Goldman, R. (1982). *A casebook in time-limited psychotherapy.* New York: McGraw-Hill.

Marmor, J. (1979). Short-term dynamic psychotherapy. *American Journal of Psychiatry, 136,* 149–155.

Mays, V. M., & Albee, G. W. (1992). Psychotherapy and ethnic minorities. In D. K. Freedheim (Ed.), *History of psychotherapy* (pp. 552–570). Washington, DC: American Psychological Association.

McClendon, R., & Kadis, L. B. (1983). *Chocolate pudding and other approaches to intensive multiple-family therapy.* Palo Alto, CA: Science & Behavior Books.

McGoldrick, M., Pearce, J. K., & Giordano, J. (Eds.). (1982). *Ethnicity and family therapy.* New York: Guilford Press.

McMullin, R. E. (1986). *Handbook of cognitive therapy techniques.* New York: Norton.

McNeel, J. (1976). The parent interview. *Transactional Analysis Journal, 6,* 61–68.

Meichenbaum, D. (1977). *Cognitive behavior modiciation.* New York: Plenum Press.

Meichenbaum, D. (1993). Stress inoculation training: A 20-year update. In P. M. Lehrer & R. L. Woofold (Eds.), *Principles and practices of stress management* (2nd ed., 373–406). New York: Guilford Press.

Meichenbaum, D. (1994). *A clinical handbook/practical therapist manual for assessing and treating adults with post-traumatic stress disorder (PTSD).* Waterloo, Ontario, Canada: Institute Press, University of Waterloo.

Melges, F. T. (1982). *Time and the inner future: A temporal approach to psychiatric disorders.* New York: Wiley.

O'Hanlon, W. H. (1987). *Taproots: Underlying principles of Milton H. Erickson's therapy and hypnosis.* New York: Norton.

O'Hanlon, W. H., & Hexum, A. L. (1990). *An uncommon casebook: The complete clinical work of Milton H. Erickson, M.D.* New York: Norton.

O'Hanlon, W. H., & Martin, M. (1992). *Solution-oriented hypnosis: An Ericksonian approach.* New York: Norton.

O'Hanlon, W. H., & Weiner-Davis, M. (1989). *In search of solutions: A new direction in psychotherapy.* New York: Norton.

O'Hanlon, W. H., & Wilk, J. (1987). *Shifting contexts: The generation of effective psychotherapy.* New York: Guilford Press.

Parad, H. J. (Ed.). (1965). *Crisis intervention: Selected readings.* New York: Family Service Association of America.

Peak, T.H., Borduin, C. M., & Archer, R. P. (1988). *Brief psychotherapies: changing frames of mind.* Newbury Park, CA: Sage.

Perls, F. S., Hefferline, R. F., & Goodman, P. (1951). *Gestalt therapy.* New York: Julian Press.

Persons, J. B. (1989). *Cognitive therapy in practice: A case formulation approach.* New York: Norton.

Phillips, M. (1988). Changing early life decisions using Ericksonian hypnosis. *Ericksonian Monographs, 4,* 74–87.

Pinsker, H., Rosenthal, R., & McCullough, L. (1991). Dynamic supportive psychotherapy. In P. Crits-Christoph & J. P. Barber (Eds.), *Handbook of short-term dynamic psychotherapy* (pp. 220–247). New York: Basic Books.

Prochaska, J. O., DiClemente, C. C., & Norcross, J. C. (1992). In search of how people change. *American Psychologist, 47,* 1102–1114.

Rasmussen, A., & Messer, S. B. (1986). A comparison and critique of Mann's time-limited psychotherapy and Davanloo's short-term dynamic psychotherapy. *Bulletin of the Menninger Clinic, 50,* 163–184.

Robinson, P. J. (1991). Providing couples' therapy in prepaid health care. In C. S. Austad & W. H. Berman (Eds.), *Psychotherapy in managed health care* (pp. 171–184). Washington, DC: American Psychological Association.

Rosen, S. (1982). *My voice will go with you: The teaching tales of Milton H. Erickson.* New York: Norton.

Rosenbaum, R. (1990). Strategic psychotherapy. In R. A. Wells, & V. J. Giannetti (Eds.), *Handbook of the brief psychotherapies* (pp. 351–403). New York: Plenum Press.

Rosenbaum, R. (1993). Heavy ideals: Strategic single-session hypnotherapy. In R. A. Wells & V. J. Giannetti (Eds.), *Casebook of the brief psychotherapies* (pp. 109–129). New York: Plenum Press.

Rosenbaum, R. (1994). Single-session therapies: Intrinsic integration? *Journal of Psychotherapy Integration, 4,* 229–252.

Rosenbaum, R., Hoyt, M. F., & Talmon, M. (1990). The challenge of single-session therapies: Creating pivotal moments. In R. A. Wells & V. J. Giannetti (Eds.), *Handbook of the brief psychotherapies* (pp. 165–189). New York: Plenum Press.

Schuyler, D. (1991). *A practical guide to cognitive therapy.* New York: Norton.

Selvini-Palazzoli, M., Cecchin, G., Prata, G., & Boscolo, L. (1978). *Paradox and counterparadox.* New York: Jason Aronson.

Shectman, F. (1986). Time and the practice of psychotherapy. *Psychotherapy, 23,* 521–525.

Shoham, V., Rohrbaugh, M., & Patterson, J. (1995). Problem- and solution-focused couple therapies: The MRI and Milwaukee models. In N. S. Jacobson & A. S. Gurman (Eds.), *Clinical handbook of couple therapy* (pp. 142–163). New York: Guilford Press.

Siddall, L. B., Haffey, J. A., & Feinman, J. A. (1988). Intermittent brief treatment in an HMO setting. *American Journal of Psychotherapy, 42,* 96–106.

Sifneos, P. E. (1972). *Short-term psychotherapy and emotional crisis.* Cambridge, MA: Harvard University Press.

Sifneos, P. E. (1987). *Short-term dynamic psychotherapy: Evaluation and technique* (rev. ed.). New York: Plenum Press.

Sifneos, P. E. (1992) *Short-term anxiety-provoking psychotherapy: A treatment manual.* New York: Plenum Press.

Spoerl, O. H. (1975). Single-session psychotherapy. *Diseases of the Nervous System, 36,* 283–285.

Stewart, I., & Joines, V. (1987). *TA Today.* Chapel Hill, NC: Lifespace Publishing.

Strupp, H. H., & Binder, J. L. (1984). *Psychotherapy in a new key: A guide to time-limited dynamic psychotherapy.* New York: Basic Books.

Stuart, R. B. (1981). *Helping couples change: A social learning approach to marital therapy.* New York: Guilford Press.

Sue, D. W. (1990). *Counseling the culturally different: Theory and practice* (2nd ed.). New York: Wiley.

Sullivan, H. S. (1954). *The psychiatric interview.* New York: Norton.

Talmon, M. (1990). *Single-session therapy.* San Francisco: Jossey-Bass.

Talmon, M. (1993). *Single session solutions.* Reading, MA: Addison-Wesley.

Talmon, M., Hoyt, M. F., & Rosenbaum, R. (1990). Effective single-session therapy: Step-by-step guidelines. In M. Talmon, *Single-session therapy* (pp. 34–56). San Francisco: Jossey-Bass.

Ticho, E. A. (1972). Termination of psychoanalysis: Treatment goals, life goals. *Psychoanalytic Quarterly, 41,* 315–333.

VandenBos, G. R., Cummings, N. A., & DeLeon, P. H. (1992) A century of psychotherapy: Economic and environmental influences. In D. K. Freedheim (Ed.), *History of psychotherapy* (pp. 65–102). Washington, DC: American Psychological Association.

Walter, J. L., & Peller, J. E. (1992). *Becoming Solution-Focused in Brief Therapy.* New York: Norton.

Walter, J. L., & Peller, J. E. (1994). "On track" in solution-focused brief therapy. In M. F. Hoyt (Ed.), *Constructive therapies* (pp. 111–125). New York: Guilford Press.

Watzlawick, P., Beavin, J. H., & Jackson, D. D. (1967). *Pragmatics of human communication: A study of interactional patterns, pathologies, and paradoxes.* New York: Norton.

Watzlawick, P., Weakland, J. H., & Fisch, R. (1974). *Change: Principles of problem formation and problem resolution.* New York: Norton.

Weeks, G. R. (Ed.). (1991). *Promoting change through paradoxical therapy.* New York: Brunner/Mazel.

Weiner-Davis, M. (1992). *Divorce busting.* New York: Fireside/Simon & Schuster.

Weiner-Davis, D., de Shazer, S., & Gingerich, W. J. (1987). Building on pretreatment change to construct the therapeutic solution: An exploratory study. *Journal of Marital and Family Therapy, 13,* 359–363.

Wells, R. A. (1982). *Planned short-term treatment.* New York: Free Press/Macmillan.

Wells, R. A., & Giannetti, V. J. (Eds.). (1990). *Handbook of the brief psychotherapies.* New York: Plenum Press.

Wells, R. A., & Giannetti, V. J. (Eds.). (1993). *Casebook of the brief psychotherapies.* New York: Plenum Press.

Wells, R. A., & Phelps, P. A. (1990) The brief psychotherapies: A selective review. In Wells, R. A., & Giannetti, V. J. (Eds.), *Handbook of the brief psychotherapies* (pp. 3–26). New York: Plenum Press.

Whitaker, C. A. (1989). *Midnight musings of a family therapist.* New York: Norton.

White, M., & Epston, D. (1990). *Narrative means to therapeutic ends.* New York: Norton.

Wilson, G. T. (1981). Behavior therapy as a short-term therapeutic approach. In S. H. Budman (Ed.), *Forms of brief therapy* (pp. 131–166). New York: Guilford Press.

Wolberg, L. R. (Ed.). (1965). *Short-term psychotherapy.* New York: Grune & Stratton.

Wolpe, J. (1958). *Psychotherapy by reciprocal inhibition.* Stanford, CA: Stanford University Press.

Wolpe, J., & Lazarus, A. A. (1966). *Behavior therapy techniques.* New York: Pergamon.

Worchel, J. (1990). Short-term dynamic psychotherapy. In R. A. Wells & V. J. Giannetti (Eds.), *Handbook of the brief psychotherapies* (pp. 193–216). New York: Plenum Press.

Yapko, M. D. (Ed.) (1989). *Brief therapy approaches to treating anxiety and depression.* New York: Brunner/Mazel.

Yapko, M. D. (1990). Brief therapy tactics in longer-term psychotherapies. In J. K. Zeig & S. G. Gilligan (Eds.), *Brief therapy: Myths, methods, and metaphors* (pp. 185–195) New York: Brunner/Mazel.

Yapko, M. D. (1992). Therapy with direction. In S. H. Budman, M. F. Hoyt, & S. Friedman (Eds.), *The first session in brief therapy* (pp. 156–180). New York: Guilford Press.

Zeig, J. K. (Ed.). (1982). *Ericksonian approaches to hypnosis and psychotherapy.* New York: Brunner/Mazel.

Zeig, J. K. (Ed.). (1987). *The evolution of psychotherapy.* New York: Brunner/Mazel.

Zeig, J. K. (1990). Ericksonian psychotherapy. In J. K. Zeig & W. M. Munion (Eds.), *What is psychotherapy? Contempo-*

rary perspectives (pp. 371–377). San Francisco: Jossey-Bass.

Zeig, J. K., & Gilligan, S. G. (Eds.). (1990). *Brief therapy: Myths, methods, and metaphors.* New York: Brunner/Mazel.

Zeig, J. K., & Lankton, S. R. (Eds.). (1988). *Developing Ericksonian therapy: State of the art.* New York: Brunner/Mazel.

Zois, C. (1992). *Think like a shrink.* New York: Warner.

13

Group Psychotherapies

ROBERT R. DIES

[Group psychotherapy refers to a] psychosocial process wherein an experienced . . . psychotherapist . . . utilizes the emotional interaction in small, carefully planned groups to "repair" mental ill health, i.e., to effect amelioration of personality dysfunctions in individuals specifically selected for this purpose. . . . The participants are cognizant of the psychotherapeutic purpose and accept the group experience as a means to obtain relief from distress and modify their pathological mode of functioning.
—SCHEIDLINGER (1982, p. 7)

Since its modest beginnings nearly nine decades ago, the field of group psychotherapy has demonstrated a remarkable evolution. Presently, there are approximately 15,000 articles published in hundreds of different journals and thousands of books on various aspects of group intervention. Although these figures are impressive, it is clear that they grossly underestimate the actual prevalence of group treatments because the vast majority of group psychotherapists do not contribute to the theoretical, empirical, or applied literature. It is not known how many clinicians actually conduct therapy groups regularly, but findings from a wide range of surveys of training programs, treatment facilities, and professional organizations for group psychotherapists suggest that literally tens of

thousands of psychologists, psychiatrists, social workers, and other mental health practitioners, as well as millions of patients, spend portions of their time in group psychotherapy or group counseling each week (Dies, 1986, 1992a).

Shapiro (1978) has suggested that there are three reasons for the prominence of group treatments. The first of these is expediency, namely the need to compensate for the paucity of clinicians in the face of the growing number of individuals who seek alleviation of their mental health problems. Second, is a cultural demand prompted by the desire to counteract the social alienation engendered by impersonal scientific and technological advancements. Finally, there is the demonstrated success of this modality for patients experiencing a wide spectrum of personal and interpersonal conflicts. Although the validity of Shapiro's explanations may be questioned, there is little doubt that the foundations for group psychotherapy are indeed multifaceted and include practical considerations, theoretical conceptualizations, and empirical documentation of effectiveness.

BACKGROUND OF THE APPROACH

Practical Foundations

Group psychotherapy was first and foremost a pragmatic approach to treatment. Historical accounts generally credit Joseph Pratt for originating group therapy in 1906 as a psychosocial intervention for tuberculosis patients who were unable to afford inpatient treatment (Shaffer & Galinsky, 1989). Pratt assembled patients into large groups and exhorted them to adopt a positive attitude toward their illness. His optimistic outlook was communicated to his participants and this, along with the patients' recognition that they were not alone in their suffering, apparently contributed to their sense of betterment. Other physicians and psychiatrists soon followed Pratt's initiative and within a few years the group lecture approach was extended to patients experiencing a variety of psychological disorders (MacKenzie, 1992). It was clear, however, that "practical procedures for starting and leading groups had taken precedence over formal theory, with the result that the theoretical rationale for what transpired in groups tended to be subsumed under a common-sense framework emphasizing the usefulness of instruction, advice, support, and mutual identification among members" (Shaffer & Galinsky, 1989, p. 3). Three advantages of group psychotherapy were regarded as most central at that time: expediency, cost-effectiveness, and staff efficiency.

Pratt's application of the lecture approach, for example, was based largely on the notion of *expediency*, that is, presenting information simultaneously to numerous patients who shared a common malady. Yet, early clinicians who adopted this psychoeducational strategy soon learned that it may not have been the passive assimilation of information delivered by an inspirational leader that was beneficial but rather the patients' opportunity to share with fellow sufferers the experience of their debilitating condition. This discovery influenced clinicians to become less interested in the sheer convenience of treating multiple people concurrently in favor of proper matching of patients in groups to maximize treatment effectiveness. Currently, it is clear that sound clinical judgment ought to take priority over practicality in selecting patients for groups (Dies, 1986). Thus, it has been shown that careful attention to screening, pregroup preparation, group composition, and minimizing the risks inherent in the cavalier assignment of patients to group treatments can lead to significant improvements in group functioning and therapeutic gains for individual patients (Dies, 1986, 1993; Dies & Teleska, 1985). The former "let's place them in a group, it's more convenient" attitude has been replaced by a more articulated rationale based on the unique merits of group interventions for the particular patients who have been referred for treatment.

The second pragmatic justification for the early use of the group method was based on *cost-effectiveness*. Pratt, for instance, worked with indigent patients who could not bear the expense of institutional care. Today, the concept of cost-effectiveness has a variety of overtones that extend far beyond the initial reasons formulated by Pratt and other clinicians during his era. Now, the choice is not so much between inpatient and outpatient treatment, although that, too, is critical but rather involves decisions among alternative treatment modalities. For the individual client, there is no question that group psychotherapy is much more affordable than one-to-one methods, usually about half the cost (Dies, 1986). The current question, however, is not how much the individual is expected to pay for treatment but rather the willingness of third-party payers to subsidize a major portion of this cost. Fortunately, in the face of mounting pressures from legislators, insurance underwriters, and even patient-consumers for cost containment, there is ample evidence that group psychotherapy is indeed more economical than individual treatments and generally just as effective in terms of clinical outcome (Dies, 1993). Such findings bode well for the future of group treatments (Dies, 1992a).

The third practical advantage of group psychotherapy espoused by early workers in the field relates to *staff efficiency*, that is, the capacity of understaffed mental health agencies to accommodate more patients by assigning them to a group conducted by one or two therapists. At first glance, this rationale for group treatments appears to have merit, but in actuality several problems have been noted with this practice. Elsewhere, I have suggested that many clinical settings use groups to compensate for the lack of adequately trained personnel (Dies, 1986). Patients may be informed that there is a waiting list for individual therapy but that they could join a group almost immediately. Unfortunately, this message conveys the unjustified bias that individual therapy is at a premium (implicitly because it is better) and that group psychotherapy is a secondary form of intervention. The regrettable consequence is that expectations regarding therapeutic effectiveness may diminish, thereby in-

fluencing the rate of treatment progress and hampering the group's potential. A sizable body of literature confirms the importance of positive expectations in the overall impact of psychological interventions (Yalom, 1995).

A related problem is that many agencies reserve "precious" individual therapy time for their more experienced practitioners and allow their less seasoned clinicians to conduct the group treatments. This practice is inconsistent with the degree of complexity of the therapeutic modalities. If anything, the group situation is more demanding and requires more specialized training and experience (Dies, 1986, 1994b). In fact, the skills learned as an individual therapist may not transfer readily to the group psychotherapy situation and may, indeed, interfere with the therapist's capacity to intervene effectively (Dies, 1980, 1994a).

Although group psychotherapy was established, in large part, in response to a host of pragmatic issues, these advantages seem far less salient by contemporary standards. More compelling justification for group treatments can be found in the theoretical and empirical literature.

Theoretical Foundations

As early group psychotherapists attempted to understand the powerful curative forces operating within the group context, they began to impose a theoretical framework on their experiences. Initially, psychoanalytic theory was most influential, and clinicians sought to transpose the concepts of individual psychoanalysis into the group setting. But this juxtaposition was not always compatible and many of the basic concepts and methods (e.g., free association and dream interpretation) had to be modified or set aside. Despite the need for compromise and concession, the psychoanalytic model continued to exert the primary thrust in the evolution of group treatments for many decades, and even today it remains as one of the most prominent models of group psychotherapy. At this time, however, proponents of virtually every theoretical persuasion endorse group psychotherapy as a viable and vital treatment modality (Dies, 1992a).

Contemporary theories of group therapy may be contrasted along a number of critical dimensions. Parloff (1968), for instance, has differentiated theories in terms of the focus of the therapist's interventions: individual (intrapersonalists), interpersonal (transactionalists), and the group-as-a-whole (integralists). Each perspective argues for the unique benefits of group treatments over other modalities. *Intrapersonalists* generally seek to resolve intrapsychic conflicts and view the group as especially effective in facilitating the interpretation of resistance and transference phenomena. Shaffer and Galinsky (1989) summarize other unique benefits of group psychotherapy from this perspective, including the opportunities for patients to (1) witness that they are not isolated and alone in experiencing problems; (2) discover personal resources for listening to and understanding others; (3) demonstrate, not just talk about, patterns of interpersonal relating; (4) gain insight into the effects of characterological style more quickly and forcefully; (5) experience the safety of expressing feelings through peer support and modeling; and (6) avoid the increasingly dependent patient–therapist relationship that can occur in individual treatment.

Parloff (1968) states that the second group of theorists, the *transactionalists*, are mainly interested in member-to-member relationships, and view the group as furnishing unique opportunities for understanding individual patterns of relating to others. Kaul and Bednar (1978) cite four sources of learning that are special to group treatments for these interpersonally oriented clinicians:

1) members may profit as a consequence of learnings based upon their participation in, and evaluation of, a developing social microcosm; 2) group members may benefit as a consequence of giving and receiving feedback in the group; 3) individuals may improve as a result of consensual validation derived from the group; and 4) individuals may profit from the relatively unique opportunity to be reciprocally involved with other group members as both helpers and helpees. (p. 179)

Similarly, Fuhriman and Burlingame (1990), based on their extensive review of the literature, conclude that the distinctive benefits from group treatments "rely heavily on the presence of (vicarious learning), observance of (universality), and engagement with (role flexibility, altruism, family reeanactment) others" (p. 51).

Parloff's (1968) third vantage point, the *integralists*, places primary emphasis on group-as-a-whole processes. Participation in a therapy group ostensibly evokes shared unconscious conflicts or motivations around issues of dependency (especially in relationship to the authority of the leader), aggression, sexuality, and intimacy. By attending to such shared group concerns, the therapist is reportedly able to treat each patient in the group. Theoretically, by interpreting to the group rather than to the individual, the impact of the therapist's interventions will be wider and more appropriate because each patient will find most interpretations pertinent to some extent. The overall goal of treatment is to help patients become more effective in the groups to which they belong on the outside. Thus, learning more adaptive and task-oriented styles in the here and now of group therapy is presumed to generalize to important groups in the patients' life beyond the immediate treatment setting. The group is thought to have more potential than one-to-one therapy for the exposure of unconscious conflicts and to be more capable of providing a supportive and efficient learning environment through which to facilitate the working through of these individual and shared problems.

In actual practice, the vast majority of clinicians incorporate interpretations at each level of analysis, although they vary substantially in their emphasis (Rutan & Stone, 1984). Nonetheless, each perspective regards tl•e group modality as uniquely suited for the activation, exploration, and resolution of the maladaptive behavioral patterns that led patients to seek treatment in the first place (Dies, 1986). Of course, there are other critical dimensions that differentiate the most popular models of group intervention: therapist *style* in terms of activity level, openness, and structuring; therapist *focus* (e.g., past–present–future, affect–behavior–cognition, process–content, ingroup–out-of-group); and *nature* of therapist verbalizations (e.g., confrontation, encouragement, interpretation) (Rutan & Stone, 1984). Although a recent analysis of contemporary models of group psychotherapy shows that there is considerable confusion in the field about how to best distinguish among the various perspectives, there is considerable consensus that group treatments provide a powerful medium for therapeutic change (Dies, 1992b). Indeed, the theoretical justifications for group treatments are even more compelling than those based on simple pragmatics.

Empirical Foundations

Over five decades passed before it was possible to offer sufficient research evidence to document the value of group treatments proposed by the originators of this approach. The earliest reviews in the 1960s, based on the few outcome studies that had accumulated by that time, offered highly tentative conclusions about the efficacy of group interventions (Rickard, 1962; Stock, 1964). Nevertheless, within the span of just a few years, it had become clear that "the converging evidence is consistent with the view held by many practitioners that group therapy is a valuable tool of the helping professions" (Bednar & Lawlis, 1971, p. 814). Subsequent reviews of the empirical literature displayed even more confidence in the generalization that various group formats were largely beneficial in their impact on group members (Dies, 1979, 1993).

The issue of therapeutic efficacy for group treatments has been explored through a variety of methods. Smith, Glass, and Miller (1980), for example, applied a quantitative technique called meta-analysis (based on average improvement scores on pre–postchange measures) in their comprehensive critique of psychotherapy outcome in hundreds of studies conducted across a wide range of clinical settings. These authors concluded that group psychotherapy was just as effective as individual treatments in the alleviation of psychological disorders. This observation has generally been supported in subsequent meta-analytic reviews (Shapiro & Shapiro, 1982; Lyons & Woods, 1991; Tillitski, 1990; Weisz, Weiss, Alicke, & Klotz, 1987).

Toseland and Siporin (1986) cautioned that generalizations derived from meta-analysis are based on studies using different therapeutic approaches rather than investigations making direct comparisons among the treatment modalities. That is, "average effects sizes" for studies of different one-to-one treatment approaches have been compared with other investigations examining outcome effects for different forms of group intervention. Toseland and Siporin, therefore, scanned the literature for published reports in which individual and group treatments were directly contrasted. They identified 32 studies that satisfied their standards for experimental design. The authors discovered that in 24 of these investigations, no significant differences in effectiveness were identified between the two treatment modalities. In all the eight remaining studies, group psychotherapy was established as more effective than one-to-one treatment (and more cost-efficient). Orlinsky and Howard (1986) came to the same conclusion of comparatively little differential outcome of individual and group treatments based on their systematic and thorough review of the psychosocial treatment literature; their generalization was based on a broader sampling of studies.

It is clear from these meta-analytic reviews and comprehensive surveys of the literature that group psychotherapy is indeed an effective form of treatment intervention. Although evidence relating group therapeutic outcome to particular patient diagnoses must be regarded as tentative, there is an increasing number of empirical reviews documenting the value of group treatments for patients suffering from alcoholism (Solomon, 1982), sexual dysfunctions (Mills & Kilmann, 1982), depression (Lewinsohn & Clarke, 1984), schizophrenia (Kanas, 1986), anxiety (Galloucis & Kaufman, 1988), bereavement (Lieberman, 1990), bulimia (Oesterheld, McKenna, & Gould, 1987), bipolar disorders (Kanas, 1993), and other conditions. Moreover, a number of literature reviews have shown that the risk of negative outcome from group treatments is generally quite negligible (Dies & Teleska, 1985; Erickson, 1987; Orlinsky & Howard, 1986).

Although group psychotherapy was initiated by Joseph Pratt and other early clinicians to address matters of convenience and expediency, there is little question that the theoretical and empirical foundations for group treatments

have assumed much greater importance in contemporary practice. Once thought to be a secondary form of treatment, group interventions have now become the treatment of choice for many practitioners. Before we examine how participation in an intensive, change-oriented group can foster therapeutic growth, it may be useful to highlight general concepts of personality and psychopathology to better understand the rationale for group intervention.

THE CONCEPT OF PERSONALITY

There are a variety of conceptualizations of personality among clinicians who conduct therapy groups. Certainly, no one theoretical perspective can be said to embrace a monopoly in the field of group treatments. The traditional distinctions among psychodynamic, cognitive-behavioral, humanistic, and other viewpoints regarding the important formative, maintaining, and modifying factors that influence personality functioning are just as prevalent in the group treatment literature as they are elsewhere. Although critical dimensions for differentiating among various theories of personality have been outlined (e.g., conscious–unconscious, past–present, person–situation, holistic–analytic, purposive–mechanistic), it is clear that such "either–or" distinctions do not hold up under careful scrutiny (Hall & Lindzey, 1985).

To illustrate, a recent survey requested highly experienced group psychotherapists to identify the major theoretical orientations that best represent the contemporary practice of group psychotherapy, as well as the principal theorists aligned with each position (Dies, 1992b). The 111 clinicians who responded to the questionnaire furnished nearly 50 unique orientations and approximately 200 different names. Efforts to classify these responses into clear-cut theoretical positions proved to be rather difficult. Concepts used to describe models often overlapped or appeared in combination. For instance, "psychodynamic" was hyphenated with psychoanalytic, interpersonal, object relations, and group-as-a-whole approaches by varying numbers of respondents. Similarly, the names recommended as representatives of the various theoretical viewpoints were often highly inconsistent. Many of the names appeared under several categories (e.g., "psychodynamic" and "object relations" or "interpersonal" and "existential"). While these dual identities may reflect an accurate portrayal of how the experts attempt to integrate their own perspectives, it is quite apparent that they reflect considerable confusion as well. Thus, Yalom (1995), whose book is the most widely used text for training group psychotherapists, was cited most frequently, but his name appeared under six different categories, including interpersonal, existential, psychodynamic, group-as-a-whole, object relations, and short-term.

Ten models of group psychotherapy emerged as being most popular from this survey (they appear in order of endorsement): psychodynamic–psychoanalytic, group-as-a-whole–systems, Transactional Analysis–Gestalt, interpersonal–interactional, cognitive-behavioral, object relations, group analysis, psychodrama, existential–humanistic, and self psychology. The conceptualizations of personality espoused by adherents of these theoretical models are highly divergent, as are their strategies for effecting therapeutic change. For example, the psychodynamic models (psychoanalytic, object relations, and self psychology approaches) stress the importance of early developmental phenomena, unconscious motivation, the role of defense mechanisms, repetition, and transference. As a result, these therapists adopt the position

of therapeutic neutrality and strive to help patients explore individual dynamics and interpersonal transactions, making connections between manifest content and unresolved/unconscious conflicts that become activated within the treatment context but have as their foundation earlier experiences within dysfunctional family systems. The principal goals of these clinicians are to foster insight and cathartic relief as means for promoting behavioral change.

In contrast, cognitive-behavioral and other action-oriented approaches (e.g., Transactional Analysis–Gestalt and psychodrama) emphasize basic learning processes in the formation of personality, current situational factors maintaining behavioral consistency, and the importance of the person's conscious assumptions in guiding behavioral choices. Based on the belief that "it is easier to act yourself into a new way of thinking than to think yourself into a new way of acting," these methods emphasize active structuring by the therapist and direct efforts to modify current dysfunctional thoughts and maladaptive behaviors.

Finally, the interpersonal–existential theorists place considerable importance on positive growth tendencies, subjective experience, and relationships in shaping personality. In group treatment, they encourage honest expression, genuine encounter, and the role of the therapist as a transparent model of effective interpersonal functioning, yet it is the quality of relationships established among the members that is primarily responsible for individual change (Dies, 1992b).

Although dramatic differences exist in the models of personality that form the basis for the various systems of group psychotherapy, they inevitably share certain common assumptions. Thus, most theorists would agree with the definition provided by Phares (1991), "Personality is that pattern of characteristic thoughts, feelings, and behaviors that distinguishes one person from another and that persists over time and situations" (p. 4). Two aspects of this definition are central—stability of personality and that of distinctiveness.

Fundamental to the notion of stability or *consistency* is the premise that individuals who seek group psychotherapy will enter the treatment situation displaying their central personality attributes, whether these are conceptualized as traits, learned habits, or unconscious drives. While it may take some time for these cardinal features to become manifest, inevitably each person's "essence" will surface during the group interactions. The treatment setting provides a unique opportunity both to observe and to modify the stable aspects of personality that have proven to be counterproductive. In group psychotherapy, there is much less "talking about" outside interpersonal difficulties and more "living through" relationship issues within the context of treatment. The group therapy situation is less contrived and, therefore, more likely to approximate the patient's day-to-day reality, that is, to stimulate the very conflicts that prompted the patient to seek treatment in the first place.

The group modality also has the potential to evoke uniquely powerful processes (e.g., consensual validation, shared unconscious fantasies, and multiple transferences) to effect changes in those maladaptive patterns. Sharing self-doubts, angry feelings, or inhibitions in the area of intimacy *with* a group of contemporaries is considerably different than disclosing those same feelings *to* an individual therapist who does not reciprocate. Similarly, struggling with peers to understand common interpersonal dilemmas, while striving to construct facilitative group norms (e.g., learning how to express helpful feedback, giving support, sharing time responsibly), represents a unique learning environment with charac-

teristics not found in the one-to-one treatment setting. The correspondence of these interpersonal processes to external relationships increases the likelihood that learning will generalize beyond the immediate context of treatment.

The second feature that personality theories have in common relates to *distinctiveness* or to the idea that each person's unique or idiosyncratic features will emerge in everyday interactions. Once again, the value of group psychotherapy is that it provides a unique and powerful forum for exploring these individual differences. The group is viewed as a "social microcosm," or miniaturized society (Yalom, 1995), in which patients may not only learn a great deal about how different people think, feel, and behave in common situations (e.g., through observational learning) but also discover how their own qualities and actions affect others through interpersonal feedback. In some sense, each patient serves as a therapist for others, not as an expert in psychopathology or group dynamics but as someone who, along with the other participants, can provide emotional support and consensual validation about interpersonal styles. In the individual treatment setting, a therapist who comments, "many people feel that way," can be dismissed as someone whose job it is to be supportive or confrontational, but in the group situation it is much more difficult to minimize the shared input from multiple peers (Dies & Dies, 1993a). Most contemporary group psychotherapists attend to patient selection and group composition to ensure that their groups are sufficiently diversified to provide alternative models for coping and at the same time that there is adequate commonality among members to guarantee group maintenance (Dies, 1993; Melnick & Woods, 1976).

As we have seen from this discussion, and from the earlier summary of empirical findings on treatment efficacy, participation in a therapy group can have highly positive effects on the amelioration of distress and on the modification of dysfunctional interpersonal patterns. Although it may seem counterintuitive that individuals who enter therapy because they cannot cope effectively in their relationships in the "real world" can be of considerable assistance to each other in the group treatment setting, that is precisely what happens. This observation that "patients can be therapists" requires an examination of basic assumptions about psychopathology and dysfunction.

THE PATHOLOGICAL OR DYSFUNCTIONAL INDIVIDUAL

Group psychotherapists do not share a common understanding about the nature of psychopathology any more than they adhere to identical models of personality. Moreover, their allegiance to group methods does not lead them to adopt perspectives different from their individual therapy colleagues' on how subjective distress or defective interpersonal patterns are developed or displayed. Depression and anxiety are still viewed as potentially unhealthy or debilitating emotional states, and exploitation of others and self-defeating lifestyles continue to be conceptualized as personality disorders.

Yet, group psychotherapists of all persuasions will definitely search for the *interpersonal* foundations or manifestations of psychopathology. If the focus is on etiology, the therapist will explore how faulty relationships have contributed to the establishment of dysfunctional feelings or actions. If the emphasis is on symptomatic expression, the clinician will highlight how anguish and characterological deviance persistently undermine effective coping and the individual's sense of personal integrity. Thus, the common mind-set is to interpret maladjustment in interpersonal terms and to regard the group situation as uniquely suited for the modification of pathological conditions.

According to psychodynamic theory, for example, "flaws in earlier developmental stages can be repaired if that stage can be recalled, relived, and affectively reexperienced correctively in the here and now" (Rutan, 1992, p. 21) of group treatment. Similarly, interpersonal theorists assume that in "drawing attention to patients' interpersonal worlds, and the centrality of interaction within the group, as both a mechanism for illumination and for repair of interpersonal disturbance, a powerful modality is accessed" (Leszcz, 1992, p. 60). Finally, a cognitive-behavioral theorist would state that patients

> usually give advice to each other, show how others' behavior had better be changed outside the group, and check to see if their homework suggestions are actually being carried out. Again, they normally interact with each other in the group itself, comment on each other's in-group behaviors, and give themselves practice in changing some of their dysfunctional interactions. (Ellis, 1992, pp. 77–78)

Implicit in each of these descriptions is a second common bond among group psychotherapists: their faith that individual patients, in spite of their disabilities, have the *potential to contribute constructively* in creating a powerful therapeutic environment for effecting meaningful clinical change. Many patients initially fear that participation in a therapy group with other "disturbed" people might only exacerbate their own problems, but research findings clearly demonstrate that groups exert a positive influence on improved functioning for a vast majority of the participants (Dies, 1992a). This is even the case when the patients are regarded as seriously mentally ill (e.g., Kanas, 1986). Thus, individuals who are labeled as schizophrenic, borderline, anxiety disordered, or even antisocial are not completely maladjusted or incapacitated. "Psychopathology" is not an all-or-none phenomenon. The ability of patients to offer emotional support and understanding, to share painful feelings, to furnish interpersonal validation, and/or to challenge distorted ideas or inappropriate behaviors can be enormously helpful.

THE ASSESSMENT OF DYSFUNCTION

One purpose of assessment is to ensure adequate understanding of the patient's problems so that a proper assignment to treatment can be established. Unfortunately, clinicians have tended to rely too heavily on traditional diagnostic interviews and psychological tests that have not allowed this patient–treatment "match" to be made most effectively (Woods & Melnick, 1979). Although there has been increased emphasis on the development of interpersonal measures that predict social behavior in group situations (e.g., Benjamin, 1984; Keisler, 1986; Wiggins, Trapnell, & Phillips, 1987), as well as efforts to employ "pretherapy group trials" (e.g., Mayerson, 1984; Yalom, 1995), results are too limited to be of much practical value (Dies, 1993).

Patients carrying a full range of diagnostic labels have been successfully treated with group methods, but the central issue is whether a particular treatment group is suitable for a specific patient at a given point in time. Thus, while some authors have argued that paranoid, drug-addicted, acutely psychotic, antisocial, or organically impaired individuals are poor candidates for group treatment, others have taken the opposite stance

based on the position that homogeneous groups could be designed to work effectively with such patients (Unger, 1989).

It has become evident that therapists do not actually select patients for group psychotherapy but rather deselect or exclude those who seem to be inappropriate. Vinogradov and Yalom (1989), for example, offer guidelines that are not based on traditional diagnostic criteria. Their standards for exclusion highlight the patient's inability to tolerate the group treatment situation, the likelihood of assuming a deviant role within the group, extreme agitation, potential noncompliance with group norms, and marked incompatibility with one or more of the other group members. Their inclusion indices consist of the capacity to perform the group task, motivation to participate in treatment, commitment to attend sessions regularly, and congruence of the patient's problems with the goals of the group. Klein (1985) also notes that patients who have circumscribed complaints, acute onset of symptoms, and a history of good premorbid adjustment will generally benefit most from short-term treatment.

Other clinicians have explored factors contributing to premature dropouts from group therapy to identify potential factors relevant to selection. Thus, Roback and Smith (1987) chose to highlight characterological defenses that result in major interpersonal deficits: "Included in this category are problems with self-disclosure, difficulties with intimacy, generalized interpersonal distrust, excessive use of denial, and a tendency to be either verbally subdued or hostile" (p. 427). Other considerations include patients with unrealistic expectations, persons in situational crises who are too preoccupied to engage effectively in group therapeutic work, and borderline, narcissistic, schizoid, or acutely disturbed patients who are placed in group therapy prematurely (Dies & Teleska, 1985).

It is clear that assessment goes far beyond the issue of finding a proper "diagnosis" and includes a more comprehensive understanding of the patient's personality and preoccupations, as well as an adequate evaluation of the nature of treatment and the context in which it occurs. Thus, while a particular depressed patient may be very suitable for group therapy, it would not be wise to place this individual in a group composed predominantly of antisocial personalities. Nor would it be prudent to assign a schizophrenic young woman to a group composed of less troubled anxiety-disordered individuals. In both cases, we may have made an adequate "diagnosis" of the patient, but in neither instance is there an adequate match between the patient and the group. The depressed and schizophrenic patients might become misfits in their respective groups, have difficulty keeping pace with fellow members, and risk becoming either scapegoated, or even worse, group casualties. Furthermore, these two patients might require so much attention that the progress of the other group members would be stalled needlessly. Therefore, it would be more appropriate to find a reasonable alternative, such as individual therapy or a different treatment group.

At present, there is increased emphasis on how assessment tools may be used to augment treatment and to understand the variables that might improve the quality of service delivery. Elsewhere, the author has proposed a comprehensive model to illustrate how measures may be used during four phases of group treatment (Dies & Dies, 1993b). For example, in the *negotiation* phase, when patients are making decisions about entering treatment, assessment procedures are used to identify unrealistic expectations about group therapy, to educate patients about therapeutic factors and patient roles, to establish concrete treatment objectives, and to facilitate proper assignment to treatment options. One of the major deterrents to adequate commitment to therapy relates to patients' misunderstandings about the process. It has been shown that by addressing these misconceptions early clinicians may substantially enhance their patients' involvement in the treatment process (Tinsley, Bowman, & Ray 1988).

Group therapy may be especially intimidating for many individuals. Fear of attack, embarrassment, emotional contagion or coercion, and misgivings about actual harmful effects in the group setting (Slocum, 1987; Subich & Coursol, 1985) may lead certain patients to avoid the very treatment that could best address their interpersonal conflicts. The clinician who fails to understand these pervasive anxieties may lose many prospective patients who could be attracted to treatment if only they would be permitted to discuss these issues before a specific therapy was recommended.

During the *retention* phase of group psychotherapy, when there is a risk that patients will terminate prematurely, assessment is used to identify treatment obstacles, to uncover continuing misunderstandings about therapy, and to strengthen the therapeutic bond through more effective dialogue (Dies & Dies, 1993b). Many of the evaluation procedures solicit feedback from patients about their perceptions of group process and the therapist's interventions. Thus, assessment is clearly not just used to diagnose symptomatology or dysfunction in patients but may also be applied to "diagnose" problems in the group system. For example, patients may complete a Group Climate Questionnaire to evaluate their perceptions of the group environment along such dimensions as engagement, conflict, and avoidance (MacKenzie, 1983). The Group Atmosphere Scale (Silbergeld, Koenig, Manderscheid, Meeker, & Hornung, 1975) and the Group Environment Scale

(Moos, 1986), and the Group Leader Behavior Instrument (DePalma, Gardner, & Zastowny, 1984; Phipps & Zastowny, 1988) have also been used to understand group members' perceptions of important group events that may affect their participation in treatment.

There is a twofold purpose to this type of assessment. The first, is a focus on the group system to identify dysfunction at that level (e.g., insufficient cohesion, too much avoidance). The second goal is to detect particular individuals whose ratings of the group are discrepant from those of other patients, suggesting a failure to bond effectively with comembers or expressing discomfort about the level of a friction within the group. This information may allow the clinician to work more specifically with these patients to overcome the problems that interfere with adequate alliance with the group and/or to confront obstacles that impede the development of a more constructive group atmosphere.

In the remaining two stages of group development, *enhancement* and *evaluation*, assessment instruments are once again introduced to understand patient and treatment variables that may affect therapeutic progress (Dies & Dies, 1993b). Many clinicians have discovered that the periodic administration of self-report measures can add greatly to their understanding of their patients *and* of their group treatments, with the full cooperation of their patients and without any significant investment of additional time (Dies, 1983a, 1987, 1992a).

This broadened view of assessment is spurred in part by a variety of pressures placed on clinicians to justify the nature of their therapeutic interventions and to document treatment efficacy. This renewed interest in evaluation is apparent in the proliferation of articles and books on how practitioners can incorporate instruments into their clinical work, not only to improve their objective understanding of diagnostic (Wetzler, 1989) and treatment issues (Barlow, Hayes, & Nelson, 1984; Krishef, 1991) but also to enhance the quality of their therapeutic interventions (Corcoran & Fischer, 1987; Dies & Dies, 1993b). The fact that many of the most popular diagnostic and personality instruments have been revised and renormed, and that sophisticated new tests have been introduced, also fuels this growing interest in assessment in the psychotherapy literature (e.g., Costa & McCrae, 1992; Exner, 1993; Graham, 1990; Millon, 1987; Morey, 1991).

THE PRACTICE OF THERAPY

There are wide variations in the application of group psychotherapy that relate to differences in theoretical orientation, the style of the individual practitioner, and perhaps most important, the setting within which the treatment is conducted.

Basic Structure of Therapy

The once-a-week, $1\frac{1}{2}$-hour session appears to be the most common group format, but the professional context will determine how this is modified. Certainly, in most private practice and outpatient agencies, this arrangement is most likely to occur. For clinicians who work in institutional settings, however, groups may meet several times each week and may even be scheduled daily. Hospitalized patients are also more likely to be exposed to a variety of adjunctive treatments, including recreational and occupational therapies and psychodrama, as well as drug treatments.

Historically, combined treatments have been shown to be more effective than single interventions (e.g., Parloff & Dies, 1977), but clinicians have differed in their view on how best to achieve this integration. At present, there appears to be more attention devoted to the effective melding of treatment components to ensure that the special advantages of each method dovetail congruently with the unique strengths of the other interventions (Dies, 1992a). The once prevalent psychotherapy-versus-psychobiology schism, for instance, shows signs of waning, and there are increased hints of complementarity in the group literature (Rodenhauser, 1989; Zaslav & Kalb, 1989). Authors are addressing more specific interface issues (Fink, 1989) and discussing how to circumvent roadblocks preventing successful combined psychopharmacological and group treatments (Salvendy & Joffe, 1991). This type of integration appears to have generalized interdisciplinary support (Stone, Rodenhauser, & Markert, 1991).

There are signals of revived interest in the *integration of other treatment modalities* as well. For example, although Wong (1983) observed that fewer publications on combined individual and group therapy appeared in the 1970s and 1980s than in the prior two decades, recent publications show that more attention is currently placed on concrete guidelines for achieving successful synthesis (Gans, 1990; Lipsius, 1991). This observation seems valid for marital and group modalities as well (Coche & Coche, 1990).

Another structural variation in the application of group methods relates to *treatment duration*. Although concern has been expressed that brief forms of therapy may furnish only transitory or circumscribed relief for many individuals whose conflicts are long-standing and deeply ingrained (Dies, 1992a), predictions by experts in the mental health field suggest that the popularity of short-term group treatments will increase substantially in the foreseeable future; in contrast, more conventional time-extended and one-to-one approaches are expected

to decline in importance (Norcross, Alford, & DeMichele, 1992). "Short term" generally refers to treatments that extend no more than 25 sessions (Dies & Dies, 1993a). Several strands of influence encourage the widespread acceptance of brief group interventions: pressures from legislators, insurance companies, and patient-consumers for safe and cost-efficient psychological treatments; the promise of relatively rapid relief from painful emotional states without substantial commitment of time and money; and the actual demonstration of the effectiveness of time-limited groups (Dies, 1992a).

There is general agreement that brief forms of psychosocial treatment require the establishment of more modest goals, greater attention to task focus, prompt interventions, and more active participation on the part of the therapist (Koss & Butcher, 1986). Given the time-limited nature of treatment, clinicians are more likely to focus on symptomatic relief, improvement of self-esteem, reduction of interpersonal apprehensions, development of social skills and problem-solving strategies, and efforts to ensure that patients gain a basic sense of peer acceptance (Dies & Dies, 1993a). As the duration of therapy increases, more attention can be directed to conflicts that are less accessible to conscious awareness, to maladaptive behavioral patterns that are more rigidly entrenched, and to a greater understanding of the pathogenic developmental experiences that predispose patients to personal suffering and interpersonal strife.

To enhance the efficiency and effectiveness of short-term group treatments, clinicians are inclined to compose groups more homogeneously. Groups composed of members who share common life experiences (e.g., recent loss of a loved one, transition back to the community after hospitalization, and sexual victimization) and/or similar symptoms (e.g., depression, bulimia, alcoholism, and agoraphobia) are generally defined as homogeneous, although other considerations would include age, gender, and occupational status. Melnick and Woods (1976) concluded from their review of the literature that homogeneous groups appear to "coalesce more quickly, offer more immediate support to members, have better attendance, less conflict, and provide more rapid symptomatic relief. However, they are seen as remaining at more superficial levels of interaction and are less effective in producing more fundamental interpersonal learning" (p. 495).

These authors suggest that group composition should be guided toward furnishing an optimal balance between conditions maximizing interpersonal learning (heterogeneity) and considerations ensuring group preservation (homogeneity). They propose a support-plus-confrontation model favoring moderate diversity in composition, avoiding extreme demographic differences and patients with high potential for becoming group misfits, and attempting to create a reasonable balance in terms of interpersonal styles and coping resources. Recent evidence suggests, however, that these concerns are probably most critical for longer-term groups because the active structuring inherent in abbreviated formats may serve to moderate the influence of composition to some extent (Waltman & Zimpfer, 1988).

Another factor in structuring group treatments relates to the distinction between *open and closed groups*. Usually, open-ended groups continue indefinitely and maintain a consistent size (usually six to eight members) by replacing patients as they conclude their therapy (Yalom, 1995). The ebb and flow of membership has a significant affect on the group process, however, which can be detrimental if the therapists and patients do not address the issues productively. The loss of members, especially if the departures are premature, can undermine the integrity of the group system by raising questions about trust, commitment, and shared responsibility. Invariably, the addition of new patients serves to recycle unresolved issues such as those concerning confidentiality, competition, and conflicts over control and intimacy. On the other hand, if these dilemmas are addressed effectively, patients may gain valuable insights into how to communicate feelings honestly and directly, to cope with loss meaningfully, and to respond to awkward transitions more adaptively.

The closed group format has been recommended as a way to circumvent the adverse consequences of rotating membership. Although closed groups are perhaps only feasible in short-term treatment, the stability of group composition is believed to facilitate cohesion and commitment and to allow patients to remain more constructively focused on their individual goals because they are less likely to become "sidetracked" by group-level concerns prompted by the loss of old members and the addition of new ones.

Goal Setting

During the selection process, the clinician attempts to ensure that patients are viable candidates for group treatment: distressed but not too agitated, impulsive, or manipulative to disrupt treatment; willing to cooperate with others; and generally compatible along important symptomatic and interpersonal dimensions. The paramount issue is that of "matching," that is, in evaluating the individual's preparedness for group treatment (selection) and his/her compatibility with the other group members (composition). A corollary issue is that of contracting, which is designed to enhance the therapeutic "fit" by refining individual goals and teaching patients about treatment parameters (Dies, 1993).

Numerous reviews of the literature have shown that various interventions to prepare patients for psychotherapy (e.g., audio and videotapes, verbal instructions, printed materials, and interviews) have been quite productive in generating greater patient investment in treatment and fostering improved therapeutic outcomes (Mayerson, 1984; Orlinsky & Howard, 1986; Tinsley et al., 1988). These pretreatment interventions have attempted to mollify negative anticipations regarding treatment while instilling positive role and outcome expectations and by educating patients about constructive interpersonal behaviors, group developmental issues, and helpful therapeutic factors (Dies, 1993). Research shows that multiple strategies for informing patients about treatment are generally superior than single methods (Kivlighan, Corazzini, & McGovern, 1985), and that more realistic interventions (e.g., videotapes or practice session) are more productive (Tinsley et al., 1988).

Researchers have evaluated efforts to provide specific information to patients about role behaviors and group process. Kivlighan and his colleagues (1985), for example, demonstrated the value of teaching prospective group members about role-related behaviors such as self-disclosure, interpersonal feedback, anxiety management, and here-and-now interaction. Others have illustrated the merits of educating patients about various dimensions of group process (Mayerson, 1984; Yalom, 1995). Most critical, of course, given the patients' diffuse anxieties about group interventions, is the need to furnish a solid rationale for treatment in the group format. Mayerson (1984) tells patients the "group therapy setting is one which provides a special opportunity to interact with others so as to gain insight into one's current interac-

tional patterns and to experiment with new ones" (p. 194). The interpersonal nature of psychopathology is emphasized, if not in its etiology at least in terms of its manifestation and resolution. Also highlighted in pregroup training are general ground rules (e.g., confidentiality and regular attendance), developmental trends, and a general description of therapeutic factors or central interpersonal processes that foster individual gain. These pretreatment interventions are designed to provide a coherent framework for understanding individual experiences and events within the group and to minimize the likelihood of premature attrition and therapeutic casualties (Dies & Teleska, 1985).

Considerable attention is also given to the patients' individual goals for therapy. One facet of the assessment process described earlier in this chapter was to help patients identify specific treatment objectives. A variety of instruments may be introduced to facilitate this process, including standard symptom checklists, personality tests, and individualized target goal forms (Dies & Dies, 1993b). When patients are able to define their goals more concretely, they are much more likely to remain in treatment (Garfield, 1986) and to make meaningful strides in overcoming the problems that initially prompted them to seek the guidance of a mental health practitioner.

Techniques and Strategies

Careful selection of individual patients, proper assignment to appropriate treatment groups, and pregroup training and goal setting provide the foundation for effective group intervention. Nevertheless, the real "work" of therapy begins once the patient enters the group. How this work is accomplished, though, is virtually impossible to sketch without a few words about the therapist's theoretical orientation and whether the group format is open or closed, brief or long term, or conducted within an inpatient or outpatient facility.

The therapist's *conceptual framework* will obviously influence the choice of leadership strategies and the target of interventions. Table 13.1, for example, summarizes some of the differences that were recently found in a survey of experienced group psychotherapists representing different theoretical models (Dies, 1992b). These clinicians were requested to indicate the types of leadership issues that were important for therapists to understand during the working phases of group treatment.

Obviously, there are clear differences among the three different perspectives examined, with the action-oriented therapists (e.g., cognitive-behavioral) being distinctly different from both the interpersonal and psychodynamically oriented group psychotherapists. Thus, clinicians who are grounded in learning theory are more likely to embrace the centrality of such leadership strategies as cognitive reframing, behavioral practice, and role-playing, and to deemphasize process commentary, interpretation, and exploration of underlying group themes. Conversely, psychodynamic therapists eschew the importance of action-based techniques (e.g., teaching problem-solving skills, behavioral practice, and reframing) and highlight the merits of interpreting transference and countertransference phenomena, resistance, and latent group process. Those clinicians who favor the interpersonal approach share some of these considerations, but, as expected, they are uniquely inclined

TABLE 13.1. Leadership Issues during the Working Phase of Group Psychotherapy

Psychodynamic	Interpersonal	Action-oriented
	Important considerations	
Countertransference	Cohesiveness	Cognitive reframing
Transference	Countertransference	Facilitating feedback
Identifying underlying group process	Facilitating self-disclosure	Goal setting
Resistance	Here-and-now activation	Here-and-now activation
Boundary management	Identifying underlying group process	Facilitating behavioral practice
Interpretation	Transference	Role-playing
Nonverbal communication	Therapist openness	Fostering generalization
	Unimportant considerations	
Reinforcement methods	Agenda setting	Boundary management
Cognitive reframing	Reinforcement methods	Norm building
Fostering generalization	Cognitive reframing	Identifying underlying group process
Role-playing	Facilitating behavioral practice	Interpretation
Structured exercises	Fostering generalization	Process commentary
Teaching problem-solving skills	Interpretation	Subgroup formation
Facilitating behavioral practice	Teaching problem-solving skills	Therapeutic factors

to endorse the importance of group cohesion and therapist self-disclosure. The specific implications of these differences are less important for this presentation than the simple fact that they demonstrate that generic models of group intervention do not exist.

Other structural and contextual variations also shape the nature of therapeutic practice. For example, in a *closed group* all of the patients share a similar understanding of the scheduled number of sessions and have agreed to remain in treatment until that facet of the contract is fulfilled. They are aware of how much time is available to work on individual problems and are less likely to be diverted by issues relating to premature dropouts and/or departures due to other patients' successful completion of therapy. The stability of membership and common time frame will give the group system a greater sense of integrity. Although members will invariably progress at their own pace, there will be a more or less predictable sequence of themes revolving around such issues as engagement, differentiation, individuation, intimacy, mutuality, and, finally, dissolution of the group (MacKenzie & Livesley, 1983). In an *open-ended group*, however, these developmental hurdles will be expressed uniquely as a function of who, when, and how members join or leave the group system. Thus, in the ongoing group there will not be a shared ending but a series of terminations that will require more individualized attention. Similarly, the addition of each new member will necessitate preparation of both the individual patient and the group system for the reactions that are likely to be stimulated by these changes. Thus, group "process" issues may demand more attention than individual "content" concerns in the open-ended group. This is not to suggest that closed groups are more effective (because an experienced group therapist can use these group

events to create opportunities for individual growth), but rather to convey that these system-level transitions will clearly influence the clinician's decisions about leadership strategies.

Corresponding arguments could be offered for the contrasts between *short-term* and more *time-extended* treatments. We noted earlier that abbreviated treatments demand more attention to task efficiency. It is ill-advised, for example, for the therapist in the brief group setting to remain passive based on the hope that patients will readily assume responsibility for structuring the group experience or that they will promptly learn how to confront difficult relationship issues effectively, without some active guidance from the clinician. Indeed, a majority of the patients who enter treatment have volunteered because they have been unable to manage their own "interpersonal lives" without substantial discomfort or conflict. If patients had the skills to negotiate the complex exchanges in creating a viable group system, they probably would not be seeking treatment. The group therapist on the other hand, has received specialized training and usually has years of experience in how to promote facilitative group processes that are conducive to individual change.

Finally, there are likely to be dramatic differences in *context* between groups conducted within inpatient and outpatient facilities. Residential groups may convene more times each week, there are more likely to be disruptions due to the need for ancillary treatments, and patients will be more symptomatically disturbed. Issues of confidentiality take on new meaning because patients interact in so many other formal and informal ways (e.g., recreational therapy, psychodrama, and in the dining hall). More structured interventions such as social skills training and more confrontational leadership styles may be possible or even necessary. Thus, an inpatient therapist who forcefully challenges a particular patient's counterproductive interpersonal behaviors knows that other ward personnel are available after the group session to follow through and to comfort the distressed group member. The private practitioner, however, cannot trust that a supportive friend will be there to "pick up the pieces" after the patient has been placed on the therapeutic "hot seat" and then sent home. Therapists in the hospital setting may also make different decisions about how to share their own feelings in therapy because seriously disordered patients may have greater conflicts around "boundary issues" and misinterpret the more transparent clinician's intentions in revealing personal experiences (Dies, 1983b).

Clearly, the nature of the therapist's interventions is influenced by a broad spectrum of factors. Nonetheless, it may be possible to suggest several considerations that are reasonably common across treatment settings. Earlier in this chapter we noted that therapists vary in their *focus of intervention*—individual, interpersonal, or group-as-a-whole—as a function of their theoretical perspective. Despite these variations, most therapists will attend more to group-level (process) issues in the beginning phases of group development, switch to more individual patient concerns (content) in the "working phases" of the group, and then revert back to group-as-a-whole themes as the group nears termination or as individual patients conclude their treatment.

Before group therapy can be effective there must first be a group. Simply convening eight patients in the same room is no guarantee that constructive interaction fostering individual improvement will transpire. Patients must have incentive for discussing personal problems and some assurance that risk taking may produce beneficial consequences. For this to happen, a basic rationale for group treatment must be conveyed and a climate

conducive to personal disclosure must be established. Such group-level considerations as "culture building" and "norm setting" must be addressed (Yalom, 1995), and certain procedural and process guidelines must be instituted (e.g., confidentiality, ground rules about outside socializing, active listening, shared responsibility, and supportiveness). Initial structuring that clarifies the nature of the therapeutic task and builds supportive norms and highlights positive member interactions is generally essential (Dies, 1994a, 1994b; Dies & Dies, 1993a).

Once patients have established a common framework for personalized interaction, experienced a sense of bonding with others (cohesion), and made at least a tentative commitment to the group, it is possible to shift the focus of intervention to more individualized therapeutic work. As patients share painful feelings and self-doubts, test faulty assumptions, risk new behaviors, and provide mutually supportive or constructively critical feedback, the level of group cohesiveness increases and even more intensive individual exploration is possible. This working phase may last for quite some time, depending on the nature of the therapeutic arrangement. Inevitably, certain patients will decide that their "work" is finished and that it is time to discontinue their treatment; in short-term groups this ending point is built into the contract. When termination occurs it is generally necessary for the clinician to refocus on group-as-a-whole issues to some extent. The meaning of termination for the individual patient is obviously examined, but it is often necessary for the clinician to resume a more active role to ensure that other members deal effectively with the emotional impact of the "loss" and that they discuss the implications for the group system as well (K. Dies & Dies, 1993). Although there are wide variations in how different therapists address these group developmental issues, virtually all clinicians modify their focus on individual-, interpersonal-, or group-level concerns as a function of transitional events that impact upon the entire system.

Another common ingredient across treatment settings is the *effort to translate problems into interpersonal concepts.* Whether the therapist is psychodynamic, cognitive-behavioral, or systems-oriented, the group is inherently interpersonal. For example, although depression can be viewed from a strictly individual or intrapsychic point of view, it is much more profitable to explore the social contexts that precipitate the negative affect or dysfunctional thoughts, the interpersonal consequences of feeling sad and gloomy (e.g., social withdrawal, irritability, and excessive dependency), and particularly the interpersonal processes within the group that may be applied to alter the maladaptive condition (i.e., mutual support, feedback, altruism, and imitative learning) (Dies, 1994a).

Similarly, most clinicians will accentuate the *activation of the here and now.* A basic premise is that their patients' troubling feelings and inadequate coping skills will be "replayed" within the group context in ways that parallel how they are manifest in relationships in the "outside" world. Thus, a patient who complains of being unable to trust others will display that cautious and guarded stance within the group. Another who has trouble with self-assertion will most likely assume a passive role in group interactions. The depressed patient who cannot understand why he/she continues to be rejected by friends and family will undoubtedly engage in comparable self-defeating and other-alienating behaviors within the group (e.g., pessimism, whining self-centeredness, and insensitivity to others' feelings). In each instance, it will not be necessary to furnish reports about problems that happen "out there" because they will be abundantly illustrated "in here." Moreover, the cohesive interpersonal forum that has been established within treatment will allow these dysfunctional patterns to be explored, confronted, and worked through in ways that are not feasible in routine social interactions (Yalom, 1995).

Finally, a majority of group psychotherapists will generally "think group." For most clinicians, treatment is conducted *through* a group, not *in* a group. Group treatment is not one-on-one therapy with an audience, with members taking turns working exclusively with the clinician, but it is more commonly a complex interactive process in which the quality of relationships among members is much more critical to therapeutic gain than the nature of the therapist–patient bond; it is the group that is the agent of change not the therapist (Dies, 1983b). Another way in which this group focus is reflected is in the therapist's choice of interventions. Most clinicians attempt to maximize the therapeutic impact of their techniques by searching for common "core" issues that unite patients around the shared human dilemmas that brought them to treatment (e.g., damaged or deflated self-esteem and recurring self-defeating patterns) (K. Dies & Dies, 1993). Moreover, most group therapists will weigh the impact of interventions in terms of individual needs versus benefits available for the remaining members. In rare instances (e.g., potential suicide) will the needs of the majority be sacrificed for the sake of an individual. Fortunately, this immediate decision is seldom faced because virtually every condition is pertinent to at least some of the other members, but there are times when an individual patient will be removed from a group when he/she is an obvious "misfit," or when the pathology is too acute or intrusive.

Process of Therapy

Group psychotherapists devote a significant portion of their time to ensure that the group climate is prepared for important individualized work. Thus, the group system is nurtured so that the patients' understanding of how change occurs is reasonably clear and that the emotional atmosphere is experienced as supportive (Dies, 1994b). When these conditions prevail, group members are more inclined to reveal intimate material, to attempt new behaviors, and to offer meaningful interpersonal feedback. These represent the "mediating goals" for group treatment. The "ultimate" goal, of course, is the amelioration of the distress and/or modification of the deviant interpersonal patterns that precipitated entrance into treatment.

As the principal standard bearer of the "group culture," the group leader facilitates a focus on developmental obstacles that might limit group cohesion or impede constructive interpersonal work (e.g., premature dropouts, irregular attendance, breaches in confidentiality, outside socializing, and subgrouping). This "social engineering" function highlights similarities among members, reinforces behaviors that indicate risk taking, encourages and supports members who model appropriate actions, confronts counternormative behavior, activates a here-and-now focus, and offers process commentary to illuminate undercurrents that are potentially detrimental (Yalom, 1995).

The formative *stages* of group development are negotiated so that members feel accepted and recognize the value of compliance with group norms without the need for rebellion or the fear of losing their individuality (MacKenzie, 1987). The various *roles* that members adopt are addressed to foster their constructive contribution to group development, whether they are the emotional or task-oriented members or those who represent more discrepant roles (e.g., the cautious or guarded individual who may help to elilcit feelings that others are reluctant to share) (Bahrey, McCallum, &

Piper, 1991; Dies & Teleska, 1985; Livesley & MacKenzie, 1983).

Members will not enter therapy with a clear comprehension of how group treatments can promote individual improvement, and it may take them some time to reach this understanding. Their notions about how individuals overcome personal dilemmas and interpersonal conflicts are frequently based on faulty impressions gained from such sources as the old *Bob Newhart* show or popularized accounts of individual therapy depicting intensive uncovering of childhood traumas until flashes of insight are achieved and pent-up emotions are released, thereby effecting therapeutic "cure." Thus, from the patients' viewpoint, the goal is to discuss personal problems that are evident in outside relationships, many of which derive from earlier experiences (i.e., the so-called skeletons in the closet) so they must be reviewed in historical perspective. Furthermore, patients assume that it is the therapist's responsibility to intervene to promote therapeutic change through deft questioning, sage interpretations, and other techniques to guide the uncovering process. The other group members are viewed as clearly ancillary, and their roles are generally confined to asking questions, giving advice, and sharing similar experiences. They in turn will have their opportunities for therapeutic change, as the focus rotates around the membership. Often, the expectation is that with sufficient probing and self-examination, "insight" will be gained and emotional "catharsis" will then be possible (see Table 13.2).

Most therapists will have a different view of how group treatments foster individual growth. While some discussion of outside and even historically based problems is inevitable, the vital importance of interpersonal translations, here-and-now activation, and the "group as agent of change" must be brought to light. It is the process of mutual explora-

TABLE 13.2. "Theories" of Change in Group Treatments

Patients' view	Therapists' view

Share an "outside" problem
  Personal/individual
  Historical ("skeletons" in closet)
	Manifest problems in the group
	  Interpersonal/interactional
	  Here-and-now reactivation

Therapist as "healer"	Group as "healer"

Question-and-answer format
  Advise
  "Psychologize"
  Turn taking
	Mutual exploration
	  Self-disclosure
	  Interpersonal feedback
	  Behavioral practice

Insight acquired ("aha")	Increased understanding

Cathartic relief
  (personal emotional release)
	Corrective emotional experience
	  (interpersonal encounter)

Symptomatic "cure"	Improved coping and symptomatic relief

tion and sharing, not turn taking, advising (psychologizing), and staccato-style question and answering that facilitates therapeutic understanding and improvement. The complementary processes of self-disclosure and interpersonal feedback are pivotal in the pursuit of self-awareness, cognitive restructuring, insight into others, and behavioral change.

Strong affective expression (catharsis) *may* indeed lead to a sense of release, especially *if* the patient is met with genuine support, efforts to understand, and mutual sharing by others. The care and acceptance from comembers may foster greater self-acceptance, and "putting the feelings on the table" might permit more objective exploration and sorting through confusion, which in turn can result in increased self-understanding. Patients can be encouraged to explore the intensity of their feelings, to revise their biased assumptions, to place their reactions in a more realistic perspective, and to weigh the value of holding onto such feelings in view of how their lives have changed over the years. Patients might also explore whether there are other courses of action they might take in situations before their feelings escalate disproportionately; instead of permitting

anger to mount to a sense of rage, they might learn to respond more promptly when significant others engage in behaviors that trigger dissatisfaction.

Similarly, the *group* can be used to allow patients to "test their interpersonal assumptions." Thus, group members might first share what they want most from others in their lives (e.g., respect, affection, and recognition) or how they wish to be viewed by others as people (e.g., friendly, competent, and sincere). They can describe how they attempt to generate those reactions and then consider how that style has been evident within the group. Then, the desired results can be evaluated. "How have others responded?" "Have you indeed been judged as friendly or sincere?" For example, a patient who has worked "so hard" to show genuine interest in others, and thus gain their respect and admiration, may discover that in actuality fellow group members have been "turned off" by the "phony display" of concern. The very outcome she has diligently pursued has eluded her, as it probably does in many relationships, and will continue to do so until she realizes how her own actions undermine the goals she strives so earnestly to achieve. Constructive feedback from comembers may allow her to discover new ways to express herself and thereby gain interpersonal acceptance. She might even be given specific "homework assignments" to practice in outside situations. As a follow-up she could be asked to share how her "outside experiments" worked and, depending on the outcome, encouraged to practice alternative behaviors within treatment. One of the essential skills of a group therapist is to assist patients in generalizing learning from the treatment setting to external circumstances; "inside" material is translated into outside applications, and "outside" problems are explored for their here-and-now relevance.

When group members are invited to reflect on the factors that have contributed to their improvement through group psychotherapy, they typically assign most of the credit to the quality of the relationships they established with their comembers (Dies, 1983b, 1993). The therapist's contributions to treatment outcome are generally regarded as less direct (e.g., process commentary, and providing structure) or less impactful. Although the group therapist may be supportive, his/her efforts are just not as powerful as the combined input from multiple caring peers. Similarly, clinicians may be open and self-disclosing, but they will seldom reveal at the same level of intimacy as the group members. Feedback from the therapist is usually regarded as useful but will rarely have the same influence as the feedback from a panel of peers.

Nevertheless, two aspects of the group psychotherapist's role may be unique in helping patients to accomplish their goals (Dies, 1993). The first of these has already been highlighted, and that is the clinician's task orientation. Yalom (1995) notes that only the group leader can perform this function: "Forces prevent members from fully sharing that task with the therapist. One who comments on process sets oneself apart from the other members and is viewed with suspicion as 'not one of us'" (p. 146). Given the therapists' designated responsibility to ensure that all members progress toward individually defined objectives, as well as their specialized knowledge of group dynamics, they are in the best position to manage the group system.

The second distinct role of group psychotherapists is their capacity for effective confrontation and interpretation. Beutler, Crago, and Arizmendi (1986) found that more effective therapists tend to confront and interpret patient affect more often than their less helpful counterparts. Moreover, clinicians who do not shy away from demonstrations of patients' anger promote "more realistic and goal-directed expressions of affect on the part of their clients. Indeed, evidence from many sources suggests that rousing patient affect and motivating them to confront their fears enhances both cognitive and behavioral changes" (p. 294). Because group members may be reluctant to challenge, at least initially, potentially volatile feelings, and are disinclined to deliver negative feedback (Kivlighan, 1985), the group psychotherapist should shoulder this responsibility by modeling this behavior and prompting, reinforcing, and shaping members' willingness and ability to engage in constructive confrontation (Dies, 1993).

There is considerable evidence that interpretation is a principal vehicle for therapeutic change: "Providing concepts for how to understand, explaining, clarifying, interpreting, and providing frameworks for how to change" (Lieberman, Yalom, & Miles, 1973, p. 238) foster significant levels of patient improvement. Group members may provide some of this function for each other, but this contribution is more specifically within the province of the psychotherapist who has "acquired and perfected the skill over many years of professional training and experience" (Scheidlinger, 1987, p. 348).

THE STANCE OF THE THERAPIST

We have already noted broad variations in therapist style as a function of theoretical orientation, structure of therapy (e.g., short-term or time-extended and open or closed), stage of group development (e.g., more group-centered earlier and individually focused in the working phases), and context of treatment (e.g., inpatient vs. outpatient). Three other issues seem important to address, and these relate to the levels of activity and self-disclosure that are appropriate for clinicians within treatment and the topic of cotherapy.

Therapist Activity

Although debates about the nature of therapist activity have a long history in the literature, the popularity of short-term group treatments has prompted a renewed interest in this topic (Dies, 1985). The pressure to move the group along at a faster pace through more proactive interventions has caused many clinicians to worry about the implications of "control" inherent in their role. Clearly, the action-oriented clinicians (see Table 13.1), who incorporate such techniques as role-playing, cognitive reframing, and selective reinforcement, would favor a more active therapeutic stance. On the other hand, most psychodynamic group therapists would prefer less structure and a more reactive leadership posture focusing on the interpretation of transference and resistance phenomena (Rutan, 1992). Each clinician must decide which style feels most comfortable and productive within his/her own treatment context.

The concern about increased structure or direction by clinicians, however, seems overplayed. There is very little evidence to suggest that patients will necessarily experience more active or planned interventions as controlling: directiveness should not be equated with manipulation, at least in the pejorative sense of that term. Indeed, active therapists who are viewed as supportive, dedicated to guiding the group's development for the sake of meaningful individual work, and open about their interventions and personal feelings about events within treatment are seldom depicted as manipulative (Dies, 1985).

On the other hand, patients seem to experience greater tension and feel more critical toward therapists who are viewed as inactive, aloof, distant, and judgmental. This leadership style frequently stimulates confrontations around issues of authority and perhaps may even facilitate the working through of problems in this area (Dies, 1983b); ironically, it is also felt by many patients to be manipulative.

As therapists become more actively negative in their focus, the risks of harmful effects to patients increase. Understandably, some degree of confrontation and tension-inducing challenge by the therapist may be essential for individual change, after a climate of trust has been developed within the group, but when the therapist "comes on too strong," patients may drop out of treatment prematurely or actually become therapeutic casualties (Dies, 1983b, 1994b; Dies & Teleska, 1985; Roback & Smith, 1987).

Therapist Self-Disclosure

Perhaps even more controversial is the issue of *therapist self-disclosure* (Dies, 1977). Once again, the debate revolves around the clinicians' theoretical predilections. Whereas both interpersonal and action-oriented clinicians may endorse therapist "transparency" for the modeling that such behavior represents, the psychodynamically oriented group therapists prefer a more neutral position based on their belief in the fundamental importance of understanding transference projections.

There is no "right" perspective on this topic because therapists of all persuasions can be very effective. While there is evidence that therapist self-disclosure does indeed foster greater openness among group members, it is also clear that there are other means to facilitate patient self-revelation (e.g., invitations for personal sharing, modeling by other members, and prompting and supporting such expression). Moreover, there is no evidence that therapist self-disclosure contributes to more constructive change for individual members (Dies, 1983b, 1993, 1994b). Once again, group psychotherapists must decide for themselves which stance is most compatible with their own general approach. For many, that position reflects a willingness to be selectively open about feelings generated by events within the sessions but to avoid revealing much about their personal lives. What most patients seem to want is an assurance that their therapist is "real" (i.e., can experience a range of normal feelings and reactions such as anxiety, sadness, and compassion), and that they can relate to the therapist on a affective level (Dies, 1983b, 1993).

Cotherapy

When groups are co-led, as is the case within a significant proportion of treatment settings, the issues of therapist activity and openness require a delicate balancing act between the two clinicians (Dies, 1983b). Although the cotherapists may differ or alternate naturally over the course of group development, it is important that there is reasonable harmony within the team. The literature suggests that compatibility despite dissimilarity is the key consideration, and that the capacity to model an open and positive relationship within sessions is central in maintaining an effective team. Interestingly, there is little evidence that co-led groups are any more productive than groups conducted by one therapist (Dies, 1983b, 1994b).

While the notion that cotherapists can use their own relationship to "model" or demonstrate effective interpersonal behaviors, such as self-disclosure, mutual support, or conflict resolution, is quite appealing, this has never been documented through research. In fact, a recent empirical evaluation of the idea that mutual self-disclosure between the cotherapists serves to model such behavior for group members suggests that "modeling" may be largely a myth (McNary & Dies, 1993). Nevertheless, this does not negate the importance of coleadership because other benefits for the clinicians (and indirectly the patients) may be the sharing of responsibility and the opportunities for professional growth through communication about individual patients and treatment process. Perhaps research measures have not been sensitive enough to detect the subtle coleadership effects that are apparent in group treatments.

CURATIVE FACTORS OR MECHANISMS OF CHANGE

A majority of group psychotherapists are well aware of the principal "therapeutic factors" proposed by Yalom (1995) that have now received widespread attention in the literature (e.g., Bloch & Crouch, 1985; Fuhriman & Burlingame, 1990; MacKenzie, 1987):

1. Interpersonal input or feedback from group members
2. Catharsis or open expression of affect by patients
3. Group cohesiveness
4. Self-understanding
5. Interpersonal output or learning new social skills
6. Existential factors (e.g., acceptance of ultimate responsibility, aloneness, and freedom)
7. Universality (sense of commonality among patients)
8. Instillation of hope
9. Altruism toward others within the group
10. Family-of-origin reenactment
11. Guidance, advice, or suggestions from the therapist or comembers
12. Identification or imitative behavior among group members

The importance of these therapeutic factors varies in relationship to structural, contextual, and individual matters. For example, certain elements are most salient in the formative phases of group development (a structural matter). MacKenzie (1987) labeled these as "nonspecific" morale factors, such as hope, altruism, universality, and cohesiveness, because they are mainly important in establishing a safe atmosphere in which patients can take individual risks. In high-turnover inpatient groups, short-term outpatient therapy, and self-help groups (a contextual matter) these factors may play a central role in the overall evaluation of treatment. However, in most therapy groups for moderately distressed individuals, these factors rarely emerge as most salient in patients' judgments about outcome. Quite the contrary, the variables that appear with greatest regularity are cohesiveness, interpersonal input (feedback), catharsis, and self-understanding (Yalom, 1995). A fifth factor, interpersonal output (learning social skills), is also mentioned frequently.

There are clearly no universal mechanisms of change but rather a range of key dimensions that interact with clinical settings, diagnostic compositions, and forms of group therapy. Different patients (an individual matter) may benefit from various therapeutic ingredients within the same group (Lieberman, 1989), and the availability of multiple sources of learning within sessions may be even more important than any limited set of common dimensions (Lieberman, 1983). There appears to be a confluence of nonspecific factors (e.g., cohesiveness) working in concert with cognitive, affective, and behavioral ingredients to facilitate therapeutic gain (i.e., self-understanding, catharsis, and interpersonal learning and social skills acquisition, respectively) (Dies, 1993). There is no simple formula for treatment benefit.

The literature is consistent in showing that Yalom's (1995) therapeutic factors of family reenactment, guidance, and identification are seldom viewed as important by group members. It is not especially difficult to figure out why advice and imitation are not foremost in intensive group work, but the failure of family reenactment to appear as a nuclear therapeutic dimension runs counter to much of the writing about the importance of transference in the treatment context. Conceivably, the short-term nature of most of the groups evaluated in the literature precludes the emergence of this factor as pertinent. On the other hand, the emotional reliving of earlier family dynamics has been found to be decisive for a group of incest victims (Bonney, Randall, & Cleveland, 1986) and in a long-term group treatment context (Tschuschke & Dies, 1994). It is likely that minor variations across studies of therapeutic factors can be accounted for by virtue of the specialized nature of the treatment groups employed. For example, universality (i.e., the recognition by patients that they share many problems) was understandably unimportant for a male felony offender group (Long & Cope, 1980), whereas "existential awareness" was regarded as quite significant (MacDevitt & Sanislow, 1987).

Although most of the research on therapeutic factors looks at these dimensions from the point of view of patients who have completed treatment, the consistency of the findings lends considerable credence to their central importance.

TREATMENT APPLICABILITY

It should be evident at this point that "group treatments come in all shapes and sizes." A chapter could easily be filled just itemizing the various populations and contexts in which group psychotherapy can be found. Recently, the author published a compilation of reviews, that is, a simple listing of articles that integrate major bodies of *research* on various aspects of group treatments over a 15-year period of time (Dies, 1989). Nearly 100 review articles are summarized under headings covering surveys of process and outcome, research methodology, diagnostic groups, specialized populations, life-span development, training, and various group formats. Were the thousands of theoretical and applied publications to be added to this list, it would be clear that virtually no potential target of intervention has escaped the attention of group psychotherapists.

In the beginning of the chapter, I mentioned Pratt's work in 1906 with tuberculosis patients as the earliest psychoeducational foundation for group work. Today group treatments are employed for a wide range of medical illnesses, including heart disease and cancer, gastrointestinal conditions, neurological impairment, hypertension, asthma and chronic emphysema, and many others (e.g., Stern, 1993).

Various special populations have benefited from group treatments: men's and women's groups, gay and lesbian support groups, and similar homogeneously composed groups for family caregivers, individuals in midlife career change, displaced workers, visually impaired people, victims of incest, or children from alcoholic families, to mention just a few (Alonso & Swiller, 1993; Dies, 1992a; Seligman & Marshak, 1990). The entire age range has been covered: children (Riester & Kraft, 1986), adolescents (MacLennan & Dies, 1992), and the elderly (MacLennan, Saul, & Weiner, 1988).

The practice of group psychotherapy is international in scope. Although there may be differences in how practitioners in various countries conduct their treatments (Dies, 1993), there is no question that the popularity of group therapy is universal.

The brief clinical vignettes that follow can provide only a glimpse at this fascinating but extraordinarily complex field of practice.

CASE ILLUSTRATION

This short-term group consists of eight members who have been meeting weekly for one month in a community mental health facility. Their problems are varied, but most of these young adults have reported feeling quite unhappy about the quality of their relationships and with their own inability to handle interpersonal problems more effectively. Attendance has been regular and they have all shared, at least superficially, the basic reasons they sought treatment. The therapist realizes that the group members have a rudimentary understanding about how group interaction fosters change (through the pregroup contracting) but also knows that they have not truly *experienced* this awareness through their interactions with each other. The fourth session begins:

THERAPIST: Does anyone have any feelings carried over from our last session?

ANDY: No, but something happened to me that I'd like to talk about . . . (*without waiting for others*) . . . the girl I've been dating just decided that our relationship wasn't working out so she ended it . . . without even trying to talk it through!

BRENDA: What happened? [In early groups members frequently get into a question-asking mode to get "the story."]

ANDY: [He explains how his "girlfriend" just "dumped" him and refused to talk about it, so he went over to her place to confront her about how unfair she was being. Because he had always been so open about his feelings, he could not understand her refusal to offer an explanation.]

Andy receives supportive comments from others, because he has indeed been very open about his feelings within the group, usually being the first to volunteer problems for discussion, and because the rejection did seem so unjust and insensitive. After a few minutes, however, the topic shifts to the theme of distrust; others, too, have been "burned" in relationships.

BRENDA: It's real difficult for me to trust guys, because they only seem to want one thing . . .

CATHY: Yeah, I know what you mean. I've avoided any serious dating for two years because I was really hurt by someone I truly cared about . . . I found out he was sleeping with my best friend while he was supposedly going with me.

DON: That stinks. Who do you hate worse . . . the guy or the friend?

CATHY: Probably both . . . it hurt a lot . . . since then I've really put up a wall so I don't get hurt again.

ELLEN: I can't trust people either . . . I'm afraid to get close to others because I'm not sure about their intentions.

For several minutes there is a general discussion about how members have erected defensive "walls" and become reluctant to take risks in relationships because "people can't be trusted," "you never know if they're really interested in who you are as a person," "I'm afraid to get close, because I don't want to go through all that pain again," and similar remarks focused on "people" in outside relationships. The therapist has listened because members have been interacting spontaneously but senses that this externally focused conversation may be an indirect or metaphorical communication (Gans, 1991) about the members' concerns about trust within this relatively new group.

THERAPIST: Does any of this relate to what is going on in here?

ANDY: No, it's different in here . . . people really care and are interested in each other. [Others generally confirm this impression through their own comments.]

THERAPIST: [Despite the members' collusive denial, the clinician persists with the interpretation of here-and-now relevance but realizes that the first intervention was ineffective; members are reluctant to confront their distrust of each other directly.] It would certainly be understandable if you didn't trust each other fully yet, because this is only our fourth session. But I would guess that many of you are not sure that *if* you were to really share the pain and self-doubts that brought you here, you'd be confident that others would understand or be that interested. Some of you have been fairly quiet, and others have begun to share, but none of you has really gotten into qualities you don't like about yourself and want to change. Let's look at what makes it difficult to take those kinds of risks in here?

The members launch into a meaningful discussion about both *group process* issues and *individual concerns* that have contributed to their reluctance to share more completely (e.g., how the silence of some members has led others to feel judged, how some members have felt after their initial disclosures were ignored by others who switched the topic to their own problems, the fear of monopolizing group time or being faced with challenging questions, fears of crying and then feeling stupid or vulnerable, and similar worries). The expression of these previously unverbalized feelings frees members to move into a discussion of desired "norms" around support, reciprocity, and shared responsibility. Thus, the clinician's positive structure and constructive confrontation of the members' veiled preoccupation about a natural theme in the group's development served to pave the way toward greater group cohesion and increasingly intense individual work. This same group can be examined in the tenth session of treatment.

Once again Andy begins the session. In the prior two meetings he briefly described a relationship that seemed to be going quite smoothly. Earlier, in session 4 (above), he was the lone dissenter when others described the "walls" they had constructed for self protection. His position was that when relationships fail, you "move on . . . think of what was good and how you enjoyed each other . . . but when it ends you can't just crawl into a shell."

ANDY: I don't understand it, but Lisa seems to be pulling away from me. . . . I've called several times, but she makes up excuses for not being able to talk. I'm really upset, because I've been so open and honest with her, and really treated her well. We were really getting close, and even slept together. It was a mutual decision, so it wasn't that I took advantage of her or anything like that. . . . (*He turns to the side, and in "macho pose" says quietly to the men, "It was special because I was her first."*)

ELLEN: (*irritated*) I don't blame her . . . I hope she dumps you just like Peggy and the others did!

FRED: And you're proud of that Andy? You probably sweet-talked her into it and she felt used afterwards.

Several of the other members express their disapproval, not only at Andy's insensitive display but also because of his seeming lack of insight into how his behavior might be contributing to his repeated failure in heterosexual relationships. The therapist seizes this opportunity to make this a here-and-now issue.

THERAPIST: Andy, how are you feeling about how the others are responding to you right now? [This intervention is just to check in with Andy before creating the opportunity for more meaningful work.]

ANDY: I don't understand why everyone is so intense . . . I guess I'm *hurt* by the attack. I thought people would know I was just kidding when I flexed my muscles and joked . . . I'm not that kind of person. You all know how open I am about my feelings and how hard I try to be sensitive to everyone. It was okay with Lisa . . . we talked about it first before going to bed.

THERAPIST: (*to the other members*) I have a sense that Andy doesn't really understand the strength of your reactions.

Maybe it would help if we looked at what's going on in here right now. One way to understand this is that Andy is being rejected by you just like he gets "dumped" in relationships outside. What has he done in the group sessions over time to bring this rejection about?

BRENDA: Andy, it's not so much the "macho act" you did before . . . although I didn't like that either . . . but just the attitude you have about relationships . . . you always talk about how interested you are in the other person's feelings. I sure don't feel that way in here. We spend a lot of time talking about your problems and you rarely ask about ours.

ELLEN: I feel the same way . . . you usually start the sessions before any of us have a chance to get into our problems . . .

GORDON: (*interrupting*) . . . Yeah, and when we've tried to give you feedback about that you get real defensive. It's hard for you to take criticism.

ANDY: (*flushed*) . . . But I've really worked in here . . . I express my feelings and work on my problems.

CATHY: I think Gordon is right . . . when we confront you, you just give us that "but I'm such a great guy routine" about how open and honest you are.

THERAPIST: What do you think it would be like to be in a relationship with Andy?

BRENDA: (*jumping in*) I'd feel smothered . . . I don't want to hurt your feelings Andy, but you work too hard to be "Mr. Open" . . . like you're trying to prove how likable you are, but lately it's been pushing me away from you. It's like you're *so* wonderful that you never do anything wrong, but you screw up a lot!

HAL: One of the reasons I've been so quiet in here is because of you, Andy . . . it's always *your* feelings this and *your* feelings that . . . where is there room for me? The smothering that Brenda talked about really fits for me too . . . as I think about it, it feels like you're really needy and self-centered.

ELLEN: There's one more thing for me . . . and that is your attitude that if things don't work out in a relationship, it's too bad and maybe time to move on. I'm afraid that could happen in here, too . . . like if you don't like the feedback, you'll just stop coming.

THERAPIST: Andy, people have been pretty direct in their reactions to you. I hope you can take in what they've said because it looks like there is a direct parallel between what happens in relationships and what has gone on in the group. You *have* been very open in here, but perhaps it hasn't given others the room they need in this group relationship. Your openness and desire to be such a nice guy has felt intrusive and pushed people away from you . . . they've gotten lost in this relationship and felt like they weren't very important to you. But Ellen's comment tells me that she, and I'm sure others, are concerned about you, and want to help, because they see you "shooting yourself in the foot" in relationships and not understanding why women pull away from you.

Andy is very distressed, but with the support of the therapist and other group members he is able to work with the feedback and gain increased awareness of how his style is counterproductive. His intense need for social acceptance is explored and he is helped to define alternative ways to earn recognition. In future sessions he will explore more openly the rather fragile sense of "self" that drives his defensiveness, the condescending attitude toward women (e.g., his use of the pejorative "girl" description and his sense of conquest at being the first), and his narcissism.

The here-and-now, interpersonal work with Andy was quite individual in its focus; frequently in groups several patients are working on a common theme together. For example, other patients may resort to different interpersonal styles as a result of their vulnerable self-esteem. Cathy who was so wounded when she discovered that her lover was sleeping with her best friend, and Hal who remained so quiet throughout many of the sessions, may have much in common with Andy. Although the three of them approach relationships so differently, they may share a common bond that brings each of them to treatment, and that is their fundamental dissatisfaction with who they are as people. The ability to communicate with others through intensive interaction in the group setting is one of the reasons that *group* treatments are so powerful.

CONCLUSION

There is little doubt that the group psychotherapies will continue to play a pivotal role in the mental health field. The confluence of economic and social pressures, theoretical and practical justifications, and empirical support virtually guarantee this outcome (Dies, 1992a). The complex interpersonal processes that are influential in group treatments provide a unique forum for the exploration, understanding, and alleviation of the personal suffering and maladaptive patterns of relating to others that prompt people to seek professional guidance. Further refinement in the practice of group psychotherapy is likely to be reflected in more

appropriate matching of specific group interventions and clients' needs and more effective integration along with other treatment modalities (e.g., individual, family, and biologically oriented approaches).

SUGGESTIONS FOR FURTHER READING

Books

Fuhriman, A., & Burlingame, G. M. (1994). *Handbook of group psychotherapy*. New York: Wiley. This text is the latest update on the clinical implications of group psychotherapy research.

MacKenzie, K. R. (1990). *Introduction to time-limited group psychotherapy*. Washington, DC: American Psychiatric Press. The author furnishes practical guidelines for conducting short-term group psychotherapy.

Shaffer, J., & Galinsky, M. D. (1989). *Models of group therapy* (2nd ed.). Englewood Cliffs, NJ: Prentice Hall. This volume provides a comparative analysis of different theories of group intervention.

Vinogradov, S., & Yalom, I. D. (1989). *A concise guide to group psychotherapy*. Washington, DC: American Psychiatric Press. This is a cogent overview of the interpersonal approach to group treatments.

Yalom, I. D. (1995). *The theory and practice of group psychotherapy* (4th ed.). New York: Basic Books. This is the most popular text in the field of group psychotherapy.

Articles or Chapters

Dies, K. R., & Dies. R. R. (1993). Directive facilitation: Short-term group treatments, Part 2. *The Independent Practitioner, 13,* 177–184.

Dies, R. R., & Dies, K. R. (1993). Directive facilitation: Short-term group treatments, Part 1. *The Independent Practitioner, 13,* 103–109.

REFERENCES

Alonso, A., & Swiller, H. I. (Eds.). (1993). *Group therapy in clinical practice.* Washington, DC: American Psychiatric Press.

Bahrey, F., McCallum, M., & Piper, W. E. (1991). Emergent themes and roles in short-term loss groups. *International Journal of Group Psychotherapy, 41,* 329–345.

Barlow, D. H., Hayes, S. C., & Nelson, R. O. (1984). *The scientist–practitioner: Research and accountability in clinical and educational settings.* New York: Pergamon Press.

Bednar, R. L., & Lawlis, F. (1971). Empirical research in group psychotherapy. In A. E. Bergin & S. L. Garfield (Eds.), *Handbook of psychotherapy and behavior change* (pp. 812–838). New York: Wiley.

Benjamin, L. S. (1984). Principles of prediction using structural analysis of social behavior. In R. A. Zucker, L. Arnoff, & A. J. Rabin (Eds.), *Personality and the prediction of behavior* (pp. 227–241). New York: Academic Press.

Beutler, L. E., Crago, M., & Arizmendi, T. G. (1986). Research on therapist variables in psychotherapy. In S. L. Garfield & A. E. Bergin (Eds.), *Handbook of psychotherapy and behavior change* (3rd ed., pp. 257–310). New York: Wiley.

Bloch, S., & Crouch, E. (1985). *Therapeutic factors in group psychotherapy.* Oxford: Oxford University Press.

Bonney, W. C., Randall, D. A., & Cleveland, J. D. (1986). An analysis of client-perceived curative factors in a therapy group of former incest victims. *Small Group Behavior, 17,* 303–321.

Coche, J., & Coche, E. (1990). *Couples group psychotherapy: A clinical practice model.* New York: Brunner/Mazel.

Corcoran, K., & Fischer, J. (1987). *Measures for clinical practice: A sourcebook.* New York: Free Press.

Costa, P. T., & McCrae, R. R. (1992). *NEO PI-R: Professional manual.* Odessa, FL: Psychological Assessment Resources.

DePalma, D. M., Gardner, K. G., & Zastowny, T. R. (1984). The development of an instrument for measuring leadership behaviors in therapy. *Group, 8,* 3–16.

Dies, K. R., & Dies, R. R. (1993). Directive facilitation: A model for short-term group treatments, Part 2. *The Independent Practitioner, 13,* 177–184.

Dies, R. R. (1977). Group therapist transparency: A critique of theory and research. *International Journal of Group Psychotherapy, 27,* 177–200.

Dies, R. R. (1979). Group psychotherapy: Reflections of three decades of research. *Journal of Applied Behavioral Science, 15,* 361–373.

Dies, R. R. (1980). Group psychotherapy training. In A. K. Hess (Ed.), *Psychotherapy supervision* (pp. 337–366). New York: Wiley.

Dies, R. R. (1983a). Bridging the gap between research and practice in group psychotherapy. In R. R. Dies & K. R. MacKenzie (Eds.), *Advances in group psychotherapy: Integrating research and practice* (pp. 1–16). New York: International Universities Press.

Dies, R. R. (1983b). Clinical implications of research on leadership in short-term group psychotherapy. In R. R. Dies & K. R. MacKenzie (Eds.), *Advances in group psychotherapy: Integrating research and practice* (pp. 27–78). New York: International Universities Press.

Dies, R. R. (1985). Leadership in short-term group therapy: Manipulation or facilitation? *International Journal of Group Psychotherapy, 35,* 435–455.

Dies, R. R. (1986). Practical, theoretical, and empirical foundations for group psychotherapy. In A. J. Frances & R. E. Hales (Eds.), *The American Psychiatric Association annual review* (Vol. 5, pp. 659–567). Washington, DC: American Psychiatric Press.

Dies, R. R. (1987). Clinical application of research instruments: Editor's introduction. *International Journal of Group Psychotherapy, 37,* 31–37.

Dies, R. R. (1989). Reviews of group psychotherapy research. *International Association of Group Psychotherapy Newsletter, 7,* 8–11.

Dies, R. R. (1992a). The future of group therapy. *Psychotherapy, 29,* 58–64.

Dies, R. R. (1992b). Models of group psychotherapy: Sifting through confusion. *International Journal of Group Psychotherapy, 42,* 1–17.

Dies, R. R. (1993). Research on group psychotherapy: Overview and clinical applications. In A. Alonso & H. I. Swiller (Eds.), *Group therapy in clinical practice* (pp. 473–518). Washington, DC: American Psychiatric Press.

Dies, R. R. (1994a). The therapists' role in group treatments. In H. Bernard & K. R. MacKenzie (Eds.), *Basics of group psychotherapy* (pp. 60–99). New York: Guilford Press.

Dies, R. R. (1994b). Therapist variables in group psychotherapy research. In A. Fuhriman & G. M. Burlingame (Eds.), *Handbook of group psychotherapy* (pp. 114–154). New York: Wiley.

Dies, R. R., & Dies, K. R. (1993a). Directive facilitation: A model for short-term group treatments, Part 1. *The Independent Practitioner, 13,* 103–109.

Dies, R. R., & Dies, K. R. (1993b). The role of evaluation in clinical practice: An overview and group treatment illustration. *International Journal of Group Psychotherapy, 43,* 77–105.

Dies, R. R., & Teleska, P. A. (1985). Negative outcome in group psychotherapy. In D. T. Mays & C. M. Franks (Eds.), *Negative outcome in psychotherapy and what to do about it* (pp. 118–141). New York: Springer.

Ellis, A. (1992). Group rational–emotive and cognitive-behavioral therapy. *International Journal of Group Psychotherapy, 42,* 63–80.

Erickson, R. C. (1987). The question of casualties in inpatient small group psychotherapy. *Small Group Behavior, 18,* 443–458.

Exner, J. E. (1993). *The Rorschach: A comprehensive system. Volume 1: Basic foundations* (3rd ed.). New York: Wiley.

Fink, P. J. (1989). The marriage of psychobiology and psychotherapy: A discussion on the papers by Rodenhauser, Zazlav and Kalb. *International Journal of Group Psychotherapy, 39,* 469–474.

Fuhriman, A., & Burlingame, G. M. (1990). Consistency of matter: A comparative analysis of individual and group process variables. *The Counseling Psychologist, 18,* 6–63.

Galloucis, M., & Kaufman, M. E. (1988). Group therapy with Vietnam veterans: A brief review. *Group, 12,* 85–102.

Gans, J. S. (1990). Broaching and exploring the question of combined group and individual therapy. *International Journal of Group Psychotherapy, 40,* 123–137.

Gans, J. S. (1991). The leader's use of metaphor in group psychotherapy. *International Journal of Group Psychotherapy, 41,* 127–143.

Garfield, S. L. (1986). Research on client variables in psychotherapy. In S. L. Garfield & A. E. Bergin (Eds.), *Handbook of psychotherapy and behavior change* (3rd ed., pp. 213–256). New York: Wiley.

Graham, J. R. (1990). *MMPI-2: Assessing personality and psychopathology.* New York: Oxford University Press.

Hall, C. S., & Lindzey, G. (1985). *Introduction to theories of personality.* New York: Wiley.

Kanas, N. (1986). Group therapy with schizophrenics: A review of the controlled studies. *International Journal of Group Psychotherapy, 36,* 339–351.

Kanas, N. (1993). Group psychotherapy with bipolar patients: A review and synthesis. *International Journal of Group Psychotherapy, 43,* 321–333.

Kaul, T. J., & Bednar, R. L. (1978). Conceptualizing group research: A preliminary analysis. *Small Group Behavior, 9,* 173–191.

Keisler, D. J. (1986). Interpersonal methods of diagnosis and treatment. In J. O. Cavenar (Ed.), *Psychiatry* (Vol. 1, pp. 1–23). Philadelphia: Lippincott.

Kivlighan, D. M. (1985). Feedback in group psychotherapy: Review and implications. *Small Group Behavior, 16,* 373–385.

Kivlighan, D. M., Corrazzini, J. G., & McGovern, T. V. (1985). Pregroup training. *Small Group Behavior, 16,* 500–514.

Klein, R. H. (1985). Some principles of short-term group therapy. *International Journal of Group Psychotherapy, 35,* 309–330.

Koss, M. P., & Butcher, J. N. (1986). Research on brief psychotherapy. In S. L. Garfield & A. E. Bergin (Eds.), *Handbook of psychotherapy and behavior change* (3rd ed., pp. 627–670). New York: Wiley.

Krishef, C. H. (1991). *Fundamental approaches to single subject design and analysis.* Melbourne, FL: Krieger.

Leszcz, M. (1992). The interpersonal approach to group psychotherapy. *International Journal of Group Psychotherapy, 42,* 37–62.

Lewinsohn, P. M., & Clarke, G. N. (1984). Group treatment of depressed individuals: The "Coping with Depression" course. *Advances in Behavior Research and Theory, 6,* 99–114.

Lieberman, M. A. (1983). Comparative analyses of change mechanisms in groups. In R. R. Dies & K. R. MacKenzie (Eds.), *Advances in group psychotherapy: Integrating research and practice.* New York: International Universities Press.

Lieberman, M. A. (1989). Group properties and outcome: A study of group norms in self-help groups for widows and widowers. *International Journal of Group Psychotherapy, 39,* 191–208.

Lieberman, M. A. (1990). A group therapist perspective on self-help groups. *International Journal of Group Psychotherapy, 40,* 251–278.

Lieberman, M. A., Yalom, I. D., & Miles, M. B. (1973). *Encounter groups: First facts.* New York: Basic Books.

Lipsius, S. H. (1991). Combined individual and group psychotherapy: Guidelines at the interface. *International Journal of Group Psychotherapy, 41,* 313–327.

Livesley, W. J., & MacKenzie, K. R. (1983). Social roles in psychotherapy groups. In R. R. Dies & K. R. MacKenzie (Eds.), *Advances in group psychotherapy: Integrating research and practice* (pp. 117–135). New York: International Universities Press.

Long, L. D., & Cope, C. S. (1980). Curative factors in a male felony offender group. *Small Group Behavior, 11,* 389–397.

Lyons, L. C., & Woods, P. J. (1991). The efficacy of rational–emotive therapy: A quantitative review of the outcome research. *Clinical Psychology Review, 11,* 337–369.

MacDevitt, J. W., & Sanislow, C. (1987). Curative factors in offenders' groups. *Small Group Behavior, 18,* 72–81.

MacKenzie, K. R. (1983). The clinical application of a group climate measure. In R. R. Dies & K. R. MacKenzie (Eds.), *Advances in group psychotherapy: Integrating research and practice* (pp. 159–170). New York: International Universities Press.

MacKenzie, K. R. (1987). Therapeutic factors in group psychotherapy: A contemporary view. *Group, 11,* 26–34.

MacKenzie, K. R. (Ed.). (1992). *Classics in group psychotherapy.* New York: Guilford Press.

MacKenzie, K. R., & Livesley, W. J. (1983). A developmental model for brief group therapy. In R. R. Dies & K. R. MacKenzie (Eds.), *Advances in group psychotherapy: Integrating research and practice* (pp. 101–116). New York: International Universities Press.

MacLennan, B. W., & Dies, K. R. (1992). *Group counseling and psychotherapy with adolescents* (2nd ed.). New York: Columbia University Press.

MacLennan, B. W., Saul, S., & Weiner, M. B. (1988). *Group psychotherapy for the elderly.* Madison, CT: International Universities Press.

Mayerson, N. H. (1984). Preparing clients for group therapy: A critical review and theoretical formulation. *Clinical Psychology Review, 4,* 191–213.

McNary, S. W., & Dies, R. R. (1993). Cotherapist modeling in group psychotherapy: Fact or fantasy? *Group, 17,* 131–142.

Melnick, J., & Woods, M. (1976). Analysis of group composition research and theory for psychotherapeutic and growth-oriented groups. *Journal of Applied Behavioral Science, 12,* 493–512.

Millon, T. (1987). *Manual for the MCMI-II.* Minneapolis: National Computer Systems.

Mills, K. H., & Kilmann, P. R. (1982). Group treatment of sexual dysfunctions: A methodological review of the outcome literature. *Journal of Sexual and Marital Therapy, 8,* 259–296.

Moos, R. H. (1986). *Group Environment Scale manual* (2nd ed.). Palo Alto, CA: Consulting Psychologists Press.

Morey, L. C. (1991). *Personality Assessment Inventory: Professional manual.* Odessa, FL: Psychological Assessment Resources.

Norcross, J. C., Alford, B. A., & DeMichele, J. T. (1992). The future of psychotherapy: Delphi data and concluding observations. *Psychotherapy, 29,* 150–158.

Oesterheld, J. R., McKenna, M. S., & Gould, N. B. (1987). Group psychotherapy of bulimia: A critical review. *International Journal of group psychotherapy, 37,* 163–184.

Orlinsky, D. E., & Howard, K. I. (1986). Process and outcome in psychotherapy. In S. L. Garfield & A. E. Bergin (Eds.), *Handbook of psychotherapy and behavior change* (3rd ed., pp. 311– 381). New York: Wiley.

Parloff, M. B. (1968). Analytic group psychotherapy. In J. Marmor (Ed.), *Modern psychoanalysis* (pp. 492–531). New York: Basic Books.

Parloff, M. B., & Dies, R. R. (1977). Group psychotherapy outcome research 1966–1975. *International Journal of Group Psychotherapy, 27,* 281–319.

Phares, E. J. (1991). *Introduction to personality* (3rd ed.). New York: HarperCollins.

Phipps, L. B., & Zastowny, T. R. (1988). Leadership behavior, group climate and outcome in group psychotherapy: A study of outpatient psychotherapy groups. *Group, 12,* 157–171.

Rickard, H. C. (1962). Selected group psychotherapy evaluations studies. *Journal of General Psychology, 67,* 35–50.

Riester, A. E., & Kraft, I. A. (Eds.). (1986). *Child group psychotherapy: Future tense.* Madison, CT: International Universities Press.

Roback, H. B., & Smith, M. (1987). Patient attrition in dynamically oriented treatment groups. *American Journal of Psychiatry, 144,* 426–431.

Rodenhauser, P. (1989). Group psychotherapy and pharmacotherapy: Psychodynamic considerations. *International Journal of Group Psychotherapy, 39,* 445–456.

Rutan, J. S. (1992). Psychodynamic group psychotherapy. *International Journal of Group Psychotherapy, 42,* 19–35.

Rutan, J. S., & Stone, W. N. (1984). *Psychodynamic group psychotherapy.* Lexington, MA: Collamore Press.

Salvendy, J. T., & Joffe, R. (1991). Antidepressants in group psychotherapy. *International Journal of Group Psychotherapy, 41,* 465–480.

Scheidlinger, S. (1982). *Focus on group psychotherapy: Clinical essays.* New York: International Universities Press.

Scheidlinger, S. (1987). On interpretation in group psychotherapy: The need for refinement. *International Journal of Group Psychotherapy, 37,* 339–352.

Seligman, M., & Marshak, L. E. (1990). *Group psychotherapy: Interventions with special populations.* Boston: Allyn & Bacon.

Shaffer, J., & Galinsky, M. D. (1989). *Models of group therapy* (2nd ed.). Engelwood Cliffs, NJ: Prentice Hall.

Shapiro, D. A., & Shapiro, D. (1982). Meta-analysis of comparative therapy outcome: A replication and refinement. *Psychological Bulletin, 92,* 581–604.

Shapiro, J. L. (1978). *Group psychotherapy and encounter.* Itasca, IL: Peacock.

Silbergeld, S., Koenig, G. R., Manderscheid, R. W., Meeker, B. F., & Hornung, C. A. (1975). Assessment of environment–therapy systems: The Group Atmosphere Scale. *Journal of Consulting and Clinical Psychology, 43,* 460–469.

Slocum, Y. S. (1987). A survey of exspectations about group therapy among clinical and nonclinical populations. *International Journal of Group Psychotherapy, 37,* 39–54.

Smith, M. L., Glass, G. V., & Miller, T. I. (1980). *The benefits of psychotherapy.* Baltimore: Johns Hopkins University Press.

Solomon, S. D. (1982). Individual versus group therapy: Current status in the treament of alcoholism. *Advances in Alcohol and Substance Abuse, 2,* 69–86.

Stern, M. J. (1993). Group therapy with medically ill patients. In A. Alonso & H. I. Swiller (Eds.), *Group therapy in clinical practice* (pp. 185–199). Washington, DC: American Psychiatric Press.

Stock, D. (1964). A survey of research on T-groups. In L. P. Bradford, J. R. Gibb, & K. D. Benne (Eds.), *T-group theory* and laboratory method: Innovation in re-education. New York: Wiley.

Stone, W. N., Rodenhauser, P., & Markert, R. J. (1991). Combining group psychotherapy and pharmacotherapy: A survey. International Journal of Group Psychotherapy, 41, 449–464.

Subich, L. M., & Coursol, D. H. (1985). Counseling expectations of clients and nonclients for group and individual treatment modes. Journal of Counseling Psychology, 32, 245–251.

Tillitski, C. J. (1990). A meta-analysis of estimated effect sizes for group versus individual versus control treatments. International Journal of Group Psychotherapy, 40, 215–224.

Tinsley, H. E. A., & Bowman, S. L., & Ray, S. B. (1988). Manipulation of expectancies about counseling and psychotherapy: Review and analysis of expectancy manipulation strategies and results. Journal of Counseling Psychology, 33, 99–108.

Toseland, R. W., & Siporin, M. (1986). When to recommend group treatment: A review of the clinical and reserach literature. International Journal of Group Psychotherapy, 36, 171–201.

Tschuschke, V., & Dies, R. R. (1994). Intensive analysis of therapeutic factors and outcome in long-term inpatient groups. International Journal of Group Psychotherapy, 44, 185–208.

Unger, R. (1989). Selection and composition criteria in group psychotherapy. Journal for Specialists in Group Work, 14, 151–157.

Vinogradov, S., & Yalom, I. D. (1989). A concise guide to group psychotherapy. Washington, DC: American Psychiatric Press.

Waltman, D. E., & Zimpfer, D. G. (1988). Composition, structure, and duration of treatment: Interacting variables in counseling groups. Small Group Behavior, 19, 171–184.

Weisz, J. R., Weiss, B., Alicke, M. D., & Klotz, M. L. (1987). Effectiveness of psychotherapy with children and adolescents: A meta-analysis for clinicians. Journal of Consulting and Clinical Psychology, 55, 542–549.

Wetzler, S. (Ed.). (1989). Measuring mental illness: Psychometric assessment for clinicians. Washington, DC: American Psychiatric Press.

Wiggins, J. S., Trapnell, P., & Phillips, N. (1987). Psychometric and geometric characteristics of the revised Interpersonal Adjective Scales (IAS–R). Unpublished manuscript, Department of Psychology, University of British Columbia, Vancouver, British Columbia.

Wong, N. (1983). Combined individual and group psychotherapy. In H. I. Kaplan & B. J. Sadock (Eds.), Comprehensive group psychotherapy (3rd ed.). Baltimore: Williams & Wilkins.

Woods, M., & Melnick, J. (1979). A review of group therapy selection criteria. Small Group Behavior, 10, 155–174.

Yalom, I. D. (1995). The theory and practice of group psychotherapy (4th ed.). New York: Basic Books.

Zaslav, M. R., & Kalb, R. D. (1989). Medicine as metaphor and medium in group psychotherapy with psychiatric patients. International Journal of Group Psychotherapy, 39, 457–468.

Author Index

Subject Index

530